THE
ASSISI PROBLEM
AND THE
ART OF GIOTTO

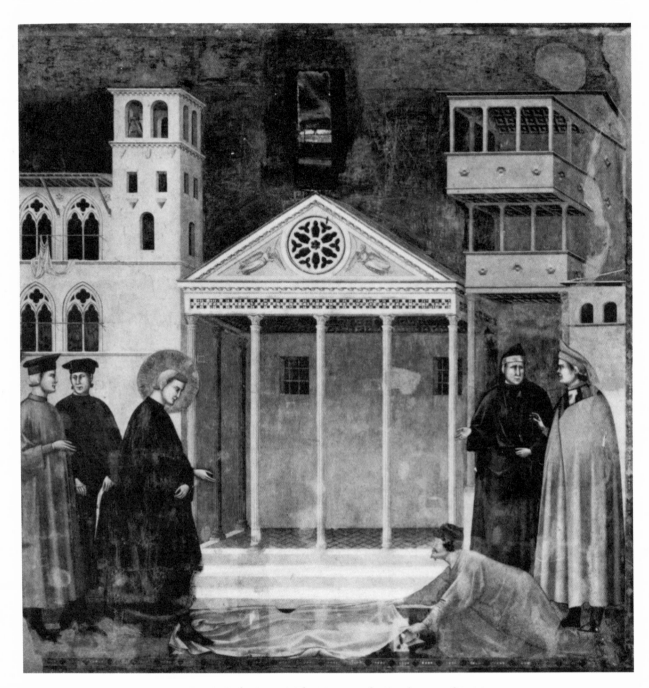

St. Francis Cycle, Scene I: The Homage of a Simple Man of Assisi

THE
ASSISI PROBLEM
AND THE
ART OF GIOTTO

═══

A STUDY OF THE
LEGEND OF ST. FRANCIS IN THE
UPPER CHURCH OF
SAN FRANCESCO, ASSISI

═══

ALASTAIR SMART

WITH A NEW PREFACE BY THE AUTHOR

1983
HACKER ART BOOKS
NEW YORK

First published by Oxford University Press
London, 1971

© Oxford University Press 1971

Reprinted by Hacker Art Books, Inc.
New York, 1983

Library of Congress Catalogue Card Number 81-81724
International Standard Book Number 0-87817-283-1

Printed in the United States of America

FOR

MARITA

PREFACE

THE SERIES OF TWENTY-EIGHT SCENES of the *Legend of St. Francis* in the nave
of the Upper Church at Assisi is among the best known of all the great fresco-
decorations of Italy: the cycle has inspired a vast literature, and every year these
familiar compositions are admired by countless thousands of visitors to Assisi.
Yet it is questionable whether any other single work of comparable importance has
been so strangely misunderstood. On the one hand the *Legend* has been regarded, in the
main, as a simple narrative sequence, with the consequence that its religious meaning
has been obscured; and on the other its purely stylistic qualities have been seen, by most
writers, through the distorting glass of Vasari's attribution of the frescoes to Giotto.

In fact, the question of content and the larger problem of style are interwoven; and
I have attempted in this book to show how the aesthetic principles that underlie the
pictorial language of the cycle assist not only in the unfolding of the narrative but also
in the realization of a theological programme embodying certain fundamental tenets of
Franciscan thought. In discussing the stylistic qualities of the frescoes I have resisted
a now fashionable tendency to play down the value of close compositional analysis. Few
aspects of stylistic criticism seem to me to be more interesting, or potentially more
rewarding, than the study of what I have here called the 'abstract imagery' of art: by this
I simply mean the choice by an artist (which is often unconscious) of specific patterns
of form which tend to recur in his work independently of the nature of the subject-
matter, and which, while having no necessary relation to representational content, yet
assume the value and recognizability of a personal imagery. (If the term itself should be
thought self-contradictory, I would add in partial defence of it that the word *image* is in
common use in contemporary criticism to denote non-figurative as well as figurative
elements in modern works of art.) Such an approach to the Assisi frescoes only serves
to underline the profound differences between the aesthetic ideals of Giotto as they are
expressed in the Arena Chapel and elsewhere and those shared by the various authors of
the *Legend*.

Although this is not a book about Giotto but a study of the *St. Francis* cycle at Assisi,
it has seemed essential to devote some space to a discussion of the nature and extent of
Giotto's authentic *œuvre* and to analyse (however briefly and inadequately) the character of his art and of his genius. In recent years the *corpus* of works attributed or

reattributed to Giotto has been inflated to such a degree that the sublime renovator of European painting has been presented to us as a curiously wayward and divided personality: the present book supports the conclusions of those doubters who cannot believe in this picture of Giotto, and who would certainly dismiss him from the Upper Church at Assisi, or at any rate (if I may adapt Ghiberti's phrase) from the *parte di sotto*. The 'Assisi Problem' has always divided critical opinion, and it would be too much to hope that this book will make converts from among those who are already convinced of Giotto's authorship (or part-authorship) of the *St. Francis* cycle; but perhaps it will help others who have an open mind on this question to assess the evidence anew, whether or not they agree with my own interpretation.

The 'Problem' itself branches out into a complex of related questions, to many of which the meagreness of the hard facts at our disposal allows, at best, only provisional answers to be given; and in a number of cases, therefore, hypotheses must be hedged around with qualifications. In accepting the necessity of this sceptical approach I am very conscious of having posed far more questions than I have been capable of answering; but, the nature of the evidence being as it is, I am content that it should be so. Possibly, but not probably, a document will one day be discovered that will enable us to give the St. Francis Master a name.[1] Until then, one can only hope to define as clearly as possible the nature of his artistic personality and his relationship to other painters of the period. In attempting this task, I have emphasized, throughout, the reflections of his style in Florentine painting in the Age of Giotto and, in particular, its importance to the development of Pacino di Bonaguida. It may be added that since this book went to press the indebtedness of Pacino's early style, as it is represented especially by *The Tree of Life* in the Accademia, to that of the 'Giotto' of the *Legend* has begun to receive a wider recognition (as the compiler[2] of the catalogue of the exhibition *Omaggio a Giotto*, held in Florence in 1967, has expressed it, there is to be discerned in this work 'una cultura giottesca basata sul periodo assisiate (Storie di San Francesco)'). The evidence here is cumulative, and therefore a fairly wide range of illustrations has been chosen, some of which are more significant than others.

The text was completed before the convening of the International Congress on Giotto held in Italy in 1967 and before the publication of the most recent work bearing upon the Assisi Problem, Professor Giovanni Previtali's monumental *Giotto e la sua bottega*. It has, however, been possible to include brief references in the notes to a very few of the more important points raised at the Congress and in Professor Previtali's book. I hope to be able to comment more fully upon the new insights of recent scholarship in a book on Giotto (as distinct from the Assisi Problem) which is now in preparation.

[1] The designation 'St. Francis Master' is used in this book instead of the more cumbersome 'Master of the St. Francis Cycle'.   [2] Paolo Dal Poggetto.

In acknowledging the help that I have received from others I would mention first my deep indebtedness to the work of two distinguished American scholars, the late Professor Richard Offner and Professor Millard Meiss. It is again to Professor Meiss that I owe an invitation to spend two semesters at the Institute for Advanced Study at Princeton, where I was able both to pursue my study of the Assisi problem in an atmosphere of idyllic quietude and also to profit from Professor Meiss's unequalled knowledge of this period of Italian art and from the many insights that he was so generously willing to share. My visit to Princeton was made possible by the grant of sabbatical leave by the University of Nottingham, and it was assisted by the award of a Fulbright Scholarship.

Among those who have been kind enough to take an interest in my work, I have been particularly indebted to the late Erwin Panofsky and to Professor Ernst Kitzinger for various helpful suggestions. My thanks are also due to Miss Rosalie Green, Director of the Index of Christian Art at Princeton, to the staff of the Marquand Library at Princeton University, and, for help especially with external loans, to the staff of the University Library at Nottingham. A number of the translations from Latin and Italian texts in this book were improved, respectively, by Professor Julian Brown and Dr. Barbara Reynolds. My debt to Professor Brown, who has been generous of his help and encouragement, is particularly great.

It would be impossible for me to forget that, during a much earlier visit to the United States as a Commonwealth Fund Fellow, I had the good fortune to attend a series of seminars on Giotto at Columbia University conducted by Professor Howard Davis: it was then that my eyes were opened to the nature and complexities of the Assisi problem, and that I felt for the first time that I was beginning to understand the art of Giotto. To that inspiration I owe more than I can adequately acknowledge.

I wish to record a particular debt of gratitude to the Very Reverend Dr. Giuseppe Zaccaria, O.F.M., prior and Ispettore Onorario of the Basilica of S. Francesco at Assisi, for the provision of special facilities in the Upper Church which enabled me to make a close inspection of the frescoes in the summer of 1958. Many of the photographs reproduced in this book, including the views showing the articulation of each bay, were specially taken by the firm of Andrea de Giovanni at Assisi, always with the greatest care and attention to quality. For permission to reproduce other photographs my thanks are due to the Trustees of the Pierpont Morgan Library, New York; to the Trustees of the British Museum; and to the authorities and officers of the following libraries, institutions, and photographic collections: the Vatican Library; the Louvre, Paris; the Frick Art Reference Library, New York; the German Archaeological Institute, Rome; the Soprintendenze ai Monumenti in Florence and Perugia; Messrs. Alinari and Brogi; the Gabinetto Fotografico Nazionale, Rome; and the Cassa di Risparmio, Florence. For help in the obtaining of a number of photographs I wish to thank Professor Craig Hugh Smyth and Professor Harry Bober, of the Institute of Fine Arts, New York University; Dr. John Plummer, Keeper of Manuscripts at the Pierpont Morgan Library, New York; Professor Roberto Salvini, of the University of Florence; Mr. John Sunderland, Witt Librarian at the Courtauld Institute of Art, University of London; Dr. Jennifer Montagu, of the Warburg Institute, University of London; and Professor Millard Meiss. The drawing from the Dal Pozzo Collection at Windsor Castle is reproduced by gracious permission of Her Majesty The Queen. The task of obtaining various photographs from abroad was made lighter by the efforts of Miss Louie Boutroy, of the Mansell Collection, London, Miss Diana Diemer, Mrs. Betty Peck, and Mr. R. H. Boothroyd; and Miss Patricia Andrews and Mrs. M. E. Bennett have been of the greatest help in the preparation of the typescript for the press. From that point I was fortunate to be guided by the most sympathetic and understanding of publishers.

The University of Nottingham provided a most handsome grant towards the cost of the illustrations, and every art historian will know how deep my gratitude must be. The substance of Chapter II was published in the Nottingham University journal *Renaissance and Modern Studies*, vol. vii (1963), and my thanks are due to the Editors, Dr. R. S. Smith and Professor James Kinsley, for allowing me to incorporate this material in the present book. An Italian version of part of the same chapter was read at the above-mentioned conference *Giotto e il suo tempo* (Congresso Internazionale per la Celebrazione del VII Centenario della Nascita di Giotto) convened in September 1967 at Assisi, Padua, and Florence under the presidency of Professor Mario Salmi. In providing modern translations of texts from Bonaventura's *Legenda maior*, I have been indebted on occasion to E. G. Salter's excellent translation of 1904, republished in 1910 (London and New York). Where the Latin text is couched in biblical language, the Revised Version of the English Bible has normally been taken as the appropriate model.

PREFACE TO THE PRESENT EDITION

During the twelve years that have passed since this book was first published I have had no cause to change the views expressed in it, except in relation to a few minor matters and peripheral questions. Even if it had been otherwise, it would not have been practicable now, in what is essentially a reprint, to revise the text or to incorporate new material. All that is possible are a few comments on certain issues, especially some that have been raised in recent studies, together with a list of *errata* and *corrigenda*.

Least of all has there been any weakening in my conviction that a true understanding of the *Legend of St. Francis* in the Upper Church at Assisi is possible only if we reject Vasari's attribution of the frescoes to Giotto and accept the cycle as the work of a group of associated painters whose aesthetic principles were fundamentally different from Giotto's own. How, for example, would we account for the stylistic character of Taddeo Gaddi's frescoes in the Refectory of Santa Croce in Florence, or of what survives of Spinello's decorations in the Carmine, or of Segna di Bonaventura's Arezzo crucifix, or of the portrait of Dante introduced by Pietro da Rimini into a fresco in San Francesco at Ravenna, if we naïvely accepted Vasari's belief that these works by different masters were all from the hand of Giotto? And in the Upper Church itself, what sense could we make of the Old and New Testament cycles in the nave (including the scenes by the "Isaac Master") if we assumed, with Vasari, that they were painted by Cimabue? Nor is the Vasarian tradition regarding Assisi quite what the proponents of Giotto's authorship of the *St. Francis* cycle like to imagine it to be; for (as I have pointed out in this book) Vasari believed that the cycle had been begun by Cimabue and was then completed by Giotto many years later.

Every student of the period is aware that the opinions of a sixteenth-century writer such as Vasari must often be in conflict with modern knowledge and modern methods of criticism. Yet in one area of inquiry, and in one alone—that relating to the "Assisi Problem,"—there has developed among Italian scholars, however eminent, a curious resistance to what in any other area of Dugento or Tracento studies is accepted as a very necessary skepticism. The explanation appears to be a simple one. Assisi has come to be associated with two names above all others—that of St. Francis, her most celebrated son, and that of Giotto, the supposed author of the most famous of all pictorial illustrations of the Poverello's life. The greatest of medieval saints and the greatest of medieval artists have thus been joined together within a hallowed tradition which is now so deeply embedded in the cultural history of Italy that it has become virtually impious to question it. Hard though it must be for any lover of Italy to know that what he writes causes offense in a country dear to his heart, it is understandable that this book was never likely to find much favour there, or even—as Frederick Hartt has charmingly regretted in a kindly notice—to be read in Italy with an open mind.

Nevertheless there is not the same disagreement about the thesis presented here in some detail that the cycle reveals, in the words of Cristina De Benedictis, a *"straordinaria connessione stilistica con lo stile di Pacino di Bonaguida"* (*Antichità Viva,* Anno XI, No. 3 (1972), 63f.); and indeed the connexion had already been noted by Salmi and others. The question that arises is one of interpretation. The late T.S.R. Boase wondered whether Vasari's reference to Pace da Faenza, supposedly a pupil and assistant of Giotto who painted some lost frescoes in the chapel of Sant' Antonio at Assisi, "represents some tradition of a Pacino who worked there" (*The Journal of the Royal Society of Arts,* CXIX, No. 5184 (November, 1971), 580f.). In my *Dawn of Italian Painting 1250–1400* (Cornell University Press and Phaidon Press, Oxford, 1978) I have emphasized the point that the stylistic connexions with Pacino are at their strongest in Scenes XIV-XVI, at the entrance end of the nave. By a curious irony this area of the decoration includes the one passage of painting which Vasari extolled in praising the expressive naturalism of Giotto.

As to the St. Cecilia Master, the publication of Luciano Bellosi's *Buffalmacco e il Trionfo della Morte* (Turin, 1974) has made less plausible older attempts to identify that great painter with the celebrated Florentine master Buonamico, known as Buffalmacco. Among other important publications of recent years, Hans Belting's *Die Oberkirche von San Francesco in Assisi: ihre Dekoration als Aufgabe und die Genese einer neuen Wandmalerei* (Berlin, 1977) contains a learned account of papal interest in the basilica and a valuable reassessment of the entire programme of decoration: it is somewhat unusual among works by non-Italian scholars on account of its author's willingness to concede to Giotto a designing role in respect of the *St. Francis* cycle.

Many reviewers of *The Assisi Problem,* on its first appearance, seemed to read Chapter II as though it were merely a survey of the literary tradition rather than, principally, a demonstration that the earliest reference to the location of Giotto's work in the double church—the notice in Ghiberti's *Commentaries*—locates it firmly in the Lower Church, and that Vasari himself fully understood Ghiberti's meaning. As I argued further, it was on other and indeed very insecure grounds that Vasari inferred that Giotto had also worked in the Upper Church. If my arguments have remained unchallenged, it is possibly because they have not always been understood. I would now draw attention to the studies by Bellosi and Gilbert which have established Ghiberti's general accuracy in matters of attribution (L. Bellosi, *op, cit.*; Creighton Gilbert, "The Fresco by Giotto in Milan," *Arte Lombarda,* XLVII-XLVIII (1977), 31ff.).

The investigations undertaken independently by Maginnis and Simon into the sequence of decoration in the Lower Church (H.J.B. Maginnis, "Assisi Revisited: Notes on recent observations"; R. Simon, "Towards a Relative Chronology of the Frescoes in the Lower Church of San Francesco at Assisi," *The Burlington Magazine,* CXVII (1975), 511ff.; CXVIII (1976), 361ff.) have provided important new evidence essential to any attempt to date the "Giottesque" frescoes in the right transept and in the Magdalen Chapel, or to consider their authorship. We even have a new document, published by Martinelli (V. Martinelli, "Un documento per Giotto ad Assisi," *Storia dell' Arte,* 1973, pp. 193ff.), which hints at Giotto's presence in Assisi in or about the year 1308—a possible date for the inception of the lovely cycle of *The Infancy of Christ* in the right transept and perhaps for the subsequent execution of the profoundly Giottesque *Crucifixion* below it. There is a growing *consensus* that the Lower Church decorations, so far from being disparate works commissioned separately from a number of painters who all happened to have been pupils of Giotto, show us Giotto's *bottega* in operation. Regarded in that light, they would fully account for Ghiberti's reference to extensive works by Giotto in the "lower part" of the basilica. The extent of Giotto's personal participation in their execution is in this sole respect a secondary question; for one thing is absolutely clear: as we stand near the high altar of the Lower Church and look into the right transept and towards the entrance to the Magdalen Chapel, we know that we are in the presence of the spiritual world created by Giotto and by him alone; whereas in the Upper Church we enter an entirely different world, and only in that great *anonimo* the Isaac Master do we encounter a mind with some affinities with his own.

One of the most challenging and interesting studies to have appeared since this book was written is Gardner's attempted rehabilitation of the Stefaneschi altarpiece, painted for Old St. Peter's, as an autograph work executed by Giotto and his assistants on the occasion of the Jubilee of 1300 (J. Gardner, "The Stefaneschi altarpiece: a reconsideration," *Journal of the Warburg and Courtauld Institutes,* XXXVII (1974), 57ff.). More recently this thesis has been subjected to searching criticism by White (J. White, *Duccio: Tuscan Art and the Medieval Workshop* (London, 1979), pp. 140ff.). The controversy cannot detain us here; but it seems appropriate to make the point that the question of the status of the altarpiece would be directly relevant to the "Assisi Problem" only if Gardner's views were proved to be correct. In that case, the difficulties already inherent in the idea that either the Isaac Master or the St. Francis Master, or both of them, can be identified with Giotto would be seen to be greater than ever; for, given that the *Isaac* scenes and the *St. Francis* cycle were painted within the period 1295–1307, and probably on either side of the year 1300, it is impossible to reconcile the style of the altarpiece with that of either series of frescoes, let alone both of them. A "Giotto" who first painted the *Isaac* scenes in one style, and then the altarpiece for St. Peter's in a second style, and finally the *St. Francis* cycle (or a great part of it, though not the more advanced parts) in a third style, while taking in the commission for the Arena Chapel at Padua along the way, presents a picture that must surely be beyond the power of the most extreme form of *pangiottismo* to accommodate.

Gardner's further reassessment of the Pisa *Stigmatization* in the Louvre (J. Gardner, "The Louvre Stigmatization and the problem of the narrative Altarpiece," *Zeitschrift für Kunstgeschichte,* 45, 1982, 3, 217ff.) as a work of innovating genius has, naturally, a direct bearing upon the "Assisi Problem." As Gardner shows, the Louvre panel "takes up the convention of the Vita-retable and recasts it in the form of an altarpiece equipped with a predella. This bold solution is assuredly the invention of a great artist." The panel is inscribed with Giotto's name, but opinion has long been divided on the question whether he executed it himself or entrusted the work to his assistants. While I no longer think that it is adequate to describe it as a mere product of Giotto's workshop, even if assistants shared in its execution, I have never doubted Giotto's responsibility for its design. The iconographical connexions between the four scenes on the panel and their counterparts in the *Legend* at Assisi have often been enlisted as evidence in favour of Giotto's authorship of the cycle (or of most of it); but it now seems clearer than ever that the Louvre compositions, as is argued in the present book, represent radical revisions by Giotto of the Assisi canon: once again we are confronted by the fundamental stylistic differences that invariably distinguish the art of Giotto from that of the St. Francis Master and his associates in the Upper Church.

As Gardner points out, the remarkable representation of the Lateran façade in the first of the three predella scenes of the Pisa altarpiece (*The Dream of Innocent III*) indicates that its author had been in Rome. This astonishing piece of realism exemplifies in itself Giotto's surpassing originality of mind: but elsewhere the iconographical traditions that underlie both the Pisa altarpiece and the Assisi cycle might be clearer to us if we could see the lost frescoes of the Life of St. Francis painted by Cavallini in the church of San Francesco a Ripa in Rome—a series to which Paeseler has drawn attention (W. Paeseler, "Cavallini e Giotto: Aspetti cronologici," in *Giotto e il suo tempo: Atti del Congresso Internazionale per la celebrazione del VII Centenario della nascita di Giotto* (Rome, 1971), pp. 35ff.). Paeseler suggests that the Assisi frescoes may to a large extent have been copies of the Roman scenes—a hypothesis that might go some way to explain their workshop character, but which in the absence of records of Cavallini's composi-tions remains unprovable. Even so, allowance would still have to be made for the addition of entirely new subjects—a case in point being Scene I (by the St. Cecilia Master), in which the representation of the central piazza of Assisi is likely to have been quite unprecedented, and whose originality of conception bears comparison with that of Giotto's depiction of the Lateran basilica on the Pisa altarpiece. That fresco is exceptional among the scenes on the north wall; and were I writing this book today I would certainly pay closer attention to the "Cavallinisms" in the representations of architecture in the frescoes of the St. Francis Master: an example is the apparent echo of the upper "storey" of the strange building on the right side of Cavallini's mosaic of *The Presentation in the Temple,* at Santa Maria in Trastevere in Rome, which is to be found in the lower structure of the visionary palace in Scene III at Assisi.

Here we touch upon one of the most striking anomalies produced by the discordance between the Vasarian tradition and the findings of modern criticism: it is an unassailable fact that those features of the *Legend* that are stylistically the most "advanced"—from the treatment of the human figure and the representation of architecture to the rendering of light and cast shadow—are all to be found, not in the frescoes by the St. Francis Master (the so-called "Giotto" of the Vasarian tradition), but in those by the two painters—the Master of the Obsequies and the St. Cecilia Master—who brought the decoration to a conclusion on the south wall. There are similar differences in quality and in technique. Therefore (if I may repeat what I have said elsewhere) if the St. Francis Master was Giotto, then Giotto was a "primitive" among the painters of the *Legend* (and that is *not* to play down the St. Francis Master's greatness as an artist). History has failed to record any trace of such a Giotto. And there is a further paradox: it is only in areas of the decoration not painted by the St. Francis Master that we discern signs of Giotto's ultimate influence on the style of the cycle.

More fundamentally, the most serious consequence of the perpetuation of what many students of the period now regard as a baseless and discredited myth is that, besides giving a misleading impression of the character of Giotto's mind and art, it gravely distorts our picture of the development of early Italian painting. Confusion, I believe, is all the more likely to continue so long as the "Assisi Problem" is still thought of as being simply concerned with Vasari's opinion that Giotto was the principal author of the *Legend of St. Francis* in the Upper Church. It should rather be redefined as the question of the whereabouts in the double church of the work by Giotto mentioned by the early writers. That inquiry leads us to the Lower Church, where four centuries ago Vasari was also led by his reading of Ghiberti.

Alastair Smart
Nottingham, March 1983

ERRATA AND CORRIGENDA

p. 5	The Latin quotation, line 5:	*for* prelatios *read* prelatos
p. 5	The Latin quotation, line 5:	*for* subspecie *read* sub specie
p. 26	The Latin quotation, line 3:	*for* Moyses, quo *read* Moyses, qui
p. 61	Footnote 4, last line:	*for* p. 24. *read* p. 24).
p. 64	Lines 16–17:	*for* the series of 'famous men' commissioned by King Robert of Naples for a chapel at Castelnuovo? *read* the series of 'famous men' in the 'Sala' at Castelnuovo in Naples and the frescoes commissioned by King Robert for the royal chapel?
p. 70	Footnote 4:	*for* (1658) *read* (1568)
p. 86	Line 13:	*for* soppellito *read* seppellito
p. 128	Second paragraph, line 8:	*for* the three *Miracles of St. Francis* in the right transept *read* the cycle of *The Infancy of Christ* in the right transept
p. 128	Second paragraph, lines 9–10:	*for* Among these, the *Miracles* contain passages worthy of Giotto himself, and *read* The three *Miracles of St. Francis* on the north wall seem to reflect a later stage in the evolution of the Giottesque style, although
p. 203	Second paragraph, line 4:	*for* it is the time of Lent *read* it is shortly before Holy Cross Day (14 September)

CONTENTS

LIST OF PLATES

PART ONE

THE *LEGEND* IN THE
AGE OF GIOTTO

I

THE *ST. FRANCIS* CYCLE
AND THE DECORATION OF THE
UPPER CHURCH

1. *The Programme of Decoration in the Upper Church*

THE FRANCISCAN BASILICA AT ASSISI is more than the shrine of the most beloved of medieval saints: it is no less the cradle of a new and revolutionary art. Founded in 1228, the year of the Poverello's canonization, the great edifice that was to grow into the double church of San Francesco arose on the Collis Paradisi as the first and most splendid of all the monuments of that cultural renaissance which the memory of the Saint's life and ministry was to nurture. Centuries later, it could still strike a traveller as being 'a temple more magnificent and more beautiful than any other in Italy'.[1] And yet in this splendour there lies a paradox—a paradox as old as the struggles between the Conventuals and the Spirituals in the early history of the Franciscan Order, and one that in modern times did not escape the ironic notice of Henry James when, standing in the Upper Church and looking around him at its frescoed walls, he marvelled that 'the apostle of beggary, the saint whose only tenement in life was the ragged robe which barely covered him', should have been made the hero of so imposing a structure.[2] It may well seem remarkable, in view of early Franciscan prejudices against church ornaments and embellishments of all kinds, that within a century of their founder's death the friars of the Sacro Convento at Assisi could boast the most superbly decorated church in Italy, the repository of the works of the greatest masters of their age.

In conformity with the simple ideal of St. Francis, who had forbidden his followers to build any but the humblest churches, successive General Chapters of the Order had issued explicit directives against the use of costly ornamentation 'in picturis, caelaturis, fenestris,

---

[1] Biondo da Forlì [Flavius Blondus], *Roma Instaurata, et Italia Illustrata* (mid-15th century) (Venice, 1543 edition), p. 115.

[2] Henry James, *Italian Hours* (Boston, 1909).

columnis et huiusmodi aut superfluitas in longitudine, latitudine et altitudine';[1] in 1260 the Chapter of Narbonne, presided over by St. Bonaventura as Minister-General, proscribed all representations of sacred subjects on stained glass windows, except on the principal window behind the main altar, which might include figures of the Crucified, the Virgin Mary, St. John, St. Francis, and St. Anthony; and the equally strict stipulations against excessive pictorial decoration, although less specific, were presumably intended to apply to all forms of painting, including frescoes. Yet, despite the angry protests of the Spirituals, not least at Assisi, these injunctions were soon to be ignored, and the interval between the Chapters held at Assisi in 1279 and 1304, at both of which the regulations of Narbonne were reaffirmed, was the very period in which the vast enterprise of the decoration of the Upper Church was being carried out. It was also in this period that there came to a head the revolt of the Spirituals against the lax party, which almost invariably had the support of the Papacy; a period of division and uncertainty within the Order which even the wise and conciliatory terms of Clement V's Bull of 1312, the famous *Exivi de Paradiso*, failed to resolve.[2]

It was against this background of strife and contention that the greatest of all pictorial interpretations of the work and ministry of the Poverello, the fresco-cycle of the *Legend of St. Francis* in the Upper Church, was undertaken. The cycle is based chiefly upon the official biography of St. Francis written at the direction of the Chapter of Narbonne, the *Legenda maior* of Bonaventura, passages from which are paraphrased in inscriptions below the scenes;[3] and it is a measure of its faithfulness to its principal source that in interpreting the character of the Saint the cycle should reflect so little of that fervent self-immolation and independence of spirit which shine, for instance, from the pages of the *Speculum perfectionis*, a work compiled from the reminiscences of the ardent Brother Leo. The commission given to Bonaventura to write the official *Life*, together with the decrees of Narbonne and of the Parisian Chapter of 1266 that all earlier accounts of the Saint were to be destroyed, constituted a deliberate act of repression aimed at the strict party, which desired only to return to the pure ideal set forth in the Rule *sine glossa* and in the Testament of St. Francis. In all probability this was not the first attempt to suppress or to discredit early writings that encouraged opposition to the policy of Rome towards the Order, and above all to the support given by the Papacy to the Conventuals in their interpretation of Franciscan poverty: there can be little doubt that Sabatier was right in suggesting that the *Vita Secunda* of Thomas of Celano represents a careful editing, at

---

[1] Franz Ehrle, 'Zur Vorgeschichte des Concils von Vienne', *Archiv für Litteratur- und Kirchengeschichte des Mittelalters*, iii (1887), 64 n.; P. Michael Bihl, O.F.M., 'Statuta Generalia Ordinis edita in Capitulis Generalibus Celebratis Narbonae An. 1260, Assisii An. 1279 Atque Parisiis An. 1292', *Archivum Franciscanum Historicum*, xxxix (1941), 13 ff.

[2] David Saville Muzzey, *The Spiritual Franciscans* (New York, 1907), p. 33; L. Wadding, *Scriptores Ordinis Minorum* (Rome, 1650), *ad ann.* 1312; M. D. Lambert, *Franciscan Poverty* (London, 1961), pp. 184 ff.

[3] See Appendix.

the injunction of Gregory IX, of such early material.[1] Certainly the Spirituals regarded Gregory IX as an enemy to the true Franciscan cause, and they especially resented his lax interpretation of the Rule in his Bull *Quo elongati* of 1230, which also declared the Testament of St. Francis to be not universally binding upon the Order. It is not without significance that Gregory IX figures prominently in the Assisi cycle: as the pope who performed the ceremony of St. Francis's canonization he was, of course, represented in the fresco devoted to that event (the now fragmentary Scene XXIV) (Plate 85); but he also appears again in the following scene (Plate 88), an unusual one in Franciscan iconography, in which he is given special emphasis as the recipient of a unique vision of the stigmatized Saint. Still more important, however, is the choice in the *Legend* of episodes from the Saint's life that stress his deference to the Papal Curia, so that he is presented no less as the servant of the Popes than as the spouse of Lady Poverty.[2] The same object had been the care of Bonaventura in composing his official interpretation of the tradition, and the *St. Francis* cycle can be regarded as fundamentally a translation of the *Legenda maior* into the terms of painting.

The early Franciscan chronicles say nothing explicit about the decoration of the great mother church of the Order; but in the writings of the Spirituals in the years around 1300 there are frequent allusions, echoing the injunctions of the General Chapters, to the growing taste for 'sumptuous' architecture and superfluous ornamentation, including the *curiositas in picturis* first condemned at Narbonne. This is one of the themes of Ubertino da Casale's *Arbor Vitae Crucifixae*, written in exile at La Verna in 1305;[3] and in the famous examination of abuses subsequently prepared by Ubertino at the request of Clement V we find still stronger criticisms of the splendour of the Franciscan churches:

Item contra hanc paupertatem altissimam est abusus et excessus effrenatus pannorum aureorum et sericorum in paramentis et aurifrizationes excessive, curiose et care cum margaritis et aliis gemmis et excessus auri et argenti in calcibus et crucibus et turibulis et tabulis et aliis curiositatibus et ornamentis ecclesie, qui in multis locis tantus est, quod superat incomparabiliter magnas ecclesias cathedrales et monasteria ditissima et prelatos divites; in quibus ex pura vanitate sub specie devotionis fatue a parvo tempore et citra est introductus excessus contra expressa statuta patrum nostrorum antiquorum, que omnia talia prohibuerunt. . . . Item contra hanc paupertatem est curiositas picturarum, caelaturarum, librorum et vestium . . .[4]

(Other things that are contrary to this most exalted poverty are the abuse and excessive use of gold and silk stuffs in apparel; excessive, elaborate, and costly orphreys adorned with pearls and other gems; and excess of gold and silver in chalices, crosses, thuribles, altar-tables, and other church ornaments and embellishments. In some places this excess is so great that it far surpasses

---

[1] Paul Sabatier, *Life of St. Francis of Assisi* (trans. L. S. Houghton, London, 1904), p. 386.

[2] Cf. E. Battisti, *Giotto* (Milan, 1960), p. 53.

[3] Ubertinus de Casali, *Arbor Vitae Crucifixae Jesu*, with an Introduction by Charles T. Davis (Turin, 1961).

[4] Ehrle, op. cit. ('Die von Ubertino von Casale gegen die Communität aufgestellten Anklageartikel und Raymunds von Fronsac Widerlegung derselben'), p. 116.

what is customary in the great cathedral churches and in the richest monasteries, as [it outdoes] also the luxury of rich prelates; and whether recently or not so recently it has been foolishly introduced out of sheer vanity, under colour of devotion, against the express injunctions of our early fathers, which forbade all such things. . . . Also contrary to this [ideal of] poverty is the taste for decoration in the form of pictures, carvings, books, and clothing . . .)

The reply of the Community to these charges, which survives in a somewhat evasive statement drawn up by Raymond of Fronsac and Bonagrazia of Bergamo, while stressing the crucial point that, as the Roman Church had taken over the possession of all Franciscan buildings and their contents, there could be no question of the friars' enjoying proprietary rights but only the simple use (*usus simplex*) of such property, also defends the construction of beautiful churches as an act of devotion 'per seculares ad laudem dei et cultum divinum ampliandum'. The authors of this document go on to maintain that beautiful churches promote a more devout form of divine worship and at the same time encourage a greater attendance on the part of the laity.[1] In answer to this Ubertino refers to the situation 'in duobis locis in Assizio et in sancto Francisco'; it is very rarely, he says, that the laity present themselves at such churches; and he now launches into a violent assault upon the whole practice of collecting money that might have been reserved for the poor and the infirm, in order to construct these 'scandalous and monstrous buildings'.[2] Here Ubertino was making a scarcely veiled attack upon Gregory IX, who had laid the foundation stone of the new Basilica and had granted indulgences to all those who contributed to the cost of its erection.

But there were other issues of equal or greater moment, and it would be too sanguine to expect to find anywhere in the very considerable body of early Franciscan literature any direct allusion to the busy artistic activity centred upon the Assisi workshops. The tracts and chronicles of the early fourteenth century offer us vivid enough glimpses into the life of the community, even if, in the writings of the Spirituals, more attention is paid to the friars' shortcomings than to their virtues—to their practice of cultivating land for profit, their acceptance of gifts of horses and arms, and their fondness for costly vestments and habits. But inevitably the chief preoccupations of the Franciscan writers were of a theological nature, and the often graphic narratives of the chroniclers are exclusively concerned with religious concepts and practices: visits to the Upper Church are described in the context of stories about confession or devil-possession, and there is never occasion to allude to any aspect of its interior, apart from incidental references to the high altar or to the choir; the records preserve the names of many of the friars who

---

[1] Ehrle, op. cit. ('Die Erwiderung Raymunds und Bonagrazias auf die von Gaufredi eingereichte Beantwortung der vier Fragepunkte'), pp. 146 ff.
[2] Ibid. ('Die Replik Ubertinos von Casale'), pp. 164 f.

lived at the Sacro Convento in the years around 1300, but there is no mention of the great painters who worked there.

It is the less surprising, therefore, that the identity of many of the artists who painted in the Basilica should eventually have been forgotten, and that the hand of the master whom the early authorities all recognized as the principal renovator of Italian painting should have been seen, in uncritical times, in large areas of the decoration that can now be ascribed only to his followers or contemporaries: the Romanesque gloom of the Lower Church conceals the names of disciples of Giotto that are now lost to us, while the clear light of the Upper Church reveals the identity of only one known master whose activity there is universally accepted—the Florentine Cimabue. Such problems of authorship, however, do not disguise a consistent pattern of stylistic development. Along the nave of the Lower Church, a great Umbrian *anonimo* of the middle years of the thirteenth century, the so-called 'Maestro di S. Francesco', attempted to dress the legend of St. Francis in a worn-out Byzantine clothing; and in the apse and transepts of the Upper Church, filled with the vast apocalyptic frescoes of Cimabue, we observe the dying splendours of the old style. As we walk back along the nave of the Upper Church towards the entrance we seem to pass into another age; it is as though we had laid aside the *Summa Theologica* and opened the colourful pages of the *Meditationes*: we pass from the age of Cimabue to the age of Giotto.

For at least five centuries the twenty-eight scenes of the *Legend of St. Francis* painted around the three walls of the nave have attracted more attention than any other part of the decorations in the Upper Church. Since the beginning of the ninteenth century, when Vasari's ascription of the frescoes to Giotto was first seriously challenged,[1] the question of their authorship has probably given rise to more argument than any other work of the period.[2] Here, indeed, lies the central problem concerning the art of Giotto:

[1] By K. Witte, 'Der Sacro Convento in Assisi', in *Kunstblatt*, 1821, pp. 64, 166 f., 175 f., 178 ff.; and by K. F. von Rumohr, *Italienische Forschungen* (Berlin and Stettin, 1827–31), ii. However, von Rumohr also denied Giotto's authorship of the frescoes in the Arena Chapel, so that his criticism has little value. On this see G. Previtali, *La fortuna dei primitivi dal Vasari ai neoclassici* (Turin, 1964), Pl. VIII and commentary.

[2] Scholarly opinion is still divided on this fundamental issue. The classic arguments against Giotto's authorship of the cycle are stated in F. Rintelen, *Giotto und die Giotto-Apokryphen* (Leipzig, 1912 and 1923); O. Sirén, *Giotto and Some of his Followers* (trans. F. Schenk, Cambridge, Mass., 1917); C. Carrà, *Giotto* (London, 1925); and R. Offner, 'Giotto, Non-Giotto', *The Burlington Magazine*, lxxiv (1939), 259 ff., and lxxv (1939), 96 ff. Grave doubts about Giotto's authorship of the frescoes were also expressed by G. B. Cavalcaselle in his great *History of Painting in Italy* (London, 1864), ii. For more recent arguments cf. T. Hetzer, *Giotto: Eine Stellung in der europäischen Kunst* (Frankfurt am Main, 1960); Millard Meiss, *Giotto and Assisi* (New York, 1960); Alastair Smart, 'The St. Cecilia Master and his School at Assisi', *The Burlington Magazine*, cii (1960), 405 ff. and 431 ff.; and J. White, *Art and Architecture in Italy, 1250 to 1400* (Pelican History of Art, Harmondsworth, 1966), pp. 227 ff.

Within the last half-century there has been a steadily increasing reaction in favour of Giotto's authorship: see in particular B. Berenson, *Italian Pictures of the Renaissance* (Oxford, 1932), p. 233; M. Salmi, 'Le origini dell'arte di Giotto', *La Rivista d'arte*, xix (1937), 193 ff.; C. Brandi, 'Giotto', *Le Arti*, i (1938–9), 5 ff. and 116 ff.; L. Coletti, *I Primitivi* (Novara, 1941–7), i (1941); E. Cecchi, *Giotto* (Milan, n.d.); G. Sinibaldi and G. Brunetti, *Pittura italiana di Duecento e Trecento: Catalogo della Mostra Giottesca di Firenze del 1937* (Florence, 1943); P. Toesca, 'Gioventù di Giotto',

the acceptance or rejection of the Vasarian attribution must fundamentally affect our view of the nature of Giotto's style and of the character of his genius; furthermore, if Giotto is excluded from any share in the painting of the cycle the traditional picture of the development of Trecento painting is in need of some revision, since the *Legend* has usually been hailed as the first important manifestation of the new style.

In one respect the modern preoccupation with the stylistic problems relating to the *Legend* has proved an obstacle to a just evaluation of the frescoes and of their place in the decorative scheme of the Upper Church as a whole. It is questionable whether in the fourteenth century the cycle could have held quite the pre-eminent position that it was to hold in later times. Damage to other frescoes in the nave, and to those in the choir and transepts, has given it a deceptive prominence. It must be borne in mind that the *St. Francis* frescoes constitute but one part of an immense scheme of decoration, which embraces not only the colossal masterpieces of Cimabue—the Michelangelo of that age —but also the scarcely less important Biblical series painted in two rows in the upper registers of the nave, immediately above the *Legend*, and numbering originally as many as thirty-four scenes (Plates 1*a*, 2*a*). It is doubtful whether, even in the home and resting-place of St. Francis, the narratives of his life and miracles would have seemed to the fourteenth-century worshipper or pilgrim more worthy of attention than the scenes from the Old Testament and from the Life of Christ represented above them. Certainly at that time the grandeur and sublimity of the two Biblical cycles would have made an even more powerful impression upon the beholder than their present condition allows.

The *St. Francis* cycle represents the last of four main stages in the decoration of the Upper Church. The earliest frescoes (apart from the vestigial remains of some ancient decorations in the north transept) are those by Cimabue and his assistants in the apse and transepts (Plate 1*b*), datable probably in the late 1270s.[1] There then followed, perhaps

Civiltà, iii, 8 (1942), 29 ff.; idem, *Giotto* (Turin, 1941); idem, *Il Trecento* (Turin, 1951); F. J. Mather, 'Giotto's *St. Francis* Series at Assisi Historically Considered', *Art Bulletin*, xxv (1943), 97 ff.; A. Nicholson, 'Again the *St. Francis* Series', *Art Bulletin*, xxvi (1944), 193 ff.; R. Longhi, 'Giudizio sul Duecento', *Proporzioni*, ii (1948), 49 ff.; R. Salvini, *Tutta la pittura di Giotto* (Milan, 1952 and 1962); R. Oertel, 'Wende der Giotto-Forschung', *Zeitschrift für Kunstgeschichte*, ii (1943–4), 1 ff.; idem, *Die Frühzeit der italienischen Malerei* (Stuttgart, 1953); K. Bauch, 'Die geschichtliche Bedeutung von Giottos Frühstil', *Mitteilungen des Kunsthistorischen Instituts in Florenz*, vii (1953), 43 ff.; C. Gnudi, *Giotto* (Milan, 1958); D. Gioseffi, *Giotto architetto* (Milan, 1963); and G. Previtali, *Giotto e la sua bottega* (Milan, 1967).

[1] There can be no absolute certainty about this date. Brandi associated Cimabue's work in the Upper Church with the papacy of Nicholas IV (1288–92), a former Minister-General of the Order of Friars Minor and the first Franciscan to become pope. Brandi's argument rests upon the fact that the building representing the Campidoglio in Cimabue's fresco of *St. Mark*, on the vault of the crossing, is decorated with shields bearing the Orsini arms, and that there were three Orsini senators during this period. Cf. C. Brandi, *Duccio* (Florence, 1951), pp. 127 ff. However, as White has pointed out, other members of the Orsini family were in office in the years 1277, 1280, 1286, 1289, 1293, and 1300: cf. J. White, 'The Date of *The Legend of St. Francis* at Assisi', *The Burlington Magazine*, xcviii (1956), 351; and idem, *Art and Architecture in Italy, 1250–1400*, pp. 126 f. On grounds of style the frescoes are more plausibly to be dated in the 1270s, at some period after Cimabue's presumed visit to Rome, documented in 1272. Battisti suggests that the representations of Greece, Palestine, and Asia on the crossing allude to the Franciscan missions in the East, inaugurated in 1278: cf. E. Battisti, *Cimabue* (Milan, 1963), p. 39.

from the late 1280s, the decoration of the nave with the two Biblical cycles—the Old Testament cycle on the north wall and the New Testament cycle on the south and entrance walls. The early scenes in these two cycles are mostly the work of a Roman or Romanizing master who can almost certainly be identified with Jacopo Torriti: but at some later date, in the early or middle 1290s, the so-called 'Isaac Master' repainted some of the Biblical scenes towards the east, or lower, end of the nave[1]—the altar being at the west end—and completed the two cycles in a markedly different and more modern style, so introducing the third phase of the programme.[2] Finally, before the year 1308, the long work of decoration was brought to a close with the execution, by a group of associated painters, of the twenty-eight scenes of the *Legend of St. Francis*, occupying the lower areas of the three walls of the nave. These famous scenes, which Vasari in the mid-sixteenth century was to ascribe to Giotto,[3] are now generally accepted as being the work of at least three masters, aided by several assistants. Even Vasari may have detected in them the presence of more than one hand, for he asserts, somewhat obscurely, that the frescoes were begun by Cimabue.[4] At all events the question is not now whether Giotto was the author of the whole cycle, but whether he was responsible for the designs and for the first group of scenes to be painted. The usual view is that his hand is to be recognized in Scenes II–XV on the north and east walls and in some of the early scenes on the south wall. There is, however, little justification for such an assumption.

2. *The Frescoes by Cimabue in the Choir and Transepts*

It is not necessary to submit the ruined frescoes in the apse and transepts to a detailed scrutiny to respond to an exalted, and profoundly Franciscan, mysticism which at once distinguishes their religious content from the simple rationality and clarity of the narratives of the *Legend*.[5] The prominence given to representations of the Virgin, St. Michael, St. Peter, and St. Paul and to scenes from the Apocalypse reflects some of the deeper preoccupations of early Franciscan theology; the choice of subjects has its roots in

[1] J. White, 'The Date of *The Legend of St. Francis* at Assisi', loc cit.

[2] The Biblical cycle in the nave of the Upper Church was probably one of the fruits of Nicholas IV's Bull of May 1288, in which it was ordained that some of the alms offered by the faithful should be reserved for the expense of repairing and redecorating the Basilica ('facere conservare, reparari, aedificare, emendare, ampliare, aptari et ornari praefatas ecclesias'). It is conceivable that the apparent interruption of the work and its subsequent completion by the Isaac Master have some connection with the election in 1289 of Raymundus Gaufridi, a vigorous supporter of the Zealots, as Minister-General of the Order. In 1295 Boniface VIII compelled Gaufridi to resign; and this date brings us close to the probable moment of the Isaac master's intervention in the decoration of the nave.

[3] Giorgio Vasari, *Le Vite de' più Eccellenti Pittori, Scultori ed Architettori* (ed. G. Milanesi, Florence, 1878–85), i, 377 f.

[4] Ibid., i, 253 f.

[5] For the thematic content of Cimabue's frescoes see especially A. Nicholson, *Cimabue* (Princeton, 1932). There is an admirable account of the style and compositional arrangement of the cycle in J. White, *Art and Architecture in Italy,*

Franciscan meditations upon the significance of the Poverello's ministry and of his divine mission within the larger context of God's plan for man's salvation: the commission did not require any new emphasis upon the humanity of St. Francis. The frescoes can be related directly to that mystical tendency in Franciscan thought which found hidden allusions to St. Francis in sacred scripture and especially in the Book of Revelation. St. Francis was already being identified with the angel of the Apocalypse who bore 'the seal of the living God', just as his life was compared with that of Christ. We find such ideas in the writings of Bonaventura, but they also appear in much earlier literature, for example in the hymn *Caput Draconis* composed by Gregory IX, where Francis is hailed as another St. Michael sent by Christ to wage war against the dragon of untruth—as a *novus legatus* bearing on his body the standard of the Cross, the sacred *stigmata*.[1]

The tradition of the Saint's special devotion to the Virgin, to St. Michael and the Angels, to the chief Apostles, and above all to the Crucified Christ, whose wounds he had himself borne, is again an ancient one, although it is given in its most emphatic form in the *Legenda maior*. There is perhaps no need to look beyond it for an explanation of the existence of two *Crucifixions* side by side on the east walls of the two transepts (Plate 1*b*): it must have been intended that the friars, as they sat in the choir-stalls behind the altar, should always have the image of their crucified Lord before their eyes; moreover, each fresco includes a representation of St. Francis passionately embracing the foot of the Cross.[2]

The place of honour, the apse itself, was reserved for narratives from the Life of Mary, whom (in the words of Bonaventura) St. Francis 'loved with an unspeakable affection . . ., forasmuch as that she had made the Lord of Glory our Brother, and that through her we have obtained mercy'.[3] The *Mary* cycle in the apse bears witness to the growing cult of the Virgin among the Franciscans: St. Francis had himself initiated the practice of reciting the *Angelus* three times a day, at morning, noon, and evening; and at the Chapter held at Assisi in 1269—not long, that is to say, before Cimabue began work in the Upper Church—it was ordained that a Mass should be celebrated in honour of the Virgin Mary every Saturday.[4] This was considered a matter of some importance, especially as it conformed to the wishes of St. Francis, and a later decree, issued at the Chapter of Paris of 1292, insisted that if the Mass could not be celebrated conveniently on a particular Saturday it must be transferred to another day of the week.[5]

The subjects taken from the Book of Revelation are represented in the south transept. The west wall, immediately to the left of the apse, is dominated by a figure of St.

---

[1] 'Sequentiae in honorem S. Francisci', *Analecta Franciscana*, x (1926–41), 401.
[2] The frescoes are fronted by altars, dedicated respectively to St. Michael and to St. Peter.
[3] Bonaventura, *Legenda maior*, ix, 3.
[4] Raphael M. Huber, *A Documented History of the Franciscan Order* (Washington, 1944), p. 159.
[5] *Miscellanea Francescana*, xxxiii (1933), 27 f.; Huber, op. cit., p. 187.

Michael, triumphant over the dragon. The apocalyptic imagery characteristic of much early Franciscan thought has already been touched upon; it need only be added that the significance assumed by the mystical figure of St. Michael had its origins in the Poverello's own teaching and example: St. Francis had always reserved for the knight-errant of the angelic host a special place in his devotional life, and it had been in honour of St. Michael that he had offered his solitary prayers upon the mountain at La Verna. The elaboration of ideas connecting St. Francis with passages in the Apocalypse was soon to follow. The frescoes of Cimabue at Assisi are saturated with these concepts: on the south wall, for example, the central fresco is devoted to the account in the 7th chapter of the Book of Revelation of the angel who prevents the destruction of the world before the gathering-in of the Elect; a choice of subject due to the fact that this was the angel who was identified with St. Francis himself, the 'seal of the living God' which he bore being interpreted as the *stigmata*.[1] Beneath the *St. Michael* on the west wall, and above the *Crucifixion* on the wall opposite, on the same level, there appear ranks of angels: their counterparts in the corresponding areas of the north transept, containing scenes from the Lives of St. Peter and St. Paul, are the twelve Apostles, whom St. Francis 'held in the highest devotion for their fervid love of Christ'.[2] The whole scheme of the decoration is ordered and unified; but its coherence is not of a purely pictorial nature, for the thread uniting the diverse themes that are illustrated is a specific view of world history, deriving from meditations upon the coming of St. Francis, as one who had given mankind a new revelation.

3. *The Nave Frescoes*

The concern of the Sacro Convento to preserve, as far as it was possible, an over-all unity in the decoration of the Upper Church is evident from the repetition in the nave of certain ornamental features of the frescoes in the choir and transepts. Around the whole course of the Upper Church there runs a narrow, and for the most part open, corridor or cat-walk, immediately above the level of the *St. Francis* cycle and the main scenes of Cimabue's decorations. Below this corridor, throughout the apse and transepts, with the sole exceptions of the east walls (dominated by the two *Crucifixions*), Cimabue had introduced a continuous band of painted consoles supporting a coffered ceiling, so creating the illusion that this ceiling is actually the underside of the corridor seen from below. This is precisely the function of the similar consoles painted above the scenes of the *Legend*. Again, both in the choir and transepts and in the nave, painted hangings cover the lower areas of the walls, beneath the scenes (Plate 1*b*) (although the present choir-stalls obscure large areas of them). These decorative motifs, running round the

---

[1] *Legenda maior*, Prologus, 1.   [2] Ibid., ix, 3.

interior of the church, lay the foundations of a harmonious unity which is completed by a number of further correspondences, chiefly of a thematic character.

On the ceiling of the nave, the vaulting of the first bay (nearest the entrance) is filled with representations of the *Four Doctors of the Church*, monumental in scale and elaborate in design; solemn figures which provide a counterweight to the imposing images of the *Four Evangelists* painted by Cimabue on the crossing of the transepts. The choice of subject was possibly connected with the Decretals issued by Boniface VIII in the year 1297, in which the cult of the *doctores* was officially promulgated, giving the Doctors of the Church a place of honour beside the Evangelists,[1] for in more than a purely decorative sense the effect of this addition to the ceiling decorations was to balance the *Four Evangelists* and the *Four Doctors* about the centrally placed medallions, containing figures of Christ, the Virgin, the Baptist, and St. Francis, which were already in existence on the vaulting of the third bay. More archaic than the *Four Doctors*, which date from the period of the Isaac Master's intervention in the decoration of the Upper Church, these medallions belong to the phase of the execution of the earlier Biblical scenes: theologically, their significance is that to the traditional *personae* of the *deësis* there is added a new image—that of St. Francis, showing in his hands the imprint of the *stigmata*, and paired with Christ himself.

The New Testament cycle overspills on to the entrance wall, of which the upper areas were reserved for the scenes of *The Ascension* on the right and *Pentecost* on the left.[2] In the small spaces above, two roundels were introduced containing heads of *St. Peter* and *St. Paul*, incidents from whose lives had been illustrated in the north transept. Thus the Apostles represented in the scene of *Pentecost* are found on the same side of the church as the *Apostles* of Cimabue, and his *St. Michael* (in the south transept) corresponds in a similar manner to the angel of *The Ascension*, who was identified with St. Michael in medieval thought. These last associations may well have been fortuitous, but it is difficult to think that the subsequent addition of a representation of the *Madonna and Child* (Plate 5) over the entrance was not affected by the presence, at the opposite end of the church, of the scenes from the life of the Virgin painted by Cimabue in the apse.

Nothing better illustrates the reverence felt by the early Franciscan writers for the person of their founder than the frequency with which they liken him, on the one hand, to such Old Testament prophets as Moses and Elijah and, on the other, and more daringly, to Christ himself. Many of these comparisons are already implicit in the first written accounts of the Saint's life. The story, for instance, of the friars' vision of Francis's ascent in the fiery chariot (cf. Plate 55) refers back to the ascension of Elijah; and

[1] Cf. A. Schmarsow, *Kompositionsgesetze der Franziskuslegende in der Oberkirche zu Assisi* (Leipzig, 1918), pp. 103 ff.; Gnudi, *Giotto*, p. 237.

[2] Charles Mitchell (cf. p. 17, note 2) sees in the prominence given to these two scenes a reflection of Joachimite deas.

inevitably the references in the early literature to this wondrous event, such as the verses in the *Officium Sancti Francisci*, tend to be imbued with the language and imagery of the Book of Kings:

O stupor et gaudium,
O index homo mentium:
Tu nostrae militiae
Currus et auriga;
Ignea praesentibus
Transfiguratum fratribus
In solari specie
Vexit te quadriga.[1]

(O wonder and joy, O thou man, that inspirest our minds; thou art the chariot and horseman of our army; a fiery chariot bore thee up in the presence of the brethren, as one transfigured in the likeness of the sun.)

Where such comparisons are woven into the fabric of the *St. Francis* cycle at Assisi, the allusions to Old Testament figures appear on the north side of the nave, in the vicinity of the Old Testament frescoes, and those to Christ on the south side, beneath the New Testament scenes, with the sole exception of the *Ecstasy* (Scene XII).

In one important respect, however, the organization of the *St. Francis* cycle differs radically from that of the Biblical cycles above it: whereas in the two Biblical cycles the historical movement carries back along the nave from the altar to the entrance, reaching its climax in the scenes of *The Ascension* and *Pentecost* on the east wall, the narra-tive of the *Legend* runs clockwise around the three walls of the nave, beginning at the west end of the north wall and finishing at the west end of the south wall. Thus the two frescoes beneath the *Pentecost* and *The Ascension* do not in any sense form the climactic point of the narrative: nevertheless, these two scenes—*The Miracle of the Spring* and *The Sermon to the Birds*—are related compositionally, as we shall see, to the *Madonna* over the doorway, and as St. Francis, in *The Miracle of the Spring* (Scene XIV), extends his hands in prayer towards the *Madonna*, the momentum of the narrative is temporarily stayed (Plate 5). It would seem that those who planned the decorations were conscious of this distinction, and wished to compensate for it; for the compositional movement of the scenes on the south wall runs for the most part counter to the narrative sequence, and almost invariably the figures that are given the most emphasis face towards the entrance.

4. *The Compositional Organization of the* St. Francis *Cycle*

The painting of the *Legend* posed quite different problems from those that confronted Giotto in the Arena Chapel at Padua. The Arena Chapel is a simple, box-like structure

---

[1] Iulianus de Spira, 'Officium Rhythmicum Sancti Francisci', in *Analecta Franciscana*, x (1926–41), 377.

in which the wall-spaces of the nave are interrupted only by narrow windows on the south side and by a large window high over the entrance. Although the south windows reduce the wall-areas on one side of the nave, producing a slight imbalance, Giotto did not have to take account of any structural complications at all comparable with those presented in the Upper Church at Assisi by the columns that divide the side walls into separate bays. At Padua the treatment of perspective in the scenes from the Life of Christ and in the *Virtues* and *Vices* demonstrates that Giotto related the decoration as a whole to a central point in the middle of the nave. This conception is also carried into the painted cornice running along each wall above the *Virtues* and *Vices*. Standing in the centre of the nave, the visitor to the Arena Chapel can take in the entire scheme, composed though it is of tier upon tier of frescoes, knit together in a complex system of compositional and theological relationships.

At Assisi, on the other hand, the painters of the *Legend* were concerned solely with a single row of scenes which could never have been related very closely to the Old and New Testament frescoes above them: all that was possible was a lateral harmony within the *Legend* itself; but as the nave is divided on each side into four distinct fields by the clustered columns which support the vaulting, and as the columns project a considerable distance from the wall (Plates 1*a*, 2*a*), so that wherever one stands parts of the decoration will always be obscured, the problem confronting the painters of the *Legend* was, in effect, the composition not so much of single wall-areas as of separate bays. Since the north and south walls each contained four bays, with the east wall providing a further field of comparable size (divided at the centre by the doorway), this gave a total of nine separate areas (Plate 2*b*). At the same time it was necessary to preserve a general unity. The solution arrived at is both simple and satisfying.

The frescoes were planned, in the first place, to form distinct groups within each bay. Except for the first bay of each wall (nearest the entrance), which, because of a structural variation at this end of the nave, is much larger than the others, leaving room for four scenes, every bay contains a unified group of three frescoes; and, as we have observed, two further scenes, linked together by the fresco of the *Madonna* with its flanking roundels of *Angels*, fill the narrow areas on the east wall to the left and right of the entrance. To a far greater extent than in the Arena Chapel, illusionistic perspective is employed to assist in the unifying process: indeed early Italian fresco-painting shows nothing to compare with the heavy emphasis placed in the Upper Church upon the painted cornices which run horizontally above and below the scenes of the *Legend*. These cornices are treated in a simple, converging perspective, which relates, not to the central point of the nave as in the Arena Chapel, but to the central point of each distinct field or bay. A similar perspective system is applied to the painted columns that separate one fresco from the next and which are imagined as supporting the upper cornice: these combine with the cornices to form the framing around each scene. The spectator's viewpoint, then, is conceived as being at the centre of each bay (Plates 3*a*–7*b*).

It is not impossible that the splendid architectural framework of the Assisi cycle was inspired by some fragment of Hellenistic wall-painting which might have been visible in Rome around 1300.[1] Whatever its sources, it differs markedly in character and function from the reserved use of architectural detail in the ornamental parts of the Arena Chapel cycle and of other works by Giotto.[2] In the Arena Chapel, for instance, the cornice painted above the *Virtues* and *Vices* is introduced solely in order to give the appearance of actual stonework seen in perspective: it does not serve the function of a decorative border separating one fresco from its neighbour. The borders around the frescoes, which enclose varied floral designs, are conceived as flat decorations laid on the surface of the wall, preserving its two-dimensional character and providing a foil to the spatial 'windows' of the scenes themselves. The pictorial space within each individual scene is imagined as lying behind this two-dimensional framework: it is as though we were looking through an extensive lattice. At Assisi this process is virtually reversed, since the effort to create a credible space is concentrated upon the architectural framework: exploring the spatial world of the scenes beyond, the eye that assumes the presence of Giottesque principles of composition must be alternately excited and disappointed, for here the impulse towards the realization of a three-dimensional world remains subservient to the overriding requirements of an essentially two-dimensional conception of design.

The true nature of the compositional principles that lie behind the Assisi frescoes is revealed above all by the treatment of perspective in the representations of buildings: again and again we find that the orthogonals resulting from the rendering of a building from a particular angle are so contrived that they establish ascending or descending lines across the picture-plane, creating surface-rhythms which are consistently employed to relate one fresco to another within each bay and to impose upon every group of scenes a harmonious two-dimensional pattern. This approach to design differs fundamentally from that of Giotto in the Arena Chapel, where so thoroughgoing an insistence upon the values of surface-pattern would be unthinkable. It is not the least important of the many stylistic features of the *Legend* that remove the cycle far from Giotto's world of ideas.

Equally fundamental to the style of the *Legend* is its measured symmetry. Its coherence and unity largely depend upon the presence throughout the cycle, notwithstanding the diversity of its authorship, of the same ideal of order and balance; and it seems clear that from the beginning the cycle was planned in terms of a symmetrical arrangement of

---

[1] Cf. D. Gioseffi, op. cit., p. 21.

[2] The classic exposition of the differences between the framings at Assisi and at Padua is to be found in Offner, art. cit., p. 267 f.

the various scenes within its main divisions. In bays containing three scenes, the two outer frescoes are balanced—virtually as mirror-images—about the central scene, which always has a centralized design. For example, in the third bay of the north wall (Scenes IV–VI, Plate 3*b*), the third scene repeats in reverse the general pattern of the first, and the composition of the second is centralized. A symmetrical order is thus imposed upon the group of three scenes, which may be likened to a triptych, with the central scene as the main panel and the outer scenes as the wings. We can see very clearly how this system was adapted to the two bays containing four scenes, if we consider the organization of the frescoes in the opening bay on the south wall (Scenes XVI–XIX, Plate 6*a*). Here we find a triad of three indoor scenes, the second of which is given a centralized design, followed by an outdoor scene (*The Stigmatization*). At the same time all four scenes cohere together within a larger unity based upon an ideal of symmetry and pattern-repetition: in Scene XVI the figure of St. Francis begins a rising movement which is carried by the jutting support of the loggia into the architectural forms which dominate the next two scenes; whence it is carried down by the inclined orthogonal of the roof of the chapter-house represented in Scene XVIII (*The Appearance at Arles*) until it comes to rest in the backward-swaying form of the Saint in *The Stigmatization*. This larger unity of the bay is assisted by many other relationships between one fresco and another; but the basic principle is the pairing of the two outer and the two inner scenes: thus the vast linear movement which opens in the first is closed in the last; the towering architectural forms that bracket the figure of St. Francis in Scene XVI find their analogies in the rising verticals established by the mountain and the Seraph in Scene XIX; while various similarities of design, both in the treatment of the architectural detail and in the grouping of the figures, harmonize the compositions of the two inner frescoes (Scenes XVII and XVIII). The principles underlying the organization of the bay opposite (Scenes X–XIII, Plate 4*b*) are exactly the same, but in the context of three outdoor scenes followed by one indoor scene. Throughout the cycle, the symmetrical ordering of each bay is emphasized, finally, both by the perspectival rendering of the illusionistic cornices, which establishes orthogonals directed inwards towards the centre, and also by the symmetrical lighting of the capitals of the painted columns.

When we turn from the examination of individual bays to a consideration of the decoration as a whole, we find that the same principle, the same ideal of a perfected symmetry, governs the relationship between opposite bays. Aspects of the design of individual bays on the north wall are echoed in the corresponding bays on the south wall, creating a symmetrical balance between the two main wall-areas which is completed by the symmetry of the east wall, dominated by the tondo of *The Virgin and Child* at its centre (Plate 5). How carefully this concordance between the north and south sides of the decoration was planned can be judged from its presence in the purely ornamental features of the cycle. As Tintori and Meiss have pointed out, the design of the capitals and piers of the fictive columns between the scenes varies from one bay to another, but the same sequence occurs on both walls.[1] With one curious exception, the same rule applies to the painted hangings below the scenes: the ornament on these hangings again varies from one bay to the next, but, except in the third bays, precisely the same sequence unfolds on both walls, from the altar to the entrance. In the third bay of the north wall (Plate 3*b*), the ornament on the tapestry is more severely geometric than it is in the bay opposite (Plate 7*a*). Otherwise there is an absolute concordance between the two walls; and this symmetrical ordering of the cycle is carried, no less conscientiously, into the treatment of light in the various scenes. In respect of all the scenes, except those in the fourth bay of each main wall and the two scenes on the entrance wall, the imagined source of light is at the east end of the nave: therefore in all the scenes on the north wall, save the first three, the light is represented as flowing from the right, and in all the scenes on the south wall, save the last three, it is represented as flowing from the left. In the scenes in the altar bays (Scenes I–III on the north wall and Scenes XXVI–XXVIII on the south wall), the source of light is at the west end of the church.

5. *The Theological Structure of the* St. Francis *Cycle*

The significance of this ideal of symmetry would not be fully apparent if it were understood only in aesthetic terms, as though the *Legend* could be appreciated simply as a work of art in the modern sense, without reference to its religious meaning. Even when it has been read as a narrative sequence the cycle has been misunderstood, for the disposition of the frescoes relates far more profoundly to certain concepts of Franciscan piety than to the requirements of mere storytelling. The underlying theme of the *Legend* is the theological significance of the Saint's life, rather than the drama of that life in itself, and it is this most important aspect of the Assisi cycle that brings it so close in spirit to its principal literary source, the *Legenda maior*;[2] for Bonaventura had also been concerned to trace, with the utmost clarity, the theological patterns which he discerned in the tradition. Therefore, behind the human interest of the story unfolded in the Upper

---

[1] Leonetto Tintori and Millard Meiss, *The Painting of* The Life of St. Francis *in Assisi* (New York, 1962), p. 49.

[2] Charles Mitchell finds the key to the 'triple articulation' of the cycle in Bonaventura's concept of the three stages of illumination, as propounded in the *Itinerarium* (1259): see the *Atti* of the International Congress of 1967, *Giotto e il suo tempo* (still unpublished at the time of going to press). These three stages are, first, the recognition of God's Creation by the external eye; secondly, the going inside, to recognize spiritual things; and, thirdly, the rising above the created world, to see God. Thus in the opening bay the external pomp of Scene I is followed by representations of inward charity (Scene II) and an ecstatic vision (Scene III). Difficulties, however, are presented by the quadruple articulation of the two long bays and by the diverse characteristics of the entrance wall and the three final bays. Nevertheless, it is quite possible that the ideas contained in the *Itinerarium*, which reflect Bonaventura's meditations at La Verna, contributed to the programme of the cycle, especially in its initial stages. But the primary literary source of the cycle must obviously be the *Legenda maior*, paraphrased in the *tituli* below the scenes.

C

Church, there runs a sublime theme—that this man, through the depths of his humility and the heights of his love, became the pattern of the *imitatio Christi*.

This conception of St. Francis as an *alter Christus* is already stated explicitly in the Prologue to the *Legenda maior*; while the author of the *Meditationes* (one of the most influential of all Franciscan writings of the late thirteenth century) gives expression to the same evaluation of the Saint's ministry when he describes him as one 'so ardently attached to the life of Christ that his own life became a picture of it. For', he declares, 'he imitated it in the practice of all virtues as perfectly as he could; and at length Jesus, it is said, completed and perfected the likeness by the imprint of His Sacred Wounds, so that he became wholly transformed into Him.'[1] It is this theme that is expounded in the Upper Church in the very substance and fabric of the designs.

The combination in the *Legend* of spirited storytelling and an often exquisite decorativeness lends the frescoes something of the appearance of vastly enlarged manuscript illuminations, and the cycle unfolds like a sequence of illustrations to Bonaventura's text. The narrative reaches its climactic point in the central area of the nave, in the frescoes in the second bay of the south wall (Scenes XX–XXII, Plate 6*b*), illustrating the Exaltation of St. Francis, of which the narratives in the bay opposite (Scenes VII–IX, Plate 4*a*) are prophetic. The religious meaning of the *Legend* may be said to turn upon this central declaration of the glory of St. Francis, as one raised with Christ and exalted to a heavenly throne among the angels. On either side of these central bays the decoration divides itself into two areas of roughly equal weight—the upper area of the nave, in the vicinity of the altar, and the lower area bounded by the east wall, an area considerably smaller than the other, but one that includes the two large bays, the two scenes on the east wall, and the additional fresco of *The Virgin and Child* with its flanking roundels of *Angels* (Plate 2*b*). (Even if the *Madonna* is excluded, the frescoes in the lower part of the nave number as many as ten scenes, in comparison with the twelve scenes in the area of the altar.)

The significance of this arrangement becomes clear as we follow the narratives around the three walls of the nave. The opening bay on the north wall (Scenes I–III, Plate 3*a*) offers us a prelude to the story of the Saint's life and ministry: here Francis remains as yet unconscious of his future calling, which is merely announced, in three successive episodes, by a divinely inspired prophecy (Scene I), by an impulsive act of charity on the part of the Saint (Scene II), and by Christ's appearance to him in a dream (Scene III). In the next bay, however (Plate 3*b*), he is represented in a new and positive relationship to the Crucified Christ (Scene IV), to the Father (Scene V), and to the Pope (Scene VI). The opening episode of the following bay (Scene VII, Plate 4*a*) is concerned with the

---

[1] *The Life of Christ by S. Bonaventura*, trans. and ed. by the Rev. W. H. Hutchings (London, 1881), p. xxx. On the authorship, cf. L. Cellucci, 'Le "Meditationes vitae Christi" e i poemetti che ne furono ispirati', *Archivum Romanum*, xxii (1938), xvii, 30 ff.

sanction given by the Church to the life of poverty and obedience ordained by the Franciscan Rule; and the remaining two frescoes show the glory to which St. Francis is destined in consequence of such humility (Scene VIII) and the reward to which it will entitle him in heaven (Scene IX). The next ten scenes—those occupying the first bay of the north wall, the east wall, and the first bay of the south wall—form a compact group, illustrating aspects of the ministry of St. Francis that are particulary emphasized in the *Legenda maior*, and concluding with the last and most important event of his earthly life, the imprint of the *stigmata* at La Verna (Scenes X–XIX, Plates 4*b*, 5, 6*a*). There then follow the solemn representations of his obsequies and ascension into heaven (Scenes XX–XXII, Plate 6*b*), wherein the grief of his companions is transcended by the affirmation of his glorification and union with Christ. The third bay (Plate 7*a*) opens with the two last events mentioned in the main part of the *Legenda maior*—the triumphal funeral procession into Assisi (Scene XXIII) and the canonization of St. Francis by Gregory IX (Scene XXIV); and it concludes with another story connected with Gregory IX (Scene XXV), the account given in the *Miracula* of the Pope's vision of St. Francis confirming the reality of the *stigmata*, which Bonaventura relates directly to his canonization, and which, as it is interpreted in the Assisi cycle, takes on the character and finality of a resurrection-appearance. The episodes represented in the last bay (Scenes XXVI–XXVIII, Plate 7*b*) are all taken from the *Miracula*, and show us three miracles of succour performed by St. Francis after his death.

To sum up, then, we may divide the cycle into the following seven chapters or 'cantos': (1) the Prelude to the ministry of St. Francis: his future sanctity is disclosed by various signs (Scenes I–III); (2) Francis is revealed as the destined saviour of the Church (Scenes IV–VI); (3) the prophecy of the glory of St. Francis and of the reward for his humility (Scenes VII–IX); (4) the ministry of St. Francis and the seal placed upon it by Christ by the imprinting of the *stigmata* (Scenes X–XIX); (5) the death and glorious ascension of St. Francis (Scenes XX–XXII); (6) the funeral and canonization of St. Francis and his appearance to Gregory IX (Scenes XXIII–XXV); and (7) the posthumous miracles of succour (Scenes XXVI–XXVIII).

The structure of the cycle, built upon relationships between one scene and another and between one bay and another, is such that compositional analogies and thematic parallelisms are interwoven. It is impossible, therefore, to consider design and meaning separately: the one contributes to the other; individual forms and images are enriched in symbolic significance by association; and in relation to a similar complex of associated images they acquire still further overtones of meaning. Although the thinking that underlies these associations seems subtly different from that of Giotto as it is expressed in the extensive system of theological parallelisms that has been discerned in the Arena Chapel, both cycles bring home to us in the same way the distance that separates us from the pictorial conventions of the Middle Ages, when simile and analogy belonged as much to the language of the visual arts as to that of philosophy or theology.

In a well-known passage in the *Purgatorio* Dante describes how he is led by Virgil to three sculptural reliefs symbolizing the virtue of Mildness and illustrating, respectively, themes from the New Testament, the Old Testament, and classical antiquity: Virgil then asks Dante to look attentively from one composition to another, entreating him 'non tener pur ad un loco la mente'.[1] It has been plausibly argued that the grouping of the frescoes in the Arena Chapel was intended to invite similar comparisons between paired scenes.[2] There can be no doubt that the Assisi cycle was designed to be studied in this manner: indeed to take a contrary view would force upon us the burden of explaining away an enormous number of coincidences in the choice of related forms and images in every section of the narrative. The cycle in the Upper Church is much more than a series of illustrations to Bonaventura's *Legenda maior*: it is, as nearly as possible, the *Legenda maior* and its principal arguments translated into the painter's language.

No part of the *Legend* shows more clearly the range and subtlety of that language, as it was employed by the painters of the Assisi cycle, than the central areas comprising the frescoes in the second bay of each of the nave walls (Scenes VII–IX and XX–XXII, Plates 4a, 6b). It has already been observed that these two groups of scenes are closely related, the triad on the north wall anticipating in its subject-matter the frescoes in the bay opposite. Each group, however, was designed as an entity complete in itself, as a single *canto* within the great poem of the *Legend*, upon one level displaying a narrative sequence but on a deeper level disclosing the significance of the events thus linked together.

The three compositions on the north wall (Plate 4a)—*The Sanctioning of the Rule* (Scene VII), *The Vision of the Chariot* (Scene VIII), and *The Vision of the Thrones* (Scene IX)—are so designed that the whole group is bound together by a broad pictorial movement which begins at the kneeling figure of St. Francis in the first scene, rises to a climax in the second scene, where St. Francis appears in the heavens in a chariot of fire, and descends in the third to come to rest once more in a representation of the kneeling Saint. This movement is carried forward not only by the disposition and attitudes of the principal figures—not merely, for instance, by the gestures of St. Francis in the first scene and of the angel in the third—but also by the firm direction-lines established by the perspectival treatment of architectural forms: so the eye is led upward from Scene VII, by a series of oblique orthogonals, into the upper areas of Scene VIII, where the Saint's chariot seems to be resting upon the roof of the lofty building on the left, and then down again in Scene IX through the slanting lines of the heavenly thrones and the roof of the chancel.

---

[1] *Purgatorio*, x, 28–96.
[2] M. Alpatoff, 'The Parallelism of Giotto's Paduan Frescoes', *Art Bulletin*, xxix (1947), 149 ff.

In Scene VII St. Francis is shown in an attitude of humility, as he kneels before the Pope to receive from him the authorized Rule of his new Order, and here the lowly appearance of the Poverello and his followers is contrasted with the pomp and magnificence of the papal court.[1] In the following scene, however, he is exalted in a vision prophetic of his future glory, and the friars who are vouchsafed the vision see him borne aloft like a second Elijah—as one who, in Bonaventura's words, 'had been made by God, like another Elijah, the chariot and horseman of spiritual men': 'virorum spiritualium, ut alter Elias, factus fuerat a Deo currus et auriga'.[2] In the final scene an angel shows another friar a splendid throne which has been reserved for St. Francis in heaven amidst the thrones of angels. This is the explanation of the prophetic vision of the previous scene; but the heavenly throne is also the reward for the humility set forth in the first scene, for according to the *Legenda maior* it was only by the merit of such humility that St. Francis was deemed worthy of so great a glory; it is by becoming nothing, according to the precept of the Franciscan Rule (the subject of Scene VII), that 'the truly humble shall be exalted to that excellent glory from which the proud are cast down': 'ad excellentiam gloriae, de qua superbus eicitur, vere humilis exaltetur'.[3] The *Legenda Monacensis* likewise relates the Vision of the Thrones to the humility of St. Francis.[4] This theme is underlined at Assisi by the compositional pairing of the two outer scenes, the design of the one repeating in reverse the general pattern of the other. The relationship between the two scenes is stated most emphatically in their upper areas, where the heavenly thrones of Scene IX recall the forms and even the colours of the vaulting over the papal hall in Scene VII, suggesting a comparison between the earthly glory of the Church and the heavenly glory of her saints.

In the bay opposite (Scenes XX–XXII, Plate 6*b*), St. Francis is no longer likened to Elijah, but to Christ himself. The central fresco (Scene XXI) echoes certain features of *The Vision of the Chariot* (Scene VIII), the central fresco in the north bay. The subject is again a vision of St. Francis ascending into the heavens, a vision which in this case is experienced independently by a Franciscan friar and by the Bishop of Assisi—the friar and his companions corresponding to the standing friars in Scene VIII, and the sleeping bishop to the friars huddled in sleep within the building in the other fresco. The composition is dominated by towering architectural forms similar in character to those in Scene VIII (although executed by a painter of greater refinement); their severe lines are modified by the curvilinear shapes produced by a cluster of arches and semi-arches; and these echo the circles and implied circles stated in Scene VIII in the chariot-wheels, the

---

[1] This contrast is implicit in the *Legenda maior*, iii, 9.   [2] Ibid., iv, 4.   [3] Ibid., vi. 6.

[4] 'Legenda Monacensis Sancti Francisci', vii, 21, in *Analecta Franciscana*, x, 701. Here the friar is assured by the Holy Spirit that his vision was a true one: 'Cognosce veram fuisse visionem, quoniam sedem per superbiam perditam humilitas humillimo conservavit.' The *Legenda Monacensis*, composed in the monastery of Oberaltaich, in Bavaria, is to be dated *c.* 1275.

Saint's halo, and the prancing horses. The relationship of the two compositions remains fundamentally unaffected by pronounced stylistic differences arising from the fact that the frescoes were executed by different hands.

The subject of the friar's vision appears in the preceding fresco (Scene XX), where St. Francis ascends into heaven flanked on either side by ranks of angels, who thus confront the angels' thrones in Scene IX. The action of the friar, as he extends his hands towards the vision, leads the eye back into Scene XX, just as the movement of the horses in Scene VIII carries forward in the same direction into Scene IX. The two outer frescoes (Scenes XX and XXII) are again paired together, and like their counterparts in the opposite bay they show strong similarities of design which emphasize their relationship. Once more the chief stress, in this respect, is placed upon the associated upper areas, containing (in Scene XX) the ascension-image and (in Scene XXII) a representation of the iconostasis of a church, upon which we see a crucifix at the centre and two further devotional pictures on either side—a *Madonna and Child* and a *St. Michael*. Thus the ascension-image in Scene XX, showing St. Francis with his hands raised to reveal the signs of the *stigmata* (Plate 78*a*), is directly compared to an image of the Crucified Christ (Plate 12*b*), whose wounds the Poverello had borne. (Nor can it be accidental to this association of images that the subjects of all three pictures on the iconostasis in Scene XXII should have held a special significance in the Saint's devotional life.) Herein, then, there is stated that central conviction of Franciscan theology, that St. Francis was transformed into the likeness of Christ:

Fuit igitur tota vita eius in amaritudine compassionis, qua transformabatur per amorem compassionis, in Christum . . .[1]

(Therefore his whole life was passed in the sorrow of compassion, by which he was transformed through love of compassion into Christ . . .)

And this is his unique glory, which in the Assisi cycle is only foreshadowed on the north wall, where he is likened to Elijah—to one, that is, who in Christian tradition prefigured the Christ, and who in Franciscan thought came to prefigure the Poverello himself.[2]

The subject of Scene XXII (Plates 6*b*, 82), *The Verification of the Stigmata*, is connected in the *Legenda maior* with *The Sanctioning of the Rule*, the subject of Scene VII directly opposite (Plates 4*a*, 53): Bonaventura refers to the *stigmata* as 'the seal, as it were, of the Chief Pontiff, Christ, to sanction in all ways the Rule'.[3] The connection is emphasized

---

[1] *Tredici Sermoni in onore di S. Francesco di Assisi* (ascribed to Bonaventura), ed. D. Paolino Manciana (Rome, 1882), Sermo i, p. 4.

[2] See, for example, the passage in the *De Conformitate*, Liber i, Fructus i, Pars Secunda, 4: 'Octava figura est de Elia in curru igneo asportato, *IV Reg. 2, 11*. Sanctus Franciscus in curru igneo transfiguratus apparuit fratribus, ut dicit IV pars *Legendae*' ('*De Conformitate Vitae Beati Francisci ad Vitam Domini Iesu Auctore Fr. Bartholomaeo de Pisa*', in *Analecta Franciscana*, iv (1906), 41). This is a work of the late fourteenth century.

[3] *Legenda maior*, iv, 11.

in the Assisi frescoes by the central positions given respectively to the kneeling figures of St. Francis and the witness to the reality of the *stigmata*, the sceptical Jerome. (Where in the one scene the two principal figures are linked together by their gestures, which unite as St. Francis receives the parchment of the Rule from the Pope's hand, in the other the long torches held by the acolytes lead the eye from the dead Saint to the image of the Crucified Christ upon the iconostasis.)

Parallelisms of this nature occur throughout the *Legend*. The opening bay on the north wall (Plate 3*a*) already establishes the principle of symmetrical organization which, more than any other factor, makes possible these thematic concordances. Here the second scene is again designed as a centre-piece, and the haloed head of St. Francis, who stands in the centre foreground, becomes the focal point of the design of the whole bay. This country scene—*The Gift of the Mantle* (Plate 42)—is flanked by compositions filled with architectural forms, the first of them opening on to a view of the main piazza of Assisi, with its Roman temple and (immediately behind St. Francis) the Palazzo del Capitano del Popolo (Plate 41 and Frontispiece). The other fresco (Scene III) is dominated by the heavenly palace filled with arms and banners which Christ reveals to St. Francis in a dream: an association is therefore brought about between the *palazzo* on the left side of Scene I, symbolic of the Saint's worldly youth, and the heavenly palace which occupies the right side of Scene III (the mirror-image of the first), and which betokens his vocation as a soldier of Christ.

But the full significance of the realistic representation of Assisi in Scene I (Frontispiece) becomes clear only in the context of the relationship of this fresco to Scene XXVIII (*The Liberation of the Prisoner*), which faces it at the end of the south wall (Plates 7*b*, 93); for here the setting is Rome, identifiable as such by the inclusion of a stylized representation of Trajan's Column and perhaps also of the Septizonium:[1] the narrative of the *Legend* ends in the Holy City, but it begins in Assisi, the new *città santa*, as St. Francis himself named it; and nothing in the ordering of the cycle is more interesting than this implicit comparison between Assisi and Rome. Assisi is represented again in Scene II (Plate 42), and the church on the hill to the right is San Francesco itself, rising up over the valley which once lay between the Collis Paradisi and the city walls. The church is placed directly opposite the figure of St. Francis in Scene XXVII (*The Confession of the Woman of Benevento*), where the Saint is shown in the heavens in the act of kneeling in supplication before Christ (Plates 91, 92*a*): so also, in the church raised in his honour, we are perhaps to understand that he will join his prayers to those of the faithful.

It is possible that this emphasis upon San Francesco, however natural it may seem as a simple expression of pride in the great basilica, reflects the controversy that was

---

[1] For the proposed identification of the building on the left side of the fresco as the Septizonium (which was still in existence at the time of the painting of the *Legend*), see Roger Fry, 'Giotto, II', *Monthly Review*, Feb. 1901, p. 96.

centred upon the Portiuncula Indulgence, a dispute dating back to the opposition of the strict party to Brother Elias, the founder of the basilica, and kept alive by the later Spirituals, for whom the church of the Portiuncula, so dear to the memory of St. Francis and so intimately associated with his spiritual life, remained the true mother church of the Order. A legend had grown up that the Saint's heart was buried at the Portiuncula; and in the treatise on the Portiuncula Indulgence written early in the fourteenth century by Francesco Bartolo of Assisi we read of the many miracles that were performed in the church: at one point we are told of a woman possessed by devils who was taken by her friends to the Upper Church in the hope of a cure; when this proved ineffectual she was led to the Portiuncula, where she was at once released from her sufferings and restored to complete bodily and mental health.[1] It may well have been thought desirable to combat the views of the Spirituals by drawing attention in the Assisi cycle to the unique status of San Francesco as the *caput et mater*[2] of the whole Order. It is worth noting in addition that the General Chapter held at Assisi in 1295 issued a directive discouraging the Provincials from granting permission to members of the Order to make pilgrimages to the Portiuncula, on the grounds that they caused disturbances at the Portiuncula Convent and in the convents of other cities on the way.[3]

In the next bay on the north wall (Scenes IV–VI, Plate 3*b*), the ruined church of San Damiano represented in Scene IV (*The Miracle of the Crucifix*) is bracketed with the falling Lateran Church which St. Francis supports on his shoulders in Scene VI (*The Dream of Innocent III*): having in the first episode obeyed the command of Christ to rebuild his Church, St. Francis is revealed in the last as its chosen saviour. The thematic connection between these paired frescoes is underlined by the inscription below Scene IV, which although partly defaced can still be read. This concludes with the explanation that Christ's words referred, not, in a literal sense, to the church of San Damiano, but in a figurative sense to the Church of Rome, symbolized in Scene VI by the Lateran Basilica, the Cathedral of Rome:

> FRANCISCE, VADE REPARA DOMU[M] MEA[M] Q[UAE] TOTA [DESTRUITUR: PER HOC]
> ROMANA[M] SIG[NIFICANS] ECCLE[SI]A[M]

('Francis, go and repair my house, which is totally falling into ruins'—by this meaning the Church of Rome.)

The relationship of the two scenes is emphasized pictorially by striking similarities of design, and especially by the manner in which the weighty orthogonal produced by the perspectival treatment of the church of San Damiano in Scene IV is repeated in reverse by the tilted ground-plane of the basilica in Scene VI.

---

[1] Franciscus Bartholi de Assisio, *Tractatus de Indulgentia S. Mariae de Portiuncula*, ed. P. Sabatier (Paris, 1900), pp. 61 ff.
[2] The words are Gregory IX's, in the Bull *Is qui ecclesiam* (April, 1230).
[3] Huber, op. cit., p. 188.

Although the scenes in this bay are related in design to the corresponding scenes in the bay opposite (Scenes XXIII–XXV, Plate 7a), the main thematic connections follow the narrative sequence: each chapter of three episodes opens at San Damiano—shown in Scene IV as fallen into ruin and in Scene XXIII as rebuilt as the convent church of the Poor Clares—and each ends with an appearance of St. Francis to the reigning pope—to Innocent III in Scene VI and to Gregory IX in Scene XXV. Over and above these relationships, the *stigmata*, revealed to the doubting Pope in Scene XXV, are here associated for the first time with the Crucified Christ, who addresses St. Francis in Scene IV (directly opposite) through the medium of the miraculous crucifix of San Damiano, and St. Francis raises his hands towards the crucifix, not in a simple attitude of prayer, but as he will raise them towards the Seraphic Christ on Mount La Verna. A similar repetition appears in the same context in the *St. Francis* altarpiece in the Siena Pinacoteca by a follower of Guido da Siena,[1] which includes representations of the Miracle of the Crucifix and the Stigmatization: once again the same attitude is given to St. Francis in both scenes.

In Scene V at Assisi—the central fresco in the bay (Plates 3b, 48)—Francis renounces his father Pietro Bernardone and all earthly ties, and receives the blessing of his heavenly Father: significantly the hand of God is represented in the heavens immediately above the figure of Bernardone, who strides forward angrily as though to strike his son. To this episode, in which the future Saint suffers the scorn not only of his father but also of the people of Assisi, there is opposed at the centre of the south bay the splendid ceremony of his *Canonization* (Scene XXIV): the setting is once more Assisi, but mockery has given way to reverence, and anger to joy, and the children no longer come to throw stones. This scene, alone among the frescoes of the *Legend*, has suffered extensive damage from damp, and little of the upper area of the composition remains; but here the Pope —the spiritual father of the Church (*dominus papa*)—was represented in the act of giving his blessing from a high throne, as Francis is enrolled among the company of the Saints.

The frescoes at the lower end of the nave (Scenes X–XIX) illustrate ten of the most important episodes in the ministry of St. Francis, revealing different aspects of his sainthood to which the *Legenda maior* devotes separate chapters, and underlining his likeness to Christ. Thematic and compositional considerations required that three of these episodes should depart from the narrative order of the *Legenda maior*: according to Bonaventura's chronology (which was not, however, intended to be historically accurate), *The Miracle of the Spring* (Scene XIV) should precede the scene of *St. Francis before the Sultan* (Scene XI); *The Sermon to the Birds* (Scene XV) should follow *The Death of the Knight of Celano* (Scene XVI); and similarly *The Appearance at Arles* (Scene XVIII) should come

---

[1] Siena Pinacoteca No. 313. For this work see J. H. Stubblebine, *Guido da Siena* (Princeton, 1964), pp. 107 ff., and Fig. 61.

immediately after *The Vision of the Chariot* (Scene VIII).¹ This rearrangement of the narrative permitted in the first place the pairing on the east wall, on either side of the entrance to the nave, of the two pastoral scenes of *The Miracle of the Spring* and *The Sermon to the Birds*.² Here considerations of design may well have been decisive: certainly there is nothing in the cycle more charming than the decorative unity given to the east wall by the association of these two scenes in relation to the *Madonna and Angels* over the doorway (Plate 5). But the arrangement also had other advantages. Not only did the position accorded to *The Miracle of the Spring* afford an opportunity for an allusion to the Franciscan devotion to the Virgin, but this scene was retained on the Old Testament side of the nave, as was appropriate to a subject that was regarded as the Franciscan analogue of the story of Moses' striking of the Rock: in the words of Bonaventura, 'omnipotentis Dei famulus . . . in eductione aquae de petra conformis exstitit Moysi'³ ('The servant of almighty God . . ., when he drew water from a rock, was like Moses'); a comparison which is repeated in the *De Conformitate*:

> Quadragesimus primus actus est a beato Francisco aquae a petra eductio, scilicet in monte Alvernae, quando homini, cuius asello vehebatur, aquam oratione propinavit. Hunc figuravit Moyses, qui bis aquam de petra virga percutiendo eduxit, Ex. 17, 6; Num. 20, 11.⁴

> (The forty-first act of St. Francis was the drawing of water from a rock, when, on Mount La Verna, he provided through prayer a drink of water for the man on whose ass he was riding. This act was prefigured by Moses, who twice drew water from a rock by striking it with his staff (Exodus 17 : 6; Numbers 20 : 11).)

At the same time *The Sermon to the Birds* took its place near two other scenes of preaching, *The Sermon before Honorius III* (Scene XVII) and *The Appearance at Arles* (Scene XVIII). On the other hand *The Appearance at Arles* was assigned to the south wall for a more important reason. The story of St. Francis's miraculous appearance at the Chapter of Arles has a direct connection with the preaching of the Cross of Christ, of which the analogue in the Franciscan legend is the miracle of the Stigmatization on Mount La Verna, whereby St. Francis experienced the sufferings of the Crucified: accordingly, *The Appearance at Arles* was placed next to *The Stigmatization* at the end of the first bay (Plate 6a).

We have noted that the group of four frescoes in the first bay of the north wall (Scenes X–XIII, Plate 4b) comprises three open-air scenes followed by an indoor scene, and that this pattern is simply reversed on the south wall (Scenes XVI–XIX, Plate 6a). In this section of the decoration, as in the third bays (Scenes IV–VI and XXIII–XXV),

---

¹ The sources for the scenes are as follows: *Legenda maior*, iv, 4 (Scene VIII); *Leg. maior*, iv, 10 (Scene XVIII); *Leg. maior*, vii, 12 (Scene XIV); *Leg. maior*, ix, 8 (Scene XI); *Leg. maior*, xi, 4 (Scene XVI); *Leg. maior*, xii, 3 (Scene XV).

² On this see J. White, *The Birth and Rebirth of Pictorial Space* (London, 1957), pp. 43 f.

³ *Legenda maior*, vii, 13.   ⁴ *De Conformitate*, Liber i, Fructus i, Pars Secunda, 3.

the principal thematic connections between the scenes on the north wall and those on the south wall follow the narrative sequence. The first episode in each chapter of four scenes is concerned with the supernatural gifts bestowed upon St. Francis by virtue of his zeal in prayer—in Scene X (*The Exorcism of Arezzo*) with his power over the evil spirits, in Scene XVI (*The Death of the Knight of Celano*) with his gift of prophecy. The second is concerned with his preaching ministry—in Scene XI (*St. Francis before the Sultan*) within the citadel of unbelief, and in Scene XVII (*The Sermon before Honorius III*) in the presence of the Papal Curia.[1] The third shows St. Francis in the similitude of the Crucified, with his arms extended as upon a cross—in Scene XII (*The Ecstasy of St. Francis*) miraculously borne heavenward in a shining cloud, and in Scene XVIII (*The Appearance at Arles*) miraculously carried in spirit from Assisi to Arles during the sermon on the Cross of Christ preached by St. Anthony before the assembled Chapter. Finally, as in Scene XIII (*The Christmas Crib at Greccio*) St. Francis celebrates the birth of Christ, by means of a tableau symbolizing, according to Celano, his mystical union with the Lamb of God, so in Scene XIX (*The Stigmatization*) he shares in the Lord's Passion and Death.

This last analogy, between the sufferings of the Poverello upon Mount La Verna and the sufferings of Christ upon Golgotha, provides the most constantly recurring theme of early Franciscan literature, and, as we have seen, it is already anticipated in the *Legend* in three of the narratives (Scenes IV, XII, and XVIII). Within the group of ten scenes which we have been considering, this profound conviction about the significance of the miracle of La Verna, which is to be given its ultimate, triumphant expression in the second bay of the south wall (Scenes XX, XXII), is stated with absolute clarity in Scenes XVIII and XIX, where the figure of St. Francis, represented in *The Appearance at Arles* with his arms extended in the form of the Crucified ('extensis velut in cruce manibus'),[2] echoes the attitude of the Seraphic Christ of *The Stigmatization*. This association of images is anticipated in the bay opposite in Scenes XII and XIII, the similar attitude given to St. Francis in the scene of his *Ecstasy* being echoed in *The Christmas Crib at Greccio* by a large crucifix surmounting the rood-screen of a church. Once again we observe how the scenes on the north wall prepare the way for the explicit statement on the south wall of the central Franciscan affirmation that the 'little poor man' of Assisi became an *alter Christus*.

Indeed, as we follow the narratives of the south wall, we are reminded in turn of one passage after another from the Gospel accounts of Christ's Passion, Death, and

---

[1] The quotation from Luke 21 : 15, 'I will give you a mouth and wisdom', with which Bonaventura illustrates the story of the visit to the Sultan (*Legenda maior*, ix, 8) (Assisi, Scene XI), is fulfilled still more strikingly in the story of the sermon before Honorius III (Assisi, Scene XVII), where St. Francis, having forgotten his prepared address, finds new words coming to his lips through the inspiration of the Holy Spirit (*Leg. maior*, xii, 7).

[2] *Legenda maior*, iv, 10. The words EXTE[N]SIS MANIB[US] occur in the inscription beneath the fresco (Scene XVIII).

Resurrection.[1] The Stigmatization, of course, had been associated from the first with the Crucifixion of Christ,

> Cuius in sancto vulnera
> Francisco renovantur

('Whose wounds are renewed in St. Francis'), as Julian of Speyer had sung in the metrical *Offices* which he had composed for the use of the friars;[2] and there was an obvious analogy between the story of the unbelieving Jerome and that of the doubting Thomas in the Fourth Gospel.[3] A comparison between the bearing home of the Saint's body into Assisi (the subject of Scene XXIII, Plate 83) and Christ's Entry into Jerusalem is implicit in Bonaventura's narrative in the *Legenda maior*, and it is significant that the figure of the boy climbing a tree in the Assisi fresco (Plate 96) is borrowed from the iconography of the Gospel story.[4] The Poor Clares' lament over the body of the Saint, in the same fresco, strongly recalls a *Pietà*, and it is interesting to find an Umbrian pupil of Meo da Siena making use of the Assisi composition in a painting of *The Lamentation over the Dead Christ*.[5] All in all, such resemblances to the Gospel narratives bring to mind the striking declaration of a sermon ascribed to Bonaventura:

Item Beatus Franciscus fuit creatus ad similitudinem Humanitatis Christi, videlicet quantum ad tria: quantum ad *vitam*, quantum ad *passionem*, et quantum ad *resurrectionem*.[6]

(Further, the Blessed Francis was created in the likeness of the Humanity of Christ, and that in three ways: in his Life, in his Passion, and in his Resurrection.)

From the many stories collected by Bonaventura in the *Miracula*, three representative examples of the Saint's power to assist his spiritual children were selected to complete the great cycle in the mother church (Plate 7b). The first of these, the story of the recovery of a wounded man (Scene XXVI), comes from the opening section of the *Miracula*, which is devoted to the curative virtues of the sacred *stigmata* themselves.[7] It follows in the *Miracula* shortly after the account of the appearance of St. Francis,

---

[1] Bonaventura's account of St. Francis's last exhortation to his followers from his death-bed strongly recalls Christ's own words to his disciples as the shadow of the Cross approached. Before the Passover (in Mark's version) Jesus warns them of what lies ahead: 'Ye shall be hated of all men for my name's sake: but he that shall endure unto the end, the same shall be saved.' St. Francis says to his own disciples: 'Since temptation will come, and trials draw nigh, blessed are they who shall continue in the works that they have begun' (*Legenda maior*, xiv, 5). And immediately before his death St. Francis requests that the 13th chapter of St. John's Gospel be read to him, from the opening verse, which reads: 'Now before the Feast of the Passover, when Jesus knew that his hour was come that he should depart out of this world unto the Father, having loved his own which were in the world, he loved them unto the end' (John 13 : 1). This passage from John 13 is already cited in *Leg. maior*, xiii, 2, with reference to the Stigmatization.

[2] Iulianus de Spira, 'Officium Rhythmicum Sancti Francisci', in *Analecta Franciscana*, x, 378. The *Officium* is datable before 1236. The *Stigmatization* and *Crucifixion* are of course frequently paired together in paintings of the 13th and 14th centuries.

[3] Bonaventura himself says that Jerome had been 'an unbeliever like Thomas' (*Legenda maior*, xv, 4).

[4] Cf. M. R. Fisher, 'Assisi, Padua, and the Boy in the Tree', *The Art Bulletin*, xxxviii (1956), 47 ff.

[5] R. Van Marle, op. cit., v: *Local Schools of Central and Southern Italy* (1925), Fig. 23.

[6] *Tredici Sermoni*, Sermo vi.   [7] *Legenda maior*, Miracula, i, 5.

bearing a phial of blood drawn from the wound in his side, to Pope Gregory IX. The story of the Pope's vision is told in the *Miracula*, where it heads the list of miracles wrought by St. Francis by virtue of the *stigmata*.[1] In the story of the wounded man (Scene XXVI) it is the touch of the *stigmata* upon the man's wounds that effects his cure: this subject follows naturally, therefore, after *The Appearance to Gregory IX* (Scene XXV), with which event it is connected in Bonaventura's text.

The two other miracles represented (Scenes XXVII and XXVIII) seem to have been chosen in order to emphasize St. Francis's power to give succour both in this life and in the life to come. They were among the best known of the miracle-stories, for the first appears again in the *Vita Sancti Francisci* of Jacopo da Voragine,[2] and the second in the *Legenda Choralis Umbra*;[3] they both derive ultimately from the *Tractatus de Miraculis* of Thomas of Celano. Both are stories about liberation from bondage: in the one the beneficiary is a woman, in the other a man. In Scene XXVIII a disciple of St. Francis, Peter of Alifia, is freed by the intervention of the Saint from the prison in which he has been incarcerated on a suspicion of heresy. In Scene XXVII, which is accorded the central position in the bay, a woman of Benevento who has died without making a good confession is liberated by St. Francis from the prison of hell itself; in the words with which the resurrected woman addresses her priest, 'Ego enim mortua duro eram carceri mancipanda, quoniam peccatum, quod tibi pandam, necdum confessa fueram'[4] ('For when I died I was to be confined in a grim prison, because I had not yet confessed the sin that I am about to reveal to you'). It is, then, on a note of triumphant affirmation in the merits of St. Francis, in the supernatural gifts bestowed upon him after his death and ascension, and in the efficacy of his prayers as a mediator between man and God, that the sublime narrative of the *Legend* draws to a close. But before the end one final comparison between St. Francis and Christ is placed before our eyes: in Scene XXVI, as the Saint kneels in supplication before Christ, their communing hands reveal the same wounds (Plate 92*a*).

6. *The Date of the* St. Francis *Cycle*

If the lofty religious symbolism of the *Legend* may be described as its essential language, the vocabulary of that language is a developed naturalism which has misled some writers into proposing a date for the cycle long after the Paduan period of Giotto: its style has even been categorized as 'late-Trecento Giottesque'. That the *Legend* had either been completed or was nearing completion by 1307 is virtually proved by the influence

---

[1] *Legenda maior, Miracula*, i, 2.   [2] Jacobus de Voragine, *Vita Sancti Francisci*, 49.
[3] *Legenda Choralis Umbra, Miracula*, 23. This is a compilation of the mid-thirteenth century.
[4] *Legenda maior, Miracula*, ii, 1.

of the fresco of *The Stigmatization* (Scene XIX) upon the treatment of this subject by Giuliano da Rimini in his Urbania altarpiece (now in the Gardner Museum at Boston), which was painted in that year.[1] This *terminus ante quem* is confirmed by the presence of a still more striking borrowing from the Assisi cycle in an anonymous Umbrian panel dated 1308, the altarpiece of *The Virgin and Child with Angels and Saints* in the church of Santa Maria at Cesi, where the figures of the Virgin and Child are copied from the *Madonna* represented on the iconostasis in Scene XXII of the *Legend*.[2]

Further evidence in support of an early date for the cycle is possibly provided by the representation of the Torre del Comune at Assisi in Scene I (Frontispiece). It is known that the tower was not completed before 1305: thereafter it was heightened and castellated, assuming the elegant proportions we see today (Plate 41); its finished appearance is already recorded in a fresco in S. Damiano at Assisi datable between 1305 and 1315.[3] In the fresco by the St. Cecilia Master in the Upper Church the tower appears as a stunted, uncastellated structure rising little above the roof of the adjacent Palazzo del Capitano del Popolo, and it has been argued that the artist did not know it in its finished state. However, in view of the imaginative treatment of the Temple of Minerva in the same fresco and of the Column of Trajan in Scene XXVIII (Plate 93), it cannot be taken for granted that the St. Cecilia Master would have been interested in the accurate rendering of a particular building or monument.

The commencement of the *St. Francis* cycle is usually placed within the last years of the thirteenth century, and sometimes as early as 1295 or 1296. The chief difficulty in accepting so early a date lies in the necessity of allowing sufficient time for the immediately preceding phase in the decoration of the Upper Church. As we have seen, a plausible *terminus post quem* for the execution of the *Isaac* group of frescoes is provided by the ceiling frescoes of the *Four Doctors* at the east end of the nave. The possible connection between these frescoes and the Decretals of 1297 has already been mentioned. As the substance of the Decretals had already been communicated by the Pope to the Dominicans and to the Archbishop of Rheims in two Bulls of September 1295, it may be that their contents had been made known to the Franciscans a little before the new decree became absolute throughout the Church in the year 1297. If, then, we are to assume that the *Four Doctors* were painted during the pontificate of Boniface VIII (1294–1303), and that the decoration of this part of the ceiling immediately preceded the completion of the Biblical cycles by the Isaac Master and his associates, it becomes impossible to date the *Isaac* group before the middle 1290s. On these grounds a date nearer the year 1300 for the *St. Francis* cycle must appear more plausible. Unfortunately, however, the

---

[1] J. White, 'The Date of *The Legend of St. Francis* at Assisi', *The Burlington Magazine*, xcviii (1956), 344 ff.

[2] M. Meiss, *Giotto and Assisi* (New York, 1960), pp. 3 f.

[3] P. Leone Bracaloni, O.F.M., 'Assisi Medioevale: Studio Storico-Topografico', *Archivum Franciscanum Historicum*, vii, 3 ff.

connection with the Decretals of 1297 remains speculative, since before that date the cult of the Doctors had unofficial recognition.

The only certain *terminus post quem* for the *Legend* is the date 1291 deducible from the iconography of one of the frescoes in the Upper Church, *The Dream of Innocent III* (Scene VI, Plate 52). It can be shown that the representation in this fresco of St. Francis supporting the Lateran basilica was adapted in its iconography to the extensive rebuilding of the Lateran portico by Nicholas IV (1288–92).[1] Regrettably, damage to the fresco has destroyed much of the building as the Assisi painter represented it, but what remains conforms to two sixteenth-century accounts of the portico which describe the mosaic decorations, including the heads in the frieze. The emphasis in the fresco upon the portico itself, which is the part of the building that St. Francis actually supports, makes a break, as far as we can tell, with earlier iconographic tradition, and it is significant that an inscription of 1291 inside the Lateran church connects the work of rebuilding undertaken by Nicholas IV with the story of Innocent III's dream that he saw St. Francis supporting the church and preventing it from falling. Nicholas IV was the first Franciscan pope, and it is evident that he regarded his work at the Lateran as the fulfilment of a prophecy. Moreover, shortly after his election, he issued a Bull, dated 14 May 1288, in favour of further expenditure on the Franciscan basilica at Assisi, including whatever might be required for the decoration of the church. It has therefore been concluded that *The Dream of Innocent III* in the Upper Church must be dated shortly after the year 1288, and probably about 1291 (the date of the Lateran inscription) or slightly later.[2] But on stylistic grounds alone there are strong arguments against so early a dating for the cycle. And if the cycle was not, after all, executed during the pontificate of Nicholas IV, we may have to find some additional reason for so precise a depiction of the Lateran basilica.

It would be dogmatic to assert that the impulse of stylistic development would not have been sufficient in itself to account for this vivid evocation of an actual building (even in terms of the curiously 'abstracted' architecture preferred by the painters of the *Legend*); but it is possible that other factors entered in. Nicholas IV would naturally have been remembered both as the first Franciscan to become pope and as the benefactor of the Sacro Convento: yet it was not until the pontificate of Boniface VIII that the Lateran church assumed a place of special importance in the religious life of the Franciscan Order. At the General Chapter held at Lyons in 1299 and presided over by the Minister-General Giovanni da Murrovalle (who according to Vasari commissioned Giotto to paint the *St. Francis* cycle), observance of the Feast of the Dedication of the Lateran Basilica was made obligatory throughout the Order, and a rubric to that effect

[1] Peter Murray, 'Notes on Some Early Giotto Sources', *Journal of the Warburg and Courtauld Institutes*, xvi (1953), 58 ff.   [2] Ibid., pp. 72 f.

was inserted in the liturgy.[1] The decree was reaffirmed at the Chapter of Genoa of 1302.[2] This addition to the Franciscan liturgy would undoubtedly have given further point to an unmistakable representation of the basilica in a painting of the Dream of Innocent III; and although the evidence is no more than suggestive it is in conformity with other arguments favouring a date for the *Legend* closer to the year 1300.

There is even a possibility that the cycle was executed at about the same time that Giotto was engaged in decorating the Arena Chapel at Padua. The Arena frescoes are datable with reasonable certainty within the years 1303–6,[3] and although it may well be that the Assisi cycle was begun before them it is possible that the two enterprises overlapped. A General Chapter of the Franciscan Order was held at Assisi in 1304, and perhaps it was required that the decoration of the Upper Church should be completed by then. On such matters we can only speculate; but there is one iconographical argument which, if correct, would make it certain that at least Scene XXIII (*St. Francis Mourned by St. Clare*, Plate 83) was painted after Giotto had begun work in the Arena Chapel.

As we have observed, the Assisi fresco includes the figure of a boy climbing a tree (Plate 96). A similar figure, in an almost identical attitude, appears in *The Entry into Jerusalem* in the Arena Chapel, and the question at once is raised of the possible dependence of one of these two compositions upon the other.[4] While the motif of the 'boy in the tree' is traditional in scenes of the Entry into Jerusalem, there was no such iconographic tradition for the Franciscan scene, which was an entirely new subject for painters. Nevertheless, in telling the story of the lament of the Poor Clares and of the bearing home of the body of St. Francis, Bonaventura implicitly suggests a comparison with Christ's triumphant entry into Jerusalem, and his words are plainly reminiscent of the appropriate passage in the Gospel of Matthew: 'When morning came', he tells us, 'the crowds that had come together, carrying branches of trees and many wax lights, brought the holy body to the city of Assisi.'[5] We may compare St. Matthew (21 : 8): 'And the most part of the multitude spread their garments in the way; and others cut branches from the trees, and spread them in the way.' The Assisi master has grasped the analogy between the two stories, which was already indicated in his literary source, and has proceeded to translate the comparison into pictorial terms by adapting to his subject an iconographical motif proper to representations of the Biblical scene.

[1] P. M. Giuseppe Abate, O.F.M., 'Memoriali, Statuti ed Atti di Capitoli Generali dei Frati Minori dei Secoli XIII e XIV', *Miscellanea Francescana*, xxxiii (1933), 29.

[2] Idem, 'Memoriali, Statuti ed Atti di Capitoli Generali dei Frati Minori', *Miscellanea Francescana*, xxxv (1935), 237. In one codex listing the statutes of the Chapter of Lyons (1299) the ordinance regarding the Feast of the Dedication of the Lateran Basilica is given as a statute of the Chapter of Genoa (1302).

[3] See especially Meiss, *Giotto and Assisi*, p. 4; Gioseffi, op. cit., pp. 35, 114 ff.

[4] M. R. Fisher, op. cit., 47 ff. Gioseffi (op. cit., p. 105) feels that the figure at Padua is less convincing than the Assisi figure, and argues that in the Arena Chapel Giotto was merely repeating an image that he had first introduced into Scene XXIII of the *St. Francis* cycle (of which, according to Gioseffi, he was the author).

[5] *Legenda maior*, xv, 5.

Yet Giotto's 'boy in the tree' is of an unprecedented type, being shown from the back, whereas in all previous representations that are known such figures are always seen from the front or side. It has been well said that 'the figure has been altered by an innovating intelligence, which transforms a rather standard iconographical detail into something very new';[1] and this is precisely the kind of visual experimentation in which the Arena Chapel abounds. At Assisi the 'boy in the tree' is again seen from the back, and since an innovation of this nature is most likely to have taken place within the iconographical tradition to which it properly belongs—namely, in a scene of the Entry into Jerusalem—the natural inference is that the Arena fresco was painted before the composition in the Upper Church, and that Giotto's design was known to the Assisi painter. A weakness in the argument is that the Padua figure may repeat an image first evolved by Giotto in some earlier composition now lost to us. Nevertheless, we should not expect such an innovation before the early years of the new century.

Further, the developed naturalism of the frescoes on the south wall at Assisi and their close stylistic relationship with the *St. Peter Enthroned* (Plate 40) at S. Simone, which must belong to the immediate following of the St. Cecilia Master, and which bears the date 1307, make it difficult to remove the frescoes too far from that year. It is equally suggestive that the *Madonna* represented in Scene XXII seems to reflect the influence of the statue of the *Madonna and Child* executed by Arnolfo di Cambio for Florence Cathedral (Plate 37c, d). Arnolfo is recorded as *capomaestro* at Santa Reparata in 1300. The foundation stone of the new building had been laid some years before—in September 1296—and it can reasonably be assumed that the *Madonna* and Arnolfo's other sculptural work for the façade were executed between that date and the year 1302, by which time he appears to have been no longer alive. Once again, therefore, a date closer to 1300 seems to be indicated. It must, however, be emphasized that the question is still an open one: what is important is that by the years around 1300 we are confronted with a style that makes its own decisive break with the *maniera greca*.

7. *The Execution of the* St. Francis *Cycle: Technical Procedures and Chronology*

It was normally the practice, in decorating the nave of a church, for the painter and his assistants to begin work in the area of the altar, moving back along both walls towards the lower end: this method of working would have allowed the altar to be freed as soon as possible for the conduct of services. The evidence, however, that has been brought to light by the technical examination of the *St. Francis* frescoes undertaken by Tintori and Meiss shows that this procedure was not adopted in the execution of the cycle in the Upper Church.[2] By examining the joins between adjacent patches of the

---

[1] M. R. Fisher, op. cit., p. 52. For the history of this motif cf. G. Millet, *Recherches sur l'iconographie de l'Évangile* (Paris, 1916), pp. 281 ff.   [2] Tintori and Meiss, op. cit., pp. 43 ff.

intonaco in the *St. Francis* frescoes Tintori and Meiss have been able to determine, with a remarkable degree of accuracy, the successive stages in the execution of each scene and of groups of scenes within their respective bays. The evidence regarding the chronology of adjacent bays is less conclusive, since the joins on the plaster of the columns that divide one bay from another are rougher than those elsewhere, and it is not usually clear from adjacent patches which overlies the other.[1] Nevertheless, the total evidence supports the conclusion that the first fresco to be painted was Scene II, and that thereafter the painters executed the frescoes (with the exception of Scene I) in their narrative order, working in a generally clockwise direction around the three walls of the nave. There were, however, certain variations in this procedure, especially where work was being carried out on more than one fresco at the same time.

The distribution of the *intonaco* patches suggests that the scaffolding upon which the painters stood supported three platforms on different levels, and that the scaffolding may have been wide enough to embrace three or even four scenes. In all probability, therefore, it would have been possible throughout the operation for work to proceed simultaneously on separate areas of the same fresco and on more than one scene in any one bay. In all fresco-painting, however, the general movement is necessarily downward, since the completion of the upper areas before the lower parts of the composition avoids the dripping of paint upon newly finished passages. This consideration apart, there is a natural tendency for a painter to work from left to right (as in writing), and this was the normal rule at Assisi: but certain interesting exceptions to it are to be found.

It would have been difficult, if not impossible, to undertake a work of fresco-decoration as elaborate as the *St. Francis* cycle in the Upper Church, in which so much depended upon intricate relationships of form, without some recourse to compositional drawings giving (perhaps in considerable detail) the design of each scene and its place in the whole scheme. Such drawings would presumably have been prepared by the *capomaestro* in consultation with a theological adviser at the Sacro Convento or in Rome. It would seem logical to suppose that this master was the author of Scene II, the first fresco to be painted. The only real alternative would be to assume the presence from the beginning not so much of a single master surrounded by a band of assistants as of a number of associates of perhaps equal status. The chief difficulty inherent in this hypothesis lies in the presence in the cycle of definite breaks in the continuity of style, where one

---

[1] Tintori and Meiss, op. cit., p. 45. More recently Tintori and Meiss have pointed out that it would have been possible to attempt to provide more complete evidence about the sequence of bays only by the use of micro-photographs, 'difficult to make and difficult to read': cf. L. Tintori and M. Meiss, 'Additional Observations on Italian Mural Technique', *Art Bulletin*, xlvi (1964), 380, note 11. Gioseffi (op. cit., pp. 112 ff.) rejects the conclusion of Tintori and Meiss regarding the sequence of bays, arguing that the evidence of the *intonaco* patches proves only that the painters worked from left to right in individual bays. Gioseffi suggests that the work proceeded, bay by bay, from the entrance to the west end of the nave, and he thus explains the St. Cecilia Master's intervention in the execution both of the fourth bay on the south wall and of the corresponding bay on the north wall, when he was brought in to complete the cycle.

painter apparently disappears from the scene and another takes his place: that is to say, the total evidence strongly favours the view that the three principal authors of the *Legend* worked in the Upper Church in succession, rather than simultaneously.

According to the findings of Tintori and Meiss, the decoration was begun with the painting of the illusionistic cornice above Scene II, and thence with its continuation, to left and right, along the whole width of the bay (Plate 3*a*). As elsewhere in the cycle, this initial stage corresponded to the highest level of the scaffolding. The area thus covered included a narrow strip of sky[1] at the top of each of the three scenes, the sky being everywhere finished *a secco* in azurite over a grey fresco preparation. Next, the remainder of the sky in Scene II was prepared, together with the little town on the left and the church on the right. The column on the left was executed along with the scene itself, and therefore by this stage about half of the column, including the capital, had been completed. The next parts to be painted were the remainder of the hill on the left, the haloed head of St. Francis, and the hill on the right, the three areas being executed in succession. It is possible that at this point attention was given to the painting of the architectural forms in the upper half of Scene III, together with the adjacent parts of the fictive columns on either side. The general organization of the bay as a whole, except for Scene I, would thus have been established around its focal point, the head of St. Francis at the centre of Scene II: work might even have been begun immediately upon the uppermost areas of the following bay. All that remained to be done in Scene II, apart from a narrow strip at the very bottom which was left until later, was the painting of the foreground areas, including the horse, the body of St. Francis together with the cloak which he offers to the impoverished nobleman, the head and body of the nobleman, and the small hillock on the far right: this operation occupied five *giornate*, one of which was devoted to the nobleman's head. The painting of Scene I, of which only the topmost strip of *intonaco* and perhaps its overlying wash of azurite had as yet been attended to, was for some reason delayed: a possible reason is that the iconostasis, which until recent times spanned the nave from the top of Scene I to the corresponding point in Scene XXVIII (see Plate 1*a*), may not yet have been fixed in position.[2]

Except in the case of Scenes I and XIII, it was the rule on the north wall to leave the painting of a narrow strip of foreground at the bottom of each composition until the remainder of every scene in the bay in question had been completed. The painting of this lower strip, together with the corbel-table and its tapestry hangings, formed the final operation in the decoration of the bay. Thus in the third bay (Plate 3*b*), for example, the foreground of Scene IV (*The Miracle of the Crucifix*), which is the first fresco in the bay, was painted after the completion of the figures and architecture in Scene VI (*The Dream of Innocent III*), save those small portions—such as the Saint's left foot and the

---

[1] Its lower edge can be clearly seen in Plate 42 (near the church spire).   [2] G. Gnudi, *Giotto* (Milan, 1958), p. 66.

bases of the columns of the papal palace—that extend into the foreground of that scene. In the same way it would have been feasible for the uppermost strip, containing the entablature and part of the sky, to have been executed in advance of the scenes below, provided that the composition of each individual scene was known. The lower edge of this upper strip often defines some feature of the design, such as the position of St. Francis's halo in Scene VIII, *The Vision of the Chariot* (Plates 4a, 55), or the pinnacles of the green building and the canopy of the throne in Scene XI, *St. Francis before the Sultan* (Plates 4b, 61). Since this strip never itself contains figures or architectural forms, there is no reason why it should not have been entrusted to the care of assistants who could have proceeded with this journeyman's labour independently of the masters working on more important tasks below them. On the south wall, however, there were certain differences in the procedure, the most important of which was the abandonment of the earlier practice of executing the foregrounds along with the console-table and tapestry hangings. In the scenes on the south wall, therefore, the lowest *intonaco* patches are always contiguous with the lower edge of the composition: as all the patches that comprise the structure of each composition are confined within the pictured area, the painting of the console-table, with its tapestries, became an entirely separate operation.

The *giornate* throughout the decoration (apart from the *Madonna and Angels* on the east wall) have been fully tabulated and interpreted by Tintori and Meiss.[1] It is not necessary at this stage to examine their evidence further, except perhaps to draw attention to one other feature of the decoration of the south wall. It is interesting to find that in beginning their work in the first bay (Plate 6a) the painters fixed the position of the central painted column—that is to say, the column that separates Scenes XVII and XVIII —before proceeding with the first two compositions in the bay (Scenes XVI and XVII): in executing the topmost areas, containing the entablature and the narrow strip of sky, they moved outwards from the centre of the bay, working in a leftward direction in Scenes XVI and XVII. Moreover, the whole of the architecture in the top half of Scene XVII, above the tapestry represented at the back of the papal hall, was almost certainly completed before work continued on the figures in the preceding scene. Thus the procedure in the initiation of the decoration on the north wall was perhaps not quite as exceptional as it might first appear: there too the decoration had commenced at the centre of the opening bay; a decision that might seem entirely logical in itself. Nevertheless, an important difference between the two cases must be allowed, if it is assumed that Scene I was painted at much the same time as the last three compositions in the cycle, Scenes XXVI–XXVIII. As has long been recognized, these four frescoes, which show a common style, are the work of the great *anonimo* whom we know from his

---

[1] The reader interested in studying in greater detail the technical procedures adopted in the Upper Church is referred to the diagrams published by Tintori and Meiss and to the accompanying commentaries.

Santa Cecilia altarpiece (Plate 8) in the Uffizi as the St. Cecilia Master;[1] and the conclusions reached by Tintori and Meiss support the generally accepted view that the St. Cecilia Master's frescoes in the Upper Church were the last scenes in the cycle to be executed.[2] The inference is that for a long period of time the space reserved for Scene I remained vacant.

Unfortunately we possess no information that would throw light upon the reason for the postponement of the painting of this scene. Was it because work on the iconostasis had not been finished? Or was this scene reserved for the St. Cecilia Master by the terms of the commission? Or did it replace an earlier fresco by the author of Scene II, which for some reason was found to be unsatisfactory? Was it perhaps only at a late stage in the execution of the cycle that the idea was conceived of setting the opening narrative in the Piazza del Comune, and so glorifying the city of Assisi? To these questions there is no certain answer; but they raise problems to which it will be necessary to return.

8. *The Stylistic Character of the* St. Francis *Cycle*

Until comparatively recently our picture of the development of late Dugento and early Trecento painting was a grossly oversimplified one, and it is still easy to think too rigidly in terms of such major personalities as Cavallini in Rome, Duccio in Siena, and Giotto in Florence. What the early histories disguised was the complexity of the artistic currents of the period. At the same time increasing knowledge has only revealed the depths of our ignorance: we have records of a large number of contemporary masters whose work no longer survives or is no longer identifiable; and the *anonimi* of the period are legion. Indeed, the Sacro Convento at Assisi itself called into its service several great

[1] For the St. Cecilia Master see especially R. Offner, *A Corpus of Florentine Painting*, III, i (1931), and W. Suida, 'Einige florentinische Maler aus der Zeit des Übergangs vom Duecento ins Trecento', *Jahrbuch der K. Preuß. Kunstsamml.*, ii (1905), 89 ff. As early as 1791 Della Valle had expressed the doubt whether all the frescoes in the cycle could be ascribed to Giotto: cf. *Vite de' Più Eccellenti Pittori, Scultori ed Architetti Scritte da M. Giorgio Vasari*, ed. Guglielmo della Valle, ii (1791), 80, n. 3. In 1864 Cavalcaselle recognized that the first fresco and the concluding scenes of the Assisi cycle were by the same painter, attributing to this master, besides Scene I, Scenes XXIV–XXVIII: cf. J. A. Crowe and G. B. Cavalcaselle, *A New History of Painting in Italy* (London, 1964–6), i, 219, 227, 235. In 1875, in the Italian edition of this work, Cavalcaselle identified in these scenes the stylistic characteristics of the *Santa Cecilia* altarpiece (*Storia della Pittura in Italia dal Secolo II al Secolo XVI* (Florence, 1875–87), i, 313 f.). Today there is general agreement with Offner's attribution to the St. Cecilia Master of only Scene I and Scenes XXVI–XXVIII: cf. R. Offner, 'A great Madonna by the St. Cecilia Master', *The Burlington Magazine*, l (1927), 97. There has, however, been a tendency among some writers who still accept Giotto's authorship of the majority of the frescoes to credit Giotto himself with the painting of Scene I: see, for instance, Enzo Carli, *I Grandi Maestri del Trecento Toscano* (1955); E. Cecchi, op. cit., where the fresco is ascribed to 'Giotto and assistants'; and Gnudi, op. cit. This position is manifestly so untenable that it scarcely requires refutation.

[2] My earlier hypothesis that the St. Cecilia Master initiated the decoration and that the work proceeded in the accustomed manner along both side walls, from the altar end of the nave towards the entrance, must therefore be abandoned (*The Burlington Magazine*, cii (1960), 405 ff. and 431 ff.). The new evidence does not, however, affect my insistence upon the intimate connections between the St. Cecilia Master's style and that of the main author of the cycle.

painters whose identities remain obscure, including the authors of the *Franciscan Allegories* in the choir of the Lower Church, the New Testament scenes and the *Miracles of St. Francis* nearby, the Giottesque decorations in the Magdalen Chapel, and the *St. Nicholas* cycle in the Cappella Orsini. All these works are datable within the first quarter of the fourteenth century, and the *St. Nicholas* frescoes were certainly in existence by the year 1307.[1] The double church at Assisi not only reveals the successive stages and some of the variations in the evolution of a new pictorial treatment of the visible world, but also brings home to us the fact that this revolution in the art of seeing was the work of many minds.

It is therefore futile to suggest, as it has often been suggested, that only a Giotto could have conceived so original a work as the *Legend*. Moreover, it is questionable whether the character of the cycle would have been substantially different if Giotto had never lived, for it shows no essential dependence upon his vision. On the other hand many of the artistic principles that are fundamental to the *Legend* and many of the formal idioms that are most typical of it are already seen at a developed stage in a number of paintings of the late thirteenth and early fourteenth century which seem to stand mainly outside the Giottesque tradition.

Not the least important of these works is the great Crucifix at Santa Maria Novella in Florence (Plate 12*a*), at one time accepted as the cross commissioned for the church from Giotto in the year 1312, but attributable rather to an anonymous painter who evidently had close contacts with the St. Cecilia Master and who was possibly the author of the well-known *Madonna* at S. Giorgio alla Costa (Plate 15*b*).[2] It has long been recognized that the crucifix (Plates 12*b*, 82) represented on the iconostasis of the Portiuncula church in Scene XXII of the *Legend* (*The Verification of the Stigmata*) closely resembles the crucifix at Santa Maria Novella, and owing to the confusion over the authorship of the latter work this resemblance has been adduced as evidence of Giotto's authorship of the Assisi cycle. Once, however, the Santa Maria Novella Cross is detached from Giotto's *œuvre* and recognized for what it is, the same evidence leads in a quite different direction, and the similarity of the *Madonna* (Plate 15*b*) at S. Giorgio alla Costa to the fresco of the *Madonna and Child* (Plates 5, 16*a*) on the east wall at Assisi is no less suggestive. As we shall see, there are also reflections of the style of the *St. Francis* cycle in the work of that still-neglected master Pacino di Bonaguida.

These affinities raise the question whether the cycle as a whole, so far from belonging to the world of Giotto, is not rather to be related to that independent development in Florentine painting in our knowledge of which we owe so much to the pioneering

[1] Meiss, op. cit., pp. 3 f.

[2] For the Santa Maria Novella Cross, cf. R. Offner, *Corpus*, III, vi (1956), 3 ff. Offner ascribed the S. Giorgio *Madonna* to the same hand (ibid., loc. cit.), having previously attributed it to the St. Cecilia Master (ibid., III, i (1931), 32). It is questionable, however, whether the two works show an absolute identity of style.

investigations of the late Richard Offner.[1] The *Legend* abounds in stylistic features that are especially characteristic of this group of painters, from the fundamental principles of design to the treatment of the human figure, of architecture, and of landscape forms. Among these painters, according to Offner's reconstruction, the mysterious St. Cecilia Master emerges as the dominant personality, but to what extent he may be regarded as the founder of a style and to what extent he simply contributed to a general tendency must remain in considerable doubt, especially in view of the impossibility of giving to more than a few of the works assigned by Offner to this stylistic group even a very approximate date. It is questionable, for example, whether the author of the Santa Maria Novella Cross, which was evidently painted before 1302 and probably within the last years of the thirteenth century, is to be considered as precisely the St. Cecilia Master's pupil: he may rather have been an artist of the same generation, with perhaps a similar or identical training, whose relation to the St. Cecilia Master resembled (let us say) that of Titian to Giorgione.

One of the most suggestive of the stylistic certainties bearing upon the Assisi problem is the presence in the Upper Church of the St. Cecilia Master himself, as one of the painters of the cycle, and, beyond that, the apparent adherence of the various masters who helped to execute the frescoes to a common artistic tradition. The St. Cecilia Master's four frescoes at Assisi (Scene I and Scenes XXVI–XXVIII) are closely related, although not identical, in style to his most important painting on panel, the *Santa Cecilia* altarpiece in the Uffizi (Plate 8), a work commissioned for the church of Santa Cecilia in Florence, presumably before the year 1304, when the church was gutted by the great fire which swept through the city. Most of the St. Cecilia Master's works were painted for churches in or near Florence, but the only frescoes certainly by him are those at Assisi. His impact upon Florentine painting in the early fourteenth century is shown by the number of his followers, who included, in addition to a host of *anonimi*, such masters as Pacino di Bonaguida, Jacopo del Casentino, and Bernardo Daddi.[2] It is tempting to speculate upon the identity of so influential a master, and the place that he seems to fill in the history of Florentine painting has given rise to the suggestion that he was none other than the celebrated Buonamico Buffalmacco who figures in some of the *novelle* of Boccaccio and Sacchetti, and whom Ghiberti eulogizes in the *Commentarii* as one of the greatest artists of his age.[3] If there are crucial difficulties inherent in this

[1] The scepticism recently expressed by Professor White about the validity of Offner's reconstruction of this non-Giottesque tendency in Florentine painting does not seem to me to be soundly based, although the question is worth raising (cf. J. White, *Art and Architecture in Italy . . .*, pp. 258 f.).

[2] Cf. Offner, *Corpus*, III, i (New York, 1931), xxxv ff., and III, ii (1930), 1 ff.

[3] A. Venturi, *Storia dell'arte italiana* (Milan, 1901–48), v (1907), 290; O. Sirén, 'The Buffalmacco Hypothesis: Some Additional Remarks', *The Burlington Magazine*, xxxvii (1920), 183. A bibliography of works relating to this question, a summary of the relevant documents, and a list of past attributions to Buffalmacco are given in Offner, *Corpus*, III, i, 41 ff. See below, p. 258, note 1.

hypothesis (notably the irreconcilability of his style with that of the one surviving work among those ascribed to Buonamico by Ghiberti—the much-damaged fresco-cycle in the Badia at Settimo), the St. Cecilia Master was undoubtedly a painter worthy of Ghiberti's encomiums, and he reveals himself at Assisi as one of the supreme masters of fresco in the history of early Italian painting.

His four frescoes in the Upper Church exhibit a quality of elegance and refinement which is approached elsewhere in the cycle only in some of the scenes on the south wall. Their miniaturist delicacy presents a forcible contrast to the more 'monumental' style prevalent on the north wall, where the forms are more largely conceived and the drawing and modelling less subtle. Nevertheless, all the frescoes in the cycle clearly belong to the same stylistic family, whatever the variations from one part of the decoration to another, and in many respects the main author of the frescoes on the north and east walls—the 'Giotto' of the Vasarian tradition—shows much closer stylistic affinities with the St. Cecilia Master than with the real Giotto of the Arena Chapel in Padua. It is not enough to attempt to explain such affinities merely in terms of the St. Cecilia Master's compliance at Assisi with a specific programme; and Offner's view that the St. Cecilia Master's style was largely formed by his experience at Assisi, as the artist called in to complete the *St. Francis* cycle, is open to the objection that he clearly arrived in the Upper Church as an already mature and practised master whose technical proficiency in fresco-painting was in fact superior to that of any of the other painters employed there.

The question can be put in another way. The resemblances between the fresco of the *Madonna and Child* on the east wall of the Upper Church (Plate 16a) and the altarpiece of the *Madonna Enthroned* at S. Giorgio alla Costa (Plate 15b) have frequently been pointed out, and their common authorship—accepted as axiomatic by most scholars who see Giotto's hand in the *St. Francis* cycle—has also been proposed by others who refuse both works to Giotto. There can be no doubt that Offner was correct in denying all possibility of Giotto's authorship of the S. Giorgio panel and in placing it within the milieu of the St. Cecilia Master, and the same considerations must apply to the frescoed *Madonna*, if we accept the common authorship of the two works. Even if we do not, the Assisi *Madonna* still has a much closer resemblance to the type of *Madonna* produced in the St. Cecilia Master's circle (see Plate 15a) than to any *Madonna* by Giotto. The relationship already touched upon between the *St. Francis* cycle and the Santa Maria Novella Cross seems to lead to similar conclusions. Furthermore, a connection of some kind between the main author of the cycle and the St. Cecilia Master would go some way to account for the latter's presence in Assisi as one of the painters entrusted with the execution of the frescoes.

It is clear that the stylistic origins of the *Legend* lie very largely in Rome—the Rome of

Pietro Cavallini and Arnolfo di Cambio. The Roman training of at least its principal authors is reflected not only in a fundamental indebtedness to Cavallini but also in such reminiscences of the city of Rome as the representations of the Lateran Basilica in *The Dream of Innocent III* (Scene VI) and Trajan's Column in *The Liberation of the Prisoner* (Scene XXVIII). The *baldacchino* (Plate 37*a*) in *The Christmas Crib at Greccio* (Scene XIII) closely resembles Arnolfo's *ciborium* (Plate 37*b*) at S. Paolo fuori le mura, while the columned parapet or loggia surmounting the house in *The Death of the Knight of Celano* (Scene XVI, Plates 10*c*, 70) recalls the balustraded superstructure of the Fieschi Monument in S. Lorenzo fuori le mura[1] (Cavallini had introduced a similar structure into one of his frescoes at S. Paolo[2]). The lavish use of Cosmati-work in many of the representations of buildings in the Assisi cycle indicates no less clearly the Roman orientation of its style.

At the same time many of the architectural structures in the *Legend* are quite manifestly inventions of a highly imaginative and even fantastic nature, and seem to have no known precedents in earlier painting, unless after all the *Santa Cecilia* altarpiece predates the Assisi cycle; for here certainly there are close parallels with the architectural taste reflected in the cycle as a whole and with other aspects of its style.[3] The pilasters and voluted consoles supporting the jutting roof of the Knight of Celano's house (Scene XVI, Plate 10*c*) may be compared, for instance, with the similar features that dominate the seventh compartment of the altarpiece (*St. Cecilia before the Prefect Almachius*, Plate 10*a*). Again, the construction of the papal hall in *The Sanctioning of the Rule* (Scene VII, Plate 53) has various features in common with that of the lofty rooms represented in the second and fifth scenes of the altarpiece (*St. Cecilia urges Valerian to Conversion* and *The Baptism of Tiburtius*, Plates 8, 81), and in each case the architecture has the function of imposing the same kind of geometric order upon the composition, creating an ideal space for the figures. The fifth scene on the altarpiece (Plate 81) may also be set alongside the fresco on the south wall of *The Vision of the Ascension of St. Francis* (Scene XXI, Plate 80). The two compositions have more in common than certain architectural forms reduced to much the same degree of abstraction: more fundamentally, these forms establish clear-cut divisions within the picture-space, which define the fields reserved for the various figures. Within these fields the human actors remain for ever fixed, and here we touch upon one of the essential differences between the compositional principles that underlie the *St. Francis* cycle as a whole and Giotto's own practice in the Arena Chapel, where the designs are compounded of fluent rhythms of form, and where mass is weighed against mass in a free space.

[1] D. Gioseffi, *Giotto architetto*, p. 30, Fig. 24*a*, *b*.

[2] Cf. J. White, 'Cavallini and the Lost Frescoes in S. Paolo', *Journal of the Warburg and Courtauld Institutes*, xix (1956), 84 ff., Fig. 25*d* ('Devotional Scene').

[3] A. Smart, 'The St. Cecilia Master and his School at Assisi', *The Burlington Magazine*, cii (1960), 405 ff. and 431 ff.

Although on the north wall of the Upper Church, after Scene I, and especially in the second and third bays, there is an almost invariable tendency towards a massiveness of form untypical of the St. Cecilia Master, the treatment of the human figure in the cycle as a whole conforms to conventions that are still closer to his own than to those of Giotto in the Arena Chapel. Thus the bystander who raises his right hand in surprise in *The Christmas Crib at Greccio* (Scene XIII, Plate 63) would scarcely seem out of place in one of the St. Cecilia Master's frescoes in the Upper Church, such as *The Homage of a Simple Man of Assisi* (Scene I, Frontispiece), while the guest who rises from the table (Plate 38b) in *The Death of the Knight of Celano* (Scene XVI) could almost be a parody of the refined gentleman (Plate 38a) standing immediately behind St. Francis in Scene I and turning to converse with a companion. Further along the south wall, the nun represented in full face within the central doorway of the church (Plate 84a) in Scene XXIII (*St. Francis Mourned by St. Clare*) approaches still nearer to the 'Cecilian' type, and the configuration of her features corresponds very closely to the same figure in Scene I and to the angel in Scene XXVI (Plate 84b). Indeed, the transitions within the cycle from one style to another are the less abrupt on account of such resemblances. It is this harmony that lends a general unity to the frescoes in the opening bay, and which surely accounts in large measure for the fact that even today many proponents of Giotto's authorship of the greater part of the cycle also see his hand in Scene I.

When we compare the *Legend* at Assisi with Giotto's frescoes at Padua, we become aware that the figures represented in the Upper Church do not *behave* like those in the Arena cycle. The Assisi figures express themselves in nervous, *staccato* gestures somewhat akin to the vocabulary of a sign-language, much as we find in the Uffizi and Montici altarpieces of the St. Cecilia Master and in the manuscript illuminations of Pacino di Bonaguida, but as we never find in the authentic work of Giotto, where the articulation of the figure is invariably smooth and flowing and the gestures largely conceived and often magisterial in character. The gestures, for instance, that are given to St. Cecilia in the fifth compartment of the Uffizi altarpiece (*The Baptism of Tiburtius*, Plate 81), to St. Francis in Scene I of the *Legend* (by the St. Cecilia Master (Frontispiece)), and to the friar on the extreme left in Scene XXI (*The Vision of the Ascension of St. Francis*, Plate 80) all conform to the same pattern, which is characterized by the crossing of the right arm over the left, in such a way that the right hand sticks out at an abrupt angle from the body: it is a gesture that seems eloquent of a sudden thought, which awakens a quick bodily response.[1] A similar gesture distinguishes the figure of St. Francis (Plate 16b) in *The Sermon to the Birds* (Scene XV) from Giotto's figure (Plate 27b) in his version of the same subject on the predella of the Louvre *Stigmatization*; and it is with such gestures that one figure discourses with another in the Assisi cycle as a whole, however much the

---

[1] A. Smart, 'Reflections on the Art of Giotto', *Apollo*, lxxxi (1965), 263.

proportioning and general treatment may vary from one part of the decoration to another—from the massive forms found in areas of the north wall to the more delicate forms prevalent on the south wall.

The stylistic variations within the cycle will be studied in due course, and it is desirable at this point to indicate only their main divisions. It is clear that the principal painter of Scenes II and III, on the north wall, was also chiefly responsible for the frescoes in the following bay (Scenes IV–VI). Here it may be noted that nowhere on the north wall, after Scene I, does the style of the decoration approach more closely to that of the St. Cecilia Master than in the opening bay: in Scene III (*The Vision of the Palace*, Plate 45) the lofty room on the left, crowned by a diminutive storey, more strongly resembles the rooms represented by the St. Cecilia Master in the opposite bay (Scenes XXVI and XXVII, Plates 90, 91) than any of the other interiors included in scenes on the north wall, where the structural elements are lacking in the same elegance of proportioning; while the buildings (Plate 10*d*) outside the city wall in Scene II (*The Gift of the Mantle*), with their cube-like simplifications of form, recur in the second scene (*St. Margaret Brought before Olybrius*, Plate 10*b*) of the *Santa Margherita* altarpiece (Plate 9), although it should be borne in mind that this work may be very considerably later in date than the *St. Francis* cycle.[1]

The general uniformity of the style of the architectural forms which dominate the compositions in the three succeeding bays (Scenes IV–XIII) indicates the controlling hand of one master, who was unquestionably the painter in charge of the execution of Scenes II and III. This painter, whom it is convenient to refer to as the 'St. Francis Master', therefore initiated the great enterprise with the painting of Scene II, and his control over the succeeding phases of the work would seem to have continued into at least the first stages in the decoration of the south wall. But by the time of the execution of the second bay on the north wall (Scenes VII–IX) the intervention of other hands is increasingly noticeable in the figures. Several painters, for example, worked together on Scene VII (*The Sanctioning of the Rule*, Plate 53); another would seem to appear for the first time in Scene VIII (*The Vision of the Chariot*, Plate 55), being responsible for the standing friars and perhaps for other parts of this fresco, and the same artist goes on to paint the kneeling friar (Plate 57*c*) in Scene IX (*The Vision of the Thrones*); the Sultan and his retinue in Scene XI (*St. Francis before the Sultan*, Plate 61), together with the figure of Christ in Scene XII (*The Ecstasy of St. Francis*, Plate 62), disclose the presence of yet another assistant, or possibly two; while the friars in Scene XII and the bystanders in Scene XIII (*The Christmas Crib at Greccio*, Plate 63) are treated with a refinement that distinguishes them from any of the figures represented in Scenes II–XI, although this

[1] For the *Santa Margherita* altarpiece, cf. Offner, *Corpus*, III, i, 36 ff., and Giulia Sinibaldi and Giulia Brunetti, op. cit., pp. 389 ff. The altarpiece is generally regarded as a very late work of the St. Cecilia Master.

variation is not, perhaps, sufficient to exclude the possibility that they were executed, or partly executed, by the St. Francis Master himself.

The execution of Scene XIII, at the lower end of the north wall, was in fact entrusted to several painters, and the bystanders on the left and the priest on the right are clearly not the work of the same hand. The general dumpiness characteristic of the priest and of the kneeling Saint, with their large heads and awkward gestures, is entirely new in the cycle, but it reappears in the figures of St. Francis and his companion in *The Sermon to the Birds* (Scene XV, Plate 68) on the east wall and in some of the figures in Scenes XVI–XVIII on the south wall. These differences, which embrace the treatment of landscape as well as the figure-style, as is evident from a comparison between Scenes II and XIV (Plates 42, 64), are sufficiently great to raise the question whether a painter distinct from the St. Francis Master was not chiefly responsible for the execution of the frescoes at the lower end of the nave, especially Scenes XIV–XVIII. The only alternative is to assume that the St. Francis Master underwent a considerable stylistic evolution at Assisi.

After Scene XVII (*The Sermon before Honorius III*, Plate 74), in the first bay of the south wall, a further stylistic change is apparent, this time one that affects the treatment of the architecture, which becomes more elegant and graceful and more harmonious in its proportioning. This change announces the intervention of a new and skilful painter, whose delicate style is already detectable in the figures of St. Francis in Scene XVIII (*The Appearance at Arles*, Plate 75) and Scene XIX (*The Stigmatization*, Plates 29a, 76), and who thereafter becomes the dominant personality in the execution of the frescoes in the second and third bays (Scenes XX–XXV). As the main author of the scenes relating to the Saint's death, this interesting painter may conveniently be referred to as the 'Master of the Obsequies of St. Francis': he shows in many ways a close kinship with the St. Cecilia Master,[1] and has in the past been confused with him, but his vision was a very personal one, and there is nothing elsewhere in the cycle quite comparable with his exquisite draughtsmanship, his feeling for the textures of materials, and the gentle resonance of his colour. Other lesser painters also took a hand in the execution of the frescoes on the south wall: the handiwork of such assistants is particularly in evidence in the group of women in Scene XVI (Plate 70) and in many of the figures in Scene XXIV (*The Canonization of St. Francis*, Plate 85). Finally, the St. Cecilia Master completed the cycle with his three frescoes in the fourth bay of the south wall (Scenes XXVI–XXVIII), having, presumably, first executed Scene I in the bay opposite.

It is difficult to form any very definite opinion upon the length of time that would have been required for the operation as a whole. The total number of *intonaco* patches in the cycle is about 300; but this figure cannot be simply equated with the number of

---

[1] Tintori and Meiss (*The Painting of the* Life of St. Francis *in Assisi*, p. 133) say of this master: 'He must . . . have been one of the prominent painters of the time, closely related to the St. Cecilia Master but independent of him.'

working days involved, for we must take into account various complicating factors—on the one hand the extra time required for the preparation of the designs and (if they existed) the *sinopie*, and on the other the saving of time that would have been made possible by the simultaneous execution of separate passages (even in different scenes), and by the fact that considerable areas, including the sky and the framing columns, were painted *a secco*, so that work could have proceeded on them independently of the execution of the main areas in true fresco. A further consideration is the difficulty and inconvenience of undertaking a work of this nature, especially in the medium of fresco, during the cold and damp of winter. The successive stylistic changes within the cycle seem themselves to be indicative of a fairly protracted programme of work, and perhaps also of unforeseen interruptions. A period, therefore, of about two years appears likely, although it could conceivably have been less, and indeed the employment of so many painters might equally be interpreted as evidence of haste.

The participation of several masters and their assistants in a single work was not unusual in the thirteenth and fourteenth centuries, during which the workshop tradition developed so strongly in Italy, and such co-operative enterprises are still met with in Renaissance times. Nevertheless there is no exact parallel outside Assisi to so extensive a distribution of the work, although in the sister art of sculpture a not dissimilar procedure was shortly to be employed in decorating the façade of Orvieto Cathedral.[1] What is especially puzzling about this aspect of the Assisi cycle is the *successive* employment of so many painters, suggesting difficulties of one kind or another of which we can now know nothing. Yet, despite the diversity of the workmanship, which varies considerably in quality even within individual scenes, nothing is more striking in the Upper Church than the unity of idea which a great conception imposed upon a family of styles.

[1] For the stylistic divisions of the Orvieto reliefs see J. White, 'The Reliefs on the Façade of the Duomo at Orvieto', *Journal of the Warburg and Courtauld Institutes*, xxxii (1959), 254 ff.

II

THE LITERARY TRADITION AND VASARI'S
ATTRIBUTION OF THE *LEGEND* TO GIOTTO

IOTTO'S AUTHORSHIP of some important work for the Franciscans at Assisi is alluded to in the almost contemporary *Compilatio chronologica* of Riccobaldo da Ferrara; and his employment in the Basilica is mentioned again in Ghiberti's *Commentarii*, written about the middle of the fifteenth century: but the tradition that Giotto was the author of the *Legend* in the Upper Church can be traced back only to the second edition of Vasari's *Lives*, published in 1568, in which he is credited also with the *Franciscan Allegories* in the Lower Church. The earliest of our sources, Riccobaldo's *Compilatio*, completed in the second decade of the fourteenth century, merely states that Giotto painted in the Basilica, without specifying whether it was in the Upper or Lower Church, while the ambiguity of Ghiberti's phraseology has only exacerbated and confused the controversy surrounding the *St. Francis* cycle.

According to Ghiberti, Giotto 'dipinse nella chiesa d'Asciesi nell'ordine de' frati minori quasi tutta la parte di sotto'[1] (Giotto 'painted in the church of the Order of Friars Minor at Assisi almost all the lower part'). Presumably Ghiberti cannot have been unaware that the Basilica at Assisi comprises two churches, the one built over the other, and both lavishly adorned with fresco decorations: yet it is difficult to see how he could have expressed himself more obscurely; and opinion is still divided as to whether he meant the lower part of the Upper Church or the lower part of the whole edifice. If he meant the former, he would seem to have had in mind the *St. Francis* cycle (although, as we shall see, even this presumption is open to doubt); and, if the latter, some or all of the Giottesque frescoes in the Lower Church. But what Ghiberti himself meant is only one half of the problem: it is scarcely less important to attempt to discover the meaning that Vasari, a century later, attached to Ghiberti's words; for it was Vasari who first definitely associated Giotto's name with the *St. Francis* cycle, and thus

---

[1] Lorenzo Ghiberti, *I Commentarii*, Bibl. Nazionale, Florence, Magliabecchiana Cod. XVII, 33; Julius von Schlosser, 'Lorenzo Ghibertis Denkwürdigkeiten: Prolegomena zu einer künstigen Ausgabe', *Kunstgeschichtliches Jahrbuch der K.-K. Zentral-Kommission für Erforschung und Erhaltung der Kunst- und Historischen Denkmale*, IV (1910), xv.

established the long tradition of Giotto's authorship of the frescoes which, despite the stylistic evidence against it, is still accepted by many historians.

It is generally held that Vasari interpreted the words 'quasi tutta la parte di sotto' as in fact a reference to the *St. Francis* cycle, on the grounds that the frescoes occupy the lowest register of the nave of the Upper Church, and that the use of a similar expression in the first edition of the *Lives*—'tutta la chiesa dalla banda di sotto'—provides, in the words of one writer, 'very strong linguistic evidence that in Vasari's day Ghiberti's phrase . . . was understood in its obvious sense—"almost all the lower range of frescoes" —and not as meaning "lower church" '.[1] This assumption, however, is not borne out by a careful examination of the texts. It can be demonstrated that the passage in the *Commentarii* was the basis for Vasari's attribution to Giotto of the *Franciscan Allegories* in the Lower Church, and that it was on other grounds that he came to believe that Giotto was the author of the *St. Francis* cycle. It is, indeed, difficult to resist the conclusion that Vasari's attribution of the *Legend of St. Francis* to Giotto was the result of a logical, but unwarranted, deduction from the two most important written sources that were known to him in addition to the *Commentarii* of Ghiberti.

These were the *Libro di Antonio Billi*, written in the early sixteenth century, and the slightly later manuscript containing lives of Italian artists by the unknown author usually referred to as the Anonimo Magliabechiano.[2] The author of the *Libro*, who evidently did not know the *Commentarii*, says briefly that Giotto 'cominciò ad acquistare fama per la pittura grande in S.to Francesco, da Sciesi, cominciata da Cimabue'[3] (Giotto 'began to achieve fame through the great work of decoration in S. Francesco at Assisi, begun by Cimabue'). The Anonimo, however, collates this statement with that of Ghiberti, as follows: 'Dipinse assaj, il che fu da Cimabue cominciato; et per tale opera cominciò acquistare fama. La onde poi per l'opere sue sempre s'accrebbe. E nella chiesa de' frati Minorj quasi tutta la parte di sotto della chiesa dipinse.'[4] ('He painted much that had been begun by Cimabue; and by such work he began to achieve fame; whence thereafter through his own works it continually increased. And in the church of the Friars Minor he painted almost all the lower part of the church.')

The phraseology used in the *Libro* of Antonio Billi suggests that the author may have intended no more than that Cimabue and Giotto were successively employed at S. Francesco, and that Giotto's work there established his reputation. That is to say, it cannot be assumed that he was necessarily referring to a particular series or group of

[1] P. Murray, 'Notes on Some Early Giotto Sources', *Journal of the Warburg and Courtauld Institutes*, xvi (1953), 66. Murray has also suggested that the word *parte* in the text of the *Commentarii* is a misreading of *parete*, 'wall', 'wall-surface' (idem, *An Index of Attributions Made in Tuscan Sources before Vasari* (Florence, 1959), p. 80).

[2] Or Anonimo Gaddiano.   [3] *Il Libro di Antonio Billi*, ed. K. Frey (Berlin, 1892), p. 6.

[4] C. de Fabriczy, 'Il Codice dell'Anonimo Gaddiano nella Biblioteca Nazionale di Firenze', in *Archivio storico italiano*, xii (1893), 36; R. Salvini, *Giotto: Bibliografia* (Rome, 1938), p. 22.

frescoes begun by Cimabue and completed by Giotto. Moreover, if he knew only that both Cimabue and Giotto had painted in the Basilica, nothing would have been more natural than that he should recollect Dante's famous allusion to the two masters in the eleventh Canto of the *Purgatorio*,[1] where, meditating upon the transitoriness of earthly fame, the poet cites as an example the eclipse of the great fame of Cimabue by that of Giotto:

> Credette Cimabue nella pintura
> tener lo campo; ed ora ha Giotto il grido,
> si che la fama di colui è oscura.[1]

(Cimabue thought to hold the field in painting; and now it is Giotto's name that is on everybody's lips, so that the other's fame is obscured.)

Dante's words may seem today to be of little historical consequence; but before the publication in 1550 of the first edition of Vasari's *Lives* they were undoubtedly the best-known of all literary references to Giotto, as the attention they received from the early commentators on the *Divine Comedy* sufficiently indicates;[3] indeed, they appear to lie behind Ghiberti's own account of Giotto's apprenticeship to Cimabue: 'Concedet-tegli el fanciullo e Cimabue meno seco Giotto et fu discepolo di Cimabue, tenea la maniera greca, in quella maniera ebbe in Etruria grandissima fama: fecesi Giotto grande nell'arte della pictura.' ('The boy having been entrusted to his care,[4] Cimabue took him with him, and so Giotto became the pupil of Cimabue; he followed the Greek [i.e. Byzantine] style, in which manner he enjoyed very great fame in Tuscany; Giotto made himself great in the art of painting.') Once again when the names of Cimabue and Giotto are brought together the word 'fame' makes its appearance, as though Ghiberti himself could not help thinking of the well-known passage in the *Purgatorio*.

It may, then, be doubted whether Antonio Billi was in possession of any positive information beyond the tradition that both Cimabue and Giotto had worked at Assisi in the Franciscan church. It is, however, still possible that he knew that Giotto's frescoes there were early works, and even that they had brought him a great reputation.[5] On the other hand, it is quite clear that the Anonimo Magliabechiano had no knowledge of

---

[1] Strzygowski suggested that the similar remark about Giotto's fame in the *Libro di Antonio Billi* was based upon a passage in Landino's *Commentario della Divina Commedia*: cf. J. Strzygowski, *Cimabue und Rom* (Vienna, 1888), p. 26.

[2] *Purgatorio*, xi. 94–6.

[3] Cf. Murray, 'Notes on Some Early Giotto Sources', p. 64. It may be noted that Vasari himself quotes Dante's lines in his Life of Cimabue, in both editions of the *Vite*. For a survey of the earliest Dante commentaries see L. Rocca, *Di alcuni commenti della Divina Commedia composti nei primi vent'anni dopo la morte di Dante* (Florence, 1891).

[4] Literally, 'He [Giotto's father] entrusted the boy to him.'

[5] Meiss thinks that Billi's statement 'has a claim to authenticity precisely because its conveys the kind of fact that is normally so little regarded at the time': cf. M. Meiss, *Giotto and Assisi* (1960), p. 24. Meiss suggests that Billi was refer-ring to the *Isaac* frescoes and the related Biblical scenes at the east end of the Upper Church. Cf. also A. Smart, 'The St. Cecilia Master and his School at Assisi, II', *The Burlington Magazine*, cii (Oct., 1960), 436, where the same suggestion was put forward independently.

his own to add to the statements of Billi and Ghiberti. He simply quotes them, the one after the other, with minor stylistic variations, only inserting between them the rather gratuitous comment: 'La onde poi per l'opere sue sempre s'accrebbe.' But this addition, superfluous and meaningless in itself, has the important effect of contributing to the impression that two distinct works by Giotto are being referred to, one a continuation of a work by Cimabue, and another, evidently painted later, after his fame had 'increased', which occupied 'quasi tutta la parte di sotto della chiesa'. At the same time, the addition of the words *della chiesa*, immediately after *di sotto*, strongly suggests the Lower Church. It was thus, at all events, that Vasari evidently interpreted the Anonimo's information.

It is possible that neither the Anonimo, nor Vasari at the time that he was writing the first version of his *Lives*, felt that he understood Ghiberti's meaning very clearly. In the first edition of the *Vite*, published in 1550, Vasari relies wholly upon the two traditions preserved by Ghiberti and Billi, which, as we have seen, the Anonimo brings together. Vasari begins with a sentence which obviously echoes Billi: 'Fu condotto ad Ascesi a finir l'opera cominciata da Cimabue.' ('He was called to Assisi to finish the work begun by Cimabue.') Six lines later he repeats this in a slightly different form, after having said that on his way to Assisi Giotto undertook certain works at Arezzo: 'Finite queste opere si condusse ad Ascesi, a l'opra [*sic*] cominciata da Cimabue, dove acquistò grandissima fama, per la bontà delle figure, che in quella opera fece; nelle quali si vede ordine, proporzione, vivezza, et facilità donatagli dalla natura, et dallo studio accresciuta. Perciochè era Giotto studiosissimo, et di continuo lavorava. Et allora dipinse nella Chiesa di Santa Maria de gli Agnoli, et nella Chiesa d'Ascesi de' frati minori tutta la Chiesa dalla banda di sotto.'[1] ('On the completion of these works he proceeded to Assisi, to [continue] the work begun by Cimabue; whence he achieved the greatest fame, on account of the excellence of the figures which he made in that work; which is marked by a sense of arrangement and proportion, truth to life, and a facility of execution given him by Nature and increased by study. For Giotto was most diligent in his studies, and was continually working. And then he painted in the Church of Santa Maria degli Angeli, and in the Church of the Friars Minor at Assisi the whole of the church on the lower level.')

This passage is identical in form with the statement of the Anonimo. Although certain words have been altered and a modicum of 'padding' introduced, the construction remains essentially unchanged, and Vasari follows the Anonimo in combining the two traditions handed down by Billi and Ghiberti respectively—the first ending at *di continuo lavorava*, and the second beginning thereafter with the words *Et allora dipinse*.

[1] Giorgio Vasari, *Le Vite de' più eccellenti Architetti, Pittori, et Scultori Italiani, da Cimabue insino a' Tempi Nostri* (Florence, 1550), p. 141.

The principal alteration in the first section is the replacement of the Anonimo's remark about the continual increase of Giotto's fame by a catalogue of qualities (*ordine, proporzione, vivezza, et facilità*), which may be regarded simply as Vasari's explanation of the *reasons* for Giotto's fame. More important is the expansion of the word 'and' in the Anonimo's final sentence ('E nella chiesa de' frati Minorj . . .') into 'and then': 'Et allora dipinse . . . nella Chiesa d'Ascesi de' frati minori tutta la Chiesa dalla banda di sotto.' This change now makes it absolutely clear that two separate works by Giotto in the Basilica are under discussion. It is a crucial stage in the development of the tradition regarding Giotto's activities at Assisi, and in the second edition of the *Vite* Vasari is to identify the first of these two works (mentioned by Billi) with the *St. Francis* cycle, and the second (the work mentioned by Ghiberti) with the *Allegories* and some other scenes in the Lower Church. That the expression *dalla banda di sotto* replaces Ghiberti's *quasi tutta la parte di sotto* is confirmed by Vasari's allusion to work in Santa Maria degli Angeli, which is mentioned in the *Commentarii* (and also by the Anonimo, where he quotes from Ghiberti), but not by Billi—the whole passage in the *Commentarii* relating to Giotto's work at Assisi reading as follows: 'Dipinse nella chiesa d'Asciesi nell'ordine de' frati minori quasi tutta la parte di sotto. Dipinse a Sta Maria degli Angeli in Ascesi.' Vasari excludes the reference to Santa Maria degli Angeli from his second edition.

Vasari may well have had no clear idea what the two works by Giotto in the Basilica consisted of, and the virtues which he extols in one of them are too general to convince us that he was not indulging in the kind of guesswork that came so easily to him when lack of positive information impeded him in his great task of charting the forgotten history of Italian art. That at this time he knew little about the decoration of S. Francesco is further suggested by the difference between his two accounts, in the first and second editions of the *Vite*, of the unfinished work which, according to Ghiberti, Stefano Fiorentino had painted in the Basilica. In the first edition Vasari simply transcribes the information given by Ghiberti and repeated by the Anonimo; but in the second edition he provides an entirely new account, noting both the position and the subject-matter of the fresco, while preserving something of the phraseology of his two sources: Stefano's fresco is referred to by Ghiberti as a *gloria* ('a heavenly glory'), by the Anonimo as a *historia* ('a narrative'), in Vasari's first edition as a *storia*, and in his second edition as a *storia della gloria celeste*. In the same way the accounts in the second edition of all the other frescoes in the Basilica which he mentions are quite clearly written from first-hand knowledge.

These differences between the two editions have a simple explanation. In the interval —in the year 1563—Vasari had paid a visit to Assisi, so that when he came, shortly afterwards, to prepare the second edition of the *Lives*, he was able to write much more fully about the frescoes which he believed that Giotto had painted in the Basilica. During his stay in Assisi he appears to have studied the decorations with some care, even if he did miscount the number of scenes in the *Legend*, giving it as 32 rather than 28—a useful mistake, as it happens, since Ridolfi's repetition of it ten years later indicates that Vasari was his sole authority for his own ascription of the frescoes to Giotto.[1]

If, before his visit, Vasari was ignorant of the precise nature of Giotto's work at Assisi, all would have seemed clear to him when he stood inside the Upper Church and looked around him at the ruined frescoes of Cimabue in the choir and transepts and at the Biblical scenes in the upper ranges of the nave, which he believed to be also by Cimabue: here, assuredly, was the 'pittura grande . . . cominciata da Cimabue', or, as the Anonimo had put it, 'il che fu da Cimabue cominciato'; and below, in the lower registers of the nave, was its completion by Giotto, the scenes of the *Legend of St. Francis*. In his life of Cimabue he even states that the *Legend* itself had been begun by Cimabue: 'When these works were finished Giovanni [Cimabue] set about painting the walls beneath, namely those below the windows, and he did some things there, but as he was summoned to Florence on some affairs of his own, he did not pursue the task, which was finished by Giotto many years after, as will be related when the time comes.'[2] There is no evidence here of anything but speculation arising out of Vasari's knowledge of the statements of Billi and the Anonimo and his natural inference at Assisi that the great work begun by Cimabue could only be the decoration of the Upper Church. Cimabue's personal affairs (doubtless imaginary, for how could Vasari know about them?) are dragged in as a means of explaining Cimabue's failure to proceed with the *St. Francis* cycle, and also in order to get the artist to Florence so that Vasari may discuss his work for Santo Spirito and Santa Maria Novella.

'When the time comes'—that is to say, in his life of Giotto—Vasari defines Giotto's share in the decoration of the nave of the Upper Church as the 'series of thirty-two scenes in fresco of the Life of St. Francis', having said previously (as in the first edition) that Giotto had set out from Florence to Assisi in order to finish what Cimabue had begun there ('per andare a finir in Ascesi l'opere cominciate da Cimabue'): here, of course, he is quoting once more from Billi. He then tells us (again as in the first edition) that on his way to Assisi Giotto painted some frescoes at Arezzo. Having mentioned these, he comes to what he regards as Giotto's first work at Assisi, the *Legend of St. Francis* in the Upper Church:

Finite queste cose, si condusse in Ascesi, città dell'Umbria, essendovi chiamato da Fra Giovanni di Muro della Marca, allora generale de' Frati di San Francesco; dove, nella chiesa di sopra, dipinse a fresco, sotto il corridore che attraversa le finestre, dai due lati della chiesa, trentadue storie della

---

[1] Pietro Ridolfi da Tossignano, *Historiarum seraphicae religionis libri tres* (1578), ii, 185.

[2] G. Vasari, *The Lives of the Painters, Sculptors and Architects*, trans. by A. M. Hinds (London, 1927), i, 24; idem, *Le Vite de' Più Eccellenti Pittori, Scultori et Architettori* (1568), ed. Gaetano Milanesi (1878–85), i, 253 f.

vita e fatti di San Francesco, cioè sedici per facciata, tanto perfettamente, che ne acquistò grandissima fama. E nel vero, si vede in quell'opera gran varietà non solamente nei gesti ed attitudini
di ciascuna figura, ma nella composizione ancora di tutte le storie; senza che fa bellissimo vedere
la diversità degli abiti di que' tempi, e certe imitazioni ed osservazioni delle cose della natura.
E fra le altre, è bellissima una storia dove uno assetato, nel quale si vede vivo il desiderio dell'acque,
bee stando chinato in terra a una fonte, con grandissimo e veramente maraviglioso affetto, in tanto
che par quasi una persona viva che bea. Vi sono anco molte altre cose degnissime di considerazione;
nelle quali, per non esser lungo, non mi distendo altrimenti. Basti che tutta questa opera acquistò
a Giotto fama grandissima, per la bontà delle figure, e per l'ordine, proporzione, vivezza e facilità
che egli aveva dalla natura, e che aveva mediante lo studio fatto molto maggiore, e sapeva in tutte
le cose chiaramente dimostrare. E perchè, oltre quello che aveva Giotto da natura, fu studiosissimo,
ed andò sempre nuove cose pensando e dalla natura cavando, meritò d'esser chiamato discepolo
della natura, e non d'altri.[1]

(On completing these things he proceeded to Assisi, a city of Umbria, having been summoned
there by Fra Giovanni di Muro della Marca, at that time General of the Friars of St. Francis; where,
in the upper church, he painted in fresco, under the gallery which runs below the windows, on
the two sides of the church, thirty-two scenes of the life and miracles of St. Francis, namely sixteen
on each side, and with such perfection that he thereby achieved very great fame. And in truth there
is to be seen in that work great variety, not only in the gestures and attitudes of all the figures, but
also in the composition of every subject; besides which it is very captivating to see the various
costumes of those times and several imitations and observations of natural forms. And among the
scenes there is one that is particularly beautiful, in which a thirsty man, whose desire for water
is vividly represented, stoops to the ground as he drinks from a spring, with so great and so truly
marvellous a conviction of reality that he appears almost like a real person drinking. There are,
besides, many other things eminently worthy of consideration; into which, for the sake of brevity,
I shall not enter. Let it suffice to say that this whole work acquired for Giotto very great fame,
because of the excellence of the figures and because of its sense of arrangement and proportion,
its truth to life and that facility of execution with which he had been endowed by Nature, and
which he had greatly increased through study, and which he put to good purpose in all that he did.
And because, not content with his natural gifts, Giotto was most diligent in his studies, and was
always inventing new things and taking his ideas from Nature, he deserved to be called the pupil
of none but Nature herself.)

A comparison with the first edition will demonstrate that in remodelling this passage
Vasari did not abandon its original form, but was content to pour new wine into an
old bottle. The new elements are in fact only three in number—first, the assertion that
Giotto was called to Assisi by Fra Giovanni, which, as Murray has shown, was probably
no more than a guess;[2] secondly, the identification of Giotto's first work at Assisi with
the *St. Francis* cycle in the nave of the Upper Church; and, thirdly, the eulogy upon the
figure of the thirsty muleteer in *The Miracle of the Spring* (Scene XIV, Plate 65a). This
whole passage, therefore, hangs upon the brief notice in the *Libro* of Antonio Billi,

---

[1] G. Vasari, *Le Vite. . . .,* ed. cit., i, 377 f.   [2] Murray, op. cit., pp. 66 ff.

which the Anonimo had expanded. Even the concluding sentence, which at first sight seems to express an independent observation, belongs to the same tradition. Not only are the words *fu studiosissimo* an echo of the *era Giotto studiosissimo* of the first edition, but what follows is no less than a disguised allusion to Cimabue, whom Vasari has earlier mentioned as Giotto's master, and whose work at Assisi, according to Billi and the Anonimo, Giotto had completed: Giotto, Vasari is telling us, was in a deeper sense the pupil of Nature. Vasari's attribution of the *St. Francis* cycle to Giotto rests, then, upon his deductions from the statements of Antonio Billi and the Anonimo Magliabechiano, neither of whom mentions it.

Vasari now turns to the Lower Church: 'Finite le sopradette storie, dipinse nel medesimo luogo, ma nella chiesa di sotto, le facciate di sopra dalle bande dell'altare maggiore, e tutti quattro gli angoli della volta di sopra, dove è il corpo di San Francesco.'[1] ('On completing the scenes just mentioned, he painted in the same place, but in the lower church, the upper parts of the walls by the High Altar, and all four sections of the vaulting over the place where lies the body of St. Francis.') Of these frescoes, Vasari clearly identifies only the four *Franciscan Allegories* on the vault over the High Altar. These are now described at some length, and Vasari concludes with a brief mention of the paintings on the side walls, one of which, he says, contains an excellent portrait of Giotto himself: presumably he is here referring to the fresco of *The Resuscitation of a Dead Child* near the entrance to the Orsini Chapel. The passage quoted replaces the somewhat obscure statement in the first edition of the *Vite* that Giotto painted 'tutta la chiesa dalla banda di sotto': an echo of this lingers in the expressions *bande* and *di sotto*, which do not occur in the passage on the *St. Francis* cycle. The Anonimo had possibly intended to clarify matters when he had altered Ghiberti's 'quasi tutta la parte di sotto' to 'quasi tutta la parte di sotto della chiesa'; but in Vasari's hands the words 'di sotto della chiesa' become 'nella chiesa di sotto'. The Anonimo's statement, and hence Ghiberti's which it reflects, are now unequivocally interpreted as referring to the Lower Church, or, rather, to its central part, the Presbytery. Thus the cryptic note in the *Commentarii*, as mediated by the Anonimo, can be seen to be Vasari's ultimate authority for his attribution of the *Franciscan Allegories* to Giotto.

Indeed, this development would appear to have been virtually inevitable, once the Anonimo, by repeating the statements of Billi and Ghiberti, the one after the other, had given the impression that two separate works by Giotto existed in the double church, of which the first was an offshoot of Cimabue's great masterpiece and established Giotto's fame, and the second the fruit of a more mature phase in his career. Vasari believed that Cimabue was the author not only of the frescoes in the choir and transepts of the Upper Church (as we believe today) but also of the two rows of Biblical scenes

[1] Vasari, op. cit., ed. cit., i, 378.

in the upper areas of the walls of the nave, a cycle now accepted as being the joint work of a Roman master (probably Torriti) and a more progressive painter, the so-called 'Isaac Master'. All this, together with the entire decoration of the ceiling, was, for Vasari, the *pittura grande* of Cimabue. According to his information this vast scheme of decoration had been completed later on by Giotto; and consequently Giotto's share in this work could only have consisted in the painting of the scenes of the *Legend of St. Francis* below, the sole remaining frescoes in the Upper Church, which, besides, had also been 'begun by Cimabue'. Since all the frescoes in the Upper Church were now accounted for, Giotto's later work in the Basilica must be in the Lower Church: it was to this that the other tradition passed on by the Anonimo must have referred—the tradition, that is to say, deriving from the *Commentarii*—even if it seemed to Vasari that Ghiberti's words were in need of correction, inasmuch as his information about Santa Maria degli Angeli was not to be relied upon.

Thus Vasari appears to have reasoned. Yet there is no evidence that originally two traditions, relating to two distinct works, actually existed; no evidence that Ghiberti and Billi were not referring to the same work;[1] no evidence that the presence of two works by Giotto in the double church was more than a myth created by the Anonimo when he copied out the two passages that he found in the *Libro* of Antonio Billi and the *Commentarii* of Ghiberti respectively, and when he inserted between them a gloss upon Billi's remark about the fame of Giotto. It is easy to understand how meaningful the addition of that one word 'and', with which the Anonimo had prefixed his version of Ghiberti's 'dipinse nella chiesa d'Ascesi . . . quasi tutta la parte di sotto', must have seemed to Vasari as he pondered the documents before him: Giotto, the Anonimo was saying, had not only painted the frescoes mentioned by Billi, but had also painted the frescoes known to Ghiberti.

Once, then, we have traced the growth and expansion of the tradition regarding Giotto's work at Assisi, it becomes clear that in the first version of his *Lives* Vasari did not depend upon Ghiberti, but upon Billi and the Anonimo, for his information about the work which Cimabue had begun and Giotto had completed, and which in the second edition he was to identify with the *St. Francis* cycle; and that, in the second edition, his further attribution to Giotto of the *Franciscan Allegories* and other frescoes 'nella chiesa di sotto'—this phrase replacing the 'tutta la chiesa dalla banda di sotto' of the first edition —derives from the Anonimo's 'quasi tutta la parte di sotto della chiesa', which in turn depends upon Ghiberti's 'quasi tutta la parte di sotto'. Vasari, in fact, could have associated the statement in the *Commentarii* with the *St. Francis* cycle only by accepting the 'quasi tutta la parte di sotto' of Ghiberti and the virtually identical 'quasi

---

[1] It may be noted here that, as Fabriczy demonstrated, the author of the *Libro* did not know Ghiberti's *Commentarii* (Fabriczy, op. cit., p. 314). It is possible, therefore, that the information in Ghiberti and Billi derives independently from a common source.

tutta la parte di sotto della chiesa' of the Anonimo as references to two distinct works.

Vasari's reasons, therefore, for ascribing the *Legend* to Giotto can easily be understood: they were in fact founded upon the very imprecision of the earlier writers. As to Ghiberti's own statement, it is no matter for surprise that those who see Giotto's hand in the *St. Francis* cycle should interpret the words 'quasi tutta la parte di sotto' as meaning 'almost all the lower part of the walls of the Upper Church' (although they did not mean this either to Vasari or, evidently, to the Anonimo), and that those who deny Giotto's authorship of the *Legend* should generally assume that they refer to the decoration of the Lower Church, much of which is associated with Giotto's name by a long local tradition. There is, however, one further possibility—that Ghiberti meant 'the lower part of the nave', that is to say the part furthest from the choir or upper end—just as Vasari, in noting the position of Masaccio's *Trinity* in Santa Maria Novella in Florence (where the nave runs from north to south, with the choir at the north end), described it as 'sotto [that is, south of] il tramezzo della chiesa, una Trinita, che è posta sopra [that is, north of] l'altar di St. Ignazio'.[1] In this event, Ghiberti would most probably have meant the Biblical scenes by the Isaac Master, which occupy the east end of the nave. Indeed, 'quasi tutta la parte di sotto' would be a very fair description of the area of the Upper Church decorated by the Isaac Master and his assistants.

Nevertheless, the weight of probability favours the supposition that Ghiberti was referring to the Giottesque frescoes in the Lower Church, as Vasari himself believed. That by the *chiesa d'Asciesi* Ghiberti meant not the Upper Church but the whole Basilica is, moreover, suggested by his allusion, some thirty lines later, to Stefano's *Gloria* in the Lower Church (upon which, as we have seen, Vasari also comments). In referring to this fresco (which is now lost, although a recent attempt has been made to reconstruct its composition),[2] Ghiberti uses the same expression—*nella chiesa d'Ascesi*—without any differentiation between the Upper and the Lower Church. We should scarcely expect exactly the same words to be used of the Lower Church if only a few lines earlier Ghiberti had applied them exclusively to the Upper Church. If it is now legitimate to take the apparently logical step of paraphrasing the whole passage 'nella chiesa d'Asciesi . . . quasi tutta la parte di sotto' as 'in the double church at Assisi . . . almost all the lower part', it becomes extremely difficult to interpret this as an allusion to the Upper Church. Certainly, Ghiberti's reference to the fresco by Stefano Fiorentino makes nonsense of the argument, sometimes advanced, that, since the Upper Church was the more famous and important of the two, he would have felt it necessary to distinguish between them only in writing about the Lower Church.

---

[1] Cf. A. Smart, 'Giotto and Assisi' (review of M. Meiss, *Giotto and Assisi*), *The Burlington Magazine*, cii (1960), 541.

[2] Cf. Margherita Gabrielli, 'La "Gloria Celeste" di Stefano Fiorentino', *Rivista d'arte*, xxxi (1956), 3 ff.

The fame of Giotto may, as Dante declared, have obscured that of Cimabue; but at Assisi the truth seems to have been that the fame of both masters quickly eclipsed that of the other painters who are known to have laboured in the Basilica, including Simone Martini, Pietro Lorenzetti, and Puccio Capanna. By the late sixteenth century it had evidently become customary to ascribe almost anything in both churches either to Cimabue or to Giotto. One writer of the early eighteenth century, Antonio d'Orvieto, went so far as to say that Giotto decorated the whole of the Upper Church, and Cimabue the whole of the Lower Church.[1] Such is the magic of these two names that even to this day it is not unknown for well-meaning guides to inform visitors to the Upper Church that all the frescoes in the choir and transepts are by Cimabue, and all those in the nave by Giotto.

It is not sufficient to argue from the position of the critical standards of modern scholarship and to affirm—as it has been affirmed—that Ghiberti is not likely to have meant the Lower Church, 'where there is no fresco that can be attributed to Giotto'.[2] One might as lightly say that the *Legend* in the Upper Church cannot be attributed to Giotto (a statement which would be equally true), and leave the matter at that. The fact remains that the greater part of the fourteenth-century decoration of the Lower Church is the work of Giotto's pupils and immediate followers, and represents the largest corpus in any one place of frescoes of his School. By the middle of the fifteenth century, when Ghiberti wrote his *Commentarii*, these could well have been believed to be largely by Giotto himself.[3] An interesting analogy is provided by the reference in the *Commentarii* to Giotto's work at Santa Croce, where Ghiberti says that Giotto painted four chapels, meaning those of the Bardi, Peruzzi, Giugni, and Tosinghi families. Albertini, however, writing in 1510, appears to have based himself upon a sounder tradition when he ascribed to Giotto the decoration only of the first two of these chapels.[4] The frescoes in the other two have been destroyed, but the *Assumption* which still remains over the entrance to the Tosinghi Chapel is certainly not by Giotto but by the so-called 'Maestro di Figline' (also known as the 'Master of the Fogg Pietà').[5] On the analogy of *The*

---

[1] Antonio d'Orvieto, *Cronologia della Provincia Serafica Riformata dell'Umbria o d'Assisi divisa in tre libri* (Perugia, 1717), p. 31; cited by Murray, op. cit., p. 67.

[2] R. Salvini, *Giotto* (1952), p. 28: 'È più probabile infatti che lo scrittore intendesse indicare la parte bassa della Chiesa Superiore piuttosto che la Chiesa Inferiore, dove nessun affresco può attribuirsi a Giotto.'

[3] As was suggested by Sirén (*Giotto and Some of his Followers*, p. 28).

[4] Francesco Albertini, *Memoriale di molte statue et picture sono nella inclyta Cipta di Florentia* (1510), ed. H. P. Horne (Letchworth, 1909); P. Murray, *An Index of Attributions before Vasari* (Florence, 1959), p. 82.

[5] The fresco was first recognized as a late work of the 'Maestro di Figline' by Graziani (A. Graziani, 'Affreschi del Maestro di Figline', *Proporzioni*, i (1943), 74 ff.). This attribution is now generally accepted and is in fact indisputable. Graziani still held, however, that Giotto himself painted the lost frescoes in the interior of the Tosinghi Chapel, holding the tradition to that effect to be too strong to be denied; he suggested that the 'Maestro di Figline' worked at Santa Croce as an assistant of Giotto, and this hypothesis led him to assume that the *Stigmatization* over the entrance to the Bardi Chapel was delegated to another pupil (op. cit., p. 77). For the Santa Croce *Assumption* see also Offner, *Corpus*, III, vi (1956), 96 ff.

Stigmatization (Plate 29b) painted by Giotto over the entrance to the Bardi Chapel, the interior decoration of which is unquestionably from his hand, we may provisionally assume that the 'Maestro di Figline' was the author of the lost frescoes in the Cappella Tosinghi.[1] It appears, therefore, that Ghiberti believed Giotto to have been responsible for a fresco-decoration that in fact was the work of one of his followers.[2]

Nevertheless, it is within the bounds of possibility, although it seems most improbable, that Ghiberti was, after all, referring to the *St. Francis* cycle in the Upper Church:[3] in which case, we are confronted with a conflict between conclusions arrived at by stylistic analysis and the opinion of an early writer, the source of whose information we have no means of knowing; and when all is said it is stylistic criticism that has generally proved itself to be the safest guide through the wildernesses of art history, where documents of any kind are few and contemporary documents fewer still; and it may be appropriate in this context to recall the wise words of Richard Offner upon the problem of the Santa Maria Novella Cross, which, as it happens, has its own bearing upon the question of the authorship of the *St. Francis* cycle: 'We must remember that its style is the master's own, whilst the documents are the products of other hands. It is the style, therefore, that must be accorded the primary authority.'[4]

About the time that Ghiberti was writing his *Commentaries* Assisi became involved in the war of succession which broke out on the death of Alfonso of Sicily, and the city, which was a dependency of the Papacy, was temporarily occupied by the forces of Jacopo Piccinino, a general in the service of Alfonso's son Ferrante. In 1459, after the restoration of Assisi to the Church, Pope Pius II—the famous humanist and poet Enea Piccolomini—visited the city and stood for the first time in the Basilica. Unfortunately, this learned man had little to say about the frescoes that he saw there, and his diary contains

---

[1] For an attempt to reconstruct the compositions of the Tosinghi Chapel frescoes, cf. Giuseppe Marchini, 'Gli affreschi perduti di Giotto in una cappella di S. Croce', *Rivista d'arte* (1938), Serie ii, Anno X, 216 ff. Marchini's thesis is founded upon the assumption that the frescoes were by Giotto.

[2] An unconvincing attempt has recently been made to reattribute the *Franciscan Allegories* to Giotto, on the basis of their stylistic affinities with the Stefaneschi Altarpiece in the Vatican Gallery: cf. M. Gosebruch, 'Giottos römischen Stefaneschi-Altar und die Fresken des sog. "Maestro delle vele" in der Unterkirche S. Francesco zu Assisi', *Kunstchronik*, ii (1958), 288 f. The Stefaneschi Altarpiece is not by Giotto but by a pupil, as almost all authorities are agreed, although it may well have been painted in Giotto's workshop. Giotto's authorship of the altarpiece was first denied by Friedrich Rintelen, 'Das Altarwerk in der Sakristei von S. Peter in Rom', Supplement to the *Allgemeine Zeitung* (Munich), 13 Dec. 1905. Adolfo Venturi held that it was painted in Giotto's workshop, chiefly by his pupils, and pointed out that Gothic triptychs of this type were unknown in the early years of the 14th century. Berenson believed the altarpiece to be an early work of Bernardo Daddi. For a further discussion cf. C. Carrà, *Giotto*, pp. 53 f. This, however, is not to deny the stylistic connections between the frescoes and the altarpiece to which Supino was the first to draw attention (I. B. Supino, *Giotto*, p. 38). Still more recently, Cesare Gnudi has advanced the hypothesis that Giotto was personally responsible for the execution of two of the four *tondi* on the vault of the Cappella della Maddalena in the Lower Church (those representing the *Magdalen* and *Lazarus*), and he even states categorically that it is 'absolutely certain' that Giotto was given the commission for the decoration of the chapel (although according to his thesis the work was undertaken mainly by pupils): cf. Cesare Gnudi, *Giotto* (Italian edn., 1958), p. 182.

[3] Even so, 'almost all the lower part' would have been a curious phrase by which to distinguish the frescoes in the nave from those by Cimabue in the apse and transepts.   [4] Offner, *Corpus*, III, vi (1956), 11.

but one brief comment upon them: 'Assisi', he writes, 'was made glorious by St. Francis, the founder of the Order of the Minorites, to whom there were no riches greater than poverty. A noble church was erected to him in which they say his bones now lie. It is in fact a double church [*duplex ecclesia*], the one above the other, decorated with paintings by the Florentine Giotto, who is acknowledged to have been the greatest painter of his time.'[1] Even Cimabue remains uncelebrated. Taken at their face value, Pius's words suggest that by this time Giotto's share in the decoration of the entire building was believed to have been fairly extensive. It is a pity that the construction of the original Latin gives no indication as to whether Pius was alluding to the Upper Church, the Lower Church, or both together. But a little more than a century later the Franciscan historian Pietro Ridolfi da Tossignano, basing himself upon Vasari, was able to give to Giotto the *Legend*, the *Allegories*, the scenes from *The Infancy of Christ*, and most of the remaining decorations in the right transept, admitting, however, that others ascribed some of the frescoes to Puccio Capanna.[2] Moreover, Fra Ludovico da Pietralunga, writing a few years earlier, observed that there were even conflicting opinions as to whether *The Passion of Christ* in the left transept of the Lower Church, which is by Pietro Lorenzetti (and assistants), should be attributed to Giotto or not.[3] By this time, therefore, the extent of Giotto's supposed activity at Assisi had grown to considerable proportions; and the way was open to further accretions in the centuries to come. It may be wondered how far the process had gone, in the Sacro Convento itself, at the time of Pius II and Ghiberti.

No Franciscan document anterior to Vasari's *Lives* mentions Giotto's work in the Basilica, and although some such source, now lost to us, has often been presumed to lie behind Vasari's assertion that Giotto was called to Assisi 'by Fra Giovanni di Muro della Marca, at that time General of the Friars of St. Francis', it has been convincingly demonstrated that there are no grounds for this assumption. As Murray points out,[4] Fra Giovanni's real name was Giovanni Mincio da Murrovalle, but Vasari uses the unusual form given in the *Chronica XXIV Generalium*, a history of the Franciscan Order compiled in the late fourteenth century, where Fra Giovanni is described as *Iohannes de Murro, magister in theologia, de Provincia Marchiae*:[5] yet although this work devotes considerable attention to Fra Giovanni, who was an important figure in the Franciscan movement at

[1] *Pii Secundi Pontificis Max. Commentarii Rerum memorabilium, quae temporibus suis contigerunt* (1584), Lib. ii, 75: 'Nobilitauit hanc vrbem diuus Franciscus ordinis Minorum inuentor, cui nihil paupertate ditius fuit. Huic nobile templum erectum est, in quo ferunt sua ossa iacere: & duplex ecclesia est, altera super alteram picturis illustrata Ciocti Florentini, quem constat sui temporis omnium pictorum fuisse nobilissimum.' An English translation by F. Gragg and L. Gabel is published in *Smith College Studies in History*, xxii (1936) and xxv (1940).

[2] Pietro Ridolfi da Tossignano, op. cit., ii, 185.

[3] Fra Ludovico da Pietralunga, 'Descrizione della Basilica di S. Francesco in Assisi', in B. Kleinschmidt, *Die Basilika S. Francesco in Assisi* (Berlin, 1915), iii, 8 ff.

[4] P. Murray, 'Notes on Some Early Giotto Sources', *Journal of the Warburg and Courtauld Institutes*, xvi (1953), 66 ff.

[5] *Chronica XXIV Generalium Ministrorum Ordinis Fratrum Minorum*, in *Analecta Franciscana*, iii (1897), 1 ff.

a time when the peace of the Order was threatened by controversies over the Rule of Poverty and by the increasing complaints of the Spirituals, it makes no mention of his patronage of Giotto. Fra Giovanni was Minister-General from 1296 until December 1302, when his appointment as Cardinal-Bishop of Oporto compelled him to resign; but at the request of the Pope he continued to rule over the Order as Apostolic Vicar until the year 1304. Now if Vasari assumed that the *St. Francis* cycle was painted around the year 1300—as he must have done, since he believed it to be an early work (and he gives Giotto's date of birth as the year 1276)—then it is more than possible that he simply embellished his account with the name of the Minister-General who was in office at that time; and he would have found the name of Fra Giovanni in the *Chronica XXIV Generalium*. It seems significant that Ridolfi, in his *Historiarum seraphicae religionis libri tres*, published in 1578, is the first Franciscan writer to connect Giotto's work at Assisi with Fra Giovanni, and that he betrays the fact that the source of his information about Giotto was none other than the second edition of Vasari's *Lives*; for, like Vasari, he makes the mistake (as we have seen) of describing the *St. Francis* frescoes as being thirty-two in number.[1] Furthermore, the almost contemporary *Descrizione della Basilica di S. Francesco in Assisi* written by Fra Ludovico, who lived and died in the Sacro Convento, while accepting Vasari's attribution of the *Legend* to Giotto, lacks any reference to Fra Giovanni—a curious omission if there had been any document at the convent connecting his name with that of Giotto.[2]

One other early source bearing directly upon the problem of the Assisi frescoes—the earliest source of all to mention Giotto's work in the Basilica—remains to be examined. This is the celebrated passage about Giotto in the *Compilatio chronologica* of Riccobaldo da Ferrara, which is datable in the second decade of the fourteenth century.[3] The *Compilatio* is known, with slight differences between one text and another, in various manuscripts and printed editions. Being a chronicle of contemporary events, it occupied its author over a period of many years, and in the past there has been considerable disagreement about the dating of the passage in question. Rintelen, questioning the Latinity of the passage in the texts known to him, even suggested that it might be a later interpolation.[4] These doubts, however, have now been resolved by Gnudi's careful examination and comparison of all the extant versions in manuscript and print.[5] Gnudi shows that Riccobaldo almost certainly wrote the passage in question in 1312 or 1313, and that the original text ran as follows: 'Joctus pictor eximius florentinus agnoscitur.

---

[1] The mistake is repeated a century later by Baldinucci: cf. Filippo Baldinucci, *Notizie de' Professori del Disegno . . .* (Florence, 1681), p. 46.　　　　　　　　　　　　　　　　[2] Cf. Murray, loc. cit.

[3] Riccobaldo da Ferrara, *Compilatio chronologica*, in L. A. Muratori, *Rerum italicarum Scriptores* (Milan, 1726), ix, 235*a*.

[4] F. Rintelen, *Giotto und die Giotto-Apokryphen* (2nd edn., 1923), pp. 152 ff.

[5] C. Gnudi, 'Il passo di Riccobaldo Ferrarese relativo a Giotto e il problema della sua autenticità', *Studies in the History of Art dedicated to William E. Suida* (London, 1959), pp .26 ff.; and idem, *Giotto*, ed. cit., pp. 241 ff.

Qualis in arte fuerit testantur opera facta per eum in ecclesiis minorum Assisii Arimini Padue et in ecclesia Arene Padue.' ('Giotto is acknowledged to be the outstanding Florentine painter. The works executed by him in the churches of the Friars Minor at Assisi, Rimini, and Padua and in the church of the Arena at Padua testify to what he was in his art.')

It seems almost certain from the context that Riccobaldo was referring in each case to frescoes, and Gnudi's dating of the passage in the *Compilatio* is generally held to support the view that Riccobaldo must have been writing about the *St. Francis* cycle in the Upper Church. This, however, is by no means a safe assumption. Riccobaldo could equally well have been referring to the Biblical scenes by the Isaac Master at the east end of the nave; and in the view of many scholars the Isaac Master was none other than the young Giotto.[1] We must also consider whether this work by Giotto could have been in the Lower Church.

If by the year 1312 or 1313 there did exist in the double church a group of frescoes accepted as the work of Giotto, it seems clear that these decorations must be sought either among the later Biblical narratives in the Upper Church or in some area of the Lower Church. There are in the Lower Church five groups of frescoes attributable either to followers of Giotto or, more directly, to his *bottega*—the *St. Nicholas* cycle in the Cappella Orsini; the *Franciscan Allegories* on the vault of the crossing; the scenes from the *Infancy of Christ*, together with a *Crucifixion* (Plate 36b) of separate authorship, in the north transept; the *Miracles of St. Francis* nearby; and the episodes from *The Life of Mary Magdalen* in the Cappella Maddalena. Among these compositions, the *Crucifixion* in the transept and the *Raising of Lazarus* and *Noli me tangere* in the Magdalen Chapel are variants of the designs of the corresponding scenes in the Arena Chapel at Padua, and the style approximates at times very closely to that of Giotto himself (Plate 36a, b). A series of frescoes executed by members of a painter's *bottega* might certainly be described at the time as works by the master himself, who would have been the recipient of the commission, and who would then have contracted the work out to his pupils. If this was the case in the Lower Church at Assisi, there may be no need to account for Riccobaldo's reference to Giotto's work in the Basilica in any other way. On the other hand, it is uncertain whether any of the Giottesque frescoes in the Lower Church, with the exception of the *St. Nicholas* cycle in the Cappella Orsini, can be dated as early as the year 1313. We shall return to this question later.

The further possibility cannot altogether be excluded that Riccobaldo was misinformed.[2] One important argument against his reliability is that a Florentine source

[1] This thesis was first argued by Thode: cf. H. Thode, *Franz von Assisi und die Anfänge der Kunst der Renaissance in Italien* (Berlin, 1885), pp. 239 ff. See below, p. 107 n.

[2] Riccobaldo's reliability was questioned by Carrà on the grounds that the passage in the *Compilatio* must refer to the *St. Francis* cycle, which Giotto cannot have painted (Carlo Carrà, *Giotto* (1924), pp. 66 f.). Carrà also thought it

not very much later in date, the *Ottimo Commento* of about 1333, gives a list of the cities in which Giotto worked—Rome, Naples, Avignon, Florence, and Padua—but fails to mention either Assisi or Rimini.[1] As far as we know, the list is an accurate one, for although it is impossible now to verify the tradition, which originated here, concerning Giotto's summons to Avignon, there is no positive reason to question it, and we have certain knowledge that Giotto executed important works in the four other cities mentioned. On the other hand, it would be unwarrantable to conclude, on this evidence, that Giotto undertook no commissions in other Italian cities.

It has also been objected that in his brief catalogue of Giotto's works Riccobaldo includes no reference to the mosaic of the *Navicella*, which may well have been in existence before the year 1312, and which was undoubtedly one of the most celebrated works of the age:[2] but one could as well cast doubt upon the reliability of Filippo Villani because he mentions the *Navicella* in Rome but not the Arena Chapel in Padua, or, for that matter, Giotto's frescoes at Santa Croce in Florence, which is perhaps a still more surprising omission on the part of a Florentine chronicler of those times. In the case of Riccobaldo the relative isolation of Rome immediately after the removal of the Papal Curia to Avignon may well have a bearing upon the matter; but if there is a genuine problem here there is another possible solution to it. It is extremely likely that Riccobaldo's information came to him from some Franciscan source, perhaps on the occasion of the General Chapter of the Franciscan Order which was held in Padua in 1310,[3] the Paduan origin of his list of Giotto's works being suggested by his particular mention of the Arena Chapel cycle. His allusion to Giotto appears in the context of work undertaken for Franciscan communities, and it would have been quite natural, once he had mentioned the Franciscan church at Padua, to add a reference to Scrovegni's private commission for the decoration of the Arena Chapel in the same city.[4] On this premiss, there would have been no reason whatsoever to mention the *Navicella*, even if his informant knew of its existence; nor can the *Navicella* be certainly dated before 1310.

suspicious that 'no chronicle of the fourteenth century, which speaks of Giotto's works, makes any mention of work at Assisi'; and he even went so far as to suggest that 'the silence of Ghiberti on the Legend of St. Francis . . . is a direct testimony against the Chronicler of Ferrara'.

[1] On this question see especially J. White, *Art and Architecture in Italy, 1250–1400* (1966), p. 229.

[2] This point is discussed in I. B. Supino, *Giotto* (1920), p. 60, and Pier Liberale Rambaldi, 'Postilla al passo di Riccobaldo', *Rivista d'arte* (1937), Serie ii, Anno IX, 355 f. The absence of any reference to the *Navicella* in the *Compilatio* was enlisted by Lionello Venturi in support of a late dating of the mosaic (*c.* 1320): cf. Lionello Venturi, 'La data dell'attività romana di Giotto', *L'Arte*, Anno XXI (1918), 229 ff. For the *Navicella* see especially Wilhelm Paeseler, 'Giottos Navicella und ihr spätantikes Vorbild', *Römisches Jahrbuch für Kunstgeschichte*, v (1941), 51 ff.

[3] Schmeidler suggested that Riccobaldo's source of information was the Franciscan community at Ravenna (B. Schmeidler, *Italienische Geschichtschreiber des XII. und XIII. Jahrhunderts* (Leipzig, 1909), p. 58). This view is repeated in F. Jewett Mather, 'Giotto's *St. Francis* Series at Assisi Historically Considered', *Art Bulletin*, xxv (1943), 97 ff.

[4] It is possible that Riccobaldo intended to suggest a definite chronology—first Assisi, then Rimini, and finally Padua. Meiss thinks it significant that the three towns are not given in alphabetical order, the *Arimini* of the original text following rather than preceding the reference to Assisi (Millard Meiss, *Giotto and Assisi* (1960), p.24).

As we survey the written accounts of Giotto's work at Assisi, from Riccobaldo in the early fourteenth century to Ridolfi in the late sixteenth, we can scarcely avoid the conclusion that what we are witnessing is a gradual and almost inevitable process of accretion, founded not upon the substance of solid fact but upon the very exiguity of the tradition.[1] Perhaps Fra Ludovico felt just this when, standing in the Basilica and seeing around him so many works about which there was so much uncertainty, he vainly endeavoured, with the help of his artist friend Adone Doni, to wrest from the walls the secrets which had been sealed too long for recovery. By then, apparently, all that was known for certain was that Cimabue, Giotto, Puccio Capanna, and Stefano Fiorentino had worked in the double church. What these masters had painted there was no longer remembered with accuracy, save that it was assumed that only Cimabue could have been the author of the frescoes in the choir and transepts of the Upper Church. Even the great Sienese masters Pietro Lorenzetti and Simone Martini had been forgotten. Stefano Fiorentino and Puccio Capanna, celebrated in their own lifetime, were now shadowy figures: according to Ghiberti and the Anonimo, Stefano had left no finished work at Assisi; and the difficulty was to distinguish Puccio's frescoes from those now associated with the greater name of Giotto. And if much was attributed to Giotto that in reality was not his, was this not how the very legends of the saints had always grown, appropriating to themselves the mighty works that had originally surrounded other names?

[1] Flavius Blondus, writing long before the publication of the first edition of Vasari's *Lives*, refers to Giotto in his section on Florence (as a master worthy of comparison with Apelles), but makes no mention of him in his account of Assisi: cf. Biondo da Forli, *Roma Instaurata, et Italia Illustrata*, trans. by Lucio Fauno (Venice, 1543), p. 115.

III

THE ACTIVITY OF GIOTTO

1. *Works Attributable to Giotto*

THE REASONS FOR VASARI'S ATTRIBUTION of the *Legend* at Assisi to Giotto appear perfectly comprehensible: not only did the literary tradition point to the existence of some major work by him in the Basilica, but the vivid naturalism of the frescoes, epitomized by the figure of the thirsty muleteer in *The Miracle of the Spring* (Scene XIV, Plate 65a), which Vasari singled out for special praise, would have seemed to him to conform precisely to Giotto's historic place in the revival of painting in Italy. The early writers had all stressed Giotto's return to Nature: in Ghiberti's words, he had broken away for the first time from the *rozzezza dei Greci*, the 'roughness of the Byzantines';[1] a view anticipated by Cennino Cennini when he wrote that Giotto had 'translated the art of painting from Greek into Latin, and made it modern'.[2] Earlier still, in a famous passage in the *Decameron*, Boccaccio had summed up the significance that the *arte nuova* of Giotto must have had for his own age:

His genius was of such excellence that there was nothing produced by Nature, the mother and operator of all things, in the course of the perpetual revolution of the heavens, that he could not reproduce with his stylus, pen or brush, so that his painting, rather than being similar to his model, appeared as the model itself; so much so that his works often misled the eyes of men, who took what was painted to be real. And so he restored to the light an art that had been buried for centuries under the errors of those who painted to please the eyes of the ignorant rather than to satisfy the minds of the knowledgeable; on which account he deserves to be called one of the lights of the glory of Florence; furthermore, he was so humble that, although he lived as a master of others, he always refused to be called master.[3]

To the modern student, however, the definition of Giotto's place in the history of Florentine painting must be less simple than this. We are aware of other impulses at this time towards a 'naturalism' broadly comparable with his but in no sense to be confused

[1] Lorenzo Ghiberti, *I Commentarii*, loc. cit.

[2] Cennino d'Andrea Cennini, *Il libro dell'Arte*, ed. D. V. Thompson (New Haven, 1932), p. 2: *il quale Giotto rimutò l'arte del dipignere di grecho in latino* (Cap. i).

[3] Giovanni Boccaccio, *Decameron*, vi, 5. The translation given here is based on that of Panofsky (Erwin Panofsky, *Renaissance and Renascences in Western Art* (Stockholm, 1960), pp. 12 f.).

with it, and our first necessity is to distinguish between his authentic work and all that has been doubtfully ascribed to him. Of all the controversial attributions, none can be regarded as more important than Vasari's attachment of Giotto's name to the *Legend* at Assisi, and in the absence of documentation the only sound approach to the problem of its authorship lies first through a detailed stylistic analysis based upon comparisons with authenticated works. A difficulty, however, presents itself, for our knowledge of Giotto is extremely limited: relatively little from his hand has survived, and the full range of his art remains for ever unknowable. The early writers record numerous works by Giotto that have since disappeared, including fresco-cycles in Florence, Rome, and Milan and many paintings on panel, such as those formerly in the Florentine churches of Santa Maria Novella and S. Giorgio alla Costa. Only one of his major works in fresco, the great cycle in the Arena Chapel at Padua, has come down to us in its entirety, and what has been preserved of his frescoes in Santa Croce in Florence offers no more than a partial insight into the nature of his later development. What should we not give to be able to see the great fresco-decoration devoted to astrological themes which once embellished the great hall of the Palazzo della Ragione in Padua,[1] or the series of 'famous men' commissioned by King Robert of Naples for a chapel at Castelnuovo?[2] The losses are vast, and they are in proportion to the augmentation of the canon by works of uncertain authenticity.

The list of works securely attributable to Giotto can be briefly given. It comprises: frescoes of *The Life of the Virgin* and *The Life of Christ* in the Arena Chapel at Padua; the Padua Crucifix (Plate 11b), painted for the Arena Chapel (now in the Museo Civico at Padua); the *Navicella* mosaic at St. Peter's in Rome (entirely restored in the sixteenth and seventeenth centuries); the Ognissanti *Madonna*, now in the Uffizi in Florence (recorded at the Ognissanti church by Ghiberti); frescoes of *The Lives of St. John the Baptist and St. John the Evangelist* in the Peruzzi Chapel at Santa Croce, Florence (recorded by Ghiberti); frescoes of *The Life of St. Francis* in the Bardi Chapel in the same church, together with a *Stigmatization* (Plate 29b) over the entrance to the chapel (recorded by Ghiberti); a panel of *The Dormition of the Virgin* in the Staatliches Museum in Berlin (recorded by Ghiberti as being in the church of Ognissanti). To these works we must add a number of panels produced by Giotto's *bottega*: among the most important of these are the Louvre *Stigmatization of St. Francis* (Plates 27a, b, 28), with three scenes from the Saint's life on the predella (signed *Opus Jocti Florentini*, and recorded by Vasari as being in the church of S. Francesco at Pisa); the Crucifix at S. Felice in Florence; the altarpiece of *The Virgin and Child Enthroned, with Saints*, in the Pinacoteca at Bologna (signed *Opus*

---

[1] G. Fabris, 'La Cronaca di Padova di Giovanni da Nono', *Bollettino del Museo Civico di Padova*, N.S., x–xi (1932–40), 20. This work dates from the 1320s.

[2] L. Ghiberti, op. cit., loc. cit.

magistri Jocti de Florentia, and executed for the church of Santa Maria degli Angeli at Bologna); and the altarpiece of *The Coronation of the Virgin* at Santa Croce in Florence (signed *Opus magistri Jocti*, and recorded by Ghiberti). A panel of *The Stigmatization of St. Francis* in the Fogg Art Museum (Cambridge, Mass.) may also be a workshop product.

A considerable number of other paintings have been ascribed to Giotto or his workshop, but few of these attributions are worth considering.[1] Of the more notable works in this category, the seven *tavolette* representing scenes from the Life of Christ, three of which are now in the Alte Pinakothek at Munich and the remainder in the Metropolitan Museum in New York, the Gardner Museum at Boston, the National Gallery in London, and Villa I Tatti in Florence, and which evidently come from an altarpiece commissioned for some Franciscan church, would seem to have been executed by a direct pupil, possibly a member of Giotto's workshop in Florence. The beautiful *Madonna* in the National Gallery of Art in Washington, originally the central panel of a polyptych to which a half-length *St. Stephen* in the Horne Museum in Florence and a *St. John the Evangelist* and a *St. Lawrence* in the Musée Jacquemart-André at Châalis also belonged, reflects the late style of Giotto as we know it from the Santa Croce frescoes;[2] and there is some reason to suppose that the polypytch in the Kress Collection (North Carolina Museum of Art, Raleigh) representing *The Saviour, with the Virgin, St. John the Evangelist, the Baptist, and St. Francis*—a work probably executed in Giotto's *bottega*—once stood over the altar of the Peruzzi Chapel.[3]

There is no need to doubt the seventeenth-century tradition that the mosaic fragment of an *Angel* in tondo now in the church of S. Pietro Ispano at Boville Ernica, together with a similar tondo in the Museo Petriano, originally formed part of the *Navicella* in Old St. Peter's. Where—as in the Boville Ernica fragment—the hand of the restorer has not complicated the issue, there is much to remind us of the physiognomic types found in the Arena Chapel frescoes, and such affinities are scarcely less striking than the almost obtrusive indications of the influence of Cavallini.

An important event of recent years was the recovery of portions of a fresco-cycle in the main chapel of the Badia of Florence, consisting of scenes from the life of the Virgin.[4] Ghiberti believed these frescoes to be by Giotto, and according to Vasari, who singled out *The Annunciation* for special praise, they were his earliest works. Their fragmentary

[1] A complete and fully illustrated survey of attributions to Giotto is admirably presented in G. Vigorelli and E. Baccheschi, *L'opera completa di Giotto* (Milan, 1966).

[2] In Longhi's view the *tavolette* belonged to the *predella* of the Horne–Washington–Châalis polyptych: cf. R. Longhi, 'Progressi nella reintegrazione d'un polittico di Giotto', *Dedalo*, xi (1930), 285 ff., and 'Giudizio sul Duecento', *Proporzioni*, ii (1948), 5 ff.

[3] W. Suida, *Paintings and Sculptures from the Kress Collection* (Washington, 1951), pp. 21 ff.

[4] For the Badia frescoes see especially C. Gnudi, *Giotto* (Milan, 1958), p. 241 (with a provisional dating between the *Isaac* scenes at Assisi and the Arena Chapel cycle); U. Procacci, *Sinopie e affreschi* (Milan, 1961), p. 228; and Paolo Dal Poggetto, *Omaggio a Giotto* (Catalogue of the exhibition at Orsanmichele commemorating the seventh centenary of Giotto's birth) (Florence, 1967), pp. 12 ff.

nature and poor state of preservation make it difficult to arrive at more than very tentative conclusions about their authorship and date; but on the whole the quality of the
workmanship indicates the hand of a pupil of Giotto rather than that of the master
himself, whether we assume that the cycle was commissioned from Giotto but largely
entrusted to assistants, or whether we accept it as an independent work by one of his
followers. Moreover, the freedom and fluidity of the draughtsmanship—most apparent
in the only complete head to have survived, that of a young shepherd represented in
profile—would be hard to account for except in terms of Giotto's late style; and we may
compare this head with some of the expressive profiles that are so characteristic of the
Bardi Chapel cycle. The treatment of architectural forms is equally consistent with a
dating posterior to the execution of the Santa Croce frescoes: virtually all that survives
of the scene of *The Presentation in the Temple* is a perspectival view of the façade of an
imposing church, fronted by a portico raised on elegant classical columns; a building
which has no counterpart in the Arena cycle but which recalls, in its gracility and soaring
lightness, the lofty structures that dominate such scenes as *The Appearance of the Angel to
Zacharias* in the Peruzzi Chapel or, in the Bardi Chapel, *The Renunciation of Worldly
Goods*. It certainly cannot be assumed that Vasari was in possession of any positive
information regarding the early date of the Badia frescoes.

Giotto must be considered, in addition, as an architect and sculptor. Between 1334
and 1337, the year of his death, he held the office of *magister et gubernator* of the Opera di
Santa Reparata and of other building works in the city of Florence: during this period
he began the Campanile of the Cathedral, and what may be his original design is preserved in a coloured drawing in the Museo dell'Opera del Duomo at Siena; and he may
also have superintended the construction of the new Ponte alla Carraia on the Arno.[1]
According to Antonio Pucci, he designed some of the sculptural reliefs on the lower
part of the Campanile; and according to Vasari he had been responsible, at an earlier
date, for the designs for the reliefs on the Tarlati Monument in the Cathedral at Arezzo,
representing a series of New Testament subjects which were executed by Agostino di
Giovanni and Agnolo di Ventura.[2] But as there is no secure evidence of his employment
as an architect or as a sculptor before the last few years of his life, his work in either
capacity can be regarded as only marginally relevant to problems of attribution relating
to his early paintings.

It is a striking fact that of all the works that can be ascribed to Giotto with absolute
certainty the earliest for which we have a definite *terminus ante quem* is the Arena Chapel
cycle at Padua. As we have seen, the passage in the *Compilatio* of Riccobaldo da Ferrara,

---

[1] For the Siena drawing and the Ponte alla Carraia cf. D. Gioseffi, op. cit., pp. 74 ff., Plates XIII, XIV, Figs. 67, 70,
79, 80, 81, 82; and pp. 67 ff., 124 ff., Fig. 65.
[2] Giorgio Vasari, *Le Vite* . . . (1568), ed. Milanesi, i, 395; D. Gioseffi, op. cit., pp. 62 ff.

in which the frescoes are first mentioned, was written in 1312 or 1313; and the same *terminus ante quem*, the year 1313, is supplied by another early source, the *Documenti d'amore* of Francesco da Barberino, a work that refers in passing to Giotto's fresco of *Envy*, and which was completed by 1313.[1] A *terminus post quem* is provided by documentary evidence that the chapel had been begun by the year 1303.[2] Thus we are left with a fairly extensive period, the years 1303–13, within which the decoration of the Arena Chapel must have been executed: the precise date cannot be determined, but various considerations make it unlikely that the frescoes were painted later than 1309, and probable that they had been completed by the year 1306.[3] Yet even this date brings us into the period of Giotto's maturity as an artist, whether we accept as the year of his birth the traditional date of 1276 or whether, following most recent writers, we place it ten years earlier, in 1266 (1267 according to the modern Calendar). Since, therefore, we first encounter the 'authentic' Giotto relatively late in his career, the problem of his artistic origins presents particular difficulties, which are aggravated by the uncertainty over the exact date of his birth.

The Arena Chapel cycle, the greatest of Giotto's surviving works, creates a natural division in his life, and it is convenient to distinguish broadly between a pre-Paduan and a post-Paduan period. If the works mentioned in the *Compilatio* were listed by Riccobaldo in their chronological order, then within the pre-Paduan phase we can assume an activity first at Assisi and subsequently at Rimini, although not all scholars regard the Crucifix in the Tempio Malatestiano at Rimini as a work by Giotto from this period. However, the Paduan Cross, painted for the Arena Chapel, would no doubt have been executed at the same time as the frescoes or shortly afterwards.[4] A Florentine, and, according to a long tradition, the pupil of Cimabue, Giotto must have become known as a painter in his own city—where he is first documented in the year 1301—well before his visit to Padua, but the Badia frescoes, which Vasari believed to be his first paintings, cannot be securely dated within the pre-Paduan period. It is possible, however, that the Ognissanti *Madonna* dates from these early years. Certain characteristics of the frescoes in the Arena Chapel, especially their reflection of the influence of Cavallini and the antique, suggest the likelihood of a youthful visit to Rome: it should, however, be added that according to Vasari the work of Cavallini was known in Florence[5] and that not all the apparent borrowings from the antique in the Arena Chapel can be associated with Roman monuments.

[1] Francesco da Barberino, *Documenti d'amore*, ed. F. Egidi (Rome, 1905–27), ii, 165: 'unde Invidiosus invidia comburitur intus et extra hanc padue in arena optime pinsit Giottus.'

[2] A. Moschetti, *La Cappella degli Scrovegni e gli affreschi di Giotto in essa dipinti* (Florence, 1904), pp. 15 ff.; idem, 'Questioni cronologiche Giottesche', *Atti e Memorie della R. Accademia in Padova*, ccclxxx (1920–1), 181 ff.; U. Schlegel, 'Zum Bildprogramm der Arena-Kapelle', *Zeitschrift für Kunstgeschichte*, xx (1957), i, 125 ff.; C. Gnudi, *Giotto*, pp. 241 ff.

[3] See especially M. Meiss, *Giotto and Assisi*, pp. 4, 10, and D. Gioseffi, op. cit., pp. 35, 114 ff.

[4] For a dating c. 1317, cf. C. Gnudi, *Giotto*, p. 188.   [5] Giorgio Vasari, *Le Vite . . .* (1568), ed. Milanesi, i, 539.

On stylistic and other grounds we can assign to the post-Paduan period, besides the fresco-cycles in the Bardi and Peruzzi Chapels at Santa Croce, which have generally been dated in the 1320s, a number of other Florentine works—the Santa Croce *Coronation of the Virgin*, the Peruzzi Chapel altarpiece, and the Berlin *Dormition of the Virgin* (painted for Ognissanti). The Bologna altarpiece, originally at Santa Maria degli Angeli, must be very late, since the church was not erected until after 1328. To the last period of Giotto's life belong his works for King Robert of Anjou at Naples, of which nothing now survives, but which documents place within the years 1329–33, and those for Azzone Visconti in Milan, where he is recorded in 1336, the year before his death.

Thus we may sketch the outline of Giotto's working life, so far as it is known; and somewhere within this outline must be placed his visit to Rome to design, and perhaps to execute, the great mosaic of the *Navicella* for the atrium of St. Peter's. It is scarcely a *curriculum vitae*: it is the merest sketch and no more; and any attempt to fill out the details of his development, and to trace the origins of his art, must lay particular weight upon the stylistic evidence supplied by the cycle in the Arena Chapel, the earliest datable work unquestionably from his hand. Here we see the *arte nuova* of Giotto in all its clarity; here we have a yardstick by means of which we may measure the claims advanced for his authorship of other works, such as the *Jubilee* fresco at S. Giovanni Laterano in Rome, the crucifix traditionally ascribed to him at Santa Maria Novella in Florence, and not least the *Legend of St. Francis* at Assisi. It is equally on the basis of our knowledge of Giotto's style as it is revealed to us in the Arena Chapel that we must approach the important problems posed by the Louvre *Stigmatization*, in respect not only of its date but more especially of its evident iconographic dependence upon the Assisi cycle.

2. *Giotto in Rome: the* Navicella *and the Stefaneschi Altarpiece*

That Giotto was in Rome before the year 1313 is proved by a document of that date in which he empowers an agent to recover certain household goods still in the care of his former landlady in Rome.[1] Although there are indications that he was resident in Florence in 1311 and 1312[2] this document suggests a date for the Roman visit not long before 1313. However, there is no documentary evidence that it was at this time that he executed the celebrated mosaic of the *Navicella* for Old St. Peter's or any of the other Roman works attributed to him in the early sources, of which there now survive only the Stefaneschi altarpiece (in the Vatican Museum) and a small fragment of the frescoes once in the apse—the scenes from the Life of Christ ascribed to Giotto by Ghiberti.

The Stefaneschi altarpiece and the *Navicella* are first recorded in a *Martyrologium* of the

[1] A. Chiappelli, 'Nuovi documenti su Giotto', *L'Arte*, xxvi (1923), 132 ff.
[2] Ibid., loc. cit.; I. B. Supino, *Giotto* (Florence, 1920), p. 316.

benefactors of St. Peter's.[1] The entries in the *Martyrologium* referring to the benefactors are given under the dates on which they died, and under 22 June 1343 we find the following notice of Cardinal Stefaneschi:

There died master Jacobus Caetani de Stephanescis, of holy memory, deacon of St. George, Cardinal, and canon of our church, who brought us much good, for he had the apse painted, in which work he spent fifty florins of gold. He gave the picture painted by the hand of Giotto, above the High Altar of this same basilica, which cost 800 gold florins. In the roof of the same basilica he had the mosaic made in which Christ upholds the blessed Apostle Peter, by the hand of the same eminent painter, for which work he expended two thousand and two hundred florins, and many other works which it would take too much space to mention . . .[2]

Unfortunately this important document gives no date for either work. It was Filippo Villani, writing at the beginning of the following century, who first connected the *Navicella* with the Jubilee of 1300, asserting that Giotto executed the mosaic in time for the Jubilee in order to demonstrate his genius to the world, which was flocking to Rome for the festival.[3]

Other errors followed. Evidently through a misreading of the entry in the *Martyrologium*, Giotto's name was attached, not merely to the *Navicella* and the Stefaneschi altarpiece, but also to the frescoes in the apse.[4] Thus Ghiberti writes of Giotto: '. . . lavorò di mosayco la nave di San Piero in Roma, et di sua mano dipinse la capella e'lla tavola di S. Piero in Roma.' Secondly, Vasari, in attempting to collate the sources known to him, deduced by a false process of reasoning that the scenes from the Life of Christ, as well as a further series of frescoes of Old and New Testament subjects, were commissioned from Giotto by Pope Benedict: the name appears in Vasari's text as Benedict IX, but this must be a slip of the pen or a printing error for Benedict XI.[5] The pontificate of Benedict XI spanned but a few months of the years 1303–4, the period immediately preceding the removal of the Papal Court to Avignon under his successor Clement V. However, Vasari does not specifically date the *Navicella* within the same period, although his reference to it follows directly upon his description of Giotto's other work at St. Peter's—an account entirely mythical in character, but memorable for being prefaced by the famous story of Giotto's O.

The reasons that lie behind this dating of Giotto's sojourn in Rome seem sufficiently clear. Platina, writing in the 1470s, had mentioned in his *Liber de vita Christi ac Pontificum*

[1] Cf. P. Egidi, *Necrologi e libri affini della Provincia romana* (Rome, 1908), pp. 167 ff.

[2] This translation of the Latin text is taken from C. Carrà, op. cit., p. 53, n. 1.

[3] Filippo Villani, *De famosis civibus* (c. 1404): 'Unde ampliandi nominis cupidine per omnes fere Italie civitates famosas locis spectabilibus aliquid pinxit Romeque presertim in foribus ecclesie Sancti Petri Transtiberim, ubi ex musivo periclitantes navi apostolos artificiosissime figuravit, ut confluenti orbi terrarum ad urbem indulgentiarum temporibus de se arteque sua spectaculum faceret.'

[4] Cf. Lionello Venturi, 'La data dell'attività romana di Giotto', *L'Arte*, xxi (1918), 230.

[5] Ibid., pp. 231 f.; Murray, 'Notes on Some Early Giotto Sources', *Journal of the Warburg and Courtauld Institutes*, xvi (A53), p. 78. See Vasari, *Le Vite . . .* (1568), ed. Milanesi, i, p. 382.

omnium that Benedict XII, who was pope from 1334 to 1342, had expressed a desire to summon Giotto to Avignon: 'Zotum pictorem illa aetate egregium ad pingendas martyrum historias in aedibus a se structas [*sic*] conducere in animo habuit.'[1] However, the source used by Vasari in respect of this circumstance was evidently the well-known guide to Rome of Francesco Albertini, the *Opusculum de Mirabilibus novae urbis Romae*, published in 1510, which gives an erroneous transcript of Platina's information. Here the sentiments of Benedict XII described by Platina are attributed to Benedict XI: 'a Benedicto XI pont. max. in Avenionem ad pingendum martyrum historias accitus, ingenti pretio; morte interveniente opus omisit.'[2] Vasari must have been aware that Clement V, rather than his predecessor Benedict XI, was the Avignon pope: it seems therefore that he proceeded to connect Benedict XI with Giotto's papal commissions in Rome, and Clement V with the story about Avignon. Indeed, according to the *Chronicle* of Fra Jacopo Filippo da Bergamo, Giotto had not only gone to Avignon, but had died there, leaving unfinished the fresco-cycle devoted to the history of the Martyrs to which Albertini also refers.[3] Vasari, on the other hand, knew that Giotto had died in Florence, and so at the end of his story of the visit to Avignon he brings him home covered with glory:

... Soon after, Pope Clement V was elected at Perugia, on the death of Pope Benedict IX [*sic*], and Giotto was obliged to accompany the new pontiff to his court at Avignon to execute some works there. Thus, not only in Avignon, but in several other places of France, he painted many very beautiful frescoes and pictures, which greatly delighted the Pope and all his court. When he at length received his dismissal, he was sent away kindly with many gifts, so that he returned home no less rich than honoured and famous. ... The date of this return to Florence was the year 1316.[4]

In the seventeenth century the *Navicella* came to be associated once again with the Jubilee year of 1300. Baldinucci, in his *Notizie de' Professori del Disegno*, published in 1681, made an attempt to correct some of the errors and inventions of Vasari; but he was far from being free from error himself, and a new date now finds its way into print: according to Baldinucci the *Navicella* was commissioned by Cardinal Stefaneschi in the year 1298.[5] There can be no doubt that Baldinucci's source was an unfounded statement —an invention worthy of Vasari himself—in a manuscript treatise written by the painter Giulio Mancini.[6] Since Baldinucci gives the impression that he discovered this date in a document of the fourteenth century—in a version, in fact, of the *Martyrologium* of 1343 —subsequent writers generally accept it, assuming that the *Navicella* was required to be

[1] B. Platina, *Liber de vita Christi ac Pontificum omnium* (Venice, 1479), c. 172[v].
[2] Francesco Albertini, *Opusculum de Mirabilibus novae urbis Romae* (Heilbronn, 1886), p. 40.
[3] Cited by L. Venturi, loc. cit.   [4] Vasari, *Lives* ... (1658), trans. A. M. Hinds, i, 74.
[5] Filippo Baldinucci, *Notizie de' Professori del Disegno* ... (Florence, 1681), i, 44 f.
[6] L. Venturi, op. cit., pp. 232 ff.

ready in time for the Jubilee. This reading of the sequence of events represents a return, approximately, to the position of Filippo Villani, save that the urgent motives of ecclesiastical policy now replace the artist's desire for personal glory.

Stylistic considerations apart, there is nevertheless one strong argument against a date in or before the year 1300: so long as Rome was still the seat of the Papacy, one would expect that a commission of this importance, instead of coming from Cardinal Stefaneschi, would have been the prerogative of the Pope himself; but it would have been a different matter during the period of the exile at Avignon, when Stefaneschi was placed in charge of St. Peter's.[1] On these grounds, therefore, it seems more plausible to propose a date for the *Navicella* within the period 1304–13.[2] This dating would place Giotto's visit to Rome either immediately before or, more probably, soon after his visit to Padua to decorate the Arena Chapel. We are left with no further guidance except that afforded by the internal evidence of style. This, however, is not very sure, for the original appearance of the *Navicella* can be deduced only approximately from copies and derivations. Nevertheless, the general character of the figure-composition shows a fairly close relationship with the Arena Chapel cycle, where also we find heads (for example, in *The Last Judgement*) which are consistent with Giotto's authorship of the unrestored tondo at Boville Ernica. On the other hand, no aspect of the *Navicella* recalls any feature of the *Legend of St. Francis* at Assisi, unless it is the reflection, apparent in both works, of the pervasive influence of Cavallini.

The Stefaneschi altarpiece[3] falls into a different category. Although there can be little doubt that the existing work in the Vatican Museum is to be identified with the picture recorded in the *Martyrologium* as having been commissioned from Giotto by Cardinal Stefaneschi, the execution is far inferior to that of any autograph work by Giotto, and only the figure of the donor in the central front panel (*The Redeemer Enthroned*) approaches the quality of his painting. A glance at the figures in the lateral scenes on the wings (*The Martyrdom of St. Peter* and *The Beheading of St. Paul*) is alone sufficient to raise doubts about the authorship of the altarpiece. Moreover, this elaborate form of Gothic triptych suggests a taste closer to that of Bernardo Daddi than to Giotto's own. In a deeper sense the triptych has affinities also with the *Franciscan Allegories* and with the other frescoes painted by the 'Maestro delle Vele' in the Lower Church at Assisi, although

---

[1] C. Gnudi, *Giotto*, p. 247.

[2] The date proposed by Lionello Venturi—*c.* 1320—seems far too late, although it might explain Riccobaldo da Ferrara's failure to mention the *Navicella* in his brief account of Giotto's works. Paeseler has proposed a date around 1310: cf. W. Paeseler, 'Giottos Navicella und ihr spätantikes Vorbild', *Römisches Jahrbuch für Kunstgeschichte*, v (1941), 49 ff. White thinks that the style is less developed than in the Arena Chapel, and he therefore prefers a date before the Paduan period: cf. J. White, *Art and Architecture in Italy . . .*, pp. 217 f.

[3] For this work see E. Müntz, 'Il tesoro della Basilica di San Pietro in Vaticano dal XIII al XV secolo', *Archivio della R. Società Romana di Storia Patria*, vi (1883), 81 ff.; M. Gosebruch, 'Giottos römischer Stefaneschi-Altar und die Fresken des sog. "Maestro delle Vele" in der Unterkirche zu Assisi', *Kunstchronik*, xi (1958), 288 ff.

it is not certainly by the same hand.[1] On the whole it is safest to assume that it is a product of Giotto's Roman workshop: this hypothesis is not irreconcilable with the notice in the *Martyrologium*, on the assumption that, having accepted the commission from Cardinal Stefaneschi, Giotto was content to entrust one or more of his pupils with its execution. That this was Giotto's frequent practice in respect of altar-paintings on panel is indicated by the diverse stylistic qualities of his signed altarpieces, which must in the main be workshop products. Given that the picture in the Vatican Museum is the work commissioned by Cardinal Stefaneschi, its exceptional qualities are the less puzzling in that many of them reappear in the vault frescoes in the Lower Church at Assisi, which are unquestionably by one of Giotto's direct pupils. Further affinities with the Bologna polyptych, which have long been recognized, suggest the participation of the same assistant in the painting of both altarpieces.

3. *Works Falsely Ascribed to Giotto*

(a) The Jubilee *Fresco*

In February 1300 a splendid ceremony was performed in the Loggia of Benediction which Boniface VIII had built on to his new palace at the Lateran: in the presence of the Pope and the assembled Curia, a Bull of Indulgence was published proclaiming to the people the institution of the Jubilee. Shortly afterwards the Loggia was decorated with frescoes commemorating this event and glorifying Boniface VIII as a worthy successor to the Emperor Constantine, the founder of the Lateran Basilica. Three subjects were represented: The Baptism of Constantine; The Founding of The Lateran Church; and The Proclamation of the Jubilee. There has survived from this extensive scheme of decoration a fragment of the last of these three scenes: at the time of the rebuilding of the Lateran Palace, in the late sixteenth century, the central upper portion of the fresco was detached from the wall and transferred to the cloisters; later it was fixed to a pillar inside the church, where it can still be seen today; recent restoration has removed layers of repaint.[2]

Boniface VIII is represented in the fresco in the act of giving his blessing to the populace from a high portico; a clerk standing beside him has just finished reading the text of the Bull; the impressive-looking dignitary on the other side of the Pope is traditionally supposed to be a portrait of Cardinal Stefaneschi; on the far right, beyond one of the pillars supporting the canopy, can be seen a bearded attendant represented in profile.

---

[1] B. Khvoshinsky and M. Salmi, *I pittori toscani dal XIII al XVI secolo* (Rome, 1912–14), i, 11; M. Gosebruch, op. cit., pp. 118 ff.; R. Van Marle, *The Development of the Italian Schools of Painting*, iii (The Hague, 1924), 201 ff.

[2] The account of the Lateran fresco given here is largely based upon the study by Charles Mitchell, 'The Lateran Fresco of Boniface VIII', *Journal of the Warburg and Courtauld Institutes*, xiv (1851), 1 ff. For the restorations see C. Brandi, 'Giotto recuperato a San Giovanni Laterano', in *Scritti di Storia dell'Arte in onore di Lionello Venturi* (Rome, 1956), i, 55 ff. For the Year of Jubilee of 1300 see T. S. R. Boase, *Boniface VIII* (London, 1933), pp. 231 ff.

Over the balcony there hangs a rich tapestry, flanked by the papal arms. Although only this small fragment of the fresco has survived, the rest of the composition is known to us from an old coloured drawing in the Ambrosiana. This shows, on either side of the canopy, ranks of Cardinals and other clerics, and, rising above their heads, an *ombrellino*, a pastoral cross, and the halberds of the papal guard. The balcony upon which all these figures stand is decorated with a frieze bearing alternately the Caetani arms[1] and the papal keys and tiara, and it is supported by three magnificent Corinthian columns, placed immediately beneath the papal canopy. Below, an excited crowd reacts joyfully to the new decree. It is an impressively ordered design. The square form of the canopy, the long horizontal of the balcony, and the disposition of the columns divide the composition into regular geometric areas: in this and in other respects the design owes much to an ancient relief on the obelisk of Theodosius at Constantinople;[2] but it sounds an entirely modern note in the realism of its presentation of the imposing scene and in the vivacity of its treatment of the human figure.

The date of the fresco must be close to the year 1300. It is still widely accepted as an early work by Giotto, but the attribution has no foundation whatsoever.[3] No early source mentions it, nor does it help to swell the list of attributions to Giotto supplied by Vasari. In fact Vasari ascribed the fresco to Giottino,[4] while Panvinio, writing in 1570, gave it to Cimabue.[5] It was not associated with Giotto's name until the middle of the seventeenth century, when his authorship was proposed by Cardinal Rasponi, the compiler of a history of the Lateran.[6]

There are, undoubtedly, certain stylistic affinities between the *Jubilee* fresco and the *Legend of St. Francis* at Assisi, and it has even been argued that the Lateran fresco establishes Giotto's authorship of the Assisi cycle:[7] it need only be said that it is a poor case that rests upon such insecure foundations. Moreover, the closest resemblances at Assisi to the style of the *Jubilee* fresco are found in some of the scenes on the south wall, which

[1] For the arms of Boniface VIII and for an account of the development during his reign of the triple-crowned tiara see D. L. Galbreath, *A Treatise on Ecclesiastical Heraldry*, Part I: *Papal Heraldry* (Cambridge, 1930), pp. 18 ff. Like those represented in the *St. Francis* cycle at Assisi, the tiara seen in the Lateran fresco belongs to the earlier type, which had only one circlet.

[2] C. Mitchell, op. cit., p. 5, and Pl. 3*b*.

[3] The authorship is discussed in F. Rintelen, op. cit. (1st edn., 1912), pp. 224 f.

[4] Giorgio Vasari, *Le Vite . . .* (1568), ed. Milanesi, i, 626.

[5] Onofrio Panvinio, *De praecipuis urbis Romae sanctioribusque basilicis* (Rome, 1570), p. 113. See also P. Lauer, *Le Palais du Latran; étude historique et archéologique* (Paris, 1911), pp. 233 ff.

[6] Cesare Rasponi, *De Basilica et Patriarchio Lateranensi libri quattuor* (Rome, 1656), pp. 327 f.

[7] Cf. Salvini, op. cit., i, 22: 'In 1300 Giotto returned to Rome where he painted, in the Lateran Basilica, *Boniface Proclaiming the Jubilee*. The recently recovered fragments . . . provide unquestionable proof that Giotto painted *The Legend of St. Francis* and that he did so in the last years of the thirteenth century'; and again, p. 53: ' . . . This fragment is extremely important in that it confirms beyond any possibility of error both the attribution to Giotto of *The Legend of St. Francis* and its date of execution before 1300.' More recently the fresco has been ascribed by Previtali (op. cit., p. 369) to one of Giotto's Roman assistants.

even the proponents of Giotto's responsibility for the cycle as a whole assign to other hands. The Lateran composition surely reflects nothing of Giotto's mind: it is quite impossible to suppose that the painter of this fresco, which must have been executed in 1300 or very shortly afterwards, developed within the space of two or three years into the author of the Arena Chapel cycle. Moreover, a glance at the modelling of the heads and hands is sufficient to show that the style of the fresco is less advanced than that of the *Legend* at Assisi, so that it becomes equally impossible to imagine a 'Giotto' who, having conceived and largely executed the Assisi cycle, reverted immediately afterwards to older, Roman traditions. The fresco is probably by a Roman artist whose manner is not identifiable in other surviving works, but who may possibly have had contacts with the St. Francis Master and his associates at Assisi.

(b) *The Santa Maria Novella Cross*

No single work has a more crucial place in the arguments advanced on behalf of the 'inclusive' view of Giotto's early development, which ascribes to him both the *Isaac* group of frescoes at Assisi and the *Legend of St. Francis*, than the large crucifix which hangs today in the sacristy of Santa Maria Novella in Florence (Plate 12a).[1] Giotto's execution of a large crucifix for Santa Maria Novella is established by documents of 1312 and 1315, and Ghiberti refers to a crucifix in the church which he believed to be by Giotto: furthermore, what appears to be the crucifix now in the sacristy is mentioned as a work by Giotto in other sources dating from the early sixteenth century. It has generally been assumed, therefore, that the existing crucifix must be the work commissioned from Giotto; attention has been drawn to the remarkably similar cross represented in Scene XXII of the *St. Francis* cycle (*The Verification of the Stigmata*, Plate 12b); and certain stylistic affinities have been noted not only with the *St. Francis* cycle but also with the *Isaac* scenes.[2] On the other hand a considerable body of opinion has refused the crucifix to Giotto on the grounds of its marked stylistic divergences from the S. Felice and Padua crosses and others executed by Giotto or his pupils, such as

---

[1] For the Santa Maria Novella Cross see especially R. Offner, *Corpus*, III, vi, 9 ff., and G. Sinibaldi and G. Brunetti, op. cit., pp. 301 ff. Gioseffi (op. cit., p. 105) calls the crucifix the 'vero ponte tra i due momenti [of Giotto's activity at Assisi]'.

[2] Coletti, for example, notes 'le straordinarie affinità morfologiche e tipologiche fra le prime storie di Assisi — anzi anche fra quelle della zona superiore dell'ultima campata — e il Crocefisso di Sta Maria Novella, specialmente i Dolenti che è del tutto irragionevole negare a Giotto'; cf. L. Coletti, *Gli affreschi della Basilica di Assisi* (Bergamo, 1949), pp. 96 f. Elsewhere Coletti remarks that to deny the Assisi frescoes to Giotto involves also the negation of the Santa Maria Novella Cross, which he relates both to the 'identico Crocefisso' represented in Scene XXII of the *St. Francis* cycle and to the *Pietà* by the Isaac Master ('dove una delle Marie è identica alla Vergine del "Crocefisso"'); he adds that the Santa Maria Novella Cross is recorded as a work by Giotto in the document of 1312: cf. L. Coletti, *I Primitivi* (Novara, 1941–7), i, xlv f. See also K. Bauch, 'Die geschichtliche Bedeutung von Giottos Frühstil', *Mitteilungen des Kunsthistorischen Instituts in Florenz*, vi (1953), 43 ff. (originally given as a paper read at the Kunsthistorisches Institut of Florence on 1 June 1942).

those at Rimini and at S. Marco in Florence, concluding as a necessary corollary of this rejection that the documents must refer to another crucifix which has since disappeared.[1]

There are two extant documents referring to Giotto's crucifix. The first of these, the document of 1312, contains the provision made in the will of one Riccuccio Pucci for the cost of the oil for the perpetual lamp hung in front of the crucifix at Santa Maria Novella 'painted by the celebrated painter Giotto di Bondone'.[2] A second document, of 1315, notes the payment of 5 lire and 4 soldi by the Company of the Laudesi for an ounce of oil, in accordance with the terms of Pucci's will, for the 'lampada del crocifixo grande di Giotto'.[3] There can, therefore, be no doubt that Giotto did paint a large crucifix for Santa Maria Novella; and the existence of a crucifix by Giotto at the church is mentioned in the Commentarii:[4] but whether this was the crucifix now in the sacristy is quite another matter.

Until fairly recently the existing crucifix hung over the central doorway of the nave. According to Cavalcaselle, it was moved there from a side-chapel after the restorations carried out in the church in 1861;[5] but Cavalcaselle may well have been in error on this point, or perhaps the crucifix had been housed only temporarily in the side-chapel during the restorations, for a reference to a 'large crucifix' by Giotto 'sopra la porta di mezo [sic]' already appears in the Libro di Antonio Billi, compiled in the early sixteenth century;[6] a reference repeated by the Anonimo[7] and elaborated by Vasari, who adds that Giotto painted the crucifix with the assistance of Puccio Capanna.[8] The existing crucifix, however, cannot have been designed from the beginning to hang over the doorway: most probably it stood originally over the old marble choir-screen—or ponte, as it was

---

[1] The attribution to Giotto was first questioned by Cavalcaselle: cf. J. A. Crowe and G. B. Cavalcaselle, *A New History of Painting in Italy . . .*, ii, 282. It has since been denied by Frey, Rintelen, Sirén, Weigelt, Berenson, Offner, Dorothy Shorr, and others; for the literature see Offner, *Corpus*, III, vi, 9 ff.

[2] 'Anno ab eius incarnatione millesimo trecentesimo duodecimo ind. decima die quintodecimo mensis Junij. Discretus uir Ricchuccius filius quondam Puccii de populo Sce. Marie Nouelle de Florentia . . . disposuit . . . dare et soluere sacristie fratrum Predicatorum dicte ecclesie Sce. Me. Nouelle libras quinque flor. paru. pro emendis annuatim duobus urceis olei, ex quo oleo unus urceus sit pro tenenda continue illuminata lampada crucifixi entis in eadem ecclesia Sce. Me. Nouelle, picti per egregium pictorem nomine Giottum Bondonis, qui est de dicto populo Sce. Me. Nouelle, coram quo crucifixo est laterna ossea empta per ipsum testatorem' (Archivio di Stato, Florence: Archivio Diplomatico, Santa Maria Novella). Published in Vasari, *Le Vite . . .*, ed. K. Frey (Munich, 1911), i, 458 n.; Offner, *Corpus*, III, vi, 10; quoted inaccurately in F. Vincenzio Fineschi, *Memorie Istoriche che possono servire alle vite degli Uomini Illustri del Convento di S. Maria Novella di Firenze* (Florence, 1790), i, 321.

[3] Offner, *Corpus*, loc. cit.; first published by R. Oertel in *Zeitschrift für Kunstgeschichte*, vi (1937), 224.

[4] Lorenzo Ghiberti, *I Commentarii*; in *Denkwürdigkeiten . . .*, ed. Julius von Schlosser (Berlin, 1912), i, 36.

[5] G. B. Cavalcaselle, *Storia della pittura in Italia . . .*, i (Florence, 1875), 478 f.

[6] *Il Libro di Antonio Billi e le sue copie nella Biblioteca Nazionale di Firenze*, ed. Cornelio de Fabriczy, in *Archivio Storico Italiano*, vii (Florence, 1891), 319: 'Dipinse in S.ta Maria Novella uno crocifisso grande, che è oggi sopra la porta di mezo; et uno s.to Lodovico sopra il tramezo da mano destra. . . .'

[7] C. de Fabriczy, 'Il Codice dell'Anonimo Gaddiano nella Biblioteca Nazionale di Firenze', in *Archivio Storico Italiano*, xii (Florence, 1893), 46 f.

[8] Giorgio Vasari, *Le Vite . . .* (1568), ed. Milanesi, i, 394.

called—which was to be dismantled by Vasari in 1565.[1] But, as Offner pointed out, a church of the size and importance of Santa Maria Novella is likely to have contained more than one crucifix, even at this early date: at Santa Croce, for example, there were certainly by the early fourteenth century at least two large crucifixes—the great crucifix by Cimabue (all but destroyed in the tragic floods of 1966) and the crucifix by the 'Maestro di Figline' which still hangs in the choir of the church.[2] The early sources refer to many pictures by Giotto and his contemporaries that have since disappeared without trace from the churches they once adorned. Ghiberti, for instance, mentions a crucifix by Giotto at S. Giorgio alla Costa,[3] but no such work is now to be found there. He also says that Giotto painted for Santa Maria Novella itself, in addition to the crucifix, 'a panel and many other things',[4] none of which is known to us. Again, Vasari refers to a crucifix there by Stefano Fiorentino, 'which has since been much damaged by other painters in restoring it'.[5] Might this not even have been Giotto's crucifix, and was it subsequently removed from the church because of its damaged condition? We cannot tell; but at all events we do know for certain of the disappearance from Santa Maria Novella of several unspecified works which were ascribed to Giotto by Ghiberti, together with a crucifix ascribed by Vasari to Stefano: it becomes all the more difficult, therefore, to argue with any confidence that the crucifix now in the sacristy *must* be the work referred to in the documents.

Both the style and the iconography of the existing crucifix point to a date not far from 1300; and attempts have been made to explain its lack of resemblance to the Padua cross in terms of the rapid evolution of Giotto's style. According to this view, then, the Santa Maria Novella Cross reflects Giotto's pre-Paduan or (as we may conveniently call it) his 'Assisan' style, and even provides a link between the *Isaac* frescoes and the *St. Francis* cycle.[6] Naturally enough, particular stress is placed upon the fact that the crucifix conforms precisely to the type of cross represented in Scene XXII of the *Legend*, from which it differs only in the greater thickness given in the fresco to the beams of the cross —a variation that might be explained by the painter's attempt to render the crucifix in perspective. Moreover, in Scene XIII (*The Christmas Crib at Greccio*, Plate 63) we find a further representation of a crucifix: we see it from the back, and it stands upon a marble rood-screen such as that formerly at Santa Maria Novella. It seems to offer suggestive

---

[1] See J. Wood Brown, *The Dominican Church of Santa Maria Novella* (Edinburgh, 1902), p. 119; Giovanni Gaye, *Carteggio inedito d'artisti dei secoli XIV, XV, XVI* (Florence, 1839-40), ii (1840), 480; Stefano Orlandi, '*Necrologio*' *di S. Maria Novella* (Florence, 1955), ii, 402; W. Paatz, *Die Kirchen von Florenz* (Frankfurt am Main, 1952-5), iii (1952), 674, 734 f.

[2] Offner, *Corpus*, III, vi, 11, n. 14.

[3] '. . . È in sto. Georgio una tavola e uno crocifixo . . .'

[4] '. . . una tavola perfectissima di sua mano: ancora vi sono molte altre cose . . .'

[5] Giorgio Vasari, *Le Vite . . .* (1568), ed. Milanesi, i, 449.

[6] See, for example, Gioseffi, op. cit., p. 105.

evidence in support of the view that the Santa Maria Novella Cross was known to the designer of the cycle and provided the model for the crucifix represented in Scene XXII. Understandably, this connection has been regarded as proof of the common authorship of the cycle and the existing crucifix at Santa Maria Novella, and, both the cycle and the crucifix having a traditional attribution to Giotto, the style of each work has appeared to confirm the paternity of the other. Furthermore, Giotto's authorship of a crucifix for Santa Maria Novella is not merely recorded in literary tradition, but securely documented: what greater proof, it has been asked, could there be of his authorship of the *St. Francis* cycle, especially in view of the testimony of Riccobaldo da Ferrara to Giotto's employment in the Basilica?[1]

Nevertheless, even on documentary grounds, this inference that the attribution of the *St. Francis* cycle to Giotto is given support by the documents of 1312 and 1315 is open to one serious objection, which is no less crucial than the failure of Riccobaldo to indicate the nature of Giotto's work at Assisi; for the argument ignores an important document, now no longer extant but known to Fineschi in the late eighteenth century, which dates Giotto's crucifix at Santa Maria Novella within the post-Paduan period. This document referred unequivocally to payment made to Giotto for a crucifix completed by him for Santa Maria Novella in the year 1312:[2] nor, it may be added, do the surviving documents take us back beyond this date.

If, therefore, the existing crucifix is an early work, from the 'Assisan' period, it cannot be the cross painted by Giotto in 1312. Alternatively, if it is argued that it is a late work by Giotto, painted in that year, then we are confronted with the impossible task of reconciling it with his post-Paduan style; for it is inconceivable that, as a work by Giotto, it can postdate either the Arena Chapel *Crucifixion* (Plate 36a) or the Padua Cross itself. As it happens, supporting evidence of the early date of the Santa Maria Novella Cross is supplied by its apparent influence upon a crucifix by Deodato Orlandi in the Convent of St. Clare at S. Miniato al Tedesco (Plate 13a), which is dated 1301:[3] the figure of Christ in this work is almost identical in pose and general conception with the Christ of Santa Maria Novella, whereas in an earlier cross by the same artist at Lucca, dated 1288, the figure still conforms entirely to the older Romanesque type.[4] So radical a change in the style of a minor master of the period would seem inexplicable without some powerful external influence, such as the example of the crucifix in the great Dominican church would have afforded. If, then, Fineschi's information is correct—and

[1] L. Coletti, *I Primitivi*, i, p. xlvi.

[2] Cf. V. Fineschi, op. cit., i, 321, n. 2. This document stated that in the year 1312 Giotto 'finì di dipignere il Crocifisso'. See also Offner, *Corpus*, III, vi, 10, n. 12, referring to a manuscript volume in the Biblioteca Moreniana in Florence containing excerpts from various documents, one of which includes the statement that Giotto 'dipinse un Crocifisso l'anno 1312 per la chiesa di S. Maria Novella'.

[3] E. B. Garrison, *Italian Romanesque Panel Painting: An Illustrated Index* (Florence, 1949), No. 535.

[4] Ibid., No. 534.

it is hard to see on what grounds it could be doubted—the documentary evidence when taken as a whole, so far from supporting Giotto's authorship of the crucifix now to be seen at Santa Maria Novella, would seem to exclude all possibility of it. In no sense can it be maintained that the stylistic criticism which refuses the crucifix to Giotto is in conflict with the documents.

It is questionable, indeed, whether serious stylistic criticism can fail to remove the crucifix from Giotto's *œuvre* and to transfer it, following the lead given by Offner, to the circle of the St. Cecilia Master. The fact remains that the crucifixes attributable without question to Giotto and his pupils[1] all follow a single pattern and reveal similar artistic preoccupations; while those attributable to the pupils or associates of the St. Cecilia Master[2] are no less consistent in style. We are concerned with two distinct types of crucifix, reflecting two distinct traditions; and to ascribe the Santa Maria Novella Cross to Giotto is to accept an anomaly which requires explanation.

Both types, of which the Santa Maria Novella Cross (Plate 12a) and Giotto's Paduan Crucifix (Plate 11b) are the prime exemplars, show important differences from the older, late-thirteenth-century tradition of the *Christus patiens* as it is found, for instance, in the crucifixes of Cimabue (Plate 11a). Cimabue stresses the sheer, insupportable weight of Christ's body, which hangs outwards from the cross to the spectator's left, while the upper part of the torso is pulled the other way by the muscles of the left shoulder. The Padua Cross, on the other hand, clearly derives from a simpler, less dramatic conception of the crucifix, not uncommon in Tuscany in the late thirteenth century, which visualizes the weight of the body as being distributed equally between the two arms, with the consequence that the thorax no longer swings to the left, and the bulging left shoulder is replaced by a form of finer and more natural proportioning; at the same time Giotto places greater emphasis upon the articulation of the legs, which are set further apart and allowed to assist more in bearing the weight of the body; and a generally softer modelling within the figure tones down the sharpness of such features as the ribs and the clavicle, which in the typical thirteenth-century representations are prominently drawn. The quality that distinguishes Giotto's image of the Crucified from all previous interpretations is his profoundly sculptural treatment of form, according to which the figure is visualized as a plastic mass protruding from the flat plane of the cross, like a figure sculptured in bronze or wood. And whereas in the Cimabuesque Crucifix the body of Christ curves two-dimensionally in a large arc which is reversed in the tilt of the head, in the Giottesque Crucifix the head and the knees thrust forward, and the whole figure, from head to foot, obeys a spatial rather than a linear rhythm: the

---

[1] Arena Chapel, Padua; Ognissanti, Florence; S. Felice, Florence; S. Marco, Florence; Tempio Malatestiano, Rimini.

[2] Santa Maria Novella, Florence; Convento delle Oblate, Careggi, Florence (Plate 13b); Corsi Collection, Florence; Accademia, Florence, No. 436; S. Qurico, Ruballa; Oberlin College, Ohio; Museo dell'Opera di Santa Croce, Florence, No. 15.

head and the knees are brought into a new relationship, not merely as shapes that detach themselves from the verticality of the figure seen as a design on the flat, but more essentially as the only forms that protrude outwards from the plane of the torso.

It is in its contradiction of such principles that the Santa Maria Novella Cross differs most radically from the crucifixes of Giotto and his School. While it also avoids the position of the figure characteristic of the Cimabuesque type—although still emphasizing the muscles of the left shoulder—and draws the body back towards the upright beam of the cross, it carries this process so far that the figure now bends markedly at the waist and the hips bulge out to the spectator's right. Whereas in the Cimabuesque crucifix the thorax swings outwards to the left, in the crucifix at Santa Maria Novella it is pulled in the opposite direction. Clearly a determining factor in the evolution of this type of cross, which may conceivably be of Roman origin, was the desire to achieve a perfect harmony between the rounded forms of the figure and the simple rectilinear framework enclosing it, which is never replaced in any works of the School by the elaborate mould-ings and quatrefoil framings that are so notable a feature of the Cross at Padua. In the Santa Maria Novella Crucifix the rounded mass of the hips balances the inclined head, with its halo, about the upright of the cross, so that within the rectangle formed by the patterned apron behind the figure a delicate equipoise of comparable shapes is attained. Yet this harmony, however beautiful, is essentially two-dimensional in conception, in the sense that a receding form is weighed against one that comes forward, as though in the painter's mind their similarity of shape gave them an equal value. This is not to deny that the figure itself is represented three-dimensionally, but simply to question whether spatial concepts materially affected the design: on the other hand, there can be no doubt that in the Arena Chapel Crucifix they determined its principal features. Nor, it may be added, were Giotto's innovations upon the traditional crucifix confined to the central figure. In the Padua Crucifix the figures of the Virgin and St. John the Evangelist represented on the terminals are brought into a dramatic and spatial relationship with the Crucified: their bodies turn inwards, and their expressions betray extreme anguish as they gaze upon their Lord, whereas in the Santa Maria Novella Cross they remain passive witnesses, grieving within themselves, and are precluded by their frontal placing from taking the same active part in the drama of Golgotha.[1]

A significant difference between the Christs of the Santa Maria Novella and Arena Chapel Crucifixes was pointed out by Kurt Bauch when he noted that the one was a sleeping, and the other a dead figure;[2] a distinction elaborated by Offner in his masterly analysis of the style of the Crucifix of Santa Maria Novella:

---

[1] The gestures of the terminal figures in both crucifixes have their ultimate origins in classical antiquity. On this question in general see Dorothy C. Shorr, 'The Mourning Virgin and St. John', *Art Bulletin*, xxii (1940), 61 ff.

[2] Kurt Bauch, op. cit., p. 43.

The figure of Christ hardly suggests death, still less any of the noble aspects of spiritual martyrdom. It represents a body of muscular build and bone, more suited to rustic exertion than moulded by the divine spirit, much less a body by such a master as Giotto to whom it is often attributed. We need only compare the Sta Maria Novella Cross with Giotto's Paduan Cross to see that where Giotto sustains an inner exaltation, the Sta Maria Novella Cross is restless and bristles with animal energy. There is not one feature of the clumsily foreshortened head or of his mortal body that reflects the greatness of the moment. The muscles are taut with physical strains and the lungs expanded in breathing. The gushing blood (supplied in part by a later brush) fails to provide a drop of evidence of that cessation of life which in the Paduan instance sustains the semblance of eternal peace. Whereas Giotto's figure carries us invariably towards the region of ideas, here it is an object taken directly from life . . .

The type, the elongated, slender proportions of Giotto's figures of the Crucified, their kinetic implications, consistently diverge from those of the Sta Maria Novella Cross. But most of all the divergencies inhere in the evocation of the third dimension. In Giotto this is accomplished by means of light and shade which encircles the solid, without the superimposition of so arbitrary an element as an outline which mars the illusionism of the Sta Maria Novella Cross. Here, as never in Giotto, the line is used descriptively as a boundary, not in its plastic function, and has been given a rhythmic character independent of its specific purpose and conforming to the larger structural articulations of the body.[1]

This analysis does less than justice, perhaps, to the beauty of the crucifix, which resides no less in the gracefulness of its design than in its simple harmonies of colour (as in the deep blues and light reds of the draperies of the Virgin and St. John, these reds being echoed in the upper part of the cross and in the pinkish notes in Christ's loincloth): yet there can be no doubt that Offner is correct in making a clear and absolute distinction between its author's artistic aims and those of Giotto. And if stylistically the Santa Maria Novella Cross appears quite irreconcilable with the Paduan Cross or with the Arena Chapel *Crucifixion*, it seems equally far removed from the spiritual world of the Isaac Master at Assisi.

The stylistic case so far advanced for the common authorship of the crucifix and the *Isaac* frescoes rests almost entirely upon a supposed resemblance between the figure of St. John the Evangelist (Plate 14d) on the right terminal and the figure of Esau (Plate 14c) in the fresco of *The Rejection of Esau* in the Upper Church.[2] It is doubtful, however, whether the likeness can be regarded as more than superficial. The St. John belongs essentially to an earlier culture as yet untouched by the profound rethinking upon which the style of the *Isaac* scenes is so clearly founded. It is closer to that late-thirteenth-century Florentine evolution which culminates in the more 'advanced' mosaics in the lower registers of the vault of the Florentine Baptistery;[3] and a comparison between the St.

[1] Offner, *Corpus*, III, vi, 9.   [2] M. Meiss, op. cit., p. 24.
[3] For the Baptistery mosaics cf. A. de Witt, *I mosaici del Battistero di Firenze* (Florence, 1954); C. L. Ragghianti, *Pittura del Dugento a Firenze* (Florence, 1955); M. Salmi, 'I mosaici del "Bel San Giovanni" e la pittura del secolo XIII a Firenze', *Dedalo*, xi (1930–1), 543 ff.

John of the Santa Maria Novella Cross and the representation of the young Baptist (Plate 14*b*) in the scene in the Baptistery of *St. John's Retirement to the Desert* reveals affinities of a more than general nature which only serve to emphasize the relative remoteness of the figure of Esau in the Assisi fresco.

The resemblance between the two heads is most obvious in the treatment and styling of the hair, which flows over the forehead from the crown in a heavy fringe, concealing half the brow, and which elsewhere is broken up into separate, mop-like thatches of curl. The hair lies loosely upon the head, adding to its apparent size, and creates effects of pattern within the outline. The Isaac Master's treatment, on the other hand, is more functional: the hair is not broken up in the same way, but falls in long waves from the crown to the shoulder; the thick fringe common to the other two heads, forming a kind of cap over the forehead, is replaced by shorter and finer curls which leave most of the brow uncovered; and the hair, rather than obscuring the shape of the skull beneath, accentuates it. As we shall see, the whole figure seems to have been inspired by a classical model. Nor is the Isaac Master's triumphant solution of the problem of representing a solid form in space to be confused with the partial understanding of such problems evinced in the other two heads, where, for instance, the plane of the brow wholly lacks the recession suggested in the same form in the head of Esau. And to compare the St. John of the crucifix first with the Esau of the fresco and then with the Baptist of the mosaic is to be struck as much by the dissimilarities of actual feature that are disclosed by the first comparison as by the similarities revealed by the second. Above all, perhaps, the author of the crucifix and the 'proto-Giotto' of the *Isaac* scenes differ from one another in their feeling for the proportioning of a head: a typical example of distinctions of this kind can be seen in the unusually long upper lip which is so striking a feature of the St. John; a feature that has no parallel in the physiognomy of any figure by the Isaac Master; nor can such proportions be discovered in a single head in the Arena Chapel cycle or in any other authentic work by Giotto, where the upper lip is invariably much shorter than the distance between mouth and chin: indeed, except possibly in some passage entrusted to an assistant, so manifest a contradiction of recognized principles of proportion and measure is scarcely conceivable in his art. Similar proportions are, however, found in several of the figures in the *Legend* at Assisi.

(c) The S. Giorgio Madonna

The same type of head reappears in the *Madonna* at S. Giorgio alla Costa in Florence (Plate 15*b*), a work that has been ascribed to Giotto on the insubstantial grounds that Ghiberti refers to a painting by Giotto in the church, although he does not give its subject.[1] Possibly by Ghiberti's day the *Madonna* was thought to be by Giotto, but, as

---

[1] L. Ghiberti, *I Commentarii*, loc. cit.; Sinibaldi and Brunetti, op. cit., p. 357.

Offner has demonstrated, its style is close to that of the Santa Maria Novella Cross, even if Offner's view that it must have been painted by the same master is open to some doubt.[1] Stylistically the S. Giorgio *Madonna* depends either directly upon the type of the 'Cecilian' *Madonna*, as it is seen, for example, in the *Madonna* at Montici (Plate 15a), or upon the same traditions that moulded the St. Cecilia Master's own development. The origins of this type of *Madonna* can be traced back through the lovely *Madonna* in the church of S. Andrea at Mosciano (Plate 110c), by an anonymous painter working towards the end of the thirteenth century, to a small group of other Florentine panels of the late Dugento; but there is also present in the work both of the St. Cecilia Master and of the Master of the Santa Maria Novella Cross a reflection of a distinctly Arnolfian culture which is combined with a no less evident indebtedness to Cavallini. The S. Giorgio *Madonna* possesses much of that conjunction of monumentality and elegance which characterizes the work of Arnolfo as a sculptor; like the Santa Maria Novella Cross, it is highly naturalistic in intention, while at the same time preserving a decorativeness and a certain passivity in the characterization which contrasts strongly with the more forceful qualities of the Ognissanti and Bologna altarpieces and the *Virgin* roundel on the ceiling of the Arena Chapel. More consciously charming than these grave *Madonnas* by Giotto, it also differs from them in every detail of execution, from the rendering of the limp and boneless hands to the flowing, curvilinear rhythms that harmonize the Virgin's features. The configuration of particular features obeys formulae foreign to the style of Giotto, and no Morellian analysis can produce any other conclusion but that we are here in the presence of a sensibility far removed in character from his. On the other hand the S. Giorgio *Madonna* has obvious qualities in common with the frescoed *Madonna* in the Upper Church at Assisi (Plates 5, 16a), where we find close similarities in the rounded form of the Virgin's head, in the thick, column-like neck, and in the flowing calligraphy of the mouth and the rather open eyes.[2] There are also interesting resemblances between the angels standing behind the Virgin's throne in the S. Giorgio altarpiece (Plate 16c) and certain figures in some of the scenes of the *Legend*, for example in *The Death of the Knight of Celano* (Scene XVI, Plate 16d), where one of the grieving women conforms quite closely in type to the left-hand angel in the *Madonna*, not least in that haphazard proportioning of the features that has already been noted in the figure of St. John on the Santa Maria Novella Cross.[3]

[1] Offner, *Corpus*, III, vi, 3 ff. Previously Offner had ascribed the S. Giorgio *Madonna* to the St. Cecilia Master himself: cf. Offner, *Corpus*, III, i, 32.

[2] A. Smart, 'The St. Cecilia Master and his School at Assisi', *Burlington Magazine*, cii (1960), 431; see also J. White, *Art and Architecture in Italy* . . ., p. 143, n. 7. Such are the stylistic connections between the two works that Toesca, for example, assumed the influence of the fresco (which he accepted as being by Giotto) on the altarpiece (which he ascribed to the St. Cecilia Master): cf. P. Toesca, *Il Trecento*, p. 606.

[3] A. Smart, loc. cit.

(d) The Badia Polyptych

Another *Madonna* generally ascribed to Giotto on the authority of Ghiberti, the polyptych of *The Virgin and Child with Four Saints* in the Museo dell'Opera di Santa Croce,[1] which originally stood over the main altar of the Badia of Florence, must clearly be retained within Giotto's immediate circle; but it reflects tendencies that lie outside the main development of the Giottesque tradition, and which are discovered again in the *St. Nicholas* frescoes in the Orsini Chapel at Assisi. In fact the similarities that the Badia polyptych bears to the frescoed *Madonna* in the Orsini Chapel entitle us to postulate their common authorship.[2] The early date of the frescoes, which were certainly in existence by the year 1307, indicates that their author was among the first of Giotto's direct pupils; and from their style it is evident that the St. Nicholas Master was acquainted either with the Arena Chapel cycle or with a slightly earlier work by Giotto of a similar character.[3] While evincing great curiosity about spatial and perspectival problems, and demonstrating his understanding of the sculptural qualities of Giotto, the St. Nicholas Master shows a fondness for the decorative and the delicate which in some ways brings him close to the 'Master of the Obsequies' in the Upper Church, and it is interesting to observe the resemblance of a building represented in one of the scenes in the *St. Nicholas* cycle (*St. Nicholas forgives the Repentant Judge*) to the splendidly decorated church in Scene **XXIII** of the *Legend* (*St. Francis Mourned by St. Clare*, Plate 83).[4] This suggests that Scene **XXIII** was already in being before the decoration of the Orsini Chapel. On the other hand, if work on the two cycles overlapped, the St. Nicholas Master could well have been the channel by means of which Giotto's work in the Arena Chapel became known to the painters of the *Legend*; for it is the same scene in the *St. Francis* cycle that includes the motif of the 'boy in the tree', very possibly borrowed from the fresco in Padua of *Christ's Entry into Jerusalem*.

4. *The Date of Giotto's Birth*

According to the *Commento a Dante* written about 1376 by Benvenuto da Imola, Giotto was still quite young (*adhuc satis iuvenis*) at the time that he was working in the Arena Chapel.[5] On this point, however, there is conflicting testimony: but it is one that it is essential to examine in any consideration of Giotto's early development. The *Libro* of

[1] U. Procacci, 'La tavola di Giotto dell'Altar Maggiore della chiesa della Badia Fiorentina', in *Scritti di Storia dell'Arte in onore di Mario Salmi* (Rome, 1960), ii, 9 ff.

[2] O. Sirén, 'Some Paintings by a Follower of Giotto', *Burlington Magazine*, xliii (1923), 259; G. Vitzthum and W. F. Volbach, *Die Malerei und Plastik des Mittelalters in Italien* (Wildpark-Potsdam, 1924), p. 272; Offner, *Corpus*, III, ii, I (New York, 1930), v.   [3] M. Meiss, op. cit., p. 4.

[4] D. Gioseffi, op. cit., pp. 105 f. Gioseffi argues for the priority of the fresco in the Upper Church.

[5] Benvenuto da Imola, *Comentum super Dantis Aldigherij Comoediam* (Florence, 1887), iii, 313. Cf. P. Murray, op. cit., p. 65, n. 5.

Antonio Billi, followed by Vasari, gives Giotto's date of birth as 1276,[1] which would be consistent with the statement in Benvenuto da Imola's *Commentary*. This date has nevertheless been widely rejected on the grounds that it is not in accord with the earlier testimony of Antonio Pucci, who tells us in his *Centiloquio*,[2] a rhymed version, completed in 1373, of the *Cronica* of Giovanni Villani (c. 1340), that Giotto died in 1336 (New Style, 1337) at the age of 70, thus implying that he was born in 1266 (N.S., 1267). The context of Pucci's reference to Giotto is the building of the Campanile, for which the earliest of the reliefs, as the author tells us, were made by Giotto, the work being continued after his death by Andrea Pisano, who made 'la bella porta a San Giovanni' (the present south door of the Baptistery):

> Nell'anno, a dì dicennove di Luglio,
>   della Chiesa maggiore il Campanile
>   fondato fu, rompendo ogni cespuglio,
>
> per maestro Giotto, dipintor sottile,
>   il qual condusse tanto il lavorio
>   ch'i primi intagli fe' con bello stile.
>
> Nel trentasei, siccome piacque a Dio,
>   Giotto morì d'età di settant'anni,
>   e 'n quella chiesa poi si soppellìo.
>
> Poscia il condusse un pezzo con affanni
>   quel solenne Maestro, Andrea Pisano,
>   che fe' la bella porta a San Giovanni.[3]

It has been suggested that a copyist made an error in transcribing the original manuscript, and as one of the two oldest manuscripts gives the number 70 in Roman numerals the possibility that the figure X was added by mistake to an original LX cannot be discounted.[4] The further possibility exists that *settant'anni* represents a misreading of *sessant'anni*: in fact an instance of the reverse process is to be found in *Centiloquio* xci, 1, where the date 1373 (*settantatre*) appears in one manuscript as 1363 (*sessantatre*).[5] The whole question has been raised again by Brandi, who agrees with Cavalcaselle in doubting Pucci's reliability. On the assumption that the Arena Chapel was decorated in or around 1306, Giotto would then have been about 40 years of age if he was 70 at the time of his death in 1337. As Brandi points out, it is difficult to think that in the four-

---

[1] C. de Fabriczy, loc. cit.; R. Salvini, *Giotto: Bibliografia* (Rome, 1938), p. 20.

[2] The only complete edition of the *Centiloquio* is to be found in the *Poesie di Antonio Pucci* (4 vols., Florence, 1712–75). The oldest manuscripts of the *Centiloquio* are those preserved in the Biblioteca Nazionale in Florence—cod. Gaddi II. iii. 83 (formerly Magliab. xxv. 327) and II. iii. 84 (formerly Magliab. xxv. 548).

[3] Antonio Pucci, *Centiloquio*, lxxxv, 83–6.

[4] See the discussion of this question in Crowe and Cavalcaselle, *Storia*, i, 375 ff.

[5] Cf. K. McKenzie, 'Antonio Pucci on Old Age', *Speculum*, xv (1940), 160 ff.

teenth century the expression *adhuc satis iuvenis* would have been applied to a man who was about 40 years old.[1]

Indeed there are sufficient grounds for an even more radical scepticism.[2] The most significant fact about Antonio Pucci is that he was a versifier, composing an enormous poem in *terza rima* which purports to be a faithful rendering of a prose history. Such a thing is surely an impossibility. Were there never occasions when the historical material could not be forced into a metrical mould? Was it always easy for Pucci to transcribe Villani accurately without infringing the rules of prosody? Was he never troubled by the difficulty of finding a rhyme? An examination of the many instances where Pucci differs from Villani shows that such poetic pains were only too real to him. Again and again the only plausible explanation of his extensive departures from Villani's text is that they were determined by poetical rather than historical considerations; that is to say, in order to preserve a correct scansion or in order to rhyme. To take one example out of many, in *Centiloquio* lxxxv, 41, Pucci alters Villani's '31st March' (*a' dì 31. di Marzo*)[3] to '19th March' (*del detto Marzo, ed a' dì dicennove*), evidently in order to rhyme *dicennove* with *dove* four lines earlier and with *Giove* two lines earlier.

Suspicion is also aroused by the fact that Villani himself makes no mention of Giotto's age at the time of his death.[4] Now in any *terzina* there is always likely to be one key-word at the end of a line, which occurs to the poet first and for which he now has to find two other rhymes. The context of the reference to Giotto in the *Centiloquio* suggests that in this case it was *Giovanni*, since an allusion to Andrea Pisano's 'bella porta a San Giovanni' would have seemed a natural, and indeed convenient, adjunct to any reference

---

[1] C. Brandi, 'Giotto recuperato a San Giovanni Laterano', op. cit., p. 83.

[2] The conclusions that follow were originally contained in a paper which I read at a seminar on Giotto conducted by Professor Howard Davis at Columbia University in the summer of 1955. See also A. Smart, 'The St. Cecilia Master and his School at Assisi', *The Burlington Magazine*, cii (1960), 437, n. 21.

[3] Giovanni Villani, *Cronica*, xi, 6. Two further examples may be cited: in *Centiloquio*, lxxi, 12, the date '17th May' (*a' dì diciasette*) replaces Villani's '14th May' (*a' dì 14*), presumably in order that *diciasette* can be rhymed with *perfette* and *stette*; and in lvi, 9, Villani's '160 horsemen' (*cento sessanta*) are increased to 500 (*cinquecento*), allowing *cinquecento* to rhyme with *argomento* and *ardimento*. As a typical instance of an alteration evidently determined by metrical requirements, we may consider *Centiloquio*, lxxx, 4, where Villani's '18 months' becomes '19 months', *diecinnuove* replacing *dieci otto*: here *dieci otto* would not have scanned, since the elision of the open vowels would have upset the metre. It must be emphasized that these examples are only a selection from a large number of instances where Pucci departs from Villani's text. A list of over sixty such discrepancies is given in Ferruccio Ferri, *La poesia popolare in Antonio Pucci* (Bologna, 1909), pp. 117 f.

[4] *Cronica*, xi, 12. The passage reads: 'Nel detto anno, a dì 18 di Luglio, si cominciò a fondare il campanile nuovo di santa Reparata, di costa alla faccia della chiesa in sulla piazza di santo Giovanni. E a ciò fare a benedicere la prima pietra fu il vescovo di Firenze con tutto il chericato e co' signori priori e l'altre signorie con molto popolo a grande processione; e fecesi il fondamento infino all'acqua tutto sodo; e soprastante, e provveditore della detta opera di santa Reparata fu fatto per lo comune maestro Giotto nostro cittadino, il più sovrano maestro stato in dipintura che si trovasse al suo tempo, e quegli che più trasse ogni figura e atti al naturale; e fugli dato salario dal comune per remunerazione della sua virtù e bontà. Il quale maestro Giotto tornato da Milano, che 'l nostro comune ve l'avea mandato al servizio del signore di Milano, passò di questa vita a dì 8 di Gennaio 1336, e fu seppellito per lo comune a santa Reparata con grande onore.'

to the building of the Campanile, a work which Andrea Pisano had continued after Giotto's death. Moreover, at the beginning of the passage which Pucci is here paraphrasing, Villani mentions that the Campanile stands in the 'piazza di santo Giovanni', and there are few instances in the *Centiloquio* where Pucci does not seize upon a *Giovanni* in the relevant passage in the *Cronica* as an apparently welcome rhyme-word; and as often as not he will introduce *anni* as one of the other two rhymes, even if the word is absent from Villani's text.

Frequently, therefore, Pucci must resort to what can only be termed 'padding'. A good example is to be found in the account of the death of Pope John XXI, who was killed by a falling roof. We read in the *Cronica*:

. . . fu eletto papa maestro Pier Spagnuolo cardinale, il quale fu chiamato papa Giovanni ventesimo primo, e non vivette papa che otto mesi e dì; che dormando in sua camera in Viterbo gli cadde la volta di sopra addosso e morìo, e fu soppellito in Viterbo.[1]

Pucci gives the following:

> Qual ebbe nome Messer Martin Pietro,
>   chiamato fu ventun Papa Giovanni,
>   e'n capo d'otto mesi come vetro,
>
> la vita sua si ruppe con affanni
>   perch' una volta addosso gli cadette,
>   ch'era abitata prima per molti anni.[2]

It is obvious that the last line has no value apart from Pucci's compulsion, as a poet, to complete his rhyme-scheme. There are a very large number of other examples of the same kind.

Throughout his vast poem Pucci employs the rhyme *-anni* 74 times (in each case he must find three rhyming words); and in all but twelve cases he selects the three rhyming words that he requires out of the following six words: *anni*, *inganni*, *affanni*, *panni*, *danni*, and *Giovanni*. The twelve exceptions are cases where he uses either *tiranni* (5 cases) or a proper noun other than *Giovanni*. There are even instances where we find *affanni* in one manuscript and *inganni* in another, as though the scribe, or the poet himself, was fully aware of the mechanical nature of these rhymes. Returning now to the passage on Giotto, we discover that only seven verses (or 21 lines) earlier Pucci has already employed the same rhyme (*-anni*), using the words *Giovanni*, *inganni*, and *panni*:[3] he is here referring to the altar of San Giovanni, so that *Giovanni* must be the key-word in the *terzina*. We should consequently expect him to introduce two entirely different words when he comes to rhyme with *Giovanni* again in the passage relating to Giotto; and this we find

---

[1] *Cronica*, vii, 50.   [2] *Centiloquio*, xx, 45 ff.   [3] Ibid., lxxxv, 76 ff.

to be the case, since he now uses *anni* and *affanni*. Indeed, the only possible alternatives would have been the somewhat intractable *danni* and the still more unsuitable *tiranni*. What would have been more natural than to be tempted by the simplest of the limited possibilities open to him—the word *anni*, which has so often served him well—and to bestow upon Giotto a conventional 'threescore years and ten'? Certainly a careful comparison between the *Centiloquio* and Villani's *Chronicle* demonstrates that rhyme and metre frequently took precedence in Antonio Pucci's mind over historical truth—a failing not uncommon among poets. He cannot, therefore, be regarded as the most trustworthy of witnesses. Pucci's intention in composing what has been described as this 'long, wearisome work' was to provide a mnemonic aid which might help his compatriots to remember the history of their city.[1] It is doubtful whether he would have considered absolute accuracy essential to his purpose.

But the chief difficulty in accepting the year 1267 as the date of Giotto's birth lies in the over-long period of time which it necessarily entails for his early development and maturation.[2] His earliest independent works, on this assumption, must have been executed towards 1290, perhaps in the late 1280s, whereas all the evidence suggests that the new style developed by Giotto did not make its appearance until the closing years of the century. At the earliest it is to be traced in the *Isaac* scenes in the Upper Church, where we seem to see it in process of growth; but not until the first decade of the new century does its impact make itself felt; by which time we may properly speak of a School of Giotto. It would appear, therefore, that the great cycle in the Arena Chapel belongs to a relatively early stage in the evolution of Giotto's style, when the master was indeed 'still quite young'. Perhaps originally called to Padua by the Franciscans, Giotto may well have undertaken some work in the Franciscan basilica of Sant'Antonio before receiving Scrovegni's commission to decorate his private chapel. But for the modern student the Arena Chapel remains the *locus classicus* of his art: it is also, more than any other work, the touchstone by which the validity of less certain attributions to Giotto may be tested.

[1] K. Speight, 'Resources for Italian Studies . . .', *Journal of Documentation*, x, No. 2, 66.

[2] The 'inclusivists' among Giotto scholars require on the other hand a longer period for the master's early development than the date 1276 (or some date near 1276) would allow. No doubt this consideration, more than any other factor, has been responsible for the general acceptance of the date 1266 implicit in Antonio Pucci's verses.

IV

THE ARENA CHAPEL AND THE
REBIRTH OF PAINTING

1. *The Revolutionary Nature of Giotto's Art*

THE PICTORIAL LANGUAGE CREATED BY GIOTTO represents but one among various responses to the challenge of the new age, but it was by far the most important and the most influential, and the early writers were not mistaken when they recognized in him the founder of modern painting. By the time that he received from Enrico Scrovegni the commission to decorate his private chapel at Padua (which then adjoined the magnificent Scrovegni Palace)[1] Giotto's style was fully mature; the revolution, we may say, had been accomplished; and thus we meet him in his first authenticated work in fresco as a painter already formed, as the complete master of his art.

In the Arena Chapel we no longer look up at remote images of heavenly splendour hung upon the vault, but around us at the pictured stories on the walls, unfolding like the successive scenes of a sacred drama. The new style, foreshadowed to some extent in the lost fresco-cycle by Cavallini at S. Paolo fuori le mura in Rome, and already emergent in the frescoes by the Isaac Master at Assisi, came into existence at a time of spiritual and social change which demanded the presentation of ideas inexpressible through the old forms. The growing desire for the vivid evocation of sacred legend, which is reflected in the rich pictorialism of much of the devotional literature of the period, and especially in the writings of the Franciscans, could no longer be satisfied within the terms of the Italo-Byzantine tradition of the Dugento: a new art was needed, at once more intimate, more human, and more realistic; and it is significant that it is in this period that fresco-painting succeeds mosaic as the most appropriate medium for large-scale church decoration.

---

[1] For the history of the Arena Chapel see A. Moschetti, *La Cappella degli Scrovegni e gli affreschi di Giotto in essa dipinti* (Florence, 1904); A. Tolomei, *Scritti varii* (Padua, 1894); P. E. Selvatico, 'L'oratorio dell'Annunziata nell'Arena di Padova', in *Scritti d'arte* (Florence, 1859), pp. 220 ff.; D. M. Federici, *Istoria de' Cavalieri Gaudenti* (Treviso, 1787).

The stylistic innovations of Giotto can be seen as running parallel to the beginnings of a subtle spiritual revolution: whether in the *Meditationes Vitae Christi* or in the religious dramas of the period, a new realism makes itself felt in the interpretation of the story of Salvation, a new attempt to penetrate to the inner thoughts and feelings of the Gospel figures; a change that even affects the conception of the Person of Christ, as it also enriches the popular devotion to the Mother of God. It is evident at once to the visitor to the Arena Chapel that, as Giotto represents him, Christ is no longer the unapproachable Judge and heavenly King of Byzantine art, but one with whom it would be possible to converse—still the divine Son of God, but also a man wearing the vesture of humanity. According to his dramatic role in each narrative, the Christ of the Arena Chapel reveals different aspects of his nature, showing in his countenance now inspiration, as in *The Baptism*; now majesty, as in *The Entry into Jerusalem*; now foreknowledge, as in *The Last Supper*; now patient humility, as in *The Trial before Caiaphas* (Plate 19*b*); and now compassion, as in *The Carrying of the Cross*, where he turns in pity to look at his Mother. The actual means consist of modifications of expression so slight that it seems incredible that such simplicity could conceal such art.

In such a scene as *The Kiss of Judas* (Plate 17*b*), Giotto reveals himself as the master dramatist, conscious of the individual responses of all his actors. Sometimes, as in the portrayal of the High Priest in this fresco, the interpretation of character is forced up to a pitch of exaggerated harshness, but never in such a way that it loses conviction. And what could be more convincing as a portrait of an individual person than the representation of the young man in light olive-green who stands nearby, holding a long torch and looking dreamily towards Christ? His profile is exquisitely drawn, and his physical beauty is enhanced by the contrast offered to it by the odd appearance of the man walking beside him, a figure surely taken straight out of life, with his sloping forehead and receding chin. The Arena Chapel cycle is full of such marvels of characterization.

An art that attempted, for the first time since classical antiquity, to conjure up the visible world—or, rather, a world of the imagination created out of a desire to visualize an event as it might have appeared to the sense of sight—required, above all, a radically new concept of pictorial space. It was therefore not enough for Giotto to represent individual forms three-dimensionally, in the manner of Cavallini; for he knew that it was the space inhabited by all visible forms that determined their pictorial treatment. In his practice this is always a relatively shallow space, akin to that of a bas-relief or a narrow stage; but within its confines all the forms represented are consistently realized in terms of defined spatial relationships. In *The Kiss of Judas*, in which Christ and Judas confront one another amid a crowding mass of humanity, the spatial positions of these two central figures can be exactly determined: set in a little from the picture-plane, they stand not merely at the central point of the design, seen on the flat, but also in the central space of the box-like area of Giotto's stage. This new sculptural conception of form results in a marked heightening of the sense of reality, and it creates the conditions for a vast enrichment of painting as an expressive language. The envelopment of the figure of Christ in Judas's great yellow cloak (in its colour symbolic of evil) produces at one level of experience an impressive form which can be appreciated virtually in abstract terms; more than that, it lingers in the memory as an unforgettable image of a dramatic encounter; and, still further, it suggests, in a symbolic manner, Christ's surrender to the fate prepared for him by the betrayer and now closing in upon him.

The decisive nature of the revolution effected by Giotto becomes clear to us when we compare this fresco with *The Kiss of Judas* (Plate 17*a*) ascribed to Jacopo Torriti in the Upper Church at Assisi.[1] The Assisi fresco must be accounted one of the supreme masterpieces of late Dugento painting: sublime in its expression of the spiritual content of the subject, it reaches out at the same time towards a new naturalism in the rendering of individual forms, which must, however, be clearly distinguished from the realism of Giotto; for it is plain that the fateful encounter of Christ and Judas, as a visual event, still remains far less important to the painter than purely spiritual realities. Since every figure or group of figures has its own iconographic significance, it is sufficient to give each its appropriate place in the design so that its meaning will at once strike the beholder. The iconography was long established: Judas must be seen to be about to kiss the Lord, and yet not to touch him with his lips; St. Peter, usually placed in the foreground, as here, must stoop to sever the ear of the kneeling Malchus, the high priest's servant, and simultaneously look up at Christ; and Christ himself must extend one hand towards him in a gesture of reproach, according to the Matthean account of his rebuke to St. Peter: 'Put up again thy sword into its place: for all they that take the sword shall perish with the sword'; at the same time his gesture refers to the miracle of his healing of Malchus's ear. This tradition stresses Christ's passive surrender to his enemies; but if the spiritual eye is satisfied, the outward eye suspends its disbelief: for St. Peter must be represented in the act, on the one hand, of performing his gruesome operation upon Malchus, and, on the other, of turning his head towards Christ; and Christ also must perform two simultaneous acts, in addressing St. Peter and surrendering himself to Judas.

In Giotto's fresco, on the other hand, everything contributes to the idea of a unity that neither mocks the senses nor offends the intellect. The main movement is directed towards the centre, where Christ and Judas meet face to face in a moment of silence. The lateral movement from left and right is provided chiefly by the violent action of St. Peter, on the far left, and by the agitated gesture of the priest, on the far right, who has suddenly observed the deed done to his servant and raises his hand in horror and

---

[1] A. Venturi, op. cit., p. 179.

anger. The relationship thus set up between the priest and St. Peter at once connects the two sides of the composition, which would otherwise have been separated by the central figures of Christ and Judas, as in the Assisi fresco. Significantly, Giotto chose an alternative iconographic tradition, according to which St. Peter and Malchus stand behind Christ's back, so that he is not immediately aware of St. Peter's act: the severing of Malchus's ear ceases to be a separate incident taking place in the foreground, and becomes part of the general action; and St. Peter no longer looks up at Christ, but concentrates his whole attention upon his violent deed. The same iconographic pattern appears at an earlier stage of development in the scene of *The Kiss of Judas* represented on Salerno di Coppo's Crucifix in Pistoia Cathedral, which provides (in reverse) the germ of Giotto's composition.[1] But Giotto was the first to create out of the given tradition a convincing unity of dramatic action, and it may be observed that even in Duccio's rendering of the subject on the Siena *Maestà*, where the iconography is similar, St. Peter and Malchus are still placed further to the front of the composition than any of the other figures, as though they existed on a different plane: in the Arena fresco, on the other hand, the two figures have entirely lost their appearance of separateness, and stand upon the central stage of the action. Every form inhabits a real space, upon which the frescoed area seems to open like a window. The conception of pictorial composition has undergone a radical change, which is due primarily to a new awareness of three-dimensional space as the necessary environment of all visible forms: whereas in the Assisi fresco space is still treated descriptively, at Padua it is first experienced by the senses.

In the fresco at Padua the art of a great composer is concentrated upon the presentation of a single dramatic moment. Such properties of the tradition as the lances, staves, and lanterns carried by the soldiery, which in the Assisi fresco have a largely descriptive purpose, become in Giotto's hands the agents of a dynamic thrust into the central area, pointing inwards, like the ribs of a fan, towards the heads of Christ and Judas, and emphasizing the drama of this stupendous encounter. Conforming to the same inward movement, the crowd begins to close around the principal protagonists in the drama. It could not be so in the fresco at Assisi, for there Christ remains aloof from the action, a majestic, Johannine figure who, so far from being involved in the events taking place around him, preserves his divine separateness, and refuses even to turn to look at his betrayer: it is as though there had been transferred to this scene of action an image of the Christ Pantocrator. Nor would the representation of Judas have satisfied the imagination of Giotto. The mastery of the profile, which was to be consummated in the work of Giotto, still belonged to the future. While the profile is not, of course, unknown to Dugento painting, there is often a tendency for the head to be turned slightly towards the spectator, as though the person represented were aware of an audience. But Giotto's revolutionary

[1] Sinibaldi and Brunetti, op. cit., Figs. 59*a*, *b*.

conception of pictorial space, linked inextricably as it was with his desire to create an art of dramatic realism in which the various actors on his stage would be placed in a meaningful and convincing relationship to each other, led him to attempt the representation of human beings from a wide variety of angles, including what was still rarer than the profile, if not completely unprecedented, the rendering of the figure from the back.

Just as there could be nothing more powerful in its effect than his use of the profile in *The Kiss of Judas*, where the two central figures gaze hard and long into one another's eyes, so also the enclosure of Christ's body in the *Pietà* (Plate 18a) by the huddled figures of grieving women, two of whom turn their backs to us, as though forgetful of the outside world within which we stand as spectators looking on, contributes immeasurably to the solemn dignity of the scene, seeming to deepen the sense that we have of sorrow too heavy to be shown. And where in other scenes such innovations in the representation of the visible world carry overtones of meaning less intense than this, they are never introduced merely for their own sake, as though Giotto had been concerned only, in Boccaccio's phrase, to 'mislead the eyes of men': the new mastery of form and space is put to a higher end—the creation of an ideal stage for the interpretation of human life. It is a disciplined art, never permitting the addition of unnecessary detail: in *The Kiss of Judas* the impression is given of a large crowd of people surrounding the central protagonists, and their noise and clamour are almost audible; but in reality this narrow stage holds relatively few figures. Nothing in Giotto's art impresses more than the economy of his means of expression; so much depends upon a concentration of essential forms, a knitting together of significant images in meaningful relationships.

Further dimensions of meaning are added to the Arena Chapel cycle by its complex and highly intellectual organization. An elaborate system of associations between one fresco and another, and among the six successive 'cantos' into which the narrative is divided,[1] establishes a pattern of thematic and compositional relationships which runs like a commentary through this sublime epic of Redemption. Thus the full meaning of the *Pietà* (Plate 18a) is disclosed only when it is contemplated in its context, and especially in relation to the fresco of *The Resurrection*, or *Noli me tangere* (Plate 19a), which follows it and with which it is paired at the centre of the north wall. Compositionally, the one scene is the mirror-image of the other, and they combine to present two successive moments of sorrow and joy: 'O death, where is thy sting? O grave, where is thy

---

[1] These are: (i) (south wall, first register) the Story of Saints Joachim and Anne; (ii) (north wall, first register) the Life of the Virgin (ending with the *Annunciation* and *Visitation* on the *tribuna*); (iii) (south wall, second register) the Nativity and Infancy of Christ; (iv) (north wall, second register) the Ministry of Christ; (v) (south wall, third resigter) the Betrayal and Trial of Christ (beginning with the *Tradimento* on the *tribuna*); (vi) (north wall, third register) the Passion, Death, and Resurrection of Christ.

victory?'[1] At the same time the *Noli me tangere* represents the fulfilment of the theme of Christ's power over death which is already stated in the scene of *The Raising of Lazarus* immediately above.[2]

The emotions of despair and grief have often been expressed in painting by forms in downward movement, corresponding to a natural impulse in our physical being, but never more effectively than in the crushing weight of the masses that press down towards the head of the dead Christ in the Arena *Pietà*. The great bulk of the rocky scarp itself, uniting the angels and the earthly mourners within a vast *Z* lying across the design, shares in this symbolic pictorial movement. Topped by a leafless tree, it contrasts in its barrenness with the corresponding landscape in the *Noli me tangere*, where shrubs are springing to life at the feet of the Resurrected Lord, and where the figure of Christ begins a rising movement that is completed in the following scene of *The Ascension*. No less meaningful in the *Noli me tangere* is Giotto's adaptation of the traditional iconography in such a way as to allow the 'horizon' dividing earth from heaven to cut across Christ's gesture of denial as he forbids Mary Magdalen to touch him, so that the two figures, while being conceived as forms that seem about to interlock, remain fixed in their separateness. It is impossible to conceive of a pictorial language capable of more profound or more complex implications.

Such an art was not created out of a void. It is clear that Giotto was an artist of an unusually broad culture who was receptive to a wide range of external influence. The dramatic intensity of his art probably owes much to Cimabue, his reputed master, and although in many respects his work represents a revolt against Cimabue's aesthetic principles, there is a quality of compression and compactness in his forms, due to the tension of the bounding outlines (as, for instance, in the sleeping figure of Joachim in the fresco of *Joachim's Dream* at Padua), which indicates the possible nature of Giotto's stylistic indebtedness to the older painter. But while expressive outline plays an important part in Giotto's language in its own right, it is used principally as a modelling agent, in combination with subtle gradations of light and shade, which must have been founded upon a searching study of the *sfumato* of Cavallini. Yet Giotto went much further than Cavallini in giving substance to his forms. In the Apostles of Cavallini's *Last Judgement* at Santa Cecilia in Trastevere, the interior modelling of each impressive head exists independently of any larger concern with the spatial 'envelope' which contains the forms so represented; and it is because of this essential difference from Giotto's practice that individual forms in Cavallini often give the impression of being flattened out: the interior modelling is not as closely related as it is with Giotto to the shaping of the form as a whole. In other respects also Giotto gave his figures a firmer structure: his knowledge of the construction of the human body was more considerable than Cavallini's, and his

[1] Cf. A. Smart, 'Reflections on the Art of Giotto', *Apollo*, lxxxi (1965), 262.   [2] M. Alpatoff, op. cit., p. 152.

figures leave no doubt that beneath the surface of the flesh there lies, if not a complete anatomy, at least an armature of bone.

But in any profound sense the Paduan decorations have no antecedents in Dugento painting, except in the Isaac Master's frescoes at Assisi.[1] Otherwise, it is easier to relate the innovations of Giotto to the comparable revival of sculpture which had been initiated by Nicola Pisano over forty years earlier in his pulpit for the Pisa Baptistery, and, more generally, with the realistic tendencies in Gothic sculpture as a whole, whether in France or in Italy. The Arena Chapel frescoes are unquestionably the work of a painter deeply versed in the art of sculpture, and the narrative scenes have much of the character of low reliefs. That the *Virtues* and *Vices* in the lowest register of the nave walls should actually simulate sculpture is no less significant: there is a quality of austerity here that recalls the severe classicism of Nicola Pisano; and if the two masters had anything in common, it was that, for both, the way to the creation of the modern style lay through the mists of antiquity.

The more obvious Gothic qualities of Giotto's style have tended to distract attention from his underlying 'classicism', and even to conceal it altogether. Yet, while it is natural to compare his work with certain aspects of northern Gothic, and even to postulate some direct connection with French cathedral sculpture, it is in the classicizing tendencies of High Gothic that the closest affinities with the art of Giotto are to be seen, as in the *Virgin* Portals of Amiens and Reims, where there are figures that anticipate Giotto's in their rhythmic grace of movement and in the classic fall of their draperies: the tender portrayal of the Virgin in *The Annunciation* at Amiens comes close to the spirit of Giotto's interpretation at Padua in such frescoes as *The Virgin's Return Home* and *The Presentation of Christ in the Temple*,[2] while some of the figures on the *Judgement* Portal at Reims[3] bring to mind Giotto's skilful use of groups of figures to enclose a defined space. But Giotto stands nearer, so to speak, to the fountainhead, and *The Virgin's Return Home* in particular reflects a sensibility that is almost Greek in its quest for the ideal and in its refined sensitivity to interval: it is difficult to think that such a work was not inspired directly by ancient relief-sculpture. There is every reason to suppose that Giotto made use of ancient models in much the same way that Nicola Pisano had done before him.

It was Vasari who first drew attention to Nicola's study of ancient art, pointing out the indebtedness of one of the reliefs on the Pisa Pulpit to the famous *Hippolytus* sarcophagus in the Camposanto.[4] We now have knowledge of at least two instances of the

---

[1] Cf. Lidia Lochoff, 'Gli affreschi dell'Antico e Nuovo Testamento nella basilica superiore di Assisi', *Rivista d'arte*, xix, 3–4, Numero speciale del Centenario Giottesco (1937), 240 ff.: M. Meiss, op. cit., pp. 21 ff.

[2] Cf. M. Meiss, op. cit., p. 20.

[3] Cf. K. Bauch, op. cit., p. 59, Fig. 6.

[4] G. Vasari, *Le Vite* . . . (1568), ed. Milanesi, i, 294 f.; G. H. and E. R. Crichton, *Nicola Pisano and the Revival of Sculpture in Italy* (Cambridge, 1938), pp. 11 f.

dependence of Nicola Pisano and Giotto upon the same classical source: a figure from a *Meleager* sarcophagus (Plate 20*a*) which was used by Nicola Pisano in the relief of *The Massacre of the Innocents* on his Siena Pulpit was transformed by Giotto into the grieving St. John of the Arena *Pietà*;[1] and a figure of the drunken Dionysus, supported by a satyr, on a Neo-Attic crater in the Camposanto, from which Nicola Pisano derived a figure of a bearded man supported by a boy in the Pisa *Presentation in the Temple*, became the model also for the melancholy Joachim in the scene of *Joachim's Withdrawal to the Sheepfold* at Padua (Plate 18*b*).[2] The number of such apparent borrowings from the antique in the Arena Chapel is considerably larger than has generally been supposed; and it is difficult to resist the conclusion that the example of ancient art exerted an influence upon Giotto's stylistic development scarcely less potent than that of any other source of inspiration.

In this respect Giotto's vision differs significantly from that of Giovanni Pisano as it is revealed, for example, in his Pistoia Pulpit, where the reliefs include some of the subjects that are treated in the Arena Chapel. As the son and assistant of Nicola, Giovanni Pisano belonged to an earlier generation, but his independent work had its beginnings in the period of Giotto's initial development, the Pistoia Pulpit being completed in the year 1301. His later impulse towards a marriage of the Gothic and the 'classical', which is detectable in his second Pulpit, made for Pisa Cathedral between the years 1302 and 1310, may have owed something to Giotto's influence. In other respects he anticipated Giotto in the realism and intimacy of his presentation of Biblical subject-matter and in his portrayal of the individual; but there is at times an almost frenetic quality in his expression of emotion that is entirely absent from Giotto's work: where Giovanni Pisano often gives vent to a highly charged emotionalism, Giotto always preserves a calm reserve and restraint; where Giovanni's forms run wild with feeling,[3] Giotto's forms contain it, making it amenable to contemplation. Indeed, among the sculptors who were Giotto's contemporaries, his fellow-countryman Arnolfo di Cambio approaches in some ways more closely to his austere and yet refined taste, although, even so, it is chiefly Arnolfo the architect whose influence can be traced in the Paduan cycle—as, for example, in the graceful style of the *baldacchino* in *The Presentation of Christ in the Temple*.[4]

[1] A. Bush-Brown, 'Giotto: Two Problems in the History of his Style', *Art Bulletin*, xxxiv (1952), 42 ff.; E. Panofsky, *Early Netherlandish Painting, its Origins and Character* (Princeton, 1953), p. 367; and idem, *Renaissance and Renascences in Western Art* (Stockholm, 1960), pp. 68, 152–3.

[2] A. M. Telpaz, 'Some Antique Motifs in Trecento Art', *Art Bulletin*, xlvi (1964), 372 ff.

[3] As Wölfflin expressed it, '[Giovanni Pisano] überstürzt sich im Ausdruck. Das Körperliche wird von dem Empfindungsausdruck förmlich aufgezehrt und die Kunst mußte verwildern' (H. Wölfflin, *Die klassische Kunst* (Munich, 1899)).

[4] For the debated question of Arnolfo's influence on Giotto see G. Fiocco, 'Giotto e Arnolfo', *Rivista d'arte*, xix, 3–4, Numero speciale del Centenario Giottesco (1937), 221 ff.; D. Gioseffi, op. cit., pp. 27 ff.

2. *Giotto and Antiquity*

When the early writers, from Boccaccio to Vasari, emphasized Giotto's rediscovery of the artistic principles of the ancients—as Politian expressed it in his memorial verses, 'Ille ego sum per quem pictura extincta revixit'—they were more exact than they knew; for, although it is uncertain whether Giotto could have acquired, even in Rome, much knowledge of ancient painting, the extent of the apparent borrowings from antique sculpture in the Arena Chapel cycle suggests an avid interest in whatever relics of ancient art were available to him. One of the strongest impulses behind such borrowings would have been the need to find a solution to new problems of representation, to which their mastery in sculptural terms in the classical works known to him could have shown the way. A case in point is the much discussed 'boy in the tree' in the left background of *The Entry into Jerusalem* in the Arena Chapel, which has been plausibly connected with a climbing figure on a *Season* sarcophagus:[1] this is certainly a striking enough example of one of Giotto's most important stylistic innovations—the attempt to represent human figures from various angles, including a back view.

But it is equally clear that a preoccupation with representational problems can account only in part for Giotto's curiosity about the art of the ancients. The graceful movement of the figures in *The Virgin's Return Home*, recalling some Roman, or even Greek, processional relief; the meditative Joachim, in the scene of his exile among the shepherds (Plate 18*b*), repeating the attitude of the Camposanto Dionysus; the huddled postures of the mourners in the *Pietà* (Plate 18*a*), suggesting a derivation from Etruscan funeral reliefs[2]—these and other explorations of the human figure in all the complexity of its movement and articulation were quite new pictorial adventures, and undoubtedly the only true precedents for them were to be found in the art of antiquity: but they indicate also that the temper of Giotto's mind responded to the spirit of the Graeco-Roman tradition on a much deeper level, above all to its heroic dignity and restraint and to its ideal of order and balance. Giotto's interpretation of the *Pietà*, which evidently draws at least two elements from the *Meleager* relief (Plate 20*a*)—the marvellous St. John,[3] hovering between earth and heaven (as though sharing in the form of his own symbol, the Eagle), and the nude figure of the dead Christ, foreshortened in a manner that is previously unknown in Italian painting but which is already implicit in the figure of the dying Meleager—not only modifies the accepted iconographic pattern for the purposes of a revolutionary realism, but also brings to the subject an equally new heroic emphasis.

In almost every instance of a borrowing from the antique in the Arena Chapel, Giotto's direct knowledge of the source in question may reasonably be presumed. The

---

[1] M. R. Fisher, op. cit., p. 51 and Fig. 5. Similar climbing figures occur, for example, on Tino di Camaino's *Tomb of Catherine of Austria* at S. Lorenzo, Naples.

[2] E. Panofsky, *Renaissance and Renascences in Western Art*, p. 154.   [3] A. Bush-Brown, loc. cit.

context of the quotation from the *Meleager* scene, an appropriate subject to assimilate to the Lamentation over Christ, virtually rules out the possibility (a remote one in any case) that Giotto derived his St. John from Nicola Pisano's earlier adaptation of the mourning figure; a conclusion that is supported by the further evidence that the figure of the dead Meleager inspired the foreshortened Christ of the fresco. Again, the elegant relief with which Giotto decorated the gable of St. Anne's house, in the scenes of *The Annunciation to St. Anne* and *The Birth of the Virgin*, cannot be anything but a direct imitation of the characteristic type of Roman funeral relief, in which two *putti* bear aloft a conch containing the image of the deceased (this being replaced in Giotto's fresco by an image of Christ):[1] it is possible, therefore, to draw a distinction between a direct classical allusion of this kind and what might seem to be the same sort of reference in such scenes as *The Homage of a Simple Man* (Frontispiece) and *The Christmas Crib at Greccio* (Plate 37a) in the Upper Church at Assisi, where Victories or *putti* decorate an architectural feature (the temple in the first scene and the *baldacchino* in the other), but where the Arnolfian inspiration of the allusion is only too evident (Plate 37b). In the same way the gateway in *The Meeting of St. Joachim and St. Anne* (Plate 24a) at Padua must surely have been fashioned out of the memory of some Roman triumphal arch, perhaps the Arch of Augustus at Rimini,[2] while the little statues of horses surmounting the arcaded forecourt of the temple in *The Expulsion of the Traders* (Plate 33a) suggest a recollection of the famous *Horses of San Marco* in Venice.

Giotto's knowledge of ancient art is nowhere more apparent than in the *grisaille* frescoes of the *Virtues* and *Vices* (the themes of which go back to the *Psychomachia* of the Latin poet Prudentius). The heroic *Virtues* of the Arena Chapel would scarcely be conceivable without the example of Roman statuary. Its influence is most evident in the noble figure of *Fortitudo* (Plate 26a): here Giotto's ultimate source was undoubtedly an ancient *Hercules with the Lion-skin*; but in adapting the image to a female figure Giotto could have found the perfect paradigm in a Roman statue of *Juno Sospita* (Plate 26b).[3] Among the *Vices*, the imaginatively conceived *Inconstantia*, one of the most original of Giotto's inventions, has a close connection with ancient representations of *Fortuna*, with her symbolic wheel:[4] it is upon such a wheel that Giotto's type of Inconstancy attempts

[1] E. Panofsky, *Renaissance and Renascences in Western Art*, p. 148 and n. 3. [2] D. Gioseffi, op. cit., pp. 47 f.

[3] For this figure, which is in the Vatican Museum, see E. S. Strong, *La scultura romana da Augusto a Costantino* (Florence, 1923–6), ii, 249, Plate XLIX.

[4] I owe this suggestion to the late Erwin Panofsky. A word of caution may be added here on the subject of Giotto's *Prudentia*, which has normally been read as a double-headed figure similar to Andrea Pisano's image of *Prudentia* on the Campanile of Florence Cathedral and other representations of the period: thus Kugler, in his *Handbook*, publishes an engraving of the Arena Chapel fresco in which the head of Prudentia is shown as being backed by that of a bearded man somewhat resembling Socrates. (Cf. F. Kugler, *Handbook of Painting, The Italian Schools*, ed. Sir Charles Eastlake (3rd edn., London, 1855), Part I.) The motif of a philosopher's head backed by a female visage is of Greek origin; but not only is the fresco now difficult to read, but it would seem highly improbable that Giotto's reinterpretation of the traditional iconography owes anything to a classical allusion of this nature.

to balance herself, and the repetition of the wheel motif at a different angle in the flying draperies that sweep up behind her increases the sense of imbalance. Giotto's knowledge of Roman portrait-busts is not merely suggested in the Pilate of the *Trial* scene (Plate 22), in the *Christ* cycle, a figure of identifiably Roman physiognomy in every chiselled feature, but seems to be imprinted in the very style, in the sculptural manner in which the forms of the head are defined (Plate 20*b*).

Some of the less obtrusive details of the frescoes of the *Virtues* and *Vices* are equally remarkable. The superbly drawn scene of banditry beneath the terrifying figure of *Injustitia* must owe much to Giotto's study of classical relief-sculpture, of which further confirmation is provided by the corresponding scene on the base of the throne of *Justitia* (Plate 20*c*). This joyous scene, also simulating a relief, includes the representation of a man who has abandoned himself to a wild dance; poised upon one foot, and with one arm flung high, he is caught in a moment of rhythmic balance: dancers in such attitudes are common in ancient bacchanalian scenes, and there can be no doubt of the classical origin of Giotto's figure.[1] Above, in the main field of the fresco, the enthroned personification of human justice holds in her hands a pair of scales, in each of which there stands a tiny figurine—'one of them', in Panofsky's words, 'threatening the violent in the typical posture of a Jupiter throwing the thunderbolt, the other a diminutive Victory rewarding the peaceful scholar'.[2] That at least the *Victory* (Plate 20*d*) was derived directly from an ancient prototype seems certain: a similar image appears, for example, on the silver cup of Boscoreale as an attribute of the Emperor Augustus (Plate 21*a*).[3]

Borrowings in Giotto from antique sources well known to the Middle Ages—such as the statue in Rome of the *Spinario* (or *Thorn-drawer*), disguised as an apostle tying his sandal in *The Washing of the Feet* in the Arena Chapel—naturally lack the significance possessed by his use of new models. Here it should be borne in mind that little distinction would have been made in the fourteenth century between classical and early Christian art, and not unexpectedly we find that some of the figures in the Paduan frescoes derive from early Christian sarcophagi. The relaxed pose of the shepherd leaning upon his staff in the scene of *Joachim's Dream* repeats a motif common in representations of shepherds on early Christian reliefs, and readily identifiable from the manner in which the shepherd's staff is tucked under his armpit.[4] In *The Washing of the Feet* the young apostle carrying a water-jug may have a similar origin, and indeed an almost identical figure is to be found in the scene of *Pilate Washing his Hands* on the sarcophagus of Junius Bassus in Rome.[5]

[1] E. Panofsky, *Renaissance and Renascences in Western Art*, p. 152, n. 2.   [2] Ibid., p. 152.

[3] For the Boscoreale Cup, see especially Ant. Héron de Villefosse, 'Le Trésor de Boscoreale', *Monuments et Mémoires* (Fondation Eugène Piot), v (1899), 134 ff., and Strong, op. cit., i, 80 ff. The figure offering the Victory to Augustus is to be identified as a *Virtus romana*.   [4] A. M. Telpaz, op. cit., p. 373, Figs. 6, 7.

[5] For an account of this sarcophagus see F. Gerke, *Der Sarkophag des Iunius Bassius* (Berlin, 1936).

In making such adaptations Giotto evidently sought to give his figures a new expressiveness and naturalness, and the rich variety of pose and gesture that characterizes the *dramatis personae* of the Arena Chapel cycle must be due as much to his understanding of ancient art as to his study of life. The precise nature of his inspiration, however, often remains elusive; and it would be absurd, as it would also be presumptuous, to exaggerate the dependence of a genius as inventive as his upon known precedents. On the other hand, we are now aware, as never before, of the extent to which art feeds upon art, and this insight into the processes of artistic creation must affect our consideration of even the most daring of Giotto's innovations. An example that springs to mind is the figure of the young groom or attendant who stands looking up at one of the camels in *The Adoration of the Kings*, with the bridle in one hand: there is no precedent in Dugento painting for a head foreshortened in this striking manner; nor does the figure suggest a derivation from relief-sculpture; but the frequency with which similar figures appear in later representations of this subject, whether in association with camels or with horses, poses an interesting if unanswerable question; for there is some evidence that at least by the fifteenth century such figures were often modelled upon one or other of the famous *Dioscuri* of Montecavallo, of which there exist Renaissance drawings giving a foreshortened view close to that of the attendant in Giotto's fresco:[1] it is possible, therefore, that Giotto originated the tradition, and that the figure in the fresco was evolved from a drawing that he had made from the *Dioscuri* during a previous visit to Rome.[2]

The larger problem of the sources of Giotto's innovations in the treatment of perspective in a more general sense presents considerable difficulties, not least because the extent of his acquaintance with ancient fresco-painting remains unknown. However, a hint of what he may have learnt from ancient relief-sculpture is provided, once again, by the silver cup of Boscoreale, in the scene showing the submission of barbarians to Augustus (Plate 21*b*). Various elements of this composition, from the abruptly turned heads of two of the soldiers represented in profile to the attitude and gesture of Augustus and the perspectival treatment of the dais upon which he is seated, come together again in other guises in Giotto's fresco of *Christ before Caiaphas* (Plate 19*b*)—in the bearded soldier standing beside Christ, in the dramatic gesture of Annas's outflung arm, and in the figure of Caiaphas himself, who is seated upon a throne represented, like the raised dais on the relief, at an oblique angle to the picture-plane. In the scene on the Boscoreale Cup the Emperor's throne defines the depth of the space between the foreground figures and the frieze-like array of heads at the back. It is not suggested that this particular relief was Giotto's precise model; and indeed the Boscoreale Cup was not discovered until the

---

[1] A list of such drawings is given in Phyllis Pray Bober, *Drawings after the Antique by Amico Aspertini* (London, 1957), p. 72.   [2] Professor Howard Davis informs me that he shares my view of the origin of Giotto's figure.

late nineteenth century (although this fact does not exclude the possibility that some version of the composition shown on the relief was known in Italy in the years around 1300, especially as one of the other subjects represented on the exterior of the cup is repeated exactly in a relief at Mantua):[1] but Giotto's study of antique compositions of this type could have profoundly affected his conception of spatial design, and, as we shall see, there are reasons for assuming the influence of Roman relief-sculpture upon the adjacent scene of *The Trial before Pilate*.

3. The Trial before Pilate *and the 'donna velata' at Padua*

Various indications of Giotto's attitude to antiquity are offered by the scene of *The Trial before Pilate* (Plate 22) in the Arena Chapel, which includes the subject of the Mocking of Christ, combining it with an allusion to another subject not treated separately in the cycle—the Flagellation, or Christ at the Column. One of the most imaginative of all Giotto's works, *The Trial before Pilate* has a title to be regarded as the greatest single composition in the entire cycle, the *Pietà* alone excepted; and, especially as in the past some of its principal qualities have been overlooked, although they probably tell us more about the mind of Giotto than almost any other fresco in the Arena Chapel, it will not perhaps be out of place to give it special attention and to examine it in some detail.

The figure of Pilate (Plate 20*b*) has already been mentioned: early Trecento painting knows no more powerful piece of characterization; and clearly Giotto intended to suggest a Roman physiognomy. His Pilate is no less sharply differentiated in type from the Jewish priest on the extreme right, pointing with skinny hand towards the Saviour, than he is from so apparent a foil as the superb figure of the negro flagellant standing at the centre of the composition;[2] but of these three figures, each of which seems to typify a different level of humanity, it is Pilate who is portrayed with the deepest sympathy. The black flagellant, with his muscular frame and clutching—almost predatory—left hand, is occupied simply with the infliction of physical pain. The Jew is engaged, not in physical action, but in fierce, dogmatic argument: his gesture is accusatory. Pilate, on the other hand, extends his open palm in quite a different gesture, suggesting expostulation; he is the reasonable man, the fair-minded judge of St. Luke's account, who can say: 'Ye have brought this man unto me, as one that perverteth the people: and, behold, I, having examined him before you, have found no fault in this man touching those things whereof ye accuse him.'

---

[1] For this relief see A. Levi, 'Rilievi di Sarcofagi del Palazzo Ducale di Mantova', *Dedalo*, vii (1926), 205 ff. (Fig. on p. 225), and idem, *Sculture Greche e Romane del Palazzo Ducale di Mantova* (Rome, 1931), pp. 86 ff., Pl. XCVII. The Mantua relief was the basis of the central group in Raphael's tapestry-cartoon of *St. Paul at Lystra* (Victoria and Albert Museum, London; collection of Her Majesty The Queen).

[2] On black flagellants in medieval art, cf. G. K. Hunter, 'Elizabethans and Foreigners', in *Shakespeare in his Age* (Oxford, 1964).

He is an unforgettable figure, without parallel in any previous representation of the subject. It was customary for Byzantine and medieval artists to portray Pilate as a young man with a beard, arrayed in costly vestments and wearing a gold-embroidered head-dress: Duccio largely preserves this tradition in the *Maestà*, save that the headdress has been replaced by a crown of bay-leaves such as we find on a number of representations on early Christian sarcophagi. Giotto, however, fashions the entire image anew: his Pilate, who is now beardless, is not only remarkably Roman in feature, but wears a garment reminiscent of a toga and adorned with Roman eagles. The consequence is a startling intensification of the sense of reality, for this could be a personage of the very time of Caesar Tiberius. Moreover, such realism of portraiture helps to point the contrast between Pilate, the vicegerent of the Imperial power, and Christ, mockingly reverenced as the King of the Jews; a contrast already implicit in the positions given to both figures at the centre of enclosing groups on opposite sides of the composition. The two figures dominate the two main subjects that Giotto here brings together within one scene—the Mocking of Christ and the Trial before Pilate. The negro unites the two groups, striding forward from the one to the other and filling the space between two equidistant profile heads, the placing of which subtly reinforces the expression of his violent action, since they lie on the circumference, as it were, of the impending sweep of his raised stick.

The group containing Pilate forms, then, a little scene on its own, composed as a distinct unit although skilfully interwoven into the design of the fresco as a whole. When it is studied in isolation it may well stir in the beholder certain memories, perhaps undefined, of something seen and possibly forgotten, some fragment of Roman art itself; for it is surely not only on the representational level—in its vivid evocation of the Roman past, to which the very forms and ornamentation of the architectural setting so effectively contribute—but also in a more profound, stylistic sense that this noble group seems to escape from the age that gave it birth into the remembered world of Imperial Rome. That in composing this group Giotto was directly influenced by ancient relief-sculpture is suggested above all by the unusual association of profile heads with one in a three-quarter frontal view. There has already been occasion to draw attention to a tendency in the representation of figures in thirteenth-century painting, whereby the face is inclined slightly towards the spectator, so that the individual represented often gives the impression of an actor who is too much aware of his audience. It was one of Giotto's tasks, so to speak, to make his actors forget that they were being observed, as it was also to define with the utmost clarity their exact spatial relationships within the narrow box of his stage; and the apparent indications in *The Trial before Pilate* that Giotto was influenced in his treatment of the figures by classical prototypes seem to confirm the general impression given by the Arena Chapel cycle as a whole that his understanding of the art of antiquity greatly assisted him in the solution of such problems.

There are two Roman reliefs that reveal quite striking affinities with this passage in Giotto's fresco. One of these is a fragment of a processional scene which has long adorned the exterior of the Villa Medici (Plate 23*b*), and which was once thought to have belonged originally to the Ara Pacis Augustae;[1] the other is the triumphal relief in the Palazzo Torlonia representing the submission of barbarians to the Emperor Hadrian, which perhaps came from the Arch of Constantine (Plate 23*a*).[2]

The first of these two reliefs shows a number of standing figures surrounding a dignified personage who wears the spiked *apex* of a *flamen*, and who is identifiable as Augustus. Both in attitude and in feature (although the face is now damaged) this figure bears a marked resemblance to Giotto's Pilate. The turn of the head and the positions of the hands—the one closed and held in front of the body and the other extended to one side with open palm—closely correspond to the pose given by Giotto to Pilate (save only that Augustus's right hand is not raised quite so high as Pilate's). A notable feature of the frescoed figure is the emphasis that is placed upon the muscular structure of the neck, which Giotto explores with great interest: the treatment is profoundly sculptural, as is also the way in which the head is chiselled out in well-defined planes, so that the very style of the figure suggests its sculptural origin.

Beside Pilate there stands a rather younger man with a bushy black beard: he looks, with a serious expression, not at Pilate himself but at an officer of the guard standing behind Pilate near the entrance to the room. The two figures exchange glances, as though weighing up the argument that is in progress between the Roman Governor and the Jewish priests. Exactly the same motif occurs in the Palazzo Torlonia relief, where two figures—one of them astonishingly like the bearded man in the fresco—exchange glances in an identical manner behind the Emperor's back. The identity of the bearded man in Giotto's fresco is not certain, but he is possibly the *assessor* who attended the judge in Roman courts of law and who is sometimes introduced into scenes of the Trial before Pilate in early Christian art. To these resemblances must be added the detail that Pilate thrusts his right arm across the body of the black-bearded man, much as Hadrian's gesture (itself very similar to that of the Villa Medici Augustus) carries across the corresponding figure in the Torlonia relief. Pilate's garment is more voluminous than Hadrian's, so that the right arm of the bearded man is largely concealed from sight:

[1] Cf. M. Cagiano de Azevedo, *Le antichità di Villa Medici* (Rome, 1951), pp. 56 ff., Cat. No. 23 (Plate 7); R. Bloch, 'L'Ara Pietatis Augustae', *Mélanges d'Archéologie et d'Histoire* (École Française de Rome), lvi (1939), 81 ff.; Giuseppe Moretti, *Ara Pietatis Augustae* (Rome, 1948), pp. 218 ff. (Fig. 165).

[2] Cf. E. S. Strong, op. cit., ii, 257 (Fig. 164); S. Reinach, op. cit., i, 249. For the drawing of this relief in the Dal Pozzo–Albani collection in the Royal Library at Windsor see Cornelius C. Vermeule, 'The Dal Pozzo–Albani Drawings of Classical Antiquities: Notes on their Content and Arrangement', *Art Bulletin*, xxxiv (1952), 40 (Fig. 15).

but a close examination will show that the pose of the Roman figure is exactly repeated.

Each figure, moreover, stands on the outside of a small group placed at the extreme right of the design. In the Torlonia relief the group in question comprises three figures; in the fresco there are two more, the one scarcely visible and the other in a three-quarter back view, so that his features are not clearly seen: these are the two Jewish priests, and their relatively unemphatic treatment ensures that the first three figures—presumably all of them representations of Romans—form a dominating group on their own, which corresponds in a striking manner to the group in the Palazzo Torlonia relief. If the Torlonia relief was indeed Giotto's principal source (although there can be no proof of this), it is easy to understand why he should have modified the attitude of the central figure and given his Pilate a somewhat different pose and aspect, recalling the Villa Medici Augustus: by turning Pilate's head round into a three-quarter frontal position, not only was he able to bring him into a positive relationship with the Jewish priests on the right, but he also avoided the representation of three profiles in close proximity.

Such adaptations of Roman relief-sculpture on Giotto's part would go far to explain the unmistakably Roman 'atmosphere' of this scene; and a further quotation from antiquity in the same area of the Arena Chapel cycle may account for the unusual character of a mysterious figure which has always puzzled commentators—that strange *donna velata*, if we may so describe her, who stands within the archway in *The Meeting of St. Joachim and St. Anne at the Golden Gate of Jerusalem* (Plate 24a). In the midst of a scene of rejoicing and reunion, which had long been associated with the popular doctrine of the Immaculate Conception of Mary, this grave personage strikes a harshly discordant note: solemn in aspect, when those around her are smiling, she has seemed to most observers a prophetess of tragedy to come, and, not unnaturally, an explanation of her presence has been sought in the proximity of the scene of *The Massacre of the Innocents* (Plate 24b), which is represented immediately below. The funereal black[1] of her hooded cloak, which she appears to be drawing still more tightly around her with her left hand, contributes to the same impression of ill omen.

The Massacre of the Innocents occupies the field directly above *The Trial before Pilate*, and the two frescoes provide a clear case of the kind of thematic pairing that characterizes the organization of the Arena Chapel cycle. In Alpatoff's words, 'the Massacre was performed according to the command of King Herod; his majestic figure appears in the upper part of the picture. The Scourging of Christ was committed in presence of imperial representatives, witnesses of the brutal scene. It is not by chance that these two most turbulent and noisy scenes of the Paduan cycle were placed by Giotto one over the other.'[2]

---

[1] The actual colour used is a deep purple.   [2] M. Alpatoff, op. cit., p. 151.

To this it may be added that by Giotto's time two distinct traditions had grown up directly associating Pilate with the Massacre of the Innocents. According to the earlier of these traditions, which is to be found in the apocryphal *Gospel of Nicodemus*, or *Acts of Pilate*, it was the Jews' relation to Pilate of the story of the massacre ordered by Herod that finally persuaded him to surrender Jesus to their mercies.[1] The second tradition is preserved in the description of Pilate's examination of Jesus in the *Golden Legend* of Jacopo da Voragine, where the author, citing as his authority the *Historia scholastica* of Peter Comestor, remarks that 'the Jews accused Pilate of having permitted the massacre of the Holy Innocents, of having set up pagan images in the Temple, and of having purloined the money from the poor-chests for his own profit'; and he adds that in consequence of these charges Pilate was exiled to Lyons (the city of his birth), where he died 'despised by his own people'.[2]

Whether or not, at the time of the decoration of the Arena Chapel, the decision to bring together the *Massacre* and the *Trial* was influenced by either of these legends, there can be little doubt that Giotto intended the spectator to compare the two events in his mind. Moreover, compositional evidence alone suggests that both scenes were designed in relation to the earlier fresco of *The Meeting at the Golden Gate* painted in the field above.[3] It is therefore possible that the dark-cloaked woman in that fresco alludes to the grim

---

[1] 'And the Jews cry out and say: We know that Caesar is king, and not Jesus. For assuredly the magi brought gifts to him as to a king. And when Herod heard from the magi that a king had been born, he sought to slay him; and his father Joseph, knowing this, took him and his mother, and they fled into Egypt. And Herod, hearing of it, destroyed the children of the Hebrews that had been born in Bethlehem.

'And when Pilate heard these words, he was afraid; and ordering the crowd to keep silence, because they were crying out, he says to them: So this is he whom Herod sought? The Jews say: Yes, it is he. And, taking water, Pilate washed his hands in the face of the sun, saying: I am innocent of the blood of this just man; see you to it. Again the Jews cry out: His blood be upon us, and upon our children.' (*The Apocryphal New Testament*, trans. M. R. James (Oxford, 1924), p. 103.)

[2] *The Golden Legend of Jacopo de Voragine*, trans. G. Ryan and H. Ripperger (New York, 1941), p. 215.

[3] The assumption that the narratives in the uppermost register (*The Story of Saints Joachim and Anne* and *The Life of the Virgin*) were added to the decoration of the nave after the completion of the scenes from the Life of Christ has encouraged the view that they form a separate entity on their own, lacking any thematic connection with the main narratives below. However, the technical examination of the frescoes carried out by Tintori and Meiss has proved that the uppermost register was painted first: cf. Tintori and Meiss, op. cit., pp. 159 ff. This new knowledge does not establish the thematic connection of the three scenes under discussion, but it does remove one possible objection to it. If there is such a relationship, we should expect similar relationships in other areas of the decoration, especially where (as on the north wall) the architecture of the chapel permitted the exact vertical alignment of the scenes in all three registers. Three examples taken from the north wall will perhaps suffice to show that calculated correspondences of this nature are by no means to be excluded. Thus each of the three scenes that open the successive narratives on the north wall is concerned with maternal love: in *The Birth of the Virgin*, St. Anne holds out her arms to receive the infant Mary from the midwife; in the scene of *Christ in the Temple*, directly beneath, the Virgin rushes eagerly forward, with outstretched arms, to embrace her lost Son; and finally, in *The Carrying of the Cross*, she attempts to reach him amid the throng, to be repulsed by a soldier. Again, *The Presentation of the Virgin in the Temple*, depicting the sacred calling of Mary, is placed directly over the *Baptism*, in which Christ accepts his divine vocation, itself fulfilled in the redemptive sacrifice of the Cross, the subject of the similarly organized composition below. Finally we may note the important part played by figures kneeling in supplication in the triad of *The Prayer of the Suitors*, *The Resurrection of Lazarus*, and the *Noli me tangere*.

consequences of this scene of reunion.[1] Serious consideration should be given to the suggestion that she represents *Synagoga*,[2] whom medieval thought imagined as one dressed in black and often veiled—in allusion to those who through their adherence to the Old Law turn away from the light of the New Dispensation. According to this identification the scene of the Meeting at the Golden Gate would have been conceived as being anticipatory of the Incarnation, which is rejected alike by the murderous Herod of the *Massacre*, by the Jews who mock and accuse Christ in the scene of *The Trial before Pilate*, and by Pilate himself, who condemns Christ to death at the insistence of the Jews—all of them types of the blindness personified by *Synagoga*. It is evident that her compositional function is very similar to that of the bearded soldier who occupies the centre of the stage in *The Massacre of the Innocents* and to that of the negro flagellant in *The Trial before Pilate*: these three figures all introduce an arrestingly dark note into the central areas of their respective scenes, and the fact that because of the displacement due to the space taken up by the windows on the south wall *The Meeting at the Golden Gate* lies off-centre in relation to the other two scenes is not perhaps of great significance. The similarity of the negro's action to that of the soldier, who is about to thrust his sword into the body of a child, is apparent enough: but what of our mysterious 'dark lady' (Plate 25*b*)?

If this figure does represent *Synagoga*, who is normally shown in medieval art blind-folded or with her eyes veiled, the iconography is somewhat unusual. Seeking her prototype, we find it rather in the iconography of one of the most horrifying stories of classical legend; for she bears an uncommon resemblance to a similarly cloaked figure on a *Medea* sarcophagus known from a Renaissance drawing (Plate 25*a*).[3] (The cloaked figure in the drawing is represented as accompanying Medea at the bridals of Jason and Creusa.) The appropriateness of what might seem to be an allusion, in the immediate vicinity of the grim subject of *The Massacre of the Innocents*, to the ancient story of Medea's infanticide may well be coincidental; but the origin of Giotto's figure in a classical prototype of this kind is not at all improbable.

It can be shown, in contradiction of certain older theories, that the frescoes in the *Joachim* and *Mary* cycles in the Arena Chapel antedate those of the *Christ* cycle in the two lower registers. It is no less evident that there is a stylistic progression in the *Christ* cycle from what must be the earlier scenes at the east end of the nave to the later ones at

[1] A. M. Telpaz, op. cit., p. 373.

[2] Laurina M. Bongiorno, 'The Theme of the Old and the New Law in the Arena Chapel,' *Art Bulletin*, L, 1 (March 1968), 11 ff.

[3] MS. Coburgensis, fol. 32. This scene was represented on a now fragmentary sarcophagus in the Museo di Anti-chità, Turin: cf. C. Robert, *Die antiken Sarkophagreliefs*, ii (Berlin, 1890), no. 190, Pl. LXI. A. M. Telpaz (op. cit., p. 373) suggests that the dark-cloaked figure in Giotto's fresco was based upon a representation of Laodamia on the *Protesilaus* sarcophagus in the Vatican. I believe that the latter work was the source for some representations of the grieving Virgin in Renaissance paintings, notably in Titian's *Entombment* in the Louvre: cf. A Smart, 'Titian and the *Toro Farnese*', *Apollo*, lxxxv, 64 (1967), 420 ff., Figs. 14–17.

the entrance end. *The Meeting at the Golden Gate*, therefore, belongs to the first phase of Giotto's Paduan style, and *The Trial before Pilate* to the last. By the time that the *Trial* had been painted, Giotto's work in the Arena Chapel would have been virtually complete, and in all probability all that remained to be done was the execution of the *grisaille* frescoes of the *Virtues* and *Vices*, a great part of which could have been entrusted to assistants. What we witness, then, is an increasing assimilation, not merely of some of the outward forms, but more significantly of the very spirit, of antique and especially Roman sculpture, culminating in such magisterial statements of this classicizing ideal as are to be found in the monumentally composed scene of *The Trial before Pilate* and the more austerely sculptural *Fortitudo* and *Justitia*. We may truly say, echoing the sentiments of Politian, that in Giotto a dead art lived again; and before the fifteenth century we can apply these words to no other Italian painter.

V

GIOTTO'S EARLY DEVELOPMENT
AND THE PROBLEM OF THE ISAAC MASTER

1. *The Hypothesis of Two Assisan Activities*

SINCE THE TIME OF CAVALCASELLE critical opinion has tended to affirm with ever-increasing confidence the intervention of the young Giotto in the Old and New Testament cycles in the nave of the Upper Church at Assisi.[1] The two *Isaac* scenes (Plates 32*a*, 33*b*), the *Pietà* (Plate 34*a*), and other frescoes at the east end of the nave anticipate to a remarkable degree the style of the Arena Chapel cycle, and their decisive break with Byzantine tradition certainly announces the revolution in painting with which history associates Giotto's name. These frescoes have thus assumed, for most modern scholars, the importance that is appropriate to Giotto's first identifiable works. Disagreements about his precise share in the execution of this part of the decoration— as to whether he painted only the two *Isaac* scenes on the north wall, or only the *Pietà* on the south wall, or (with the aid of assistants) the whole stylistic group, culminating in the scenes of *The Ascension* and *Pentecost* on the entrance wall—are less significant than the general acceptance of the view that it is in the work of the 'Isaac Master' at Assisi that Giotto's beginnings are to be traced.

Much less warrant, as we have seen, can be given to the widespread assumption that two activities of Giotto in the Upper Church are to be distinguished—an early phase during which he completed or helped to complete the Biblical narratives in the upper registers, and a later phase, during which he designed and largely executed the *Legend of*

---

[1] Thode, in 1885, following the surmise of Cavalcaselle, was the first to identify the Isaac Master with Giotto. This view has been accepted by Berenson, Fry, Toesca, Salvini, Cecchi, Gnudi, Gioseffi, and many others. A few years ago Professor Meiss and I suggested independently that the allusion by Riccobaldo da Ferrara to work by Giotto at Assisi possibly referred, not to the *St. Francis* cycle, but to the *Isaac* group of frescoes in the upper registers of the nave of the Upper Church: cf. M. Meiss, op. cit., pp. 23 f., and A. Smart, 'The St. Cecilia Master and his School at Assisi', op. cit., pp. 436 f. and n. 19. The *Isaac* scenes have been ascribed to Cavallini by Van Marle and others. Modern scholars who assign them to the young Giotto concur in deducing from them his study of the work of Cavallini after the period of his presumed apprenticeship to Cimabue. The divergences of the Isaac Master from the style of Cavallini are analysed in Cecchi, op. cit., pp. 16 ff.

St. Francis in the register below. It is this second phase that is almost universally connected with the reference by Riccobaldo da Ferrara, in his *Compilatio chronologica*, to work by Giotto in the Basilica.

Between the two Assisan periods it is customary to place the crucifix at Santa Maria Novella, as a work that supposedly marks the transition from the *Isaac* style to that of the *Legend*. Giotto's failure to complete the *Legend* is generally ascribed to his summons to Rome by Boniface VIII to paint the *Jubilee* frescoes in the Lateran. His visit to Rimini is placed either immediately before or shortly after the Paduan period,[1] and those scholars who ascribe to Giotto the crucifix in the Tempio Malatestiano at Rimini (usually dated after the Padua Cross) see in the existence of this work confirmation of the accuracy of the tradition handed down by Riccobaldo da Ferrara. Somewhere in the interval between the second Assisan phase and the Paduan period a place is usually found for three important altarpieces—the Louvre *Stigmatization*, which repeats four of the subjects of the *St. Francis* cycle at Assisi, the *Madonna* at S. Giorgio alla Costa in Florence, and the Badia polyptych.

This is the commonly accepted picture of Giotto's early development. It is a strange one. It has more the character of a kaleidoscope, contriving a different set of patterns at every shaking: so, we should have to assume, must it have been with Giotto—that virtually every new commission evoked in him a quite novel response, dissolving in an instant the previous patterns of his thought and style. On this reading, his development must have been uneven and haphazard to the point of incomprehensibility. The theory behind it possesses something of the fantastic persuasiveness of Baconian criticism: neglecting fundamental principles, it brings to bear upon each question of attribution a parcel of unsupported traditions and mistaken resemblances, and, what is still more unreasonable, it ignores the immense improbabilities inherent in a stylistic evolution that discloses at every turn a changed personality. An artist's manner may alter, but was there ever a sequence of self-contradictions of this nature? The irresolvable conflicts are several—between the *Legend* and the *Isaac* frescoes; between the *Legend* and the Arena Chapel cycle; between the Santa Maria Novella Cross and the Padua Crucifix; between the Ognissanti and S. Giorgio *Madonnas*; between the *Jubilee* fresco and the Arena Chapel cycle; between the Badia polyptych and the Ognissanti *Madonna*; and (despite the similar, although not identical, iconography) between the *Legend* and the Louvre *Stigmatization*. The list of incompatibilities could be extended still further. We have

---

[1] Riccobaldo may well have listed Giotto's work at Assisi, Rimini, and Padua in chronological order, and Meiss notes that Riccobaldo 'did not adopt an alphabetical order but placed Assisi first, before *Ariminum* and Padua' (M. Meiss, op. cit., p. 24). On the other hand, since Riccobaldo was concerned chiefly with works by Giotto in Franciscan churches, he may have chosen to give priority to the Basilica at Assisi as the mother church of the Order, while it would have been convenient to refer to the Santo at Padua last of all, so that the further reference to the Arena Chapel in Padua would not interrupt the list of Franciscan churches.

seen what little reason there is to ascribe to Giotto such works as the Santa Maria Novella Cross, the S. Giorgio *Madonna*, the *Jubilee* fresco, and the Badia polyptych. The retention of these works within Giotto's *œuvre* has served only to confuse the whole problem of his early development, and not until they are finally excluded can the way be cleared to a prospect of the real evidence. Only then can we begin to understand the uniqueness of his genius and the consistency of his ideals: face to face with the real Giotto, rather than with his shadow, we shall be in less danger of mistaking for his sublime discourse the inflections of other voices.

2. *The Louvre* Stigmatization of St. Francis

It is understandable that Vasari should have assumed that the panel of *The Stigmatization of St. Francis* (Plate 28), commissioned for the church of S. Francesco in Pisa, and now in the Louvre, was painted immediately after Giotto's work for the Franciscans at Assisi.[1] The panel is inscribed with Giotto's name, but the uneven execution, especially in the predella, marks it as a product of his *bottega*.[2] The predella contains three scenes from the Saint's life which reflect the iconography of the corresponding scenes in the *St. Francis* cycle at Assisi (Plates 52, 53, 68): but this apparent dependence upon the Assisi cycle does not provide evidence, as it is often thought to do, of Giotto's authorship of the frescoes. Inevitably the great cycle in the mother church of the Order of Friars Minor exerted a wide influence upon later representations of the hallowed stories of St. Francis's life and ministry, for which the scenes at Assisi offered the paradigms with the best title to canonical authority. Sometimes, as in the fresco-cycle in S. Francesco at Pistoia, ascribed by tradition to Puccio Capanna, the Assisi compositions were copied with relatively few alterations;[3] but the evolution of Franciscan iconography was also accompanied by certain significant changes, which were due both to modifications of the religious interpretation of the subject-matter and to the historical processes of stylistic development. For example, the representations of the Stigmatization by Pietro Lorenzetti in the Lower Church at Assisi and by Giotto at Santa Croce in Florence both reflect traditions found in the *Fioretti*, a work based on the slightly earlier *Actus Beati Francisci* and one that postdates the cycle in the Upper Church: but other differences in the treatment of the subject are explicable purely on stylistic grounds; and it must have been chiefly the impulse of style, combined with the obvious convenience of accessibility, that led

[1] G. Vasari, *Le Vite . . .* (1578), ed. Milanesi, i, 379 f.

[2] White makes the interesting suggestion that 'Giotto signed those major products of his workshop which he himself had not painted. These were the works that were in need of the protection of a signature to prove their provenance' (J. White, *Art and Architecture in Italy . . .*, pp. 204 and 223 f.). Nevertheless, the Giottesque characteristics of the designs of the Louvre scenes would seem to provide evidence of his superintendence of the work. If this was not so, we can only assume a thorough understanding of his aims on the part of a pupil.

[3] For the Pistoia frescoes see A. Chiappelli, 'Puccio Capanna e gli affreschi in S. Francesco di Pistoia', *Dedalo*, x (1929-30), i, 199 ff.

Taddeo Gaddi, one of the great innovators in the interpretation of Franciscan legend, to base the scenes on his *armadio* panels for Santa Croce[1] more extensively upon Giotto's frescoes in the same church than upon the cycle at Assisi.

The Giottesque panel of *The Stigmatization* in the Fogg Museum,[2] including as it does a representation of the cave at La Verna which is first mentioned in the *Actus* (*c.* 1325), must on this account be dated relatively late. The Louvre picture, on the other hand, suggests a much earlier moment in the development of the iconography, and stands closer to the cycle in the Upper Church: how close this relationship is can be judged from the repetition in the central scene of the predella, *The Sanctioning of the Rule* (Plate 27*a*), of so minor a detail as the motif of confronted birds which decorates the tiles of the floor in the Assisi fresco (Plate 53). Yet not one of the four subjects represented— *The Stigmatization* in the main panel and the three scenes of *The Dream of Innocent III*, *The Sanctioning of the Rule*, and *The Sermon to the Birds* (Plate 27*b*) on the predella— accepts the Assisan iconography without important modifications, which have their deepest roots in style.

Of relatively minor significance are the changes due to the association, in the predella, of three scenes which are not found together in the Assisi cycle. In the Louvre picture *The Sanctioning of the Rule*, with its centralized perspective, becomes the natural centre-piece; and the Lateran basilica represented in the first scene combines now with the tree in *The Sermon to the Birds* to form a kind of bracket at the extremities of the group of three scenes which rounds off the design of the whole. In *The Dream of Innocent III* the abolition of the curious inclined plane upon which, in the Assisi fresco (Plate 52), the Lateran basilica is placed, and upon which St. Francis himself stands, represents a funda-mental revisualization of the scene on Giotto's part which was perhaps inevitable, although this somewhat naïve device is still retained in the fresco at Pistoia: in Giotto's conception, at any rate, the building no longer heels over in one piece, like a sinking ship, and the introduction of a single broken column is sufficient to convey an immediate impression of structural collapse.

But it is in a more far-reaching sense than this that the treatment of architecture in the Louvre predella differs from that found in the corresponding scenes of the *Legend*. The massive, block-like forms at Assisi, supported upon thick columns, are quite foreign to the art of Giotto, as they are also absent from the frescoes of the Isaac Master; they are quite as uncharacteristic of Giotto's sensibility as the 'monumental' and sometimes dumpy figures, with their frequent appearance of stony immobility. While the designs of the predella scenes preserve the general layout and disposition of the buildings represented in the Assisi frescoes, we see Giotto everywhere correcting that abstracting

---

[1] Accademia, Florence, Nos. 8594–8603; Sinibaldi and Brunetti, op. cit., pp. 429 ff., Pl. 137*p–y*.
[2] F. J. Mather, 'Giotto and the *Stigmatization*', *Art Studies*, viii, 2 (1931), 49 ff. and Fig. 3.

process which is always at work at Assisi and which seeks to reduce architectural forms to an almost geometrical simplicity: thus the treatment of architectural detail in the Louvre scenes is at once more realistic and more particularized than it is in the Assisi frescoes, and shows a deeper understanding of structure and function.

As though he felt that the Assisi master had not been sufficiently precise, Giotto introduced into the façade of the Lateran basilica a remarkable copy of its mosaics, giving the church a still more unmistakable identity. A no less distinctive characteristic of the same scene, as Giotto interprets it, is the elegant proportioning of the architectural forms of the Pope's room. This is particularly noticeable in the rendering of the columns supporting the roof, which are far removed in type from the massive piers to be seen in the Assisi fresco, and which correspond to Giotto's invariable taste in the representation of architectural detail, whether in the Arena Chapel cycle, in the frescoes in the Bardi and Peruzzi Chapels at Santa Croce, or in the fragmentary decorations recovered from the Badia, as they correspond also to the ideal of the Isaac Master. Indeed, this distinction carries with it curious implications for the view that Giotto was the author of the *St. Francis* frescoes on the north wall at Assisi, in addition to the *Isaac* scenes; for his proportioning of such architectural forms on the north wall would represent a wholly exceptional and unrepeated departure from his habitual practice, and only on the south wall, in frescoes executed by other painters—the 'Master of the Obsequies' and the St. Cecilia Master—would there have been a return to an ideal approximating his own.

In designing the scene of *The Sanctioning of the Rule* (Plate 27a) on the Louvre altarpiece Giotto ingeniously adapted the basic pattern of the architecture represented in the Assisi fresco (Plate 53) to his own refined taste, giving a greater spaciousness to the room and letting in more light and air. The elaborately woven tapestry hanging at the back of the papal hall in the Assisi fresco—a decorative feature charming in itself but one that may have seemed to Giotto to distract attention from the figures—is omitted in favour of a more austere representation of bare wall-spaces, relieved only by three aumbries and a solitary doorway: the doorway itself, it will be noticed, is reduced in size, being given a scale proportionate to the height of the room, whereas in the fresco at Assisi the two doors represented reach up to the consoles below the ceiling. In this scene on the Louvre predella the treatment of the architecture strongly recalls the rendering of interiors in the Arena Chapel, as, for example, in *The Wedding at Cana* and *Christ before Caiaphas* (Plate 19b), providing strong evidence that the altarpiece is to be dated *c.* 1300–7.

The spatial organization still lacks the breadth and completeness, and the serene harmony, of *The Confirmation of the Rule* in the Bardi Chapel, where, besides, the figures have a noble and fundamentally classical simplicity absent from their counterparts in the Louvre picture, which are more finely and delicately proportioned, as they are also more particularized in their characterization. Yet, except in their repetition of a very few gestures, the figures on the altarpiece suggest a quite different vision of humanity from that of the Assisi painter (Plate 54c) (or painters, for the fresco was the work of more than one hand), and St. Francis and the other friars, the Pope, and the attendant members of the Curia all show a consistent divergence in physiognomic type from their originals in the fresco: the expressions of the Louvre figures are more mobile, more eloquent of inner response, subtler in every respect in their psychological implications; the repetitious postures of the friars kneeling behind St. Francis in the Assisi fresco are here avoided; and, like the aspirants to the Virgin's hand who kneel before the altar in *The Prayer of the Suitors* at Padua, they form a compact group as complete in the realization of solidity and depth in space as the Assisi group is deficient in it. In the same way the figures of the Pope and his retinue have been redesigned to allow the air to circulate about them: they are no longer cramped within a space that scarcely holds them; and, significantly, the cardinal on the extreme right has been brought forward so that he has room to breathe.

All three scenes heighten the dramatic tension of their models in the Upper Church. Where at Assisi St. Francis is revealed to the sleeping Pope as the passive instrument of the divine will, in Giotto's interpretation he is seen in the toils of heroic action: nothing could be more striking than this difference between the two images of the Saint—the first, that almost of a granite column supporting with ease the mighty structure tilting above, the other the picture of a man struggling to prevent the fall of the church by hurriedly interposing himself in the place of the broken column. Other divergences from the fresco in the Upper Church include the natural position given to the recumbent Pope, and, what is of greater iconographical importance, the addition of the figure of St. Peter, who draws the Pope's attention to the action of the Saint: a similar figure appears in the fresco at Pistoia.[1] His presence adds to the dramatic content of the scene, avoiding the tableau-like passivity of the fresco in the Upper Church. So also, in *The Sanctioning of the Rule* (Plate 27a), Giotto brings the two principal participants, St. Francis and the Pope, into a more active relationship: the Pope has ceased to be the stolid, impersonal image of papal authority which is presented to us at Assisi; he stoops towards the humble Francis, and his expression conveys a benign sympathy; St. Francis himself leans eagerly forward, and it is his gesture, rather than his lowly position in relation to the Pope, that is most eloquent of his humility.

In *The Sermon to the Birds* (Plate 27b), in like manner, St. Francis assumes a commanding attitude which lends to Giotto's interpretation of the story a sense of urgency and strong purpose absent from the more descriptive and far less dramatic representation in the

---

[1] G. Kaftal, *Iconography of the Saints in Tuscan Painting* (Florence, 1952), Fig. 448. Here the figure is a representation of Christ rather than St. Peter.

Upper Church (Plate 68); his whole body is tense with life, as though its rhythms had communicated themselves to the painter's brush—how clumsy and awkward by comparison the stocky figure in the famous scene in the Upper Church appears, beside this fluency, this grace and vigour! Moreover, the gesture of St. Francis in the Assisi fresco (Plate 16*b*) has nothing in common with those found in the work of Giotto: the abrupt manner in which one arm crosses over the other, at right angles to it, has already been mentioned, together with other instances of this gesture in the Assisi cycle. The design of the figure in the Louvre scene reflects a wholly different conception of the language of gesture and expression in pictorial composition.

The same distinctions between Giotto's treatment of the human figure and that common to the painters of the Assisi cycle make themselves felt in the main panel of the Louvre altarpiece. As the Stigmatization on Mount La Verna was the most important event in the Franciscan legend (which accounts for its selection as the principal subject of the altarpiece), and as it was illustrated more frequently than any other, the development of the iconography is relatively easy to trace, even if allowance has to be made for a number of lost works; and here iconography has its own light to throw upon the problem of style.

Almost all thirteenth-century representations of the Stigmatization show St. Francis kneeling on the ground; the pose varies from one version to another, although as a rule the Saint rests on both knees; but it is clear that in each case the attitude given to St. Francis was determined chiefly by the position decided upon for the Seraph. The iconographic tradition falls into two main categories—the first exemplified by the representations on the mid-thirteenth-century altarpiece in the Bardi Chapel at Santa Croce in Florence (Plate 29*c*)[1] and on Bonaventura Berlinghieri's Pescia altarpiece of 1235 (Plate 30*a*),[2] and the second by the scene on the Reliquary Shutters now ascribed to Guido da Siena (Plate 31)[3] and by a similar composition by a close follower.[4] In the works belonging to the second of these categories the Seraph is placed high over the Saint's head, whereas in those of the first category the position of the Seraph is visualized as being lower down and to one side of the composition, so that St. Francis has to raise his head relatively little to behold the vision. The latter type inevitably encouraged a representation of St. Francis from the side, with his arms held out in front of him. The Guidesque type, on the other hand, made possible a front or even a back view: in the Sienese panels the upper part of the Saint's body is twisted round as he reaches upwards in wonderment at the vision, so that his shoulders are seen from the back, and his flame-like form is

[1] Ibid., Fig. 468; Sinibaldi and Brunetti, op. cit., Pl. 55*a*.   [2] Sinibaldi and Brunetti, op. cit., Fig. 5*c*.
[3] Pinacoteca, Siena, No. 4: cf. J. H. Stubblebine, *Guido da Siena* (Princeton, 1964), pp. 21 ff., Figs. 1, 4: Kaftal, op. cit., Fig. 467.
[4] Gallerani Reliquary Shutters (School of Guido da Siena), Pinacoteca, Siena, No. 5: cf. Stubblebine, op. cit., pp. 69 ff., Fig. 35.

extraordinarily evocative of ecstatic rapture. In Guido's panel, which is datable shortly after 1255,[1] we actually see the *stigmata* in the soles of the Saint's feet, as well as in the backs of his hands: as the figure is turned away from us we scarcely notice the wound in his side.

From a theological point of view this was a less satisfactory image than Berlinghieri's or than that on the Bardi altarpiece, and it was the other tradition that contained the greater posibilities for future development. Yet in creating this figure twisting round on its axis and seeming to imply the existence of a real space around and behind it, Guido da Siena anticipated Giotto's own unequalled representation of the subject at Santa Croce (Plate 29*b*); for in Giotto's fresco the Seraph is visualized as appearing from behind St. Francis; and as the Saint is shown in a fully frontal view he must turn his head sharply over one shoulder to see the vision. It is as though Giotto had divined the spatial implications of the image on the Bardi altarpiece (Plate 29*c*)—an image repeated with only minor differences in a related panel in the Accademia in Florence (Plate 30*b*)[2] which is rather easier to read, but in which the Seraph appears slightly higher in the heavens, producing in the rays of light joining the figures of the Seraph and the Saint a steeper diagonal closer to Giotto's conception. A theological virtue, so to speak, of this image is that the Saint's raised arms recall the attitude of a figure on a cross.

Giotto's conception of the subject is that of an artist profoundly interested in the exploration of spatial problems; it is a conception that is also intensely dramatic: the imprinting of the sacred *stigmata* is conceived as an act of power which bends back the Saint's hands as far as the joints of the wrist will allow; the fingers of each hand are tensed and the thumb is pulled backward, as though by the sheer force and weight of physical impact. When we compare the version on the Louvre altarpiece (Plate 28) we find that, apart from a difference in the pose, it contains all the essential characteristics of the Santa Croce fresco—the appearance of the Seraph from behind St. Francis, the necessary turning of the Saint's head so that he can look at the apparition over his left shoulder, and the bending back of his hands (particularly the important left hand, which iconographic tradition placed next to the Seraph). These fundamental elements of Giotto's reinterpretation of the miracle are found again in the damaged fresco in the Capitolo of the Santo at Padua,[3] a work of Giottesque origin, and in the panel in the Fogg Art Museum.

---

[1] J. H. Stubblebine, loc. cit. To Professor Stubblebine is due the attribution to Guido himself, rather than to his following.

[2] Accademia, Florence, No. 8574; Sinibaldi and Brunetti, op. cit., pp. 21 f., Pl. 6*a*, *b* (as School of Bonaventura Berlinghieri); C. L. Ragghianti, *Pittura del Dugento a Firenze* (Florence, 1955), Fig. 56 (as Circle of the Bardi St. Francis Master).

[3] The frescoes in the Sala del Capitolo of the Santo at Padua, of which only fragments now remain, were devoted to scenes from the *Legend of St. Francis* and the *Passion of Christ*. They have sometimes been identified with the decorations by Giotto in the Santo referred to by Riccobaldo da Ferrara, Ghiberti and other writers: cf. Suzanne Pichon,

The Santo fresco already anticipates the dramatic rendering of the subject at Santa Croce: unfortunately the lower part of the figure of St. Francis is completely lost; but what remains is almost identical with the figure at Santa Croce (except that the left hand is not raised so high nor the right arm dropped quite so low). The Seraph is imagined once more as appearing to St. Francis from behind, and the Saint, accordingly, turns his head to look over his shoulder, much as he does in the Louvre panel. In fact, in all these Giottesque versions of the subject St. Francis is represented as one taken by surprise: in his astonishment he sways backwards, as though suddenly thrown off balance. It seems clear that the Louvre panel represents an early stage in the development of an idea to which Giotto was to give final expression in the great fresco over the entrance to the Bardi Chapel. As Panofsky has shown, it is an idea derived directly from an antique source, the memory of which survived into the late Middle Ages and which was to be adapted in the High Renaissance, notably by Dürer, to representations of Christ bearing the Cross: it is the ancient image of Orpheus in the scene of his death at the hands of the Thracian women, a figure shown crouching on one knee with his left arm raised in an attempt to ward off the blows of his executioners, who stand behind him, and with his head turned to look over his shoulder.[1]

At Santa Croce (Plate 29*b*) Giotto heightened both the dramatic and the spatial tension of the composition by representing St. Francis as kneeling away from the Seraph, with his left rather than his right knee on the ground, and by increasing the sense of the swaying motion of the torso by raising the Saint's left hand high above his head and lowering the right. The first of these changes produces a dramatic *contrapposto* unknown to Italian painting before this time, while the other frees the movement of the body from its earlier stiffness and relates its tilted axis more harmoniously to the inclined form of the Seraph.

The fresco in the Upper Church at Assisi (Plates 29*a*, 76) evidently descends from the same Florentine tradition: but the whole concept is less dramatic than Giotto's and altogether simpler in aesthetic intention. The Saint's gaze carries across the picture-plane instead of turning back into the depths of the pictorial space; there is no sense here of an almost physical incursion of divine power; and the Saint's fingers are relaxed and the palms less open than in the Santa Croce fresco or in the Louvre altarpiece. Whereas in Giotto's versions of the subject St. Francis raises his hands in surprise and wonder at the vision, in the fresco at Assisi he simply offers them for the imprint of the sacred *stigmata*.

'Gli affreschi di Giotto al Santo di Padova', *Bollettino d'arte*, iv, 2 (1924–5), 26 ff.; Pier Liberale Rambaldi, 'Postilla al passo di Riccobaldo', *Rivista d'arte*, xix, 3–4, Numero speciale del Centenario Giottesco (1937), 354, n. 2. The fresco of *The Stigmatization* and its relationship to Scene XIX in the Upper Church at Assisi are discussed in F. J. Mather, op. cit., pp. 49 ff. Mather accepted both frescoes as the work of Giotto, and held that together with the Louvre *Stigmatization* they belonged to the same iconographic tradition.

[1] E. Panofsky, *Albrecht Dürer* (Princeton, 1945), p. 32, Pls. 49 and 50.

St. Francis does, it is true, sway backwards—even further, indeed, than he does in the Louvre picture—but we receive no impression of imbalance, for the vision appears directly in front of him, and he has only to lean back with a natural movement to look up at it. The Assisi master accepts the simple, non-spatial conception preserved in the thirteenth-century Florentine tradition, and sees no reason to modify it in any radical way. There is less emphasis than in Giotto's interpretations of the subject upon the articulation of the figure, which remains passive, and the arms are largely concealed, in any case, by the voluminous sleeves of the Saint's habit. Altogether the figure is treated as a much less complex and more static mass, and the right hand, for example, does not penetrate beyond the elegant silhouette of the body; a difference partly explicable by the fact that St. Francis is represented in more of a side view than he is in the Giottesque versions. This difference in viewpoint also accounts for other dissimilarities in the treatment of the figure: in the Louvre panel, for instance, the left foot is represented on an inclined and receding plane, whereas at Assisi it is seen from the side in an exactly horizontal position.

We do not know whether Giotto had represented this subject before he received the commission for the Pisa altarpiece. If he had not, then it is reasonable to assume that the fresco in the Upper Church at Assisi provided the basis of his composition. That being so, it is evident that, no less than in the predella scenes, he felt it necessary to undertake a fundamental remodelling of the design in terms of the new spatial and dramatic considerations which were inseparable from his understanding of the painter's art. In these respects the Assisi master's interpretation of the subject must have appeared to him to stop short at the point where his own deepest interests began. This is not in any sense to disparage the fresco in the Upper Church. The aims of the two masters were basically different. The designer of the Assisi fresco was not interested in the dramatic moment as Giotto was to understand it: he was more concerned to narrate the story of the great miracle at La Verna as clearly as possible, and to illustrate its theological significance, than to penetrate very deeply into the reactions of St. Francis as a human being suddenly overwhelmed by a divine visitation; and so in the Assisi fresco the Saint raises his hands less in astonishment than in obedience to the divine will that they shall be marked with the wounds of Christ. The function of the figure in the design as a whole is, moreover, more decorative than Giotto would have allowed. It is not made to dominate the scene, as Giotto's figure dominates the Louvre composition, but rather is absorbed in the pattern of the landscape, as the central but not the strongest element in the design—for the mountain of La Verna on the left and the Seraphic Christ on the right are both weightier forms.

It is one of the notable features of Giotto's treatment of the Stigmatization that allowance is made for the distance of the Seraph from St. Francis: the visionary form appears accordingly on a reduced scale, as it also appears (although no doubt for a different reason) in most thirteenth-century illustrations. But this is far from being the most important difference from the treatment of the Seraph at Assisi. The most significant innovation made by Giotto in its representation consists of the marked tilting of its axis from the vertical, so that the Seraphic Christ now plays an active part in the drama of La Verna, seeming to invade the scene suddenly with beating wings. By contrast the figure of the Seraph in the Assisi fresco is only slightly inclined, and gives little if any impression of movement: like the figure of St. Francis in the preceding fresco in the cycle, *The Appearance at Arles* (Scene XVIII, Plate 75), it suggests rather the momentary manifestation of a spiritual presence; and the slight tilting of the Seraph's form seems to have been due primarily to the artist's desire to create a shape that would echo that of the sunlit mountain slope, and so to maintain a harmonious symmetry in the upper areas of his design (Plate 76).

This is a very different conception from that of Giotto in the Louvre *Stigmatization*. The design of the Louvre picture is based upon the dramatic relationship established between the Seraph and St. Francis, who confront one another actively across an emphatic, swinging diagonal. In the Assisi fresco the disposition of the Seraph's wings within what is essentially an equilateral triangle relates the total form less fundamentally to St. Francis than to the equally regular shape of the mountain, while the Christ-figure itself is associated with the 'theological' image of St. Francis in the previous scene (Plate 6a). Giotto's conception is dramatic and spatial before it is anything else, and the idea of the Seraph's incursion from behind St. Francis must have determined the design of both figures: but the Assisi master, while creating a very real impression of space and depth in his landscape, and succeeding admirably in setting his figures and buildings within it, still thinks two-dimensionally in establishing relationships between one form and another. And the many differences that exist between two interpretations of the same subject that are so deceptively similar to the superficial glance cannot be explained either by stylistic development or by the particular demands of patronage: they cleave to the hidden roots of style, to the spiritual and aesthetic impulses that determine its every aspect, and which distinguish one artistic personality from another.

3. *The Isaac Master*

The Upper Church at Assisi is full of contrasts, but there is none more striking than that between the linear, late-Byzantine style of the earlier scenes in the Biblical cycles, which in the main are probably to be ascribed to Jacopo Torriti, and the revolutionary art of the Isaac Master, with its unprecedented concern with volume and space. The two *Isaac* scenes and the *Pietà*, which are among the least damaged of the frescoes in the stylistic group as a whole, represent an artistic achievement unsurpassed elsewhere in the decoration of the Upper Church. The product of a sublime and profound mind, intent not merely upon the solution of new pictorial problems but also upon the rendering of subtle nuances of psychological expression, the work of the Isaac Master at Assisi, while reflecting the immediate influence of Cavallini, points beyond the traditions of the Dugento towards the *arte nuova* of the Arena Chapel; and so striking and so manifold are the anticipations in these frescoes of Giotto's Paduan style that it is difficult to resist the conclusion that it is here, amidst the ruins of the later Biblical scenes in the Upper Church, that the origins of Giotto's art are to be sought.[1]

Yet, tempting though it is to take the further step of affirming categorically that the Isaac Master can only be Giotto in an early phase of his development, such a proposition must remain a hypothesis which new evidence may compel us eventually to abandon. A close examination of the Isaac frescoes reveals differences from the Arena Chapel cycle in the brushwork and modelling and, on a purely Morellian level, in the formation of such features as eyes and ears. Such differences are taken into account by the most persuasive of all the advocates of Giotto's identity with the Isaac Master, Millard Meiss, and, in view of the possibility of substantial stylistic development and change within the ten or fifteen years that separate the Assisi frescoes from those at Padua, Meiss is clearly right to give compensatory weight to deeper spiritual values and aesthetic preoccupations. On the other hand, many periods in the history of painting have thrown up artists of like mind and intention—a Titian alongside a Giorgione, a Turner beside a Girtin—whose styles can readily be confused; and while recognizing the extraordinary affinities that exist between the Arena Chapel frescoes and the *Isaac* scenes we shall be wise to admit the validity of an alternative interpretation of the stylistic evidence, which sees the Isaac Master and Giotto as two closely related painters with common origins in Cavallini. What is certain is that the Isaac Master was one of the great innovators in the history of art.

In the two *Isaac* scenes (Plates 32*a*, 33*b*) space is treated for the first time in Italian painting as a virtually tangible entity which the human figure displaces as it penetrates it. Whereas in the *St. Francis* cycle space occurs as a void between one form and another —as the negative aspect, so to speak, of the pattern of forms of which the design of each scene is composed—the Isaac Master visualizes every form in its relationship to neighbouring forms; and it is in the completeness of his awareness of the implications of a thoroughgoing representation of the three-dimensional world that he differs most from Cavallini. The extent to which the Isaac Master surpasses Cavallini in solving the problem of relating one figure to another in space is made clear by a comparison between the second of the two *Isaac* scenes, *The Rejection of Esau* (Plate 33*b*), and Cavallini's mosaic of *The Birth of the Virgin* at Santa Maria in Trastevere, which offers a not dissimilar

[1] In addition to Meiss's recent study of the problem, see especially Lidia Lochoff, op. cit. Dr. Lochoff sees the workshop of the Isaac Master at Assisi as the place of origin of Giotto's style, the inference being that Giotto worked in the Upper Church alongside the other members of the *bottega*.

composition and at the same time indicates sufficiently clearly the Cavallinesque origins of the Isaac Master's style. Where Cavallini still tends to turn his figures into a frontal position, whatever their intended relationship, on a dramatic level, with the other actors in the scene, the *personae* of the Isaac Master, at once more substantial and more convincing as living beings swayed by human passions, both exist as physical presences whose precise relationship to the spatial envelope around them is clearly and logically defined, and also respond to each other on a deeper spiritual level, so that we become aware at once of a tense conflict of human natures. The presence in each composition of such elements as the railings on the near side of the bed, the curtains behind, and above all a female figure holding a pitcher[1] points to a close connection between the two works.[2] The advanced style of the Assisi fresco, coupled with the fact that servants with pitchers belong to the iconography of scenes of The Birth of the Virgin, makes it difficult to date the Isaac Master's fresco before Cavallini's mosaic, which was executed about 1291.

The vocabulary of gesture and expression employed in the *Isaac* frescoes strongly recalls the intensely dramatic language of Giotto in the Arena cycle, and attention has been drawn by Meiss to the important part played by the meaningful glances of Esau and his companion, in *The Rejection of Esau*, in heightening the drama of the scene. Meiss's discerning observations are worth quoting in full:

These glances are so controlled and so vivid that they establish almost tangible channels across the space. Thus the drama culminates in them while, or rather because, they participate in the geometry of the design. The character of these glances is approximated in other late Dugento works, especially those of Cimabue and Duccio, but this is the first post-antique painting in which sight is focussed to this degree and given so fundamental a role in the structure and content of a painting. From such a model the chief painter of the *Legend* learned to control and intensify the glances, but only in the Arena Chapel are they equally embedded in the design.[3]

So profound is the Isaac Master's understanding of the implications of his revolutionary conception of pictorial space that it is not necessary for him to contrive an illusion of the third dimension by devising elaborate architectural structures like those that are introduced into many of the scenes of the *St. Francis* cycle, lending a rigid and static quality to the spaces so defined. It is instructive to observe what little effect the extensive damage to the room represented in the second of the two *Isaac* scenes has upon the expression of the interior space, whereas in the other scene, where the same room is represented, and where it is the figures rather than the architectural forms that have suffered comparable damage, the impression of space is much weakened. As in the Arena Chapel, space is defined, not as a separate element, but as the necessary environment in

---

[1] Meiss, op. cit., Figs. 31, 52.   [2] Ibid., p. 18.   [3] Ibid., p. 16.

which all forms have their being; and this space takes on its deepest pictorial significance in the context of dramatic action, wherein one figure is made to impinge upon the spatial environment of another.

Entirely new possibilities are here opened up for the painter, enabling him to create a living stage upon which all the complexities of human emotion can be unfolded. History links one name, that of Giotto, with this revolutionary development in painting, and yet it would be hard to deny that the Isaac Master exhibits at an earlier stage of evolution many of the qualities of Giotto's art as we encounter it on its first certainly identifiable appearance—that is to say, in the Arena Chapel at Padua. If the Isaac Master was not the young Giotto, he must, surely, have been one of the strongest formative influences upon him: Meiss goes still further, and insists that 'if the Isaac Master is not Giotto, then he and not Giotto is the founder of modern painting'.[1]

It is clear that both in their style and in their iconography the *Isaac* frescoes have their deepest roots in Roman traditions. Certain basic elements of the first scene, *Isaac Blessing Iacob*, are already found in the fifth-century mosaic of this subject at Santa Maria Maggiore[2]—notably the semi-recumbent pose of Isaac, who extends one hand to prove the identity of his son; the parted curtains behind Isaac's bed; and the inclusion of the figure of Rebekah. In the mosaic, however, Jacob is represented as a diminutive boy, and Isaac touches his son's head instead of clasping him by the hand. Another fifth-century Roman representation, the fresco formerly at S. Paolo fuori le mura, the design of which is known from a seventeenth-century drawing,[4] approaches the Assisi composition more closely in giving the figure of Jacob, now shown as a youth, the same scale as that accorded to the other figures, and in placing him on the far side of Isaac's bed; once again the figure of Rebekah completes the group. The Isaac Master may well have had this work in mind when he designed the companion scene of *The Rejection of Esau*, a subject that occurs less commonly in earlier paintings: the Isaac in the Roman fresco (as far as we know it from the drawing) bears a quite close resemblance to his counterpart in the Upper Church, especially in the general character of the head and in the classicizing treatment of the draperies; and there is a similar, although looser, resemblance between the pose of Jacob in the Roman fresco and that of Esau at Assisi.

Beyond such connections with older traditions deriving from Rome, the *Isaac* frescoes show an intimate acquaintance with the work of Cavallini; it was from the great Roman master that their painter must have learnt how to model his forms in graded tones of light and shade, and his discipleship is reflected in lingering echoes of Cavallini's physiognomic types, while something of Cavallini's lofty spirit, his noble monumentality and *gravitas*, is also preserved in the Assisi frescoes. At the same time, and no less certainly, the Isaac Master belongs to the broad movement that culminates in Italian Gothic—and,

[1] Meiss, op. cit., p. 25.   [2] Ibid., Fig. 34.   [3] Ibid., Fig. 35.

as Meiss has shown, one important element of the iconography of the first *Isaac* scene, the combination of blessing and proving, derives from a Gothic rather than from a Roman tradition.[1] The Gothic elements in the Isaac Master's style are more pronounced in the *Pietà*, with all its passionate agony of emotion, than in the two *Isaac* scenes themselves, and everywhere they are less evolved than the Gothicisms of the Arena Chapel. Yet a development of such a kind within a single artistic personality would not be unexpected in this period, and it would have run parallel to the general development in sculpture between Nicola and Giovanni Pisano.[2] The connections with Cimabue, upon which Meiss insists, are less easy to perceive; but the expressive use of a bounding outline in the figures and the conventions used for the rendering of the folds of draperies may well derive ultimately from Cimabue, although they become transmuted by a classicizing taste formed, evidently, upon the study of antique sculpture. It may be said further that the Isaac Master develops within the context of a more 'advanced' style Cimabue's unique sense of the dramatic possibilities of painting. The Isaac Master may possibly have been a pupil of Cimabue who subsequently came under the influence of Cavallini, but his relationship to Cavallini is the more apparent, and it must have been under Cavallini that he received his essential training.

But neither to Cavallini nor to Cimabue did the Isaac Master owe the quality that most distinguishes the two *Isaac* scenes from all previous interpretations of these subjects and which informs his art as a whole—his concern with the human aspect of his subject-matter. No earlier interpretations of this strange story of deception—which sets forth in narrative form the ancient Jewish belief in the sacredness of a bond, and which in patristic and medieval thought was taken to be an allegory of the substitution of the New Covenant for the Old—shows anything comparable with the Isaac Master's insistence upon its emotional content, upon the drama of Jacob's triumph and the tragedy of Esau's loss. The first scene (Plate 32*a*), as Meiss has expressed it, 'dwells on the human situation as much as on the theological allegory, on the biblical narrative rather than its medieval exegesis'.[3] We are invited to hang upon the event, imminent but not yet consummated: Jacob still hesitates to approach his father, involved in the awareness of his own guilt, while his mother, entering the room at his side and swiftly drawing back the curtain, appears to be hurrying on the issue of their plot. To stand in the Upper Church and to look up at the half-ruined fresco and the scene beside it, and to compare them with the frescoes by other masters elsewhere in the nave, is to become aware of a close proximity to the spiritual world of the Arena Chapel, with its tense dramatic situations and subtle intimations of human emotion. Indeed much the same quality of imagination seems to be at work at Assisi and at Padua, employing similar means to similar ends.

Only in the art of Giotto do we discover a comparable concentration of personal

---

[1] Ibid., pp. 13 f.   [2] Ibid., pp. 22 f.   [3] Ibid., p. 14.

emotion in the expression and physiognomy of a head. Both the power of characterization and the economy of the means employed in the portrayal of Jacob in the Assisi fresco have much in common with Giotto's subtle evocation, in the scene of *Joachim's Withdrawal to the Sheepfold* at Padua (Plate 18b), of the confused reaction of the young shepherd, equally absorbed in interior thought; while the Rebekah may call to mind the strange *donna velata* who stands within the archway in *The Meeting at the Golden Gate* (Plates 24a, 25b), a figure possibly derived from an ancient sarcophagus:[1] the figure of Rebekah, which was perhaps inspired by a Roman portrait bust,[2] conveys a remarkably similar impression of a mysterious and fateful presence.

Certainly, the *Isaac* frescoes bear the evidence of a searching revival of antique forms which itself anticipates the 'classicism' of the Arena Chapel cycle. The impressive figure of Isaac in *The Rejection of Esau* (Plate 33b) could have been modelled directly upon the *Tiber* statue on the Capitol (Plate 32b): whatever its precise source, it is impossible to think that it was not inspired directly by some such prototype; and the chiselled draperies are alone evidence of the painter's awareness of the treatment of drapery in ancient figure-sculpture. We may consider also the figure of Esau (Plate 33b), the antique character of whose attire itself hints at a reminiscence of this nature: everything about the handling of the pleat-like folds of his garments suggests the direct influence of monumental Roman sculpture. It is no great distance from the Esau at Assisi to some of Giotto's representations of young men in the Arena Chapel: in *The Expulsion of the Traders from the Temple* (Plate 33a) the draperies of the young merchant who raises his right arm in surprise and self-defence are treated in a not dissimilar manner, although the folds are now softer and less deeply incised; nor, it may be added, would his wary glance seem out of place in one of the Assisi frescoes.

Of the subjects common to the *Isaac* group and the Arena Chapel, the two *Lamentations* (Plates 18a, 34a) show particularly interesting similarities of design. Some of the figures in the background of the Assisi fresco are of inferior quality and suggest the workmanship of an assistant; but the tragic power and humanity of the central group already foreshadow the sublime realism of the great *Pietà* at Padua. The two works could well be the product of the same creative imagination, and many of the compositional elements of the Assisi fresco are preserved in the scene in the Arena Chapel—notably the relationship of Christ's body to the diagonal slope of the hill in the background, the two forms combining with the line of mourning angels to establish a large, Z-like pattern almost embracing the entire picture-area; the interruption of the edge of the hill by the head of one of the mourners (at Assisi, one of the Marys; at Padua, the Beloved Disciple); the enclosure of Christ's body, at its extremities, by a seated or kneeling figure; and the disposition of the standing mourners—the Holy Women on the left

---

[1] See above, p. 105, and Plate 25a.   [2] Meiss, op. cit., p. 19, Fig. 53.

and Joseph of Arimathea and Nicodemus on the right—in a wide arc behind the central group. Similarly, the angels in the Assisi fresco bear a close resemblance to the 'uccelli divini' of the Arena Chapel, and differ in type from the more ethereal beings of Cimabue and of the Dugento tradition in general. Altogether the originality of the composition in the Upper Church and the similarity of the fresco at Padua make it impossible to doubt that if Giotto was not the author of the Assisi *Lamentation* he must at least have known it, whether directly or at second hand.

We find a no less striking resemblance between the Christ in the large fresco of *The Ascension* on the east wall at Assisi and the majestic figure in Giotto's version of the subject at Padua. Early medieval art provides several instances of a profile representation of the ascending Christ not so very far removed from Giotto's conception; but there is nothing in such early examples to compare with the vigorous and yet graceful rhythm of the figure as Giotto fashioned it: stylistically and imaginatively, it has only one known prototype, the similar figure in the fresco at Assisi. In both frescoes the Ascension is apprehended neither in purely symbolic terms nor under the aspect of a literal representation of a miraculous occurrence: each combines, rather, in the purest language, a credible image of a divine event with a realism of portrayal that emphasizes the humanity of Christ, much as it is emphasized in the *Meditationes*. Both conceptions are almost as far removed from the remote symbolism of the Byzantine Ascension as they are from the Baroque insistence upon the mechanics of levitation. No device could be simpler or more effective than the upward thrust of Christ's hands beyond the picture-space of the Arena fresco into the concealed region of the heavens. A similar conception is to be found in the figure of *Spes* in the Arena Chapel, which may be said to provide a link between the Christs of Assisi and Padua. Here, as in the Assisi Christ, both hands are completely visible, but they break across the framework of imitation marble, which would have cut off the hands at their extremities, precisely as in the Padua *Ascension*, if it had been represented as lying on the near side of the figure.

Like *The Ascension*, the *Pentecost* (to its left on the east wall) was evidently executed by an associate of the Isaac Master—probably the same assistant whose hand is detectable in parts of the *Lamentation* and in the fragmentary *Resurrection* on the south wall and in *The Finding of the Silver Cup* on the north wall. This last scene and the *Pentecost* are remarkable for their imposing architectural backgrounds, which remain curiously separated from the figures grouped beneath them. The elaborately conceived building in the *Pentecost*, however, represents a bold attempt to solve the perspectival problems posed by a centralized view of an interior. The floral motifs that embellish the upper walls, like those contained in the purely ornamental parts of the decoration in this part of the nave, revive antique forms, and there are hints also, in the elegant pinnacles and gables, of the influence of Arnolfo's Roman tabernacles, a factor that has no doubt been responsible for the tendency of some writers to confuse the quite distinctive taste shown here in the treatment of architectural detail with that of the main author of the *St. Francis* cycle, whose debt to Arnolfo was still more profound.

It is possible, however, that the architectural forms in such compositions as Scenes VII and XI of the *Legend* reflect the St. Francis Master's study of this fresco, just as the painters responsible for Scenes XVIII and XX may have learnt from the sculpturally conceived figures of the disciples in the *Pentecost* how to render seated figures effectively from the back and to define their forms beneath their enveloping draperies. In his grasp of the nature of this problem the author of the *Pentecost* anticipates by over a decade its easeful mastery by Giotto in his own *Pentecost* and *Last Supper* in the Arena Chapel.

The lovely head of the youthful Jesus in the fresco of *Christ among the Doctors* (Plate 35a) (the only passage, apart from portions of the figure and some architectural detail, that has survived) seems no less 'proto-Giottesque' in character. This head, at once a spiritual and a physical presence, brings to mind not so much the representation of Christ in the corresponding scene at Padua, which it surpasses, as some of Giotto's interpretations of young men in other parts of the Arena Chapel cycle, such as the shy shepherd in *Joachim's Withdrawal to the Sheepfold* (Plate 18b) and the two beardless disciples seated on the far side of the table in *The Last Supper*. Resemblances of a like nature have been seen between the heads of Esau and Jacob, in the two *Isaac* scenes, and those of Lazarus and the astonished youth who witnesses Lazarus's resurrection in the fresco at Padua.[1] The sculptural treatment of the head of Jesus in the fresco of *Christ among the Doctors* and the character of the features suggest a derivation from some actual work in sculpture, perhaps an early Christian figure of Christ Enthroned: a now damaged statue in the Museo delle Terme[2] (Plate 35c) gives us an idea of the type of ancient model of which the Isaac Master may have availed himself.

Not unexpectedly perhaps, the facial types in the Arena Chapel frescoes that most closely resemble those at Assisi are to be found in those areas of the Paduan decorations that are relatively early in date—in the *Joachim* and *Mary* cycles and in the scenes from the Life of Christ towards the east end of the Chapel.[3] The rapid evolution of Giotto's style during the period of his work in the Arena Chapel, which is unlikely to have been protracted for longer than two years, suggests a continuous development which must have proceeded uninterrupted from the days of his apprenticeship. Within the Arena Chapel, as the decoration of the central areas unfolds towards the entrance, there can be observed a gradual softening of the modelling, an enlargement of the forms, an increased interest in the portrayal of individual types, and a grander conception of design, accom-

---

[1] Meiss, op. cit., p. 22
[2] For this statue see Strong, op. cit., ii, 345 ff., Pl. LXIX.
[3] The *Last Judgement* on the entrance wall presents problems of dating that cannot be discussed here.

panied by a new adventurousness and informality of composition, including an extensive use of figures or heads that are only partly visible, some of them being almost entirely cut off by the borders framing the scenes. Such a master, for ever making new advances, might have developed from the *Isaac* style with a rapidity no less astonishing.

This is a hypothesis that is attractive for two reasons: in the first place, it offers an explanation of Riccobaldo's reference to Assisi; in the second, it supplies a plausible, if incomplete, picture of Giotto's early development, and seems to throw further light upon his debt to Cavallini. Nevertheless, it remains a hypothesis, and the affinities between Assisi and Padua are not exact enough to exclude the alternative possibility that the Isaac Master was, after all, a quite separate personality—the link, we should then have to assume, between Cavallini and Giotto.

4. *Rimini*

Of all the clues to the nature of Giotto's early activity none is more important than the statement in the *Compilatio chronologica* that he executed some work for S. Francesco at Rimini. There does indeed survive considerable evidence of Giotto's impact upon the development of the Riminese School, of which Giuliano, Neri, and Giovanni da Rimini (the latter being documented as early as 1292) can be regarded as the founders.[1] Yet the early history of Riminese painting is extremely complex, and other influences, deriving from Rome, from the Assisi workshop, and from the Romagna, helped to mould the distinctive character of this little Riminese 'renaissance'. That Giuliano da Rimini visited Assisi towards the beginning of the fourteenth century can be deduced from the extensive reflections in his Urbania altarpiece of the fresco decorations in the Upper Church and those in the Orsini Chapel. Similar influences from Assisi are detectable elsewhere in early Riminese painting, notably in the frescoes of *The Life of the Virgin* in S. Agostino at Rimini:[2] in *The Presentation of Christ in the Temple*, the most impressive of the S. Agostino frescoes, the graceful architectural forms that dominate the design are closely related to the style of the Master of the Obsequies at Assisi and more especially to that of the St. Cecilia Master in Scenes XXVI and XXVII of the *Legend*. At the same time the volumetric treatment of the figures and the assured management of space suggest direct contact with Giotto, possibly at a moment prior to the decoration of the Arena Chapel.

[1] For the Riminese School see especially Carlo Volpe, *La Pittura riminese del Trecento* (Milan, 1965), which includes a list of the relevant documents and full references to recent studies and attributions.

[2] Cf. M. Salmi, 'La scuola di Rimini', *Bollettino d'arte*, xxvi (1931-2), 256. For an attribution of the S. Agostino frescoes to Giuliano da Rimini, see D. Gioseffi, 'Lo svolgimento del linguaggio giottesco da Assisi a Padova: il soggiorno riminese e la componente ravennate', *Arte Veneta*, 1961 (dedicated to the memory of Luigi Coletti), pp. 11 ff. For the more widely accepted attribution of the frescoes to Giovanni da Rimini, see C. Volpe, op. cit., pp. 12 ff., 72.

The painter of the large fresco of *The Last Judgement*, formerly at S. Agostino but now to be seen in the Palazzo dell'Arengo,[1] clearly came under Giotto's influence to the same degree, and the character of his conscientious discipleship is not inconsistent with the chronology that has been inferred from Riccobaldo's reference to Giotto in the *Compilatio*—with the hypothesis, that is to say, that Giotto's impact was first felt in Rimini before the period of the decoration of the Arena Chapel. The Giotto reflected in *The Last Judgement* could well be Giotto in a relatively early phase in his development, a Giotto with a closer resemblance to the Isaac Master at Assisi. Some of the Apostles of *The Last Judgement* particularly recall the severe sculptural qualities of the figures in the two *Isaac* scenes, and of such heads as those of the angel in *The Ascension* and of the young Jesus in the fresco of *Christ among the Doctors*, with their finely chiselled bone structure and incised draperies, while the purely physiognomic similarities are often striking (Plates 34*b*, 35*a*, *b*).

The *Compilatio* fails to specify the nature of Giotto's work at Rimini, informing us only that it was in the Franciscan church; but since the time of Vasari it has been assumed that Giotto was commissioned to paint a fresco-cycle at S. Francesco which was destroyed in the fifteenth century when Alberti remodelled the church (thereafter to be known as the Tempio Malatestiano). It is not impossible that this putative work by Giotto consisted, entirely or in part, of a *St. Francis* cycle, perhaps coeval with the *Legend* at Assisi or even anterior to it; but if this was so it is surprising that so important a work should have cast no reflections in the stream of Riminese painting of the early Trecento. On the other hand there exist a considerable number of panels of the Riminese School, datable within the first decade or two of the fourteenth century, which contain a series of New Testament subjects evidently deriving from a common source now lost to us:[2] the Giottesque character of many of these paintings, the monumentality of the compositions, and the repetition of certain subjects not found in the Arena Chapel, such as the Flagellation, the Deposition from the Cross, and the Harrowing of Hell, suggest the presence in Rimini in the early years of the century of an important New Testament cycle which could conceivably have been executed for the Franciscan community: but, tempting though it is to identify this hypothetical cycle with the work mentioned by Riccobaldo, the evidence of its existence is clearly too slight to enable us to draw any firm conclusions from it.[3]

[1] For the fresco of *The Last Judgement* from Sant'Agostino see L. Coletti, *I Primitivi*, iii, x ff., and H. Beenken, 'The Master of *The Last Judgement* at Rimini', *The Burlington Magazine*, lxvii (1935), 53 ff.

[2] On the Riminese *tavolette* see especially R. Van Marle, *The Development of the Italian Schools of Painting* (19 vols., The Hague, 1923–38), iv (*Local Schools—North Italy*), 279 ff.; L. Coletti, op. cit., iii, xvii ff.; C. Brandi, *Mostra della pittura riminese del Trecento: Catalogo* (Rimini, 1935).

[3] One of these panels, now in the Palazzo Venezia in Rome, contains a scene of *The Entombment* in which the pose of the St. John closely resembles that of the St. John in the Arena *Pietà*. For this panel cf. Sinibaldi and Brunetti, op. cit., p. 573, Fig. 185.

There remains to be considered the damaged crucifix in the Tempio Malatestiano. This delicate work has been attributed to Giotto by several authorities,[1] and it has naturally been associated with the visit to Rimini mentioned by Riccobaldo. Others have ascribed it to a Riminese pupil of Giotto,[2] and the same hand has been detected in a small panel of *The Crucifixion* at Strasbourg.[3] The Tempio Malatestiano crucifix stands, unquestionably, at the head of that characteristic type of Riminese cross which culminates in the intense expressiveness of Pietro da Rimini. At the same time it conforms closely to the iconographic tradition reflected in the Arena Chapel and S. Felice crucifixes, and its Giottesque origin appears indisputable, even if its execution was largely carried out by a pupil. Moreover its relatively early date is confirmed by the virtual certainty that it provided the model for Giovanni da Rimini's crucifix in S. Francesco at Mercatello, which seems to bear the date 1309 (rather than 1345, as was previously thought).[4]

It would be difficult, on stylistic grounds, to date the Tempio Malatestiano cross after the crucifix commissioned from Giotto for the Arena Chapel; and the delicacy of its treatment would in any case seem to show closer affinities with the earlier narratives in the Arena Chapel than with the later: it is possible, therefore, that this much debated work reflects at least something of Giotto's style during the period of his employment by the Franciscans at Rimini, and that his visit to Rimini preceded his summons to Padua.[5]

5. *Riccobaldo da Ferrara and the Identity of Giotto's Work at Assisi*

If the information in the *Compilatio* concerning work undertaken by Giotto in the Franciscan Basilica at Assisi is accepted as trustworthy, and if it can be assumed that Riccobaldo was referring to fresco-decorations rather than to an altarpiece or some other lost work, stylistic considerations permit us to consider two possible interpretations of his meaning (which are not mutually exclusive). These are, first, that Giotto executed, or helped to execute, the *Isaac* group of frescoes in the Biblical cycle in the Upper Church, and, secondly, that before the year 1313 some of the decorations in the Lower Church, having been commissioned from Giotto, had been contracted out to members of his workshop.

[1] See, for example, L. Coletti, 'Note giottesche: il Crocifisso di Rimini', *Bollettino d'arte*, xxx (1936–7), 350 ff.; R. Longhi, 'Restauri', *La Critica d'arte*, v (1940), 123; C. Gnudi, *Giotto*, Ital. edn., p. 248; and F. Zeri, 'Due appunti su Giotto', *Paragone*, viii, 85 (1957), 78 ff.

[2] See especially G. Sinibaldi, 'Il Crocifisso del Tempio Malatestiano in Rimini', *Zeitschrift für Kunstgeschichte*, x (1941–2), 289 ff.; C. Brandi, *Mostra della pittura riminese del Trecento: Catalogo*; and idem, 'Giotto', *Le Arti*, xvii (1938–9), 128 f.

[3] G. Sinibaldi, op. cit., Fig. 2; Sinibaldi and Brunetti, op. cit., p. 585, Fig. 189a, b.

[4] C. Volpe, op. cit., pp. 13 ff.; G. Previtali, op. cit., pp. 70 ff.

[5] Cf. E. Battisti, *Giotto* (Cleveland, Ohio, 1960), p. 77.

The first of these alternatives has much in its favour. Apart altogether from the interesting historical fact that the identification of the Isaac Master with the young Giotto was made on grounds of style long before the testimony of the *Compilatio* was enlisted in its support, there is no doubt about the presence in these frescoes of quite remarkable anticipations of Giotto's Paduan style. On the other hand, there is still a considerable distance between Assisi and Padua, a stylistic gap which the supposition that the Badia fragments are early works from Giotto's hand, executed in the intervening period, does not succeed in filling; and there remains the further problem of the date of the *Isaac* scenes. If the frescoes were painted in the early 1290s, as many scholars would now propose, and if, following the tradition preserved in the *Libro di Antonio Billi*, we retain the year 1276 as the date of Giotto's birth, then his identification with the Isaac Master must be definitely excluded: only if we accepted a birth-date closer to that implied in the *Centiloquio* of Antonio Pucci—that is to say, a date in the middle or late 1260s—could the Isaac Master be the young Giotto; and we have seen that there are reasons at least to question Pucci's reliability. This difficulty is removed if the *Isaac* frescoes are assigned, as they usually have been, to the mid-1290s: according to the traditional date of his birth, as given by Billi and repeated by Vasari, Giotto would then have been a young man of about twenty embarking on his first independent works.

The second hypothesis—to the effect that Riccobaldo was referring to the Lower Church—may nevertheless prove to be the right one. As we have seen, a careful textual analysis of Vasari's sources demonstrates beyond doubt that he understood Ghiberti's allusion to works by Giotto in the Basilica to refer to the Giottesque frescoes in the Lower Church. Already by the year 1307 one of Giotto's pupils was at work in the Orsini Chapel, and there are other frescoes within the vast programme of decoration that might perhaps be datable before the year 1313—notably the *Crucifixion* (Plate 36*b*) and the three *Miracles of St. Francis* in the right transept and the scenes of *The Life of Mary Magdalen* in the Magdalen Chapel nearby. Among these, the *Miracles* contain passages worthy of Giotto himself, and they have occasionally been regarded as roughly contemporary with the *St. Nicholas* cycle;[1] but at present we have no positive clue as to their date. The dependence of the *Crucifixion* and two of the compositions in the Magdalen Chapel upon the corresponding scenes in the Arena Chapel (Plate 36*a, b*) suggests at least the possibility of a date not too distant from the period of Giotto's work at Padua:[2] these are questions to which no absolutely convincing answers have yet been found, but to which increasing attention is now being given.

[1] Cf. Martin Gosebruch, *Giotto und die Entwicklung des neuzeitlichen Kunstbewusstseins* (Cologne, 1962), pp. 100, 216.

[2] The Magdalen Chapel cycle was commissioned by Tebaldo Pontano, bishop of Assisi from 1296 (not 1314, as has long been assumed) until 1329, the year of his death: see the note in Cesare Gnudi, *Giotto*, Italian edn., p. 247, on the researches among the Assisi archives undertaken by Padre Giuseppe Abate. The recent restorations in the Magdalen Chapel have revealed the superb quality of the frescoes, and the possibility of a more direct connection with Giotto

In brief, the evidence is at present inconclusive; and we should certainly resist the temptation, not unknown to students of Giotto, to rest the foundations of historical inquiry upon hypotheses built on the shifting ground that lies between the possible and the plausible. We can affirm no more than that the frescoes in the Lower Church at Assisi are 'Giottesque', and that some of them may have been completed by the time that Riccobaldo wrote the passage on Giotto in his *Compilatio*, and, secondly, that the *Isaac* frescoes are 'proto-Giottesque', even if their descent from Cavallini is more certain than their Florentine parentage.[1]

6. *Giotto's Early Development: a Hypothetical Chronology*

The tradition that Giotto was the pupil of Cimabue may well be correct; but he owed far more to Cavallini: the Cavallinesque elements in his Paduan style suggest that early in his life he made a visit to Rome; an inference that is supported by the profundity of his understanding of ancient art and by his abundant use of classical motifs. Similar reflections of Cavallini's influence, combined once more with a strong interest in the antique, appear in the Isaac Master's frescoes at Assisi; and if we do not see here the emergence of the young Giotto himself as an independent master, we may infer Giotto's close contact with the Isaac Master, possibly as a fellow-pupil in Cavallini's *bottega*. It is unlikely that we shall ever be able to connect Giotto's name with any earlier work, and the attribution to him of the Cavallinesque roundels of *Prophets* and *Saints* in the left transept of Santa Maria Maggiore in Rome must be considered extremely doubtful.[2]

Giotto is first documented in Florence in the year 1301, but the attempts that have been made to assign the Badia fragments to this period are far from convincing. The only works that have claims to be considered as the products of Giotto's early years in Florence are the Louvre *Stigmatization*, executed by his *bottega* for S. Francesco at Pisa, and (less certainly) the Uffizi *Madonna*, painted for the church of Ognissanti in Florence. The arguments for dating the Ognissanti *Madonna* somewhere within Giotto's early period cannot be discussed here;[3] but in respect of the Louvre *Stigmatization* three

at a relatively early stage in his development became the subject of much discussion at the Giotto Congress of 1967. Since the present book went to press, Previtali has in fact proposed a date *c.* 1308–10 for these decorations, which he regards as in part autograph works by Giotto: cf. G. Previtali, op. cit., pp. 87 ff.

[1] It has not been thought necessary, in a book principally devoted to the *St. Francis* cycle in the Upper Church, to examine the decorations in the Lower Church in any detail. The author intends to discuss these frescoes at length in a book on Giotto now in preparation.

[2] The attribution to Giotto was first advanced by Roberto Longhi in 1927, in a series of lectures delivered at the University of Rome, although a possible connection with the young Giotto had been suggested earlier by Toesca. See also E. Cecchi, op. cit., pp. 7 ff., and P. Toesca, *Il Dugento* (Turin, 1927), p. 1019. Mario Salmi has ascribed the roundels to the Isaac Master and his School. Salmi distinguishes between the Isaac Master and Giotto, to whom, however, he attributes some of the Biblical scenes in the Upper Church at Assisi: cf. M. Salmi, 'Le origini dell'arte di Giotto', *Rivista d'arte*, xix, 3–4, Numero speciale del Centenario Giottesco (1937), pp. 207 ff.

[3] For recent arguments see L. Marcucci, *I dipinti toscani del secolo XIV* (*Catalogo delle Gallerie Nazionali di Firenze*) (Rome, 1965), pp. 11 ff., and G. Previtali, op. cit., p. 83.

indications of an early date may be recalled at this point—its iconographical dependence upon the *St. Francis* cycle at Assisi, the absence from the main panel of any trace of the influence of the *Fioretti*, and its close stylistic relationship to the Arena Chapel cycle.

By 1304, in all probability, Giotto would have begun the decoration of the Arena Chapel. His works for the Franciscan communities at Rimini and Padua, mentioned by Riccobaldo da Ferrara, may well have been undertaken before the painting of the Arena frescoes, although in the case of Padua Riccobaldo may have been alluding to the now fragmentary *St. Francis* cycle in the Capitolo del Santo, executed (perhaps about 1310) by pupils of Giotto. The Tempio Malatestiano Crucifix, whatever its authorship, provides confirmatory testimony to Giotto's influence in Rimini in the early years of the fourteenth century. By 1307, meanwhile, a talented pupil of Giotto had initiated in the Orsini Chapel what was to become an extensive programme for the decoration of the Lower Church at Assisi; and we must leave open the possibility that after the completion of the decoration of the Arena Chapel Giotto himself made a visit to Assisi to superintend the work entrusted to his *bottega*.

The works embraced by this outline of what is known of Giotto's early career—however tentative and incomplete it may be—all cohere together in style and are consonant with the logic of artistic development, even if much doubt still surrounds the question of the Isaac Master. With this possible exception, no place is found here for the *apocrypha* which should never have been associated with Giotto's name—not least among them the Santa Maria Novella Cross, the *Jubilee* fresco in Rome, and the *St. Francis* cycle at Assisi.

VI

THE STYLE OF GIOTTO AND THE
STYLES OF THE *LEGEND*

1. *Introductory*

HAD IT NOT BEEN FOR THE TRADITION deriving from Vasari, there would
have been no particular reason to connect Giotto's name with the *Legend
of St. Francis* in the Upper Church. Stylistically, the *St. Francis* cycle at
Assisi differs from the authentic work of Giotto as profoundly as the work
of Masolino differs from that of Masaccio. The real question posed by the *Legend* is not
whether it is by Giotto, but rather who among Giotto's contemporaries could have
been its authors. To a very large extent its historical interest lies in the fact that it
reflects an important and mainly non-Giottesque tradition which played its own part in
the stylistic revolution upon which Renaissance painting was to be founded.

We must allow the Assisi frescoes to speak to us in their own terms: if we seek in them
more than an occasional echo of Giotto's voice, we shall be disappointed. Neither the
spiritual grandeur of his world nor his profound expression of human nature is to be
found in them; but they possess other qualities that have endeared them for centuries
to countless visitors to the Upper Church, not least their narrative charm and lively
naturalism. Yet, despite the manifest absurdity of Vasari's attribution, a comparison with
the art of Giotto is still useful, since it helps to define all the more clearly the stylistic
character of the cycle and its authors' general independence of the Giottesque tradition.
That is not to deny that the painters of the *Legend* may have been—and apparently were
—touched by the art of Giotto, as Masolino was by that of Masaccio; but Giotto's impact
upon the *Legend* cannot be regarded as more than a superficial one, and it could never
be said to disguise the distinctive flavour of its style—or, rather, of the family of styles
to which it belongs.

It has long been recognized that the cycle is the work of several hands;[1] but such is its

---

[1] As long ago as 1821 Witte perceived the existence of three separate styles in the cycle, dividing the frescoes into
the following groups: (i) Scenes I–XV; (ii) Scenes XVI–XXIII; (iii) Scenes XXIV–XXVIII. Berenson ascribed

unity of conception that the existence from the beginning of a carefully prepared set of designs for all the scenes can be inferred as a probability, if not as a certainty. Although the quality of the workmanship varies considerably from one part of the cycle to another, exhibiting an extraordinarily wide diversity of talent, what is so remarkable is that such variousness should have been welded into a unity so complete.

It is one of the paradoxes of the *Legend* that the architectural divisions in the nave, formed by the clustered columns supporting the vault, themselves contribute to the unity of the whole. The reason is simply that each bay tends to be dominated by one of the styles, so that the transition from one manner to another becomes less obvious than it would be if the wall-spaces were unbroken. In fact the unity that is achieved is largely the effect of the sum of a number of similar parts. Even the ornament of the painted hangings below the scenes varies from one bay to the next, instead of supplying a constant decorative pattern throughout the nave.

2. *The Architectural Framings*

What may be called the additive basis of the total conception of the cycle is underlined by the separate system of illusionistic perspective imposed upon each bay by its feigned architectural framework. This system has often been contrasted with that preferred by Giotto in the Arena Chapel, where the frescoes are surrounded by flat decorative borders similar to those used in the Biblical cycle in the Upper Church, and it has been argued, understandably, that if Giotto was the author of the *Legend* he might have been expected to retain the system already employed in the upper registers.[1] The type of framing used by Giotto in the Arena Chapel appears again in the Bardi and Peruzzi Chapels and in the fragments of the decorations for the Badia of Florence. The question, however, is complicated by the fact that at least one feature of the illusionistic framework surrounding the scenes of the *Legend*—the painted consoles at the top, supporting a coffered ceiling—is itself a continuation and development of the similar motif introduced by Cimabue into his frescoes in the choir and transepts.[2]

Moreover, the twisted columns forming the vertical divisions of the painted framings in each bay of the nave have their precedents in the south transept, where the upper part of the arcading is decorated with feigned Corinthian pillars. These pillars, and the trilobe arches they support, enframe half-length figures of angels, just as the twisted columns and cornices of the *St. Francis* cycle enframe the individual scenes of the *Legend*. In each case the painted architecture echoes nearby structural features of the Upper Church: the

(i) Scenes II–XIX to Giotto; (ii) Scene I and Scenes XX–XXV to the St. Cecilia Master working under Giotto's direction; (iii) Scenes XXVI–XXVIII to the St. Cecilia Master working independently (B. Berenson, *Pictures of the Renaissance* (Oxford, 1932), pp. 79, 144).

[1] R. Offner, 'Giotto, Non-Giotto', *The Burlington Magazine*, lxxiv (1939), 268.

[2] Cf. A. Nicholson, 'Again the *St. Francis* Series', *Art Bulletin*, xxvi (1944), 194.

feigned Corinthian pillars in the south transept are situated immediately above the real Corinthian columns of the arcade; and the fictive columns of the *Legend* continue in little the sequence of real columns supporting the vaulting of the nave.

Yet the system of framing employed in the *Legend*, although anticipated in the earlier frescoes of Cimabue, represents an unprecedented exploitation of the possibilities of ornamental illusionism in church decoration. This splendid architectural invention is seized upon as a means of establishing the spatial unity of each bay, and, whereas the scenes themselves are given their own independent perspective, the perspective of the entire framework within each bay is related to the central point of that bay: it is towards this central point that the orthogonals of the capitals and bases of the columns, those of the consoles and coffered ceiling above the scenes, and those of the mouldings below them all recede.[1]

As the treatment of perspective in the scenes themselves contains inconsistencies arising from the dependence of spatial considerations upon an essentially linear conception of design, there is a sense in which the architectural framework gives a greater illusion of reality than the scenes upon which it opens out. There could be no greater contrast with Giotto's practice in the Arena Chapel, where the main scenes are related perspectivally to the central point of the nave, and where the framings and decorative bands, being conceived as flat ornamentation, remain quite independent of this system. One important consequence of this difference is that, whereas in the Arena Chapel the definition of space belongs only to the scenes, at Assisi it already begins in the decorative colonnade through which we penetrate to the scenes beyond. Furthermore, the scheme employed in the *Legend* shows fundamental differences, not merely from Giotto's system in the Arena Chapel, but also from that of Cimabue in all the narrative scenes in the choir and transept, which are separated from each other by flat bands of ornamentation.

The illusionistic framings of the *Legend* recall earlier Roman schemes of decoration, such as those at Santa Maria Maggiore and S. Paolo fuori le mura;[2] and we may also instance the frescoes of *The Life of St. Benedict* in the Sacro Speco at Subiaco, painted not long before the Assisi cycle, where twisted columns support illusionistically represented consoles.[3] But their ultimate origins are still more ancient. As White has expressed it, 'there is a crispness and a clarity, a decisive quality, that reaches back beyond the world of Cimabue and of Cavallini, and of the great refurbished schemes of Old St. Peter's and of S. Paolo fuori le mura which inspired them. The similar elements in the late-thirteenth-century decoration of S. Saba or in the basilicas of S. Maria Maggiore in Rome and Tivoli, and the complete foreshadowing of the scheme

---

[1] See also J. White, *The Birth and Rebirth of Pictorial Space* (London, 1957), pp. 33 ff.; and idem, *Art and Architecture in Italy . . .*, pp. 136 ff.

[2] Idem, *The Birth and Rebirth of Pictorial Space*, p. 54, n. 36.

[3] For these frescoes see E. W. Anthony, *Romanesque Frescoes* (Princeton, 1951), pp. 83 f. and Figs. 107, 108.

in S. Crisogono in Rome, appear to dwindle in importance. Even the echoes of the lost fourth-century decorations of S. Costanza or of the Temple of Junius Bassus seem to fade before the memory of the real and painted architecture of the villas and town houses of Pompeii.'[1]

The questions raised by the framings of the scenes bear upon a further difference between the *St. Francis* cycle and Giotto's frescoes at Padua. Where Giotto preserves, throughout, a horizontal format, except where this was impossible (as in *The Last Judgement* and the *Virtues* and *Vices*), at Assisi there would seem to have been a natural preference for a vertical format affording an unusually large space in the upper areas of the compositions, which are often filled with towering architectural forms. The *St. Francis* frescoes are of great size, measuring over 11 feet in height. Their proportions vary considerably, chiefly on account of the amount of space available in a particular section of the wall: thus the two scenes on the east wall are of necessity narrower than all the other frescoes in the cycle, while all the scenes in the two large bays near the entrance are wider than those in the adjacent bays. But only in the fourth bay of the south wall, where each fresco is exactly square, do we find scenes that are not taller than they are wide. In the fourth bay of the north wall they are only fractionally taller, but in all the others considerably so. The structure of the Upper Church, and in particular the great height of the wall-space that had to be covered, may well have inclined the designer of the *Legend* to adopt a predominantly vertical format, such as, indeed, we find in the *Isaac* scenes above: there is, however, no force in Mather's argument that, if the frescoes had been divided by the wide bands used in the Arena Chapel, they would have acquired 'an unmanageably tall form more proper for a Japanese Kakemono painter' than for a fresco painter of this period of Italian art;[2] for a horizontal format could still have been obtained by combining broad horizontal bands with narrower vertical ones, such as Giotto himself employed in the Bardi and Peruzzi Chapels.

The relative tallness of the *St. Francis* frescoes could not have been better suited to the compositional principles that lie at the heart of the narratives. Even where they are wider than usual—as, for example, in the final three scenes—their great height permitted the erection of those lofty architectural structures that habitually dominate the compositions of the St. Cecilia Master; and elsewhere in the cycle the vertical format conduces towards that emphasis upon the setting of an individual scene, with a consequently diminished emphasis upon the human actors, which perhaps more than anything else distinguishes the *Legend* at Assisi from the fresco-cycles of Giotto.

Nowhere is the effect of this emphasis more powerful, nowhere is the originality of the *Legend* more in evidence, than in those scenes in which an attempt was made to give

[1] J. White, *Art and Architecture in Italy . . .*, p. 137.
[2] F. Jewett Mather, 'Giotto's *St. Francis* Series at Assisi Historically Considered', *Art Bulletin*, xxv (1943), 108.

an impression of local topography. No doubt this adventure in naturalism is partly accountable, as Mather suggested, to the newness of the tradition to which the painters were giving expression: not only is the *Legenda maior* of Bonaventura circumstantial and realistic in character, but its author was largely concerned with places, towns, and buildings known to the people of Assisi, whereas the subject-matter of the Arena Chapel frescoes derived from remote antiquity, and its iconography was already crystallized by long usage. Nevertheless, this distinction cannot be used, as Mather attempted to use it, to support an argument in favour of Giotto's authorship of the *Legend*. The Franciscans at the Sacro Convento could never have insisted that the scenes of their founder's ministry and miracles were as important—or almost as important—as the events themselves, so requiring Giotto to make a radical departure from his otherwise invariable insistence upon the primacy of the human figure and of the dramatic action. We have only to compare Giotto's treatment of the story of St. Francis in the Bardi Chapel, or the four subjects represented on the workshop panel in the Louvre, to be reminded of fundamental differences of interpretation—differences arising from purely artistic considerations rather than from the character of the subject-matter or, evidently, from the nature of the patronage.

3. *The Representation of Architecture*

It would doubtless be impossible to deduce from Giotto's frescoes that besides being a great painter he was also a great architect; but, having that knowledge, we feel no surprise, for the buildings represented in the Arena Chapel and at Santa Croce, however stylized and simplified, are functional in a way in which those depicted in the *Legend* at Assisi rarely are. The painters of the *Legend* pay more attention to the external beauty of a building, to its mosaic ornamentation and to its sculptural decorations, and yet, while the interpretation of architecture is in this sense more naturalistic at Assisi than it is in the work of Giotto, it is at the same time more abstract. The fantastic nature of much of the architecture in the *Legend* arises chiefly from the tendency to turn architectural forms into geometric abstractions. Neither of the two cubic constructions represented in *The Renunciation* (Scene V, Plate 48) convinces the beholder as being a real building like the elegantly designed *palazzo* introduced by Giotto into his own version of the subject at Santa Croce (Plate 49). The strange edifice in *The Vision of the Chariot* (Scene VIII, Plate 55) at Assisi is no less an abstraction, and is oddly lacking in windows and doorways. And was ever a Roman portico fronted by five columns, like the Temple of Minerva as the St. Cecilia Master renders it in the opening scene (Frontispiece), so that one of the columns blocks the way at the centre?[1] Was such a portico ever built to lead nowhere

---

[1] There is, however, a curious parallel in the structure of the portico represented in the *Jubilee* fresco in the Lateran, as we know it from the drawing in Milan (C. Mitchell, op. cit., Fig. 3*a*): here the central porch is blocked by a Corinthian column.

(for no doorway opens into any interior beyond)? Even if we had never examined with any attention the portico of the temple in *The Expulsion of the Traders from the Temple* in the Arena Chapel (Plate 33a), we should rightly assume that no such anomaly could possibly be present there. The great gateway of Jerusalem, with its massive tower, in *The Carrying of the Cross* at Padua, is a real building treated in generalized terms. On the other hand, the church crowning the hill outside the town in *The Gift of the Mantle* (Scene II, Plate 42) at Assisi, although evidently intended to represent San Francesco itself, remains an abstraction constructed of cube-like blocks, and the *città santa*, perched on the slope of the other hill, is composed of similar forms: it is almost as though the artist had taken his models from a textbook of cubic geometry. Only perhaps in the impressive cathedral which stands outside the city in *The Exorcism of the Demons at Arezzo* (Scene X, Plate 58) do we find on the north wall at Assisi an example of architectural construction that in any way approaches the buildings in Giotto's frescoes in giving a convincing impression of actuality: yet the towers and dwellings of the city itself, notwithstanding the inclusion of a wealth of naturalistic detail, such as the representation of bells, bell-ropes, windlasses, and the timbers and slates of roofs, revert to the block-like forms characteristic of the buildings in Scene II.

Once the nature of this abstracting process has been perceived, and recognized at work throughout the cycle, the *Legend* seems even further removed than before from the world of Giotto. This principle, underlying the treatment of architecture in every scene, may be less in evidence in some of the frescoes (such as Scenes XVII and XVIII on the south wall) than it is in others, but it is overwhelmingly obvious in a very large number of them, and especially in the very area of the decoration in which the majority of critics still detect Giotto's hand. The architecture represented in the Arena Chapel and at Santa Croce never possesses this character of a reduction to basic form for its own sake, and the massing together of the cubes and slabs that compose the townships of Assisi and Arezzo in Scenes II and X of the *Legend* would be unthinkable in the work of Giotto. The projecting roof overhanging the upper storey of the house in *The Sacrifice of Zacharias* in the Peruzzi Chapel is a simplified but convincing interpretation of an architectural detail; but the solid slabs surmounting the buildings of the city in *The Gift of the Mantle* suggest, rather, the fantasies of a geometrician playing with pure form, and thinking less in terms of external reality than of ideal harmonies. There is an essential realism in Giotto's outlook akin to that of Masaccio: on the other hand there underlies the *Legend* an ideality of conception, combined with a fascination with naturalistic detail, that brings to mind certain aspects of the art of Uccello and Masolino. The difference, surely, could never be explicable in terms of natural development within a single artistic personality, but argues two minds of distinctive and independent character.

The smallest details bear out the fundamental nature of these divergences of thought and taste. No one comparing the gateway in Giotto's fresco of *The Meeting of St. Joachim and St. Anne* (Plate 24*a*) and the city wall, with its portals, in *The Exorcism of the Demons at Arezzo* (Scene X, Plate 58) at Assisi could be in any doubt as to which piece of masonry is the more soundly constructed. Nor is it possible to imagine Giotto's remaining content, even at some early moment in his development, with the spatial treatment of the chancel in *The Vision of the Thrones* (Scene IX, Plate 56) or of the episcopal palace in *The Vision of the Ascension of St. Francis* (Scene XXI, Plate 80), in both of which the logic of perspective is defiantly contradicted. There are similar anomalies in the representation of the apse of San Damiano in *The Miracle of the Crucifix* (Scene IV, Plate 46). When Giotto comes to design a flight of stairs, as in *The Presentation of the Virgin* in the Arena Chapel, he is concerned to show how the rests of the stairs disappear from sight as the stairway ascends above eye-level—a difficult perspectival problem which evidently did not interest the designer of the outer stairway in the *Renunciation* at Assisi (Scene V, Plate 48), where the stairway, with its tiled covering, is strangely represented from a bird's-eye view, despite the fact that all the other architectural forms, including the house to which the stairway belongs, are seen from below.

Another small but revealing detail is provided by the representations of curtain-rods in the *St. Francis* cycle, which are to be found in Scenes III, VI, and XXVI (Plates 45, 52, 90). In each case the rod is visualized as lying on the front plane of the room to which it belongs—as we also find in the second scene of the *Santa Cecilia* altarpiece (Plate 8). In fact it becomes one with the very fabric, or geometric metamorphosis, of the building. Curtain-rods are represented in the Arena Chapel four times—in the two compartments of *The Annunciation* on the tribune, in *The Annunciation to St. Anne*, and in *The Birth of the Virgin*—and in each instance they are clearly set back into the interior space of the room (as they also are in the *Isaac* frescoes (Plate 32*a*) in the Upper Church). The Assisi masters, we may say, isolate a naturalistic detail and blend it into the abstract harmonies of the design, whereas Giotto can never visualize any object save as a form related to other forms both functionally and spatially.

The unreal qualities of the architecture represented in the *Legend* are nevertheless not inconsistent with a sometimes lavish and detailed embellishment of the masonry with mosaics and sculpture. The reliefs on the 'Column of Trajan' (Plate 94*a, b*) in *The Liberation of the Prisoner* (Scene XXVIII, Plate 93) are among the finest passages in the entire cycle; and it would be difficult to find any representation of Gothic sculpture in early Italian painting to compare in beauty and richness of effect with the angels and prophets on the façade of the church in that noble composition *St. Francis Mourned by St. Clare* (Scene XXIII, Plates 83, 84*d*, 109). On the north wall, we may point to the reliefs on the cathedral front in *The Exorcism of the Demons at Arezzo* (Scene X, Plate 60*a*), which although less refined in drawing are remarkable for the fluid handling of their forms. The Cosmatesque decoration on the Lateran Basilica and the papal palace in *The Dream of Innocent III* (Scene VI, Plate 50) reveals the same taste for splendour of ornamentation, and suggests that the designer of the *Legend* was largely formed in Rome. Close contacts with Rome can, however, be presumed of almost every major painter in this period, and it is noteworthy that at Assisi the strongest links seem to be with the work of Arnolfo di Cambio,[1] the greatest architect of the age (the first, indeed, to be honoured in Vasari's *Lives*), and himself, although active in Rome, a Florentine. The *baldacchino* in *The Christmas Crib at Greccio* (Scene XIII) must have been modelled directly upon Arnolfo's Roman *ciboria* (Plate 37*a*, *b*); the temple in *The Homage of a Simple Man* (Scene I, Frontispiece) has been remoulded in terms of the same Arnolfian taste and its pediment decorated with motifs similar to those on the *ciborium* at S. Paolo fuori le mura; while the representation of San Damiano in *St. Francis Mourned by St. Clare* (Scene XXIII, Plate 83) may have been inspired by the façade designed by Arnolfo for Florence Cathedral. Several figures in the cycle recall Arnolfo's works in sculpture: the kneeling woman in *The Death of the Knight of Celano* (Scene XVI, Plates 70, 72) has an unmistakable affinity with the *Assetata* in Perugia,[2] and the Pope in *The Sermon before Honorius III* (Scene XVII, Plate 74) with Arnolfo's figure of *Boniface VIII* in Rome[3] (compare Plate 38*d*); and there is a strong resemblance between Arnolfo's female heads and the facial types of some of the nuns depicted in Scene XXIII, with their heavy jowls and long, thick necks (Plate 84*a*): moreover, the image of the *Madonna and Child* (Plate 37*c*) represented on the iconostasis of the church in *The Verification of the Stigmata* (Scene XXII) seems to show an iconographic dependence upon the statue of the *Madonna* (Plate 37*d*) executed by Arnolfo for Florence Cathedral.

Those who accept the frescoes as the work of Giotto take their Florentine character for granted. Others assume that they are Roman. What can be established with greater certainty is that the authors of the cycle, although unquestionably trained in Roman traditions, made a particularly strong impact upon painting in Florence. The treatment of the architectural detail as a whole leads the inquirer inevitably to Florence, but rather to the milieu of the St. Cecilia Master than to that of Giotto. It is not Giotto or any of his known pupils but the St. Cecilia Master and some of the painters within his circle who show a predilection for those massive structures raised upon voluted consoles that overhang the figures in such compositions as *St. Francis before the Sultan* (Scene XI, Plate 61) and *The Death of the Knight of Celano* (Scene XVI, Plate 70); it is in the work of this group of painters also, and especially in the *Santa Cecilia* and *Santa Margherita*

---

[1] Cf. G. Fiocco, 'Giotto e Arnolfo', *Rivista d'arte*, xix (1937), 221 ff.

[2] P. Toesca, *Il Trecento*, Fig. 182. Fiocco (op. cit., p. 234, Figs. 8, 9) also relates this work to the figure kneeling at the Knight of Celano's feet in Scene XVI at Assisi.

[3] Toesca, op. cit., Fig. 187.

altarpieces, that the characteristic slabs and blocks and geometric cubes of the Assisi cycle are to be found; and the thrones of the Montici *Madonna* (Plate 15a), the *St. Peter* at S. Simone (Plate 40), and other altar paintings by followers of the St. Cecilia Master reflect a taste close to that which informs the *St. Francis* cycle as a whole, both in their design and in the style of their ornamentation.

4. *The Representation of Landscape*

The treatment of landscape in the *Legend* is reflected no less clearly in this stream of Florentine painting. Once more the characteristic forms present a marked contrast with those preferred by Giotto and his followers. Landscape backgrounds and representations of trees appear in six of the scenes in the Upper Church; over twice that number occur in the work of Giotto that has come down to us: there is no lack, therefore, of comparative material. In common with other painters of the time, both Giotto and the painters of the Assisi cycle accepted the traditional practice—later to be described in the *Libro dell'arte* of Cennino Cennini[1]—of building up a landscape from magnified stones or rocks, only sparsely covered with vegetation; and the similarity of method might at first glance conduce to an impression of similarity of interpretation: but to mistake what was merely a convention of the period for the mark of a personal style would also be to equate the landscape of Giotto with that of Duccio or the Lorenzetti, and to ignore the distinctive character of each.

At the outset we are confronted by a basic conceptual difference which has already been touched upon: the primacy invariably given by Giotto to the human figure determines its degree of stress within a landscape; and the profound interest in dramatic expression which made it impossible for him to place as great an emphasis upon the mountain of La Verna as upon the miracle of the Stigmatization everywhere distinguishes his conception of landscape from that of the designer of the *Legend*. Never does Giotto allow the landscape to dominate the figures, or to share an equal or almost equal emphasis: on the other hand, the principles of design fundamental to the *Legend* allow a much more even distribution of weight among the pictorial forms as a whole, and in such compositions as *The Miracle of the Spring* (Scene XIV, Plate 64), *The Sermon to the Birds* (Scene XV, Plate 68), and *The Stigmatization* (Scene XIX, Plate 76) the figures hold our chief attention largely because of the lively naturalism of their representation as human beings, rather than because, as forms, they really dominate their environment.

No less significant differences disclose themselves in the actual rendering of landscape forms. Neither the character of the foliage at Assisi nor that of the rocky ground from which the trees spring can be categorized as Giottesque, and quite different formations

---

[1] Cennino Cennini, *Il libro dell'Arte*, ed. D. R. Thompson, Jr. (New Haven, 1932), pp. 55 f. (Capitolo LXXXVIII).

are found in the Arena Chapel. At Assisi, it appears, all the trees (and many are represented) belong to the same *genus*; at Padua one type of tree is clearly distinguished from another—as we see, for example, in *Joachim's Withdrawal to the Sheepfold* (Plate 18*b*) and in the *Injustitia*. Giotto's conception of a tree could be said to be almost as unlike that of the Assisi masters as Rubens's conception is unlike Claude's: where Giotto seeks to express its growth and inner structure, the Assisi painters dwell chiefly upon its beauty as a static form and upon the charm of its silhouette; the eye is not permitted to penetrate the depths of the foliage, but is left to play upon the surface-patterns formed by the manifold clusters of leaves. The splendid, green-leafed tree in *The Sermon to the Birds* (Scene **XIV**, Plate 68) is more decorative in intention and based much less upon particular observation than its counterpart in the Louvre altarpiece (Plate 27*b*) or than those beautifully proportioned trees in the *Injustitia*. The narrow trunks of Giotto's trees rise gracefully, as growing things filled with life-giving sap, to divide naturally into their upper branches: at Assisi, on the other hand, the trunks are always considerably thicker and less structural, and lack the same impression of growth, like so many Joseph's rods that have miraculously burgeoned; their outlines tend to be wavy and uneven; and we notice here and there, as in some of the manuscript illuminations of Pacino di Bonaguida, a particular curiosity about the formation of their roots. Where, again, Giotto introduces trees and plants into his landscapes with great reserve, the painters of the *Legend* scatter them in profusion.

It has been observed by Offner that, whereas 'the stony waste of the Assisi frescoes climbs in stratified stages of shining white levels, flashing back a cold light, and drops at edges of a lacerating sharpness into sheer dark declivities', in the Arena Chapel 'the edges are worn to roundness and the planes flow into one another'.[1] Indeed, while Giotto breaks up the surfaces of the rock as little as possible, and then for the most part by the softest of tonal gradations, at Assisi every opportunity is taken to variegate the mass by splitting it up into multifarious slabs and crevices, rendered usually by abrupt changes of tone, and thus to create an over-all effect of animated pattern. The treatment of landscape in the *Legend*, like the treatment of architecture, is more decorative and two-dimensional than that of Giotto. The form of a hill may be conceived as a solid volume, but attention is confined to its visible planes, little attempt being made to suggest their continuation on its other side, as in the landscape backgrounds of the Arena Chapel frescoes: thus the mountain of La Verna in Scene **XIX** of the *Legend* (Plate 76) gives the impression of being a half-slice of a mountain, much as the *palazzo* in *The Liberation of the Prisoner* (Scene **XXVIII**) remains a mere façade. At Assisi the various formations into which the total mass of a hill is broken up always tend to be reduced to flat, geometric patterns. Whereas in *Joachim's Withdrawal to the Sheepfold* (Plate 18*b*) the

[1] R. Offner, 'Giotto, Non-Giotto', *The Burlington Magazine*, lxxiv (1939), 108.

steep hill rising up on the right is cleft at the top by a little chasm, the inner surfaces of which the eye may explore, the hill occupying a similar area of *The Miracle of the Spring* (Scene XIV, Plate 64) divides at its summit into decorative star-like formations lying upon the outer surface of the rock. The contrast between these two passages, which could be paralleled by many other examples, speaks eloquently in itself of the differences between the two masters as painters of landscape.

A careful study of the treatment of Nature in the *Legend* reveals all the more clearly, then, the non-Giottesque character of the cycle. It does not, however, lead to a merely negative conclusion, for the absence from the work of Giotto of the landscape conventions followed in the *Legend* is not more striking than their presence in the work of such painters as the St. Cecilia Master and Pacino. These conventions, which are of Byzantine origin, have their *locus classicus* in Florentine painting in the scene of *The Martyrdom of St. Cecilia* on the Uffizi altarpiece (Plate 8), which makes an interesting comparison with Scene XIV of the *Legend* (*The Miracle of the Spring*, Plate 64). The same basic conception—of a larger and smaller hill meeting to one side of the principal figure, which slightly penetrates the triangular space between—underlies the two compositions; and this type of design never occurs in the surviving work of Giotto. Much the same fantasy is common to both scenes, with their steepling scarps, their ice-thin slivers of rock and similar fragmentations, as though these stony surfaces had been split into myriads of pieces by the blows of an axe; and at the edges of the cliffs there hang those characteristic rag-like trees, silhouetted against the wide expanse of the sky. Pacino, preserving the same traditions, resembles the painters of the *Legend* still more closely in his treatment of landscape, and the sharply defined crevices in the rocky foreground of such frescoes as *The Exorcism at Arezzo* (Scene X, Plate 58) and *The Miracle of the Spring* (Scene XIV, Plate 64) are exactly repeated in his miniatures (Plates 43, 67a). The manner in which he sets his figures within their landscape settings also brings the Assisi cycle to mind: we may compare, for instance, the figure of the Saviour in the Morgan *Christ at Gethsemane* (Plate 67b) with that of St. Francis in *The Miracle of the Spring* (Scene XIV, Plate 64), the two figures being posed in a very similar manner in relation to the brightly lit mountain slopes that tower above them.

5. *The Treatment of the Human Figure*

The human beings who inhabit the world of the *Legend* in the Upper Church belong no less obviously to another race than that conjured up by Giotto on the walls of the Arena Chapel and Santa Croce. Since the *St. Francis* cycle was executed by many hands, the figures vary considerably in type and proportioning, but they are all members of the same family. From the graceful women and slightly effeminate men of the St. Cecilia

Master to the robuster types that predominate on the north wall, they have in common a kind of external liveliness that never characterizes the more inwardly spiritual figures of Giotto, and which expresses itself especially in quick, curious glances and abrupt and at times nervous gestures of the hands. The elegantly dressed witness of the miracle at Greccio in Scene XIII (Plate 63) and the man who turns to question St. Francis in Scene XIV (*The Death of the Knight of Celano*, Plates 70, 72) are more heavily and more stockily built than any of the figures in the St. Cecilia Master's frescoes in the Upper Church, but their demonstrative gestures and self-conscious expressions are modelled on exactly the same pattern as those of the bystanders in the opening scene (*The Homage of a Simple Man of Assisi*, Frontispiece and Plate 38a, b). The sign-language of their hands calls attention to their surprise at the events they are witnessing, and they may remind us a little of inexperienced actors who have not yet learnt the lesson of Hamlet's advice to the Players: 'Do not saw the air too much with your hand, thus; but use all gently.' By contrast, such figures in the Arena Chapel as the soldier in *The Massacre of the Innocents* who shrinks away from the scene of carnage, or the young man who gazes in wonder at the resurrected form of Lazarus, or, at Santa Croce, the witnesses of St. John's resurrection and ascension, convince us by the spontaneity of their reactions, and if we think of them as actors it is as actors who know how to conceal their art.

The scenes of the *Legend* never approach the dramatic intensity of Giotto's compositions, and at times we are reminded of some gracious tableau in which all action has been stilled for contemplation. This, for example, is the impression created by *The Gift of the Mantle* (Scene II, Plate 42), and if any one would convince himself how far removed this work is from the world of Giotto's imagination he need only compare the figures with the group of soldiers disputing over Christ's garments in the Arena *Crucifixion*, all of whom are far too deeply involved in what they are about to give the least hint that they are aware of being observed, as the almost coy figures of the Assisi fresco do. The effect of the Assisi figures could hardly be more charming, but the whole spirit of the narrative is quite un-Giottesque. At Assisi, moreover, most of the figures outside the areas painted by the St. Cecilia Master and the Master of the Obsequies are characterized by a stiffness of articulation and even a certain disjointedness of limb never found in figures by Giotto. The Bernardone and Francis in the *Renunciation* in the Upper Church (Scene V, Plate 48) offer themselves readily for comparison with their counterparts in the fresco of the same subject in the Bardi Chapel (Plate 49), and throw into relief the vast differences in Giotto's conception and treatment of the human body.

For Giotto, as Offner has admirably expressed it, the figure

communicates chiefly a kind of noble forbearance in every line and pressure, so that we become aware of an ultimate indwelling meaning, as of a living spirit that directs the body and sets it in motion, rather than of its irreducible materiality as in Assisi. In Assisi the bodily frame is square and large-boned, of stout build and ample mould. At times it is magnified to rhetorical impressiveness—uncongenial to Giotto—as in the grandiose *St. Francis Exorcizing Arezzo* or in the papal figures. The head always sits firmly on a neck which in its posture declares a stubborn life-power as confident as the unwincing glance of the light-coloured iris. This harbours the rude knowledge of simple-souled men who live by forcing their bodily needs from the earth. But the conscience within them, like their type, is solid and impenetrable compared to the spiritually evolved creatures in Padua. Here the whole man belongs to a higher order of sentiency and his face, marked with graver human experience, betrays a deeper awareness. Full at once of passion and acquiescence, the face is of a softer consistency, the nose rounded, the mouth flexible, the features and intervening areas of a proportion that brings them into immediate physiognomic co-ordination.[1]

The so-called 'Giotto' of the *Legend*—if we may continue to speak in the singular of a composite personality—treats individual features much more in isolation, so that at times he fails to relate them properly to each other: the eyes are often placed out of alignment (as in some of the bystanders in Scene V) and the mouth set at a curious, lop-sided angle (as in the case of the girl who stretches out her arms to her dying father in Scene XVI, Plate 16*d*); and, particularly on the north wall, the proportioning of a head will occasionally go completely awry (as in the vast craniums of some of the friars in Scene VII, Plate 54*c*). The flesh tends to a polished roundness of surface, lacking the flexuous quality characteristic of Giotto's more mobile faces. In most of the frescoes on the north wall the hair is treated less as a large and soft mass, as it is in the Arena Chapel and in the altarpieces of Giotto, than as a series of separate strands of rather wiry consistency; sometimes (as in the angel in Scene IX) it is plaited in alternating bands of light and dark tone (Plate 56); in the area of the entrance (as in the Saint's companion in Scene XV, Plate 68, and in the seated friar in Scene XVI, Plate 70), it can assume a much coarser, fibrous texture: on the other hand, in the heads executed by the Master of the Obsequies, in the central area of the south wall, it becomes soft and fine, being picked out in minute strokes of the brush as though the painter had wished to rival in fresco the delicacy of tempera (Plate 102*b*).

The features never resemble those of Giotto's figures. In the frescoes of the *Legend* not executed by the St. Cecilia Master they can yet recall his own, especially on the south wall. On the north wall they are mostly drawn in firm, hard lines which can give a somewhat masklike cast to the whole face. The transitions between one form and another—for instance, between the nose and brow—are normally more abrupt than in Giotto, and contribute to a general impression of sharpness. The features lack the delicacy of the St. Cecilia Master's ideal, but they conform less to a stock type and we are aware of a generally wider range of characterization. This is particularly striking in such compositions as the *Renunciation* (Scene V, Plate 48), dominated by the choleric Pietro Bernardone and the resolute Francis, attended by a mildly disconcerted bishop,

---

[1] R. Offner, 'Giotto, Non-Giotto', *The Burlington Magazine*, lxxiv (1939), 102.

or *The Sanctioning of the Rule* (Scene VII), where an astonishing realism of portraiture attains, in the head of one Roman-featured friar (Plate 54c), an intensity of individualization scarcely to be matched elsewhere in the cycle.[1] It is in such heads that the principal author of the frescoes on the north wall (the 'St. Francis Master') reveals his true originality and declares his independence of the St. Cecilia Master's gentler and more delicate vision.

Few artists have represented human beings in a more personal manner than the St. Cecilia Master: the head, like the hands, is unusually small, and is often supported upon an exceptionally long, column-like neck; the eyes tend to be placed close together on either side of a rather pinched and delicate nose; the mouth is always small and its expression usually grave; every feature expresses the most exquisite refinement: it is as though the whole human race were composed of aristocrats. This highly individual physiognomy is common to the St. Cecilia Master's frescoes at Assisi and to the Uffizi and Montici altarpieces. Certain similarities can be found in the facial types preferred by Simone Martini and the Lorenzetti and by some of the Riminese painters of the period, although they are never so close as to give rise to any confusion between the styles of these painters and the St. Cecilia Master's own.

We discover a still closer approximation to this ideal in many of the heads represented in other areas of the Assisi cycle, although it is always modified to produce a heavier and larger type. In the *Legend* as a whole the tendency to a close setting of the eyes becomes at times more marked than at others, but it frequently asserts itself (as, for instance, in the head of Bernardone in Scene V and in that of the man in a red hat standing next to St. Francis in Scene XVI, Plate 38b). The St. Francis Master incises the creases at the corners of the eyes more deeply than the St. Cecilia Master, who expresses them by means of delicate and subtly varying lines (Plate 38a); he also deepens the shadows below the brows, and in general works in a more vigorous chiaroscuro: we may compare, for example, the children represented in Scene V (Plate 51b) (by the St. Francis Master) and the child in Scene XXVII (Plate 91) (by the St. Cecilia Master). The mouth, small and thin-lipped in heads by the St. Cecilia Master, is usually, although not always, represented by the St. Francis Master as a larger form defined with a rather harder line. The modelling about the mouth frequently lends a curiously puffy appearance to the flesh immediately beneath the lower lip (as in the angel in Scene IX)—a characteristic that is found in the St. Cecilia Master's own works, as in the Montici *Madonna* (Plate 15a) and in the angel standing next to St. Francis in Scene XXVI at Assisi (Plate 84b).

The St. Francis Master strives to give his figures volume, and hews out their rounded masses with a chiselling light, passing rapidly between extremes of tone, which he expresses by means of hatching strokes of the brush that usually follow the rotundity of

---

[1] A striking (although somewhat later) example of this type of profile 'portraiture' is provided by Pacino's comparable image of Robert of Anjou (Plate 54b).

a surface. In Giotto's practice, on the other hand, the brushstrokes normally follow the direction of a form (such as an arm or a finger), running along it rather than around it in defining its planes; the tones are subtle and liquid, and lack the abrupt transitions found on the north wall at Assisi. Indeed, the technical procedures of the two painters differed in a still more fundamental sense. White lead, for example, seems never to have been employed either in the Arena Chapel or at Santa Croce: it was known to turn black with time, and Cennino Cennini specifically warns against its use by the fresco-painter. At Assisi, on the other hand, especially in Scenes II–XXIII, it was employed quite lavishly in highlights and in many other areas. Again, while in the frescoes of the St. Francis Master the figures were first laid in with a *verdaccio* ground and then modelled up from dark to light, at Padua the *verdaccio* was covered with a light flesh-colour into which the shadows were subsequently worked. It may be added that a further variation from Giotto's technical procedures occurs in the frescoes executed by the Master of the Obsequies, where the forms were first drawn in on the *intonaco* in a yellow wash.

6. *Principles of Composition*

Notwithstanding the endeavour of the painters of the *Legend* to create the illusion of a three-dimensional world, the aesthetic principles to which they conformed placed a primary emphasis upon a linear and two-dimensional order of design. As Meiss has put it, 'the single forms are voluminous, but they are united more by lines in one plane'.[1] The predominant qualities of the Assisi frescoes as designs—their linear patterns, their insistent symmetry, and their systematic geometry—are not those of the fresco-cycles of Giotto. It is true that Giotto's late style, as it is manifested in the frescoes at Santa Croce, shows a tendency towards a spacious symmetry of design such as we do not find in the Arena Chapel. Nevertheless, it remains rooted in the same principles that govern the style of the Paduan period: it is still founded upon a conception of the function of painting radically different from that shared by the painters of the *Legend*; it still concerns itself primarily with the dynamic tension of volumes in space, rather than with static harmonies of shape. It is not that his art is innocent of geometry or linear relationships: such qualities belong to the pictorial language of every painter; but for Giotto these are never overruling principles; and the problems posed by the very different qualities of the *Legend* at Assisi are not resolved by the supposition[2] that the cycle was executed by assistants working from Giotto's designs; for the individual characteristics of the cycle are rooted in the distinctive nature of the designs themselves.

Thus the *Renunciation* in the Bardi Chapel (Plate 49), although superficially like, is fundamentally unlike the corresponding scene in the Upper Church (Plate 48). At Assisi the tension set up between St. Francis and his father arises very largely from their

[1] Meiss, op. cit., p. 7.   [2] Cf. R. Oertel, *Die Frühzeit der italienischen Malerei*, pp. 62 ff.

placing within the compositional fields enclosing them, and from the disposition of their silhouettes in relation to the rectangular gap between them: but in the Bardi Chapel we become aware at once of the opposition of two volumes within a defined space, and Bernardone, as he strains forward, seems to be bending space itself with the weight of his body. In *The Presentation of the Virgin* in the Arena Chapel the infant Mary, ascending the temple steps, moves, not simply across the pictorial space, but into its depths, to be received into a circlet of forms composed of the outstretched arms of her mother and the High Priest and of the ranged heads of the temple virgins, forms symbolic of her seclusion from the world. In *The Kiss of Judas* (Plate 17*b*) the horror of the traitor's act of betrayal is expressed above all by the enshrouding of Christ's body in the folds of Judas's great cloak; and similarly the dead Christ of the *Pietà* (Plate 18*a*) lies within a circle of grieving men and women, enclosed, as it were, in their sorrow. Such subtleties of spatial composition are never found in the *Legend* in the Upper Church: in *The Death of the Knight of Celano* (Scene XVI, Plates 70, 72), to take an example comparable with the *Pietà* at Padua, the simple movement of the design lies wholly upon the picture-plane, carrying downwards to the right from the figure of St. Francis; and even where an attempt is possibly made to come to terms with Giotto's conception of pictorial space, as in *The Death and Ascension of St. Francis* (Scene XX, Plate 77) and *The Verification of the Stigmata* (Scene XXII, Plate 82), in which the mourners surround the body of the dead Saint, the intention, if present, is largely defeated by the insistent two-dimensional rhythms that lie more deeply at the heart of each composition, and the height given to the figures standing beyond the bier prevents us from forgetting the relatively superficial character of the spatial treatment.

Nothing in fact could be more mistaken than to approach the Assisi frescoes with Giotto's artistic principles in mind: it is as though we were to judge Uccello by the ideal of Masaccio, or Matisse by that of Cézanne. The compositions in the Upper Church possess virtues of their own, and they are rare ones. We have only to stand in the nave and to look back towards the entrance at the frescoes on the east wall—the *Virgin* and *Angel* roundels over the doorway and the two country scenes on either side (Plate 5)—to respond to the charm of a style that so happily combines a fresh and innocent naturalism with a delight in pure decoration. The implicit linear movement that brings these three separate fields into harmonious unity, rising from the figure of St. Francis in *The Miracle of the Spring* (Scene XIV), passing from the sunlit mountain-top beneath which he kneels into the central field dominated by the *Madonna*, and descending through the tree on the left side of *The Sermon to the Birds* (Scene XV), to be released at last in the active gesture of the Saint, can be matched by similar rhythms in every bay and every scene.

Basically, design is conceived in terms of a highly sophisticated pattern-making, and the vivid naturalism and the lively narrative qualities of the cycle always remain sub-servient to the desire to create harmonies of related shapes within a generally symmetrical framework: thus in *The Miracle of the Spring* (Plate 64) stability is given to the composition by the inclusion of two trees immediately to the right of the centrally placed figure of St. Francis, creating a pattern of shapes analogous to the heads of the friars on his left. This pattern-making, which is capable, as in the instance just given, of establishing relationships between elements of the visible world that are fundamentally unlike in character, often provides the means by which one composition is harmonized with another, as in the repetition in reverse, in the form of the cloud that bears St. Francis aloft in Scene XII, of the semicircular shape of the canopy of the Sultan's throne in Scene XI (Plate 4b), or the balancing of the gleaming white tablecloth in Scene XVI against the shining plateau upon which St. Francis kneels in Scene XIX (Plate 6a).

Such relationships are fundamental to the design of the *Santa Cecilia* altarpiece (Plate 8), and one of the St. Cecilia Master's supreme qualities as a composer lies in the taste with which he harmonizes his figures and their architectural setting. In the various compart-ments of the Uffizi altarpiece, as in his frescoes at Assisi, a graceful geometry imposes a rhythmic unity and order upon each scene. The curved forms of the human figures find their echoes in the curve of an arch or a window; but their movements are never per-mitted to break the still perfection of the architectural framework that encloses them. Vermeer, no doubt, would have understood the nature of this art, and would have recognized in the opening narrative of the Assisi cycle (*The Homage of a Simple Man of Assisi*, Frontispiece) the sensibility that determined the isolation of the Roman temple at the centre of the composition, a pure geometric form separating and yet relating the two principal actors, St. Francis on the left and the *pazzo* on the lower right. Were these two figures to intrude any further than across the edges of this rectangle the balance of the design would be entirely upset.

A similar principle underlies the design of the *Renunciation* (Scene V, Plate 48), by the St. Francis Master, where the two buildings establish geometric fields for the two oppos-ing groups of figures, between which there lies a rectangular void, at the centre of the composition. The two chief actors in this scene are St. Francis (on the right) and his father Pietro Bernardone (on the left), and both encroach upon the empty central area, Bernardone nearly separating himself from the rectangular group formed by his sup-porters. The intrusion upon the central space is greater than in the fresco by the St. Cecilia Master, but the principle of composition is basically the same. And within the design as a whole one form repeats the pattern of another: the hand of the fat bystander on the left echoes the horizontal set up by the bishop's forearm on the right; Bernar-done's right arm and the Saint's raised forearms lead the eye up, like the equal sides of an isosceles triangle, to the very central point of the design; and below, in the middle of the empty field between the two figures, the bundle of the Saint's discarded garments, which his father holds over his left arm, hangs suspended like the central motif of some geometric ornament, having indeed much the same function in the design as that given to the centrally placed rose-window in Scene I.

It is, to this day, one of the charms of the *Legend* in the Upper Church that here, in the famous words of Gregory of Nyssa, 'dumb painting speaks from the wall', and speaks with such clarity; and it does so in large measure because the language of its style was perfectly adapted to the purity and simplicity of Bonaventura's own thought. Where Giotto is closer to the spirit of the *Fioretti*, which presents the stories of St. Francis in a frequently dramatic and even emotional manner, the designer of the *Legend* was concerned more, like Bonaventura himself, with their theological significance. To the author of the *Fioretti*, the Stigmatization was a stupendous, dramatic event, inspiring St. Francis with fear and great agony of mind; but for Bonaventura it was the manifestation of a divine sign filling the Saint with joy and wonder, and with tender compassion for the Crucified, as it was also for the designer of the Assisi fresco. And where, for instance, Bonaventura shows how the throne reserved for St. Francis in heaven was the wonderful but entirely credible reward for an incomparable humility, the Assisi master lays bare the same *exemplum* on the wall with no apparent consciousness of any difficulty in translating from the medium of literature to that of painting.

The very clarity with which St. Bonaventura presents the interrelation and yet the absolute distinctness of the earthly and the heavenly is itself implicit in the pictorial language of the *Legend*. It must, in the main, have been technical convenience that led to the execution of the frescoes in horizontal bands corresponding, presumably, to the various levels of the scaffolding: but these divisions also corresponded to a basic acceptance of the principle that the upper field of a composition denoted the heavenly world and the lower field the earthly; a convention normally discarded by Giotto in preference for a greater interpenetration of the divine and earthly spheres; and thus it is that in front of a work by Giotto we are never conscious of an absolute geometric division between these two spheres, as we are in the Upper Church. It is not, therefore, only in its purely stylistic aspects, not only in the recurring patterns of its designs, not only in its manner of depicting the physical world of tangible reality and in its portrayal of humanity, that the *Legend* at Assisi upholds ideals essentially opposed to those of Giotto: the differences in spiritual expression are scarcely less profound. Only when we discard all preconceptions deriving from the attribution of the *Legend* to Giotto do we discern its true character and discover its real virtues.

PART TWO

THE *LEGEND OF ST. FRANCIS*

VII

NORTH WALL: FOURTH BAY

(SCENES I–III)

THE NARRATIVE of the *Legend* in the Upper Church opens with a prophecy (Frontispiece). The honour done to the young Francis by a simple man of Assisi— a 'child of grace' endowed with supernatural vision—occupies an important place in early Franciscan literature from the *Legenda maior*[1] to the *De Conformitate*,[2] being regarded as one of a number of miraculous proofs that the Poverello's life of sacrifice had been predestined by God. To Bonaventura, the action of the 'simpleton' of Assisi in spreading his cloak before St. Francis's feet recalled the acclamation of Jesus as Messiah on the occasion of his triumphal entry into Jerusalem. In the *Speculum Vitae Beati Francisci* the simpleton appears again at the moment in the Saint's life when he has set out to win glory as a soldier, and once more he utters a prophecy: 'I told you a little while ago that before long he would be doing great things. Now he has begun; and you will yet see greater things than these that the Lord Jesus will do through him. What you see now are only human things; but wait till you see the spiritual ones.'[3]

The scene is set in the main piazza of Assisi at the time of Francis's prodigal youth, when, as we are reminded in the *Tres Socii*, he behaved more like a prince than the son of a merchant, the unashamed hedonism of his enjoyment of the good things of this life being manifested most obviously to the eyes of his fellow citizens by his delight in sumptuous clothing, woven, we are told, from 'stuffs more costly than it beseemed him to wear'.[4] The early biographers of St. Francis dwell with fascination upon the youthful worldliness of one who was to become the least worldly of men; and yet, according to

---

[1] *Legenda maior*, i, 1.

[2] Cf. *De Conformitate*, Lib. i, Fructus i, Pars Secunda, 5: 'Decimo, beatus Franciscus fuit declaratus, qualis esset futurus, per quendam virum simplicem de Assisio, prout dicit dominus frater Bonaventura in *Legenda maiori*, parte I, qui beato Francisco adhuc saeculari eunti per civitatem, eidem obviando, deponebat pallium, tergebat viam et sternebat ipsius pedibus vestimentum . . .' (*Analecta Franciscana*, iv (1906), 56 f.).

[3] *A New Fioretti: A Collection of Early Stories about Saint Francis*, trans. J. R. H. Moorman (London, 1946), p. 13.

[4] *The Legend of Saint Francis by the Three Companions*, trans. E. G. Salter (London, 1902), 2 (p. 9).

the *Tres Socii*, there was even at that time a hint of his subsequent rejection of this way of life. 'So wayward was his fancy,' we read, 'that at times on the same coat he would cause a right costly cloth to be matched with one of the meanest.' The writer is thinking ahead to the invention of the Franciscan habit, the prime symbol and token of the Rule of Poverty.

It is noteworthy that all three scenes in this opening chapter of the cycle are concerned with dress and adornment: in the first scene St. Francis, attired like a prince, does not decline to tread upon the poor man's cloak spread in homage at his feet; in the second scene, which marks the first stage in the development of his spiritual life, he dismounts from his horse to give his own cloak to an impoverished knight; and in the third it is revealed to him in a dream that his calling is to wear, not in earthly palaces, the very armour of Christ. The climactic point in the narration of this theme is reached in the central fresco in the next bay (Scene V), where Francis, having stripped himself naked, accepts henceforth as his only covering a hair-shirt and the rough tunic of a peasant, marked with the sign of the Cross. *The Homage of a Simple Man of Assisi* is concerned, then, with much more than mere storytelling: it states at the outset of the narrative an important contrast which the early biographers of St. Francis considered deeply significant, and which throws into relief the meaning of the subsequent events of his spiritual life.

No subject could have been better suited to the genius of the St. Cecilia Master, with his predilection for a world of aristocratic refinement. Whether in his altarpieces or in his frescoes at Assisi, this great painter reveals himself as an artist who combines the curiosity of the realist with the remoter vision of the seeker after ideal harmonies. Here the story told by Bonaventura, having no less familiar a setting than the city of Assisi itself, afforded a master capable of such novelty and adventure the opportunity of throwing open a window upon the everyday world and of creating in the process what may be described as the first modern street-scene in Italian art. The Temple of Minerva (Plate 41), so much admired by Goethe, presides over this charming townscape, which anticipates—and by more than a century—the elegant descriptiveness of Masolino's fresco of *St. Peter healing the Cripple* in the Brancacci Chapel. Yet the taste by which the St. Cecilia Master was moulded did not permit him to reproduce the classical forms of the Roman temple without fundamental alterations, and an alembic of Gothic refinement transforms the massive columns into architectural delicacies of slender and exquisite proportions: at the same time they are reduced in number from six to five. Most extraordinary of all, a rose-window between two reliefs of angels pierces the pediment, and a band of mosaic-work is introduced below, so that the Roman building is assimilated to the dreamy memory of some Gothic tympanum. The design of the pediment is especially reminiscent of the canopy of Arnolfo di Cambio's elegant tabernacle at S. Paolo fuori le mura in Rome (Plate 37*b*), completed in the year 1285: thus the forms of ancient Rome bow to the modes of a later age. In conformity with the same taste, the Romanesque windows of the Palazzo del Capitano del Popolo, which stands in the piazza to the left of the temple (Plate 41), have been redesigned in the Gothic style. No other representations of architecture in the cycle can quite compare with this elegant backdrop against which the action takes place and which contributes so effectively to the unity of the design.

The graceful figures that flit across this insubstantial stage, as though they had lightly tiptoed from the wings, belong to the same race that peoples the *Santa Cecilia* and *Santa Margherita* altarpieces: they have the same quaint proportioning, with small heads and hands and high waists; their features are delicate and their bearing aristocratic; and, as in the Uffizi and Montici narratives, we observe a tendency towards a stooping posture and a thrusting forward of the head which brings to mind the quick movements of birds. The simpleton is represented as a man of strange appearance, with staring eyes and unkempt beard; St. Francis as a young man of great beauty and refinement. The portrayal of the Saint, apart from the lack of beard, conforms to the famous description by Thomas of Celano: the slight and elegant build, the smooth but fairly low brow, the well-shaped nose and thin lips, and the slender neck and delicate hands are all carefully indicated.

As is usual with the St. Cecilia Master, the pattern of the design is essentially symmetrical; but everywhere this fundamental principle has been quietly modified. It is established unequivocally at the outset by the central position of the temple, which divides the composition vertically into three distinct fields—a large area in the centre and two narrower segments of equal width at the sides. It is within these lateral segments that the figures are placed, and in a geometric sense the composition is activated by the partial detachment of the two principal figures (St. Francis and the simpleton) from their enclosing fields, so that they slightly penetrate the large central field formed by the temple. A further division gives special prominence to St. Francis, who is aligned against the tower adjoining the *palazzo* on the left. The tower and the palace balance the houses on the far right, but their dissimilarities of shape and colour and the treatment of all the architectural forms in an oblique perspective give variety to a system that might otherwise have seemed too regular.

To know the work of a great designer is never to be in danger of underestimating the part played by the intellect in casting the mould into which true feeling may be poured. In the case of the St. Cecilia Master, and not least in the Uffizi and Montici narratives, the expression of human emotion is often intense: yet he joins that rare company of painters whose inspiration is capable of being sustained through the nicest and most prolonged calculations, although once the details of a composition had been determined his execution was rapid: in *The Homage of a Simple Man* at Assisi the entire pediment of the temple, with its exquisitely drawn rose-window and its lovely angel-reliefs, and almost the whole of the palace and the tower, including the finely observed detail of a clothes-line suspended from the palace windows, were painted in a single session, and none of the other painters of the *Legend* shows a comparable mastery of the techniques of fresco. This is no ordinary painter, and the perfection to which he aspired was possible of attainment only where every passage of the work was under his complete control. A mind not trained to the same delicate perceptions could easily have failed, for instance, to give the figure in dark red standing to the right of the temple exactly that hint of circularity, in the area bounded by the curved shoulders and the active hands, which, without being too obvious, was required to echo on this side of the composition the large circle of the Saint's halo, itself in turn repeating that of the rose-window above: a comparable example of this subtle geometrizing is to be found in the seventh compartment of the Uffizi altarpiece (*St. Cecilia before Almachius*, Plate 8), where St. Cecilia's halo, a marble inlay at the back of Almachius's judgement-seat, and a round shield in the hand of a soldier of the guard provide a similar triad of circular shapes.

Within the geometric prosody of this delicately balanced art the St. Cecilia Master delights to play upon the finest assonances of colour. Against the deep blue of the sky in this scene, the buildings which establish the main divisions in the composition provide a lightly tinted back-cloth setting off the richer colours and deeper tones of the figures in their gay attire—the yellow, dark red, and blue of the costumes of the Saint and his young companions, placed against the pink stonework of the palace and its tower; the light green of the simpleton's garment and the deep red and pale lilac of the long cloaks worn by the two bystanders, set against the soft green of the house on the right. In the centre the Temple of Minerva, which must hold its own in the design as a form unactivated by figures (if the reliefs on the tympanum are excluded), is emphasized by the picking out of certain of its principal features in white, against an over-all yellow tonality, and a further stress is provided by the deep red tiling of the portico. The St. Cecilia Master was altogether a more feminine colourist than Giotto, preferring delicate nuances to the bolder combinations and sometimes harsh contrasts of the Arena Chapel frescoes; on the other hand, his colour lacks the intensity and brilliance peculiar to the early Sienese masters: it is distinctly Florentine in character, and it charms by a purity and refinement comparable in many ways with the exquisite palette of his younger contemporary Bernardo Daddi, who may well have been his pupil.

No earlier representation of this subject is known, and it may be assumed that the iconography was entirely new. Nevertheless, it is evident that where no prototype for the representation of a particular subject was available, the painters of the Assisi cycle often drew inspiration from the iconography of some analogous scene from the Bible or from the legends of the saints, and the simpleton in the St. Cecilia Master's fresco stands in a direct line of descent from the young men and children who appear in scenes of the Entry into Jerusalem and who spread their garments in Christ's path. This association, indeed, was already embedded in the text of the *Legenda maior*, for Bonaventura's description of the simpleton's action—'sternebat ipsius pedibus vestimentum'—is itself a quotation from the account of Christ's Entry into Jerusalem given in St. Luke's Gospel.

In the same way an approximate model for *The Gift of the Mantle* (Scene II, Plate 42),[1] also a new subject in Franciscan iconography, already existed in the story of the Charity of St. Martin of Tours, with which this incident in St. Francis's life is associated in the *Legenda Monacensis*.[2] Although there are certain fundamental differences between the two stories, both subjects comprise much the same elements—a lordly young man surprised in an act of impulsive charity, a beggar or poor man, a horse, and a landscape setting. Variations upon the same theme are also found in the legends of other saints, and Pacino di Bonaguida produced a similar type of composition when he designed his charming illustration of the comparable legend related of the Blessed Gherardo da Villamagna (Plate 43).[3]

Like the preceding scene, *The Gift of the Mantle* powerfully evokes the familiar surroundings of the Saint's early life. Perched on the hill that rises upon the left can be seen the city of Assisi, with its rose-coloured walls and battlemented gates:[4] the painter made no attempt, however, at the accurate representation of any particular building. As we have seen, the spired church surmounting the smaller slope to the right must be intended for San Francesco itself, the bell-tower of the great basilica having originally been topped by a spire. The dry, rocky landscape, cleft by the deep gorge of the ancient Collis Inferni, which Gregory IX, in honour of St. Francis, renamed the Collis Paradisi, provides the main fabric of the design, the two hills converging at the Saint's head (the central point of the composition and of the decoration of the bay as a whole). The symmetrical balance all the more necessary to the scene in respect of its function as a centrepiece is completed by the horse and the poor man, both represented in a profile view and as facing inwards.

Although he played the dominant role in the painting of the cycle, the St. Francis Master lacked the technical virtuosity of the St. Cecilia Master. His draughtsmanship is clumsier, although it is bolder; his colouring is less luminous, but it is stronger; and

---

[1] *Legenda maior*, i, 2.

[2] *Legenda Monacensis S. Francisci*, 2 (*Analecta Franciscana*, x (1926–41), 696).

[3] Pierpont Morgan Library, New York: cf. M. Harssen and G. K. Boyce, *Italian Manuscripts in the Pierpont Morgan Library*, with an Introduction by Bernard Berenson (New York, 1953), pp. 13 f. (No. 22).

[4] For other early representations of Assisi, which are extremely rare, see P. Leone Bracalone, op. cit.; U. Gnoli, 'Il "Gonfalone della Peste" di Niccolò Alunno e la più antica veduta di Assisi', *Bollettino d'arte*, v (1911), 63 ff.; V. Fachinetti, *San Francesco d'Assisi nella storia, nella leggenda, nell'arte* (2nd edn., Milan, 1926), pp. 2 f.

his treatment of form, while being less subtle, is more monumental. He inclines towards strong contrasts of light and shade, which are generally absent from the work of the St. Cecilia Master, and in representing sculptural detail he shows an unusual curiosity about effects of cast shadow, an interest sufficiently rare in this period: the Victories, for example, that decorate the *baldacchino* in Scene XIII (Plate 37*a*) cast very noticeable shadows, whereas in Scene I the similar reliefs represented on the tympanum of the temple cast none.[1] The St. Francis Master gives, besides, the impression of an adventurousness and even of a certain impatience of temperament that baulks at no difficulty, even when the problem is beyond his powers to solve. Altogether he was a bolder and yet far less sophisticated painter than the St. Cecilia Master, and the difference between the two artists is manifested in their techniques. Unlike the St. Cecilia Master, and unlike Giotto, the St. Francis Master made lavish use of white lead, which by its known action of eventually turning black has ruined many passages in his frescoes in the Upper Church; and he was fond of leaving certain details—such as the horse's reins in Scene II (now scarcely visible)—to be added in tempera rather than in *buon fresco*;[2] so also, in his eager but less skilled hands, the smooth finish that characterizes the *intonaco* surfaces of Scene I—as though the brush had kissed and cosseted the plaster—gives way to a rougher and somewhat coarser treatment.

Symmetrical landscape-compositions of this type, although unknown in the work of Giotto, occur in paintings by the St. Cecilia Master and such followers of his as Jacopo del Casentino and Pacino di Bonaguida. No less characteristic of the same tendency in early fourteenth-century Florentine painting are the conventions adopted in this impressive landscape for the representation of rocks, trees, and buildings. As though Nature abhorred unbroken surfaces, the stony expanses of the hills are split into countless fissures and clefts, which serve not less than the purposes of realism an instinct for decorative pattern. The hills are treated as much as a backdrop as the buildings in Scene I, and the problem of relating them to the foregound plane has been ignored. Against this broad panorama the two human figures and the horse are placed like paper cut-outs: the deterioration of areas added in tempera (such as the Saint's blue cloak, painted over a grey fresco preparation) has increased their impression of insubstantiality, exaggerating the linear nature of the artist's conception of design and his delight in pattern-making. The use of white lead has caused the Saint's hands and the poor man's left hand to turn black, and much of the landscape has darkened for the same reason.

St. Francis and the poor man—an impoverished knight, we are told—look at one another with that odd, peering curiosity which often characterizes the expressions of the St. Cecilia Master's figures and those by his followers. The refined delineation of the Saint's features in the opening scene is lacking here, while the poor man is awkwardly

---

[1] This question is discussed more fully in Chapter XVI.   [2] Meiss and Tintori, op. cit., pp. 56 f.

drawn: his clumsy, lumpish figure is nevertheless similar in general type to those lively little personages that are represented in profile on the *Santa Cecilia* altarpiece (Plate 8), and it may be compared, for example, with the figure of Valerian in the second compartment of the altarpiece. These and other affinities between the styles of the two masters suggest one of three possibilities—first, that the St. Francis Master's stylistic origins are to be sought in the art of the St. Cecilia Master; secondly (and conversely), that the St. Cecilia Master was a pupil of the St. Francis Master; and thirdly, that the two painters had a similar training. It is questionable whether we are entitled to go beyond the last of these alternatives: despite the advanced style of the St. Cecilia Master's frescoes at Assisi, there is certainly no evidence that the St. Francis Master belonged to an older generation.

Not here the epic grandeur of the pastoral episodes in the story of Joachim at Padua (compare Plate 18*b*), but rather a quality of interpretation that reappears in the treatment of landscape by such Florentine contemporaries as the St. Cecilia Master and especially Pacino di Bonaguida. Pacino's illustration of the story of the Charity of the Blessed Gherardo da Villamagna (Plate 43), in the Morgan Library, reflects something of the same spirit, a still quietism of which the severer and more activated landscapes of the Arena Chapel show no trace. Giotto would never have given St. Francis this languid air: notwithstanding the text of the *Legenda maior*, it was not the impulsiveness of the Saint's action that impressed itself upon the painter's mind. Virtually all the drama has been drained from the story, and replaced by a simple narration of a charming incident possessing something of the timelessness of the gradual unfolding of a dream.

The buildings within the city and just outside its walls, constructed of simple blocks resembling children's bricks (Plate 10*d*), bring to mind the forms found in the second compartment of the Montici altarpiece (*St. Margaret before Olybrius*, Plate 10*b*). They are, however, rendered with less refinement, and there is a quality of particularization in some of the buildings in the Assisi fresco that was evidently foreign to the St. Cecilia Master's taste. Just as the figure-style has patently less in common with Giotto's ideal than with that of the St. Cecilia Master, so also certain youthful heads by Pacino, notably in his great *Tree of Life* in the Accademia[1] and in his miniatures, approximate more closely to the representations of St. Francis in this and the following fresco (Plates 39*a*, *b*, 44*b*, 45), with their somewhat rounded features and close-cropped hair, and to other figures in the same area of the nave (Plates 50*a–d*, 51*a–d*) than to the physiognomic types of Giotto or any other contemporary. Such affinities underline the strength of the St. Francis Master's impact upon that distinctive stream of Florentine painting of which both the St. Cecilia Master and Pacino were representative.

---

[1] For this work see Offner, *Corpus*, III, ii (Part I), 8 f. and Pls. II, II¹⁻¹⁴; ibid., III, vi, 122 ff.; Sinibaldi and Brunetti, op. cit., pp. 401 ff., Pl. 124*a–d*.

The story of the Gift of the Mantle is followed immediately in the *Legenda maior*, as it is in the Assisi cycle, by that of the Vision of the Palace:[1] as Bonaventura tells us, the vision was the reward for the mercy that St. Francis had shown to the poor man. It not only announced his destined vocation as a soldier of Christ—for the palace was filled with armour and banners adorned with the sign of the Cross—but also declared his worthiness to be received into these heavenly mansions. Yet the story as told by Bonaventura is a mere petrified abstraction of one of the Saint's most intense religious experiences, and it is understandable that the designer of the fresco (Plate 45) should have sought inspiration in the earlier and more human account given by Thomas of Celano and repeated with slight variations in the *Tres Socii*: there, Christ appears in person to the ardent Francis (as he does not do in the *Legenda maior*), visiting him 'in the sweetness of grace by a night vision', 'calling him by name', and himself leading him to the palace. By combining the two traditions, the Assisi master was able to preserve the vividness of the earlier narratives, while losing nothing of Bonaventura's lofty spirituality.

Bonaventura goes on to tell how Francis, understanding this revelation of his vocation in a literal and worldly sense, presented himself to a certain Count, 'hoping in his service to win glory in arms'. As we have noted, the real meaning of the vision is suggested in the fresco by the opposition of the heavenly palace, at one end of the bay, to the earthly palace at the other, in the opening scene of the cycle. The two frescoes are closely related in design, despite the dissimilarities in their subject-matter and the necessary reduction of the figures in Scene III to two, and their harmonization on either side of *The Gift of the Mantle* completes the decorative unity of the bay (Plate 3a).

Like Scene I, *The Vision of the Palace* is divided into three vertical fields: these are defined by the curtain behind the Saint's bed, by the palace, and by the intervening space, which the blue of the background is allowed almost to fill, and which provides a spatial vacuum similar to that created by the temple in the other fresco. Similarly, the diagonal set up by Christ's gesture as he directs the attention of St. Francis to the heavenly palace echoes, in reverse, the diagonal implicit in the Saint's encounter with the simpleton. The fresco was clearly executed by the author of Scene II; but once again, and especially in some of the architectural forms that crowd the picture-space, we observe close affinities with the style of the St. Cecilia Master.

The lofty proportions of the Saint's bedroom, which is constructed of thin wooden beams, are found again in *The Confession of the Woman of Benevento* (Scene XXVII, Plate 91)—one of the frescoes painted by the St. Cecilia Master in the bay opposite—and they reappear in *The Dream of Innocent III* (Scene VI, Plate 52), in *The Healing of the Wounded Man* (Scene XXVI, Plate 90), and in the interiors represented on the Uffizi altarpiece. The curtains, suspended from long rods that define the front and back planes of the

---

[1] *Legenda maior*, i, 3.

building, have the function, as in Scene XXVI, of providing a clearly marked division within a rectangular field; and in both frescoes one curtain is slung around a pillar to produce a curving motif that gives variety to the geometric scheme. In *The Vision of the Palace* this motif combines with the two haloed heads to repeat, within a more confined space, the play upon circular forms already present in Scene I. The house in which St. Francis lies sleeping is topped by a diminutive storey, similar to those represented in Scene XXVII and in the third compartment of the *Santa Cecilia* altarpiece (Plate 8). Features of the heavenly palace resemble architectural forms found in the fourth scene of the altarpiece. On the other hand, as in Scene II, the handling of architectural detail in *The Vision of the Palace* lacks the refinement characteristic of Scene I and of Scenes XXVI–XXVIII, and the columns, for example, tend to a squatness of proportioning that belongs to another taste.

The design of this fresco is organized according to principles which have already been analysed in relation to Scenes I and V. The gesture of Christ's left arm serves not only to explicate the narrative, and not only to establish a movement echoing the thrusting diagonal implicit in Scene I, but also to create a pictorial tension, at the centre of the composition, between a virtually empty rectangle and a form that irrupts upon it. The abrupt invasion of such empty fields by a form of this kind (usually a hand or an arm) was one of the St. Cecilia Master's favourite methods of activating his compositions, and it occurs many times in the Uffizi and Montici altarpieces: it can be seen in its most dramatic aspect in the final narrative of the *Santa Cecilia* altarpiece (*The Martyrdom of St. Cecilia*), where the saint's arms reach up across the horizon-line of a hill to penetrate the central void of sky. It is a device that seems to derive directly from Italo-Byzantine practice, and an example of its use can be seen in the fresco by Cimabue in the Upper Church representing *The Fall of Simon Magus*:[1] but what is distinctive about its exceptionally frequent employment by the St. Cecilia Master is the association of such gestures with a rigidly geometrical system of design. It is no less characteristic a feature of the *St. Francis* cycle as a whole, but in the frescoes of the St. Francis Master (as in Scenes III and V) the invading movement tends to be stronger, producing a deeper penetration of the associated field.

The treatment of perspective in this bay (Plate 3a) reflects general principles that become clearer as the cycle unfolds. The outer scenes are both visualized as being observed from a point to the right of centre. The perspective of Scene II, on the other hand, is centralized, and the orthogonals of the buildings in the background slope for the most part inwards, supporting the inward movement of the design, although in this respect the composition is exceptional in the cycle. The level of the spectator's viewpoint is equated with the height of the upright figures (such as St. Francis in the first two scenes

[1] D. Gioseffi, *Giotto architetto*, p. 21, Figs. 10, 11.

and Christ in the third): thus the upper part of the heavenly palace in Scene III, above this level, is seen from below, and the lower part, below the same line, from above. The resulting orthogonals in the lower part of the building consequently slope upwards from left to right, supporting the main movement suggested by Christ's gesture,[1] and reversing the similar movement implicit in Scene I, a movement reinforced by the red roof of the temple. At the same time the slightly stooping posture of St. Francis in Scene I begins a rising movement which is carried up by the left side of the pediment of the temple into the green building on the right and thence into the cluster of towers comprising the little town in Scene II. Already the inclined orthogonals of the green house in Scene I begin a downward movement culminating in Scene II at the Saint's head; but evidently the gentle slope of the rooftops of the town in Scene II was no less carefully calculated, for they lead the eye across the composition, and slightly downward, to the church on the right. This lateral movement is then picked up in the strong horizontals formed by the upper structure of the Saint's bedroom in Scene III. Finally, the whole broad movement bends downward into the curtain—the orthogonals of the upper part of the heavenly palace and of the bedroom itself running parallel to, and supporting, the direction of the eye's descent.

Similar linear rhythms, assisted in the same manner by the use of perspective to establish direction-lines across the surface of the design, harmonize the narratives of the St. Cecilia Master's altarpieces, bringing paired scenes into a symmetrical relationship. In the *Santa Margherita* altarpiece (Plate 9) each of the three scenes to the left of the central cult-image of the saint bears a close compositional resemblance to the corresponding scene on the right. In the two cases where an architectural scene is paired with a scene without architecture the orthogonals of the buildings echo the linear pattern of the other scene: thus the tall building represented in the second scene (*St. Margaret before Olybrius*) was designed so that the inclined orthogonal of its roof should mirror the downward slope of the hill in the first scene (*The Proposal of Olybrius*). Again, the compositions of the torture and execution scenes—paired together in the lowest row—are both based on diagonals meeting at the figure of the saint: each is of a regular, centralized design, and the perspective of the architectural background of the torture scene (which alone contains buildings) is treated in terms of the same decorative symmetry. This thoroughgoing symmetry supports, with an equal weight on either side, the long vertical field reserved for the cult-image, towards which the orthogonals of all buildings placed close to the central field lead in.

The organization of the *Santa Cecilia* altarpiece (Plate 8) is more complex, comprising

---

[1] The triangular formation of the *giornata* above Christ's head, noted by Tintori and Meiss (op. cit., p. 88 and Pl. 30), may possibly indicate that Christ was originally conceived as holding a banner in his right hand, or, perhaps, that he was to have been shown drawing the bed-curtain aside.

as it does four scenes arranged in two rows on each side of the figure of the enthroned saint; but exactly the same principles are at work. Once again orthogonals adjacent to the central field build up towards the image of the saint, supporting a general inward and ascending movement. In each scene the function given to architectural forms of establishing direction-lines across the picture-plane is paralleled by the attitudes and gestures of the figures; and it must, for example, be on account of the same concern to create an over-all linear pattern that in the final scene the figure of the saint is represented as inclining backwards at an angle. It should be added that colour is employed in an analogous manner to enhance the general symmetry: for example, the two inner scenes in the upper register are brought into a relationship with one another by predominant notes of red and pink in their architectural backgrounds, and those in the lower register by dominant greys. Similar principles underlie the whole of the *St. Francis* cycle at Assisi: throughout the *Legend*, perspective is placed at the service of the two-dimensional pattern of the design. That is not to deny its function of creating at the same time an illusion of the three-dimensional world, but in every scene the choice of a particular perspectival system evidently depended upon this fundamental decorative requirement.

VIII

NORTH WALL: THIRD BAY

(SCENES IV–VI)

THE CHAPTER OF THREE EPISODES that now follows in the third bay from the entrance recounts the well-known stories of the divine call to St. Francis at San Damiano to rebuild the Church of Christ, the Saint's rejection of his earthly father and all worldly ties and possessions, and his appearance in a dream to Innocent III as the destined saviour of Christendom (Plate 3*b*). The opening narrative, *The Miracle of the Crucifix* (Scene IV, Plate 46),[1] at once associates the future bearer of the sacred *stigmata* with the Crucified Christ, and not only do the raised hands anticipate the representation of St. Francis in *The Stigmatization* (Scene XIX, Plate 76) but the figure of Christ on the crucifix resembles that of the Seraphic Christ in the same fresco. In representing the miraculous *crocifisso che parlava* the St. Francis Master made some attempt to suggest the antique character of a Romanesque cross, but he did not copy the actual twelfth-century crucifix that originally stood over the altar in San Damiano and which is still revered as a holy relic at Santa Chiara:[2] his model must rather have been a work similar in type to the Crucifix by Alberto Sozio (dated 1187) in Spoleto Cathedral.[3] (It is perhaps this prototype, rather than the crucifix in the Assisi fresco, as has recently been suggested, that lies behind the Spoleto Crucifix by the so-called 'Cesi Master'.)[4]

If the representation of *The Miracle of the Crucifix* on one of the windows in the nave of the Upper Church antedates the fresco, then the Assisi painter may well have been influenced by its design, for it contains the basic elements of his composition.[5] It is again

---

[1] *Legenda maior*, ii, 1.

[2] E. B. Garrison, op. cit., No. 459; E. Sandberg-Vavalà, *La Croce dipinta italiana* (Verona, 1929), pp. 623 f.; E. Zocca, *Assisi and the Environs* (Rome, 1950), pp. 66 f.

[3] Sandberg-Vavalà, op. cit., pp. 613 ff.; Garrison, op. cit., No. 456.

[4] Meiss suggests that the Cesi Master may have been directly influenced by the crucifix represented in the fresco: cf. M. Meiss, 'Reflections of Assisi: A Tabernacle and the Cesi Master', *Scritti di Storia dell'Arte in onore di Mario Salmi* (Rome, 1962), pp. 104 ff. and Figs. 24 and 26.

[5] P. Egidio M. Giusto, *Le Vetrate di S. Francesco in Assisi* (Milan, 1911), Pl. XIV.

uncertain whether the somewhat archaic interpretation of the subject on an altarpiece by a follower of Guido da Siena representing *St. Francis and Eight Scenes from his Life* is definitely earlier than the fresco, but here in any case the design is quite different.[1] Probably, however, the window preserves an older thirteenth-century tradition for the rendering of this scene. What can scarcely be doubted is that one important feature of the Assisi composition—the heavy stress placed upon the crumbling masonry of the dilapidated church—was entirely original, for it is by means of this emphasis that the ruined building is associated with the tottering Cathedral of Rome represented in Scene VI. The association makes clear the true meaning of Christ's command to St. Francis, who is represented in the *Legenda maior* as taking literally what was intended in a spiritual sense, and as obediently setting to work to repair the church of San Damiano.

Within the dark square that encloses him, St. Francis kneels in front of the altar, which is set into a little apse.[2] The surface of the fresco, however, is so badly damaged that his features can now scarcely be made out. The blue of his gown has almost entirely fallen away, revealing the underpainting, which is in a red earth-colour: in consequence the balance that was no doubt intended with the figure of a blue-gowned attendant in Scene VI is now lost. Tempera was used not only for the gown but also for the crucifix, of which all that remains is the underdrawing on the *intonaco*.

St. Francis looks slightly up at the cross, and his kneeling form establishes a rising movement which is taken up and continued in the next scene by the ascending diagonal of an outer stairway: thus attention is directed to the culminating point of the central fresco, where the hand of God appears in benediction. At the same time the inclined orthogonals of the altar-wall of the church, above the little apse with its semi-dome, flow into those of the red-bricked building to which the stairway belongs. The floor of the church, receding at the same marked angle, is mirrored exactly by the base of the falling Lateran Basilica in Scene VI (Plate 3*b*). The façade of the basilica lies on the picture-plane, but the decorated architrave of the portico repeats in reverse the angle of the foreshortened crucifix in the first scene.

Supported and enframed by the two outer scenes, like the main panel of a triptych (Plate 3*b*), the central fresco (Plate 48) releases the tension of the preceding episode in an explosive conflict between two contending parties. Like some other early representations of this subject, including Giotto's composition in the Bardi Chapel (Plate 49), the Assisi fresco combines the story of the Saint's act of renunciation with a reference to the prior account in the *Legenda maior* of his friendship with the priest of San Damiano (to whom he had given money for the repair of the church and for the use of the poor), and of his increasing carelessness about his own dress and appearance, which had led to his being

[1] For this panel see J. H. Stubblebine, op. cit., pp. 107 ff. and Fig. 61.

[2] The treatment of space in Scene IV is discussed in Chapter XVI, and certain similarities in designs by Pacino are touched upon in the same chapter and also in Chapter IX.

stoned by the uncomprehending citizens of Assisi:[1] this is the meaning of the priest standing with a companion behind the bishop, and of the children on the left, who have made their voluminous garments into receptacles for stones. Bonaventura's story[2] concludes with an account of the origin of the Franciscan habit, the plain garment of sackcloth in which St. Francis is clothed in all the subsequent scenes of the *Legend* except *The Christmas Crib at Greccio* (Scene XIII, Plate 63), where he wears the vestments of an officiating priest. Hereafter, with this same exception, he also appears barefoot.

Although this important incident in his early life is omitted from the most important of the very early illustrations of the Franciscan legend—the six scenes on the altarpiece at Pescia painted in 1235 by Bonaventura Berlinghieri[3]—the essential iconography is firmly established later in the thirteenth century in the little scene on the Bardi altarpiece at Santa Croce in Florence[4] and in the damaged fresco in the Lower Church at Assisi.[5] In both these representations there is already found a clear-cut division of the composition into two groups of figures. Giotto in the Bardi Chapel and the St. Francis Master at Assisi both availed themselves, therefore, of an iconographic tradition dating back perhaps fifty years or more, although the uses to which they put that tradition were far from being identical.

The impressive scene in the mother church of the Franciscan Order inevitably set a pattern for the later treatment of the subject, and just as the Assisi fresco itself develops an earlier tradition, so in its turn it furnished the elements of Giotto's own composition in the Bardi Chapel (Plate 49). Yet the two frescoes are profoundly unlike in spirit. Where Giotto is primarily concerned with the dramatic confrontation of the two protagonists, so that Pietro Bernardone must be forcibly prevented from leaping across the space separating him from St. Francis, the Assisi painter emphasizes the division that has come about between father and son by means of an actual geometric division within his composition. At Santa Croce the bishop's palace which forms the background of the scene serves to bridge the gap between the two groups of figures, while preserving a division within the total unity by virtue of the spatial alignment of each group of figures with one of the receding planes formed by the two visible walls of the building. At Assisi an absolute void opens up between the two groups; there is no strong movement anywhere, except in the lurching form of Pietro Bernardone: the gesture of the bishop, as he covers the Saint's nakedness, has a somewhat casual air; and he betrays no more positive interest than St. Francis himself on the occasion of his charity towards the impoverished knight (Scene II). Pietro Bernardone, moreover, seems to require little pressure upon his arm to hold him back, and his action is much less convincing than that

---

[1] *Legenda maior*, ii, 1.   [2] Ibid., ii, 4.
[3] G. Kaftal, *Iconography of the Saints in Tuscan Painting* (Florence, 1952), No. 122a; Sinibaldi and Brunetti, op. cit., pp. 15 ff.   [4] Ibid., pp. 177 ff. and Pl. 55a.
[5] B. Kleinschmidt, O.F.M., *Die Wandmalereien der Basilica San Francesco in Assisi* (Berlin, 1930), Pl. 2a.

of the muscular individual who strains to be unhanded in Giotto's fresco: indeed, his forward movement is suggested less powerfully by the painter's attempt to render a human being in violent action than by the displacement of his form from the rectangular field with which it is associated.

Some of the less important heads in this scene were clearly executed by assistants; but the style of the St. Francis Master can be recognized in most of the principal figures, including the young man on the very left, his fat companion, the two children, the man holding Bernardone by the arm, Bernardone himself, St. Francis, and perhaps the bishop. Throughout the three scenes of the bay the style of the architecture corresponds no less evidently to that of the buildings represented in Scenes II and III, but here a predilection for brick-red and deep orange which is typical of the north wall as a whole begins to be more dominant. Once again there are figures by Pacino that show, on a smaller scale, marked similarities with the more monumental protagonists of the *Legend*, both in their facial characteristics and in their gestures: it is in Pacino, for example, that we find that curious disjointedness of limb to which attention has been drawn earlier and which is particularly noticeable in the figure of Bernardone; in Pacino also those tight-sleeved garments that hang loosely at the elbow; and similar chubby-faced children with large eyes and thick, flowing locks (Plates 50 *a–d*, 51 *a–d*).

In the *Renunciation* the forms of the St. Francis Master assume an unprecedented grandeur, which is summed up in the celebrated *ignudo* of the young Francis. It is this impressive figure that dominates the composition, a figure that has called forth countless eulogies upon its author's heroic conception of form. Although to some nineteenth-century eyes it could appear clumsy in drawing and deficient in life, it possesses a massive monumentality, of an almost antique character, which strongly appeals to the tastes of our own age. We recognize here, in addition, one of the first-fruits of a new interest in the representation of the nude, of which the north wall at Assisi provides other instances in the statues surmounting the Pope's palace in the next fresco (Scene VI) and in the reliefs on the cathedral in *The Exorcism of the Devils at Arezzo* (Scene X, Plates 58, 60a). In such examples, where it was a matter of introducing a minor detail of an ornamental nature, the painter evidently felt free to give rein to his inventiveness: on the other hand, the figure of St. Francis is in this respect more conservative, for there were already precedents in scenes of the martyrdom of saints for figures represented in precisely the same attitude, with the eyes turned upward in prayer and the hands raised to the heavens. Nevertheless, the scale of the fresco provided an opportunity for a searching study of the nude which may well have been assisted by the relative freshness of the iconography: otherwise it was for the most part only in such traditional subjects as the Baptism, the Flagellation, and the Crucifixion that new explorations of this kind were possible to the fresco-painter.

The Dream of Innocent III (Scene VI, Plate 52)[1] brings us again to Rome. The cycle follows the *Legenda maior* in passing over the Poverello's youthful ministry and the charming stories related of it, and presents him as one who received the immediate recognition of the Church. Other early representations of this subject, such as the predella scene on the Louvre *Stigmatization* and Taddeo Gaddi's panel in the Accademia,[2] insist still further upon this official view of the growth of the Franciscan movement by including the figure of St. Peter, who appears to the Pope and directs his attention to the Saint's symbolic action of supporting the Lateran Basilica upon his shoulders.[3] The Assisi fresco, on the other hand, stands closer to Bonaventura's text, which lacks any reference to St. Peter's role in the Pope's vision. According to the *Legenda maior*, it was as a direct consequence of his dream about the 'little poor man, of small stature and humble appearance', that Innocent III gave his official sanction to the Franciscan Rule, an event of the greatest importance in the history of the Order and the one chosen to open the sequence of three scenes in the following bay. In Benozzo Gozzoli's cycle at Montefalco the inclusion of the stories of the Pope's dream and the Sanctioning of the Rule within one composition emphasizes the close connection between the two events: at Assisi, however, the Pope's vision concludes one chapter of the narrative, and his blessing upon St. Francis and his ministry opens another.

The surface of Scene VI has suffered in the upper left-hand areas from the effects of damp, and the façade of the Lateran Basilica represented on the left side of the composition is now no longer visible: its main lines, however, have been indicated by a summary restoration which satisfactorily preserves the relationship of the basilica to the adjacent building in the preceding scene, the lines of the two structures flowing into each other so that the spectator's eye is led easily from the one scene to the other (Plate 3*b*). The original appearance of the basilica may be deduced, with a fair degree of certainty, from the version of the subject at Pistoia,[4] which closely follows the composition in the Upper Church in all other architectural details. The façade probably took the form of a plain, squarish structure pierced by three rounded windows and surmounted by a pointed roof. The accurately represented mosaics which form a notable feature of the scene on the predella panel of the Louvre *Stigmatization* are lacking in the fresco at Pistoia: indeed, the windows leave no room for them; and since, in the Assisi fresco, what appears to be part of a similar window can just be traced at the edge of the damaged area, it seems probable that here also the mosaics were not included;[5] a band of mosaic-work, however, decorates the architrave of the portico below.

The representation of S. Giovanni Laterano in the Assisi fresco may be likened in a

[1] *Legenda maior*, iii, 10.   [2] Sinibaldi and Brunetti, op. cit., pp. 429 ff., Pl. 137*q*.
[3] G. Kaftal, op. cit., col. 413, n. 11.   [4] Ibid., Fig. 449.
[5] P. Murray, 'Notes on Some Early Giotto Sources', *Journal of the Warburg and Courtauld Institutes*, xvi (1954), 58 ff.

general way to that of the Temple of Minerva in Scene I: without conforming to its original in detail, it suggests some of its essential features, such as its ancient columns, the majestic portico, and the bell-tower with its three tiers of arched windows. The Cosmati-work adorning the basilica and the papal palace on the right is typical of the ornamentation of architectural forms in the cycle as a whole, and betrays the Roman education of its designer, while the effigy-like figure of the sleeping Pope strongly recalls Arnolfo di Cambio's impassive image of Boniface VIII in St. Peter's.[1]

Innocent III reclines on a crimson couch, and one of the splendid gold bed-curtains, woven with a red pattern, has been drawn aside and draped around a column, much in the manner of the curtains represented in Scenes III and XXVI. The long, sweeping curve of the Pope's body and the white, gold, and rich red of his vestments are echoed in the shape and colouring of the palace roof. Once again, as in Scene III and elsewhere in the cycle, the room is remarkable for its lofty proportions. The nearer curtain curves down in an arc to unite with the bow-like figure of St. Francis, and where it is twisted about the column it resolves itself into a small nodular form which provides a pictorial balance to the Pope's head at the other extremity of the room. The two attendants seated on the floor beside the bed complete the ordered symmetry of the right half of the design. (A *cassone* painted in tempera between the attendants and the bed has now almost entirely disappeared.)

The elements of the iconography are present in the Guidesque panel at Siena of *St. Francis and Eight Scenes from his Life*, which has been mentioned earlier: here the relative positions of the Pope and St. Francis are approximately the same as in the Assisi fresco, although the basilica—shown as a domed Byzantine church—inclines the other way.[2] But, as we have seen, it is not clear whether the fresco postdates the Siena panel. A similar uncertainty surrounds the date of the window in the Upper Church containing scenes from the Franciscan legend, where the representation of *The Dream of Innocent III* bears a general resemblance to the Assisi fresco, while too much has been lost of the fresco in the Lower Church and the mosaic at Santa Maria in Aracoeli in Rome to allow useful comparisons with the composition in the Upper Church to be made. An important aspect of Scene VI at Assisi is the inward inclination of the basilica, which gives a tightness and compression to the design, enclosing the figure of St. Francis in a narrow triangular field and assisting in the tripartite division of the picture-area, so that the composition is brought into a closer relationship with Scene IV: thus, although Scene IV is divided vertically into three almost equal areas, and Scene VI into two, the further division of the left-hand side of Scene VI into two parts—the one occupied by the figure of the Saint and the other, on the left, by the doorway of the portico—contributes to the harmonization of the two compositions (Plate 3*b*). In each fresco St. Francis

---

[1] Compare also Plate 38*d*.   [2] J. H. Stubblebine, op. cit., Fig. 61.

gazes into the adjoining area across a dividing-line formed by a column, and the relationship between the Saint in Scene IV and the crucifix and intervening column is basically identical with his relationship to the two columns in Scene VI. Moreover, both these passages contain the same kind of play upon larger and smaller circular forms, such as are provided by the two haloes in the first scene and the halo and mosaic medallions in the other. In a still more striking manner, the related forms of St. Francis and the campanile in Scene VI reverse the pattern established in Scene IV by the thrust of the Saint's body to the right and the leftward inclination of the broken masonry above him.

By these means the whole left half of *The Dream of Innocent III*, constructed upon the inclined ground-plane of the Lateran Basilica, is brought into harmony with that area of *The Miracle of the Crucifix* which is erected on the similarly inclined orthogonal formed by the receding nave of San Damiano. It can be no accident that the remaining third of Scene IV repeats, in a somewhat looser manner, some of the main divisions of the large area in Scene VI that is reserved for the Pope's palace—the two blocks of stone that indicate the entrance to the church corresponding to the solid forms of the two attendants seated by the Pope's bed, and the large patch of sky glimpsed through the broken brickwork echoing the shape of the tied curtain. The three frescoes comprising this section of the narrative form, then, a unity no less complete than that found in the preceding bay.

IX

NORTH WALL: SECOND BAY

(SCENES VII–IX)

THE SETTING OF *The Sanctioning of the Rule* (Scene VII, Plate 53)[1] is an imposing hall hung with tapestries, where the Pope, surrounded by his cardinals, receives the kneeling Francis and his humble companions. The Pope is seated upon a high throne, and, in receiving from his hand the parchment containing the Rule of the Order, St. Francis must look up at him. The lowliness and humility of the friars, emphasized in the *Legenda maior* and expressed in the Assisi fresco as much by their attitudes as by the meanness of their plain brown habits, are simply and effectively contrasted with the splendour and power of the Curia, which in the original state of the fresco the rich attire of these grave dignitaries must have brought out still more strongly. Read as a single episode, the scene presented to us clearly bears that meaning; but within the compass of the triad of three frescoes in the bay, taken as a narrative unit, the humility of St. Francis is quickly turned to glory: indeed, the cycle offers no more striking instance of thematic and compositional unity than the sequence of three scenes which begins with *The Sanctioning of the Rule*; a unity made possible by the abstract language of planar design which welds together the three compositions in the bay into a larger whole (Plate 4*a*). So the historic event whereby the Church, in the person of Innocent III, gave her sanction to the ministry of the Poverello of Assisi is illuminated by two successive visions of his future glory (Scenes VIII and IX): this declaration that the Saint's glorification was the reward for his unique and Christ-like humility—a humility re-emphasized in Scene IX in the lowly attitude given to St. Francis as he kneels before the altar—follows with absolute fidelity the argument of the *Legenda maior*.[2]

[1] *Legenda maior*, iii, 9, 10.

[2] Compare the *Tredici Sermoni*, Sermo iii: 'Fuit nihilominus tertio elevatus a statu fructuoso ad statum gloriosum juxta illud I. Reg. 2: *Elevat pauperem, ut sedeat cum principibus*, inquam id est cum Apostolis, quibus dictum est: *Constitues eos principes super omnem terram*. Ad istum statum elevavit eum Deus per virtutem subjectivam, et per virtutem abjectivam, et per virtutem allectivam, prima est virtus obedientiae, sive humilitatis, secunda est virtus paupertatis, tertia est virtus castitatis.'

Bonaventura explains that when the friar who saw the vision of the Saint's heavenly throne had awoken from his trance he began to corverse with St. Francis about the things of God, without telling him what he had seen, and finally asked him what he thought of himself; to which question, we are told,

the humble servant of Christ answered . . .: 'I think myself the greatest of sinners.' When the Brother objected that he could not say or feel this with a clear conscience, Francis added, 'If any man, however guilty, had received such mercy from Christ as I have done, I truly think that he would have been much more acceptable to God than I.' And so, through the hearing of such marvellous humility, the Brother was assured of the truth of the vision that had been shown him, knowing by the witness of the Holy Gospel that the truly humble shall be exalted to that excellent glory from which the proud are cast down.[1]

The intention of the designer of the frescoes to bring about an explicit association between the two outer scenes is manifest above all in the similarity of function, in a compositional sense, of the thrones in Scene IX and the arches and consoles supporting the ceiling of the papal hall in Scene VII, a similarity that extends to the repetition in both these areas of a dominant note of orange-yellow. The same concern to relate the two scenes explains the high position in the design that is given to the Pope in *The Sanctioning of the Rule* in comparison with the treatment of the figure in other early representations of this subject, such as the thirteenth-century fresco at Fabriano,[2] which otherwise resembles the Assisi composition fairly closely, and the scenes on the Bardi altarpiece at Santa Croce in Florence (Plate 54a)[3] and the altarpiece at Pistoia.[4] The story itself demanded that the Pope should be placed in a lofty position in relation to St. Francis; but that he should be elevated above the members of his retinue was necessitated, it would seem, chiefly by the decision to pair the figure compositionally with that of the angel in *The Vision of the Thrones*: in earlier representations his head is placed lower in the design than the heads of all the cardinals standing behind him.

Another significant feature of the composition that is absent from previous versions of the subject, and which was also excluded from the scene on the predella of Giotto's *Stigmatization of St. Francis* in the Louvre (Plate 27a), is the introduction of a cardinal, whose head alone is visible, behind the Pope's raised arm. In consequence of this addition, the row of five heads topping the group of cardinals combines with the curve of the Pope's *pallium* to create a pattern equivalent in value to that made by the angel's wings in *The Vision of the Thrones* (Scene IX, Plate 4a). The Pope's tall tiara and the haloed head of the angel rise slightly above these related forms, and the concordance is completed by the manner in which the long, downward flow of the angel's gesture repeats in reverse that of the Pope's left arm. This creation of compositional relationships

---

[1] *Legenda maior*, vi, 6.   [2] Van Marle, op. cit., i, Fig. 235.
[3] G. Kaftal, op. cit., No. 122 *c* 13.   [4] Ibid., No. 122 *e* 13.

between scenes so different in character is extraordinarily skilful and ingenious, and it will be observed that the figures of St. Francis, the Pope, and the seated cardinal in the richly embroidered cope are arranged to make up a simple triad of forms which is echoed (again in reverse) by the more open disposition of the figures of St. Francis, the angel, and the friar in Scene IX. Indeed, it was the challenge presented by these specific creative problems at Assisi, more than any factor other than the desire to give the story of the Poverello a new conviction of reality, that transformed and enriched the Franciscan iconography, changing the older modes of representation and breaking down much that was fixed and rigid in the tradition. A case in point is the inclusion in the group of cardinals of one seated figure, which adds variety to the group as a whole. This figure was retained by Giotto, both in the Louvre predella scene and in *The Confirmation of the Rule* in the Bardi Chapel, and it is still to be found in Gozzoli's fresco at Montefalco: but its origins almost certainly lie in the desire of the Assisi Master to create a form in the corner of his composition equivalent to that of the kneeling friar in *The Vision of the Thrones* (Plates 56, 57c), a figure essential to the iconography of that scene.

A still closer examination of the means by which Scenes VII and IX have been brought into harmony, notwithstanding their dissimilarity of content, will clarify further the compositional principles and methods of the designer of the *Legend*. It has been pointed out that the main diagonal established by the relationship of the kneeling St. Francis to the Pope in Scene VII finds its mirror-image in Scene IX in the gesture of the angel's right arm: in each scene, however, this motif is crossed by a secondary movement associated with a gesturing hand—in Scene VII that of the Pope, raised in blessing; in Scene IX that of the friar, pointing upwards. In each case the result is to produce an 'axis rising diagonally from the figure in the corner. If we examine this pattern of shapes in *The Sanctioning of the Rule* (Scene VII, Plate 53) we can see how regular and ordered it is, and how abstract in character is the harmony that underlies the disposition of the figures. The pattern itself may be likened to the form of a crossbow, of which the shaft is the axis defined by the Pope's right hand and the bow the long, curving line which flows from his head to that of St. Francis through their respective left and right arms and the parchment held between them.

It is the same motif that relates the figure of the Pope to that of St. Francis in Scene VI (*The Dream of Innocent III*, Plate 52), and the shaft-like architrave of the Lateran Church in the same fresco to the equated forms of the campanile and the tensed figure of the Saint. It can be found again in Scene VIII (*The Vision of the Chariot*, Plate 55) as the means of relating the Saint's haloed head, at the top of the composition, to the gesticulating friars below; it no less obviously underlies the dramatically pointing hands that activate the designs of Scene X (*The Exorcism of the Devils at Arezzo*, Plate 58) and Scene XI (*St. Francis before the Sultan*, Plate 61); and the same concept, the same 'abstract imagery' of design, is implicit in Scene XIV (*The Miracle of the Spring*, Plate 64) in the relationship between the Saint's head, at the centre of the composition, and the arched form of the drinking muleteer.

Very frequently in the Assisi cycle this pattern of forms is based upon a hand pointing into or out from the corner of the composition (or, it may be, of some rectangular section of it)—as in Scenes VII, IX, X, XV, and XVI. It is strange, if Giotto was the creator of the *Legend* in the Upper Church, that he should invariably have avoided such a practice in the entire body of his work in the Arena Chapel and at Santa Croce. It is not perhaps insignificant that in his fresco of *The Confirmation of the Rule by Honorius III* in the Bardi Chapel, which owes much to *The Sanctioning of the Rule* at Assisi (the two subjects of the initial Sanctioning of the Rule by Innocent III and the subsequent Confirmation of the Rule by Honorius III being virtually interchangeable in this period), the Pope's hand is lowered from its position in the Assisi fresco so that its angle is not directed towards the corner of the room. Where, as in the figure of Herod in *The Massacre of the Innocents* (Plate 24*b*) in the Arena Chapel, a pointing hand might well have been aligned with one corner of the composition, it is always Giotto's practice to direct it slightly off that point. Such differences are worthy of close attention, for it is in an artist's inclination towards particular types of 'abstract imagery' that some of his deepest aesthetic preoccupations are revealed.

To isolate this particular form would be of slighter consequence if it did not recur so often in the cycle. We may also take notice of the fact that this was one of the St. Cecilia Master's favourite compositional devices. The most obvious instance of its use by the St. Cecilia Master is to be seen in the graceful figure of the man stirring the fire in the martyrdom scene on the Uffizi altarpiece (Plate 8); but it is normally associated with a pointing or gesturing hand, as in the third scene of the altarpiece, representing the crowning of Valerian by an angel, where St. Cecilia, seated to the right, gestures with one hand towards her husband, who is entering the room from the left: the implied line that connects the two figures along the angle of St. Cecilia's forearm terminates at the centre of Valerian's head, on either side of which a kind of bracket is formed by his right shoulder and upper arm and by the head and visible arm of the angel. The second scene of the altarpiece (*St. Cecilia Urges Valerian to Conversion*) shows the same principle at work, and once again the implicit line lies at an oblique angle. In the preceding scene of the wedding banquet St. Cecilia is related in an identical manner to the servant bending over the table—the gesturing hand of the woman who is conversing with her playing the shaft, so to speak, to the bow of the servant's arms. Several other examples of the use of this motif are to be found in both the Uffizi and Montici altarpieces. In general, however, the resultant pattern of forms (even when allowance has been made for the difference of scale) possesses a quality of nervous delicacy absent from the bolder forms of the St. Francis Master. This type of geometrizing has its origins in much earlier traditions, and in Florentine painting of the mid-thirteenth century a similar approach to design, in the context of a Byzantinizing style, is to be found, for example, in the 'Maestro del S. Francesco Bardi' (Plate 54a).

In the hands of the designer of the Assisi cycle, the need to impose an ordered pattern upon visible reality becomes an overriding principle, and his skill as a composer is such that it enables him to harmonize the most disparate forms. Often, his instinct for pattern leads him to give an equal emphasis to inanimate objects and human beings: he even dares to play off the apse and chancel of the church in *The Vision of the Thrones* (Scene IX) against the closely knit group of friars kneeling behind St. Francis in *The Sanctioning of the Rule* (Scene VII, Plate 4a). It is understandable that this group should often have been criticized as an example of a faulty realization of space, since the various heads are heaped up, one above another, in a manner that allows those at the back to loom up above those in front (Plate 54c): but the reason for this anomaly evidently lies in an approach to spatial problems that regards their solution as being of secondary importance to the creation of a two-dimensional harmony of design.

A similar group appears in the sixth scene of the Uffizi altarpiece (*St. Cecilia Preaching*), where a comparable heaping of the figures results in a near-oval shape, of great regularity, which lies like a disc against the rectangle formed by the lower room of a little house. The kneeling friars in the fresco in the Upper Church are compressed into precisely the same kind of formation, which overlaps the rectangular plane of the far wall of the audience-chamber. It seems clear that it was the St. Cecilia Master's purpose to relate this oval form to the arching rhythms of the figures in the other scenes in the upper register. It does not follow that a similar intention lies behind the design of *The Sanctioning of the Rule* at Assisi; but such an inference does begin to make sense of a passage that might otherwise seem inexplicable except in terms of artistic failure. Attention may first be drawn to the fact that the blue tapestry, embroidered with a pattern of rich plum, which hangs at the back of the papal hall in *The Sanctioning of the Rule* (Scene VII) is drawn aside to disclose a brilliantly lit patch of wall, and so to provide an accent of light corresponding to the outer wall of the chapel which runs parallel to the right edge of Scene IX, and which is no less strongly illuminated. The consoles supporting the vault of the papal hall in Scene VII also catch the light, so that these accented forms, in combination with the huddled group of friars in the same scene, act as a counterpoise to the brightly lit chapel in the other fresco. The piling-up of the friars' heads helps to give substance and weight to the total 'image', and the resulting curvilinear form, which is echoed by the apse in Scene IX, may well have been the fruit of very deliberate calculation. From the evidence provided by the compositional ordering of the cycle as a whole, it would undoubtedly appear that the creation of concordances between forms so unlike in character came as naturally to the designer of the *Legend* as other expected harmonies, such as that between the open expanse of sky in Scene IX and the blue tapestry in Scene VII (now greatly reduced in splendour, since much painting *a secco* has come away).

Once again, as we have observed, perspective is enlisted in the ordering of the group of three frescoes in terms of an essentially two-dimensional pattern. As in the previous two bays, the perspective system established on the right side of the first scene is carried into the left side of the next: hence the oblique perspective of the building in *The Vision of the Chariot* (Scene VIII, Plate 55). But the most striking instance of this principle of two-dimensional design is to be found in *The Vision of the Thrones* (Scene IX, Plate 56), where the perspective system seems at first sight quite arbitrary, so inconsistent is it with every logic of spatial composition. To begin with, it may be noticed that the altar and the chancel steps are seen from above, and the apse, with its roof, from below: there is no cause for puzzlement here, since the spectator's viewpoint in all the frescoes corresponds to the height of a standing figure, and the altar lies below this level. What seems so disconcerting to the modern eye is that while the apse is represented at an oblique angle as being viewed from a point to the right of centre, the thrones of heaven are seen from a point to the left of centre—an impossiblity, unless the laws of optics be transcended in that sphere.[1] Nevertheless, there is nothing in the least arbitrary about this arrangement. In accordance with the abiding principle of linear design which was the ideal of the designer of the cycle, the spectator's eye, having been led up to the chariot at the top of Scene VIII, must now, in the final scene in the bay, be guided down again to the kneeling figure of St. Francis (Plate 4a). For this purpose the angel's gesture must have been considered insufficient in itself; and a series of slanting lines, running parallel to the angel's arm, was therefore established by the representation of the five thrones in an oblique perspective determined by a viewpoint to the left of centre. But to have applied the same system to the chancel, with its projecting roof, would have been to defeat this purpose by producing orthogonals slanting the other way: the chancel, accordingly, was represented as being viewed from a point to its right. Only in the altar and the chancel steps are such orthogonals permitted to rise in the opposite direction, and they, we find, are given the function of echoing in reverse the receding lines of the Pope's footstool in Scene VII. It may be added that the same principle of linear design accounts for the representation of the heavenly thrones from above rather than from below: there is a precedent for this apparent exception to the normal rule in the outer stairway in Scene V.

[1] Professor White has suggested that the painter's intention may have been to show 'a change from one reality to another, from a material to a visionary world' (J. White, *The Birth and Rebirth of Pictorial Space*, p. 33). This interesting explanation, however, does not account for similar anomalies and spatial ambiguities in other parts of the cycle.

The principles governing the treatment of perspective in the cycle cannot be understood in terms of a thoroughgoing attempt to conquer the three-dimensional world, in a realistic sense, but only in the context of a wholly consistent and logical application of the laws of two-dimensional decoration, and the paradox is that such a task could not have been achieved by the painters of the *Legend* without their availing themselves of the very terms and elements of an emergent perspective theory. Until this aesthetic principle is recognized for what it is, the variations in the use of perspective from one fresco to another—giving a centralized view here, an oblique view there, and apparent anomalies almost everywhere—will seem arbitrary and inexplicable, and may even lead to unwarranted conclusions about the supposedly 'advanced' style of certain scenes in comparison with others. Approached as it has been from the point of view of Giotto's quite different conception of pictorial space, the cycle has inevitably been misunderstood, and critics on the one hand have strained themselves to claim for it qualities that lay outside the intentions of its authors, and on the other have failed to do justice to its actual virtues.

In fact, no style could have been better fitted to the requirements of the subject-matter, which demanded that the life of St. Francis should be treated neither as heroic drama nor as mere narrative, but as a model and pattern of the *imitatio Christi*, in which earthly events were to be shown to have both a human and a theological dimension. No purely pictorial problem, no insistence upon the logic of realistic representation, such as might have given rise to doubts concerning the validity of the conventions accepted for the treatment of space and perspective, could be allowed to obscure the clarity of that pattern. The compositional relationships established between *The Sanctioning of the Rule* and *The Vision of the Thrones* not only serve pictorial or aesthetic ends, but also expound the lesson of that great humility which entitled St. Francis to a place among the angels: the humility laid before us in the first scene and the reward promised in the other are linked together by the language of this style as effectively as in the reasoned argument of the *Legenda maior* itself.

The story of the heavenly throne reserved for St. Francis reminds us that from an early stage in the history of the Franciscan Order the Poverello of Assisi was identified with the angel of the Apocalypse who 'bore the seal of the living God'.[1] Still more significantly, he was revered as an *alter Christus* of almost divine status; and such was the cult of St. Francis by the later years of the fourteenth century that a friar attached to a Silvestrine monastery near Assisi could protest that the Saint was being made into a new god.[2] By

---

[1] Cf., for example, Jacopo da Voragine, *Serm. 2 de S. Franc.*: 'Christus ante primum adventum, qui erat misericordiae, praemisit Angelum, scilicet beatum Joannem Baptistam: ante vero secundum adventum suae justitiae, praemisit alterum Angelum, scilicet B. Franciscum.'

[2] '. . . quod fratres sic predicantes et commendantes beatum Franciscum de suis virtutibus et miraculis, fingunt et faciunt in mundo unum novum deum' (*Acta Inquisitoris Umbriae Fr. Angeli de Assisio contra Stigmata S. Francisci Negantem contra Fraticellos Aliosque, A[nno] 1361*', in *Archivum Franciscanum Historicum*, xxiv (1931), 63 ff.).

the end of the century the pious fervour that had woven so many legends about St. Francis's name had produced in the *De Conformitate* an elaborate system of comparisons between his ministry and that of Christ. It is this same belief in St. Francis of Assisi as an *alter Christus* that illumines the further comparisons that had long been drawn with such prophets as Moses and Elijah, who had themselves prefigured the Saviour.

The allusion to the ascension of Elijah implicit in *The Vision of the Chariot* should therefore be seen in the wider context of the theme of St. Francis's likeness to Christ, whom the story of the Transfiguration compares with both Elijah and Moses, and of whose Ascension the ascent of Elijah in the fiery chariot was the type. The image of the chariot and horses in the Assisi fresco itself suggests an ultimate iconographic origin in scenes of Elijah's ascension (see Plate 35*d*), so that an allusion to the story of Elijah is embedded no less in the painter's interpretation of the subject than it is in such literary accounts as those of the *Legenda maior*, the *De Conformitate*, and the *Legenda Monacensis*. In the words of the *De Conformitate*, 'Octava figura est de Elia in curru igneo asportato, IV. Reg. 2, 11. Sanctus Franciscus in curru igneo transfiguratus apparuit fratribus'[1] ('The eighth figure is of Elijah carried off in the fiery chariot, 2 Kings 2 : 11. St. Francis appeared to the brothers transfigured in a fiery chariot'); this passage being a condensation of Bonaventura's narrative in the *Legenda maior*, where also St. Francis is described as being 'transfigured':

Intellexerunt namque concorditer omnes, videntibus invicem universis in cordibus singulorum, sanctum patrem absentem corpore, praesentem spiritu tali transfiguratum effigie, supernis irradiatum fulgoribus et ardoribus inflammatum supernaturali virtute in curru splendente simul et igneo sibi demonstrari a Domino, ut tamquam veri Israelitae post illum incederent, qui virorum spiritualium, ut alter Elias, factus fuerat a Deo currus et auriga.[2]

(For truly they all with one accord understood, when they looked into each other's hearts, that although their holy father was absent in body he was present in spirit, and that through the operation of a supernatural miracle he was being shown to them by God transfigured in this way, radiant with heavenly brightness and on fire with heat, in a shining and fiery chariot, so that they, as Israelites indeed, might follow after him, since he had been made by God, like another Elijah, the chariot and horseman of spiritual men.)

To the author of the *De Conformitate* the story in the Book of Kings was prophetic not only of the Transfiguration of Christ but also of the 'transfiguration' of St. Francis himself; and, as the Franciscan equivalent of the Transfiguration, the story told by Bonaventura inevitably became one of the most important in the entire tradition. It is understandable therefore that it should have been chosen as the dominant subject in this section of the Assisi cycle (Plates 4*a*, 55).

The bronze-red colouring given to the figure of St. Francis and to the chariot and

---

[1] *De Conformitate*, Liber i, Fructus i, Pars Secunda, 4.   [2] *Legenda maior*, iv, 4.

horses denotes the fiery heat which according to the *Legenda maior* emanated from the
visionary forms: originally the radiance of the Saint's image must have been far more
splendid than it is today, for the gilt striations on his habit—similar to those on Christ's
mantle in Scene XXVII (Plate 92*a*)—as well as the gilt used to represent the rays of
light around him, have largely disappeared. In Taddeo Gaddi's panel in the Accademia
the whole image radiates incandescence, and flames leap up before and behind St.
Francis.[1]

Like the scene at Siena, on the panel by a follower of Guido da Siena referred to
earlier,[2] Taddeo Gaddi's representation of the subject omits the horses, which are not
explicitly mentioned in the *Legenda maior* but which contribute at Assisi to the comparison with Elijah. The treatment of the horses in the Assisi fresco suggests that the
artist may have been aware of a particular classical model: possibly he had in mind the
bronze horses of San Marco in Venice, or representations of *quadrigae* on ancient sarcophagi.[3] The ordered repetition of the horses' movements, scarcely thinkable in the art
of Giotto, and anticipating, rather, the measured geometrizing of an Uccello, is, however, echoed in a strikingly similar image of paired horses which is to be found in one
of the illustrations produced by Pacino's shop for a manuscript of Villani's *Chronicle*
(Plate 47*a, b*): this little scene, depicting an incident related of a miraculous crucifix at
S. Miniato, may well reflect a knowledge both of this fresco and of Scene IV at Assisi
(Plate 46), to which it is closely related in subject-matter. Although it is slight in execution, and rather poor in the quality of its draughtsmanship, the drawing faithfully
repeats several features of the Assisi horses, and the treatment of the rear legs, executed in
three tones which descend, according to their proximity to the spectator, from extreme
light to extreme dark, is virtually identical with that of the Assisi master.

Despite the sculptural roundness of their forms the horses in the Assisi fresco remain
strangely unreal, even when allowance has been made for the unearthly nature of this
epiphany, and the absence of any harness attaching them to the chariot is not less
remarkable than the ambiguity of their relationship to the surrounding space. The
chariot rests upon the roof of the friars' dormitory, and sets the beholder wondering how
it ever arrived there. Evidently the designer of the fresco was less concerned to express
the movement of the visionary horses and chariot within a real space than to create an
equilibrium of rounded and rectangular forms dominating his design.

Basically, the composition may be described as a cohesion of four distinct and almost
equal parts, comprising the top right-hand quarter of the picture-area, which contains
the figure of St. Francis and the horses, the top left-hand quarter containing the upper

---

[1] Sinibaldi and Brunetti, op. cit., Pl. 137*s*.   [2] Stubblebine, op. cit., Fig. 61.
[3] Cecchi saw in the horses a marked Hellenistic quality: cf. E. Cecchi, *Giotto*, p. 16. Cecchi also drew attention to the
antique character of the shrubs and acanthus leaves decorating the chariot.

storeys of the building, the bottom left-hand quarter containing the area of the building below the level of the chariot-wheels, and the remaining section containing the three friars who have observed the vision together. The right edge of the building forms the central vertical division, and the lower roofs of the building the horizontal division, of this partition of the design into quarters. A series of repetitions of a formal, or 'abstract', nature from one section of the design to another assists in giving an essentially symmetrical *stasis* to the whole: the great curve of the prancing horses is continued in the group of three friars below, descending through the raised arm of the central figure; the rising levels of the roofs on the left repeat, in a curious way, the upward-stepping motion of the horses; the pediment of the little alcove that abuts on the façade establishes a triangular motif which is repeated in the group of sleeping friars; and the three standing friars are so designed that they create a solid rectangular form analogous to that of the three-aisled building. Considered almost in terms of a geometrical exercise, the composition hangs together in a remarkably satisfying manner: otherwise, it would be virtually incomprehensible as a design, and still more incomprehensible as a centre-piece in the decoration of the bay.

X

NORTH WALL: FIRST BAY

(SCENES X–XIII)

THE ORGANIZATION OF THE LARGE BAY at the lower end of the north wall (Plate 4b), containing four instead of the usual three frescoes, is based on the same system of ascending and descending rhythms that underlies the decoration of the previous bay, and the linear pattern of these rhythms again accounts for the treatment of perspective in each scene. Neither here nor in the corresponding group of four scenes on the south wall, directly opposite, is there any question of a departure from the principles that give unity to each of the smaller bays containing three scenes.

The narrative opens with the story of Brother Silvester's exorcism of the demons at Arezzo (Scene X), passes to the Poverello's mission with Brother Illuminatus to the Sultan of Egypt and the confounding of the Muslim priests by the threatened test of fire (Scene XI), continues with the friars' vision of Christ's appearance to St. Francis as he is borne aloft in ecstasy in a cloud (Scene XII), and concludes with the institution of the Christmas crib, or *presepio*, at Greccio (Scene XIII). The four frescoes combine with the pair of scenes on the east wall and the four scenes in the first bay of the south wall to illustrate ten of the most important episodes in the ministry of St. Francis, revealing different aspects of his sainthood to which the *Legenda maior* devotes separate chapters, and underlining his likeness to Christ. This group of ten scenes concludes the earthly life of the Saint: the last three bays on the south wall are devoted entirely to the events surrounding his death, ascension, and canonization, and to his posthumous miracles.

The Exorcism of the Demons at Arezzo (Scene X, Plate 58)[1] is divided into two principal areas by the towering architectural forms of the cathedral,[2] decorated with some fluently drawn reliefs, which include a *putto* holding two swans by the neck (Plate 60a),

---

[1] *Legenda maior*, vi, 9.

[2] Schmarsow noted certain resemblances to Autun and other northern Gothic churches: cf. A. Schmarsow, op. cit., pp. 27 ff.

and the walled city. A rift of blue sky lies between. The centre of the stage is dominated by the figure of Brother Silvester (Plate 57*a*), who is aligned with the vertical mass of the cathedral much as Pietro Bernardone, in Scene V, is aligned with the *palazzo* behind him, and like Bernardone he strides forward to invade the empty central area. The gesture of his right arm releases a long, ascending movement which is supported by the inclined body of the kneeling Saint and continued in the ever-rising conglomeration of cube-like buildings representing the city of Arezzo. The oblique perspective of the buildings reinforces this movement, and Brother Silvester's imperious command sets the demons (Plate 60*b*)[1] flying in the same direction. Passing into the next fresco (Scene XI), the movement is carried to the right by the green building on the left side of the composition, and as this building is viewed from the same oblique angle as the city in Scene X, the inclined orthogonal of its roof slopes upwards from that scene. It then climbs still higher through the similar orthogonal defining the top of the Sultan's palace. At this point—at the exact centre of the bay—it begins to descend, the downward motion being already stated in the inclined plane formed by the visible side of the canopy of the Sultan's throne: directed by the perspectival treatment of the building in Scene XII, the eye is led down gradually to that place between earth and heaven where St. Francis communes with Christ, and it will be observed that Christ's hand is angled in exact conformity with the same slow declivity. From this scene of rapt communion the long pictorial movement descends at last through the lines of the pulpit in Scene XIII to finish its course in the lower right-hand corner of the composition, where St. Francis embraces the Christ-Child (Plate 4*b*); the perspectival rendering of the crib, the altar, and the base of the lectern in Scene XIII assists in directing the eye to this point (Plate 63). The diagonal that initiates the whole vast sweep of this linear pattern in the opening scene is thus reversed in the last; and, as in the previous bay, the movement begins and ends with a representation of the kneeling Saint.

The frescoes are harmonized further by a clear-cut division in each between an upper and a lower field, which is seen at its most obvious in the almost unbroken line of the choir-screen in *The Christmas Crib at Greccio* (Scene XIII). The corresponding division in *The Exorcism at Arezzo* (Scene X) is less apparent at first, but it is still present, for the function of the façade of the cathedral, upon which the apse abuts, and of the green roofs of the houses in the city is precisely this. As elsewhere in the cycle, the uppermost areas denote the heavenly or spiritual world, and the lower areas the earthly: so in Scenes XII and XIII the 'heavenly' region contains, respectively, the figure of Christ and a crucifix, the significance of which we shall examine presently; but in Scene X the upper field has been invaded by demons, and in Scene XI (Plate 61) the pinnacles of the building on the left, evidently intended for a Muslim temple, are surmounted by pagan statues.

---

[1] For similar demonic figures by Pacino see Plate 60*d*.

Throughout the bay, all the action takes place in the lower areas of the compositions, save only in the two passages in Scenes X and XII containing the demons and the figure of Christ (Plate 4*b*). Different eyes will no doubt interpret such matters in different ways; but it would seem that the designer of the *Legend* was anxious to disguise this imbalance in order to maintain a general symmetry of arrangement within the bay as a whole. Such an intention would explain the association that has been brought about between the demons in Scene X and the grotesques represented on the pinnacles of the temple in Scene XI, demonic figures like those bedevilling the city of Arezzo: indeed, as the demon on the very right of Scene X is partly cut off by the border and column separating the two frescoes, and the grotesque on the very left of Scene XI likewise, the one form seems to reappear in the guise of the other. But at the other end of the bay, in striking contrast to the unholy beings that preside over the temple of the Infidel, and which are so fittingly associated with the malign influences infesting the warring city of Arezzo, four tall candles, symbolic of the four Gospels, stand upon the pulpit represented in Scene XIII, in the area adjacent to the figure of Christ in Scene XII, their vertical lines echoing those of the pinnacles of the Muslim temple. The demons and the grotesques on the one hand and the heavenly Christ and the pulpit with its candlesticks on the other are thus paired together, and their association is reinforced by the use of colour: the dominant red colouring of the demonic assembly is repeated in Christ's draperies, and the clean white of the front pinnacles of the temple recurs in the candles and in much of the pulpit. In consequence of this skilful arrangement the emphasis is shifted to the centre of each of the two conjoined fields—that is to say, to the twisted columns separating the first two and the last two scenes. In this way the symmetrical balance of the whole bay is restored.

Since the bay contains four rather than three scenes, its central division coincides with the central column separating the second and third frescoes. This is accepted as the natural stress, and the two inner scenes are paired on either side of it, like blot-patterns on the pages of an open book. The Sultan's palace and canopied throne in Scene XI and the yellow building with its red and green towers in Scene XII face outwards from one another on either side of the central column, behind which the orthogonals resulting from their representation in oblique perspective are visualized as meeting. In the same way the general movement of the figures is also outwards from the centre of the bay, and the same tendency is repeated in the outer scenes by the little figures emerging from the gateways in *The Exorcism at Arezzo* and by the laymen and other figures in *The Christmas Crib at Greccio*. This outward movement is finally reversed by the enclosure of the entire scheme by figures facing inwards from the extremities of the bay.

In the *Fioretti* St. Francis is represented on several occasions as exorcizing devils by making the sign of the Cross, and, although the text of the *Legenda maior* offers no help in the matter, it is presumably that action that is expressed in the Assisi fresco by the gesture of Brother Silvester's right arm. If this is so, there is added point in the representation of a crucifix, seen from the back, in the corresponding fresco at the other end of the bay (Scene XIII, Plate 63); for it was upon the Cross that Christ, by his own 'obedience unto death', vanquished the power of Satan. It is worthy of notice also that in Scene X one of the demons fleeing from the city separates himself from his companions, flying outwards towards the centre of the composition, his red wings spread wide, his arms raised above his head, and his feet apart, so that his whole form, tilted slightly to one side, becomes a satanic parody of the inclined crucifix, with its triangular support, in the other fresco. But a still greater significance attaches to the crucifix, as an image which the spectator's eye at once associates with the figure of St. Francis in Scene XII—represented with his arms stretched out as though upon a cross.

Evidently it was the intention of the designer of the cycle to play off the city wall in Scene X, which ends in a turreted gate, against the squarish mass formed by the members of the congregation on the left-hand side of Scene XIII, behind whom there stand two friars, their heads towering above the group. The same thinking seems to have determined the shapes and proportions of many other forms in these two outer scenes: the deep fissure, for instance, that cleaves the rocky ground in front of the city wall in Scene X, as though the town had been rent by earthquake no less than by internecine strife, creates a pattern of splayed forms echoing that delightful rhythm of feet which gives such a decorative quality to the group of laymen in Scene XIII; the red spire of the cathedral in Scene X rises high above the topmost tower of the city, precisely as the red-roofed *baldacchino* in Scene XIII rises above the pulpit; the opening in the choir-screen in Scene XIII, which allows the blue of the background to invade the lower area of the composition, and in which there stand women in blue cloaks, corresponds to the central void of sky in Scene X.

The formalized character of Brother Silvester's gesture (Plate 57*a*) is made all the more emphatic by the curved sweep of the voluminous sleeve, which relates to other curvilinear motifs in the figure, similar to those present in the kneeling friar in Scene IX (Plate 57*c*). A distinctive feature of this type of gesture, which seems quite uncharacteristic of Giotto, is the emphasis placed upon the left hand, which is drawn around the figure to its near side. Variants of this idiom are found elsewhere in the cycle, and they occur also in Pacino (Plate 57*b*), just as there are figures by Pacino that discourse with pointing hand in the manner of the kneeling friar in Scene IX (Plate 98*d*). It may be added in respect of another aspect of Scene X that some of Pacino's miniatures contain architectural forms not unlike those represented in the fresco,[1] although the resemblances

---

[1] For the scenes, illustrated here, from the Vatican MS. of Villani's *Chronicle* (Plates 45, 57*a, c*), cf. Luigi Magnani, *La Cronaca figurata di Giovanni Villani* (Rome: Città del Vaticano, 1936).

are not exact (Plate 59*a–c*). Pacino's architectural tastes will be considered later in the context of his general debt to the St. Francis Master.

The figure of Brother Silvester seems to have been painted by an assistant. A similar style can be seen in the figure of the friar standing towards the centre of Scene VIII (Plate 55), in the previous bay, and in that of the kneeling friar in Scene IX (Plate 55*c*). These last two figures are unquestionably by the same hand, and the workmanship seems to be different from that of the St. Francis Master himself: the heads show a rhythmic fluidity of handling which delights in uninterrupted curves, and the formation of such features as the mouth and the ears is also quite distinctive.

Altogether there is evidence of a greater participation by assistants in the execution of the later scenes on the north wall than in the fourth and third bays (Scenes I–VI), and their intervention is particularly noticeable in Scenes XI and XIII in the first bay. Such, however, are the intricacies of the whole practice of the use of assistants in fresco-painting in this period that it is not always possible to discern their presence or to determine whether a particular passage was executed by more than one hand. It would have been perfectly possible, for instance, for the *capomaestro* to entrust an assistant with the laying in of a head or some other form, and then to go over the whole area himself, or, alternatively, to correct or modify a passage begun and brought to completion by an assistant. Nevertheless, there are certain cases at Assisi where the style and quality of the painting leave us in no doubt that what we are looking at is not the personal handiwork of the master in charge of the cycle (or of one of its three principal stylistic divisions): in the first bay on the north wall we can feel this certainty, for example, about the figures of the soldiers of the guard in Scene XI and those of the priest and the two acolytes in Scene XIII, all of which are of a markedly inferior quality.

In Scene XI (*St. Francis before the Sultan*, Plate 61)[1] the tension between the two principal figures—St. Francis, standing next to Brother Illuminatus at the centre of the composition, and the Sultan, seated on his splendid canopied throne, the base of which, it may be noted, is embossed with richly gilded figurines of lions (Plate 60*c*)—recalls the disposition of St. Francis and his father in Scene V (Plate 48). The two figures confront one another across a similar vacuum of sky, and their relationship to the architectural structures behind them follows a no less familiar pattern: like Bernardone in Scene V, St. Francis half-detaches himself from the rectangular field established by the temple, while the Sultan's arm abruptly invades the central void across a strongly defined vertical. For all its subtlety, the design as a whole is still predominantly two-dimensional. The Sultan's throne recedes into no real space, for as soon as we begin to follow its recession we are brought abruptly to a halt by the vertical plane of the sky, which, so far from being an envelope of space opening up behind the cramped solids

---

[1] *Legenda maior*, ix, 8.

of the figures and the architecture, seems in effect to be no less impenetrable than they; and it hangs, like a sheet, so far forward that its lower edge coincides almost with the front planes of the architectural forms: there is no room for the buildings in the shallow space suggested.

The composition lingers in the memory on account of the clarity and charm of the storytelling, the splendour of the colour, and the magnificence of the setting.[1] Yet the most interesting and expressive of the figures is neither St. Francis nor the Sultan but the aged Muslim priest departing in fear on the left, accompanied by three others. These figures may owe something to the representations on the Columns of Trajan and Marcus Aurelius of barbarians fleeing from the advancing Roman troops, although their immediate iconographical origin is perhaps to be sought in the group of Muslims in the scene of *St. Clare Repulsing the Saracens* on Guido da Siena's Reliquary Shutters (Plate 31), a composition that seems also to lie behind the treatment of the Clarisse in Scene XXIII (*St. Francis Mourned by St. Clare*). The figure of the white-bearded priest is remarkable for its vigorous *contrapposto* and lively movement.[2]

St. Francis's journey to the domains of the Sultan had been occasioned both by the desire to convert the unbelievers and by a longing to suffer martyrdom for Christ's sake, and the pairing of Scene XI at Assisi with *The Ecstasy of St. Francis* (Scene XII, Plate 62) at the centre of the bay may well have been intended to contain an allusion to this circumstance: the *Ecstasy* certainly anticipates the martyrdom of La Verna, and just as in the two final scenes in the first bay of the south wall, directly opposite, the Saint is likened to the Seraphic Christ, so here he is associated by analogy with the crucifix in *The Christmas Crib at Greccio*. In its most important aspect, then, the subject of Scene XII looks ahead to the glory of the *stigmata*; but it is also the conclusion of the story of the Saint's temptation in desert places, which is the counterpart in the Franciscan legend of the Temptation of Christ, and the setting of the story accounts for the suggestion of a rocky steep, surmounted by little trees, in one corner of the composition. In the *Legenda maior* St. Francis is described as 'uttering loud laments for the Lord's Passion, as though it was visibly present before him'. As the brethren watch in wonder, he appears to them in ecstatic prayer, 'his hands stretched out in the manner of a cross, his whole body uplifted from the earth and surrounded by a shining cloud, as though the wondrous refulgence that enveloped his body were the witness to the marvellous lustre of his mind'. Caught up in mystic communion with Christ, St. Francis is shown 'the dark and hidden things of the Divine Wisdom'.[3] There is a strong flavour in this passage in

---

[1] The scene is represented on the Bardi altarpiece at Santa Croce (G. Kaftal, op. cit., Fig. 460), but the fire is not shown: St. Francis and Brother Illuminatus appear on the left; the Sultan is seated on his throne on the very right, with a guard at his side; in the centre there is a large congregation, including the Muslim priests.

[2] On the Muslim priests see also E. Battisti, *Giotto*, p. 41.

[3] *Legenda maior*, x, 4.

the *Legenda maior* of the Johannine discourses of Christ with the Father: like Christ, Francis is made to understand mysteries veiled from ordinary men.

Presented in the first scene in the bay as one possessing authority, like Christ, over the legions of Satan, and in the second as having power over the elements of Nature, St. Francis is here manifested to his disciples in the very likeness of the Crucified. In the final narrative in this sequence (Scene XIII, Plate 63) he becomes the guardian of the mystery of the Incarnation, and as he kneels before the empty crib which he has placed in the church the Child Jesus miraculously appears in his arms. In Franciscan tradition the Poverello became so intimately associated with the Festival of Christmas, by virtue of the story of his institution of the *presepio*, that the legend arose that he himself had been born in a stable. But the chief object of the story of Greccio as told by Bonaventura, and as reinterpreted by the designer of the Assisi cycle, was to illustrate the Saint's devotion to the Nativity, just as in the corresponding scene at the end of the opposite bay we are shown his devotion to the Cross of Christ. This theme is underlined in the following passage in the *Speculum perfectionis*:

Nam beatus Franciscus maiorem reverentiam habebat in Nativitate Domini, quam in ulla alia solemnitate Domini, quoniam, licet in aliis eius solemnitatibus Dominus salutem nostram operaretur, tamen ex quo natus fuit nobis, ut dicebat beatus Franciscus, oportuit nos salvari.[1]

(For St. Francis showed greater reverence at the time of the Nativity of our Lord than at any other of His feasts, because, as St. Francis himself used to say, our Lord worked our salvation at other feasts, but it was inevitable that we should be saved from the moment that He was born for us.)

While Franciscan legend ascribed the institution of the *presepio* to St. Francis himself, its origins lie in fact in more ancient traditions centred upon Bethlehem and Rome.[2] The veneration of the grotto in Bethlehem where Christ, like another Mithras, was believed to have been born can be traced to the fourth century, and we are told by St. Jerome that the Christmas Crib at Bethlehem was reverently adorned with gold and silver. In Rome, meanwhile, a similar cult was made possible by the institution of the Feast of the Nativity on the 25th of December, as a festival distinct from that of the Epiphany, and by the erection of the great church later to be known as Santa Maria Maggiore, which was specially dedicated to the observance of Christ's birth. Relics consisting of pieces of wood from the crib at Bethlehem were built into one of the altars, which thus became the *praesepe* upon which, at the Christmas Mass, the celebrant laid the consecrated Host, the *Corpus Christi*. The cult was subsequently imitated in

[1] *Speculum perfectionis*, 19, in *Documenta Antiqua Franciscana*, ii, ed. Fr. L. Lemmens, O.F.M. (Ad Claras Aquas [Quaracchi], Florence, 1901).

[2] Cf. L. Gougaud, 'La Crèche de Noel avant Saint François d'Assise', *Revue des Sciences religieuses*, ii (1922), 26 ff.; K. Young, 'Officium Pastorum: A Study of the Dramatic Developments within the Liturgy of Christmas', *Transactions of the Wisconsin Academy of Sciences, Arts and Letters*, xvii, Part i (1912), 299 ff.; E. Rosenthal, 'The Crib of Greccio and Franciscan Realism', *Art Bulletin*, xxxvi (Mar. 1954), 57 ff.

other churches, and from about the eleventh century it developed into the liturgical dramas of the *Officium Pastorum* and the *Officium Stellae*, performed by members of the clergy. Nevertheless, its popularization undoubtedly owed much to the example of St. Francis, and it was the memory of the tableau which he had arranged on that Christmas night at Greccio, with a living ox and ass and perhaps an image of the Christ-Child which later legend transformed into a miraculous manifestation of the divine presence, that was responsible for the setting up, every year, in innumerable churches and *piazze* throughout Italy—and indeed throughout western Europe—of Christmas cribs, combined now with wooden figures of the Holy Family, the shepherds, and the animals, around which carols were sung.

The Assisi fresco follows the iconography of the representation of this subject on the Bardi altarpiece (Plate 65b)[1] in setting the scene within a church, although according to the *Legenda maior* it took place in the open air; and, as in the liturgical drama, the *praesepe* is associated with the altar (Plate 63). Behind St. Francis stands a tall lectern, of gold or brass, an allusion to his chanting of the Christmas Gospel. Only one of the bystanders, the dignified gentleman in the red cloak and blue hat, seen on the left raising one hand and turning his head to the side, betrays the least surprise at the miracle: presumably he is John of Greccio, the only person, according to the *Legenda maior*, who saw the vision of the Christ-Child. (A similar figure appears in the same relative position in the scene on the Bardi altarpiece, but on the right side of the composition.)

In the execution of the fresco considerable attention was paid to the task of representing the four singing friars as naturalistically as possible. Their expressions are observed with great care, and the divisions in the *intonaco* suggest that these heads were painted very slowly. The realism of their treatment seems to have made a strong impression at the time, for copies of them appear soon after in a number of works of the early fourteenth century.[2] The workmanship of more than one painter is in evidence here, and the figures of the women in the entrance of the choir-screen, the heads represented behind the standing figures on the left, and those of the servers on the far right must all be ascribed to inferior assistants. The priest also suggests the intervention of a hand not certainly identifiable before this point, and this painter was probably responsible in addition for the Christ-Child and perhaps for the kneeling Saint.

A difficulty of a technical nature attended the painting—and indeed the composition —of this scene and of the scene directly opposite (*The Death of the Knight of Celano*, Plate 70), for the wall-areas are invaded by the masonry of the vaulting. A rounded corbel supporting an applied column penetrates the upper field of each scene: these two features,

---

[1] G. Kaftal, op. cit., Fig. 462.

[2] e.g. the fresco of *The Funeral of St. Clare* at Santa Chiara, Assisi; the panel of *The Funeral of St. Clare* in the Farnsworth Museum, Wellesley College, Northampton, U.S.A. (E. B. Garrison, op. cit., No. 342), and the scene of *The Funeral of St. Louis of Anjou* on the predella of Simone Martini's *St. Louis* altarpiece at Naples (1317) (G. Kaftal, op. cit., Fig. 731).

which bulge out a considerable distance from the wall, are not of equal length—that on the north wall extending only about a third of the way down the pictured area, and the other reaching to the middle of the fresco. Such obstructions would have presented the designer of the frescoes with a more awkward problem than that occasioned by the iconostasis which formerly spanned the nave at its west end; for the iconostasis could be set up in such a way that it divided the first and last scenes of the cycle at their centres, whereas the corbels at the east end of the nave had to lie off the centres of the compositions into which they irrupt. The difficulty, however, was skilfully surmounted.

In *The Christmas Crib at Greccio* (Scene XIII) the corbel was allowed to define a rectangular field within which was placed the representation of the pulpit; and where the corbel terminates the horizontal line of the choir-screen was drawn across the composition; while in the paired scene of *The Exorcism at Arezzo* (Scene X, Plate 4*b*) an equivalent area was reserved for the lofty towers rising above the city. The same art is no less in evidence in *The Death of the Knight of Celano* (Scene XVI): in both frescoes the distracting effect of the corbels has been minimized as far as possible, not merely by their being allowed to occupy an empty area of sky, but also by their assimilation with the very fabric of the design. Unequal though the quality of the painting in Scene XIII undoubtedly is, in necessary consequence of the participation of inferior hands, there lies behind it—and behind the cycle as a whole—the sensibility of a great composer who was concerned above all to pour the magic of the Franciscan legend into the mould of a harmonious geometry.

XI

THE EAST WALL

(SCENES XIV AND XV AND THE *MADONNA* AND *ANGEL* ROUNDELS)

THE LARGE ROUNDEL of the *Virgin and Child* and the two smaller roundels of *Angels* which occupy the space between the doorway and the great rose-window of the façade wall (Plate 5) are no mere *addenda* to the cycle, but allude to the special devotion of St. Francis to the Mother of God and to the 'inseparable ties of love' that bound him to 'the angelic spirits that burn with wondrous fire to approach God'.[1] It has already been pointed out that it is the east window—or perhaps rather the fresco of the *Madonna*—that provides the imagined source of light for all the scenes of the *Legend* except those in the fourth bay of each wall, and it may well have been the intention to express the idea of the Virgin as the source of spiritual light, and so to represent the terrestrial events of the *Legend* as being enacted *sub specie aeternitatis*. A similar conception seems to be present in the system of lighting in the Arena Chapel, where the source of pictorial light in the various scenes radiates from the enthroned Christ in *The Last Judgement* on the entrance wall, immediately below the principal window: there the entrance is at the west end of the nave, so that it is the scenes on the north wall that are illumined from the left and those on the south wall from the right.

Neither of the famous compositions flanking the doorway at Assisi—*The Miracle of the Spring* (Scene XIV, Plate 64) on the left and *The Sermon to the Birds* (Scene XV, Plate 68) on the right—can be fully appreciated in isolation, any more than any other scene elsewhere in the cycle. The decoration of the whole area of the wall beneath the large frescoes of *Pentecost* and *The Ascension*, belonging to the earlier Biblical cycle, is designed as a unity which embraces the roundel of the *Virgin and Child* at the centre, and the main pictorial movement of *The Miracle of the Spring* rises up towards the *Madonna* and the *Angels*; whence that of *The Sermon to the Birds* descends on the other side. St. Francis, as he kneels in prayer in Scene XIV, in his compassion for his thirsty mule-driver, seems to aspire towards the Virgin, the fount of mercy (Plate 5).

[1] *Legenda maior*, ix, 3.

The stylistic affinities between the roundel of the *Virgin and Child* (Plate 16a) and the *Madonna Enthroned* at S. Giorgio alla Costa in Florence (Plate 15b) have already been touched upon. Common to the S. Giorgio and Assisi *Madonnas* are the rounded form of the Virgin's head, the large, petal-like eyes, the emphasis upon the cylindrical form of the neck and, indeed, the character of the features in general.[1] The fingers are exceptionally long and slender (Plate 5), and when bent take on the appearance almost of claws, being articulated separately, rather than together according to the practice of Giotto— a peculiarity found both in the *Madonna* by the St. Cecilia Master at Montici (Plate 15a) and in the enthroned St. Cecilia of the Uffizi altarpiece (Plate 8). Moreover the Assisi *Madonna*, its deep blues and reds set against a light gold background, is informed with much the same quality of quiet and passive serenity that characterizes the S. Giorgio altarpiece.

Even more interesting, perhaps, are the resemblances between *The Miracle of the Spring* (Plate 64) and the final scene of the *Santa Cecilia* altarpiece (Plate 8), representing the saint's martyrdom. In both compositions two hills of unequal size slope down to meet slightly to one side of the principal figure, which is placed in the centre of the picture with the body aligned with the mass of the larger hill. The basic conception is one of near-symmetrical balance about the central figure—of a symmetry modified by the fixing of the meeting-point of the two hills a little to one side. The fundamental thinking is quite different from that of Giotto in the Arena Chapel, where the seven or eight open-air scenes in which a similar design might have been used provide not one instance of it: there is no case of hills meeting towards the centre of a composition in this way—in fact this seems to be deliberately avoided—and therefore no question of a comparable symmetry. Equally non-Giottesque is the sensibility that relates the figure to the central vacuum of sky by making a small portion of it—the Saint's haloed head in the Assisi fresco, St. Cecilia's hands and forearms in the scene on the altarpiece— jut into this empty space across the edge of the larger hill. A similar type of design can also be found in Pacino, whose treatment of landscape forms is scarcely distinguishable from that of the Assisi master. In the Morgan illustrations, already referred to, the resemblances are particularly striking (Plates 43, 67a, b). In such compositions by Pacino we find the same jagged shelves of rock, the same channelled declivities, the same splintered surfaces as at Assisi, as we also find a very similar type of tree, of which the irregular trunk and the straggling roots are especially characteristic (Plates 39c, 43, 67a); and, while his manuscript illuminations preserve a miniaturist convention for the rendering of foliage, the treatment is quite naturalistic in his panels, as in the *Christ at Gethsemane* on *The Tree of Life* (Plate 69a).

[1] A. Smart, 'The St. Cecilia Master and his School at Assisi', *The Burlington Magazine*, cii (1960), 431, Figs. 11 and 13; J. White, *Art and Architecture in Italy . . .*, p. 407, n. 9.

It is only necessary to compare the two friars (Plate 66 *a, b*) standing beside the mule with the two shepherds who greet the melancholy Joachim in the well-known scene in the Arena Chapel (Plate 18*b*), the one turning to the other much as the friar holding the bridle turns to his companion, to become even more aware of the gulf that divides the world of Giotto from that of the Assisi master. Of all the differences that come to mind, one is perhaps more significant than the rest, and this is that, whereas in the Arena fresco the two shepherds are brought into a dramatic relationship with the meditative Joachim —their arching forms curving to meet the sorrow of his drooping head—the heads and shoulders of the two friars, cut off by the form of the mule, make a little pattern which is repeated on the other side of the composition by the silhouettes of two trees. Giotto never equates figures and landscape forms in this manner. At Assisi, however, the paired heads and trees not only help to stabilize the design of *The Miracle of the Spring* but also serve the important function of harmonizing this scene with *The Sermon to the Birds*, where a similar emphasis, in relatively the same area of the composition, is given to the heads of St. Francis and his companion, a bird flying down to the ground, and a tuft of foliage growing from the other side of the great tree which dominates the scene (Plates 5, 68). (The motif of the flying bird is found occasionally in earlier representations, for example in a late thirteenth-century calendar-obituary at Valenciennes.)[1] The over-all balance on the east wall at Assisi is achieved largely by simple repetition, and the small and large hill in Scene XIV are weighed against the small and large tree in Scene XV. Damage to *The Sermon to the Birds* has to some extent upset the intended harmony: some of the birds have been obliterated, and others reduced to shadowy wraiths; but originally the Saint's spellbound congregation must have formed a larger and weightier mass, more comparable with that of the prone figure of the muleteer (Plate 65*a*) and giving much more activation to the lower area of the composition.

The muleteer, it will be recalled, was the one figure in the cycle that Vasari, in the second edition of his *Lives*, singled out for particular mention; and since then this figure has become a symbol of the new naturalism ushered in by Giotto. In reality, however, the whole treatment is very different from that of any figure by Giotto: in the arching sweep of the pose and in the elegant rhythms of the draperies it reflects a taste for the decorative and the graceful that is far removed from Giotto's ideal. On the other hand, something of this quality is carried over into the miniaturist art of Pacino, where the figure-design often shows similarities in its emphasis upon rhythmic associations of curvilinear shapes: an example is the figure of the young man pouring water into wine-bottles in the Morgan *Wedding at Cana* (Plate 65*c*), although of course the treatment is far more formalized and the scale tiny. To make this comparison is not to ignore the differences that separate Pacino's little figure from the imposing conception of the Assisi master: at the same time

[1] Valenciennes, Bibl. Publique, 838.

the juxtaposition calls attention to aspects of the Assisi master's style that distinguish him from Giotto, but to which some of his Florentine contemporaries were evidently receptive.

The pairing of these two country scenes on the east wall required a departure from the narrative order of the *Legenda maior*, which places the Miracle of the Spring before the account of the visit to the Sultan, and the Sermon to the Birds after the story of the Knight of Celano. Yet, throughout the cycle, no association of subjects produces more delightful an effect; nor does either scene fail to do justice to the vivid narrative that inspired it. The parched and desolate terrain of *The Miracle of the Spring* (Plate 64), with its winding steeps, could not be more appropriate to the description given by Bonaventura,[1] who here followed the *Second Life* of Thomas of Celano,[2] of the Saint's journey to a place of solitude through rough mountain ways cut from the flinty rock. It is one of the charms of the Assisi cycle that the miracles associated with St. Francis are depicted as simply and unaffectedly as they are recounted by the Saint's early biographers, as though, given this sanctity, they could not fail to be the events of everyday experience. The muleteer drinks from the stream, absorbed in the simple quenching of his thirst; the two friars turn to one another, not to exclaim that these things should be possible, but as though thankfully echoing Bonaventura's words: 'O marvellous condescension of God!' For had not the grace and power given to the prophets of old been bestowed also, and in like measure, upon the Little Poor Man of Assisi?

Inevitably the Miracle of the Spring came to be likened to the story of Moses' striking of the Rock: the comparison, already stated explicitly in the *Legenda maior*, is repeated in the *Legenda Monacensis*[3] and in the *De Conformitate*.[4] The analogies that were drawn in early Franciscan literature between Francis and Moses evidently played their part in determining the iconography of the Assisi fresco, for the figure of the Saint, kneeling at the foot of the mountain—which became identified with La Verna itself, the holy mountain of Franciscan legend—recalls the representation of Moses in scenes of Moses in the Wilderness and the Giving of the Law on Mount Sinai.[5]

The preaching ministry of St. Francis—introduced in the Assisi cycle by *The Sermon to the Birds* (Scene XV, Plate 68)[6]—was not undertaken without an intense inner struggle; and its commencement seemed to Bonaventura to mark a climactic point in the pattern of a life perfected in the imitation of Christ. Accordingly, the chapter in the *Legenda maior* devoted to the preaching ministry, to which there is added an account of the Saint's miracles of healing, is saturated with implicit comparisons with the ministry of

[1] *Legenda maior*, vii, 12.   [2] ii Celano, ii, 16.

[3] *Legenda Monacensis S. Francisci*, xxi, in *Analecta Franciscana*, x, 711.

[4] *De Conformitate*, i, Fructus i, Pars Secunda, 3.

[5] The story of the Miracle of the Spring was rarely treated by later painters, but the Assisi fresco clearly inspired the composition of the panel by Taddeo di Bartolo in the Kestner Museum, Hanover (G. Kaftal, op. cit., No. 122 *n* 26, Fig. 457).

[6] *Legenda maior*, xii, 3.

Christ: as, for example, Christ on one occasion withdraws into a boat to avoid the press of the multitude gathered by the Sea of Galilee, so St. Francis is represented as escaping by boat from the crowd that had come to hear him and to touch him when he was preaching on the seashore at Gaëta; and the boat is miraculously impelled into deep water, where it stays motionless among the waves so that St. Francis may address the people.[1] The sermon to the birds, moreover, was itself associated by tradition with the preaching ministry of Christ: the birds to which St. Francis had preached at Bevagna were comparable to the Friars Minor, the chosen disciples who were to carry the teachings of their master to the four corners of the earth, possessing, like the birds of the air and the disciples of Jesus themselves, 'nothing of their own in this world'.

The Sermon to the Birds departs from the account in the *Legenda maior* in one small detail, preferring a tradition preserved in the *Fioretti*,[2] according to which the birds assembled upon the ground to hear St. Francis, whereas according to Bonaventura those that were perched on bushes remained there, 'inclining their heads as he drew near them, and looking at him in unaccustomed fashion, until he came up to them and earnestly exhorted them to hear the Word of God'. Earlier representations of this subject, certainly in Italy, show the birds gathered on the branches of trees as well as upon the ground: the most important examples are the little scene on the altarpiece by Bonaventura Berlinghieri at Pescia (Plate 69*b*),[3] the not dissimilar composition on the Bardi altarpiece at Santa Croce in Florence (Plate 69*c*),[4] and the fresco in the nave of the Lower Church at Assisi.[5] The primary Latin text of the *Fioretti* was not completed until after the year 1322, but the stories contained in it were compiled over a long period,[6] and some of these might have been known in Assisi at the time of the commissioning of the *Legend*. Alternatively, the composition may derive directly from the account of the miracle in Celano, where the trees are not mentioned, while taking over from the accepted iconographic tradition a landscape feature which could scarcely, perhaps, have been omitted.[7] Otherwise the fresco preserves the earlier tradition in its principal iconographical elements, and it stands closest of all to the composition in the Lower Church, in which St. Francis is accompanied by only one friar, and where the design is dominated by a tall tree of remarkably natural appearance. In both frescoes St. Francis is shown in a slightly stooping attitude, his head haloed by a large nimbus. But among the more

[1] *Legenda maior*, xii, 6.   [2] *Fioretti*, xvi.   [3] G. Kaftal, op. cit., No. 122 *a* 33.   [4] Ibid., No. 122 *c* 33.

[5] Compare also the early thirteenth-century fresco in the Sacro Speco at Subiaco (G. Kaftal, *Iconography of the Saints in Central and South Italian Schools of Painting* (Florence, 1965), Fig. 547), where the birds appear to be represented in the bushes as well as upon the ground.

[6] J. R. H. Moorman, *The Sources for the Life of S. Francis of Assisi* (Manchester, 1940), pp. 159 ff. In the popular version of the story used in the 13th century in liturgical readings, the trees are not mentioned, and the birds are merely described as being assembled 'in a certain field' (P. L. Lemmens, O.F.M., 'Testimonia Minora Saeculae XIII de S.P. Francesco', *Archivum Franciscanum Historicum*, i (1908), 260.

[7] The representation of this subject in the *St. Francis* cycle at S. Francesco, Pistoia, breaks with the tradition in setting the scene before the walls of a city (A. Chiappelli, op. cit., p. 213).

significant differences is the abandonment in the fresco in the Upper Church of the Byzantine gesture of blessing: this, however, is already absent from the scene by Berlinghieri, painted as early as 1235.

The lively gesture given to St. Francis in the fresco in the Upper Church (Plate 16b) is not found in earlier representations of this scene: it has an unmistakable character, bringing to mind those expressive gesticulations of the hands, akin to the vocabulary of a sign-language, that occur again and again in the figures of the St. Cecilia Master and his associates—a typical example being the gesture of St. Cecilia in the fifth scene of the Uffizi altarpiece (*The Baptism of Tiburtius*, Plate 81). Hands crossing one another in this abrupt, *staccato* manner are unknown to the work of Giotto, and the gesture has been radically altered in the version of the subject on the predella of the Louvre *Stigmatization* (Plate 27b). Similar considerations apply to the attitude of the friar who stands behind St. Francis raising one hand, palm outwards, in evident wonder, as he looks slightly to one side: it is the combination of the raised hand with the sidelong glance that is so distinctive, and once again the gesture is modified in the scene on the Louvre panel; nor does it occur in any other work attributable to Giotto or to his *bottega*.

The figure of the friar would seem to have been executed by the author of that of Brother Silvester in Scene X (Plates 57a, 58). His style is marked by large and rather cumbrous forms; he shows a predilection for a thickset figure, which he surmounts with a boulder-like head; the large eyes are overhung by bushy eyebrows and a massive forehead; the lips tend to be thick, and the jowl heavy; the hair is distinctive, being composed of somewhat coarse strands which catch the light. His manner is recognizable again in the next fresco, *The Death of the Knight of Celano* (Scene XVI, Plate 70), in the friar seated next to St. Francis. Altogether *The Sermon to the Birds* shows a certain hesitancy of execution absent from *The Miracle of the Spring*, and the fact that both of the Saint's hands were painted on separate *intonaco* patches may indicate (as Tintori and Meiss suggest) that they replaced an original pair of hands which were considered unsatisfactory and which were then cut out of the *intonaco*.[1] A similar feebleness of execution is evident in the two *Angel* roundels, although their damaged condition makes analysis difficult.

Examined closely, *The Sermon to the Birds* reveals several weaknesses in drawing and in general execution, and its damaged state cannot be ascribed wholly to external causes, such as its proximity to the doorway and its consequent subjection to extreme variations of climate and temperature. An artist more experienced in the techniques of fresco would have avoided the use of tempera in passages requiring detailed treatment, such as the flock of birds, which have deteriorated so much as now to be scarcely visible save as mere outlines, while the black patch below the tree on the right bears witness to

---

[1] Tintori and Meiss, op. cit., p. 118.

the deleterious effects of white lead. Despite these faults, however, *The Sermon to the Birds* has justly become one of the most famous and one of the best loved of all the scenes of the *Legend* in the Upper Church: few compositions of the period are more memorable than this, and a subject that was already a little stereotyped has here been quickened by the genius of a great story-teller and rephrased in the language of a new and convincing naturalism.

XII

SOUTH WALL: FIRST BAY

(SCENES XVI–XIX)

THE PROFOUND SIGNIFICANCE attached by the Franciscans to the events surrounding the death of their Founder is reflected in the large amount of space
accorded to them in the Assisi cycle. Two entire bays—the second and third
on the south wall—were reserved for this climactic chapter in the legend of
the Poverello. Thus the story of his earthly life is concluded in the four frescoes in the
first bay (Scenes XVI–XIX, Plate 6a). Even so, his death, likened as always to that of
Christ, is anticipated in two of them—first, in *The Appearance at Arles* (Scene XVIII),
in which a friar sees a vision of the Saint with his arms extended as though upon a cross,
and secondly in *The Stigmatization* (Scene XIX), in which St. Francis suffers the imprint
of the Saviour's wounds.

It is not difficult to understand why *The Appearance at Arles* should have been taken
out of its context in the *Legenda maior*, where it is associated with a much earlier moment
in the Saint's life. The reasons for the change are made clear by the subject-matter of
the frescoes on either side of it. Each of the other three episodes illustrated in the bay
is taken from a separate chapter of the *Legenda* devoted to one particular theme. The
first, *The Death of the Knight of Celano* (Scene XVI), represents an incident illustrative
of the Saint's gift of prophecy; the second, *The Sermon before Honorius III* (Scene XVII),
exemplifies his efficacy as a preacher; while the great event depicted in the last—*The
Stigmatization* (Scene XIX)—occupies a special place in the *Legenda maior*, being given a
chapter to itself, in which Bonaventura discusses the miracle and its meaning at great
length, and in which he stresses the resemblance of the sufferings of St. Francis on
Mount La Verna to those of Christ upon the Cross. These three episodes are related in
Chapters XI, XII, and XIII respectively, whereas the story of the Appearance at Arles
is to be found in Chapter IV, which is devoted to the first advancement of the Order
under the Saint's guidance: this is, however, a story about preaching, and the fresco
takes its place very satisfactorily as the neighbour of *The Sermon before Honorius III*.

There was, besides, a still more important, typological reason for this displacement. Bonaventura insists upon the fact that St. Francis appeared to the brethren at Arles 'with his hands outstretched as though upon a Cross' (*extensis velut in cruce manibus*), a phrase quoted in abbreviated form in the inscription beneath the fresco (EXTE[N]SIS MANIB[US]). Moreover, at the time of the miraculous appearance the friars were listening to a sermon by St. Anthony on the subject of the title affixed to the Cross of Christ, 'Jesus of Nazareth, the King of the Jews'. A further allusion to the Cross occurs at the end of the story, where Bonaventura adds that it was God's will that 'His servant Francis should be present at the preaching of His true herald Anthony, so that he might sanction his preaching of the truth, and especially his preaching of the Cross of Christ, of which he was both the bearer and servant'.[1] Accordingly, St. Francis appears in the Assisi fresco *extensis manibus*, that is to say in the attitude in which Christ himself appears in *The Stigmatization*—with 'his hands and his feet stretched out in the manner of a Cross'.[2] The relationship of the two figures stands out all the more plainly because this association follows a similar pairing in the first and second frescoes in the bay (Scenes XVI and XVII), where the two representations of St. Francis are virtually identical. There was a precedent for this typological use of related images in the pairing of scenes of the Stigmatization and the Crucifixion on altarpieces and especially in manuscript illuminations of the thirteenth century.

To Bonaventura,[3] as to the author of the *De Conformitate*,[4] the story of the knight of Celano, whose death St. Francis foretold, urging him before it was too late to make a good confession, was a supreme illustration of the Poverello's gift of prophecy, itself one of the fruits of his perfect imitation of Christ. Not unexpectedly, it is Thomas of Celano who first tells the story.[5] The Assisi fresco (Plate 70), however, contains several figures that are not specifically mentioned either by Celano or by Bonaventura, and which must be ascribed entirely to the fancy of the Assisi master. The knight's household is represented as being a large one, and chiefly female, but the nine women in white headdresses are presumably servants. The knight's family have instantly left the table and rushed to his side; his wife embraces him in her arms and gazes down at his face with grief-stricken countenance; three girls and one older woman—presumably his daughters and his mother—gather around him, one of them kneeling at his feet; a novice or young friar (on the very right of the group) and another man of youthful appearance press in from either side; the man in the red gown and hat—no doubt the knight's father—seems to be asking St. Francis the meaning of the tragedy, and the Saint, who has risen to his feet, to be about to answer him; the knight's confessor has alone remained seated. The sorrow of the knight's family is movingly expressed, and the principal actors in

---

[1] *Legenda maior*, iv, 10. [2] Ibid., xiii, 3. [3] Ibid., xi, 4.
[4] *De Conformitate*, i, Fructus **v**. [5] iii Celano, 41.

the tragic scene are well characterized; but the setting is curiously unconvincing: the seating arrangements, for one thing, are far from adequate, and there seems to be room at the table for no one but St. Francis, his companion, and the man in the red gown. The same anomaly occurs in the scene of St. Cecilia's marriage-feast on the Uffizi altarpiece (Plate 8), where seats are provided only for the four women, and the two scenes have other elements in common. In both we find the same long, unbroken stretch of table, placed unusually low in the picture-space, and the manner in which each table stands under a massive architectural structure, which juts forward over it upon heavy voluted supports, is no less striking. Yet the forms are heavier than those preferred by the St. Cecilia Master himself; nor is there anything in his known work that quite compares with the treatment of light and shade in this fresco: the author of the fresco was evidently fascinated by the problem of representing the fall of light upon the heavy material of the table-cloth and of showing how the side of the table recedes into deep shadow, within which stray gleams of light are picked out where the sun catches some fold or border. Comparable explorations of chiaroscuro effects in the Orsini Chapel may be due to direct influence, of which there are also hints in Umbrian painting, for example in the altarpieces of Meo di Guido and his School. A similar curiosity about such effects of light makes itself felt in the work of Pacino, and indeed two of the scenes in the Morgan series include a virtually identical table-cloth, with the same tasselled sides: in *The Supper at Emmaus* (Plate 71*c*) the left side is thrown into shadow exactly as in the Assisi fresco (Plate 71*b*). Other stylistic characteristics of this fresco with which affinities are to be found in the work of Pacino, and especially in his manuscript illuminations, will be discussed in a later chapter (see Plates 72, 73*a*, *b*).

The iconography of this scene would seem to owe much to the traditional *Pietà*, a derivation that would explain the presence of so many women: one supports the knight's head and looks intently into his face in precisely the attitude of the Virgin in a *Lamentation*; another kneels at his feet, in the place reserved in late-medieval iconography for Mary Magdalen; a third stands directly behind, her head lowered and her hands clasped together in sorrow, calling to mind the tragic figure in Giotto's *Pietà* at Padua (Plate 18*a*); while two more women join in the lament, like the other Marys of Christian legend, Mary Salome and Mary Cleophas.

The story of the knight of Celano, although important as an illustration of St. Francis's gift of prophecy, never acquired the popularity of the others narrated in this bay, and it is rarely treated in later painting.[1] On the other hand, the subject of Scene XVII (Plate 74), the inspired sermon preached by St. Francis before Honorius III and his cardinals, holds a special place in all the early *Lives* of the Saint, and both this episode and the Pope's official confirmation of the Franciscan Rule which followed directly from it are

---

[1] It is, however, included in Benozzo Gozzoli's cycle at Montefalco.

frequently represented in early Italian art. Often, however, it is difficult to distinguish a representation of the Confirmation of the Rule—an event that took place in the year 1223—from one describing the earlier incident of the Sanctioning of the Rule by Innocent III in 1209: the same basic iconography was used for both subjects, and hence the general similarities between *The Sanctioning of the Rule* (Scene VII) at Assisi and Giotto's fresco of *The Confirmation of the Rule* at Santa Croce.

Since the first of these two scenes had already been represented in the Upper Church, there was no need for the inclusion later in the narrative of an almost identical subject: it is therefore merely alluded to in the story of the sermon. According to Bonaventura, as St. Francis began to speak before the assembled Curia he discovered that he had entirely forgotten the address which he had carefully memorized for the august occasion; but, calling humbly upon the help of the Holy Spirit, he found new and more powerful words coming to his lips.[1] In the *Legenda maior*, accordingly, the story becomes a supreme example of the indwelling in him of the Holy Spirit and a proof of his divine mission.

The papal hall represented in the fresco creates an even more imposing effect than the hall in Scene VII, and the whole composition is dominated by the regular pattern of its high Gothic arches. The Pope and his cardinals are seated in a wide arc terminating at the solitary figure of St. Francis, who stands in an attitude suggestive of intense zeal. One figure alone breaks into the central space of the foreground—that of a friar who sits humbly on the floor, resting his head on his hand as he listens to the sermon. His compositional function is to echo the jutting form of the Pope's throne, and so to help preserve the general symmetry of design already established in the architecture. The effect is enhanced by the disposition of the six cardinals, three on each side of the papal throne, and two in each group dressed respectively in deep red and blue.

The attentive concentration of this little congregation, as its members hang eagerly upon the Saint's words, or meditate within themselves with lowered gaze, has frequently been remarked upon. This expression of the act of listening—a difficult thing for any painter to attempt—has a distinctive flavour of its own which is quite absent from comparable scenes by Giotto, such as the *Christ among the Doctors* in the Arena Chapel or *The Appearance at Arles* in the Bardi Chapel at Santa Croce. Giotto, like his pupil Taddeo Gaddi in his own version of *The Confirmation of the Rule* in the Accademia,[2] strives for the expression of interior feeling and response, and his figures maintain a dignified passivity. These, on the other hand, are more active in facial expression and gesture, and most of them peer quizzically at the preacher, stretching their necks forward like the birds in the story of the marvellous sermon at Bevagna. It is this mannerism, more than any other aspect of the fresco, that recalls the imagery of the St. Cecilia Master and the

---

[1] *Legenda maior*, xii, 7.   [2] Sinibaldi and Brunetti, op. cit., Pl. 137*u*.

related imagery of Pacino (compare Plate 73*a*). In the scene of *St. Cecilia Preaching*, on the Uffizi altarpiece (Plate 8), the rapt attentiveness of the congregation is rendered in precisely this way. The similarity of the conception becomes all the more striking when we compare the young cardinal seated on the very right in the fresco and the man seated in the right foreground of the St. Cecilia Master's composition. The two figures resemble one another not only in attitude but also in the treatment of the deep folds of their garments, which hang down heavily at the front, in consequence of the forward inclination of the torso, and sweep round at the back in long, graceful lines, broken here and there into regular patterns where they divide. (All that is left of the gown of the figure in the fresco is the red underpainting.)

The young cardinal also bears a strong facial resemblance to some of the younger men in the other scene, who tend to conform to a single type. His personal beauty is exceeded only by that of the other very youthful member of the Curia, who sits behind the second column with his cheek resting upon his hand. This handsome young man, with his finely drawn features and gentle, meditative expression, may call to mind the elegant soldier (Plate 92*b*) who gracefully turns his head in *The Liberation of the Prisoner* (Scene XXVIII), and the type recurs in paintings by artists influenced by the St. Cecilia Master —for example, in the beautiful angels with inclined heads who stand on either side of the Virgin's throne in the great *Madonna* in the church of Santa Maria Maddalena at Pian di Mugnone,[1] a work that may have been painted for Or San Michele in Florence,[2] and in the seated figure of St. John the Divine in a diptych by Pacino in the Straus Collection.[3] The prototype of the Assisi figure could well be the similarly posed Jacob in the fragmentary fresco of *Jacob's Dream* at Santa Cecilia in Trastevere in Rome.[4] Once again, in the figure of the cardinal immediately to the right, next to the Pope, we find an example of that characteristic gesture of the raised hand which occurs so frequently in the cycle.

To Bonaventura, the story of the miraculous appearance of St. Francis at the Chapter of Arles, when St. Anthony was preaching, exemplified above all the grace bestowed upon the Poverello in the preaching of the truth, and especially of the Cross of Christ, and it is told in a section of the *Legenda maior* devoted to the early history of the Order and describing the creation of separate Chapters within the rapidly growing brotherhood.[5] Bonaventura then goes on to narrate the history of Honorius's confirmation 'in

---

[1] For the Pian di Mugnone *Madonna* see Offner, *Corpus*, III, i, pp. xxvi and 67 f.; Sinibaldi and Brunetti, op. cit., pp. 398 f. The altarpiece was exhibited in 1961 at the Palazzo Strozzi in Florence (*Mostra di Arte Sacra Antica dalle Diocesi di Firenze, Fiesole e Prato* (Florence, 1961), No. 142).

[2] W. Cohn, 'La seconda immagine della Loggia di Orsanmichele', *Bollettino d'arte*, xlii (1957), 335 ff.

[3] Straus Collection, New York. Cf. Offner, *Corpus*, III, ii (Part i), 16, Pls. VI, VI[1].

[4] Ascribed by Parronchi to the St. Cecilia Master at an early stage in his development: cf. A. Parronchi, 'Attività del Maestro di Santa Cecilia', *Rivista d'arte*, xxi (1939), 193 ff.

[5] *Legenda maior*, iv, 10.

perpetuity' of the Franciscan Rule,[1] to which the previous Pope had given his blessing. Honorius, however, does not come out of the story at all well; for he loses the Rule 'through negligence', and St. Francis has to draw it up a second time.

The Appearance at Arles (Scene XVIII, Plate 75) has sometimes been compared unfavourably with the previous fresco for its failure to suggest quite so vividly the response of the congregation to the sermon. But this criticism misses the point of the story. The intention must have been less to depict the friars' reactions to the words of St. Anthony than to show the effect upon them of the sudden appearance of St. Francis; for, although only one of the brothers—named Monaldo—was granted the vision of the Saint, all the others, as Bonaventura tells us, knew 'a consolation of spirit' which itself testified to the 'true presence' of their Founder. The moment chosen is one at which only two of the company apart from Monaldo have become aware of this spiritual presence: these are the two friars seated side by side between St. Francis and St. Anthony. The whole drama of the scene is concentrated into this area of the composition; and the other friars, huddled together in a scarcely differentiated mass, provide little more than the necessary background to the narration of the miracle. They form a solid phalanx held to attention by the imposing, upright figure of St. Anthony (Plate 89c). This passive communing of twelve men with one is offset by the more active and dramatic rapport between Monaldo, seated apart on the very left, and the spiritual form of St. Francis, uplifted with outstretched arms within the Gothic archway of the chapter-house.[2] Monaldo gazes in rapture at the vision; between him and St. Francis are the two friars who have become aware of the Saint's spiritual presence: they also are set apart, and they are further distinguished from their fellows by the colour of their habits, which is a warm reddish-brown, contrasting with the more neutral tones, tending to blue-grey and ochre, that predominate among the rest of the company.[3] The gestures of the two friars are subtly expressive of a gently suffusing emotion, and have the more force in that they are the only active gestures in the entire gathering, and alone suggest continuing movement: Monaldo has been transfixed into immobility by the vision; St. Anthony, moveless as a rock, is immersed in the delivery of his sermon, and holds his hands together, motionless, within the sleeves of his habit; all the friars facing him sit stolidly in one still mass, and their hands are also concealed, so that no gesture activates the group; the friar facing

---

[1] *Legenda maior*, iv, 11.

[2] The Assisi fresco was perhaps the first representation of the subject to render the scene realistically as taking place in an interior. On the Bardi altarpiece (G. Kaftal, *Iconography of the Saints in Tuscan Painting*, Fig. 352) St. Anthony delivers his sermon out of doors, and St. Francis appears to him (not to Monaldo) from the heavens. The scene on the window in the Capella di S. Antonio in the Lower Church, by Giovanni di Bonino, shows an interior (Giusto, op. cit., Pls. XXXI and XXXIII).

[3] It was ordained at the Chapter of Narbonne (1260) that the colour of the Franciscan habit should be grey; but such was the lack of uniformity that as late as 1316, when a Chapter was held at Paris, it was still necessary to issue a decree forbidding the friars to wear habits of colours of their own choice.

the other way, with his back to St. Anthony, remains oblivious of everything around him; nor is St. Francis any more active a figure; no movement is implied in his raised arms, for he is present only as a visionary form suddenly manifested in the likeness of the Crucified.

As we have seen, the symbolic meaning of the Saint's attitude is reinforced by its repetition in the figure of the Seraphic Christ in Scene XIX (Plates 6a, 76). Giotto, at Santa Croce, achieved a similar end within a single composition by representing directly behind St. Francis, on the wall of a cloister, an image of *Christ on the Cross*. At the same time he modified the Saint's pose and, instead of showing his arms stretched wide apart, disposed them in a graceful curve which is continued in the Romanesque archway forming the entrance to the chapter-house. The Saint's arms do not, therefore, break across the architectural forms as they do in the Assisi fresco. A compromise between these two conceptions of the figure is to be found in Taddeo Gaddi's panel in the Accademia, where, as at Assisi, St. Francis extends his arms beyond a central Gothic archway;[1] but in other respects the composition is based upon Giotto's fresco at Santa Croce. Yet by now the precise nature of the miracle, as it had been recounted in the *Legenda maior*, seems to have become blurred: it is difficult to tell from Taddeo Gaddi's interpretation of the story which of the friars is intended to be Monaldo; nor was his decision to bring the figure of St. Francis forward, so that he floats in the midst of the congregation, quite appropriate to Bonaventura's narrative, however graceful and imaginative this conception may be. It would be impossible to imagine the designer of the *Legend* in the Upper Church making so bold a departure from his text: indeed, in all its aspects the Assisi fresco reminds us how close the cycle stands to the argument and to the spirit of the *Legenda maior*.

To Bonaventura[2] and to the early Franciscan writers in general, the Stigmatization of St. Francis was an event of supreme and wonderful significance: it was the most important of all the miracles recorded in the tradition, for it set the seal upon the Poverello's earthly mission and confirmed his divine calling, as one sent by Christ to renew the world. Bonaventura refers to the sacred *stigmata* as 'the seal of the likeness of the living God'; and the phrase is echoed by Dante when he comes in the *Paradiso* to evoke the scene at La Verna.:

> nel crudo sasso intra Tevere ed Arno
> da Cristo prese l'ultimo sigillo;[3]

a description that may also owe something to one or other of the pictorial representations known to Dante, perhaps even to the famous fresco in the Upper Church. In the eyes of the Franciscans La Verna was a holy mountain, another Sinai, but, above all, another Golgotha. It was there that Bonaventura himself withdrew from the world

---

[1] Sinibaldi and Brunetti, op. cit., Pl. 137w. [2] *Legenda maior*, xiii, 3. [3] *Paradiso*, xi, 106.

at a crucial moment in his spiritual life, in order to find the same peace and the same communion with Christ that St. Francis had experienced: 'ad montem Alverni tanquam ad locum quietum, amore quaerendi pacem spiritus, declinarem.'[1]

To the artist, meanwhile, the Stigmatization presented the challenge of a new and modern subject, with which the only true analogy in Christian art was that of Christ at Gethsemane. It was a complex subject, requiring the representation of one or more figures in a landscape—a particular landscape, dominated by La Verna—and involving also a dramatic or supernatural encounter, and hence a consideration of several different emotions, from surprise to religious awe and ecstatic contemplation: but, above all, the painter was obliged to do justice to the theological significance of the miracle; and here —to recall our earlier analysis of the composition—we touch upon one of the supreme virtues of the fresco in the Upper Church.

The story of the Stigmatization is given in its earliest form in the *First Life* by Thomas of Celano, written shortly after the Saint's canonization. Here we are told of the apparition to St. Francis on Mount La Verna of 'a man like a seraph, having six wings, with hands outstretched and feet joined together, fixed to a cross'.[2] The author describes two of the seraph's wings as being raised above his head, two as being spread for flight, and two as veiling his entire body; an image deriving from Isaiah.[3] According to Celano the three pairs of wings symbolized the three gifts of the spirit—love, mercy, and purity. Another, slightly later tradition, preserved in the *Legend of the Three Companions*, offers us a rather more complex image, distinguishing between the Seraph and the mystical figure of the Crucified at the centre of the apparition, and describing the vision as 'a seraph, within the wings of which was the form of a beautiful, crucified man'.[4] However, the most important development of this image, and the really essential one, is found in the *Legenda maior*, where the identification of the Seraph with Christ himself is now made explicit. Bonaventura calls the vision a visitation of Christ 'in the guise of the Seraph' (*sub specie Seraph*), and we may therefore refer to the visionary figure as a 'Seraphic Christ'. In his theological works Bonaventura dwells upon the mystic significance of the six wings, elaborating the ideas of Thomas of Celano: in Bonaventura's thought the number six corresponds, for example, to the six stages of Creation; to the steps of Solomon's throne; to the six days during which Jehovah veiled himself in the cloud from the eyes of Moses; to the six days preceding Christ's Transfiguration; and to the successive degrees of the soul's ascent to God.[5]

---

[1] Bonaventura, *Itinerarium mentis in Deum*, Prolog., 2; in *Doctoris Seraphici S. Bonaventurae opera omnia* . . . (10 vols., Quaracchi, 1882–1902), v, 293 ff.

[2] i Celano, 114.   [3] Isaiah 6 : 2.   [4] *Tres Socii*, xvii.

[5] *De sex aliis Seraphim* (*Doctoris Seraphici S. Bonaventurae opera omnia* . . ., viii, 131 ff.); *Breviloquium*, Prolog., ii, 1–4 (*Opera* . . ., v, 199 ff.); *Opusculum de reductione artium*, 7 (*Opera* . . ., v, 293 ff.). On this see E. Gerson, *The Philosophy of St. Bonaventure*, trans. I. Trethowan and F. J. Sheed (London, 1938), pp. 233 f.

Before the year 1263, when the *Legenda maior* became the official Life of St. Francis, we must therefore go to Celano and to the *Three Companions* for the literary sources of paintings of this subject, and (as we should expect) the visionary form in such early pictorial interpretations is that of a Seraph rather than a Christ-figure in the guise of a Seraph. In the scene on the altarpiece by Bonaventura Berlinghieri at Pescia, dated 1235 (Plate 30a), the artist insists so strongly upon the otherworldly nature of the vision that the cross is omitted altogether. Even after the publication of the *Legenda maior* the older image tended to be retained, and the fresco in the Upper Church must be one of the earliest representations of the subject to give the Seraph the form of the Crucified Christ. The Cross, however, is again omitted, possibly in order to reinforce the intended comparison with the figure of St. Francis in *The Appearance at Arles* (Scene XVIII). (It appears in the form of a Y-branched cross in the scene on Giuliano da Rimini's altarpiece at Boston, which is largely based on the Assisi fresco.) The fresco in the Upper Church shows a further iconographical change from the earlier thirteenth-century tradition: the rays of divine light emanating from the Seraph now join the two figures from wound to wound, rather than radiating from a single point.[1]

Bonaventura tells the story of the Stigmatization at great length. St. Francis, as he kneels in prayer on Mount La Verna, is pictured as a soul in rapture, aware that he has drawn closer than ever before to the Divine Presence; he knows also that he is near death; it is the time of Lent, and he experiences an overwhelming desire to share the very sufferings of Christ upon the Cross. Bonaventura goes on to describe how St. Francis, taking the book of the Gospels from the altar of the little church which has been built for him at La Verna, and giving it to a companion—identified in the *Fioretti* with the faithful Brother Leo—asks him to open it at random. This he does three times, and on each occasion the book falls open at the Lord's Passion. St. Francis understands from this that, as he has imitated Christ in his life, so before he dies is he to be made like Christ 'in the afflictions and sufferings of His Passion'. The opening of the Gospels has therefore an important place in the story, being prophetic of St. Francis's identification with Christ Crucified; and it is alluded to in the Assisi fresco in the figure of the friar in the lower right corner (Plate 95b), seated on the ground with the Gospels open before him. It is interesting to compare the panel by Sassetta in the National Gallery in London,[2] which once belonged to an altarpiece painted for the church of S. Francesco at Sansepolcro, and which must owe much to the composition at Assisi. It is not without significance that in Sassetta's picture the book of the Gospels which Brother Leo holds in his hand is placed immediately beneath a crucifix garlanded with the Crown of Thorns and bearing

---

[1] J. White, 'The Date of *The Legend of St. Francis* at Assisi', *The Burlington Magazine*, xcviii (1956), 347.

[2] National Gallery, London, No. 4760; one of a series of scenes of the Life of St. Francis, of which a central panel is in Villa I Tatti, Florence.

the Sacred Nails, and that the crucifix, in turn, occupies a place directly below the Seraphic Christ, the three images all being represented upon the same vertical. In the Assisi fresco there is no crucifix, but between the Gospels and the Seraph we find instead a little white cross, over the entrance to the Saint's cell. This cross, however, may refer to another detail mentioned by Bonaventura; for according to the *Legenda maior* the Stigmatization took place on a morning near the Feast of the Exaltation of the Holy Cross.

As in Giotto's *Stigmatization* in the Louvre, the bare landscape of *crudo sasso* contains two buildings—the Saint's cell and a little chapel (Plate 95*a*, *b*), through whose open door there can be seen an altar. Two buildings of an elaborated Byzantine design appear in Berlinghieri's painting at Pescia (Plate 30*a*); but usually thirteenth-century representations include only one: sometimes this is an imposing, tower-like edifice surmounted by a dome and rising high above the Saint (Plate 31). The simpler structures at Assisi reflect the new attitude around the turn of the century to the value of a particularized setting in enhancing the vividness of a narrative. A later stage in the growth of the tradition is represented by Giotto's fresco at Santa Croce (Plate 29*b*), where a cave replaces the Saint's cell—a reference to the hollow in the rock in which, according to the *Fioretti*, St. Francis was tried by the Devil a little while before his Stigmatization.[1]

The fresco by Pietro Lorenzetti in the Lower Church at Assisi elaborates the subject with some of the other colourful material supplied by the *Fioretti*: a great chasm, crossed by a log bridge, now separates St. Francis from Brother Leo and the rest of the community; the Saint's cell is placed within an opening in the mountain, the wildness of which is accentuated; and the falcon that awoke St. Francis every morning before matins is perched upon a high shelf of rock—a detail that also occurs in Giotto's fresco at Santa Croce.[2] Yet in all the richness of Lorenzetti's landscape there is perhaps nothing quite as beautiful as one remarkable passage in the fresco in the Upper Church, showing a solitary blue flower, together with a smaller plant nearby, growing out of the rocky ground at the Saint's feet.[3] None of the other landscape scenes in the *Legend* contains any natural form as truthfully or as exquisitely rendered as this: Ruskin himself could have

---

[1] *Fioretti*, liii. On the question of the influence of the *Fioretti* on Giotto's treatment of the Stigmatization at Santa Croce see John R. H. Moorman, *Early Franciscan Art and Literature* (Manchester, 1943), p. 18.

[2] The falcon is mentioned by Celano, but not in the context of the Stigmatization as it is in the *Fioretti* (Celano, tr. Howell, p. 300). The *Legenda maior* refers to it, not in the chapter devoted to the Stigmatization, but in a separate chapter illustrating St. Francis's love for animals and birds. Nevertheless, Bonaventura relates the story of the falcon to the Stigmatization with the comment: 'Verily, there would seem to have been a divine omen, alike in the gladness of the birds of myriad species, and in the cries of the falcon, inasmuch as that praiser and worshipper of God, upborne on the wings of contemplation, was at that very place and time to be exalted by the vision of the Seraph' (*Legenda maior*, viii, 10). A detail of the falcon in Giotto's fresco is reproduced in P. L. Rambaldi, 'Dante e Giotto nella letteratura artistica sino al Vasari', *Rivista d'arte*, numero speciale del Centenario Giottesco (1938), p. 158, Pl. 12.

[3] Attention was first drawn to this detail by Tintori and Meiss (op. cit., p. 126, Fig. 45*a*). A similar, although much larger, flower appears in the *Stigmatization* by Francesco da Rimini at the Convento di S. Francesco in Bologna (cf. M. Salmi, 'Francesco da Rimini', *Bollettino d'arte*, xxvi (1932), 253, Fig. 5).

found no fault with it. Its presence is not inexplicable, but provides one of several indications of the intervention in the painting of this bay of that sensitive and delicate master who was largely responsible for the execution of the scenes of the Obsequies of St. Francis in the bay following.

Among the various touches added by the *Fioretti* to the story as told by Bonaventura and other early writers is the information that the Stigmatization took place before daybreak and that Mount La Verna was suddenly illumined by a dazzling splendour, so that the mountain lit up all the hills and valleys round about, 'as it were the sun shining on the earth'. Of the rare attempts made by early fourteenth-century painters to express something of the wondrous incandescence of the holy mountain, none is more striking than Taddeo Gaddi's treatment of the light in his fresco in the chapter-house of Santa Croce.[1] Taddeo Gaddi conceives the sacred mountain as a complex of three mighty scarps, of which the most distant (in the centre) is partly shrouded in darkness, its forms being picked out only by isolated gleams apparently reflected from the blaze upon the other two hills. What is remarkable about this wonderfully evocative landscape is that it is no longer illuminated from one side (as in earlier representations) but from the centre: the miraculous radiance shining from the mountain, in the Saint's immediate vicinity, has been taken as the actual source of light.

This innovation broke with the Giottesque tradition of a single illumination from the right, which is common to the Louvre and Fogg panels, Giotto's fresco at Santa Croce, the version of the subject in the Santo at Padua, and Taddeo Gaddi's own panel in the Accademia. Such a convention was a natural one, since the source of light was thus identified with the Seraph—'flaming', we are told, 'and resplendent'. This tradition, however, was not followed in the Upper Church, where *The Stigmatization* belongs to the sequence of scenes that are lit from an imagined source at the lower end of the nave —that is to say, from a point to the left of the scenes. We are confronted, therefore, with a further difference between the Assisan iconography and that of the Giottesque tradition as a whole. It may not be a particularly significant one, since the fresco had necessarily to conform to a system of lighting previously determined for the entire cycle; but it may be noted that one of the early fourteenth-century *Stigmatizations* that can be shown to have been based directly upon the fresco in the Upper Church, the little scene on the altarpiece by Giuliano da Rimini, follows it in illuminating the forms from the left.

It is certain that several painters worked on the frescoes in this bay; but the precise identification of individual hands presents considerable difficulty, for the divisions between one manner and another are not always clear-cut and neighbouring stylistic areas sometimes overlap. But after Scene XVII (*The Sermon before Honorius III*) a new taste makes itself felt, both in the treatment of architecture and in the representation of

[1] Other aspects of this fresco are discussed in F. J. Mather, 'Giotto and the Stigmatization', loc. cit.

the human figure, a more delicate sensibility that gives the other three scenes in the bay, and especially the last two, a quality of refinement absent from Scenes II–XVII. This change announces the intervention in the decoration of the south wall of the painter to whom we have given the name of the 'Master of the Obsequies', and who remains the dominant personality in the painting of the next two bays (Scenes XX–XXII and XXIII–XXV). Yet in this first bay the stylistic division is by no means absolute. It is clear, for example, that the author of the figure of St. Francis in Scene XVI (Plate 70) was also responsible for the corresponding figure in Scene XVII (*The Sermon before Honorius III*, Plate 74) and for the figure of Brother Monaldo in Scene XVIII (*The Appearance at Arles*, Plate 75). The painter of the seated friar in Scene XVI (*The Death of the Knight of Celano*) has been met with before as the author of the friar standing behind St. Francis in Scene XV (*The Sermon to the Birds*), and his style is perhaps recognizable in the heads of some of the cardinals in Scene XVII (*The Sermon before Honorius III*) and possibly in that of the Pope in the same fresco. The relationship between Scenes XVI (Plate 70) and XIII (*The Christmas Crib at Greccio*, Plate 63) is evident from the general similarity of style and from the probability that the same assistant worked on some of the less important figures in the right-hand areas of both scenes, notably the figures of the servers in Scene XIII and those of the young friar and the servants in Scene XVI. Yet the participation of so many different painters in the decoration of this first bay on the south wall scarcely affects the over-all unity of the group of four scenes; a unity difficult to account for unless detailed compositional drawings existed from which each successive painter would have worked.

XIII

SOUTH WALL: SECOND BAY

(SCENES XX–XXII)

THE DEATH OF ST. FRANCIS is now presented to us in a solemn threnody
which is repeated with telling variations before its music is allowed to die
away. Here, in the central part of the nave, the narrative is slowed down and
stayed, as St. Francis receives in death the last tributes of the Order of Friars
Minor, the Church, and the world. But the deep sorrow that thrills through this climactic period of the *Legend* is attended also by great joy and thanksgiving, for, like Christ
himself, St. Francis has triumphed over death and has ascended into heaven. The first
fresco in the second bay, *The Death and Ascension of St. Francis* (Scene XX, Plate 77),[1]
stands directly opposite *The Vision of the Thrones* (Scene IX, Plate 56):[2] the prophecy
concerning the seat reserved for the Poverello in heaven has now been fulfilled; and,
whereas in the central episode of the earlier sequence (Scene VIII) Francis ascended like
Elijah, here—witnessed in the central fresco (Scene XXI, Plate 80) by a dying Franciscan and by a bishop—he ascends like Christ.

There is no more striking instance of the symmetrical ordering of the cycle, within
its various parts, than the concordance that has been brought about between the two
outer frescoes in this bay (Scenes XX and XXII, Plate 6*b*). Each composition is divided
horizontally into three clear-cut areas, the lowest of which is occupied by a representation of the dead Saint, laid upon a narrow bier, and the middle area by a crowd of
mourners: but, as elsewhere in the cycle, it is the relationship of the uppermost or
heavenly fields that is most significant theologically, and which now makes possible a
pictorial statement of the Saint's likeness to the Crucified Christ, through the association
of the ascension-image in Scene XX with the crucifix in Scene XXII. Indeed, the
presence in the Assisi cycle of this uniquely Franciscan typology gives it an important
place among the documents illustrating the evolution of such ideas about St. Francis.

[1] *Legenda maior*, xiv, 6.   [2] See Plan, Plate 2*b*.

The beginnings of a specifically Franciscan theology can already be traced in the earliest lives of the Saint. Thus we read in the *First Life* of Thomas of Celano:

Beatissimus pater Franciscus . . . Seraphim imaginem tenuit atque formam, et in cruce persevererans ad sublimium spirituum gradum meruit advolare. Semper enim in cruce fuit, nullum subterfugiens laborem atque dolorem, tantum ut posset in se et de se voluntatem Domini adimplere.[1]

(The most blessed Father Francis . . . bore the image and form of a seraph and by continuing on the Cross was found worthy to rise to the rank of the spirits on high. For he was ever on the Cross, shrinking from no toil and pain if only he might accomplish the Lord's will in himself and concerning himself.)[2]

But in the *Legenda maior* St. Francis's angelic nature and likeness to Christ are stated still more explicitly:

Hunc Dei nuntium amabilem Christo, imitabilem nobis et admirabilem mundo servum Dei fuisse Franciscum, indubitabili fide colligimus, si culmen in eo eximiae sanctitatis advertimus, qua, inter homines vivens, imitator fuit puritatis angelicae, qua et positus est perfectis Christi sectatoribus in exemplum. Ad quod quidem fideliter sentiendum et pie, non solum inducit officium quod habuit, vocandi ad fletum et planctum, calvitium et singulum sacci signandique Thau super frontes virorum gementium et dolentium signo poenitentialis crucis et habitus cruci conformis; verum etiam irrefragabili veritatis testificatione confirmat signaculum similitudinis Dei viventis, Christi videlicet crucifixi, quod in corpore ipsius fuit impressum, non per naturae virtutem vel ingenium artis, sed potius per admirandam potentiam Spiritus Dei vivi.[3]

(Now that this angel was indeed that messenger of God, beloved of Christ, our example and the world's wonder, Francis, the servant of God, we may with full assurance conclude, when we consider the heights of lofty saintliness to which he attained, and whereby, although he lived among men, he was an imitator of the purity of the Angels, and was an example to those that perfectly follow Christ. That this belief should be faithfully and devoutly held we are convinced by the vocation that he showed to call to weeping and mourning, and to the tonsure, and to girding with sackcloth, and to set a mark upon the foreheads of groaning and grieving men, by the sign of his penitent's Cross and his habit bearing the figure of a Cross. Moreover, it is also confirmed, with incontrovertible witness to its truth, by the sign of his likeness to the living God, namely to the Crucified Christ, which was stamped upon his body, not by the force of Nature or the skill of art, but rather by the wonderful power of the Spirit of the living God.)

The desire to develop these ideas pictorially would explain the rudimentary character of the church represented in Scene **XXII** (Plate 82), for any greater emphasis upon architectural detail would have distracted attention from the association of the devotional pictures on the iconostasis with the scene of the Saint's ascension in the opening narrative in the bay (Plate 77). It is true that in consequence of the use of *a secco* painting the forms of the dome and the pillar supporting it (towards the centre of the composition) are not

[1] i Celano, II, ix, 115.
[2] *The Lives of S. Francis of Assisi*, by Brother Thomas of Celano, trans. A. G. Ferrers Howell, p. 115.
[3] *Legenda maior*, Prologus, 2.

now as clearly visible as they once were; but, even so, the summary treatment of the structure of the building seems all the more striking when we recall that the famous and theologically important event which is here illustrated—the verification of the reality of the sacred *stigmata* by the sceptical Jerome—took place in no less hallowed a shrine than the Portiuncula, where the young Francis had been given the final revelation of his Christ-like mission, and where, as he lay dying, he had asked to be carried, 'that he might yield up the breath of life there, where he had received the breath of grace'.[1]

In the corresponding bay on the north wall the three scenes were linked together by an ascending and descending rhythm which reaches its apex in the upper field of the central fresco (Scene VIII), where St. Francis appears in the Chariot of Fire (Plate 4a). Here, however, the movement is reversed (Plate 6b), carrying downward from the ascension-image through the lines of the angels' garments in Scene XX, continuing into Scene XXI (*The Vision of the Ascension of St. Francis*) across the carefully disposed heads of the friars on the left, and passing through the reaching arms of Brother Augustine, who looks up towards the vision in an attitude of longing. Less urgently, it ascends once more into the uppermost field of Scene XXII (*The Verification of the Stigmata*), being taken upwards by direction-lines established in the attitudes of the central friar and the sleeping Bishop in Scene XXI and in the perspectival treatment of the episcopal palace. It is the familiar principle of planar design that accounts for the variations in the height of the friars standing on the very left in Scene XXI: they must be disposed thus in order to continue the linear movement that flows downward from the previous fresco (or, properly speaking, upward from the central fresco into Scene XX).

The central fresco, *The Vision of the Ascension of St. Francis* (Scene XXI, Plate 80), represents two distinct events which are, however, closely connected in the *Legenda maior*.[2] At first sight they seem to be taking place under the same roof, as in Giotto's version of the subject at Santa Croce; but in reality this is not so: the Bishop's room is a quite separate structure from the lofty church upon which it abuts, and lies behind it, although the spatial conception is ambiguous and obeys no discernible logic. Once again the *Legend* follows the literal sense of Bonaventura's text, which describes the two events —the vision of Brother Augustine and the dream of the Bishop of Assisi—as occurring in different localities. The inclusion of the two events in a single composition serves, nevertheless, to emphasize the simultaneity of the two visions. Although damage to the fresco surface has obscured the fact, another vision of the Saint's ascension is depicted in Scene XX: this is the vision experienced by that unnamed disciple at Assisi who beheld St. Francis, 'under the likeness of a star of shining brightness, borne on a dazzling white cloudlet over many waters and taken up in a straight course into the heavens'.[3] The friar can be seen in the lower group on the left side of the composition, gazing

---

[1] *Legenda maior*, xiv, 3.   [2] Ibid., xiv, 6.   [3] Ibid., xiv, 6.

upwards (Plate 77). No doubt it was Bonaventura's purpose to show that St. Francis had revealed himself after death to the Church as a whole, as represented by the bishop of the new *città santa*, as well as to the community at Assisi and to the Order of Friars Minor throughout the world, as represented respectively by the unnamed disciple and by Brother Augustine, a Provincial Minister. At the same time it is the story of the appearance to Brother Augustine that is more closely tied in the *Legenda maior* to the account of the Saint's death and the vision of the unnamed friar, which it immediately follows, and the Assisi cycle reflects this sequence in a quite literal manner.

The decision to place the emphasis in Scene XXI (Plate 80) upon the story of Brother Augustine, rather than upon the bishop's dream, was natural enough in view of its richer narrative content, its Franciscan setting, and its place in the *Legenda maior*. Accordingly (as in Giotto's fresco in the Bardi Chapel), this incident occupies some two-thirds of the picture-space. Yet it was necessary to preserve the centrality of design demanded by the position of the fresco at the centre of the bay, and the solution arrived at was to restore the balance by means of dominant architectural forms and subsidiary figures composed in relation to them. We look into the nave of a lofty church; tall clustered pillars—very similar to those represented in the fourth and fifth scenes of the *Santa Cecilia* altarpiece (Plates 8, 81)—support the roof; in the upper part of the building a series of Romanesque arches and pendentives offers a varied pattern of curvilinear shapes.[1] The central pillars rise higher than the others, and standing beside them in the outer aisles and facing in towards one another are two friars, the only figures in the foreground. Their active gestures, breaking slightly across the verticals formed by the central pillars, repeat in the lower area of the composition the rounded shapes of the vaulting above them. Yet the friar on the right interrupts the line of the pillars much less than his companion—scarcely, in fact, at all. The result is an emphasis upon a strong vertical almost at the centre of the design and a division of the composition into two virtually equal areas. At the same time the scene devoted to the vision of Brother Augustine remains a symmetrically arranged composition on its own, with its central point defined by the apex of the roof—a centrality emphasized by the repetition of the shape of the tympanum by the triangular form of Brother Augustine's visible leg, bent at the knee. Still more interesting, perhaps, is the use of perspective to compensate for this shift of emphasis to the left.

The apex of the roof defines the centre of one of the two scenes into which the composition is divided: but the centre of the composition as a whole lies to the right, and it is defined, as we have seen, by the central cluster of pillars, which is surmounted

---

[1] The architectural forms of the church are repeated with variations in no less than four of the nine scenes of the *Life of the Virgin* on the altarpiece by the Cesi Master at St. Jean Cap Ferrat: cf. M. Meiss, 'Reflections of Assisi: A Tabernacle and the Cesi Master', in *Scritti di Storia dell'Arte in onore di Mario Salmi*, ii, 97.

by a small statue of a prophet, one of three such figures ornamenting the church. To the left and right of this central vertical stress the lines formed by the left side of the tympanum and by the projecting roof of a square tower, represented in oblique perspective, slope downwards, to be continued on the one side in the lower roof of the church and on the other in the slightly projecting roof of a small structure, like a diminutive house, which peeps up over the bishop's palace. Once again perspective achieves the end of establishing a linear harmony.

The frescoes on either side (Scenes XX and XXII, Plates 77, 82) call for little compositional analysis, and the almost rigid symmetry of their design is patent enough. Iconographically they both adhere to the old tradition of crowding the scene of a saint's death with a large number of mourners who stand behind the bed or bier and look down at the corpse.[1] The death of St. Francis is thus depicted on the Bardi altarpiece (Plate 78b)[2] and in other thirteenth-century works.[3] But the representation in both of the Assisi frescoes of figures with their backs turned to the spectator adds a new note of informal realism to the tradition: their origin can perhaps be traced to the scene on the Bardi altarpiece, where a group of kneeling figures, represented in profile, appears on the near side of the deathbed. But the most important iconographic innovation in the Upper Church consists of the separate treatment of two subjects that were previously brought together within a single composition—the Saint's death and ascension and the verification of the reality of the *stigmata* by Jerome of Assisi. The thematic reasons for this division have already been discussed, and it need only be added that the separation of the two events both conformed to the text of the *Legenda maior* and also made it possible to lay bare on the very walls of the Basilica the same fervent devotion that inspired the pilgrims who flocked to the altar of St. Francis in the Lower Church. In these two scenes and in the opening narrative of the following bay (Scene XXIII), the circle of homage gradually widens: first the Franciscans and the clergy (Plates 77, 82), then the citizenry (Plates 82, 83), and finally the Poor Clares (Plate 83) come to venerate the remains of the dead Saint.

The exceptionally low placing of the Saint's body in Scene XXII may be taken as the final illustration in the *Legend* of that great humility which led St. Francis, before his death, to instruct the brethren to leave his body lying on the ground, naked, 'for as long a time as a man would take in a leisurely manner to cover the distance of a thousand

---

[1] In the panel of *The Funeral of St. Francis* by Bicci di Lorenzo at Laon (G. Kaftal, *Iconography of the Saints in Tuscan Painting*, No. 49, 1; Fig. 209), ten of the companions of St. Francis who are represented are identified by inscriptions: these are Silvester, Leo, Angelus, Philip, Masseus, Peter, Sabatinus, Moricus, Bernard of Quintavalle, and Barbatus. The grouping of the figures suggests direct dependence upon Scenes XX and XXII at Assisi, while the architecture is related to that of the church in Scene XXI. It does not seem possible to identify the figures in the Assisi fresco, although the elderly friar bending over the Saint's body may well have been intended for Bernard of Quintavalle.

[2] G. Kaftal, op. cit., Fig. 469; idem, *St. Francis in Italian Painting* (London, 1950), p. 87, Fig. 26.

[3] e.g., Accademia, Siena, No. 313 (G. Kaftal, op. cit., No. 122f.).

paces'.[1] It was by virtue of this extraordinary humility, Bonaventura declares, that St. Francis was proved worthy to be adorned with an outward likeness to Christ; it was by the merits of this 'exalted sanctity' that he entered 'the abode of light and peace, where he rests with Christ for ever'.

The representation of the Saint's ascension (Plate 78*a*) differs markedly from Giotto's conception of it in the Bardi Chapel. The angels (Plate 79*b*), with their cumbrous wings and long rippling dresses, have less in common with the ethereal beings imagined by Giotto, who flit and plunge out of the depths of the heavens, than with the figures represented by Pacino on *The Tree of Life* (Plate 79*a*). Giotto's angels are birdlike creatures, akin to the *uccelli divini* of Dante; the Assisi angels, on the other hand, resemble stately women, and some of them turn their beautiful faces towards us, almost self-consciously, as though to be admired. The splendid wings, of rich crimson, white, and gold, scarcely seem sufficient, despite their size, to support the opulent frames of these most corporeal spirits, who spread them out behind them as if they were elegant adornments to their persons. The angels are disposed symmetrically on either side of St. Francis to form a pattern of gently curving rhythms of great regularity. The ascending Saint is represented in a fully frontal position, his hands raised before him with their palms outwards (Plate 78*a*). Where Giotto at Santa Croce avoids absolute symmetry, the Assisi master rejoices in it; and where Giotto expresses vigorous movement, the image presented at Assisi is a static one, as it is also in the very similar type of ascension-scene found on the *Santa Margherita* altarpiece at Montici (Plate 9): it suggests not so much an ascending figure as one who has ascended and who is now revealed to us amid the company of heaven; in a sense, it is not so much an ascension as an epiphany.

The same regular symmetry characterizes the composition as a whole. Apart from St. Francis the most important figure in the lower areas of the fresco is, of course, the friar who sees the vision of the Saint's ascension. It is this figure that initiates the linear activation of the bay, for the direction of the friar's gaze—reinforced by the line of a long taper held by one of the surpliced clerics—draws the spectator's eyes up to the ascension-image; whence the principal linear movement embracing the three scenes descends through the outstretched arms of Brother Augustine in the central fresco, to rise again into the upper field of Scene XXII, and finally to descend into the inclined form of the kneeling Jerome (Plate 6*b*). In Scene XX (Plate 77) other candle-bearing acolytes appear on the right side of the composition, preserving the general symmetry and helping to connect the upper and lower fields. It is interesting to observe that in Giotto's fresco at Santa Croce the implicit line of the friar's glance is weighed against a processional cross and banner on the opposite side of the composition. Taddeo Gaddi, on the other hand, while basing his Accademia panel upon Giotto's design, brings the friar to the same side of the picture

---

[1] *Legenda maior*, xiv, 4.

as the cross, making him kneel immediately beneath it, with the consequence that his line of sight is identified with the angle of the cross itself.[1] To look in turn at these three versions of the subject is to come tantalizingly close to the discussion of such fundamental problems of composition that must have taken place in the painters' studios: it is also to be confirmed in the view that the Assisi master's aesthetic was founded upon entirely different principles from those of Giotto and his pupils; for where both Giotto and Taddeo Gaddi seize upon the friar's wonder at the vision to heighten the drama of the otherwise quiet scene, the designer of the Assisi fresco is content to bury it in the graceful fabric of his design.

The acolytes reappear in Scene XXII (*The Verification of the Stigmata*, Plate 82).[2] The repetition could scarcely be more deliberate, and once again the eye is led upwards and inwards, this time to the crucifix on the iconostasis. No two scenes were more carefully designed as a pair; but there are important variations from the one to the other: with the exception of the sceptical Jerome, the foreground figures now stand instead of kneeling or squatting; most of the figures in the right half of the composition are turned round much further to the left, so that they provide an effective closure to the sequence; and the character of the three stresses in the uppermost field has been modified by the representation of the three pictures on the iconostasis as leaning forward, so that they appear in perspective tilted to the left.

The sutures in the *intonaco* suggest that originally only the crucifix was to have been given this forward tilt (like the crucifix represented from the back in Scene XIII), and that the decision to alter the positions of the *Madonna* and the *St. Michael* was taken during the execution of the fresco.[3] The greater of the two changes was made in the representation of the *Madonna*, which inclines at a more acute angle than the *St. Michael*, so that it combines with the taper immediately below and with the cane held by the gentleman in the red hat and coat—a beautifully observed figure which could conceivably have been another afterthought—to set up a large zig-zag motif in this area of the design. But, above all, the inclined angles of the three pictures strengthen the diagonal implicit in the figure of the kneeling Jerome, which itself reverses the initial ascending movement stated in the upward glance of the friar in Scene XX.

The crucifix (Plate 12*b*) represented in Scene XXII has suffered from the deterioration of the fresco surface, which has exposed the preliminary drawing on the *intonaco*: the outlines of the drawing, however, are well preserved. The relationship of the crucifix to the Santa Maria Novella Cross (Plate 12*a*) and to other crucifixes of a similar type, such as the cross at Careggi probably attributable to Pacino's workshop[4] (Plate 13*b*), has

---

[1] Sinibaldi and Brunetti, op. cit., Pl. 137γ.

[2] *Legenda maior*, xv, 4.   [3] Tintori and Meiss, op. cit., p. 138, Pl. 48.

[4] C. Gamba, *Bollettino d'arte*, xxvii (1933), 152; Offner, *Corpus*, III, vi (1956), 176, Pls. L, L^a–c. The attribution is not accepted by all authorities.

been touched upon in an earlier chapter. The *Madonna* to the left of the crucifix (Plate 37c), which has been similarly affected by damage, falls into a rather different category. Like the miraculous crucifix of San Damiano represented in Scene IV, it was probably intended to suggest a work of a more antique character. The picture preserves the ancient type of the *Nikopoia*, in which, in allusion to the veneration of the Virgin Mary as the God-Bearer, the Christ-Child is placed directly in front of her body, being contained by its outline; it also includes the traditional footstool, generally omitted in the four-teenth century; while the throne is unmistakably Byzantine in construction and orna-mentation: there are resemblances, for example, to the *Madonna* represented on the vault of the Florentine Baptistery. At the same time the conception must owe much to the statue of the *Virgin and Child* (Plate 37d) executed by Arnolfo di Cambio for Florence Cathedral; and indeed it may be said to combine the stylistic modernity of that work with an older iconographic tradition. The attitudes of both the Virgin and the Child are repeated in the *Madonna* in the church of Santa Maria at Cesi, which bears the date 1308 and which must have been directly influenced by the *Madonna* in the fresco;[1] but the footstool has been omitted and the Byzantine throne replaced by one of Gothic type.

The brilliance and luminosity of the colouring in this bay, ranging from blue-greys and violets to warm purples and reds, together with the prevalent softness of the hand-ling and the refinement of the drawing, reveal the extensive participation in this area of the decoration of the master responsible for much of the *Stigmatization* (Scene XIX, Plates 29a, 76) and of *The Appearance at Arles* (Scene XVIII, Plates 75, 89c, 103c) in the previous bay. The same hand dominates the third bay (Scenes XXIII–XXV, Plate 7a). The Master of the Obsequies (as we have called this talented artist) painted slowly and patiently, using very fine brushstrokes, and it has been suggested by Tintori and Meiss that he was more accustomed to working on panel than in fresco.[2] For the most part the *intonaco* in this area of the decoration was laid in unusually small patches, and as many as fifty-four *giornate* were required for the execution of Scene XX, although the upper fields of the next two frescoes were painted as swiftly as in most other sections of the cycle.

The exceptional number of figures represented in the scenes of the Saint's obsequies has generally been ascribed to the individual fancy of this intriguing master. No doubt there is much truth in this view, but it is questionable whether it provides a complete explanation of these crowded compositions. The Franciscans prided themselves upon the fact that so great a concourse of people attended the funeral rites of their Founder: the *Tres Socii*, the *First Life* of Thomas of Celano, the *Legenda maior*, and other sources all bear witness to the vast gatherings of clergy and laity 'from many lands'; there seems every reason to assume that the original designs would have alluded to this universal

---

[1] M. Meiss, *Giotto and Assisi*, p. 4, Figs. 10 and 11.   [2] Tintori and Meiss, op. cit., p. 133.

tribute. Indeed, the *Legenda maior* represents the Saint's passing as an event of which the world of Christendom as a whole quickly became aware. At first it is the fame of the *stigmata* that attracts attention, and Bonaventura tells us that immediately after the death of St. Francis, when the truth of the *stigmata* became known, a large crowd of people came to witness the miracle for themselves.[1] It was on this occasion that Jerome of Assisi, the Doubting Thomas of Franciscan legend, was converted by touching the Saint's wounds. His bold act is depicted in the foreground of Scene XXII; but it is not only Jerome who verifies the reality of the *stigmata*, although he alone requires the physical proof of touch: the great concourse of believers that fills the church—the friars and clergy in the presbyterium and, on this side of the iconostasis, the laity pressing in on either hand—represents an important element in the pictorial treatment of Bonaventura's narrative.

Subsequently, Bonaventura refers to the 'crowds that had come together' to see the Saint's remains carried to their last resting-place[2]—jostling crowds that are skilfully suggested in the opening fresco of the next bay, *St. Francis Mourned by St. Clare* (Scene XXIII, Plate 83). That we are here in the presence of history is confirmed by a letter written by Gregory IX to the Bishops of Perugia and Spoleto, in which he regretted the unruliness of the people, who had fought and struggled in their attempts to secure a place of vantage, blocking the road and alarming the friars.[3] Again, although the canonization receives only a brief mention in the *Legenda maior*, the account in the *Tres Socii*[4] of this great occasion for Assisi tells of the presence of numerous prelates, princes, and barons, and of a vast gathering of people from many countries, all summoned to the city by Pope Gregory IX, while Thomas of Celano, in his ecstatic description of the ceremony, writes of a 'mighty throng of all peoples and a well-nigh countless multitude of either sex'.[5] Franciscan tradition certainly demanded a strong emphasis in the cycle upon the universality of the grief—and of the joy—occasioned by the Saint's passing, and upon the magnitude of the tribute paid to him at his death and canonization.

---

[1] *Legenda maior*, xv, 4.

[2] Ibid., xv, 5. Celano also mentions 'an extraordinary concourse of priests and clerics', and he tells us that 'the whole city of Assisi rushed in throngs, and all that region made haste to see the great things of God which the Lord of Majesty had gloriously shown in His holy servant' (II, ix, 112: trans. Howell, p. 111). Compare in addition the account in the *Liber de Laudibus Beati Francisci* (c. 1278) of Bernard of Bessa of the translation of St. Francis's body from S. Giorgio to the Lower Church, where again the size of the crowd of witnesses is emphasized: '. . . cum ingenti apparatu et veneratione translatum, tanta propter hoc ex vicinis urbibus populorum multitudine congregata, ut, civitate illos capere non valente, per campos gregum more turmatim accumberet' (*Analecta Franciscana*, iii (1897), 688). This description is copied almost word for word in the *Chronica XXIV Generalium Ministrorum Ordinis Fratrum Minorum* (late fourteenth century): '. . . unde tanta fuit propter hoc ex vicinis urbibus multitudo congregata, ut, civitate illos capere non valente, per campos gregum more accumberent' (*Analecta Franciscana*, iii, 212).

[3] *Speravimus hactenus* (16 June 1230): cf. Raphael M. Huber, op. cit., p. 89; L. Wadding, *Annales Minorum* (Quaracchi, 1931–5), ii, 234.

[4] *The Legend of Saint Francis by the Three Companions*, trans. E. G. Salter (London, 1902), 71 (p. 109).

[5] Celano (trans. Howell), iii, 124, p. 125.

XIV

SOUTH WALL: THIRD BAY

(SCENES XXIII–XXV)

THE ACCOUNT IN THE *Legenda maior* of the bearing home of the body of St. Francis and of the moving scene of farewell outside San Damiano, rebuilt now as the convent church of the Poor Clares, presents the Saint's last journey in terms of a triumph.[1] The comparison with Christ's triumphal entry into Jerusalem implicit in Bonaventura's narrative, and stated in the Assisi fresco (Scene XXIII, Plate 83) in the iconographical quotation of the 'boy in the tree', with its allusion to the description of the Entry into Jerusalem given in St. Matthew's Gospel, may originally have been suggested by the fact that St. Clare was particularly associated with Palm Sunday: it was on that day, after her flight from her parents to seek sanctuary with St. Francis, that she had taken the habit,[2] and possibly the explicit reference in the fresco to the Festival of Palms was intended to remind the visitor to the Upper Church of St. Clare's first meeting with the Poverello, whom she now looks upon for the last time.

It is a scene not only of farewell but also of rejoicing, and the division of the composition into two distinct parts, separated by the strong central vertical formed by the corner of the church, distinguishes the grief of St. Clare and her companions from the joyful mood of the citizenry with their branches and tapers.[3] St. Clare stoops to kiss the dead Saint, hanging over him in the attitude of a Mater Dolorosa; behind and above her, sculptured in high relief on the façade of the great church, the grave images of St. Damian (Plate 109) and St. Peter, attended by angels, provide a fitting background to the solemnity of the moment. On the other hand, the more festive spirit of the laity and the chanting friars is epitomized by the eager gesture of the boy climbing the tree, as he reaches up to its topmost branches (Plate 96).

Although the fresco is thus divided into two clear-cut fields, care was taken to bring

---

[1] *Legenda maior*, xv, 5.

[2] *The Life of Saint Clare ascribed to Fr. Thomas of Celano . . .*, ed. Fr. Paschal Robinson (Philadelphia, 1910), pp. 13 ff.

[3] Celano describes St. Clare and her companions as being at this moment 'divided between sorrow and joy' (Celano, trans. Howell, p. 118).

them into unison and to relate the whole scene, with all its complexities, to the much simpler composition of *The Appearance to Gregory IX* (Scene XXV, Plate 88), which closes the sequence in this bay, and to the central fresco of *The Canonization* (Scene XXIV, Plate 85). Yet of all the groupings within the bays these three compositions seem the most loosely knit together and the least harmoniously balanced (Plate 7a). Here, however, criticism should be tempered with caution, for Scene XXIV has suffered such catastrophic damage from damp and other causes that the original effect of the three scenes as a group is difficult to judge. Indeed, the most important of all the figures in Scene XXIV, that of the Pope, is now missing. Nevertheless, the composition can be reconstructed to some extent.

Bonaventura is of little help to us in this task, since he does not describe the actual ceremony: he states merely that, after the Curia had examined the Poverello's miracles in the customary manner, Gregory IX came in person to Assisi 'in the year of the Lord's Incarnation 1228, on the sixteenth day of July, a Sunday', and that, 'with ceremonies of the greatest solemnity which it would take too long to describe, he enrolled the blessed Father in the list of the Saints'.[1] It appears, therefore, that the designer of the Assisi fresco had recourse chiefly to the graphic account of the ceremony provided by Thomas of Celano; and from this and from what is known of canonization ceremonies at the time of the painting of the *Legend* the main elements of the composition can be pieced together.

The rules of procedure contained in the *Ordo Romanus* of Gaetano Stefaneschi,[2] which were based upon the author's personal experience of canonization ceremonies between the years 1304 and 1328, show that it was customary for the Pope to be seated upon an elevated throne placed before the High Altar of the appointed church (which in this case was S. Giorgio at Assisi).[3] The altar was lit with many candles, and, in addition to the cardinals, bishops, and other clergy, a large congregation of the laity would be in attendance. After a brief prayer, followed by the chanting of the *Veni Creator*, the Pope pronounced the formula of canonization; the feast-day of the new saint was then announced, and an indulgence granted to those visiting his tomb; finally, after the singing of the *Te Deum* and the offering of prayers which introduced the name of the saint, the ceremony closed with the papal absolution and the celebration of Mass. The Assisi fresco reflects contemporary practice with some accuracy; here are the cardinals, bishops, and other clergy, the congregation of the laity assembled before an altar that is decked with

---

[1] *Legenda maior*, xv, 7.

[2] Cf. Margaret R. Toynbee, *St. Louis of Toulouse and the Process of Canonization in the Fourteenth Century* (Manchester, 1929).

[3] In describing the canonization of St. Francis, Celano refers to Gregory IX's 'lofty throne': 'Descendit denique de solio excelso felix papa Gregorius' (*St. Francis of Assisi according to Brother Thomas of Celano*, ed. H. G. Rosedale (London, 1904), p. 100).

tall candles, and, rising up beyond the altar, the lofty papal throne. As in Scene XIII (*The Christmas Crib at Greccio*), we look towards the nave of the church from the apse. The upward gaze of several members of the three groups on the right, comprising the women seated in the foreground, the Church dignitaries behind them, and the crowd of laymen standing at the back, is directed at the raised *sedia*, with its costly hangings, from which the Pope was originally represented as giving his blessing. (A little below the canopy of the throne, a light patch on the ruined surface indicates the probable position of the tiara.)

The damp from which the fresco has suffered has destroyed what may well have been the most splendid passage in the composition: the designer of such frescoes as *The Sanctioning of the Rule* (Scene VII, Plate 53) and *The Sermon before Honorius III* (Scene XVII, Plate 74) would surely have done justice to Thomas of Celano's overawed description of the Pope's appearance on this occasion. 'The Supreme Pontiff is there,' he writes, '. . . with a crown of glory on his head in manifest token of sanctity. He is there adorned with a pontifical chasuble, and clad with the holy garments bound with gold and ornamented with the work of the carver in precious stones. The Lord's Anointed is there resplendent in glorious magnificence; covered with engraven jewels shining with the radiance of spring he invites the gaze of all.'[1] If we supply the figure of the Pope, together with his cardinal-deacons—who appear at the Pope's side in the little scene on the Bardi altarpiece, beneath a canopy decked at the front with rich hangings[2]—the design both of this scene and of the bay as a whole takes on an entirely new aspect. The figure of Gregory IX must have dominated the composition in much the same way that the representation of Boniface VIII dominates the *Jubilee* fresco in the Lateran, and would have provided the focal point of the bay. The emphatic diagonal formed in Scene XXIII by the group of the Poor Clares issuing from the main portal of the church, its reversal in the gesturing arms of St. Francis and the Pope in Scene XXV, and the perspective-lines stated in the façade of San Damiano and to a lesser extent in the Pope's bedchamber all lead the eye inwards to the same point (Plate 7a).

Yet the choice of subjects for this bay presented a problem of unusual difficulty, since it brought together the two scenes that are the most crowded with figures and are in other ways the most alike (Scenes XXIII and XXIV), leaving Scene XXV (*The Appearance to Gregory IX*) somewhat on its own at the end of the sequence. However, the organization of this bay in terms of two scenes that resemble one another and a final scene that is quite different in character has its precedent in the treatment of the two large bays at the east end of the nave, and especially in that of the first bay on the south wall, where three interior scenes, containing many figures, are followed by the open-air scene of *The Stigmatization*, containing only three figures (Plate 6a). Again, as in the

---

[1] Celano (trans. Howell), iii, 124 (p. 126). [2] G. Kaftal, op. cit., Fig. 472.

large bay on the north wall the adjacent buildings in Scenes XI and XII are placed back to back (Plate 4*b*), so the church in Scene XXIII and the papal throne in Scene XXIV are given a similar relationship, so that the second scene assumes the role of mirror-image of the first. This intention possibly explains the presence of the statue of St. Peter in the tabernacle set into the façade of San Damiano (Scene XXIII), for its position relates it to the figure of the Pope once represented in *The Canonization* (Scene XXIV). Unquestionably the lavish ornamentation of the façade (Plates 84*d*, 109) must have provided an effective counterweight to the splendour of the Pope's attire and of the adornments of his throne.

At the same time every attempt was made to harmonize the two outer scenes by means of the usual repetition of certain basic shapes. The triangular form of the upper part of the façade in Scene XXIII finds its echo in the canopy of the Pope's bed in Scene XXV; the position of the dead Saint is reversed in that of the sleeping Pope, whose gesture (as we have seen) is closely related to the group of nuns stooping over the Saint's bier; and, most important of all, the nuns in the first scene and the visionary form of St. Francis in the last create strong movements outwards from the centre of the bay. In the lower areas of Scene XXV the green *cassone* in front of the Pope's bed, which is richly ornamented with a geometric pattern, repeats the long rectangle of the Saint's bier, with its costly gold hangings. Even the disposition of the attendants who guard the Pope's room sets up large arching movements similar to those implicit in the figures grouped around the bier in the other scene. Nor would it have seemed unnatural to a painter preoccupied with effects of pattern to relate the intricate patterning of the hangings behind the Pope's bed to the Cosmati-work on the façade of San Damiano, and even to the heads of the bystanders spotted over the left-hand side of Scene XXIII.

None of the three scenes can be associated with any single prototype. Iconographically, the most interesting of them is Scene XXIII (*St. Francis Mourned by St. Clare*, Plate 83). This subject, as far as is known, had not previously been treated in painting, and it is instructive to examine the process by which the new composition was constructed. The crowd of laymen and friars on the left had its precedents in representations of the obsequies of saints; but these figures are in general more lively, and less formal, than their predecessors in Scenes XX and XXII, as though the newness of the subject had inspired the artist to a greater freedom of expression. The man in red holding the bier with one hand and turning his back to us must have been observed directly from life, no doubt with the example of Giotto in mind. The left-hand area of the composition is completed by the introduction of the boy climbing the tree (Plate 96), a motif borrowed, as we have noted, from the iconography of scenes of Christ's Entry into Jerusalem. It is interesting to observe that the central group of the lamenting *Clarisse* was likewise adapted from an appropriately analogous subject, in this case from the legend of St. Clare herself: the basic conception of this enchanting passage in the Assisi fresco is already found in Guido da Siena's reliquary shutters in the Accademia at Siena, where in the scene of *The Expulsion of the Saracens* St. Clare and her companions are represented as emerging, in a closely knit group, from the doorway of their convent (Plate 31); but if the origins of the Assisi figures lie here, they have none the less been transformed by the *dolce stil nuovo* of the masters of the *Legend* into living presences of flesh and blood, and nothing in the whole cycle in the Upper Church is quite comparable with this sympathetic and tender expression of womanhood (Plate 84*a*, *c*, *e*).

The head of the nun standing in the centre of the principal doorway (Plate 84*a*) bears a close resemblance of type to certain heads by the St. Cecilia Master (Plates 84*b*, 38*a*), who may well have helped to execute this fresco. In other passages, however, the differences from his style are only too evident, and the figure kneeling down to kiss the Saint's hand—with her small eyes and languorous gesture—clearly belongs to another taste (Plate 101*c*). The art of the St. Cecilia Master is also recalled by the beautifully drawn sculptures of angels decorating the façade of the church (Plates 84*d*, 109), which bring to mind the similarly posed angels on St. Cecilia's throne (Plates 8, 108).[1] The treatment of the church, with its sculptures and reliefs, compares in brilliance of draughtsmanship and fluidity of handling only with the mastery shown in the representation of the reliefs on the Column of Trajan in Scene XXVIII (*The Liberation of the Prisoner*, Plate 94*a*, *b*). Among its most remarkable qualities is the subtlety of the suggestion of effects of light and shade: the nave of the church is itself cast into deep shadow, but the painter has also sought to show how the statues surmounting the four piers of the façade are shaded from the light by their canopies.[2] There would seem to be no real precedents in European painting for such an inquiry into the role of light in Nature, and it is interesting that the painter's curiosity about this aspect of the visible world should evidently have been aroused, in the first instance, by his observation of architectural forms and sculpture, in which effects of this kind would have been particularly amenable to close and prolonged study.

The variable quality of the painting in *The Canonization of St. Francis* (Scene XXIV, Plate 85) must be due to the participation of assistants, whose handiwork is particularly evident in some of the figures of women in the right foreground, while the bishops seated further back tend to a woodenness of expression and articulation untypical of the figures in the preceding scene. One of the painters who worked in this area was probably the assistant who was responsible for the four attendants in *The Appearance to Gregory IX* (Scene XXV, Plate 88). These attendants bear a close resemblance to certain seated or crouching figures common in the work of Pacino (Plate 89*d*); and the second

[1] A. Smart, 'The St. Cecilia Master and his School at Assisi', *The Burlington Magazine*, cii (1960), 413, Figs. 39 and 40.
[2] Cf. Tintori and Meiss, op. cit., p. 140.

attendant from the right (Plates 85, 89*b*), with his long but broad nose and straggling black beard, is almost identical in feature with the figure of Moses in *The Tree of Life* in the Accademia (Plate 86). Although the authorship is evidently different, these figures and the seated attendants in Scene VI (*The Dream of Innocent III*, Plate 52) belong to the same basic type. The individual quality of the painting in Scene XXV is apparent, further, from the exquisite treatment of the geometric ornament on the rich hangings (Plate 89*a*): the refinement and intricacy of the ornamentation are quite unprecedented in the cycle, and suggest the delicate hand of a miniaturist or of a painter of small panels; and we may compare, for instance, the central compartment of the *Santa Margherita* altarpiece (Plate 9), where a similar taste is shown in the embroidery on the saint's gown.

The subject of Scene XXV (Plate 88), like the stories narrated in the final bay (Scenes XXVI–XXVIII), is taken from the *Miracula*, so that the *Canonization* (Scene XXIV, Plate 85) is the last fresco to illustrate the main part of the *Legenda maior*. As we have observed, however, Bonaventura does not describe the Saint's canonization in detail, and the full account in the *First Life* of Thomas of Celano was undoubtedly the main literary source for the Assisi fresco. Immediately after describing the canonization ceremony, Thomas of Celano goes on to relate some of the Saint's miracles of healing, and the fresco includes a reference to at least one of these. We are told by Celano that 'on the day that the hallowed and holy body of the most blessed father Francis was put away, like a most precious treasure, having been anointed rather with celestial aromas than with earthly spices, a girl was brought whose neck had for a year past been monstrously bent so that the head was joined to the shoulder, and she could only look up sideways. But after placing her head for some time under the coffin wherein the precious body of the Saint lay, forthwith she raised up her neck, through the most holy man's merits, and her head was restored to its proper position so that the girl was astounded at the sudden change in herself and began to run away, weeping excessively.'[1] The girl can be seen in the fresco (Scene XXIV) standing to the left of the altar, with her head bent forward at a curious angle, as she looks in the direction of the Saint's coffin.[2] The fresco is also faithful to Thomas of Celano's description of the scene, in including a large number of women, two of them with children in their arms.[3]

[1] Celano (trans. Howell), iii, 125 (p. 127); noted by Thode, op. cit. This incident seems to have been very popular in the thirteenth century, and it figures in several of the most important representations of the Franciscan legend, including Berlinghieri's altarpiece at Pescia; the altarpiece of the School of Giunta Pisano at S. Francesco, Pisa; the Bardi altarpiece, Santa Croce, Florence; and the panels in the sacristy of S. Francesco, Assisi, and in the Pistoia Gallery (School of Meliore): cf. G. Kaftal, op. cit., col. 405, x.

[2] In the scene on the panel at Pisa (G. Kaftal, op. cit., Fig. 481), the girl kneels at the tomb. The iconography of the Assisi fresco is in this respect closer to that of the scene on the Bardi altarpiece (Plate 78*b*), where the girl stands (although she looks upwards, rather than down as in the Assisi fresco).

[3] Similar figures occur in some earlier representations: both in the Pisa panel (G. Kaftal, op. cit., Fig. 481) and in the Bardi altarpiece (Plate 78*b*), a woman can be seen walking out of the picture to the left with a child on her shoulder.

A more important figure is the friar in the grey habit who is standing on the far side of the altar, immediately beneath the papal throne. He is apparently addressing the congregation, several members of which look up at him. This must be Riniero Capocci, a cardinal-deacon and a member of the Dominican Order, whom Thomas of Celano describes as 'a man of mighty and penetrating intellect, illustrious by his piety and character', and who, he says, preached on this occasion with such effect that the Pope and the entire assembly wept with emotion. The placing of this figure within the opening beneath the canopied throne creates a point of interest in the composition equivalent to the emphasis in Scene XXIII (*St. Francis Mourned by St. Clare*) upon the nun standing in the centre of the principal doorway of the church.

Exalted in the scene of the *Canonization* as the instrument of Francis's beatification, Gregory IX is presented in Scene XXV (Plate 88) as one vouchsafed a special revelation of the truth of the sacred *stigmata*.[1] Yet because he belonged, if only temporarily, to the company of doubters, he occupies a somewhat ambiguous position in Franciscan history and legend. His reservations about the reality of the *stigmata*—which concerned, however, only the wound in the Saint's side—could never be quite reconciled with the subsequent decree of Nicholas III allowing proceedings for heresy to be taken against any one who denied this essential miracle.[2] It was a doubt that appears to have shocked the early Franciscans; the Spirituals did not hesitate to apply to Gregory IX the name of heretic; and Bonaventura himself felt obliged to admit that such lack of faith merited severe reproof. In the *Legenda maior* St. Francis appears to the Pope 'wearing an aspect of seeming severity', and chides him for his unbelief. He then orders a vessel to be brought to receive the blood issuing from his side. The Assisi fresco shows the moment at which the Pope takes the glass vial from the Saint's hand. Despite some clumsiness of drawing in certain passages, especially in the figures of the attendants, together with the loss of a number of details that were finished *a secco* (including the blood in the vial), this is surely the finest and most convincing, as it is also the most poetic, of all the representations of miraculous appearances in the *Legend*, with the sole exception of Scene XXVI (*The Healing of the Wounded Man*), which immediately follows it at the beginning of the next bay. The spacious design and the quality of tender lyricism that pervades the composition would appear to reflect the immediate influence of the St. Cecilia Master, who now takes charge of the completion of the cycle.[3]

---

[1] *Legenda maior*, Miracula, i, 2.

[2] Cf. *Fioretti*, ii, xiii; *The Little Flowers of St. Francis*, ed. T. Okey (London, 1910), p. 134.

[3] Scene XXV has frequently been ascribed to the St. Cecilia Master himself. Tintori and Meiss (op. cit., p. 147) infer his probable influence upon its design. The composition is repeated with certain variations (such as the omission of the attendants) in the fresco by Francesco da Rimini in the Convento di S. Francesco at Bologna: cf. M. Salmi, 'Francesco da Rimini', *Bollettino d'arte*, xxvi (1932), 253, Fig. 5.

XV

SOUTH WALL: FOURTH BAY

(SCENES XXVI–XXVIII)

JUDGED IN TERMS OF UNITS OF BAYS, the cycle attains its highest peak of technical accomplishment in the altar bay on the south wall, in which all the frescoes (Scenes XXVI–XXVIII) were executed by the St. Cecilia Master, with some little help from assistants (Plate 7*b*). Up to this point no individual scene in the cycle can quite compare in the sheer quality of its painting with the first of all (*The Homage of a Simple Man*): but now on the south wall the *Legend* comes to a close on a no less exalted note.

The change is reflected not only in the consistently high quality of the drawing and in the harmoniousness of the colouring, but also in an assurance and rapidity of execution that denote a supreme and experienced master of fresco. The technical proficiency of the St. Cecilia Master was such that Scene XXVIII (*The Liberation of the Prisoner*, Plate 93), with all its complex detail and its ten figures, took no longer to complete than the relatively simple composition of *The Sermon to the Birds* (Scene XV, Plate 68), which required only two figures and no passages calling for particularly detailed treatment.[1] The St. Cecilia Master's rapidity of execution enabled him to prepare his *intonaco* patches in unusually large areas, and in Scene XXVI (*The Healing of the Wounded Man*, Plate 90) the figures of St. Francis and the two angels, together with most of the figure of the sick man, were all painted on the same patch: this is a remarkably large area to have been begun and completed on the same day.[2] Even more striking, perhaps, is the fact that no vertical join in the *intonaco* is detectable in the whole upper area of Scene XXVIII (Plate 93), containing the figure of St. Francis and the greater part of two buildings, each of which is embellished with exquisitely finished representations of sculpture: even the execution of this area over a period of two days would have been an extraordinary achievement.

One word—grace—sums up the spirit of the St. Cecilia Master's frescoes at Assisi.

---

[1] Tintori and Meiss, op. cit., pp. 56, 82, 118, 150, 154, Pls. 41 and 55, Diagrams F, J. [2] Ibid., Pl. 53.

Grace of design, grace of drawing, and grace of colouring combine here as they do nowhere else in the cycle. Nor do we find elsewhere so fine a degree of finish, except in certain passages in the areas of the decoration executed by the Master of the Obsequies. Understandably, this is a virtue little regarded today, so fearful are we of spoiling the freshness of the rapid notation: but Trecento painting knew no such thoughts, and it is one of the miracles of the period that at a time of innovation and radical change the work of the greatest masters, whatever the difficulty or complexity of the pictorial problems that concerned them, still breathes the same breath of freshness and spontaneity that we attribute today chiefly to the sketch. If this mastery is in evidence anywhere in the Assisi cycle it is in the first and in the last three scenes.

The compositional ordering of the final three narratives of the *Legend* (Plate 7*b*) conforms to the general principles established in the other bays, and the two outer frescoes—*The Healing of the Wounded Man* (Scene XXVI) and *The Liberation of the Prisoner* (Scene XXVIII)—are paired symmetrically on either side of the central fresco illustrating the story of the woman of Benevento, the Tabitha of Franciscan legend, whose rising from the dead, being the greatest miracle of all, is given pride of place in the bay. The rigid geometry that characterizes the design of the two outer scenes contains in each case two groups of figures composed of gently arching masses; above them rise lofty architectural structures which divide each composition vertically into three fields, comprising a large central space flanked by narrow, shaft-like segments; and it is this geometrizing that allows an interior scene to be related so satisfactorily to one set in the open air. In *The Confession of the Woman of Benevento* (Scene XXVII) the emphasis is placed at the centre, where the dead woman, miraculously restored to life, confesses to her priest. Here the two groups of mourners, composed respectively of five men and a child and five women and a child, and united by the long horizontal of the bed, contribute to the general symmetry of the whole conception, which is assisted by the almost central placing of the piers supporting the two levels of the roof, and by the pairing on either side of them of the forms of the angel and the demon that had claimed the woman's soul.

Although throughout the bay the main action is confined to the lower, 'earthly' areas of the designs, a rising movement initiated in Scene XXVI in the stooping form of St. Francis, and assisted by the perspectival rendering of the roof above his head, carries into the upper, 'heavenly' region of Scene XXVII, where St. Francis kneels in supplication before Christ. A similar movement ascends to the same point from Scene XXVIII, beginning in the arched figure of the liberated prisoner and continuing in that of the Saint as he flies heavenward after working the miracle. It is in the management of these upper areas that we discern most clearly the genius of a great composer. According to Bonaventura, St. Francis appeared bodily both to the wounded Giovanni d'Ilerda and to the imprisoned heretic Pietro d'Alifia, whose faith in the merits of the Poverello is rewarded in Scenes XXVI and XXVIII, but not to the woman of Benevento. It was necessary, however, to introduce the figure of the Saint into each scene, and he could be included in *The Confession of the Woman of Benevento* only in an act of intercession, such as would normally be represented in one of the upper corners of a composition. It would seem therefore that the decision to represent St. Francis in Scene XXVIII in the act, not of liberating the prisoner, but of returning to heaven after the performance of the miracle must have had the primary purpose of creating a second stress in the upper area of the design equivalent to that provided by the intercession scene in the central fresco. Yet, like the heavenly Christ and the demons of Arezzo in the large bay at the east end of the north wall, the related images do not belong to paired scenes. Once again the difficulty seems to have been resolved by an ingenious shift of emphasis.

In Scene XXVII St. Francis is shown kneeling in prayer and looking up towards Christ, the two figures being related to one another on an axis which repeats the angle of the Saint's body in Scene XXVIII. Each of these paired images belongs to a clearly defined rectangular field. In Scene XXVII St. Francis occupies the centre of an all but perfect square defined by the architectural forms of the house-top, and the inclined orthogonal produced by the rendering of the little tower to his right in oblique perspective reverses the diagonal line of Christ's arm, giving a symmetrical *stasis* to this composition within a composition. Yet a neighbouring rectangular field on the left, occupying the top right corner of the preceding scene, extends the whole area to the left, into Scene XXVI, and the painted column separating Scenes XXVI and XXVII becomes the central division of the total rectangular field (Plate 7*b*).

In Scene XXVIII, on the other hand, the emphasis is moved to the right. The figure of St. Francis is likewise contained within a clearly defined area, the vertical limits of which are indicated by the tower on his left and the support for the iconostasis which invades the composition on his right. The iconostasis and the Roman column enclose an empty field of sky, equivalent in function to the rectangular field in Scene XXVI. In this way the spectator can accept the painted column on the one hand and the iconostasis on the other as parentheses bracketing the paired images of the intercession scene and the ascending Saint, and this is made easier by the preponderance of vertical divisions in the design of the bay as a whole. In terms of the individual design of Scenes XXVI and XXVIII, the balance is restored by the repetition of identical or similar shapes in their respective upper areas: in Scene XXVI the rectangular field in the top right corner is simply repeated in the top left corner; and in Scene XXVIII the whorl-like folds of the Saint's draperies find their pictorial counterpart in the reliefs twisting round the Roman column.

The ascending movement stated in *The Healing of the Wounded Man*[1] establishes a close

---

[1] *Legenda maior*, Miracula, i, 5.

relationship between the figures of the Saint and the attendant angels in that scene and those of Christ and St. Francis in *The Confession of the Woman of Benevento*: above the angels a large window opens on to the space of sky adjacent to the intercession scene, and so contributes to the impression that St. Francis has just descended from heaven to attend the sick man, to whom, as Bonaventura says, it seemed that he had come in through the window (Plate 90). Further to the left the despairing physician, in a long cloak which was once blue, but of which only the grey underpainting now remains, is bidding farewell to the sick man's wife. She herself is attired in a rich, plum-coloured dress which flows behind her in silken folds; she wears upon her head a high, funnel-shaped hat fastened with a chin-band. Another woman, presumably a servant, stands behind her, dressed in a deep blue garment of less elegant material and a white cap: her sorrowful expression indicates that all hope of her master's recovery has been abandoned. He himself is a handsome and exotic figure of an aquiline cast of feature; his black beard is elegantly trimmed; on his head he wears a scarlet cap. It is evident that the painter wished to give him the features of a Spaniard, as the text in the *Legenda maior* demanded. To find any comparable example of this concern to express national or racial character one must turn in this period to Giotto's superb portrayal of the Sultan and his Moorish retinue in the fresco in the Bardi Chapel at Santa Croce, or to his skilful differentiations between Jewish and Roman types in the Arena Chapel at Padua.

The finely carved wooden bed, with its white sheets and pillow and its deep red coverlet, is beautifully painted to give the effect of different textures, and combines with the rich gold hangings and the nobly proportioned architecture to lend an air of aristocratic elegance to the room. The wooden base of the bed serves a threefold function in the design, establishing a horizontal stress towards the bottom of the picture-space, which is continued in the lower edge of the curtain at the back and in the hem of the physician's cloak, and which repeats similar horizontals in the other two scenes in the bay; helping to bind together into one group the figures of St. Francis and the wounded man and those of the two angels, who are separated by an intervening column; and giving variety to the central area of the composition contained within the two tall columns of the house by contributing to its division a little to the right of centre, where the foot of the bed is aligned with the right edge of the curtain: this division is half-concealed by the overlapping form of one of the angels, whose wings, tinted in soft greys, reds, and whites, are patterned against the gold material of the curtain in an exquisite variation upon the graceful silhouettes of the two women.

In this area of the decoration there is a return to the definition of a clear-cut foreground space, such as is found almost invariably on the north wall, but which for some reason was generally abandoned up to this point on the south wall. It is a return to the more rigid geometry and clarity of the earlier scenes in the cycle. In Scene XXVI the division of the picture-space by architectural forms into regular rectangular fields possesses that quality of delicate but assured tastefulness which distinguishes the individual scenes of the *Santa Cecilia* altarpiece: nowhere is the architectural detail overstated; the buildings still tower up over the human action, but being more lightly constructed than those of the St. Francis Master they do not give the same impression of bearing down upon the figures. Yet the space occupied by the figures within the total design becomes smaller, conforming to the scale preferred in the Uffizi altarpiece. A radical reduction in the scale of the human figure in relation to an architectural setting accompanied the realistic tendencies of Trecento style, and the St. Cecilia Master must be counted among the pioneers of a more convincing system of proportioning. In this respect he was more advanced than Giotto himself, although the development of Giotto's style deducible from a comparison between his decorations in the Arena Chapel and those at Santa Croce shows that he was pursuing the same path.

In Scene XXVI at Assisi (Plate 90) the scale of the figures could not have been more nicely calculated in relation to the design as a whole, which is based upon a division of the composition into quarters and halves such as we find also in the opening scene of the *Santa Cecilia* altarpiece; the division in each case being first stated in the structure of the roof of the house, with its upper and lower levels, and emphasized in the lower area of the composition by a horizontal feature—the wounded man's bed and the table set for St. Cecilia's wedding feast (Plate 8). In the fresco the geometry is all the more rigid, since the architectural divisions are carried down into the foreground by the long columns that support the roof: this severity of design has, however, been modified by the draping of one of the columns with a gold curtain, which conceals part of the column at the level of the figures and, further up, softens its outline, as it also repeats in its largest fall, where it hangs from the curtain-rod, the gracefully curving silhouette of the figure of the sick man's wife. The thin columns in this fresco and in Scene XXVII (*The Confession of the Woman of Benevento*, Plate 91) are identical with those represented in the fourth compartment of the *Santa Cecilia* altarpiece (Plate 8), and structures similar to the thicker piers supporting the upper roof of the woman of Benevento's house can be seen in the third compartment.

The Confession of the Woman of Benevento (Scene XXVII, Plate 91)[1] is by far the most solemn and grave of the episodes represented in this bay, and in general it lacks the decorative qualities of its neighbours: but once again the static geometry of the architecture imposes an abstract order upon the scene, within which the human actors are held as in a timeless moment. The huddled figures of the penitent woman and her confessor, who are associated compositionally with the central pillars of the building, and the two groups of mourners, disposed symmetrically on either side, are all kept quite

---

[1] *Legenda maior*, Miracula, ii, 1.

separate; but they are related to each other by the long yellow bed, with its light-blue covering, a form that extends the whole distance from the mourners on the left to those on the right. The same thinking lies behind the design of the second and seventh scenes of the Uffizi altarpiece (Plate 8): in the first of these, the horizontal lines of the marriage-bed join together the vertical oblongs of the front curtains, with the two figures of the saint and her husband occupying the central space; in the other scene, Almachius's throne relates the figure of the saint to that of the soldier standing on the other side of the composition; and in both these examples the two enclosing forms define an empty rectangular field in the immediate foreground. As at Assisi, what is so impressive is the dominance of superlative design over the art of the narrator.

Despite the difficulties inherent in its pictorial treatment, the subject-matter of Scene XXVII would be clear enough to any one who had no knowledge of the narrative in the *Legenda maior*: the woman's complexion has the ashen hue of death; she is quite patently making her confession to the priest; and to complete his interpretation of the story the painter felt the need to introduce only one additional image other than the heavenly figures of Christ and St. Francis—that of the angel putting to flight the devil that had taken the woman's soul before her repentance, an allusion to the 'grim prison' in Hell to which she had been consigned after death. Yet the miracle is presented with but little expression of that awe before the supernatural which characterizes Giotto's frescoes at Padua. The *Legend* as a whole stands closer to the medieval piety that finds less cause for astonishment in the incidence of a miracle than in the merits of the saint whose holiness vouchsafed it. The hushed wonderment of the crowd which contributes so much to the unearthly atmosphere of Giotto's interpretation of the Raising of Lazarus would appear out of context here. The acolytes on the left of the composition bow their heads in simple reverence; the women on the right raise or clasp their hands in pious thankfulness; the little child is not afraid to stretch out its arms to be hugged by its *nonna*. The women have been aptly likened to flowers swaying in a breeze:[1] they are grave and gentle figures, and their emotions are touchingly expressed; but they are less the participants in a drama of human life than the passive witnesses of a sacred event, or divine manifestation, in which they can have no active role; their thin, pinched features and their intense and curious expressions are precisely those of the devoted virgin martyrs of the Uffizi and Montici altarpieces who glide along the path to death and Heaven as though they were living a familiar dream.

The story of St. Francis which began at Assisi concludes in Rome, where the Saint now exerts his power in opposition even to the wishes of Pope Gregory IX himself, who is represented in the *Legenda maior* as having instructed the Bishop of Rome—shown kneeling at the centre of the Assisi fresco (Plate 93)—to imprison Pietro d'Alifia on suspicion

---

[1] Lina Duff Gordon, *The Story of Assisi* (London, 1909), p. 256.

of heresy.[1] If the subject-matter of Scene XXVII suggests the story of Tabitha, that of Scene XXVIII recalls the miraculous liberation of St. Peter from prison, and it is perhaps not insignificant that the heretic of Alifia bears the same name. The Roman setting is indicated in the fresco by that strange mixture of fantasy and realism, the representation of Trajan's Column, with its marvellously rendered reliefs;[2] a structure curious in various ways, not least because it apparently rests upon the roof of the prison.

The principal group of figures in the foreground contains some of the finest painting in the cycle. The group is activated by the graceful, rhythmic movement flowing from the figure of the prisoner, who steps from the arched entrance to the prison, the door of which has been miraculously shattered, holding in front of him, as he stoops towards the kneeling bishop, the chains that once bound his feet, while others fall from his hands. This pictorial movement passes gently across the form of the elegant soldier with the circular shield, who inclines his head in the same direction, and then curves round the shoulders of his companion in the yellow cloak, to descend through the bishop's raised arms: at this image of reverence it is halted by the clean white lines of the palace, before being allowed to continue, through the folds of the bishop's cope as it falls behind him, into the closely knit group of spectators on the left.

It was a rare sensibility that conceived the graceful relationship of the prisoner's head and arms to the rounded forms of the archway and the soldier's shield—the basic pattern underlying this passage being an arabesque line flowing around the archway and curling back through the prisoner's arms. An almost identical motif can be found in the sixth scene of the Uffizi altarpiece (*St. Cecilia Preaching*, Plate 8), where a similar relationship is set up between the arching form of a little portico and the saint's arms and halo. In the altarpiece the arabesque linking the portico with the saint's gesture provides the means whereby a linear movement embracing the entire upper register of four scenes is brought downwards from the previous scene: in all these scenes, in fact, the architectural forms are very closely related to the linear rhythms stated in the figures. Analogies with this type of compositional device are to be found in areas of the Assisi cycle not executed by the St. Cecilia Master, especially on the south wall: a similar conception, for example, underlies the relationship of St. Francis's right arm in Scene XVIII (*The Appearance at Arles*, Plate 75) to the Gothic window to his left and of the Saint's halo in

---

[1] *Legenda maior*, Miracula, v, 4.

[2] In the Middle Ages Trajan's Column was one of the best known of the ancient monuments of Rome, and like the Column of Marcus Aurelius it attracted pilgrims and travellers who wished to enjoy a prospect of the city from a lofty point. A twelfth-century decree of the Roman Senate directs that Trajan's Column 'shall never on any pretext be injured or destroyed by any one, but shall remain as it stands, whole and unharmed for the honour of the Roman people, as long as the world endures', and that 'any one attempting to harm it shall suffer the ultimate punishment and his goods be confiscated to the treasury'. Cf. James Bruce Ross, 'A Study of Twelfth-Century Interest in the Antiquities of Rome', in *Medieval and Historiographical Essays in Honor of James Westfall Thompson*, ed. J. L. Cate and E. N. Anderson (Chicago, 1938), p. 311; R. Lanciani, *The Destruction of Ancient Rome* (London, 1899), pp. 166 f.

Scene XXIII (*St. Francis Mourned by St. Clare*, Plate 83) to the arched doorway behind him. On the north wall such rhythmic movements tend to be on a vaster scale, a contrast that emphasizes the qualities shared by the St. Cecilia Master and the Master of the Obsequies.

This melodic use of line, which is essentially Gothic in character, and which is fundamental to the St. Cecilia Master's style, can nowhere be seen to greater perfection than in *The Liberation of the Prisoner*. Evidently the St. Cecilia Master was fascinated by the relationships and oppositions that are possible between the curve and the straight line, and here as elsewhere it is the straight line that provides the austere framework for the softer harmonies of the arabesque. His designs perfectly support the habitual solemnity of his thought; but although the mood is generally grave his art invariably reflects a sensuous feeling for colour and texture. The rendering of the richly embroidered vestments of the bishop's retinue in this fresco and the sumptuous treatment of the fine silk dress worn by the wounded man's wife in Scene XXVI are perhaps unsurpassed in contemporary Italian painting outside Siena.

The upper walls of the prison are decorated with two angel reliefs, one of them represented in shadow, and the niches set into the façade of the palace each contain a statue of a prophet holding a scroll (Plate 92*c*). The gleaming white wall of this building catches the full glare of the sun, but within the recesses of their niches the statues are veiled in shadow, except where certain forms catch the light and flash out in broken glints. The same interest in effects of light is evident again in the brilliant chiaroscuro of the two reliefs on the Roman column. The absence of these qualities from the representation of the temple relief in Scene I raises a question that will be discussed later.

For sheer brilliance of drawing these reliefs (Plate 94*a*, *b*) are unsurpassed even by those miracles of suggestive draughtsmanship, the two little scenes, also in monochrome, introduced below the figures of *Justitia* (Plate 20*c*) and *Injustitia* in the Arena Chapel. The upper relief (Plate 94*a*), representing an equestrian battle-scene, is particularly remarkable for its imaginative design and for its vigorous expression of violent action. Nowhere in early Trecento painting do we find animals rendered with greater truth or feeling: even in the surviving work of Giotto there is nothing quite to compare with the wounded horse at the centre, pathetically raising its head as it attempts to struggle from the ground, or with the rearing steed immediately to the right—both masterpieces of observation and fluent drawing. The lower relief (Plate 94*b*) shows a preacher addressing a group of soldiers from a low hillock or knoll; camels are being led in from the right; one of the soldiers on the left clasps his hand to his helmet as if in sudden astonishment.

The battle relief recalls contemporary representations of battles between Crusaders and Pagans; the other relief may well allude to St. Francis's own peaceful mission to the

East. A contrast was perhaps intended: certainly St. Francis's exchange of the sword for the spiritual armour of Christ was an event in his early life that is emphasized by all his biographers. This theme is elaborated in a remarkable way in the metrical Life of St. Francis known as the *Legenda Sancti Francisci Versificata*, composed in 1232 by a poet at the court of Henry III of England. Here the spiritual conquests of St. Francis are directly contrasted with the military triumphs of Alexander the Great and Julius Caesar:

> Veteris iam fama triumphos
> Saevitiis partos et materialibus armis
> Parcius extollat: plus enituere moderni!
> Nam quid respectu Francisci Iulius, aut quid
> Gessit Alexander memorabile? Iulius hostem
> Vicit, Alexander mundum, Franciscus utrumque.
> Nec solum vicit mundum Franciscus et hostem,
> Sed sese, bello vincens et victus eodem.
>   O Christi miles, qui solus stigmata Vitae
> Morte triumphantis vivens in mente latenter
> Et moriens in carne palam, Francisce, tulisti,
> Vatis opus tibi sume tui, celsaeque canendis
> Militiae titulis humilem dignare Minervam![1]

(Already Fame is more sparing with her praise of ancient triumphs won by cruelty and material arms: modern men have achieved more! For, in comparison with Francis, what did Julius Caesar, what did Alexander do that is worth remembering? Julius Caesar conquered the enemy, Alexander the world, but Francis conquered both. And it was not the world and the enemy alone that Francis conquered, but himself, victor and vanquished in the same battle.

O soldier of Christ, you who alone have borne the *stigmata* of Life triumphant over Death, as a secret hidden in your mind while you lived, but openly manifest upon your body when you died, take to yourself, O Francis, the verses of your poet, and accept his humble Muse as not unworthy to sing of the titles of honour gained in your exalted wars.)

If it was the intention to convey a similar idea in the Assisi fresco, the iconographic significance of the Roman column extends far beyond its function as a key to the location of the story of Pietro d'Alifia: the contrasted reliefs, on this reading, would contain the final statement in the cycle of the Franciscan ideal of the imitation of Christ. This opposition of the preaching of the Word to military conquest may thus have been intended to relate to the subject of Scene XXVI (Plate 90), which is a story about man's violence towards man, and there would be added point in the placing of the two frescoes opposite Scenes I and III (Plate 3a), in which St. Francis's mission as the glorious *Christi miles* is first stated.

More important, however, is the role assumed by the setting of Scene XXVIII (Plate 93) in its relation to Scene I (Frontispiece). In many respects Scene I is the most daring,

[1] Henricus Abrincensis, *Legenda Sancti Francisci Versificata*, Liber i, 8–20, in *Analecta Franciscana*, x, 407 f.

and the most revolutionary, composition in the entire cycle: never before had sacred legend been given a local habitation as it has here; never before had a painter dared to represent, with such attention to the *genius loci*, the familiar aspect of the contemporary scene. Here Assisi itself is glorified in a composition placed over against a representation of the Holy City. Of all the implicit comparisons embedded in the pictorial language of the *Legend* in the Upper Church, this conjunction may well have meant most at the time to the people of Assisi and to the friars of the Sacro Convento, mindful of how St. Francis had once blessed his native town, calling it his *città santa*.

XVI

THE PAINTERS OF THE *LEGEND*
AND THEIR INFLUENCE

VASARI'S ATTRIBUTION of the *Legend* to Giotto not only obscured the true character of its style: it also disguised the fact that the cycle is the work of several hands; for at least three painters were given major roles in the execution of the frescoes—the so-called St. Francis Master, the Master of the Obsequies of St. Francis, and the St. Cecilia Master. In addition, a number of other painters left their individual stamp upon the cycle, and were responsible for much of the distinctive flavour of such frescoes as *St. Francis before the Sultan* (Scene XI), *The Christmas Crib at Greccio* (Scene XIII), and *The Death of the Knight of Celano* (Scene XVI).

We do not know the reasons for the employment of so many masters upon this part of the decoration of the Upper Church. One of our few guides in this matter is the evidence regarding chronology, which may indicate that the work was held up at different times by unforeseen interruptions, making necessary the successive employment of the three principal masters and their assistants. On the other hand, the stylistic divisions within the cycle are of a quite different order from the absolute break that separates the pictorial language of the Isaac Master from that of the painters who preceded him in the execution of the Biblical series in the upper registers of the nave, and it is less accurate to speak of a stylistic change from one area of the *St. Francis* cycle to another than of variations within a family of styles. This aspect of the *Legend* raises the question whether the cycle does not belong entirely to the medieval tradition of the collective enterprise, according to which a group of artists of common sympathies would form an association in order to carry out a particular commission, the precise division of the labour being agreed upon from the beginning. An arrangement of this kind, stipulated by the terms of the contract, might account, for instance, for the unusual procedure whereby Scene I—according to the topological evidence—was not apparently begun until well after the completion of the neighbouring frescoes on the north wall.

Until further evidence is available such questions must be left unanswered; but they are in any case secondary to the main problem of style. Here we are faced with the difficulty that the *Legend* cannot be related very closely to any other fresco-cycle in Italy: neither in the work of the immediate pupils of Cavallini, as we know it from the extensive series of decorations in Santa Maria Donna Regina at Naples, nor in the frescoes of Giotto's School in the Lower Church at Assisi, nor in any other fresco-decoration in Umbria or beyond, do we find anything quite comparable with the distinctive pictorial language of the *Legend*. The affinities with the style of the *Legend* that have often been detected in the *Four Doctors* on the vault[1] and in some of the Biblical scenes in the *Isaac* group (such as *The Finding of the Silver Cup* and the *Pentecost*) are of a very general nature, reflecting as they do common sources of inspiration in the Rome of Cavallini, and should not be exaggerated; nor is the stylistic relationship between the Assisi cycle and the *Jubilee* fresco in Rome close enough to throw any light upon the artistic provenance of either work.

On the other hand, strong reflections of the style of the *Legend* are to be found in contemporary or near-contemporary Florentine panels and manuscripts. Of such works the Santa Maria Novella Cross (Plates 12*a*, 14*a*, *d*), the *Madonna* at S. Giorgio alla Costa (Plates 15*b*, 16*c*), the *St. Peter Enthroned* at S. Simone (Plate 40), and the altar-pieces of the St. Cecilia Master (Plates 8, 9, 15*a*) have a special importance in the history of early Florentine painting; and to these we may now add a significant part of the *œuvre* of Pacino di Bonaguida.

As Offner was the first to demonstrate, the authors of all these works developed, in the main, independently of Giotto's influence; and the decisive role played by the St. Cecilia Master in the creation of this distinctive Florentine tradition cannot be too strongly emphasized. The close stylistic relationship of his frescoes at Assisi to those of the St. Francis Master, a relationship underlined by the aesthetic unity of the opening bay of the cycle (Scenes I–III, Plate 3*a*), is no less clear. The many differences between the artistic personalities of the two masters do not disguise their adherence to certain basic conventions, whether in the approach to composition or in the solution of particular problems of representation, from the expression of human action and response to the rendering of architectural and landscape forms. It is for this reason the less surprising that Scene II (*The Gift of the Mantle*) should sometimes have been ascribed to the St. Cecilia Master, and Scene I (*The Homage of a Simple Man*) retained by others within the area of activity of the 'Giotto' of the Vasarian tradition. The unified character of the 'family of styles' of which the *Legend* is composed is further underlined by all those qualities that bring the St. Cecilia Master's frescoes in the Upper Church into harmony with those executed by the Master of the Obsequies, a painter whom Berenson identified with the St. Cecilia Master working under Giotto's direction.

[1] Previtali (op. cit., pp. 38 ff.) has recently ascribed the *Four Doctors* and the figures of *Saints* on the *sottarchi* of the vault to Giotto and Memmo di Filippuccio.

At this point, then, we may return to a question posed earlier in this book—as to whether the Assisi cycle does not itself relate to that virtually independent current of Florentine painting of the late thirteenth and early fourteenth century which produced in the St. Cecilia Master, himself one of the painters of the *Legend*, perhaps its most influential figure. To answer this question in the affirmative is not to argue that the authors of the *Legend* were necessarily Florentines, and indeed it is not even certain that the St. Cecilia Master was himself of Florentine origin, although his roots do seem to lie partly in Florentine traditions of the late thirteenth century. What is indisputable is that both the St. Francis Master and the St. Cecilia Master must have been largely formed in Rome. The figure-style of both painters has much in common with that of Cavallini, and the taste shown throughout the Assisi cycle in the representation of architecture, with its wealth of Cosmatesque ornamentation, derives, like the inlaid thrones of the Montici *Madonna* (Plate 15a) and the *St. Peter* at S. Simone (Plate 40), no less certainly from Rome. The St. Cecilia Master's relationship to Roman painting of the late thirteenth century can also be studied in the fragmentary remains of a fresco-cycle of *The Life of St. Catherine of Alexandria* formerly at Sant'Agnese in Rome, and in what has been preserved of a group of Old Testament scenes at Santa Cecilia in Trastevere, in which some of the qualities of the St. Cecilia Master's style are anticipated, notably in the Sant'Agnese frescoes, with their elongated figures and delicate architectural forms.[1]

Whether or not, like the St. Cecilia Master, the St. Francis Master was active in Florence after his Assisan period, his apparent influence in Florence and, not least, the reflections of his style in the art of Pacino di Bonaguida throw some light upon his significance in the history of early Italian painting. While it is not possible, on the present evidence, to prove any direct connection between the Assisi cycle and the development of such a master as Pacino, since it could be argued that he came under the influence of the St. Francis Master at some anterior date, whether in Rome or elsewhere, the cycle still emerges from our analysis as the major surviving example of monumental fresco-painting that relates closely to 'non-Giottesque', Florentine traditions. This evidence also adds to our knowledge of Pacino himself, one of the most important of Giotto's Florentine contemporaries. Moreover, the recognition of stylistic qualities that Pacino shares with the masters of the *Legend* serves to define the more sharply the very character of the cycle and to underline its separateness from the world of Giotto.

Pacino is documented first in 1303 and again between the years 1320 and 1330:[2] these records thus embrace a period roughly identical with that in which there is

---

[1] The Sant'Agnese frescoes are now housed in the Vatican. For an attribution of both groups of frescoes to the St. Cecilia Master himself see Alessandro Parronchi, 'Attività del "Maestro di Santa Cecilia"', *Rivista d'arte*, xxi (1939), 193 ff.

[2] Offner, *Corpus*, III, ii (Part i), 2, where all the documents are quoted.

documentation of Giotto. He was an artist who was evidently in favour with the Franciscans, and several of his most important panels and manuscript illuminations, including that great pictorial exposition of Bonaventura's *Lignum Vitae*, the *Tree of Life* in the Accademia—which was formerly in the Convento delle Monache di Monticelli, the oldest convent of the Poor Clares in Florence—were executed for Franciscan communities. Yet we know very little about him, although a Roman training may be inferred.

Damage to the inscription on his one dated painting—the polyptych in the Accademia of *The Crucifixion, with Saints Nicholas, Bartholomew, Florentius and Luke*,[1] which was formerly in the church of S. Firenze—has not made the problem of his development easier. The framing below the central Crucifixion scene bears the following *titulus*, the last part of which appears to be missing: SȲMON · R · BTER · S · FLOR̄ · FEC̄ · PĪGI · H̄ · OP · A · PACINO · BONAGUIDE · AÑO · DÑI · MCCCX . . . There remains a faint trace of what looks like the top of a further letter, which could be I, V, or X. It has been suggested[2] that the original date was MCCCXXX, and there would indeed be room for two additional X's. This reading, however, must be rejected, for it ignores the fact that the inscription is preceded by a decorative motif which must have been balanced by a similar feature at the right extremity of the *titulus*; an inference confirmed by the identical decorative motifs that bracket the names of the saints under the side panels. In fact there would not be room for more than one letter, and the narrowness of the space available makes it easier to postulate an I rather than a V or an X, although one or other of the latter alternatives cannot be ruled out. On this reading, therefore, the altarpiece is to be dated somewhere between 1311 and 1320.

The Tree of Life must be considerably earlier. The style is less developed: none of the figures possess anything of the grandeur and monumentality of those represented in the polyptych, and the format of the panel, with its simple pointed top, itself indicates a date not later than the first few years of the century. No less significant is the retention in the central figure of the Crucified Christ of an older iconographic type: witness the hands pressed flat against the beam of the Cross—to be replaced in the *Crucifixion* polyptych by the more functional and more graceful treatment which first makes its appearance in Florence in the Crucifix of Santa Maria Novella.

Between these two works, which establish the character of Pacino's early and mature style, we must assign the Morgan *Life of Christ, with Scenes from the Life of the Blessed Gherardo*, perhaps the earliest known manuscript illuminations from Pacino's hand. These comprise thirty-three scenes from the Life of Christ and five scenes from the

[1] Accademia, Florence, No. 8568. For this work see especially Offner, *Corpus*, III, II (Part I), iv, 12 f., Pls. IV, IV iv[1–4d], and Ugo Procacci, *La Galleria dell'Accademia di Firenze* (Rome, 1951), p. 25.

[2] H. Thode, op. cit., p. 503, n. 3.

legend of the Blessed Gherardo da Villamagna, a Franciscan tertiary who lived as a hermit near Castello di Villamagna (not far from Florence) and who died in the early thirteenth century. The stylistic relationships between the Morgan series and the Assisi cycle indicate a probable date within the first decade of the new century. A much damaged and repainted dossal of *The Virgin and Child, with Saints Nicholas, Lawrence, James the Greater, and Francis* in Dublin,[1] the panel of *The Virgin and Child* (Plate 51c) in the Accademia,[2] originally the centrepiece of a polyptych which was once in the Badia of Florence, and the Careggi Crucifix (Plate 13b), ascribed to his *bottega* and formerly in the church of the Spedale di Bonifazio in Florence, must all be early works, and clearly belong to the ambient that embraces the *Madonna* (Plate 15a) by the St. Cecilia Master at Montici, the S. Giorgio *Madonna* (Plate 15b), and the Santa Maria Novella Cross (Plate 12a). To a rather later period must be assigned two important works executed for Franciscan communities—the Chiarito Tabernacle[3] and the Tuscan Custodia[4]—the first of which exemplifies the clarity of Pacino's gift for story-telling before the demands made upon an overworked *bottega*, as it would seem, led to a general unevenness in quality and to an increasing reliance upon assistants. These tendencies, however, were accompanied by a more definite approach to the art of Giotto, which shows itself in the monumental style of the later paintings on panel, the *Crucifixion* polyptych in the Accademia being a notable example.

There can be no doubt that Pacino's shop was the major centre of manuscript illumination in Florence during Giotto's lifetime, and that many artists were trained and employed there. As Offner has shown, his *bottega* had a virtual monopoly in illustrations to Dante;[5] and the lively illustrations to Villani's *Chronicle* are scarcely less important. The personalities of the numerous assistants concerned with the production of this vast body of illustrative material often obscure that of Pacino himself, and thus the impression is often given of stylistic contradictions for which Pacino can himself scarcely have been responsible; but even in the very late works, such as the beautiful illuminations for the *Appeal of the City of Prato to Robert of Anjou*, now in the British Museum[6] (see Plate 73b), elements of Pacino's early manner sometimes survive. Nevertheless, the extent of the participation of other hands, together with a tendency towards eclecticism within Pacino's own style, lends to his work as a whole a quality of variousness that we scarcely

[1] Private collection, Dublin. Cf. Offner, *Corpus*, III, vi, 174, Pls. XLIX, XLIX[a].

[2] Ibid. III, vi, 164 f., Pl. XLVI.

[3] Wildenstein Collection, New York. The tabernacle contains a representation of *The Communion of the Apostles*, with a *Trinity*, a *Madonna with St. Catherine*, scenes from the Life of Christ, and scenes from the Life of the Blessed Chiarito. Cf. Offner, *Corpus*, III, vi, 148, Pls. XLII, XLII[a-c].

[4] University of Arizona, Tucson (Kress Collection): at the centre, a *Crucifixion*; on the shutters, scenes from the Life of Christ. Cf. Offner, *Corpus*, III, vi, 150 ff., Pls. XLIII, XLIII[a-b].

[5] Ibid., III, vi, 243.

[6] Cf. G. F. Warner and J. P. Gilson, *British Museum: Catalogue of Western Manuscripts in the Old Royal and King's Collections* (London, 1921), i, 159 f. (No. 6 E. ix); Offner, *Corpus*, III, vi, 213 ff., Pls. LXI[a-d].

meet in other masters of the period; and this tendency can be disturbingly in evidence within a single composition: it is, however, less prevalent in such early works as *The Tree of Life* and the Pierpont Morgan Library manuscript.

While it is difficult to offer more than a tentative sketch of Pacino's development, his stylistic relationship to the Assisi cycle sheds some light upon his origins, suggesting an artistic personality formed within the same traditions that moulded the styles of the painters of the *Legend* as a whole. If the source of his contact with these traditions, which clearly derive in large measure from Rome, is not to be identified with the Assisi workshop itself, then the new evidence would seem to confirm the postulate of an early Roman training.

The closeness of the connections between Pacino di Bonaguida and the authors of the *Legend* is perhaps summed up in the remarkable resemblance of the figure of Moses in *The Tree of Life* (Plate 86) to one of the seated attendants in Scene XXV of the Assisi cycle (Plates 87, 88, 89*b*); and in the formalized treatment of the garments of the attendant immediately to the left (Plate 88) the resemblances to the *Moses* are equally strong. Similar figures appear also in Scene VI (Plate 52) and in the series of illuminations by Pacino in the Pierpont Morgan Library (Plate 89*d*).

The stylistic connections between Pacino and the masters of the *Legend* seem particularly close in Scene XIV (*The Miracle of the Spring*, Plate 64) on the east wall and in Scene XVI (*The Death of the Knight of Celano*, Plate 70) on the south wall; but already on the north wall much of the imagery can be paralleled in his work. Within the restricted range of miniature painting, the Morgan scene of *The Blessed Gherardo Soliciting Alms from a Traveller* (Plate 43) is remarkably close in spirit to *The Gift of the Mantle* at Assisi (Scene II, Plate 42). The Morgan illuminations are among the most elegant of Pacino's productions, and we do not find in them that searching interest in volume and mass that characterizes the roundels on *The Tree of Life*, and therefore the contrast with the monumental forms in the Assisi fresco is all the greater; but such differences should not blind us to all that this scene has in common with the composition in the Upper Church, from the way in which the figures are linked by rhythms that flow across the picture-plane to the relationships established between the figures and their landscape settings: the saint's halo, for instance, has much the same function in the design as that given to Francis's halo in the Assisi fresco, and from it the hill on the left and the arched back of the rider divide upwards and outwards in a very similar manner to the two hills in the fresco; and the frontal representation of the saint and the stance of the woman who receives the traveller's gold, thrusting her head forward to peer up at her benefactor, compare in more than a general way with the attitudes of Francis and the impoverished knight. Similar attitudes, as we have seen, characterize many of the St. Cecilia Master's own figures, without, however, giving them the same quality of ungainliness.

Damage due to the use of tempera and white lead has destroyed much of the detail in the fresco, and the horse is now little more than a formless silhouette. The more elegant steed in the miniature should rather be compared with the horses that draw the Saint's chariot in Scene VIII (Plate 47*b*), where the conventions employed in the rendering of individual features and details are virtually identical: we may note in particular the similarities in the drawing of the horses' heads, with their great eyes and flared nostrils, and the distinctive treatment of the striated manes. It is as though these conventions, these specific modes of configuration, had survived the transposition into a different key, remaining quite recognizable despite the change in medium and despite the no less obvious contrast between the monumental character of the image in the fresco and the more decorative and ornamental style of the miniature. As we have seen, other features of the Assisi imagery are repeated in an illustration produced in Pacino's workshop to Villani's story of the miraculous crucifix of S. Miniato (Plate 47*a*).

Little attention has ever been given to the varying conventions adopted by the Trecento masters for the interpretation of landscape; but the distinctions that are to be drawn between one painter's approach to landscape and that of another are quite as marked as any other stylistic differences; and just as the landscape backgrounds of the Arena Chapel cycle could never be confused with the settings preferred by Duccio or the Lorenzetti, so some of Giotto's pupils made their own variations upon his practice, as can be seen from the cycles in the Magdalen Chapel and the presbyterium of the Lower Church at Assisi or from the decorations by Taddeo Gaddi in the Baroncelli Chapel at Santa Croce. The tiny landscapes of the *Santa Cecilia* and *Santa Margherita* altarpieces have much closer affinities with those represented in the *Legend* in the Upper Church than any known interpretations of landscape by Giotto or his pupils can ever be said to have; but there are still greater resemblances to be found in the landscape conventions of Pacino, whether in the Morgan illustrations or elsewhere (Plates 39*c*, 43, 67*a*). Comparing once more the scene of the Blessed Gherardo's charity with *The Gift of the Mantle* in the Upper Church, we may note the similarity of the uses to which landscape is put in the structure of the two compositions (Plates 42, 43). The smooth plateau of rock upon which the figures stand ends, in each case, in a miniature precipice at the lower edge of the picture-area, the figures being separated from this mysterious opening in the earth by only a few inches. Following now the recession of these landscapes into the background, we find that the foreground merges imperceptibly with the far distance, where rising steeps seem to hang suspended: it is this absence of a middle distance and of a clear differentiation between horizontal and vertical planes that contributes so much to the impression that the figures are in danger of slipping from the picture-space.

Like the St. Cecilia Master, Pacino habitually breaks up the surfaces of his landscapes into a multiplicity of shapes giving an effect of variegated pattern, but the individual forms tend to be larger, and he shows a particular fondness for cubic formations of an almost geometric simplicity, which he chisels out in smooth planes defined by often abrupt transitions from light to shade. The incisions in the rock at the lower edge of the Morgan illumination (Plate 43) can be exactly matched in the more richly elaborated foreground of *The Miracle of the Spring* (Scene XIV, Plate 64), while the star-like segments of rock near the top of the hill and the square blocks and declivities elsewhere show an identity of treatment with the no less simplified formations that give so distinctive a character to the shining mountain towering above the kneeling St. Francis. There also grow from the flinty terrain in both compositions similar types of ragged tree, the roots of which tend to be accentuated; and, although the Morgan illustrations preserve throughout a miniaturist convention for the rendering of leaves which is absent from the fresco, foliage more comparable with that found in representations of trees in the *Legend* can be seen, for example, in the roundel of *Christ at Gethsemane* (Plate 69a) on *The Tree of Life*. Moreover, the rendering of the famous tree in the fresco of *St. Francis Mourned by St. Clare* (Scene XXIII, Plate 96), where the cluster of leaves springing from the branch on the near side of the climbing boy has been circumscribed with an artificial outline, is of particular interest in this context, for an identical configuration occurs on *The Tree of Life*, in the scene of *The Suicide of Judas* (Plate 97a), at whose feet there springs a tree delineated in the same manner.

Comparisons between Pacino's figure-style and that of the St. Francis Master inevitably throw into relief the essential differences that separate the painter of miniatures and small panels from the painter of large-scale mural decorations; but we have only to compare the figure of St. Francis on *The Tree of Life* (Plate 86) with the representations of the Saint in kneeling attitudes in Scenes VII, IX, X, and XIV of the *Legend* (Plates 53, 56, 58, 64), or the figure of the dead Gherardo da Villamagna (Plate 97b), from the Morgan series, with the almost identical portrayals of the dead Francis in Scenes XX, XXII, and XXIII in the Upper Church (Plates 77, 82, 83, 97c), to judge the extent to which Pacino, on the scale of the altarpiece or miniature, adheres to the stylistic traditions which inform the Assisi cycle.

No less interesting is the resemblance of the two children who stand on the left side of Scene V at Assisi to the types consistently repeated by Pacino in representations of the Christ-Child and other youthful figures. The child represented in profile in the fresco (Plate 51b), with his short, turned-up nose, long upper lip, and small chin, corresponds closely in feature with the Christ-Child of Pacino's *Madonna* in the Accademia (Plate 51c); while his companion, who turns his head only slightly to one side, to reveal the full rotundity of a face at once childishly podgy and yet prematurely creased, belongs to a type that Pacino may be said to have made his own, and of which there are several examples in the Morgan illustrations alone (Plate 51*a*, *d*). Among the individual characteristics of these heads we may note especially the large, open eyes, the slightly snub nose, and the flowing mop of hair which cascades in long waves from the tight, striated fringe to curl behind the ears; the chin is unusually heavy, the neck thick and well-fleshed and marked by circling lines. Such features characterize, for instance, the Christ-Child in the Morgan *Presentation in the Temple* (Plate 51*d*), where also the drawing of the right arm and hand and the sleeves that grip the wrist but bag out at the elbow strongly recall the representation of the other child in the fresco, who points with his right hand as he talks to his wide-eyed playmate. The work of Pacino offers similar parallels with other figures in this fresco, from St. Francis at the centre (Plates 50*a*, *b*) to the bystanders on the left (Plates 50*b*, *c*), and there are heads of young men in the Morgan illustrations that possess a definite family likeness to the youthful St. Francis of the early scenes at Assisi, with his close-cropped hair and smooth, untroubled countenance (Plates 39*a*, *b*, 44*b*, 45, 46).

This is not to suggest that Pacino's figures invariably resemble those at Assisi, as we might expect them to do if we could identify him among the painters of the *Legend*: very often they are quite dissimilar; but the resemblances, when they occur, can be extremely close. Nor do we find either in his paintings on panel or in his miniatures anything quite comparable with the elaborate architectural structures typical of the *Legend*, especially on the north wall, although they do from time to time show similar forms, such as the castellated towers, the jutting, tiled storeys supported by realistically rendered beams, and the overhanging, tessellated ceilings that are all so characteristic of Pacino's architectural tastes (Plates 59*a*, *b*, *c*, 73*a*). His fondness for a type of cusped arch, which does not occur at Assisi, is apparent both in the Morgan illuminations and in the narratives of *The Tree of Life* (Plates 47*c*, 99). On the other hand, several of his interiors have certain features in common with those of the St. Francis Master and his associates in the Upper Church, both in their particularization of detail and in their spatial organization; and the treatment of perspective in such compositions as the Morgan *Prayer of the Blessed Gherardo* (Plate 47*c*) and the Vatican miniature illustrating the story of the miraculous crucifix at S. Miniato (Plate 47*a*) recalls the pictorial conventions accepted in Scene IV of the *Legend* (*The Miracle of the Crucifix*, Plate 46) as strongly as it suggests a general independence from the practice of Giotto.

The treatment of architecture in the *Legend* is not, of course, uniform, and the buildings represented on the south wall show differences from the more abstract *aediculae* that are common on the north wall. Here again the comparisons that can be made with Pacino's panels and miniatures are not numerous, and most of the similarities that exist are either of a general or of a rather minor nature, and can be matched in the work of other painters of the period: the circular windows and inlays that are to be found in this area of the decoration may be compared, for instance, with the similar motifs that occur so frequently in Pacino's representations of architecture (Plates 47*a*, 59*a*, 75, 76, 83, 95*b*, *c*). The distinctive relationship established between the superstructures of buildings and the upper borders of the scenes in such compositions as *The Sermon before Honorius III* (Scene XVII, Plate 74), *The Appearance at Arles* (Scene XVIII, Plate 75), and *The Appearance to Gregory IX* (Scene XXV, Plate 88) is, however, a noteworthy feature of the Morgan interiors (Plates 89*d*, 98*d*), and the formula for the rendering of the meeting orthogonals of the coffered ceilings in the Morgan scenes is not far removed from the solution of this problem arrived at by the painter of the coffering directly above the *Virgin* roundel on the east wall (Plates 5, 73*a*). The repetition in the Morgan *Pentecost* (Plate 71*a*) of the same type of Cosmatesque ornamentation that is to be seen, for example, in *The Death of the Knight of Celano* (Scene XVI, Plate 71*b*), while not of course establishing direct influence, is somewhat unusual in a miniature, and might be taken as evidence of Pacino's acquaintance with Roman-inspired fresco-painting.

Pacino's use of gesture as a means of unifying his compositions belongs essentially to the same pictorial language as that employed by the St. Francis Master at Assisi: the design, for example, of the central passage of Scene VII (*The Sanctioning of the Rule*, Plate 98*a*) provides an exact analogy with the organization of the principal figures in the Morgan *Christ before Pilate* (Plate 98*b*), where the head and left arm of Christ and Pilate's head and right arm make up a symmetrically balanced form which is bisected by the raised arm of a young man who turns in accusation towards Christ. Without the presence of this youthful figure the total pattern of shapes would have been monotonously regular; but his head fills the space between his raised hand and the haloed head of Christ, precisely as, in the Assisi fresco, the head of a cardinal seated beyond the Pope fills the corresponding space between the pontiff's head and raised right hand. This type of compositional arrangement has been discussed earlier at some length, and particular emphasis has been given to it as an element of design which, while being wholly absent from the work of Giotto, recurs repeatedly in the Assisi cycle. In the search for some sort of descriptive terminology the resultant pattern of shapes in such passages has been likened to the form of a crossbow, this analogy serving to isolate its main feature, which consists of the bisection of a symmetrical, curvilinear shape by a straight line.[1]

Variations of this motif occur frequently in the roundels of *The Tree of Life*, in the Morgan illuminations, and in other compositions by Pacino. A particularly close analogy with the 'abstract imagery' underlying the central passage of the Morgan *Christ before Pilate* and Scene VII at Assisi is to be found in the representations of *The Adoration of the Kings* on *The Tree of Life* (Plate 44*a*) and in the Morgan series (Plate 98*c*) (these two compositions being virtually identical)—where the rhythmic pattern of forms that knit

---

[1] See above, pp. 171 ff.

together the figures of the Virgin and the kneeling king is interrupted at its centre by the figure of the Christ-Child, the symmetrical regularity of the total 'image' being toned down, as before, by a secondary stress, which in each variant of the design is provided by the king's proffered gift. The same method of composition can be seen, for instance, in the means employed to relate the figures of Christ and St. Peter in the Morgan *Christ Washing St. Peter's Feet* (Plate 98d) and the figures of Christ and Mary Magdalen in the *Noli me tangere*. To cite all such examples of its use would be to compile a long catalogue: it cannot be denied that Pacino's use of gesture as an element in the geometry of his designs bears a strong resemblance to the habitual practice of the St. Francis Master at Assisi.

In the *Christ Washing St. Peter's Feet* (Plate 98d) Christ's discoursing right hand activates the design in a manner that recalls the function, on a purely compositional level, of the kneeling friar in Scene IX at Assisi (*The Vision of the Thrones*, Plate 56), and in each case the gesturing hand is aligned with the lower left corner of the pictorial field. There are many other examples of a like nature, among which one of the most interesting is provided by the Morgan *Christ in the House of Simon the Pharisee* (Plate 73a), where Simon's surprised reaction to Christ's words to the prostitute (identified by tradition with Mary Magdalen) is expressed by his right hand, raised with palm open in a gesture identical in character and in compositional function with that of the red-cloaked guest at the centre of Scene XVI in the Upper Church (*The Death of the Knight of Celano*, Plates 70, 72). So also, in a more general way, Pacino's profound concern with geometry of design and his particular manner of grouping his figures in relation to the underlying geometrical structure of a composition bring him far closer in spirit to the St. Francis Master than to Giotto. A typical example of his method as a composer is provided by *The Adoration of the Kings* on *The Tree of Life* (Plate 44a), where the empty field that separates the Virgin and Child from the approaching kings, but which is yet penetrated by disengaging forms, recalls the St. Francis Master's own practice in such compositions as *The Renunciation of Worldly Goods* (Scene V, Plate 48), *The Exorcism at Arezzo* (Scene X, Plate 58), and *St. Francis before the Sultan* (Scene XI, Plate 61).

Yet it is at the lower end of the nave that the affinities between Pacino and the style of the *Legend* seem to be most marked. In *The Miracle of the Spring* (Scene XIV, Plate 64), the principles of composition, the figure-style and the simple, decorative use of colour all find their echoes in *The Blessed Gherardo Soliciting Alms* (Plate 43), and here, as we have seen, the conventions employed for the treatment of landscape are repeated exactly in the Morgan illumination and in others in the series (Plates 43, 64, 65a, 67a). The Morgan *Christ in the House of Simon the Pharisee* (Plate 73a) has various points of similarity with *The Death of the Knight of Celano* (Scene XVI, Plates 70, 72), at the lower end of the south wall, and there are other passages in the Morgan series that recall features of this fresco (Plates 71*a*, *b*, *c*). Just as there are figures in the Morgan illuminations that are not far removed in character from some of those in the fresco, for example the seated friar (Plate 71*b*), so also some of Pacino's female types, such as those represented in the splendid manuscript of *The Appeal of the City of Prato to King Robert of Anjou*, in the British Museum, are not at all unlike the mourning women in the same scene (Plates 72, 73*b*). In the Morgan *Christ in the House of Simon the Pharisee* (as also in *The Supper at Emmaus* (Plate 71*c*)) the management of the recession of the table is much less advanced than in the fresco, and a similar contrast may be noted in passing between the no less primitive rendering of the table in the scene of the wedding feast on the *Santa Cecilia* altarpiece (Plate 8) and the assured treatment of perspective in the St. Cecilia Master's frescoes at Assisi; but in other respects the two compositions have much in common, from the relationship established in each design between the table and the figures behind it and the kneeling female figure in front of it to their discursive narrative spirit and the harmonics of their tonal scale, which allow of sudden transitions from lights to emphatic darks.

There has been occasion to draw attention to the stylistic qualities that make their appearance in the area of the entrance to the Upper Church—initially in the first bay on the north wall (Plate 4*b*) but more noticeably on the east wall and at the lower end of the south wall (Plates 5, 6*a*)—and to raise the question whether they denote the emergence of a new artistic personality or whether (as most proponents of Giotto's responsibility for the *Legend* would argue) all that we are witnessing is the development and maturation of a single master (albeit a master who controlled a fairly numerous band of assistants). Could the main author of Scene V (Plate 48), for example, have developed, perhaps over the space of a year, into the author of Scene XVI (Plates 48, 70)? It must be said at once that the change in style is of a different order from the clear distinctions that separate Scene I (by the St. Cecilia Master) from Scene II (by the St. Francis Master), and that Scenes I–XVI can be meaningfully retained within a single stylistic group, dominated by the personality of the St. Francis Master; but another hand seems to be at work in Scene XVI and elsewhere in the lower area of the nave: his style can be recognized especially in the frescoes on the east wall (Plates 64, 68) and in Scene XVII on the south wall (Plate 74).

It is possible that the author of Scene XVI began as an assistant on the north wall, emerging thereafter as the controlling influence upon the task of decorating the east and south walls before the arrival of the St. Cecilia Master in the Upper Church. Some of the stylistic characteristics found on the east wall and at the lower end of the south wall are undoubtedly anticipated quite early in the cycle: for example, the friar standing at the centre of Scene VIII (Plate 55) closely resembles the friar on the very left in Scene XIV (Plates 64, 66*a*) and Brother Monaldo in Scene XVIII (Plate 75); and the heavy-jowled friars of Scenes XV and XVI (Plates 68, 70, 71*a*) also have their precedents on the north wall, notably in the figure of the kneeling friar in Scene IX (Plates 56, 57*c*). There is, of course, evidence as early as Scene V (Plates 48, 50*d*) that the task of decorating the north wall was allocated from the beginning to more than one painter.

In contrast to Giotto's decorations in the Arena Chapel, the Assisi cycle must be regarded as the masterpiece of a *bottega* or, at the very least, of a group of associated painters who may well have been accustomed to working together. To this extent the difficulty that is often encountered in the attempt to distinguish one hand from another becomes less significant: where a number of artists of like mind devote themselves to the service of a common ideal, variations within the group-style are of less importance than the qualities shared by the painters concerned; moreover, in the process of execution there will be a tendency for personal idiosyncrasies to be suppressed for the sake of the unity and harmony of the whole.

The identity of none of the painters of the Assisi cycle can yet be established; and while the common authorship of the *Santa Cecilia* altarpiece and Scenes I and XXVI–XXVIII of the *Legend* is clear enough, the reflections of the Assisi style in other Florentine paintings are not sufficient to show that their authors also participated in the execution of the frescoes. We may consider again the undoubted resemblances between the Santa Maria Novella Cross (Plates 12*a*, 14*a*, *d*) and the cross represented on the iconostasis in Scene XXII (Plate 12*b*) and between the *Madonna* at S. Giorgio alla Costa (Plates 15*b*, 16*c*) and the *Virgin* roundel in the Upper Church (Plate 16*a*). Those students of Giotto who retain the Santa Maria Novella Cross and the S. Giorgio *Madonna* within his *œuvre* are surely right to emphasize their stylistic affinities with the *St. Francis* cycle. Moreover, the hypothetical identification of the Master of the S. Giorgio *Madonna* with the St. Francis Master has received some support from outside the group of scholars who accept the Vasarian attribution of the *Legend* to Giotto.[1]

This view, which has much in its favour, confronts us with a paradox. At Assisi, the dependence of the St. Cecilia Master upon the vision of the St. Francis Master has been taken for granted by most students of the cycle; yet both the S. Giorgio *Madonna* and the Santa Maria Novella Cross have been accepted on other grounds as products, to a greater or lesser degree, of the St. Cecilia Master's influence: the S. Giorgio panel has its probable prototype in the *Madonna* at Montici[2] (Plate 15*a*), and, as we have seen, the Santa Maria Novella Cross belongs rather to the circle of the St. Cecilia Master than to that of Giotto. This position is consistent with all that has been argued in the present

---

[1] As Professor White has formulated the problem—in the context of his refusal of the S. Giorgio *Madonna* to the St. Cecilia Master—'A cut-down panel of the Virgin and Child in S. Giorgio alla Costa in Florence is a much more doubtful attribution, to which the Master of the St. Francis Cycle may have better claims' (John White, *Art and Architecture in Italy, 1250 to 1600*, p. 407, n. 9, citing the hypothesis which I advanced in *The Burlington Magazine*, cii (1960), 431 ff.).   [2] Cf. Offner, *Corpus*, III, vi, 3.

book about the close relationship that exists between the styles of the St. Cecilia Master and the St. Francis Master at Assisi. Yet in view of the limited nature of the evidence and the total absence of documentation a proper caution is necessary.

There are undoubtedly strong resemblances of style between the two panels and the Assisi cycle. We have only to compare the figure of Christ on the crucifix with the ponderous *ignudo* of St. Francis in Scene V of the *Legend* (Plates 12a, 48); the Virgin of the S. Giorgio altarpiece with the *Virgin* roundel (Plates 15b, 16a); the Christ-Child on the altarpiece with his counterpart at Assisi and with the children represented in Scene V (Plate 51b); the angels standing behind the Virgin's throne with the now damaged angel in Scene IX and with other figures in the frescoes (Plates 16c, d, 39a, 56); and the treatment of the throne in the S. Giorgio panel with the taste shown in the rendering of architectural detail in the cycle as a whole (Plates 15b, 37a, 61, 83). There are similarities in both panels with the proportioning of several of the heads in the cycle, notably in the unusual length often given to the upper lip (Plates 14d, 16c, d, 50a, d); and the long, boneless fingers of the Virgin's hands in the S. Giorgio picture are found again in the Assisi roundel. Among other physiognomic resemblances, we may point to the large, open eyes, the rather blunt noses, the often heavy, rounded jowls and the emphatic striations of the hair (Plates 15b, 16a, c, 50a, d, 51b). The more delicate modelling of form in the S. Giorgio panel, the less accentuated contrasts of light and shade, and the softer fall of the draperies might all be accountable to the difference in medium.

Yet when all this has been said it must be admitted that the total evidence lacks the overwhelming force that enables us to affirm the common authorship of the *Santa Cecilia* altarpiece and Scenes I and XXVI–XXVIII at Assisi. For one thing, the comparative material at our disposal is less extensive. For another, the most rigorous application of the Morellian method still leaves the question open: if, for example, we compare the angel on the left side of the Virgin in the S. Giorgio *Madonna* with appropriate figures in the cycle, such as the girl who approaches the dying knight in Scene XVI or (to return to the north wall) the children in Scene V (Plates 16c, d, 51b), we shall note various similarities in the general shaping of the heads and in the formation of the features, from the marked lines of the creases under the eyes to the flowing calligraphy of the lips; but we shall also observe differences—an abruptness in the tonal transitions at Assisi that is absent from the panel; a greater fullness in the forms which is particularly noticeable in the frontally placed child in Scene V (Plate 51b), with his swelling cheeks, his large, rounded eyes, and his heavy mouth, features repeated in the grave countenance of the man who stands directly behind him (Plate 50d) and to a lesser degree in the Madonna on the east wall (Plate 16a); and other minute differences of feature, as, for example, in the delineation of the ears—similar but not absolutely identical (Plates 16c, 50a, 51b)—and of the eyebrows, generally rather shorter at Assisi and less finely pencilled (Plates 16*c*, *d*, 50*a*, 51*b*). Comparisons with the Santa Maria Novella Cross present similar difficulties: the St. John the Evangelist on the right terminal of the crucifix (Plate 14*d*) has clearly a much closer resemblance to some of the figures in the Assisi cycle than to any figure painted by the Isaac Master (Plate 14*c*) or by Giotto, and yet neither the small, narrowly placed eyes nor the visible ear, with its elaborate convolutions, let alone the thick, mop-like hair, can be exactly matched in the *Legend*.

In short, the nature of the evidence compels us to keep the question of authorship open, and to confine ourselves to the positive affirmation that the Assisi cycle and the two Florentine panels belong to the same stylistic tradition. The same considerations apply to those early works of Pacino, such as *The Tree of Life* and the Morgan illuminations, in which the affinities with the *Legend*, and especially with the frescoes on the east and south walls, are most marked. The *Madonna* in the Accademia (Plate 51*c*) has much in common both with the S. Giorgio panel (Plate 15*b*) and with the Assisi roundel (Plate 16*a*), just as the crucifix on the iconostasis in Scene XXII (Plate 12*b*) is to be related not only to the Santa Maria Novella Cross but also to the Pacinesque crucifix at Careggi (Plate 13*b*). The Accademia Virgin is not far removed in type from the Assisi figure, and in some respects the resemblances are even greater than those between the fresco and the S. Giorgio *Madonna*, for the head of Pacino's figure is less elongated, the chin and neck are more rounded, and the nose and upper lip more strongly chiselled; and, as we have observed, the Christ-Child particularly recalls the child represented in profile in Scene V (Plate 51*b*).

These and other stylistic connections between Pacino and the masters of the *Legend*, which have been detailed at length, are not such as to establish his presence at Assisi, although we know that he worked for Franciscan communities elsewhere. Admittedly, if he had a connection with the Assisi workshop we should not expect any record of it to have been preserved, for he was a painter without a biographer; but what is significant about the reflections in his art of so many of the stylistic qualities of the *Legend* is not only that they add to our knowledge of the St. Francis Master's influence in Florence but that this evidence runs counter to the Vasarian attribution, for it seems clearer than ever that the Assisi cycle belongs to a different artistic current from that which helped to direct the course of Giotto's development, one that nevertheless runs parallel to it, flowing in like manner from Rome to Florence.

Although neither the Master of the S. Giorgio *Madonna* nor Pacino can be positively identified at Assisi, it is still possible that the painters of the *Legend* were accustomed to working on a smaller scale. As has been suggested earlier, the frescoes bring to mind vastly enlarged manuscript illuminations: it is difficult to say whether it is the fundamental decorativeness of their designs or the particular flavour of the narration that contributes more to this impression; but this is surely one of the qualities of the *Legend* that most distinguish it from the cycle in the Arena Chapel. The principal author of Scene XX (*The Death and Ascension of St. Francis*, Plate 77), as Tintori and Meiss have surmised, seems to have come to his task inexperienced in the techniques of fresco, while the cursive decoration which embellishes the floor of the papal hall in Scene XVII (*The Sermon before Honorius III*, Plate 74) would be more expected in the border of a manuscript.

Most of the major artists of the period were, of course, masters of several media, and could evidently turn their hands with ease from one to another according to the nature of the commission: both Cimabue and Giotto executed supreme works in fresco, in tempera on panel, and in mosaic, and Simone Martini excelled equally as a painter of frescoes, altarpieces, and manuscript illuminations. On the other hand, the author of some important fresco-decoration might well be known principally, like Bernardo Daddi, as a painter of altarpieces. Nor would it be easy, from the standpoint of an artist's work in only one or two of these directions, to guess at his possible distinction in another: if, for example, the *St. Francis* cycle at Assisi had not survived, we should have no conception of the St. Cecilia Master as a fresco-painter, and we should think of him as a relatively minor although influential figure, known only from a small group of altarpieces; and yet the four frescoes by him in the Upper Church reveal him as one of the most accomplished fresco-painters of his time, and indeed of all time.

For some reason the painters chiefly responsible for the north wall at Assisi played little part in the execution of the rest of the cycle. Gradually a new personality makes itself known—that of the principal author of the central frescoes on the south wall, that artist of consummate delicacy who has been referred to in this book by the name of the Master of the Obsequies of St. Francis. Before we consider again the qualities that characterize the art of this impressive and genial master it must be emphasized that although this area of the *St. Francis* cycle bears every evidence of the participation of more than one hand (see Plates 100*c*, 103*b*), the problem of distinguishing absolutely between the work of one painter and that of another remains as difficult as ever, for it arises out of the very processes that went into the ordering and unification of each composition, and the stylistic unity of this group of frescoes remains clear.

The 'modernity' of these compositions on the south wall evidently made a powerful impression upon local Umbrian painting. In the Cesi Master's *Assumption* altarpiece in the Musée Île de France at St. Jean Cap Ferrat, four of the eight scenes of *The Life of Mary* on the wings contain architectural forms adapted from those represented in Scene XXI of the *Legend*, and there are also reminiscences of Assisi in several of the figures.[1]

---

[1] Millard Meiss, 'Reflections of Assisi: A Tabernacle and the Cesi Master', *Scritti di Storia dell'Arte in onore di Mario Salmi* (Rome, 1962), pp. 75 ff.

In a more general way the art of Meo di Guido da Siena appears to be partly rooted in the stylistic traditions represented by the frescoes in this area of the decoration, the influence of the Assisi frescoes being suggested in particular by the searching manner in which he models in light and shade. Still more interesting, however, are the echoes of the style of the Master of the Obsequies that are to be found in the large *Madonna in Majesty, with St. Paul and St. Benedict* (Plate 95a) in the National Gallery of Umbria at Perugia,[1] a work that bears the precious signature on St. Paul's sword: *Marinus P.*

A certain 'Marino d'Elemosina' is documented in Perugia in the years 1309 and 1310,[2] and one 'Marino di Oderisio' in 1318.[3] The *Maestà* came from Montelabate, some twelve miles from Perugia, where it stood over an altar in the Benedictine church of S. Paolo di Valdiponte (otherwise known as the Badia Celestina). It can probably be dated within the first two decades of the fourteenth century.[4] This is one of the most important, as it is also one of the most beautiful, of all the works of the Umbrian School of the early Trecento, and seems to show the influence both of Riminese painting of the period and of the type of *Madonna* evolved by Duccio. The name Oderisio given in one of the documents suggests a possible connection with the miniaturist Oderisi di Guido da Gubbio mentioned in a famous passage in the *Divine Comedy*.[5]

The *Maestà* by Marino shares with the frescoes in this area of the *Legend* a softness of touch and a refinement of colouring that otherwise seem unique in early Trecento painting, and both the altarpiece and the frescoes show a predilection for glowing blues and purples of a lovely and distinctive character, combined with a rich and sensuous awareness of the textures of materials and fabrics. The dainty features and minutely rendered locks and eyebrows that characterize the *St. Paul* and *St. Benedict* on the altarpiece recall several of the figures in the frescoes, where there is also a tendency (as in the *St. Paul*) to a marked aquilinity of countenance (Plate 102a, b, c, d). There are no less interesting similarities in the build of some of the figures, with their sloping shoulders and delicate hands.[6]

Many of the qualities that distinguish the frescoes in this area of the Assisi cycle are

---

[1] Galleria Nazionale dell'Umbria, Perugia, No. 14. For this work see Van Marle, op. cit., v, 16; U. Gnoli, *Pittori e Miniatori nell'Umbria* (Spoleto, 1923), pp. 192 f.; Francesco Santi, *The National Gallery of Umbria in Perugia* (Rome, 1956), p. 11.

[2] U. Gnoli, op. cit., p. 192. In the document of 1309 the name is spelt *Marinellus*: '. . . Marinellus Elemosine pictor pinxit libros domini capitanei.' See also S. Nessi, 'Documenti sull'arte umbra', *Commentari*, xviii, 1 (1967), 73 ff.; No. 18 (p. 79).   [3] U. Gnoli, op. cit., p. 193.

[4] The identity of the beardless saint represented on the altarpiece is relevant to the question of dating. It has been suggested that this figure—usually identified with St. Benedict—is in fact St. Nicholas of Tolentino. St. Nicholas, who died in 1310, was represented as a saint long before his official canonization in 1446: the process of canonization was initiated by Pope John XXII in 1325, and if this figure is indeed St. Nicholas the altarpiece is possibly datable after that year. Most authorities, however, accept a date around 1315.

[5] *Purgatorio*, xi, 79 ff.; containing the lament upon the vanity of human fame which has been discussed earlier (see Chapter II, p. 48).

[6] I drew attention to these similarities of style in *The Burlington Magazine*, cvii (1963), 372, Figs. 41–4.

summed up in the beautifully painted but now damaged figure of the officiating priest in Scene XX (*The Death and Ascension of St. Francis*, Plates 100*c*, 103*b*), with its superb rendering of the different textures of the vestments—the crossed red band of the stole and the superbly painted alb with its rich gold embroideries. Nowhere on the north wall are draperies represented with such feeling for the quality of the material. This figure and others in a less damaged state—such as that of the elderly friar near the centre of Scene XVIII (*The Appearance at Arles*)—may be compared with the *St. Benedict* on Marino's altarpiece (Plates 100*b*, 103*a*, *c*, *d*): all these figures conform to much the same physiognomic type, and attention may be drawn especially to the distinctive treatment of the hair, which is picked out in fine, softly lit strands with a delicacy of touch less surprising in a painting on panel than in fresco-decoration. The angels who hold the cloth of honour in the Perugia *Maestà* (Plates 100*a*, 101*b*) suggest a possible derivation from the angels in Scene XX at Assisi (Plate 101*d*), while the enthroned Virgin herself bears a quite striking resemblance to the Poor Clare who stoops to kiss the hand of the dead Saint in Scene XXIII (*St. Francis Mourned by St. Clare*), even to the drawing of her graceful but flaccid hands (Plates 100*a*, 101*c*).

Unfortunately, almost nothing is known about Marino, the only other work attributable to him being a now fragmentary and inaccessible fresco of a *Madonna* high up on the exterior wall of the former Ospedale della Misericordia in Perugia. He appears, however, to have been a figure of some importance in Perugia in the early years of the fourteenth century, and in 1310 he is recorded there as being Camerlengo dell'Arte dei Pittori. His origins are obscure, but if we are correct in detecting in the Perugia *Maestà* clear indications of the influence of the Master of the Obsequies, it seems very possible that his style was partly formed at Assisi, perhaps during the period of the decoration of the south wall.

There is other evidence that Marino visited Assisi, for it is difficult to think that the active Christ-Child in the *Maestà* does not owe something to the *Madonna and Child* by the St. Nicholas Master in the Orsini Chapel.[1] He would not have been the only painter of the period to study the Orsini Chapel frescoes with attention, and the copy of the St. Nicholas Master's full-length image of St. Clare (Plate 110*b*) which Giuliano da Rimini introduced into his Urbania altarpiece, now at Boston,[2] offers particularly striking proof of such interest. In the context of the question of the impact of the decorations in S. Francesco upon Umbrian painting, it is relevant to point to a further instance of the same kind of borrowing—in fact in relation to the same figure. An altarpiece of Meo's School in the National Gallery in Perugia contains an almost identical representation of St. Clare (Plate 110*a*), and this also must be presumed to be

[1] Reproduced in Meiss, *Giotto and Assisi*, Fig. 9.
[2] Ibid., p. 3, Figs. 6, 7.

a copy of the fresco in the Orsini Chapel: indeed it is an even closer copy than its counterpart in the Boston panel, and unlike Giuliano's figure it is not reversed.

It is not surprising that attention should have been directed to so powerful a portrayal of a saint whose personality and life elicited a devotion second only to that inspired by the Poverello himself, nor that Giuliano da Rimini was drawn likewise to contemplate, and to emulate, the tenderly conceived representation in the Upper Church of St. Francis at La Verna[1] (Plates 29a, 76). Once again, Giuliano was not alone in his concern to repeat the Assisan imagery: in a Florentine miniature of *The Stigmatization of St. Francis* contained in an initial letter in a Laudario now in the Biblioteca Nazionale,[2] the kneeling St. Francis is a close copy of the corresponding figure in the fresco (Plate 105), the only significant variation being the slight turn of the head towards the spectator;[3] and, like Giuliano, the Florentine painter illuminates the figure from the left, precisely as the Assisi master does, instead of allowing it to emanate from the Seraphic Christ. Again like Giuliano, he substitutes for the latter figure, as it is represented in the fresco, a more dramatic image.

So exact a repetition of the Assisan iconography is in itself striking, and with it we return both to the personality of the Master of the Obsequies and to the general question of the influence of the painters of the *Legend* in Florence. The miniature in the Biblioteca Nazionale must be dated much later than Giuliano da Rimini's altarpiece, which is signed and dated 1307: it belongs to a group of panels and manuscript illuminations, mostly datable in the 1330s and 1340s, whose author is known to us from his most celebrated work—the panel at Santa Maria Novella in Florence representing *Christ and the Virgin Enthroned, attended by Seventeen Dominican Saints* (Plate 106)—as the 'Master of the Dominican Effigies'.[4] A pupil, probably, of Pacino and the so-called 'Biadaiolo Illuminator', he was evidently employed for some time in Pacino's workshop, before coming under the influence of Jacopo del Casentino and especially Bernardo Daddi (whose vision dominates his known altarpieces).

The possibility that the Master of the Obsequies was also one of the formative

[1] J. White, 'The Date of "The Legend of St. Francis" in Assisi', *The Burlington Magazine*, xcviii (1956), 344 ff.

[2] Biblioteca Nazionale, Florence, B.R. 19 (Cod. II, i. 212), fol. 52ʳ.

[3] Photographic reproduction of this miniature is made difficult by the absence of any marked tonal distinction between the Saint's tunic and the brown hill on whose slopes he kneels, and between the hill and the deep-blue sky behind. One effect of this is to obscure the definition of the left leg and to give the false impression that it is outlined in a sequence of bulging curves.

[4] The Santa Maria Novella panel can be assigned to the period between 1336—the year of the death of Blessed Maurice of Hungary, one of the holy Dominicans depicted in the painting—and 1347, the date of the canonization of St. Ives of Brittany (Plate 104d), the inscription on whose halo describes him as beatified but not canonized. An altarpiece in the Courtauld Institute Gallery in London (Lee Collection) bears a mutilated date which is probably 1341; a Dante MS. in the Biblioteca Trivulziana in Milan which was illuminated by the same master was written in the year 1337, and another manuscript in the Biblioteca Nazionale in Florence is dated 1342. The fullest accounts of this painter and bibliographies are to be found in Offner, *Corpus*, III, ii (Pt. i) (1930), xi ff., 49 ff.; III, ii (Pt. ii) (1930), 239 ff.; and III, vii (1957), 27 ff. See also M. L. d'Ancona, *Miniatura e miniatori a Firenze dal XIV al XVI secolo* (Florence, 1962), pp. 157, 167.

influences upon his development is raised by the occasional approximation of his physiognomic types to those of the Assisi painter and perhaps, in addition, by the character of some of his compositions, especially in his miniatures. The resemblances are not profound in a purely stylistic sense, and the quality of the Florentine master's panels and miniatures is far inferior to that of the frescoes in the Upper Church. Yet there are certain heads in the Santa Maria Novella panel that are not unlike some of those on the south wall: we may instance the delicately observed St. Ambrose of Siena (standing on the very left in the middle row), whose features recall those of some of the young acolytes in Scene XXII of the *Legend* (Plate 104a, b), and there are similarities between the two painters in their preference for large, rounded heads that bulge out at the back, and which are often inclined in accompaniment to the sidelong glance of the eyes (Plates 104c, d, 105). The hypothesis, which can be only tentatively advanced, that there was some connection between the two masters might account for the closeness of the resemblance between the figure of St. Francis in the miniature in the Biblioteca Nazionale and the famous image of the stigmatized Saint in Scene XIX in the Upper Church; and, as we have seen, the Assisan iconography is quite distinctive. It might also explain certain aspects of the Florentine painter's approach to composition, notably in some of his manuscript illuminations. A splendid and typical example is a delicately coloured illumination in the Collegiata di Santa Maria at Impruneta (near Florence), representing, in an initial, *The Assumption of the Virgin*[1] (Plate 107), where many features of the design, from the crowded figures and the rugged landscape to the type of the ascension-image, can be paralleled on the south wall at Assisi.

It is possible that, like the St. Cecilia Master, with whom he has so much in common, the Master of the Obsequies worked in Florence after the completion of the Assisi cycle. The evident connection between the miniature in the Biblioteca Nazionale and Scene XIX of the *Legend* certainly does not prove that the Master of the Dominican Effigies visited Assisi, since a drawing of the figure in the fresco might well have been accessible to him in Florence. Our knowledge of the means by which particular compositions became known in other centres is lamentably slight; but designs of this kind, however transmitted, could have been used by such masters as Giotto and Taddeo Gaddi when they came to reinterpret the stories of the Franciscan legend: least of all can we assume Giotto's presence in Assisi at some moment between the completion of the *St. Francis* cycle and the execution of the altarpiece of *The Stigmatization* for the church of S. Francesco at Pisa.

There is general agreement among students of the Assisi cycle about the close ties that link the Master of the Obsequies and the St. Cecilia Master. Some of these affinities, it is

---

[1] Collegiata di Santa Maria, Impruneta, Cod. A–V, fol. 158ʳ. Below the *Assumption* there is a further representation of *The Funeral of the Virgin*.

true, can be explained by the likelihood that the St. Cecilia Master was present during the decoration of the central bays on the south wall, and there are certain passages that suggest that he may have helped in the painting of the third bay (Plates 84*a*, *b*, 108, 109); but this cannot be the whole explanation, for the kinship of the two painters is not more striking than their ultimate independence of taste: the style of the Master of the Obsequies shows many resemblances to that of the St. Cecilia Master (Plates 80, 81), and yet it remains quite distinctive in character—as can be judged, for example, by a comparison between the representation of architectural forms in the second and third bays and the more exquisite treatment in the fourth bay (Plates 6*b*, 7*a*, *b*). Even so, Scene XXV (Plate 88), the last fresco in the third bay, has so much in common with the art of the St. Cecilia Master that there is the smoothest possible transition to the style of the final bay and the concluding narratives of the cycle.

The Master of the Obsequies reveals himself at Assisi as a painter of rare quality. His supreme virtue is a refinement of sensibility which expresses itself in the delicacy of his drawing and in the tenderness of his colouring. He delights in highly wrought detail, and excels in the individual passage rather than in the larger conception: if he has a weakness as a composer it lies in his evident desire to fill every corner, although this is also one of his charms. The smaller scale of the figures in this area of the cycle, in comparison with the earlier scenes, is among the features that relate the Master of the Obsequies to the St. Cecilia Master; his figures, besides, have much of the grace of the St. Cecilia Master's, but less of their intensity; they show a serene accommodation to the situations in which they are involved, and yet they seem, perhaps, to lack the capability of the profoundest feeling: there is scarcely anything elsewhere in the *Legend* more touching than the group of Poor Clares who weep for their dead Saint in Scene XXIII (Plate 83), the whole episode being conceived in terms of a gentle, subsiding movement which is quite as meaningful as the mourners' pensive countenances; but the grave tone of Scenes XXVI and XXVII (Plates 90, 91), with their solemn intimations of the burdens of mortality, is absent from it; nor on the other hand is it to be compared with the much starker expression of human tragedy in *The Death of the Knight of Celano* (Scene XVI, Plate 70), and indeed the more abandoned grief of the knight's household could well have offended our master's delicacy.

His figures tend to the exquisite, and much attention is lavished upon particular details, from the fine hair to the neatly formed nails. The facial expressions are frequently animated by flashing glances of the eyes, and mention has already been made of the way in which these glances are often associated with a gentle inclination of the head. The gestures are sometimes lively, although they tend to conform to set patterns, which rarely produce large compositional movements. But what is of special interest is this painter's concern with effects of light, which is particularly in evidence in Scene XXIII (Plate 83) in the treatment of the sculptural decoration of the imposing church.

The quality of draughtsmanship revealed in the rendering of architectural forms in this area of the nave is exceptionally high, and the buildings represented in Scenes XXI and XXIII (Plates 80, 83) are notable for their clean lines and clarity of drawing. The treatment of capitals and finials shows a refinement of taste that is new in the cycle. It may be added that some of the architectural motifs introduced into these frescoes—such as the floral decorations above the side doors of the church in Scene XXIII and the diamond-shaped openings in the tympanum—are also unprecedented. The one landscape (Scene XIX, Plate 76), while conforming in general to the conventions established earlier in the cycle for the representation of Nature, shows certain subtle differences, the most striking of which is the jagged sharpness of the rocky foreground; and attention has been drawn earlier to the delicate beauty of the flower at the Saint's feet, far surpassing in the quality of its observation the more summarily rendered plants in Scene II (Plates 10*d*, 42).

The contribution of the Master of the Obsequies to the great task of completing the decoration of the Upper Church was a notable one, and is worthy of special attention. The advanced style of his frescoes would seem in itself to set a question-mark against the view that the *St. Francis* cycle was commissioned in the early 1290s, unless there was a very considerable delay rather more than half-way through the programme. But there is no evidence of an interruption of this kind. The frescoes at the lower ends of the north and south walls are related to each other both by general affinities of style and by the probability that the same assistant worked on some of the subsidiary figures in Scene XIII (on the north wall) and Scene XVI (on the south wall). Moreover, the evidence provided by the joins in the *intonaco* in the first bay of the south wall shows that Scenes XVI and XVII were undertaken together,[1] and it is clear in any case that the representations of St. Francis in these two frescoes are by the same hand. Furthermore the same painter must have been responsible at least for the figure of Monaldo seated on the left in Scene XVIII; and with this scene we are already within the area of activity of the Master of the Obsequies (see Plate 103*c, d*), who then goes on to participate in the execution of Scene XIX. It cannot be emphasized too strongly that there seem to be no absolute breaks in the stylistic continuity of the cycle such as the hypothesis of a substantial interruption in the programme of decoration would require, for the stylistic groups overlap.

As well as introducing us to a rare and distinctive artistic personality, the frescoes painted by the Master of the Obsequies at Assisi provide a bridge between the scenes at the lower end of the south wall, which have their own stylistic character, and the three

[1] Cf. Tintori and Meiss, op. cit., Diagram G (pp. 198 f.).

scenes executed by the St. Cecilia Master in the vicinity of the altar. Here on the south wall at Assisi there is surely a harmony of styles, not a sequence of conflicting tendencies reflecting opposite ideals. Whatever their differences in style and technique, the various painters of the south wall had a great deal in common: the over-all impression given by the first bay (Plate 6a), upon which a number of artists collaborated, is one of unity, not of discord; and, as we have observed, there is a particularly close relationship of style between one of these painters—the Master of the Obsequies—and the St. Cecilia Master. As the link, therefore, between the first and last phases of the total programme of decoration, the Master of the Obsequies has a special importance among the painters of the *Legend*. He may be said indeed to have prepared the way for the St. Cecilia Master, whose frescoes in the fourth bay of the south wall take their place so harmoniously beside his own. Here it may be added that a comparison between the hangings on the Saint's bier in Scene XX (Plate 73) and the bishop's cope in Scene XXVIII (Plate 93), where the same style of ornamentation is repeated, suggests that at least one of the painters employed in the area of the south wall controlled by the Master of the Obsequies worked also as the St. Cecilia Master's assistant in the fourth bay.

Little can be determined for certain about the St. Cecilia Master's development from his few extant works, although the view that the *Santa Cecilia* altarpiece (Plate 8), together with his frescoes at Assisi, stands towards the beginning of his career, and the *Santa Margherita* altarpiece (Plate 9) towards its close,[2] is on the whole plausible, if speculative. One indication that the Uffizi altarpiece, painted for the church of Santa Cecilia in Florence, was executed before the church was burnt down in 1304, rather than after its rebuilding in 1341, is provided by the panel of *St. Peter Enthroned* (Plate 40), which bears the date 1307. The *St. Peter Enthroned* is very close in manner to the Uffizi altarpiece, as it is also to the St. Cecilia Master's frescoes at Assisi, and even as a work of his School it must reflect his style at a mature stage in its development. His origins are probably to be sought in Florentine traditions of the late Dugento, and the Montici *Madonna*, for example, is already anticipated in the exquisite *Madonna* (of unknown authorship, Plate 110c) in the church of S. Andrea at Mosciano,[3] which in its turn derives partly from the type of *Madonna* evolved by the 'Maestro della Maddalena'—in particular the *Madonna* at Compiobbi (Plate 110d) and the late *Madonna* at Remole.[4]

The importance and achievement of the Maestro della Maddalena, whose masterpiece is the altarpiece in the Accademia representing *Mary Magdalen with Eight Scenes from her Life*,[5]

[1] Cf. Tintori and Meiss, op. cit., p. 147.   [2] Offner, *Corpus*, III, i, xxi.

[3] As was pointed out by Offner: cf. R. Offner, 'The Mostra del Tesoro di Firenze Sacra, i', *The Burlington Magazine*, lxiii (1933), 80. For the Mosciano *Madonna* see Sinibaldi and Brunetti, op. cit., p. 293, Pl. 92, and E. Sandberg-Vavalà, *L'Iconografia della Madonna* (Siena, 1934), p. 68.

[4] Sinibaldi and Brunetti, op. cit., p. 241, Pl. 75a–c (as School of the Maestro della Maddalena).

[5] For this work see especially Ugo Procacci, *La R. Galleria dell'Accademia di Firenze* (Rome, 1936), p. 20; Sinibaldi and Brunetti, op. cit., pp. 229 ff., Pl. 70a–c; C. L. Ragghianti, *Pittura del Duecento a Firenze* (Florence, 1955),

have been obscured only by the impact made upon the period by such greater contemporaries as Duccio and Cimabue, but he was undoubtedly one of the dominant artistic personalities in Florence towards the end of the thirteenth century and the beginning of the fourteenth. His linear and highly decorative art is, however, insufficient to account for more than the general tradition out of which the more advanced style of the St. Cecilia Master seems to have emerged. It must be assumed that the St. Cecilia Master came at an early period of his life under the influence of Cimabue in Florence and of Cavallini and Arnolfo in Florence or Rome. Nevertheless, the pattern of development represented by the *Madonna*s at Remole, Mosciano, and Montici is a clear and consistent one. The stylistic origins of the *Madonna* at S. Giorgio alla Costa (Plate 15*b*) are evidently similar, and the ultimate connection between this work and the art of the Maestro della Maddalena is epitomized by the half-length figures of angels with crossed stoles represented as standing behind the Virgin's throne, which develop a motif found, for example, in the *Madonna* by the Maestro della Maddalena at Rovezzano.[1]

At Assisi we meet the St. Cecilia Master in a guise unfamiliar to us from his Florentine works: at Assisi, indeed, he is revealed to us in a different dimension—no longer, that is, as the painter of relatively small devotional panels, but as a great master of fresco. The assurance with which he approached his task at Assisi makes it all the more difficult to believe that his beginnings lie there: his style, surely, was already formed.

It is a style, as we have seen, that marks itself out from that of the St. Francis Master and which yet possesses a number of qualities in common with it. What the two masters share is evident from the unity that was achieved in the opening bay (Plate 3*a*), a unity that would be still more perfect if the inferior technique of the St. Francis Master had not been responsible for a deterioration in the paint-surfaces of Scenes II and III: yet the distinctive character of Scene I is equally unmistakable.

As the author of this fresco, painted after the completion by the St. Francis Master of Scenes II and III, the St. Cecilia Master appears, seemingly, in a secondary role in the decoration of the bay; and indeed he was given responsibility for only three other frescoes in the cycle—the three last, in the bay opposite (Plate 7*b*). There is no means of knowing whether Scene I was reserved for the St. Cecilia Master under the terms of the contract or whether its execution was delayed for some other reason, such as the possibility, first adduced by Gnudi, that at the time of the commencement of the *Legend* the iconostasis (which spanned the nave between Scenes I and XXVIII) had not yet been fixed in position. But if our reading of the relationship between Scenes I and III is valid, then it seems probable that the composition of Scene I was known by the

pp. 100 ff. Ragghianti argues that the Maestro della Maddalena, together with the 'Maestro del S. Francesco Bardi' (the author of the altarpiece of *St. Francis and Scenes from his Legend* in the Bardi Chapel at Santa Croce, Florence), initiated the mosaic decoration on the vault of the Florentine Baptistery.

[1] In the church of S. Michele: cf. Sinibaldi and Brunetti, op. cit., p. 227, Pl. 69.

time that the cycle was begun, for according to our analysis the heavenly palace on the right side of Scene III was meaningfully associated with the palace on the left side of Scene I—that is to say, with an actual building which there was no question of inventing for the occasion, but which stood, and still stands, in the main piazza of Assisi to the left of the Temple of Minerva, precisely as it is represented in the fresco.

Nevertheless, there is so much that is distinctive about the conception of Scene I that it is difficult to suppose that the St. Cecilia Master was merely working from a design by the St. Francis Master: if such a design existed from the beginning, he must have interpreted it with some freedom. But if, on the other hand, the conception was his, might he not, after all, have played some part in the general design of the opening bay? The refinement of the treatment of architecture in Scene III, where the simple structural elements of the Saint's room, on the left, possess an elegance that is never found again on the north wall at Assisi, and which is more characteristic of the St. Cecilia Master's frescoes in the opposite bay, might itself be explained by this hypothesis, which would leave open the possibility that there were two moments of the St. Cecilia Master's participation in the cycle—during the first of which he executed Scene I, and during the second of which he completed the cycle by painting Scenes XXVI–XXVIII (Plate 7*b*), perhaps taking some part also in the work of decorating the previous bay (Plate 7*a*).

But while it seems important to put this question, the arguments against such a hypothesis are fairly persuasive. In the first place, it is simpler to assume that Scene I was painted at about the same time as the other frescoes for which the St. Cecilia Master was responsible, especially in view of the established fact that this scene was painted after Scene II. In the second place, if the St. Cecilia Master was present in the Upper Church at an early stage in the execution of the cycle, it is surprising that during this phase he intervened only in the painting of Scene I. Thirdly, the 'advanced' style of Scene I suggests in itself a late stage in the stylistic evolution which can be traced in the *Legend* as a whole, and which already distinguishes the style of the Master of the Obsequies from that of the St. Francis Master.

At the same time there is a case for the view that Scene I (Frontispiece) antedates Scenes XXVI–XXVIII (Plates 90, 91, 93), from which it differs not only in its figure style but, more significantly, in the treatment of light. That nascent interest in effects of light and shade, and especially of cast shadow, which characterizes some of the later frescoes of the St. Francis Master, and which is developed further by the Master of the Obsequies, is a feature also of Scenes XXVI–XXVIII but not to the same degree of Scene I. We have observed already that whereas cast shadows are introduced into the representation of the sculptural reliefs on the *baldacchino* in Scene XIII (Plates 37*a*, 63), they are absent from those decorating the pediment of the temple in Scene I (Frontispiece). Yet in

Scene XXVIII the statues of prophets occupying the niches on the façade of the palace (Plate 92c), the reliefs on the walls of the prison, and those on the Roman column (Plate 94a, b) are all remarkable for their brilliant effects of lighting and chiaroscuro. This interest, stimulated no doubt by earlier adventures in the cycle in the treatment of light and shade (above all in Scene XXIII (Plate 83)), is also reflected in an increased subtlety in the rendering of the character of a head, as we see if we compare the man standing next to St. Francis in Scene I (Plate 38a) and the right-hand angel in Scene XXVI (Plate 84b).

Altogether the representation of the human figure is more accomplished in the frescoes on the south wall: for example, the figures in Scene I (Frontispiece) lack the fluency of treatment that characterizes those in Scene XXVIII (Plate 93); nor is the relatively simple organization of colour in Scene I quite comparable with the melodious orchestrations of the bay opposite. The larger scale of the figures in Scene I must have been determined by the need to harmonize them with the figures in Scenes II and III; but in any case the preference shown for more *petite* forms in the last three frescoes in the cycle is consonant with the general development of the St. Cecilia Master's style; for the same progression, together with an enhanced appreciation of the value of light, distinguishes the *Santa Margherita* altarpiece at Montici, which would appear to be a late work, from the *Santa Cecilia* altarpiece in the Uffizi, which cannot have been painted long after the frescoes at Assisi.

It would be difficult to challenge Offner's thesis that the St. Cecilia Master[1] was the

---

[1] I intend to discuss on another occasion the question of the problematic Buonamico Buffalmacco, whose identification with the St. Cecilia Master was first proposed by Adolfo Venturi (*Storia dell'arte italiana* (Milan, 1901–40), v, 290). A bibliography of the main literature relating to the Buffalmacco–St. Cecilia Master hypothesis, a summary of the relevant documents and a list of traditional attributions to Buffalmacco are given in Offner, *Corpus*, III, i (1931), 41 ff. For more recent literature see Pier Paolo Donato, 'Proposta per Buffalmacco', *Commentari*, Anno XVIII, iv (Oct.–Dec. 1967), 296.

The name *Bonamichus magistri Martini* appears in the *Matricola dell'Arte de'Medici e Speziali* of Florence for the year 1320, and a document of 10 March 1336, preserved in the Archivio dello Spedale Nuovo della Misericordia at Pisa, records an accusation of breach of contract brought against *Bonamicus pictor*. A further document of 1341 mentions certain unspecified decorations in Arezzo Cathedral, which had apparently been in existence for some time, as having been painted *per Bonamicum pictorem*. Ghiberti says that Buonamico painted frescoes at S. Paolo a Ripo d'Arno at Pisa and 'many works' in the Camposanto, while Sacchetti and Vasari refer to decorations by him in Arezzo Cathedral. Only one work mentioned in pre-Vasarian sources, the now ruined *St. James* cycle in the Badia at Settimo (outside Florence), now survives, apart from two full-length figures of saints painted on opposite sides of one of the pillars of the nave of S. Paolo a Ripo d'Arno at Pisa, which may have belonged to the decorations by Buonamico cited by Ghiberti. The extended list of attributions to Buffalmacco contained in the second edition of Vasari's *Lives* includes a number of works that cannot have been painted by Buonamico, including the *St. Catherine* cycle in the Cappella del Cardinale Spagnuolo in the Lower Church at Assisi, which are known to have been commissioned in 1368 from Andrea da Bologna.

After Vasari's time the canon was considerably expanded, and Padre Angeli, in his work on the Sacro Convento at Assisi, published posthumously in 1704, while recognizing that Buffalmacco could not have painted the frescoes in the Cappella del Cardinale Spagnuolo, proceeded to ascribe to him the decoration of three other chapels in the Lower Church—the Cappella di Santa Maddalena, the Cappella di S. Martino Vescovo, and the Cappella di S. Lodovico (cf. Francesco Maria Angeli, *Collis Paradisi Amoenitas, sen Sacri Conventus Assisiensis Historiae Libri II* (1704), I, xxiv,

dominant influence upon the development, during the age of Giotto, of an independent tendency in Florentine painting, in which the virtues of spirited narrative are combined with the decorative qualities of the miniaturist, but which remains scarcely touched either by the heroic grandeur of Giotto's ideal or by the fundamental rethinking of pictorial problems upon which his art was based. At the same time it would be misleading to assert that such painters as the St. Cecilia Master, Jacopo del Casentino, Pacino di Bonaguida, and the Master of the Santa Maria Novella Cross were not influenced by Giotto in some degree: but it should be stressed that these masters appear to have developed initially from older Florentine and, to some extent, Roman traditions, so that their styles were already formed before they came into fruitful contact with Giotto's austere 'monumentalism'. Their impact upon the age is recognizable most obviously in the stimulus that they gave to the development of Florentine panel-painting, and it is a short step from the exquisiteness of the St. Cecilia Master to the comparable refinement of Bernardo Daddi: indeed, the St. Cecilia Master and his associates may be said to have prepared the ground for that assimilation of Sienese *eleganza* with which the art of Daddi has always been associated.

Outside Tuscany, there are traces, as we have seen, of the St. Cecilia Master's influence in Rimini in the early years of the fourteenth century, above all in the *Virgin* cycle at S. Agostino. Like Giuliano da Rimini, the author of these tasteful decorations may well have visited Assisi: the alternative hypothesis, advanced by Coletti, that the St. Cecilia

35; xxv, 36). These attributions were clearly prompted by Vasari's statement that Buffalmacco worked on two occasions at Assisi, the first of these supposed visits taking place in 1302 ('dicesi che, l'anno 1302, fu condotto in Ascesi'). Among subsequent attributions to Buffalmacco, the most important is that of the panel of *St. John the Baptist Enthroned* now at Christ Church, Oxford, of which an engraving was published in Lastri's *Etruria pittrice* of 1791. The engraving describes this picture as a work by Buonamico Buffalmacco, and according to Lastri the panel came from the church of Santa Maria degli Ughi in Florence.

As Offner and others have pointed out, the chief difficulty in accepting Venturi's thesis is the incompatibility of the monumental style of the Settimo decorations with the St. Cecilia Master's own fresco-style as it is known to us at Assisi. Sirén's attempt to demonstrate that the two styles can in fact be reconciled (O. Sirén, 'The Buffalmacco Hypothesis: Some Additional Remarks', *The Burlington Magazine*, xxxvii (1920), 176 ff.) is not convincing, although it does succeed in suggesting certain connections between the two masters. The same objections apply to Longhi's ascription of the vault frescoes at Santa Chiara, Assisi, to Buffalmacco (cf. R. Longhi, 'In traccia di alcuni anonimi trecentisti', *Paragone*, 167 (1963), 12 f.).

The whole question of the nature of Buffalmacco's style has recently been reopened by the publication by Donati of a group of frescoes in Arezzo Cathedral. Donati associates these frescoes with the decorations mentioned by Vasari, and he argues that their style is far from being incompatible with that of the Settimo cycle (cf. P. P. Donati, op. cit., pp. 290 ff. and Figs. 1–7). The Arezzo decorations, which are to be found in a chapel on the right-hand side of the nave, represent a *Madonna and Child Enthroned, with Saints*, below a lunette containing a half-length figure of *The Redeemer*. Although much of the fresco has been lost, what remains is in a good state of preservation, and there can be no doubt that, if this is the work of Buffalmacco, the possibility of our being able to identify him with the St. Cecilia Master can be definitely ruled out. On the other hand, there seems to be nothing against Donati's suggestion that the same artist might have executed the Settimo frescoes; and it may be added that there are resemblances between the Arezzo *Madonna* and the panel, formerly in the Badia at Settimo, of *The Virgin and Child with St. Peter and St. Lucy*, which is now in the Fondazione Horne in Florence (for this work cf. Offner, *Corpus*, III, i, 57 f., Pls. XIV–XIV³, and III, vi, 51). The indebtedness of the author of the Horne panel to the St. Cecilia Master is equally clear.

Master was himself active in the Romagna, remains unproven.[1] No less suggestive are the apparent reflections of the *St. Francis* cycle at Assisi in a panel now ascribed to Giovanni da Rimini in the collection of the Duke of Northumberland at Alnwick:[2] among the various scenes represented, the *St. Catherine Preaching before the Emperor* seems to derive in part from Scene XI of the *Legend* (*St. Francis before the Sultan*), although the iconography can be traced back to the ruined fresco of this subject formerly at S. Agnese in Rome,[3] while the adjacent scene of *The Stigmatization of St. Francis* closely follows the Assisan iconography.

Among the non-Florentine masters who are known to have worked at Assisi, the Sienese Simone Martini must surely have studied the great cycle in the Upper Church with attention: in Simone's *St. Martin* cycle in the Lower Church the design of *The Renunciation of the Sword* may owe something to Scene II of the *Legend*, and the treatment of *The Obsequies of St. Martin*, with its numerous figures, suggests a reminiscence of the comparable subjects on the south wall of the Upper Church. Still more striking is the apparent imitation in *The Obsequies of St. Martin* of the singing friars represented in *The Christmas Crib at Greccio* (Scene XIII)—a borrowing that occurs again in the scene of *The Funeral of St. Louis* on the predella of Simone's *St. Louis* altarpiece of 1317[4]—and which suggests a date for Simone's visit to Assisi much closer to that year than the period in the late 1320s or 1330s that has often been proposed.

We are concerned here with the stylistic impact of the *Legend* and its authors, and only secondarily with its influence upon Franciscan iconography, which has been touched upon in passing in earlier chapters—an influence still strong in the fifteenth century, as is evident from Gozzoli's luminous frescoes at Montefalco. The style itself, however, cannot be dissociated entirely from the iconography; and one of the marvels of the Assisi cycle is the perfect manner in which the pictorial language expresses the sublime themes expounded in the *Legenda maior*. Indeed, to imagine that events had taken a different course, and that Giotto had in fact been called to Assisi to execute the frescoes, as Vasari and others would have us believe, is to be conscious of an intimation of profound loss.

[1] L. Coletti, *I Primitivi*, iii (Novara, 1947), x.

[2] The attribution to Giovanni da Rimini is due to Ellis Waterhouse, who noted that the Alnwick picture originally formed the companion-piece to the panel of *Six Scenes from the Life of Christ* in the Museo del Palazzo Venezia in Rome (Sinibaldi and Brunetti, op. cit., p. 569, Fig. 183), already ascribed to Giovanni by Longhi: cf. E. K. Waterhouse, 'Exhibitions of Old Masters at Newcastle, York and Perth', *The Burlington Magazine*, xciii (1951), 261, Fig. 17; C. Volpe, op. cit., Fig. 26.

[3] See above, p. 235.

[4] Capodimonte Museum, Naples: cf. G. Kaftal, *Iconography of the Saints in Tuscan Painting*, Fig. 731. See above, p. 186.

APPENDIX

APPENDIX

THE TEXTS FROM THE *LEGENDA MAIOR*

THIS Appendix contains the texts in the *Legenda maior* which provided the principal literary sources for the twenty-eight scenes of the *Legend of St. Francis* in the Upper Church at Assisi, together with the partly defaced paraphrases of these texts inscribed beneath the frescoes and Marinangeli's reconstructions of them. The Latin texts from the *Legenda maior*, to which English translations are added, follow the standard edition, published at Quaracchi: S. Bonaventurae, *Legendae Duae* (Quaracchi, 1898 and 1923). The reconstructions of the Assisi inscriptions were first published in B. Marinangeli, 'La serie di affreschi giotteschi rappresentanti la Vita di S. Francesco', *Miscellanea Francescana*, XIII, iv (1911), 97 ff. They were partly based upon transcripts made by Fra Ludovico da Città di Castello in the late sixteenth century, when considerably more of the original wording was legible.

SCENE I: *The Homage of a Simple Man of Assisi* (Frontispiece)

Legenda maior, i, 1:

Quidam sane vir de Assisio valde simplex, ut creditur, eruditus a Deo, cum aliquando per civitatem eunti obviaret Francisco, deponebat pallium, *sternebat* ipsius pedibus *vestimentum*,[1] asserens omni fore Franciscum reverentia dignum, utpote qui esset in proximo magna facturus et ob hoc ab universitate fidelium magnifice honorandus.

(A certain man from Assisi who was held to be of great simplicity of mind, but who was yet inspired by God, whenever he met Francis going through the city, would take off his cloak and spread the garment before his feet, declaring that Francis was worthy of all reverence, as one who before long would perform great works, and that by reason of this he should be splendidly honoured by all the faithful.)

Assisi, Sc. I:

. . . . . BEATO FRANCISCO FU . . . . RES IPSI E . . TI . . . E . H . . . CREDIT . . . . ERUDIT . . . . ASSERE*N*S

O . . . . I FRANCISCU . . . . REVERENTIA DIGNU . . . . T I . . . . XIMO MAGNA . . . . FACTUR

. . . . ET I*DEO* AB O*MNIBUS* . . . . HONO . . . .

[1] Cf. Luke 19 : 36.

Marinangeli:

CUM VIR SIMPLEX DE ASSISIO STERNIT VESTES BEATO FRANCISCO FUDITQUE HONORES IPSI EUNTI, SUPER HOC, CREDITUR, ERUDITUS A DEO, ASSERENS OMNI FRANCISCUM REVERENTIA DIGNUM, QUIA ESSET IN PROXIMO MAGNA FACTURUS, ET IDEO AB OMNIBUS HONORANDUS.

SCENE II: *The Gift of the Mantle*   (Plate 42)
Legenda maior, i, 2:

Cumque, resumptis corporis viribus, sibi vestimenta decentia more solito praeparasset, obvium habuit militem quemdam generosum quidem, sed pauperem et male vestitum, cuius pauperiem pio miseratus affectu, illum protinus, se exuto, vestivit, ut simul in uno geminum impleret pietatis officium, quo et nobilis militis verecundiam tegeret et pauperis hominis penuriam relevaret.

(Now when he had recovered his bodily strength, and had provided himself in his customary fashion with comely apparel, he met a certain knight of noble birth but poor and miserably clad; whose poverty inspired him with such tender compassion that he immediately took off his garments and clothed him with them, so that at one and the same time he fulfilled a twofold service of love, in that he both concealed the shame of a noble knight and relieved the penury of a poor man.)

Assisi, Sc. II:

[obliterated]

Marinangeli:

CUM BEATUS FRANCISCUS OBVIUM HABUIT MILITEM QUEMDAM GENEROSUM SED PAUPEREM ET MALE VESTITUM CUIUS, PAUPERIEM PIO MISERATUS AFFECTU, ILLUM PROTINUS, SE EXUTO, VESTIVIT.

SCENE III: *The Vision of the Palace*   (Plate 45)
Legenda maior, i, 3:

Nocte vero sequenti, cum se sopori dedisset, palatium speciosum et magnum cum militaribus armis crucis Christi signaculo insignitis clementia sibi divina monstravit, ut misericordiam pro summi Regis amore pauperi exhibitam militi praeostenderet incomparibili compensandam esse mercede. Unde et cum quaereret, cuius essent: illa omnia sua fore militumque suorum, superna fuit assertione responsum.

(Now on the following night, when he had surrendered himself to sleep, the divine mercy showed him a vast and splendid palace, with armour within marked with the sign of the Cross of Christ, so that he might be given to understand that the mercy that he had shown to the poor knight for love of the King Most High deserved to be recompensed by an incomparable reward: whereupon, when he sought to inquire whose these things were, answer was made to him by a celestial voice that they were all his own and his soldiers'.)

Assisi, Sc. III:

[obliterated]

Marinangeli:

CUM BEATUS FRANCISCUS NOCTE SEQUENTI SE SOPORI DEDISSET, PALATIUM SPECIOSUM ET MA-GNUM CUM MILITARIBUS ARMIS CRUCIS CHRISTI SIGNACULO INSIGNITIS VIDIT, ET CUM QUAERERET CUIUS ESSENT, ILLA OMNIA SUA FORE MILITUMQUE SUORUM SUPERNA FUIT ASSERTIONE RE-SPONSUM.

SCENE IV: *The Miracle of the Crucifix* (Plate 46)

Legenda maior, ii, 1:

Dum enim die quadam, *egressus ad meditandum in agro*,[1] deambularet iuxta ecclesiam Sancti Damiani, quae minabatur prae nimia vetustate ruinam, et in eam, instigante se spiritu, causa orationis intrasset; prostratus ante imaginem Crucifixi, non modica fuit in orando spiritus consolatione repletus. Cumque lacrymosis oculis intenderet in dominicam crucem, vocem de ipsa cruce dilapsam ad eum corporeis audivit auribus, ter dicentem: 'Francisce, vade et repara domum meam, quae, ut cernis, tota destruitur!' Tremefactus Franciscus, cum esset in ecclesia solus, stupet ad tam mirandae vocis auditum, cordeque percipiens divini virtutem eloquii, mentis alienatur excessu.

(For on a certain day, having gone out to meditate in the fields, he was walking near the church of San Damiano, which on account of its excessive age was threatening to fall into ruins, and prompted by the Spirit he went inside to pray. Lying prostrate before a crucifix, he was filled as he prayed with no small consolation of spirit; and as with tear-filled eyes he gazed upon the Lord's Cross he heard with his bodily ears a voice proceeding from that very Cross which said to him three times: 'Francis, go and repair my house, which, as you see, is falling totally into ruin!' All a-tremble, since he was alone in the church, Francis was astonished at the sound of that wondrous voice; then, experiencing in his heart the power of the divine utterance, he was carried out of his senses in a rapture of the spirit.)

Assisi, Sc. IV:

. . . . CRUCE TE . . . . C . . . . S. FRANCISCE, VADE REPARA DOMU . . . . MEA . . . . Q . . . . TOTA . . . . ROMANA . . . . SIG . . . . ECCLESIAM.

Marinangeli:

CUM BEATUS FRANCISCUS ORARET ANTE IMAGINEM CRUCIFIXI, VOX DILAPSA EST DE CRUCE TER DICENS: FRANCISCE, VADE REPARA DOMUM MEAM QUAE TOTA DESTRUITUR: PER HOC ROMANAM SIGNIFICANS ECCLESIAM.

SCENE V: *The Renunciation of Worldly Goods* (Plate 48)

Legenda maior, ii, 4:

Tentabat deinde pater carnis filium gratiae pecunia iam nudatum ducere coram episcopo

[1] Gen. 24 : 63.

civitatis, ut in ipsius manibus facultatibus renuntiaret paternis et omnia redderet, quae habebat. Ad quod faciendum se promptum exhibuit verus paupertatis amator, perveniensque coram episcopo, nec moras patitur nec cunctatur de aliquo, nec verba exspectat nec facit; sed continuo depositis omnibus vestimentis, restituit ea patri. Inventus est autem tunc vir Dei cilicium habere ad carnem sub vestibus delicatis. Insuper ex admirando fervore spiritu ebrius, reiectis etiam femoralibus, totus coram omnibus denudatur, dicens ad patrem: 'Usque nunc vocavi te patrem in terris, amodo autem secure dicere possum: *Pater noster, qui es in caelis,*[1] apud quem omnem thesaurum reposui et omnem spei fiduciam collocavi.' Hoc cernens episcopus et admirans tam excedentem in viro Dei fervorem, protinus exsurrexit et inter brachia sua illum cum fletu recolligens, uti erat vir pius et bonus, pallio, quo erat amictus, operuit, praecipiens suis, ut aliquid sibi darent ad membra corporis contegenda. Oblatus est autem ei mantellus pauper et vilis cuiusdam agricolae servientis episcopi, quem ispse gratanter suscipiens, cum caemento quod sibi occurrit, ad modum crucis manu propria consignavit, operimentum formans ex eo crucifixi hominis et pauperis seminudi.

(Then his father according to the flesh was minded to bring this son of grace, now stripped of his property, before the bishop of the city, so that he might in his hands surrender his title to his father's estate and give back all that he possessed. This the faithful lover of poverty showed himself very ready to do, and coming into the presence of the bishop he neither allowed any delay nor paused for any one, he neither waited for words to be spoken nor uttered any himself, but immediately took off all his clothes and restored them to his father. The man of God was then found to have a hair-shirt next to his skin beneath his fine clothes. Moreover, as though made drunk by his wondrous fervour of spirit, he cast aside even his breeches, and made himself naked in the presence of all, saying to his father: 'Hitherto I have called you my father on earth, but henceforth I can truly say, "Our Father which art in heaven"; with whom I have laid up my whole treasure, and upon whom I have placed my whole trust and hope.' The bishop, seeing this and marvelling at such surpassing fervour in the man of God, rose at once and, taking him with tears into his arms, for he was a devout and good man, covered him with the cloak in which he was himself attired, directing his servants to give him something to cover his limbs. And there was offered him a poor and mean tunic belonging to a farm-labourer in the service of the bishop, which he accepted gratefully, and using a piece of chalk that he happened to find he marked it with his own hand with the form of the Cross, making out of it a garment fit for a crucified, poor, and half-naked man.)

Assisi, Sc. V:

. . . . RESTITUIT PAT . . . . O . . . . E . . . . IM . . . . TIAVIT BONIS . . . . NIS ET MUT . . . . RE . . . . AMODO SEC . . . . ERE POSSU . . . . PATER NOSTER . . . . I . CELIS . . . . PETR . . . . NADONIS.

[1] Matt. 6 : 9.

Marinangeli:

CUM RESTITUIT PATRI OMNIA, ET, VESTIMENTIS DEPOSITIS, RENUNTIAVIT BONIS PATERNIS ET
MUTABILIBUS, DICENS AD PATREM: AMODO SECURE DICERE POSSUM 'PATER NOSTER QUI ES IN
COELIS' CUM REPUDIAVERIT ME PETRUS BERNADONIS.

SCENE VI: *The Dream of Innocent III*   (Plate 52)

Legenda maior, iii, 10:

Sed et visionem, quam tunc temporis e caelo perceperat, in hoc viro fore complendam,
Spiritu divino suggerente, firmavit. Videbat namque in somnis, ut retulit, Lateranensem
basilicam fore proximam iam ruinae, quam quidam homo pauperculus, modicus et despec-
tus, proprio dorso submisso, ne caderet, sustentabat. 'Vere', inquit, 'hic ille est, qui opere
et doctrina Christi sustentabit Ecclesiam.' . . .

(Moreover, he affirmed, through the inspiration of the Divine Spirit, that a heavenly
vision which he was vouchsafed at that time would be fulfilled in this man. For, as he
recounted, he saw in a dream the Lateran Basilica on the point of falling into ruins, while
a little poor man, of small stature and humble appearance, supported it with his own back
to prevent it from falling. 'Truly', he said, 'this is he who by his work and teaching shall
sustain the Church of Christ.')

Assisi, Sc. VI:

. . . . PAPA VID . . . AT LATERANEN . . . . M BASILICAM FORE PROXIMAM IAM RUINE QUAM . . . . .
. . . . SCU . . . .

Marinangeli:

QUOMODO PAPA VIDEBAT LATERANENSEM BASILICAM FORE PROXIMAM IAM RUINAE, QUAM
QUIDAM PAUPERCULUS, SCILICET BEATUS FRANCISCUS, PROPRIO DORSO SUBMISSO, NE CADERET,
SUBSTENTABAT.

SCENE VII: *The Sanctioning of the Rule*   (Plate 53)

Legenda maior, iii, 9, 10:

9. Cum autem ad Romanam curiam pervenisset et introductus esset ante conspectum
Summi Pontificis, exposuit suum propositum, petens humiliter et instanter, supradictam
sibi vivendi regulam approbari. Videns autem Christi Vicarius, dominus Innocentius tertius,
vir utique sapientia clarus, admirandam in viro Dei simplicis animi puritatem, propositi
constantiam ignitumque voluntatis sanctae fervorem, inclinatus animo est, ut pium suppli-
canti praeberet assensum. Distulit tamen perficere quod Christi postulabat pauperculus, pro
eo quod aliquibus de cardinalibus novum aliquid et supra vires humanas arduum videretur.
. . .

10. . . . . Inde praecipua devotione repletus, petitioni eius se per omnia inclinavit ac Christi
famulum speciali semper amore dilexit. Proinde postulata concessit et adhuc concedere plura

promisit. Approbavit regulam, dedit de poenitentia praedicanda mandatum et laicis fratribus omnibus, qui servum Dei fuerant comitati, fecit coronas parvulas fieri, ut *verbum Dei*[1] libere praedicarent.

(9. Now when he had come to the Roman Curia and had been led into the presence of the Supreme Pontiff, he explained his purpose, humbly and earnestly petitioning him to sanction the above-mentioned Rule of their manner of life. Then the Vicar of Christ, the Lord Innocent III, a man most renowned for his wisdom, perceiving in the man of God the marvellous purity of a simple heart and the constancy of purpose and the burning fervour of a holy will, was inclined in his mind to give his pious assent to the suppliant. He put off, however, the performance of what the little poor one of Christ requested, because to some of the Cardinals it seemed to be something both unprecedented and difficult, to the extent of being beyond human strength . . .

10. . . . Being inspired from that time by a special devotion to him, he became favourably disposed in every way towards his petition, and always loved the servant of Christ with a particular affection. Accordingly, he granted his requests, and promised to grant him still more. He sanctioned the Rule, gave him a mandate to preach repentance, and made all the lay brethren who had come with the servant of God wear narrow tonsures, so that they might freely preach the Word of God.)

Assisi, Sc. VII:

. . . . FR . . . . VE . . . . DICARENT.

Marinangeli:

CUM PAPA APPROBAVIT REGULAM ET DEDIT DE POENITENTIA PRAEDICANDA MANDATUM, ET FRATRIBUS, QUI SANCTUM FUERANT COMITATI, FECIT CORONAS FIERI, UT VERBUM DEI PRAEDICARENT.

SCENE VIII: *The Vision of the Chariot*   (Plate 55)
Legenda maior, iv, 4:

Contrahentibus autem fratribus moram in loco praefato, vir sanctus die quadam sabbati civitatem intravit Assisii, praedicaturus mane diei dominicae, ut moris erat, in ecclesia cathedrali. Cumque in quodam tugurio sito in horto canonicorum vir Deo devotus in oratione Dei more solito pernoctaret, corporaliter absentatus a filiis; ecce, fere media noctis hora, quibusdam ex fratribus quiescentibus, quibusdam perseverantibus in orando, currus igneus mirandi splendoris, per ostium domus intrans, huc atque illuc per domicilium tertio se convertit, supra quem globus lucidus residebat, qui solis habens aspectum, noctem clarere fecit. Obstupefacti sunt vigilantes, excitati simul et exterriti dormientes, et non minus senserunt cordis claritatem quam corporis, dum ex virtute mirandi luminis alterius alteri conscientia nuda fuit. Intellexerunt namque concorditer omnes, videntibus invicem universis in cordibus singulorum, sanctum patrem *absentem corpore, praesentem spiritu*[2] tali

[1] Luke 11 : 28.   [2] Cf. 1 Cor. 5 : 3.

transfiguratum effigie, supernis irradiatum fulgoribus et ardoribus inflammatum supernaturali virtute in *curru* splendente simul et *igneo*[1] sibi demonstrari a Domino, ut tamquam
veri Israelitae[2] post illum incederent, qui virorum spiritualium, ut alter Elias, factus fuerat a
Deo *currus et auriga*.[3] Credendum sane, quod ille horum simplicium *aperuit oculos*[4] ad preces
Francisci, ut viderent *magnalia Dei*,[5] qui *oculos* quondam *aperuerat* pueri ad videndum *montem plenum equorum et igneorum curruum in circuitu Elisei*.[6]

(Now while the brethren were abiding in the place aforesaid, the holy man went on a
certain Sunday into the city of Assisi, intending to preach in the Cathedral church, as was
his wont, on the Sunday morning. And while the man devoted to God was passing the night
in his accustomed manner in prayerful communion with God, in a certain hut situated in
the canons' garden, being therefore absent in body from his children, lo, about midnight,
when some of the Brethren were resting and others keeping vigil in prayer, a chariot of fire
of marvellous splendour, entering by the door of the house, turned three times hither and
thither through the dwelling, and above it there rested a ball of light, in appearance like the
sun, which made the night shine. Those who were keeping watch were astonished, and those
who were sleeping were awakened and terrified at the same time, and experienced the brightness no less in their hearts than with their bodily senses, while by the power of that wonderful
light the conscience of each was laid bare to his companions. For truly they all with one accord
understood, when they looked into each other's hearts, that although their holy father was
absent in body he was present in spirit, and that through the operation of a supernatural
miracle he was being shown to them by God transfigured in this way, radiant with heavenly
brightness and on fire with heat, in a shining and fiery chariot, so that they, as Israelites
indeed, might follow after him, since he had been made by God, like another Elijah, the
chariot and horseman of spiritual men. Indeed, we must believe that He opened the eyes
of these simple men in answer to the prayers of Francis himself, so that they should see the
strength of the majesty of God, Who had once opened the eyes of the young man so that he
might see the mountain full of horses and chariots of fire round about Elisha.)

Assisi, Sc. VIII:

. . . . URIO . . . . CUM S . . . . ALIO . . . . RIO EXTRA . . . . PAUL . . . . FRANCI
. . . . CURRU IGNE . . . . LUCIDO . . . . O . . . . DIA . . . . CE TUGUR . . . .

Marinangeli:

CUM BEATUS FRANCISCUS ORARET IN QUODAM TUGURIO ET CUM SUI FRATRES ESSENT IN ALIO
TUGURIO EXTRA CIVITATEM, QUIBUSDAM QUIESCENTIBUS ET QUIBUSDAM PERSEVERANTIBUS
IN ORANDO, ET ILLE CORPORALITER ABSENTARETUR A FILIIS ECCE ISTI VIDERUNT PAULO POST
BEATUM FRANCISCUM IN CURRU IGNEO ET PERLUCIDO, PER DOMUM, FERE MEDIA NOCTIS
HORA, VOLITARE, DUM MAGNA LUCE TUGURIUM RESPLENDUIT, UNDE OBSTUPEFACTI SUNT
VIGILANTES, EXCITATI ET EXTERRITI DORMIENTES.

---

[1] Cf. 2 Kgs. 2 : 11.   [2] Cf. John 1 : 47.   [3] 2 Kgs. 2 : 12.
[4] John 9 : 32.   [5] Eccles. 18 : 5.   [6] Cf. 2 Kgs. 6 : 17.

SCENE IX: *The Vision of the Thrones*   (Plate 56)

Legenda maior, vi, 6:

Et quoniam humilitatem tam in se quam in subditis cunctis praeferebat honoribus, amator humilium Deus[1] altioribus ipsum dignum iudicabat fastigiis, secundum quod uni fratri, viro virtutis et devotionis praecipuae, visio caelitus ostensa monstravit. Cum enim esset in comitatu viri Dei et una ipso in quadam ecclesia deserta ferventi oraret affectu, in ecstasi factus, vidit inter multas in caelo sedes unam ceteris digniorem, pretiosis ornatam lapidibus et omni gloria refulgentem. Miratus intra se praecelsi refulgentiam throni, anxia coepit cogitatione perquirere, quis ad illum deberet assumi. Audivit inter haec vocem dicentem sibi: 'Sedes ista unius de ruentibus fuit et nunc humili servatur Francisco.' Reversus demum frater ad se ab orationis excessu, virum beatum exterius prodeuntem solito fuit more secutus. Cumque incedentes per viam, de Deo invicem loquerentur, frater ille, visionis suae non immemor, solerter ab eo quaesivit, quid de se ipso sentiret. Ad quem humilis Christi servus: 'Videor', ait, 'mihi maximus peccatorum.' Cui cum frater diceret ex adverso, quod hoc nec posset sana conscientia dicere nec sentire, subiunxit: 'Si quantumcumque sceleratum hominem tanta fuisset Christus misericordia prosecutus, arbitror sane, quod multo quam ego Deo gratior esset.' Confirmatus fuit frater ex tam admirabilis humilitatis auditu de veritate visionis ostensae, Evangelio sacro testante[2] cognoscens, quod ad excellentiam gloriae, de qua superbus eicitur, vere humilis exaltetur.

(And since in himself as well as in those under his authority he placed humility above all honours, God, Who loves the humble, judged him to be worthy of loftier heights, as was demonstrated by a heavenly vision that was vouchsafed to one of the Brethren, a man of particular virtue and devoutness. For while he was in the company of the man of God and was fervently praying with him in a certain deserted church, he saw, in a transport of ecstasy, one among many seats in heaven that was worthier than the others, adorned with precious stones and shining with great splendour. Marvelling within himself at the splendour of this lofty throne, he began to ask himself with an inquiring mind who might be destined to fill it. In the midst of these deliberations he heard a voice saying to him: 'This was the seat of one of the fallen angels, and now it is reserved for the humble Francis.' At length, when the Brother had returned to himself from the flights of prayer, he followed the holy man as he went out in his accustomed manner. And as they walked along the road, speaking each in his turn about the things of God, that Brother, not unmindful of his vision, discreetly inquired of him what he thought of himself. The humble servant of Christ answered him, 'I think myself the greatest of sinners.' When the Brother objected that he could not say or feel this with a clear conscience, Francis added: 'If any man, however guilty, had received such mercy from Christ as I have done, I truly think that he would have been much more acceptable to God than I.' And so, through the hearing of such marvellous humility, the Brother was assured of the truth of the vision that had been shown him, knowing by the

[1] Ps. 137 : 6.   [2] Matt. 23 : 12.

witness of the Holy Gospel that the truly humble shall be exalted to that excellent glory from which the proud are cast down.)

Assisi, Sc. IX:

[obliterated]

Marinangeli:

CUM UNI FRATRI VISIO COELITUS OSTENSA MONSTRAVIT MULTAS IN COELO SEDES ET UNAM PRAE CETERIS DIGNIOREM OMNI GLORIA REFULGENTEM, ET AUDIVIT VOCEM DICENTEM SIBI: SEDES ISTA UNIUS DE RUENTIBUS ANGELIS FUIT, ET NUNC HUMILI SERVATUR FRANCISCO.

SCENE X: *The Exorcism of the Demons at Arezzo*   (Plate 58)

Legenda maior, vi, 9:

Contigit ipsum aliquando **Aretium** devenire, cum tota civitas intestino bello quassata propinquum sui minabatur excidium. Hospitatus vero in suburbio, vidit supra civitatem exsultantes daemones ac perturbatos cives ad caedem mutuam succendentes. Ut autem seditiosas illas effugaret aëreas potestates, fratrem Silvestrum, columbinae simplicitatis virum, quasi praeconem praemisit, dicens: 'Vade ante portam civitatis et ex parte Dei omnipotentis daemonibus in virtute obedientiae praecipe, ut exeant festinanter.' Accelerat verus obediens patris iussa perficere, et praeoccupans in laudibus faciem Domini, ante portam civitatis coepit clamare valenter: 'Ex parte omnipotentis Dei et iussu servi eius Francisci procul hinc discedite, daemones universi!' Redit ad pacem continuo civitas, et civilitatis in se iura cives omnes cum magna tranquillitate reformant. Expulsa quippe daemonum furibunda superbia, quae civitatem illam velut obsidione vallaverat, superveniens sapientia pauperis, videlicet Francisci humilitas, pacem reddidit urbemque salvavit. Humilis enim obedientiae ardua promerente virtute, super spiritus illos rebelles atque protervos tam potestativum fuerat assecutus imperium, ut et ipsorum feroces protervias premeret et importunas violentias propulsaret.

(It once came to pass that he arrived at Arezzo at a time when the whole city was shaken by a civil war that threatened its immediate destruction. Indeed, while he was lodging in the outskirts, he saw the demons exulting over the city and inflaming the impassioned citizens into mutual slaughter. Thereupon, in order to put to flight those factious powers of the air, he sent forth as his herald Brother Silvester, a man of dovelike simplicity, saying: 'Go out before the gate of the city and in the name of Almighty God command the demons, in the power of obedience, to depart with all speed.' The other with true obedience hastened to perform his father's commands, and offering his praises before the Divine Presence he began to cry with a loud voice in front of the city gate: 'In the name of Almighty God and by command of his servant Francis, depart far hence, all ye demons!' Forthwith the city returned to its former peace, and all the citizens, in complete accord, undertook the revision of their civil laws. Undoubtedly, when the demons, in their rage and arrogance, were put to flight, having held the city as though by siege, there came to its aid the wisdom of the poor, namely the humility of Francis, which restored peace and saved the city. For by the power of the difficult virtue of humble obedience he gained such potent authority over those rebellious and violent spirits that he was able to curb their fierce arrogance and drive out their insolent violence.)

Assisi, Sc. X:

. . . . U . . . . . . SO TIBI PRAESCR . . . . I . . PORTA. UT . . . . PA . . . . FACTA EST.
Marinangeli:

CUM BEATUS FRANCISCUS VIDIT SUPRA CIVITATEM ARETII DAEMONES EXULTANTES ET AIT SOCIO: VADE, ET IN VIRTUTE DEI DAEMONES EXPELLE, SICUT IN DOMINO IPSO TIBI PRAESCRIPTUM EST, CLAMANS IN PORTA. UT AUTEM ILLE OBEDIENS CLAMAVIT, DAEMONES AUFUGERUNT, ET PAX ILLICO FACTA EST.

SCENE XI: *St. Francis before the Sultan*   (Plate 61)
Legenda maior, ix, 8:

Assumpto igitur socio fratre, Illuminato nomine, viro utique luminis et virtutis, cum iter coepisset, obvias habuit oviculas duas; quibus visis exhilaratus, vir sanctus dixit ad socium: '*Confide*, frater, *in Domino*,[1] nam in nobis evangelicum illud impletur: *Ecce, ego mitto vos sicut oves in medio luporum*.'[2] Cum autem processissent ulterius, occurrerunt eis satellites Saraceni, qui, tamquam lupi celerius accurrentes ad oves, servos Dei feraliter comprehensos, crudeliter et contemptibiliter pertractarunt, afficientes conviciis, affligentes verberibus et vinculis alligantes. Tandem afflictos multipliciter et attritos ad Soldanum, divina disponente providentia, iuxta viri Dei desiderium perduxerunt. Cum igitur princeps ille perquireret, a quibus et ad quid et qualiter missi essent et quomodo advenissent, intrepido corde respondit Christi servus Franciscus, non ab homine, sed a Deo altissimo se fuisse transmissum, ut ei et populo suo viam salutis ostenderet et annuntiaret Evangelium veritatis. Tanta vero mentis constantia, tanta virtute animi tantoque fervore spiritus praedicto Soldano praedicavit Deum trinum et unum et Salvatorem omnium Iesum Christum, ut evangelicum illud in ipso claresceret veraciter esse completum: *Ego dabo vobis os et sapientiam, cui non poterunt resistere et contradicere omnes adversarii vestri*.[3] Nam et Soldanus admirandum in viro Dei fervorem spiritus conspiciens et virtutem, libenter ipsum audiebat et ad moram contrahendam cum eo instantius invitabat, Christi vero servus superno illustratus oraculo: 'Si vis', inquit, 'converti tu cum populo tuo ad Christum, ob ipsius amorem vobiscum libentissime commorabor. Quodsi haesitas propter fidem Christi legem Mahumeti dimittere; iube ignem accendi permaximum, et ego cum sacerdotibus tuis ignem ingrediar, ut vel sic cognoscas, quae fides certior et sanctior non immerito tenenda sit.' Ad quem Soldanus: 'Non credo, quod aliquis de sacerdotibus meis se vellet igni propter fidem suam defensandam exponere, vel genus aliquod subire tormenti.'

[1] Cf. Eccles. 11 : 22.   [2] Cf. Matt. 10 : 16.   [3] Luke 21 : 15.

Viderat enim, statim quemdam de presbyteris suis, virum authenticum et longaevum, hoc audito verbo, de suis conspectibus aufugisse. Ad quem vir sanctus: 'Si mihi velis promittere pro te et populo tuo, quod ad Christi cultum, si ignem illaesus exiero, veniatis, ignem solus intrabo; et si combustus fuero, imputetur peccatis meis; si autem divina me protexerit virtus, *Christum, Dei virtutem et sapientiam,*[1] *verum Deum*[2] et Dominum *Salvatorem*[3] omnium agnoscatis.' Soldanus autem optionem hanc accipere se non audere respondit, quia seditionem populi formidabat.

(Taking therefore as his companion a Brother named Illuminatus, a man assuredly of great virtue and spiritual lustre, and setting out on his journey, he happened to encounter two lambs on the way; at the sight of which the holy man rejoiced, and said to his companion: 'Brother, trust in the Lord, for in us is fulfilled the Gospel saying, "Behold, I send you forth as sheep in the midst of wolves."' And when they had proceeded further, they were met by Saracen bands, who, like wolves swiftly falling upon sheep, brutally seized the servants of God and cruelly and insolently dragged them away, loading them with abuse, tormenting them with blows and binding them in fetters. At length they led them, wretched and worn out by so much suffering, into the presence of the Sultan; and this came to pass according to the desire of the man of God and the will of Divine Providence. When that prince inquired of them from whom, to what end and in what manner they had been sent, and how they had come, the servant of Christ, Francis, replied with intrepid heart that he had been sent, not by man, but by the Most High God, so that he might show him, and show his people, the way of salvation, and that he might preach the Gospel of truth. With such steadfastness of mind, with such strength of soul and with such fervour of spirit did he preach to the Sultan God Three in One and Jesus Christ the Saviour of all that in him was truly fulfilled that Gospel saying, 'I will give you a mouth and wisdom, which all your adversaries shall not be able to withstand or to gainsay.' And indeed the Sultan, seeing in the man of God such wondrous fervour of spirit and courage, not only listened to him willingly but gave him a pressing invitation to prolong his visit to his court. But the servant of Christ, inspired by divine guidance, said to him: 'If you, together with your people, will be converted to Christ, for his love's sake I will most gladly remain among you. But if you are hesitant as to whether to give up the law of Mahomet for the faith of Christ, command that a great fire be lit, and I will enter the fire with your priests, so that even thus you may come to know which faith deserves to be regarded as the more certain and holy;' to whom the Sultan replied: 'I do not believe that any of my priests would be willing to expose himself to the fire or to undergo any kind of torture in defence of his faith.' For he had seen that one of his priests, an aged man in a position of authority, had at once fled from his sight on hearing what was being said. The holy man then answered him: 'On condition that you are willing to promise me, on behalf of yourself and your people, that you will accept the religion of Christ if I come out of the fire uninjured, I will enter the fire alone; and if I am burned, let it be imputed to my sins; but if the power of God should protect me, you will know that Christ, who is the

[1] Cor. 1 : 24.   [2] John 17 : 3.   [3] John 4 : 42.

Power of God and the Wisdom of God, is very God and the Lord and Saviour of all.' The Sultan, however, replied that he did not dare to accept these terms, for he feared an insurrection of the people.)

Assisi, Sc. XI:

. . . . . . VOLUIT I . . . . RE IG . . . . CERDOTIBUS SOLDANI BABILONIE SET NULLUS EORUM VOLUIT INTRARE CU . EO . . . T STATIM DE SUIS CONSPECTIBUS AUFUGERUNT.

Marinangeli:

CUM BEATUS FRANCISCUS OB CHRISTI FIDEM VOLUIT INTRARE IGNEM MAGNUM CUM SACER-DOTIBUS SOLDANI BABILONIE, SED NULLUS EORUM VOLUIT INTRARE CUM EO, SED STATIM DE SUIS CONSPECTIBUS AUFUGERUNT.

SCENE XII: *The Ecstasy of St. Francis*   (Plate 62)

Legenda maior, x, 4:

Vir autem Dei solitarius remanens et pacatus, nemora replebat gemitibus, loca spargebat lacrymis, pectora manu tundebat, et quasi occultius secretarium nactus, confabulabatur cum Domino suo. Ibi respondebat iudici, ibi supplicabat patri, ibi colloquebatur amico, ibi quoque a fratribus ipsum pie observantibus aliquoties auditus est clamorosis gemitibus apud divinam pro peccatoribus interpellare clementiam, deplorare etiam alta voce quasi coram positam dominicam passionem.—Ibi visus est nocte orans, manibus ad modum crucis pro-tensis, toto corpore sublevatus a terra et nubecula quadam fulgente circumdatus, ut illustra-tionis mirabilis intra mentem mira circa corpus perlustratio testis esset.—Ibi etiam, sicut certis est comprobatum indiciis, *incerta* sibi *et occulta* divinae *sapientiae*[1] pandebantur, quamvis illa non vulgaret exterius, nisi quantum *Christi urgebat caritas*[2] et proximorum utilitas exigebat.

(But the man of God, remaining alone and at peace, filled the woods with his sighs, bedewed the ground with his tears, beat his breast with his hand, and, like one who has found a secret sanctuary, conversed familiarly with his Lord. There he answered to his Judge; there he offered supplications to his Father; there he engaged in conversation with his Friend; and there also he was heard several times by the Brethren (who in their devotion would watch over him) invoking with deep sighs the divine mercy for sinners, and uttering loud laments for the Lord's Passion as though it was visibly present before him. There he was seen praying at night, his hands stretched out in the manner of a Cross, his whole body uplifted from the earth and surrounded by a shining cloud, as though the wondrous refulgence that enveloped his body were the witness to the marvellous lustre of his mind. There, moreover, as has been attested by sure proofs, the dark and hidden things of the Divine Wisdom were revealed to him, although he did not publish them abroad, except in so far as the love of Christ con-strained him and the needs of his children demanded.)

[1] Ps. 51 : 6.   [2] 2 Cor. 5 : 14.

Assisi, Sc. XII:

QUAL . . . . DO BEATUS . . . . FERVEN . . R ORARET VISUS E . . A FRATRIB . . TO COR . . RE SUBLE . . . S A TERRA . . . . CULA QUAEDA . . LUCIDISSIMA C . . . . FULSIT . . . .

Marinangeli:

QUALITER CUM ALIQUANDO BEATUS FRANCISCUS FERVENTER ORARET VISUS EST A FRATRIBUS TOTO CORPORE SUBLEVATUS A TERRA, MANIBUS PROTENSIS, ET NUBECULA QUAEDAM LUCIDISSIMA CIRCUMFULSIT EUM.

SCENE XIII: *The Christmas Crib at Greccio* (Plate 63)

Legenda maior, x, 7:

Contigit autem anno tertio ante obitum suum, ut memoriam nativitatis pueri Iesu ad devotionem excitandam apud castrum Graecii disponeret agere, cum quanto maiore solemnitate valeret. Ne vero hoc novitati posset adscribi, a Summo Pontifice petita et obtenta licentia, fecit praeparari praesepium, apportari foenum, bovem et asinum ad locum adduci. Advocantur fratres, adveniunt populi, personat silva voces, et venerabilis illa nox luminibus copiosis et claris laudibusque sonoris et consonis et splendens efficitur et solemnis. Stabat vir Dei coram praesepio pietate repletus, respersus lacrimis et gaudio superfusus. Celebrantur missarum solemnia super praesepe, levita Christi Francisco sacrum Evangelium decantante. Praedicat deinde populo circumstanti de nativitate pauperis Regis, quem, cum nominare vellet, puerum de Bethlehem prae amoris teneritudine nuncupabat.—Miles autem quidam virtuosus et verax, qui, propter Christi amorem saeculari relicta militia, viro Dei magna fuit familiaritate coniunctus, dominus Ioannes de Graecio, se vidisse asseruit puerulum quemdam valde formosum in illo praesepio dormientem, quem beatus pater Franciscus, ambobus complexans brachiis, excitare videbatur a somno.

(Now three years before his death it came to pass that he had a mind to celebrate, at the town of Greccio, the memory of the Nativity of the Infant Jesus with all possible solemnity, for the purpose of encouraging devotion. So that this should not be thought to be a mere novelty, he sought and obtained permission from the Supreme Pontiff, and then asked for a manger to be prepared and for some hay, an ox, and an ass to be brought to the scene. The Brethren were summoned, the populace assembled, the wood echoed with their voices, and that sacred night was made both splendid and solemn by numerous brilliant lights and melodious hymns resounding in praise. The man of God, filled with pious devotion, stood before the manger, bathed in tears and overcome by joy. The solemnities of the Mass were celebrated over the manger, Francis, the Levite of Christ, chanting the Holy Gospel. Then to the people that stood around he preached a sermon about the birth of the pauper King, whom, whenever he came to name him, he referred to as the Boy of Bethlehem, on account of the tenderness of his love for him. Now a certain gallant and true knight, Messer John of Greccio, who for the love of Christ had abandoned his military calling, and who was bound by close ties of friendship with the man of God, affirmed that he saw a little Child of surpassing beauty sleeping in that same manger, Whom the blessed Father Francis embraced in both arms, so that He was awakened from His sleep.)

Assisi, Sc. XIII:

. . . . . . SC . . . I . . MEMO . . . . NATALIS X . . FECIT PREPARARI PRESEPIUM APPORTARI . . . .
AV . . . . IT . . . . . . RO ORA . . . . ATTULERAT.

Marinangeli:

QUOMODO BEATUS FRANCISCUS IN MEMORIAM NATALIS CHRISTI FECIT PRAEPARARI PRAESEPIUM, APPORTARI FOENUM, BOVEM ET ASINUM ADDUCI, ET DE NATIVITATE PAUPERIS REGIS PRAEDI-CAVIT, ITEMQUE SANCTO VIRO ORATIONEM HABENTE, MILES QUIDAM VIDIT PUERUM IESUM LOCO ILLIUS QUEM SANCTUS ATTULERAT.

SCENE XIV: *The Miracle of the Spring*   (Plate 64)

Legenda maior, vii, 12:

Alio quoque tempore vir Dei ad quamdam eremum transferre se volens, ut ibi liberius con-templationi vacaret, quia debilis erat, cuiusdam viri pauperis vectebatur asello. Cumque diebus aestivis famulum Christi sequendo vir ille montana conscenderet, asperioris et longioris viae itinere fatigatus nimioque sitis ardore deficiens, instanter coepit clamare post sanctum: 'En, morior', inquit, 'siti, nisi poculi alicuius beneficio continuo refociller.' Absque mora vir Dei prosilivit de asino, et fixis in terra genibus, palmas tetendit in caelum, orare non cessans, donec se intellexit auditum. Oratione tandem finita: 'Festina', inquit viro, 'ad petram et illic aquam vivam invenies, quam tibi hac hora misericorditer Christus de lapide biben-dam produxit.' Stupenda Dei dignatio, quae servis suis tam facile se inclinat! Bibit sitiens homo *aquam de petra*[1] orantis virtute et poculum hausit *de saxo durissimo*.[2] Aquae decursus ibidem ante non fuit, nec, ut est diligenter quaesitum, deinceps potuit inveniri.

(At another time the man of God, wishing to remove himself to a certain desert place, so that he could devote himself more freely to contemplation, was riding out upon an ass belonging to a certain poor man, for he was weak in body. It was the heat of summer, and as the man followed the servant of God up the mountainous ascents, he became weary of a journey that took them on a path ever rougher and longer, and, fainting with exceeding and burning thirst, he began to cry out loudly after the Saint: 'Behold,' he said, 'I shall die of thirst if I do not have at once the benefit of some refreshing draught.' Then without delay the man of God got off the ass, and, kneeling down and stretching his hands towards heaven, he did not cease praying until he knew that he had been heard. His prayer at length ended, he said to the man: 'Hasten to yonder rock, and you will find there running water, which Christ in his compassion has at this hour brought forth from the rock so that you may drink.' O marvellous condescension of God, that so willingly inclines towards His servants! The thirsty man drank the water that issued from the rock through the merits of the

---

[1] Ps. 78:16.   [2] Deut. 32:13.

suppliant, and drained a draught from the stony ground. Before then there was no spring of water there, nor, as has been diligently ascertained, could any be found there afterwards.)

Assisi, Sc. XIV:

CUM BEATUS FRANCISCUS *CAUSA* INFIRMITATIS IN ASINO UNIUS PAUPERIS HOMINIS ASCENDERET QUEMDAM MONTEM EIDEM HOMINI SITI PERICLITANTI ORANDO AQUAM PRODUXIT DE PETRA Q . . . . . . POSTEA . . . . .

Marinangeli:

CUM BEATUS FRANCISCUS CAUSA INFIRMITATIS IN ASINO UNIUS PAUPERIS HOMINIS ASCENDERET QUEMDAM MONTEM, EIDEM HOMINI SITI PERICLITANTI ORANDO AQUAM PRODUXIT DE PETRA, QUAE NEC ANTEA FUERAT NEC POSTEA VISA EST.

SCENE XV: *The Sermon to the Birds* (Plate 68)

Legenda maior, xii, 3:

Cum igitur approprinquaret Bevanio, ad quemdam locum devenit, in quo diversi generis avium maxima multitudo convenerat. Quas cum sanctus Dei vidisset, alacriter cucurrit ad locum et eas velut rationis participes salutavit. Omnibus vero exspectantibus et convertentibus se ad eum, ita ut quae in arbustis erant, inclinatis capitibus, cum appropinquaret ad eas, insolito modo in ipsum intenderent, usque ad eas accessit et omnes ut verbum Dei audirent, sollicite admonuit, dicens: 'Fratres mei volucres, multum debetis laudare Creatorem vestrum, qui plumis vos induit et pennas tribuit ad volandum, puritatem concessit aëris et sine vestra sollicitudine vos gubernat.' Cum autem eis haec et his similia loqueretur, aviculae modo mirabili gestientes coeperunt extendere colla, protendere alas, aperire rostra et in illum attente respicere. Ipse vero cum spiritus fervore mirando per medium ipsarum transiens, tunica contingebat easdem, nec tamen de loco aliqua mota est, donec, signo crucis facto et licentia data cum benedictione viri Dei omnes insimul avolarunt. Haec omnia contuebantur socii exspectantes in via.

(Now when he drew near Bevagna he came to a place where a great multitude of birds of different kinds was assembled. When the holy man of God saw them, he ran quickly to the spot and greeted them as though they shared his faculty of reason. They themselves all awaited him and turned towards him, those that were perched on bushes inclining their heads as he drew near them, and looking at him in unaccustomed fashion, until he came up to them and earnestly exhorted them to hear the Word of God, saying: 'My brothers the birds, much should you praise your Creator, Who has clothed you in feathers and provided you with wings to fly with, Who has granted you the pure element of air as your domain, and Who watches over you without your having to make any provision for yourselves.' While he was addressing them in these and other such words, the little birds, behaving in a manner wonderful to behold, began to stretch out their necks, to spread their wings, to open their beaks and to gaze at him intently. He, on his part, passing through the midst of them with wondrous fervour of spirit, touched them one after another with his habit; nor did any of them move from the spot until he had made the sign of the Cross and given them dispensation; whereupon, having received the blessing of the man of God, they all flew away together. His companions who awaited him by the way were witnesses to all these things.)

Assisi, Sc. XV:

CUM BEATUS FRANCISCUS IRET BEVANIUM . . . . ES EXTENDEBANT COLLA PROTENDEBANT ALAS APERIEBANT ROSTRA TUNICAM EIUS TANGEBANT ET ISTA OMNIA VIDEBANT SOCII EXPECTANTES IN VIA.

Marinangeli:

CUM BEATUS FRANCISCUS IRET BEVANIUM PRAEDICAVIT MULTIS AVIBUS QUAE GESTIENTES EXTENDEBANT COLLA, PROTENDEBANT ALAS, APERIEBANT ROSTRA, TUNICAM EIUS TANGEBANT, ET ISTA OMNIA VIDEBANT SOCII EXPECTANTES IN VIA.

SCENE XVI: *The Death of the Knight of Celano*   (Plate 70)

Legenda maior, xi, 4:

Alio quoque tempore, cum post reversionem ipsius de ultra mare Celanum praedicaturus accederet, miles quidam supplici eum devotione cum instantia magna invitavit ad prandium. Venit itaque ad militis domum, omnisque familia pauperum hospitum exsultavit ingressu. Ante vero quam cibum sumerent, iuxta solitum morem vir mente devotus offerens Deo preces et laudes, oculis stabat elevatis in caelum. Oratione completa, benignum hospitem familiariter advocatum in partem sic allocutus est: 'Ecce, frater hospes, tuis victus precibus, ut manducarem, domum tuam intravi. Meis nunc cito monitis acquiesce, quoniam non hic, sed alibi manducabis. Confitere nunc peccata tua, verae poenitentiae dolore contritus, nec in te remaneat quidquam, quod veridica confessione non pandas. Reddet tibi Dominus hodie vicem, quoniam tanta devotione suos pauperes suscepisti.' Acquievit continuo vir ille sermonibus sancti, socioque ipsius universa peccata in confessione detegens, *disposuit domum suam*[1] et ad mortem suscipiendam se, quantum valuit, praeparavit. Intraverunt tandem ad mensam, et incipientibus aliis manducare, hospes subito spiritum exhalavit, iuxta verbum hominis Dei repentina morte sublatus. Sicque factum est, hospitalitatis misericordia promerente, ut iuxta verbum Veritatis *Prophetam recipiens, mercedem Prophetae acciperet*;[2] dum per sancti viri praenuntiationem propheticam miles ille devotus sibi contra mortis subitationem providit, quatenus, armis poenitentiae praemunitus, perpetuam damnationeme evaderet et in *aeterna tabernacula*[3] introiret.

(When on another occasion, after his return from beyond the seas, he had gone to Celano to preach, a certain knight with humble supplication and pressing importunity invited him to dinner. And so he came to the knight's house, and the whole family rejoiced at the arrival of their poor guests. But before they partook of the repast the devout man, according to his usual custom, stood with his eyes raised to heaven, offering prayers and praises to God. His

---

[1] Cf. Isa. 38:1.   [2] Matt. 10:41.   [3] Luke 16:9.

prayer ended, he called aside his good host in friendly fashion and thus addressed him: 'Behold, my host and brother, yielding to your entreaties I have entered your house to eat. Do you now attend to my prophetic words, for you shall eat not here but elsewhere. Confess now your sins; be contrite with the grief of true repentance; nor let anything remain in your heart that you will not reveal in truthful confession. The Lord will reward you today for having received His poor with such devotion.' The other at once assented to the Saint's words, and having laid bare all his sins in confession to Francis's companion, he set his house in order and prepared himself, as far as he could, to meet death. At length they sat down at the table, and just as the others were beginning to eat the host suddenly gave up the ghost, carried off by sudden death according to the word of the man of God. And thus, in fitting recompense for the kindliness of his hospitality, it came to pass that, according to the Word of truth, 'he that receiveth a prophet shall receive a prophet's reward'; for through the prophetic warning of the holy man that devout knight made himself ready against the sudden arrival of death, in that, being protected by the armour of penitence, he escaped everlasting damnation and entered into the eternal tabernacles.)

Assisi, Sc. XVI:

. . . BEATUS FRANCISCUS IMPETRAVIT SALUTEM ANIME CUIDAM MILITI DE CELANO QUI EUM DEVOTE AD PRANDIUM INVITAVIT QUI ET POST CONFESSIONEM ET DOMUS SUE DISPOSITIONEM ALIIS INCIPIENTIBUS MANDUCARE IPSE STATIM SPIRITUM EXALAVIT ET IN DOMINO OBDORMIVIT.

Marinangeli (corrected):

CUM BEATUS FRANCISCUS IMPETRAVIT SALUTEM ANIMAE CUIDAM MILITI DE CELANO QUI EUM DEVOTE AD PRANDIUM INVITAVERAT, QUI ET POST CONFESSIONEM ET DOMUS SUAE DISPOSITIONEM, ALIIS INCIPIENTIBUS MANDUCARE, IPSE STATIM SPIRITUM EXHALAVIT ET IN DOMINO OBDORMIVIT.

SCENE XVII: *The Sermon before Honorius III* (Plate 74)

Legenda maior, xii, 7:

Nam cum semel, praedicaturus coram Papa et cardinalibus, ad suggestionem domini Ostiensis, sermonem quemdam studiose compositum commendasset memoriae stetissetque in medio, ut aedificationis verba proponeret, sic oblivioni tradidit omnia, ut effari aliquid omnino nesciret. Verum, cum hoc veridica humilitate narrasset, conferens se ad sancti Spiritus gratiam invocandam, tam efficacibus subito coepit verbis affluere tamque potenti virtute illorum mentes virorum sublimium ad compunctionem inflectere, ut aperte clareret, quod non ipse, sed *Spiritus* Domini *loquebatur*.[1]

(For on a certain occasion, being due to preach before the Pope and the Cardinals, at the suggestion of the Lord Bishop of Ostia, he had committed to memory a certain carefully composed sermon; and, standing up in their midst to deliver his discourse for their edification, he found that he had so completely forgotten it all that he was unable to utter a word of it.

[1] Cf. Acts 6:10.

But when with truthful humility he had explained this, and had bent his will to invoke the grace of the Holy Spirit, he immediately began to pour forth a stream of words so penetrating and of such power to move the minds of those eminent men to repentance that it was patently manifest that it was not he that spoke but the Spirit of the Lord.)

Assisi, Sc. XVII:

. . . . BEATUS FRANCISCUS CORAM DOMINO PAPA ET CARDI . . . . . TA DEVOTE ET EFFICACITUR PREDICAVIT UT PATENTER CLARESCERET QUOD IPSE NON IN DOCTIS HUMANE SAPIENTIE VERBIS SET DIVINO SPIRITU LOQUERETUR.

Marinangeli:

CUM BEATUS FRANCISCUS CORAM DOMINO PAPA ET CARDINALIBUS ITA DEVOTE ET EFFICACITER PRAEDICAVIT, UT PATENTER CLARESCERET QUOD IPSE NON IN DOCTIS HUMANAE SAPIENTIAE VERBIS SED DIVINO SPIRITU LOQUERETUR.

SCENE XVIII: *The Appearance at Arles*   (Plate 75)

Legenda maior, iv, 10:

Dum enim egregius praedicator, qui et nunc Christi praeclarus confessor Antonius de titulo crucis: *Iesus Nazarenus, rex Iudaeorum*,[1] in Arelatensi capitulo fratribus praedicaret, quidam frater probatae virtutis, Monaldus nomine, ad ostium capituli divina commonitione respiciens, vidit corporeis oculis beatum Franciscum in aëre sublevatum, extensis velut in cruce manibus, benedicentem fratres. Tanta vero et tam insolita fratres omnes consolatione spiritus repletos se fuisse senserunt, ut de vera sancti patris praesentia certum eis intra se Spiritus *testimonium perhiberet*,[2] licet postmodum id non solum per evidentia signa, verum etiam per eiusdem sancti patris verba exteriore fuerit attestatione compertum.—Credendum sane, quod omnipotens Dei virtus, quae Ambrosium, sacrum antistitem, tumulationi gloriosi concessit interesse Martini, ut pium pontificem pie veneraretur officio, etiam servum suum Franciscum praedicationi praesentavit veracis sui praeconis Antonii, ut approbaret veritatis eloquia, praecipue crucis Christi, cuius erat et baiulus et minister.

(For while that illustrious preacher Anthony, who is now a glorious Confessor of Christ, was preaching to the Brethren at the Chapter of Arles on the subject of the superscription on the Cross, 'Jesus of Nazareth, the King of the Jews', a certain Brother of proven virtue named Monaldo, looking back by divine inspiration towards the door of the chapter-house, saw with his bodily eyes the Blessed Francis uplifted in the air, blessing the Brethren, his hands outstretched as though upon a Cross. Indeed all the Brethren felt that they had been filled with a consolation of spirit so great and so strange that the Spirit bore them certain witness within themselves of the true presence of the holy Father, although this was later established also from external evidence, both by manifest signs and by the words of that same holy Father. We must truly believe that the almighty power of God, which suffered the

---

[1] John 19:19.   [2] John 1:7.

holy bishop Ambrose to be present at the burial of the glorious Martin, so that he might honour that pious pontiff with his pious ministry, also ordained that His servant Francis should be present at the preaching of His true herald Anthony, so that he might sanction his preaching of the truth, and especially his preaching of the Cross of Christ, of which he was both the bearer and servant.)

Assisi, Sc. XVIII:

CUM BEATUS ANTONIUS IN CAPITULO ARELATENSI DE TITULO CRUCIS PREDICARET BEATUS FRANCISCUS ABSENS CORPORE APPARUIT ET EXTENSIS MANIBUS BENEDIXIT FRATRES SICUT VIDIT QUIDAM FRATER MONALDUS ET ALII FRATRES CONSOLATIONEM MAXIMAM HABUERUNT.

Marinangeli:

CUM BEATUS ANTONIUS IN CAPITULO ARELATENSI DE TITULO CRUCIS PRAEDICARET, BEATUS FRANCISCUS ABSENS CORPORE APPARUIT, ET EXTENSIS MANIBUS, BENEDIXIT FRATRES, SICUT VIDIT QUIDAM FRATER MONALDUS, ET ALII FRATRES CONSOLATIONEM MAXIMAM HABUERUNT.

SCENE XIX: *The Stigmatization of St. Francis* (Plate 76)

Legenda maior, xiii, 1–3:

1. . . . Biennio itaque, antequam spiritum redderet caelo, divina providentia duce, post labores multimodos perductus est in locum *excelsum seorsum*,[1] qui dicitur Mons Alvernae. Cum igitur iuxta solitum morem quadragesimam ibidem ad honorem sancti Archangeli Michaelis ieiunare coepisset, supernae contemplationis dulcedine abundantius solito superfusus ac caelestium desideriorum ardentiore flamma succensus, supernarum coepit immissionum cumulatius dona sentire. Ferebatur quidem in altum, non ut curiosus *maiestatis perscrutator opprimendus a gloria*,[2] sed tamquam *servus fidelis et prudens*,[3] investigans beneplacitum Dei, cui se conformare omnimode summo peroptabat ardore.

2. Immissum est igitur menti eius per divinum oraculum, quod in apertione libri evangelici revelaretur ei a Christo, quid Deo in ipso et de ipso maxime foret acceptum. Oratione itaque cum multa devotione praemissa, sacrum Evangeliorum librum de altari sumptum in sanctae Trinitatis nomine aperiri fecit per socium, virum utique Deo devotum et sanctum. Sane cum in trina libri apertione Domini passio semper occurreret, intellexit vir Deo plenus, quod sicut Christum fuerat imitatus in actibus vitae, sic conformis ei esse deberet in afflictionibus et doloribus passionis, antequam *ex hoc mundo transiret*.[4] Et licet propter multam austeritatem vitae praeteritae crucisque dominicae baiulationem continuam imbecillis esset iam corpore, nequaquam est territus, sed ad martyrii sustinentiam vigorosius animatus. Excreverat quidem in eo insuperabile amoris incendium boni Iesu in *lampades ignis atque flammarum*, ut *aquae multae caritatem* eius tam validam *exstinguere non* valerent.[5]

3. Cum igitur seraphicis desideriorum ardoribus sursum ageretur in Deum et compassiva dulcedine in eum transformaretur, qui ex *caritate nimia*[6] voluit crucifigi: quodam mane circa festum Exaltationis sanctae Crucis, dum oraret in latere montis, vidit Seraph unum sex alas

---

[1] Matt. 17:1.   [2] Cf. Prov. 25:27.   [3] Matt. 24:45.
[4] Cf. John 13:1.   [5] Song of Songs 8:6–7.   [6] Cf. Eph. 2:4.

habentem, tam ignitas quam splendidas, de caelorum sublimitate descendere. Cumque volatu celerrimo pervenisset ad aëris locum viro Dei propinquum, apparuit inter alas effigies hominis crucifixi, in modum crucis manus et pedes extensos habentis et cruci affixos. Duae alae super caput ipsius elevabantur, duae ad volandum extendebantur, duae vero totum velabant corpus. Hoc videns, vehementer obstupuit, mixtumque moerore gaudium cor eius incurrit. Laetabatur quidem in gratioso aspectu, quo a Christo sub specie Seraph cernebat se conspici, sed crucis affixio compassivi doloris *gladio ipsius animam pertransibat.*[1]— Admirabatur quam plurimum in tam inscrutabilis visionis aspectu, sciens, quod passionis infirmitas cum immortalitate spiritus seraphici nullatenus conveniret. Intellexit tandem ex hoc, Domino revelante, quod ideo huiusmodi visio sic divina providentia suis fuerat praesentata conspectibus, ut amicus Christi praenosset, se non per martyrium carnis, sed per incendium mentis totum in Christi crucifixi similitudinem transformandum. Disparens igitur visio mirabilem in corde ipsius reliquit ardorem, sed et in carne non minus mirabilem signorum impressit effigiem.—Statim namque in manibus eius et pedibus apparere coeperunt signa clavorum quemadmodum paulo ante in effigie illa viri crucifixi conspexerat. Manus enim et pedes in ipso medio clavis confixae videbantur, clavorum capitibus in interiore parte manuum et superiore pedum apparentibus, et eorum acuminibus exsistentibus ex adverso; erantque clavorum capita in manibus et pedibus rotunda et nigra, ipsa vero acumina oblonga, retorta et quasi repercussa, quae de ipsa carne surgentia carnem reliquam excedebant. Dextrum quoque latus quasi lancea transfixum, rubra cicatrice obductum erat, quod saepe sanguinem sacrum effundens, tunicam et femoralia respergebat.

(Accordingly, two years before he surrendered his spirit to heaven, the divine counsel guiding him, he was brought after many and varied toils to a high mountain apart, that is called Mount La Verna. When, according to his usual custom, he began to keep a Lent there in honour of the Blessed Archangel Michael, being filled even more abundantly than before with the sweetness of heavenly contemplation and kindled with a still more burning flame of celestial longings, he began to be aware of a still more copious outpouring of divine gifts. He was truly carried up to the heights, not as an inquisitive searcher into the divine majesty who is weighed down by its glory, but even as a faithful and wise servant seeking out the will of God, to which he ardently desired to conform himself in every way.

2. It was therefore instilled into his mind by the divine oracle that through the opening of the Book of the Gospels it would be revealed to him by Christ what would be most acceptable to God in him and from him. And so, having prayed very devoutly, he had the holy Book of the Gospels taken from the altar and opened, in the name of the Holy Trinity, by his companion, a man truly devoted to God and holy. When in the threefold opening of the Book the pages always fell open at the Lord's Passion, the God-filled man truly understood that, just as he had imitated Christ in the deeds of his life, so also it was required of him, before the hour came that he should depart out of this world, that he should become like Him in the afflictions and sufferings of His Passion. And although on account of the great

---

[1] Cf. Luke 2:35.

austerity of his past life and his continual bearing of the Lord's Cross he was by now frail in body, he was in no way afraid, but was the more courageously inspired to suffer martyrdom. For in him the inextinguishable burning of love of the good Jesus had increased into flashes of fire, into a very flame, so that many waters could not quench a love so strong.

3. When, therefore, he had been lifted up towards God by the seraphic ardour of his longings and transformed by the sweetness of his compassion into the likeness of Him Who, in His great love wherewith He loved us, willed to be crucified,—on a certain morning about the Feast of the Exaltation of Holy Cross, while he was praying on the side of the mountain, he saw a Seraph with six wings, flaming and resplendent, descending from the heights of heaven. And when in his most swift flight he had reached the space of air in the vicinity of the man of God, there appeared between his wings the image of a Crucified Man, having his hands and his feet stretched out in the manner of a Cross and fastened to a Cross. Two wings were raised above his head and two spread out for flight, while two hid his whole body. Seeing this, Francis was mightily astonished, and joy, mingled with grief, possessed his heart. He rejoiced, that is, in the gracious aspect with which, as he perceived, he was regarded by Christ (in the guise of the Seraph), but His Crucifixion pierced through his soul with a sword of compassionate grief. He marvelled greatly at the appearance of so inscrutable a vision, knowing that the infirmity of suffering was in no way conformable to the immortality of a Seraphic Spirit. At length the friend of Christ understood from this, the Lord revealing it to him, that this vision had been presented thus before his eyes by the Divine Providence so that he might have foreknowledge that he was to be wholly transformed into the likeness of Christ Crucified, not by the martyrdom of the flesh, but by the kindling of the mind. As it disappeared, therefore, the vision left in his heart a wondrous glow, but it imprinted in his flesh also a no less wondrous likeness of its tokens. For immediately the marks of the nails began to appear in his hands and his feet, just as a little earlier he had observed them in that figure of the Crucified Man. For his hands and his feet seemed to be transfixed through the middle by nails, the heads of the nails showing in the palms of the hands and on the upper part of the feet, and their points standing out on the other side; and the heads of the nails in both hands and feet were round and black, but the points were longish, twisted, and as it were bent back, and they rose out of the flesh itself and projected beyond it. And furthermore, as though it had been pierced by a lance, his right side was marked with a ruddy scar, which as it shed the sacred blood would often stain his habit and breeches.)

Assisi, Sc. XIX:

CUM *BEATUS* FRANCISCUS ORARET *IN* LATERE MONTIS ALVERNE VIDIT XP̄M *IN SPECIE* SERAPYN CRUCIFIXI QUI *IMPRESSIT IN* MANIBUS ET PEDIBUS ET ETIAM *IN* LATERE DEXTRO STIG . . . . RUCIS EIUSDEM DOM . . . . IES . . . .

Marinangeli:

CUM BEATUS FRANCISCUS ORARET IN LATERE MONTIS ALVERNAE, VIDIT CHRISTUM IN SPECIE SERAPHIM CRUCIFIXI, QUI IMPRESSIT IN MANIBUS ET PEDIBUS ET ETIAM IN LATERE DEXTRO STIGMATA CRUCIS EIUSDEM DOMINI NOSTRI IESU CHRISTI.

SCENE **XX**: *The Death and Ascension of St. Francis*   (Plate 77)

Legenda maior, xiv, 6:

Tandem cunctis in eum completis mysteriis, anima illa sanctissima carne soluta et in abyssum divinae claritatis absorpta, beatus vir *obdormivit in Domino.*[1]—Unus autem ex fratribus et discipulis eius vidit animam illam beatam, sub specie stellae praefulgidae a candida subvectam nubecula super aquas multas in caelum recto tramite sursum ferri, tamquam sublimis sanctitatis candore praenitidam et caelestis sapientiae simul et gratiae ubertate repletam, quibus vir sanctus promeruit locum introire lucis et pacis, ubi cum Christo sine fine quiescit.

(At length, when all the mysteries had been fulfilled in him, and that most holy spirit was loosed from the flesh to be received into the depths of the divine glory, the blessed man fell asleep in the Lord. And one of his Brethren and disciples saw that blessed soul, under the likeness of a star of shining brightness, borne on a dazzling white cloudlet over many waters and taken up in a straight course into the heavens, as though refulgent with the radiant whiteness of his exalted sanctity and filled with the bounty of heavenly wisdom and grace, through which the holy man became worthy to enter the abode of light and peace, where he rests with Christ for ever.)

Assisi, Sc. XX:

QUOMODO IN HORA TRANSITUS BEATI FRANCISCI UNUS FRATER VIDIT ANIMAM EIUS SUB SPECIE STELLE PREFULGIDE IN CELUM ASCENDERE.[2]

Marinangeli:

QUOMODO IN HORA TRANSITUS BEATI FRANCISCI UNUS FRATER VIDIT ANIMAM EIUS SUB SPECIE STELLAE PRAEFULGIDAE IN COELUM ASCENDERE.

SCENE **XXI**: *The Vision of the Ascension of St. Francis*   (Plate 80)

Legenda maior, xiv, 6:

Minister quoque fratrum in Terra Laboris tunc erat frater Augustinus, vir utique sanctus et iustus, qui in hora ultima positus, cum diu iam pridem amisisset loquelam, audientibus qui astabant, subito clamavit et dixit: 'Exspecta me, pater, exspecta, ecce, iam venio tecum!' Quaerentibus fratribus et admirantibus multum, cui sic loqueretur audacter, respondit: 'Nonne videtis patrem nostrum Franciscum, qui vadit ad caelum?' Et statim sancta ipsius anima, migrans a carne, patrem est secuta sanctissimum.—Episcopus Assisinas ad oratorium Sancti Michaelis in Monte Gargano tunc temporis peregrinationis causa perrexerat, cui beatus Franciscus, apparens nocte transitus sui, dixit: 'Ecce, *relinquo mundum et vado ad* caelum.'[3] Mane igitur surgens, episcopus sociis narravit quae vidit, et Assisium rediens, cum sollicite perquisisset, certitudinaliter comperit, quod ea hora, qua sibi per visionem innotuit, beatus Pater ex hoc mundo migravit.

[1] Acts 7:60.   [2] See note 1 on p. 285.   [3] John 16:28.

(Furthermore, the Minister of the Brethren in Terra di Lavoro at that time was a Brother named Augustine, a man both holy and honest, who, having reached his last hour, suddenly cried out in the hearing of those that stood by, although a long while before he had entirely lost the power of speech, and said: 'Wait for me, Father, wait! look, now I am coming with you!' When the Brethren, marvelling greatly, inquired who it was that he spoke to so boldly, he answered them: 'Do you not see our Father Francis, who is going to heaven?' And immediately his holy soul, departing from his body, followed the most holy Father.

At that time the Bishop of Assisi had gone on a pilgrimage to the Oratory of St. Michael on Monte Gargano, and the Blessed Francis, appearing to him on the night of his passing, said to him: 'Behold, I leave the world, and go unto heaven.' Accordingly, when he rose in the morning, the Bishop related to his companions what he had seen, and, returning to Assisi, he learnt for certain, after making careful inquiries, that at the very hour at which this became known to him through the vision, the blessed Father had departed from this world.)

Assisi, Sc. XXI:

MINISTER TERRE LABORIS *CUM* LABORARET *IN* EXTREMIS ET DIU IAM PERDIDISSET LOQUELAM[1] . . . . AV*IT* ET DIX*IT*: EXPECTA ME PATER ECCE VENIO TECU*M*. ET STATIM DEFU*N*CTUS SECUTUS EST S*A*NCTUM PATREM. EP*ISCOPU*S INSUPER ASISII CUM ESSET IN MONTE SANCTI . . . . ENTEM SIBI: ECCE VADO AD CELUM. ET[2] TA . . . . HORA ITA I*N*VENTUM EST.

Marinangeli:

MINISTER TERRAE LABORIS CUM LABORARET IN EXTREMIS ET DIU IAM PERDIDISSET LOQUELAM, CLAMAVIT ET DIXIT: EXPECTA ME, PATER, ECCE VENIO TECUM ET STATIM DEFUNCTUS SECUTUS EST SANCTUM PATREM. EPISCOPUS INSUPER ASSISII CUM ESSET IN MONTE SANCTI MICHAELIS ARCHANGELI VIDIT BEATUM FRANCISCUM DICENTEM SIBI: ECCE VADO AD COELUM. ET TALI HORA ITA INVENTUM EST.

SCENE XXII: *The Verification of the Stigmata* (Plate 82)

Legenda maior, xv, 4:

Audito siquidem transitu Patris beati, et fama diffusa miraculi, accelerans populus confluebat ad locum, ut id cerneret oculis carnis, quod a ratione dubium omne repelleret at affectioni gaudium cumularet. Admissi sunt itaque Assisinates cives quam plurimi ad stigmata illa sacra contemplanda oculis et labiis osculanda.—Unus autem ex eis, miles quidam litteratus et prudens, Hieronymus nomine, vir utique famosus et celeber, cum de huiusmodi sacris signis dubitasset *essetque incredulus* quasi Thomas,[3] ferventius et audacius coram fratribus et aliis civibus movebat clavos Sanctique manus, pedes et latus manibus propriis contrectabat, ut, dum vulnerum Christi veracia illa signa palpando contingeret, de sui et omnium cordibus omne dubietatis vulnus amputaret.

---

[1] This passage is inscribed below Scene XX.   [2] The words that follow are inscribed below Scene XXII.
[3] John 20:24 ff.

(When the passing of the Blessed Father became known, and the rumour of the miracle was spread abroad, the people flocked together in haste to the scene, so that they could perceive with their bodily eyes that which might remove every doubt from their reasons and add joy to their feelings. Very many of the citizens of Assisi were therefore permitted to examine those sacred Stigmata with their eyes and to kiss them with their lips. Now one of them, a certain learned and intelligent knight named Jerome, a man of great fame and renown, because he had had doubts concerning those sacred tokens and was indeed an unbeliever like Thomas, the more eagerly and boldly moved the nails in the presence of the Brethren and the other citizens, and handled with his own hands the Saint's hands, feet, and side, so that, as he tenderly touched those authentic tokens of the wounds of Christ, he cut away every wound of unbelief from his own heart and from the hearts of all.)

Assisi, Sc. XXII:

IN PORTIUNCULA ET CUM IAC . . . . ORTUUS DOMINUS YERONI . . . . LITTER . . . . . .
ELEBER MOVEBA . . . . TR . . .

Marinangeli:

IN PORTIUNCULA ET CUM IACERET BEATUS FRANCISCUS MORTUUS, DOMINUS HIERONYMUS DOCTOR ET LITTERATUS CELEBER MOVEBAT CLAVOS, SANCTIQUE MANUS, PEDES ET LATUS MANIBUS PROPRIIS CONTRECTABAT.

SCENE XXIII: *St. Francis Mourned by St. Clare* (Plate 83)

Legenda maior, xv, 5:

Mane vero facto, turbae quae convenerant acceptis arborum ramis et cereorum multiplicatis luminibus, cum hymnis et canticis sacrum corpus ad civitatem Assisii detulerunt. Transeuntes quoque per ecclesiam Sancti Damiani, in qua virgo illa nobilis Clara, nunc gloriosa in caelis, tunc inclusa cum virginibus morabatur, ibique aliquantulum subsistentes sacrum corpus, margaritis caelestibus insignitum videndum et osculandum sacris illis virginibus obtulerunt. Pervenientes denique ad civitatem cum iubilo, pretiosum thesaurum, quem portabant, in ecclesia Sancti Georgii cum omni reverentia condiderunt.

(When morning came, the crowds that had come together, carrying branches of trees and many wax lights, brought the holy body to the city of Assisi, with hymns and chants. Moreover, passing by the church of San Damiano, where at that time the noble virgin Clare, now glorified in heaven, lived cloistered with her virgins, and halting there for a little while, they set the holy body, adorned with its heavenly pearls, before those holy virgins, so that they might behold it and kiss it. Arriving at last at the city with jubilation, they buried the precious treasure which they were bearing in the church of S. Giorgio, with all reverence.)

Assisi, Sc. XXIII:

. . . . ASISI . . . . . . ORUM ET CEREORUM MULTIPLICATIS LUMINIBUS SACRUM CORPUS

MARGARIT . . . . D . . . . . CLARE . . . ALIIS SACRIS . . . .

Marinangeli:

CUM TURBAE QUAE CONVENERANT DEFERRENT AD CIVITATEM ASSISII CUM RAMIS ARBORUM ET CEREORUM MULTIPLICATIS LUMINIBUS SACRUM CORPUS MARGARITIS COELESTIBUS INSIGNITUM, EUM VIDENDUM BEATAE CLARAE ET ALIIS SACRIS VIRGINIBUS OBTULERUNT.

SCENE XXIV: *The Canonization of St. Francis* (Plate 85)

Legenda maior, xv, 7:

Ad omnem quoque certitudinem faciendam orbi terrarum de glorificatione viri sanctissimi inventa miracula et conscripta et testibus idoneis approbata examinari fecit per illos qui minus inter cardinales favorabiles negotio videbantur. Quibus diligenter discussis et ab omnibus approbatis, de fratrum suorum et omnium praelatorum, qui tunc erant in curia, concordi consilio et assensu canonizandum decrevit. Veniens itaque personaliter ad civitatem Assisii anno dominicae Incarnationis millesimo ducentesimo vigesimo octavo, decimo septimo kalendas Augusti, die dominico, cum maximis quae longum foret enarrare solemniis, beatum Patrem catalogo Sanctorum adscripsit.

(So that every assurance concerning the glorification of that most holy man might also be made available to the whole world, he ordered that after his known miracles had been written down and approved by trustworthy witnesses they should be examined by those of the Cardinals who seemed less favourable to the business than others. When they had been diligently discussed and approved by all, with the unanimous counsel and assent of his Brethren and of all the prelates who were then in the Curia, he decreed that he should be canonized. Coming therefore in person to the city of Assisi in the year of the Lord's Incarnation 1228, on the sixteenth day of July, a Sunday, with ceremonies of the greatest solemnity which it would take long to describe, he enrolled the blessed Father in the list of the Saints.)

Assisi, Sc. XXIV:

. . . . ANONIZA . . . . LOGO SANCTORUM ASSCRI . . . .

Marinangeli:

CUM DOMINUS PAPA PERSONALITER VENIENS AD CIVITATEM ASSISIO, MIRACULIS DILIGENTER DISCUSSIS, DE CONSILIO FRATRUM SUORUM BEATUM FRANCISCUM CANONIZAVIT ET CATALOGO SANCTORUM ASCRIPSIT.

SCENE XXV: *The Appearance to Gregory IX* (Plate 88)

Legenda maior, Miracula, i, 2:

Felicis namque recordationis dominus Gregorius Papa Nonus, de quo vir sanctus prophetando praedixerat, quod ad dignitatem foret apostolicam sublimandus, antequam crucis signiferum catalogo Sanctorum ascriberet, scrupulum quemdam dubitationis in corde gerebat de vulnere laterali. Nocte vero quadam, sicut ipse felix antistes referebat cum lacrimis, beatus ei Franciscus, quadam faciei praetensa duritia, *in somnis apparuit*[1] et haesitationem cordis ipsius redarguens, elevavit brachium dextrum, detexit vulnus phialamque poposcit ab ipso, ut scaturientem reciperet sanguinem, qui ex latere defluebat. Obtulit in visione Summus Pontifex phialam postulatam, quae usque ad summum sanguine profluente de latere videbatur impleri. Ex tunc ad illud sacrum miraculum tanta coepit devotione affici et aemulatione fervere, ut nullo modo pati posset, quod aliquis praefulgentia illa signa superba praesumeret impugnatione fuscare, quin eum severa increpatione feriret.

(Now, before he enrolled the standard-bearer of the Cross in the list of the Saints, Pope Gregory IX, of blessed memory, whose elevation to the apostolic office the holy man had foretold in a prophecy, nursed in his heart a scruple of doubt concerning the wound in the Saint's side. On a certain night, then, as the Pontiff himself used to relate with tears, the Blessed Francis, his countenance wearing an aspect of seeming severity, appeared to him in a dream, and, thus refuting the lingering doubt in his heart, raised his right arm, uncovered the wound and asked him for a vessel to receive the gushing blood that flowed from his side. In his dream the Supreme Pontiff, as he had been commanded, offered him the vessel, which seemed to be filled up to the brim with the blood flowing from the Saint's side. From that time onwards he was inspired by so great a devotion to that sacred miracle and burned with so great a desire for discipleship that he could never suffer any one to presume to denigrate those shining tokens in arrogant contentiousness without administering a severe rebuke.)

Assisi, Sc. XXV:

CUM DOMINUS PAPA G . . . . RIUS ALIQUANTULUM DUBITARET DE PLAG . . . . LATERALIS. DIXIT EI IN SOMNIS BEATUS FRANCISCUS: DA MIHI PHIALAM VACUAM QUAM CUM SIBI DARET SANGUINE LATERIS VIDEBATUR IMPLERI.

Marinangeli:

CUM DOMINUS PAPA GREGORIUS ALIQUANTULUM DUBITARET DE PLAGA VULNERIS LATERALIS, DIXIT EI IN SOMNIS BEATUS FRANCISCUS: DA MIHI PHIALAM VACUAM; QUAM CUM SIBI DARET, SANGUINE LATERIS VIDEBATUR IMPLERI.

SCENE XXVI: *The Healing of the Wounded Man*   (Plate 90)

Legenda maior, Miracula, i, 5:

In Cathalonia quoque apud Ilerdam accidit, virum quemdam nomine Ioannem, beato Francisco devotum, quodam sero per quamdam incedere viam, in qua pro inferenda morte latitabant insidiae, non quidem ipsi, qui inimicitias non habebat, sed alteri cuidam, qui videbatur similis eius et tunc erat in comitatu ipsius. Exsurgens autem quidam de insidiis, cum hostem suum hunc esse putaret, tam letaliter eum plagis pluribus gladiavit, ut nulla prorsus

---

[1] Matt. 1 : 20.

superesset spes recuperandae salutis. Siquidem primo inflicta percussio humerum cum brachio pene totum absciderat, et ictus alius sub mammilla tantam reliquerat aperturam, ut flatus inde procedens circa sex candelas simul iunctas exstingueret. Cum igitur iudicio medicorum ipsius impossibilis esset curatio, pro eo quod, putrescentibus plagis, ex eis foetor tam intolerabilis exhalaret, ut etiam ipsa eius uxor vehementer horreret, nullisque iam humanis iuvari posset remediis, convertit se ad beati Patris Francisci patrocinium quanta poterat devotione poscendum, quem et inter ipsos ictus una cum beata Virgine fidentissime invocarat. Et ecce, misero in lectulo calamitatis solitario decubanti, cum Francisci nomen vigilans et eiulans frequentius replicaret, adstitit quidam in habitu fratris Minoris, per fenestram, ut ei videbatur, ingressus. Qui *vocans* eum *ex nomine*,[1] dixit: 'Quia fiduciam habuisti in me, ecce, Dominus liberabit te.' A quo cum aeger, quis esset, inquireret, Franciscum ille se esse respondit et statim appropians vulnerum illius ligaturas resolvit et eum unguento per omnes plagas, ut videbatur, perunxit. Statim autem, ut sensit illarum sacrarum manuum stigmatum Salvatoris virtute sanare valentium suavem contactum, expulsa putredine, restituta carne et vulneribus solidatis, restitutus est integre pristinae sospitati. Quo facto, beatus Pater abscessit. Et ipse sentiens se sanatum et in vocem divinae laudis et beati Francisci laetanter erumpens, vocavit uxorem. At illa celerius currens et stare iam videns quem sepeliendum credebat in crastino, cum esset stupore vehementer perterrita, viciniam totam clamore complevit. Accurrentes autem sui, cum illum niterentur tamquam phreneticum in lecto reponere, et ille econtra renitens assereret et ostenderet se sanatum; tanto sunt stupore attoniti, ut quasi sine mente omnes effecti, phantasticum esse crederent quod videbant, quia quem paulo ante conspexerant plagis atrocissimis laniatum et totum iam marcidum, plena cernebant incolumitate iucundum. Ad quos ille qui factus fuerat sanus: 'Nolite timere', inquit, 'nolite credere inane quod cernitis, quia sanctus Franciscus modo a loco recessit et illarum sacrarum manuum tactu me integre ab omni plaga curavit.' Crebrescente tandem huius fama miraculi, accelerat populus omnis et videntes in tam aperto prodigio stigmatum beati Francisci virtutem, admiratione simul et gaudio replebantur Christique signiferum magnis laudum praeconiis extollebant.—Digne quidem beatus Pater, carne iam mortuus et vivens cum Christo, praesentiae suae ostensione mirabili et manuum sacrarum palpatione suavi vulnerato letaliter viro sanitatem concessit, cum illius in se stigmata tulerit, qui misericorditer moriens et mirabiliter surgens, vulneratum genus humanum et *semivivum relictum* plagarum suarum virtute sanavit.[2]

(And at Lerida, in Catalonia, it happened that a man named John who was devoted to St. Francis was walking at a late hour along a road where an ambush had been set to kill some one—not, in fact, himself, for he had no enemies, but another who looked like him and who was in company with him at the time. A man rushed upon him from the ambush, thinking him to be his enemy, and wounded him many times with his sword, so mortally that no hope remained of his recovery. Indeed, the first stroke had cut off almost all his shoulder

---

[1] Isa. 40 : 26.   [2] Luke 10 : 30.

along with his arm, and another blow under the nipple had left such a wide opening in his chest that the breath issuing from it would have blown out half a dozen candles joined together. And so, after the physicians had pronounced that a cure was impossible, because his wounds were festering and the smell was so unbearable that even his wife was horrified by it, and when therefore he was already past being helped by any human remedies, he set himself with all the devotion that he knew to claiming the protection of the Blessed Father Franci , whom, together with the Blessed Virgin, he had most confidently invoked even as the blows were falling. And behold, as the poor man lay lamenting in distress on his solitary bed of affliction, and repeated over and over again the name of Francis, one stood beside him in the habit of a Friar Minor, having, as it seemed to him, come in by the window, and, calling him by his name, said to him: 'Because you have had faith in me, behold, the Lord will deliver you.' When the sick man asked him who he was, he replied that he was Francis, and, drawing near, he at once untied the bandages on his wounds and, as it seemed, anointed all his injuries with an ointment. And as soon as he felt the sweet touch of those holy hands that had power to heal by virtue of the Stigmata of the Saviour, the rottenness was driven out, the flesh made good and the wounds closed, and he was completely restored to his original state of health. When this had come to pass the Blessed Father withdrew. And the other, knowing that he was healed and crying out joyfully in praise of God and Saint Francis, called his wife. But when, quickly running in, she saw him already on his feet, whereas she had thought that he would have to be buried on the morrow, she was utterly astonished and terrified, and began to fill the whole neighbourhood with her cries. Moreover, when his servants rushed in and tried to put him back into bed, as though he was out of his mind, he resisted, declaring himself, and showing himself, to be healed: they were so amazed that they thought that they had seen a phantasm, as if they had lost their wits, because they beheld him rejoicing in perfect health when a little earlier they had seen him lacerated with frightful wounds and reduced to total weakness. The man who had been made well said to them: 'Do not be afraid; and do not imagine that what you see is an empty vision; for Saint Francis has just left this place and has completely healed me of all my wounds by the touch of those holy hands.' When at length the news of this miracle was spread abroad, all the people hastened to the spot, and when they witnessed the power of the Stigmata of St. Francis in this manifest miracle, they were filled with wonder and joy together, and extolled the standard-bearer of Christ with loud proclamations of praise. Indeed, it was fitting that our Blessed Father, when already dead in the flesh and living with Christ, should have granted health to a mortally wounded man by the wonderful revelation of his presence and by the sweet touch of his sacred hands, since he bore in himself the Stigmata of Him Who, dying pitiably and wondrously rising again, healed mankind by the merits of His Sacred Wounds when the human race was itself wounded and had been left half dead.)

Assisi, Sc. XXVI:

BEATUS FRANCISCUS IOHANNEM DE CIVITATE YLERDA VULNERATUM AD MORTEM ET A MEDICIS

DESPERATUM, ET SE DUM UULNERARETUR, DEVOTE INVOCANTEM STATIM PERFECTISSIME LIBERA-
VIT SACRIS SUIS MANIBUS LIGATURAS SOL . . . . VISSIME TANGENS.

Marinangeli:

BEATUS FRANCISCUS IOANNEM, DE CIVITATE YLERDA, VULNERATUM AD MORTEM ET A MEDICIS
DESPERATUM, ET SE, DUM VULNERARETUR, DEVOTE INVOCANTEM, STATIM PERFECTISSIME LIBERA-
VIT, SACRIS SUIS MANIBUS LIGATURAS SOLVENS ET PLAGAS SUAVISSIME TANGENS.

SCENE XXVII: *The Confession of the Woman of Benevento*   (Plate 91)

Legenda maior, Miracula, ii, 1:

In castro Montis Marani prope Beneventum mulier quaedam sancto Francisco peculiari
devotione cohaerens, viam universae carnis intravit. Convenientibus autem clericis nocte ad
exsequias et vigilias cum Psalteriis decantandas, subito, cunctis cernentibus, erexit se mulier
super lectum et unum de adstantibus sacerdotem, patrinum videlicet suum, vocavit dicens:
'Volo confiteri, pater, audi peccatum meum! Ego enim mortua duro eram carceri mancipanda, quoniam peccatum, quod tibi pandam, necdum confessa fueram. Sed orante', inquit,
'pro me sancto Francisco, cui, dum viverem, devota mente servivi, redire nunc ad corpus
indultum est mihi, ut, illo revelato peccato, sempiternam promerear vitam. Et ecce, vobis
videntibus, postquam illud detexero, ad promissam requiem properabo.' Trementer ergo
sacerdoti trementi confessa, post absolutionem receptam quiete se in lecto collegit et in
Domino feliciter obdormivit.

(At Montemarano, near Benevento, a certain woman who had a special devotion to Saint
Francis went the way of all flesh. When the clergy had assembled at night to attend to her
obsequies and to keep a vigil with psalms, suddenly, while every one looked on, she rose
up on her bed and called to one of the officiating priests, who was her godfather, and said:
'Father, I wish to make my confession: hear my sin! For when I died I was to be confined
in a grim prison, because I had not yet confessed the sin that I am about to reveal to you.
But Saint Francis, whom I served with devotion while I was alive, prayed for me, and now
I have been permitted to return to the body, so that I may reveal that sin and merit eternal
life. And behold, as you shall see, after I have uncovered it I shall hasten to my promised
rest.' And so she tremblingly confessed to the trembling priest; and, when she had received
absolution, she lay down on the bed and slept peacefully in the Lord.)

Assisi, Sc. XXVII:

BEATUS FRANCISCUS SUSCITAVIT ISTAM DOMINAM MORTUAM QUE FACTA CONFESSIONE UNIUS
PECCATI QUOD NONDUM CONFESSA. VIDENTIBUS CLERICIS ET ALIIS QUI ASTITERUNT, ET ITERUM
DEFU . . . . DOMINO ET DIABOLUS CONFUSUS A . . . .

Marinangeli:

BEATUS FRANCISCUS SUSCITAVIT ISTAM DOMINAM MORTUAM, QUAE, FACTA CONFESSIONE UNIUS

PECCATI QUOD NONDUM FUERAT CONFESSA, VIDENTIBUS CLERICIS ET ALIIS QUI ASTITERUNT, ET ITERUM DEFUNCTA OBDORMIVIT IN DOMINO ET DIABOLUS CONFUSUS AUFUGIT.

SCENE XXVIII: *The Liberation of the Prisoner*   (Plate 93)

Legenda maior, Miracula, v, 4:

Residente in sede beati Petri domino Gregorio Nono, quidam Petrus nomine de civitate Alifia, de haeresi accusatus, Romae captus est et de mandato eiusdem Pontificis, ad custodiendum traditus episcopo Tiburtino. Quem sub poena episcopatus accipiens, compedibus alligavit obscuroque ipsum carcere, ne posset effugere, fecit includi, *panem* ei praebens *in pondere et* poculum *in mensura*.[1] Coepit autem homo ille beatum Franciscum ad sui miserendum multis precibus et fletibus invocare, eo quod audierat solemnitatis eius iam adesse vigiliam. Et quoniam fidei puritate omnem abdicaverat haereticae pravitatis errorem totaque cordis devotione adhaeserat fidelissimo Christi servo Francisco, intercedentibus ipsius meritis, a Domino meruit exaudiri. Instante enim iam nocte suae festivitatis, circa crepusculum beatus Franciscus in carcerem miseratus descendit et illum suo nomine vocans, ut cito surgeret, imperavit. Qui timore perterritus, quisnam esset, interrogans, beatum Franciscum adesse audivit. Cumque virtute praesentiae viri sancti vincula pedum suorum confracta conspiceret cecidisse, et tabulas carceris clavis ultro prosilientibus aperiri, et apertum iter sibi ad exeundum praeberi: solutus tamen et obstupefactus fugere nesciebat, sed ad ianuam clamans, custodes omnes perterruit. Qui cum eum liberatum a vinculis episcopo nuntiassent, post intellectum ordinem rei, ad carcerem pontifex devotus accessit, et manifeste Dei virtutem cognoscens, ibidem Dominum adoravit. Vincula quoque coram domino Papa et cardinalibus delata fuerunt, qui, videntes quod factum fuerat, admirati plurimum benedixerunt Deum.

(When Pope Gregory IX occupied the chair of Saint Peter, a man named Peter, from the city of Alifia, who had been accused of heresy, was arrested in Rome and, on the Pontiff's orders, placed in the custody of the Bishop of Tivoli. The bishop, having accepted his charge under pain of losing his bishopric, put him in irons and shut him up in a dark prison to prevent his escape, giving him bread by weight and drink by measure. Then, with much prayer and weeping, the wretched man began to call upon Saint Francis to take pity upon him, for he had heard that it was just then the vigil of his feast-day. And because in the purity of his faith he had renounced all the error of his wicked heresy and with complete devotion of heart had clung to Francis, that most faithful servant of Christ, the Lord granted his petition, through the intervention of the Saint's merits. For, as the night of his feast-day approached, Saint Francis in his pity came down towards dusk to the prison, called him by his name, and commanded him to rise at once. The other was terrified and asked him who he was; and he was told that Saint Francis was present at his side. And he saw that the fetters on his feet had been broken by the power of the Saint's presence and had fallen away, that the door-nails had leapt out of their own accord, so that the gates of the prison were open,

---

[1] Ezek. 4 : 16.

and that a way to escape was being offered him: yet, although he was free, he was so astounded that he did not know how to run away, but stood shouting in the doorway and terrifying all the guards. When the bishop was informed by them that Peter had been freed from his chains, and when he understood how it had happened, he went devoutly to the prison, openly acknowledged a miracle of God, and in that very place worshipped the Lord. And the chains were taken before the Pope and the Cardinals, and when they saw what had come to pass they were filled with wonder and praised God.)

Assisi, Sc. XXVIII:

BEATUS FRANCISCUS LIBERAVIT ISTUM CAPTIVUM ACCUSATUM DE HERESI ET DE MANDATO DOMINI PAPE RECOMMENDATUM SUB PENA EPISCOPATUS EPISCOPO TIBURTINO. ET HOC FUIT IN FESTO IPSIUS BEATI FRANCISCI CUIUS VIGILIAM IPSE CAPTIVUS . . . . SIE IEIUNAV . . . .

Marinangeli:

BEATUS FRANCISCUS LIBERAVIT ISTUM CAPTIVUM ACCUSATUM DE HAERESI ET DE MANDATO DOMINI PAPAE RECOMMENDATUM SUB POENA EPISCOPATUS EPISCOPO TIBURTINO, ET HOC FUIT IN FESTO IPSIUS BEATI FRANCISCI CUIUS VIGILIAM IPSE CAPTIVUS DE MORE ECCLESIAE IEIUNAVERAT.

SELECT BIBLIOGRAPHY

THE literature on the Assisi frescoes is too vast to be listed here. A comprehensive bibliography on Giotto up to the year 1937 is given in R. Salvini, *Giotto: Bibliografia* (Rome, 1938). A new edition of this essential work is now in preparation. For more recent literature see especially R. Oertel, 'Wende der Giotto-Forschung', *Zeitschrift für Kunstgeschichte*, 1943–4, pp. 1 ff.; C. Gnudi, *Giotto* (Milan, 1958); D. Gioseffi, *Giotto architetto* (Milan, 1963); and G. Previtali, *Giotto e la sua bottega* (Milan, 1967); and, for thirteenth- and early fourteenth-century Italian painting as a whole, G. Sinibaldi and G. Brunetti, *Pittura Italiana del Duecento e Trecento: Catalogo della Mostra Giottesca di Firenze del 1937* (Florence, 1943). The best and fullest accounts of the St. Cecilia Master, Pacino di Bonaguida, and other related painters are to be found in R. Offner, *A Corpus of Florentine Painting* (New York, 1930–). The standard works on the Basilica of S. Francesco at Assisi are: B. Kleinschmidt, *Die Basilika San Francesco in Assisi* (Berlin, 1915–28), and E. Zocca, *Assisi . . .: Catalogo delle cose d'arte e di antichità* (Rome, 1936). A splendid series of photographs of the *St. Francis* frescoes at Assisi was published by Toesca in 1946: P. Toesca, *Gli affreschi della Vita di S. Francesco* (Artis Monumenta photographice edita III, Florence, 1946).

The following is a brief list of other important works bearing directly upon the Assisi problem:

F. RINTELEN, *Giotto und die Giotto-Apokryphen* (Leipzig, 1912 and 1923).

O. SIRÉN, *Giotto and Some of his Followers*, trans. F. Schenk (Cambridge, Mass., 1917).

A. SCHMARSOW, *Kompositionsgesetze der Franziskuslegende in der Oberkirche zu Assisi* (Leipzig, 1918).

C. CARRÀ, *Giotto* (London, 1925).

L. MARTIUS, *Die Franziskuslegende in der Oberkirche von S. Francesco in Assisi und ihre Stellung in der Kunstgeschichtlichen Forschung* (Berlin, 1932).

R. OFFNER, 'Giotto, Non-Giotto', *The Burlington Magazine*, lxxiv (1939), 259 ff., and lxxv (1939), 96 ff.; recently reprinted in J. H. STUBBLEBINE (ed.), *Giotto: The Arena Chapel Frescoes* (London, 1969).

F. J. MATHER, 'Giotto's *St. Francis* Series at Assisi Historically Considered', *Art Bulletin*, xxv (1943), 97 ff.

P. TOESCA, *Il Trecento* (Turin, 1951).

E. CECCHI, *Giotto* (Milan, n.d.).

P. MURRAY, 'Notes on Some Early Giotto Sources', *The Journal of the Warburg and Courtauld Institutes*, xvi (1953), 58 ff.

K. BAUCH, 'Die geschichtliche Bedeutung von Giottos Frühstil', *Mitteilungen des Kunsthistorisches Institut in Florenz*, vii (1953), 43 ff.

R. OERTEL, *Die Frühzeit der italienischen Malerei* (Stuttgart, 1953).

J. WHITE, 'The Date of "The Legend of St. Francis" in Assisi', *The Burlington Magazine*, xcviii (1956), 344 ff.

—— *The Birth and Rebirth of Pictorial Space* (London, 1957; 2nd edn., 1967).

—— *Art and Architecture in Italy, 1250 to 1400* (Pelican History of Art, Harmondsworth, 1966).

C. GNUDI, 'Il passo di Riccobaldo Ferrarese relativo a Giotto e il problema della sua autenticità', in *Studies in the History of Art dedicated to William E. Suida* (London, 1959), pp. 26 ff.

M. MEISS, *Giotto and Assisi* (New York, 1960).

L. TINTORI and M. MEISS, *The Painting of* The Life of St. Francis *in Assisi* (New York, 1962).

H. SCHRADE, *Franz von Assisi und Giotto* (Cologne, 1964).

INDEX

Principal entries are indicated by bold type; Plate references are given in italics.

PLATES

PLATE 1

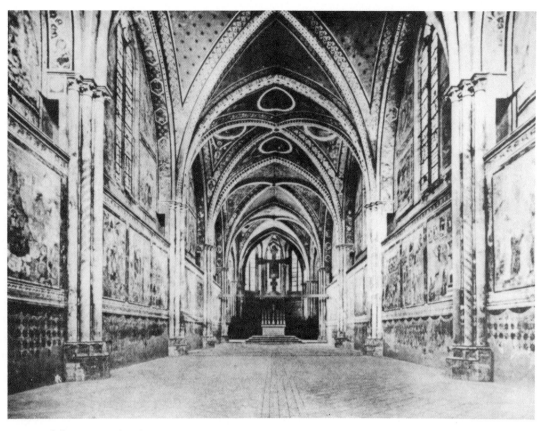

a. Nave of the Upper Church, Assisi, looking west (showing the iconostasis—now dismantled—and its crucifix)

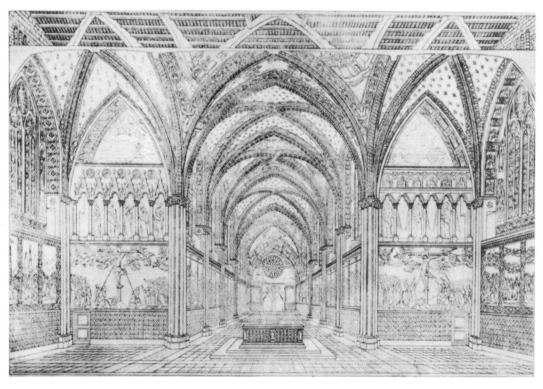

b. Choir and nave of the Upper Church, Assisi, after a drawing of the 19th century (from Kleinschmidt, *Die Basilika*)

PLATE 2

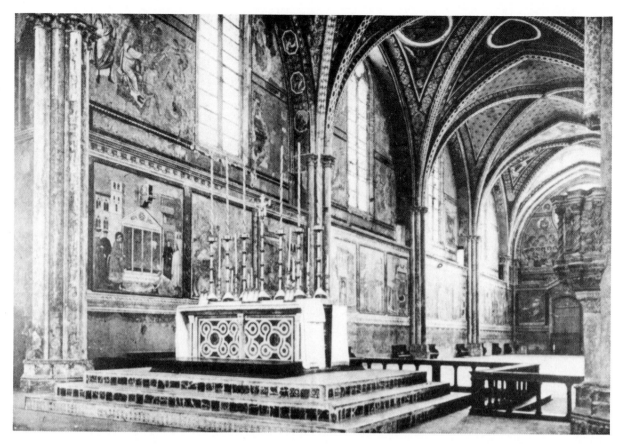

a. Nave of the Upper Church, Assisi (showing the north and east walls)

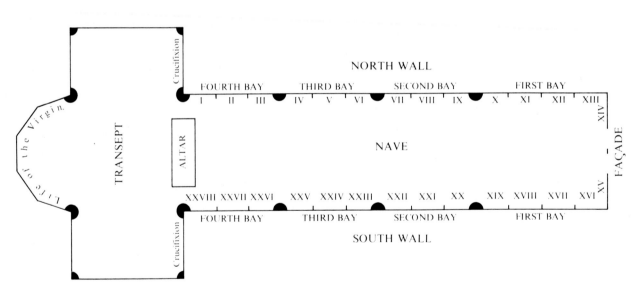

b. Plan of the frescoes of the *Legend of St. Francis*

PLATE 3

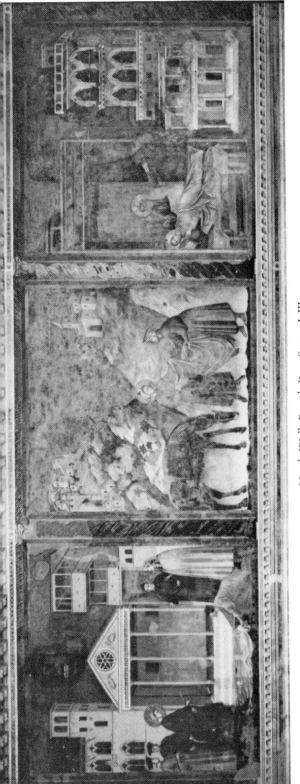

a. North Wall, Fourth Bay: Scenes I–III

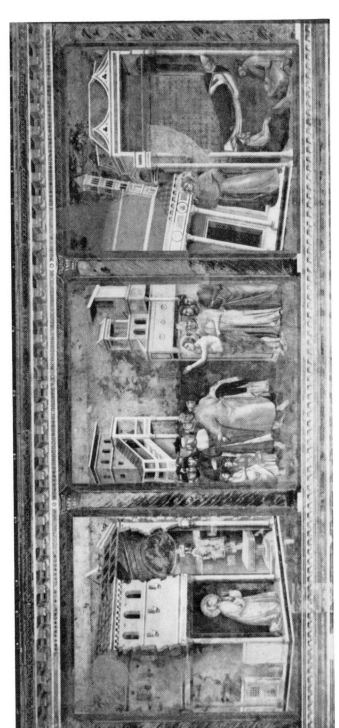

b. North Wall, Third Bay: Scenes IV–VI

PLATE 4

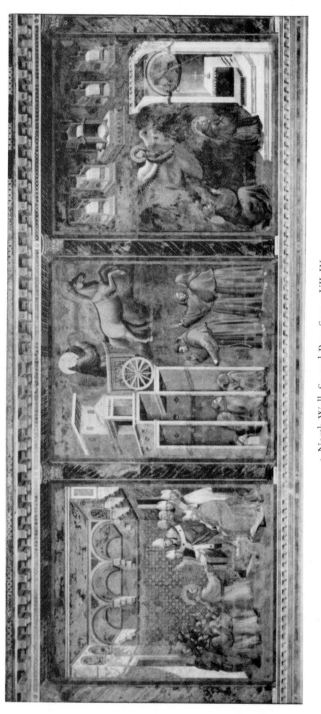

a. North Wall, Second Bay: Scenes VII–IX

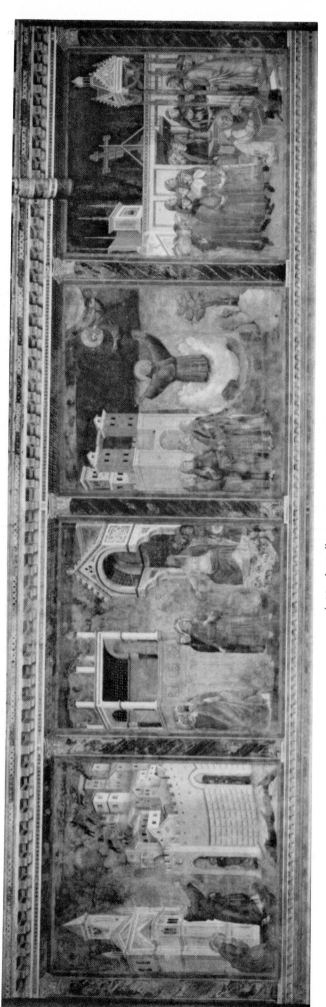

b. North Wall, First Bay: Scenes X–XIII

PLATE 5

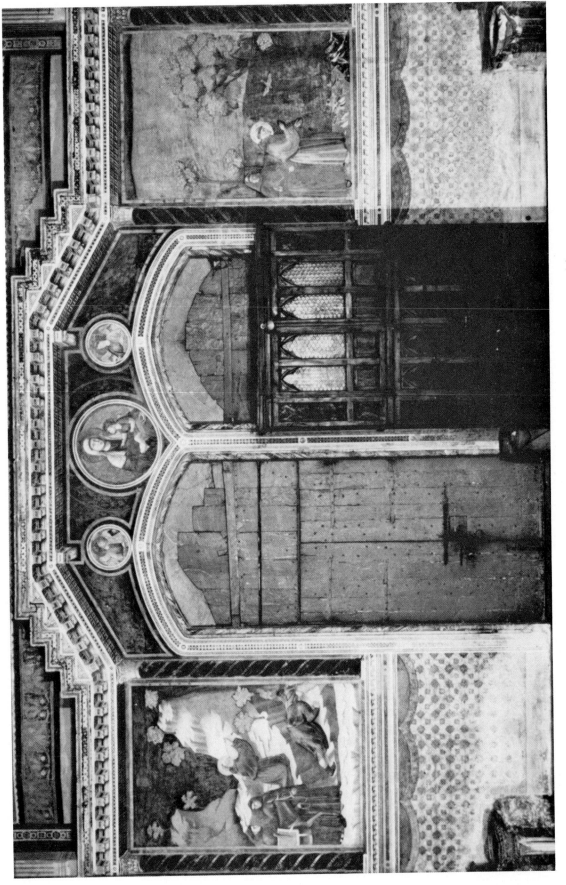

The East Wall: Scenes XIV and XV and the *Madonna* and *Angel* roundels

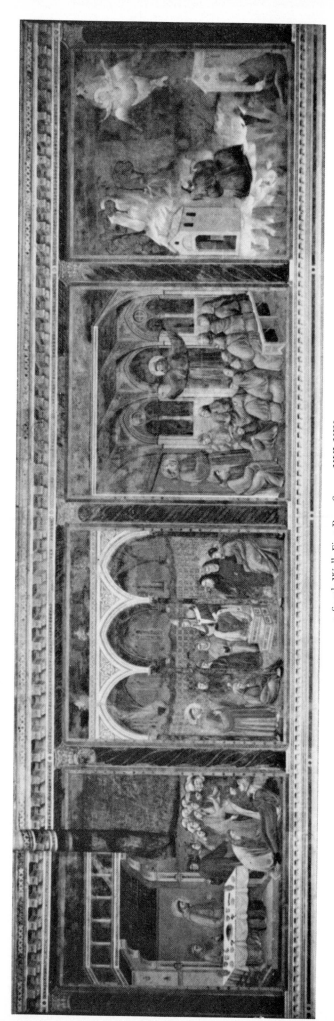

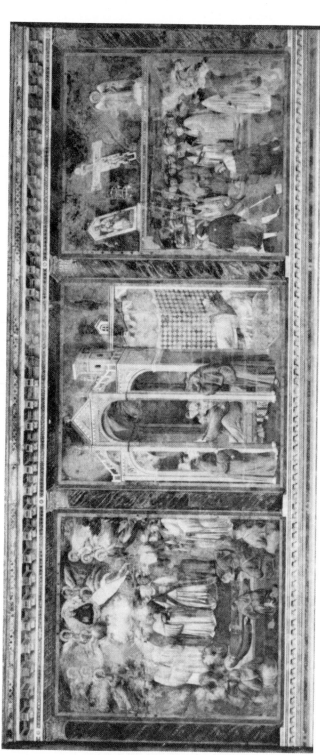

PLATE 6

a. South Wall, First Bay: Scenes XVI–XIX

b. South Wall, Second Bay: Scenes XX–XXII

PLATE 7

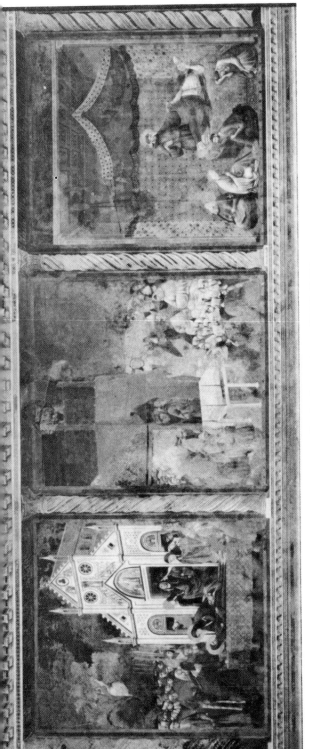

a. South Wall, Third Bay: Scenes XXIII–XXV

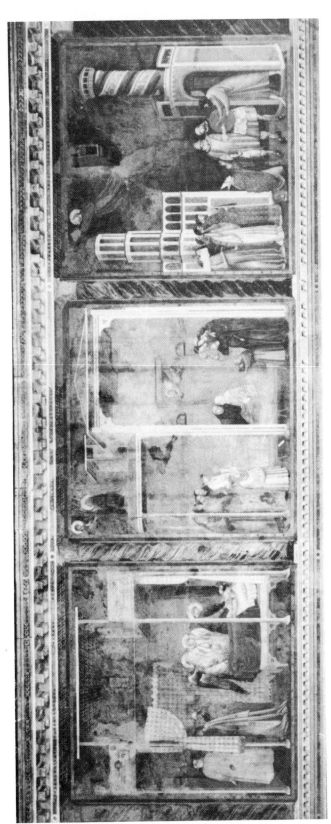

b. South Wall, Fourth Bay: Scenes XXVI–XXVIII

PLATE 8

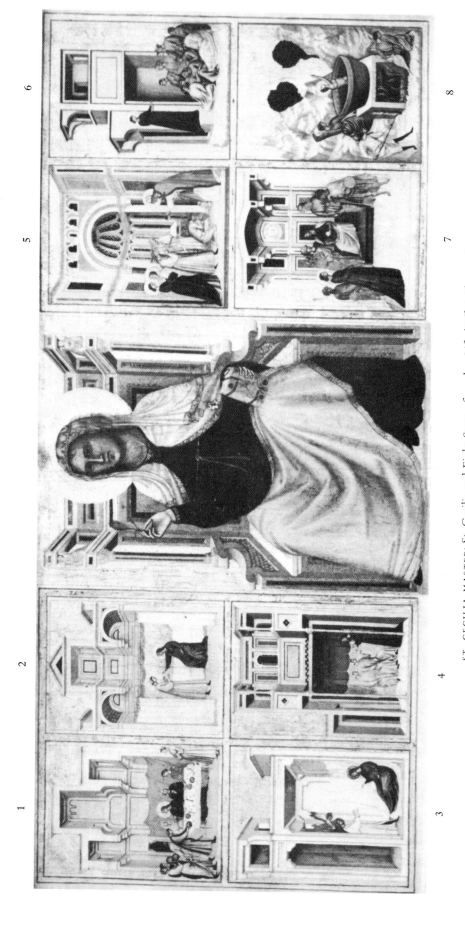

ST. CECILIA MASTER: St. Cecilia and Eight Scenes from her Life (Uffizi, Florence)

(1) The wedding feast of St. Cecilia and Valerian; (2) St. Cecilia urges Valerian to conversion; (3) Valerian crowned by an angel; (4) St. Cecilia preaching before Valerian and his brother Tiburtius; (5) the baptism of Tiburtius; (6) St. Cecilia preaching; (7) the trial of St. Cecilia before the prefect Almachius; (8) the martyrdom of St. Cecilia.

PLATE 9

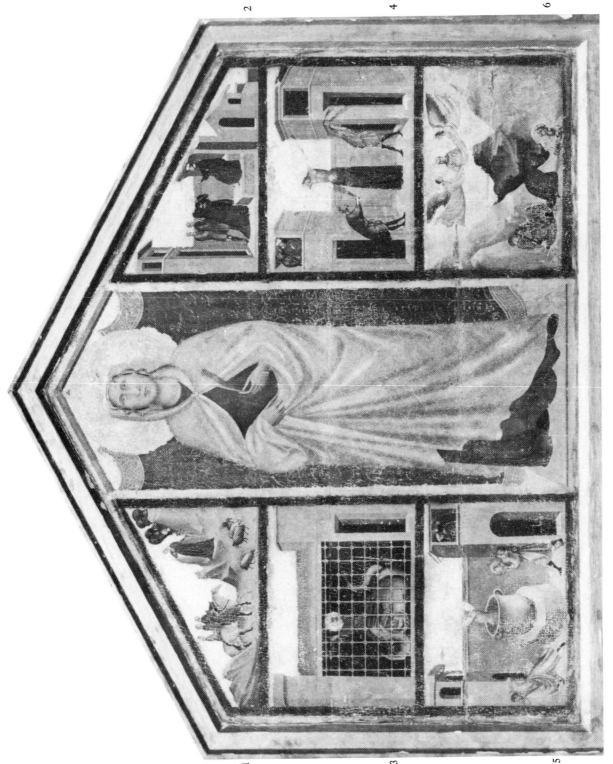

ST. CECILIA MASTER: St. Margaret and Six Scenes from her Life (Santa Margherita a Montici, Florence)

(1) St. Margaret rejects the proposal of the prefect Olybrius; (2) St. Margaret before Olybrius; (3) St. Margaret overcomes the dragon; (4) the flagellation of St. Margaret; (5) the torture of St. Margaret; (6) the martyrdom and ascension of St. Margaret.

PLATE 10

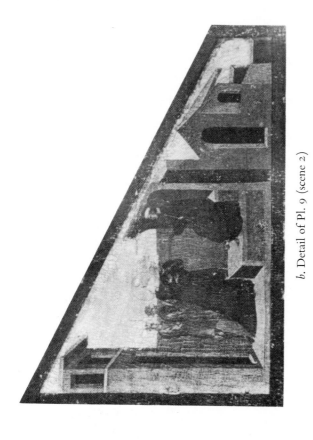

b. Detail of Pl. 9 (scene 2)

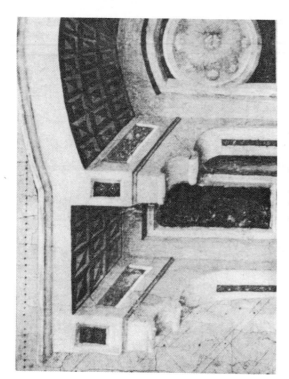

a. Detail of Pl. 8 (scene 7)

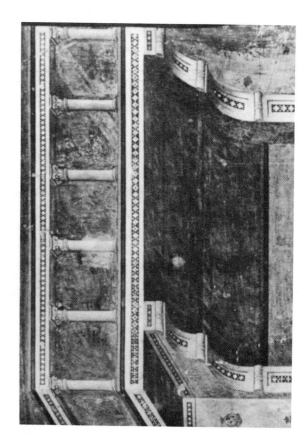

c. St. Francis Cycle, Scene XVI: detail of architecture

d. St. Francis Cycle, Scene II: detail of buildings

PLATE 11

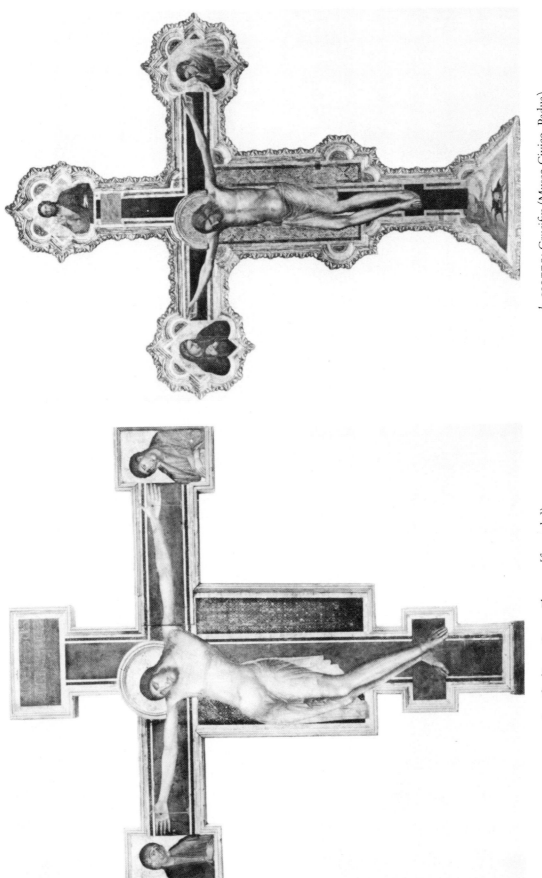

b. GIOTTO: Crucifix (Museo Civico, Padua)

a. CIMABUE: Crucifix (Santa Croce, Florence [formerly])

PLATE 12

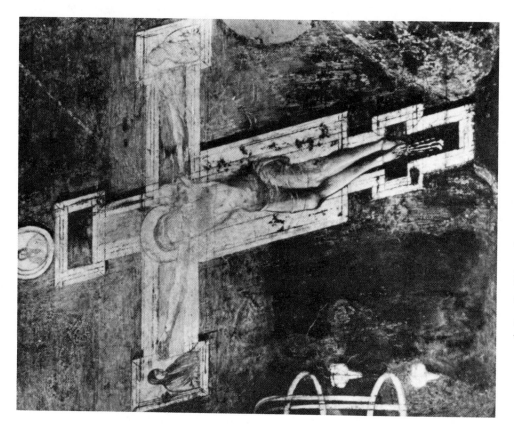

b. Detail of Pl. 82 (*St. Francis* Cycle, Scene XXII)

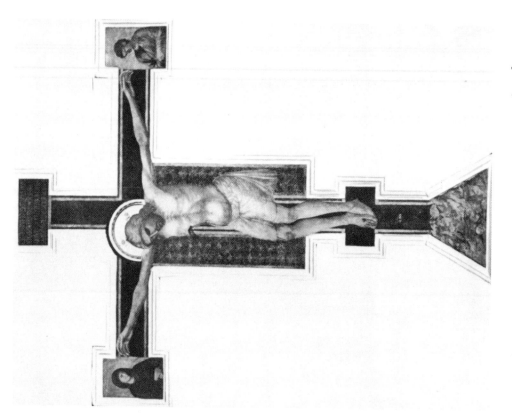

a. MASTER OF THE SANTA MARIA NOVELLA CROSS: Crucifix
(Santa Maria Novella, Florence)

PLATE 13

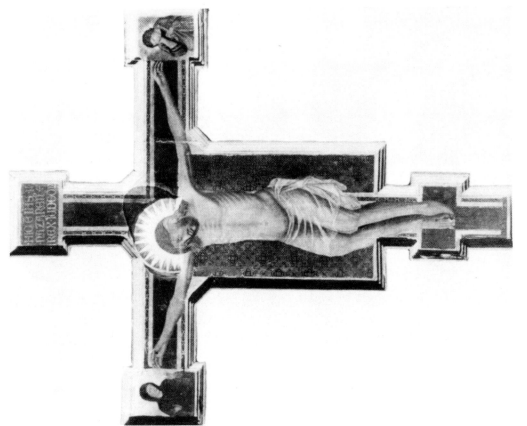

b. PACINO DI BONAGUIDA (Workshop): Crucifix
(Convento delle Oblate, Careggi)

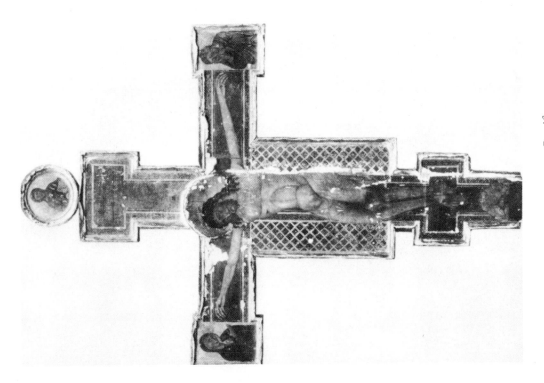

a. DEODATO ORLANDI: Crucifix
(Santa Chiara, San Miniato al Tedesco)

PLATE 14

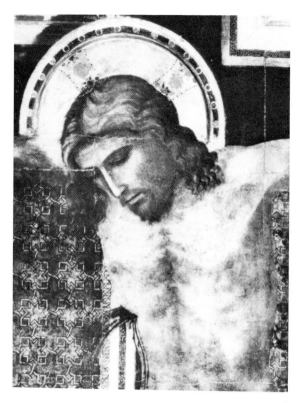

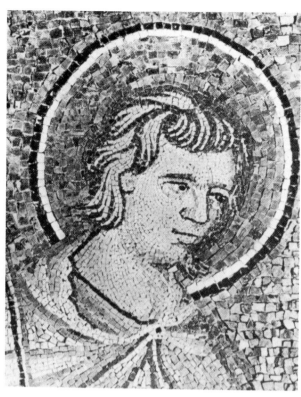

a. MASTER OF THE SANTA MARIA NOVELLA CROSS: The Crucified: detail of Pl. 12*1*

b. St. John the Baptist: detail of mosaic, The Departure of the Baptist for the Desert (Baptistery, Florence)

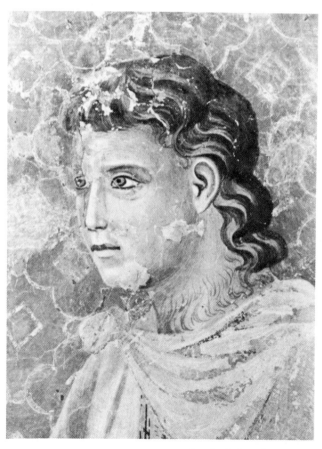

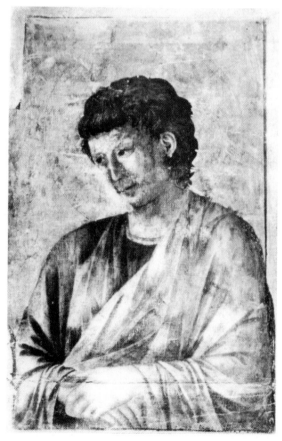

c. ISAAC MASTER: Esau: detail of Pl. 33*b* (Upper Church, Assisi)

d. MASTER OF THE SANTA MARIA NOVELLA CROSS: St. John the Evangelist: detail of Pl. 12*a*

PLATE 15

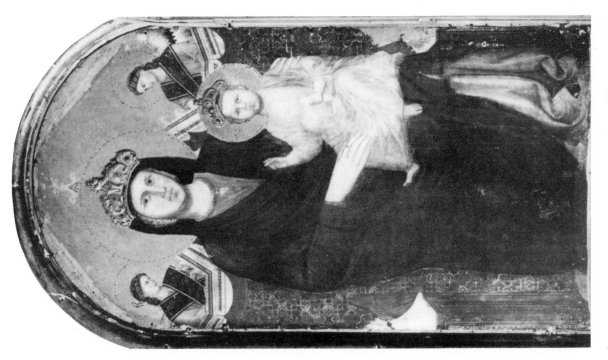

b. MASTER OF THE S. GIORGIO MADONNA: Madonna and Child
(S. Giorgio alla Costa, Florence)

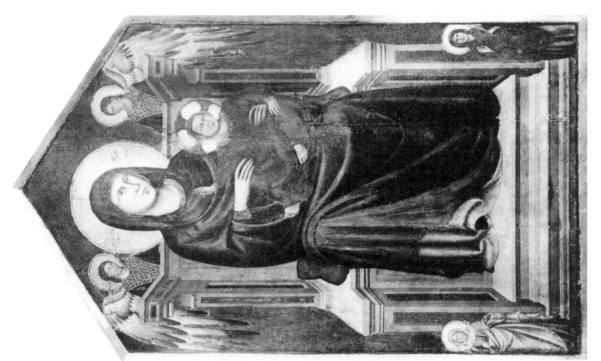

a. ST. CECILIA MASTER: Madonna and Child with Saints (Santa
Margherita a Montici, Florence)

PLATE 16

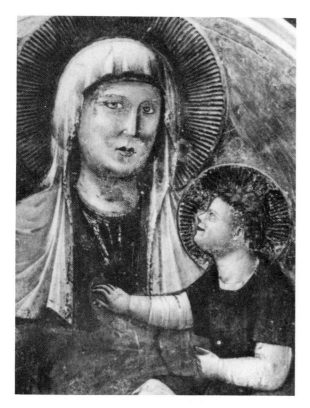

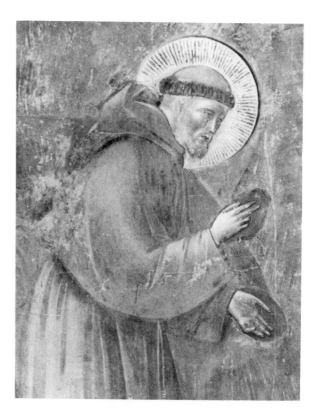

a. Madonna and Child (Upper Church, Assisi)

b. St. Francis: detail of Pl. 68 (*St. Francis* Cycle, Scene XV)

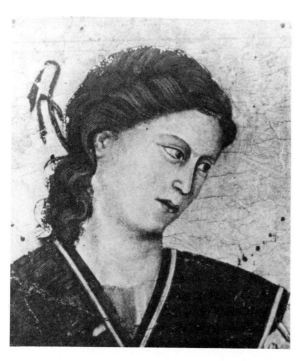

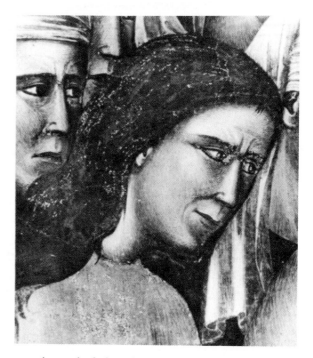

c. MASTER OF THE S. GIORGIO MADONNA: Angel: detail of Pl. 15*b*

d. Detail of Pl. 70 (*St. Francis* Cycle, Scene XVI)

PLATE 17

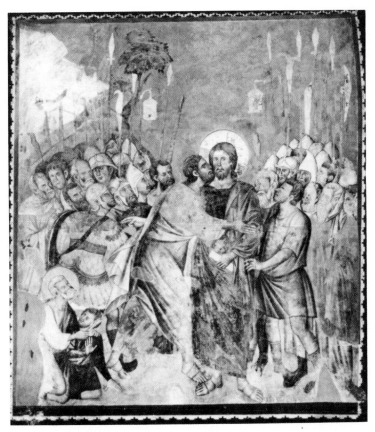

a. JACOPO TORRITI (?): The Kiss of Judas (Upper Church, Assisi)

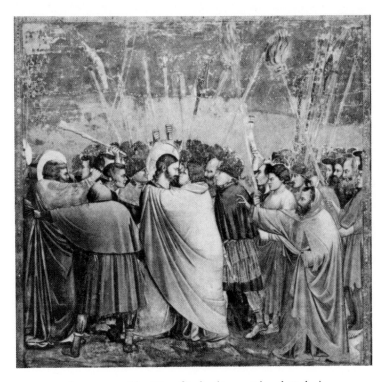

b. GIOTTO: The Kiss of Judas (Arena Chapel, Padua)

PLATE 18

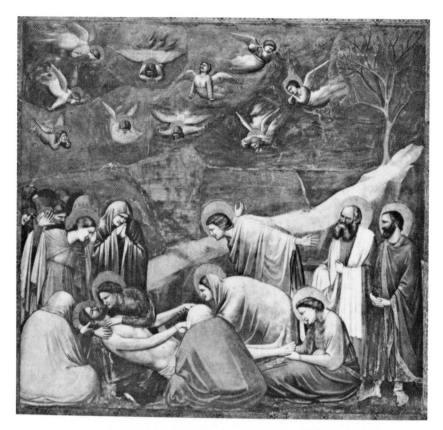

a. GIOTTO: Lamentation over the Dead Christ (Arena Chapel, Padua)

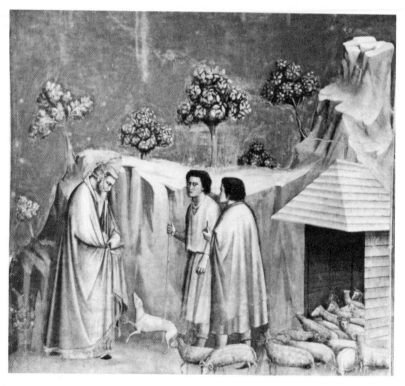

b. GIOTTO: The Withdrawal of St. Joachim to the Sheepfold (Arena Chapel, Padua)

PLATE 19

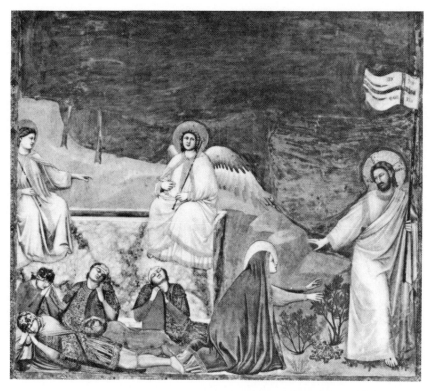

a. GIOTTO: *Noli me tangere* (Arena Chapel, Padua)

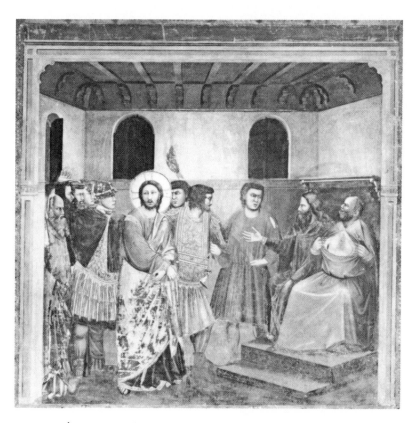

b. GIOTTO: Christ before Caiaphas (Arena Chapel, Padua)

PLATE 20

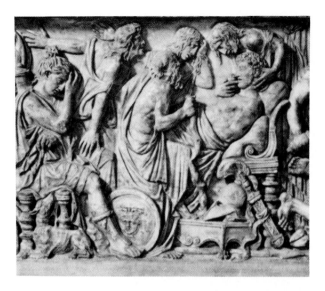

a. The Death of Meleager: detail of a sarcophagus-relief (Louvre, Paris)

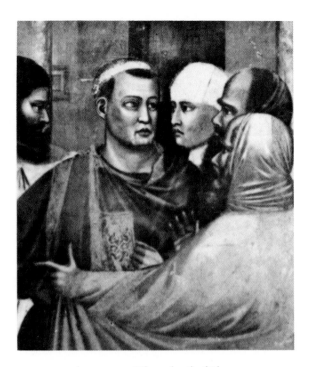

b. GIOTTO: Pilate: detail of Pl. 22

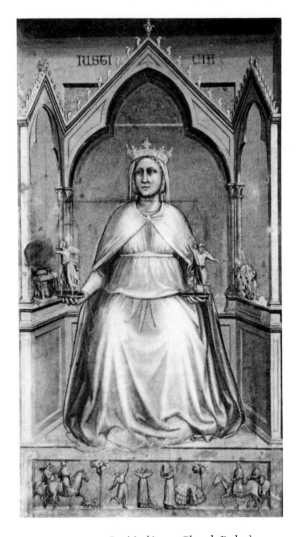

c. GIOTTO: Justitia (Arena Chapel, Padua)

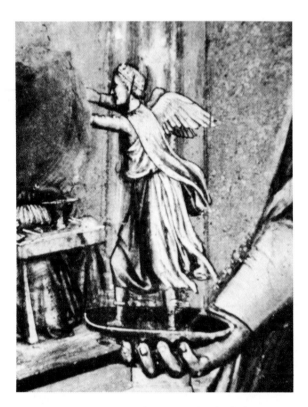

d. GIOTTO: Winged Victory: detail of Pl. 20c

PLATE 21

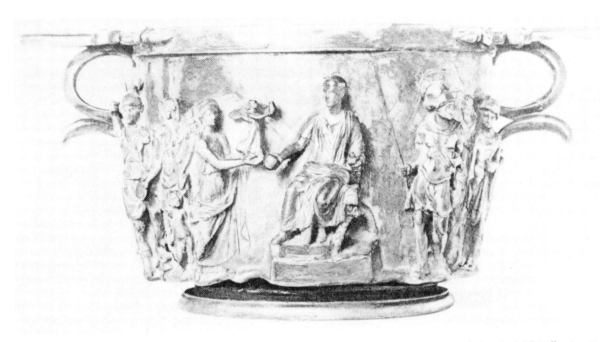

a. Augustus enthroned as Master and Pacifier of the Universe: detail of the Silver Cup of Boscoreale (Rothschild Collection, Paris)

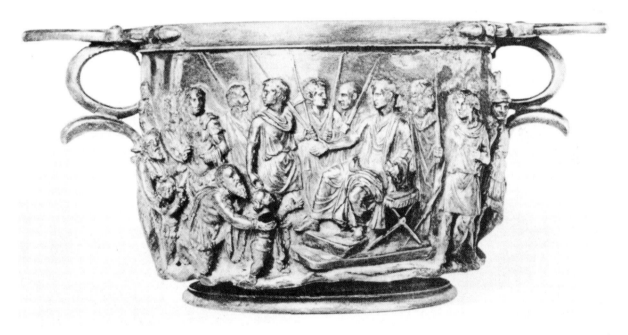

b. The Submission of Barbarian Captives to Augustus: detail of the Silver Cup of Boscoreale (Rothschild Collection, Paris)

PLATE 22

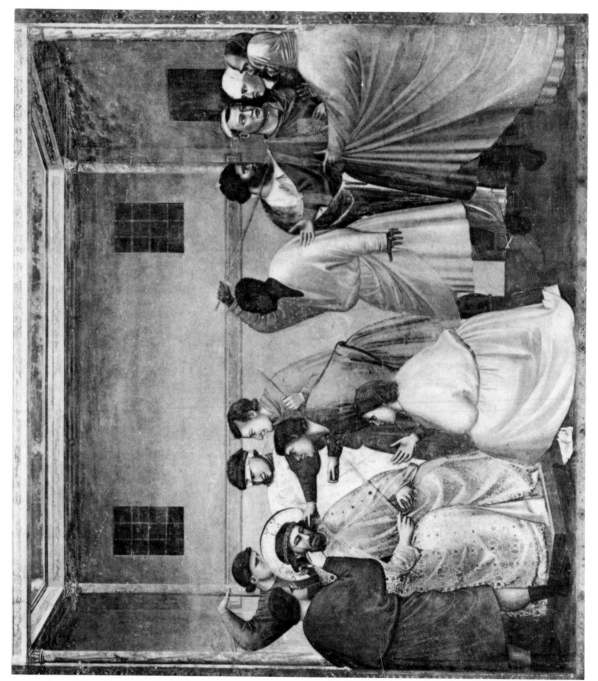

GIOTTO: The Trial before Pilate (Arena Chapel, Padua)

PLATE 23

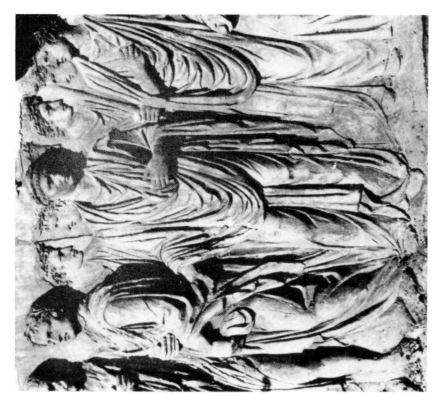

b. Roman processional relief (Villa Medici, Rome)

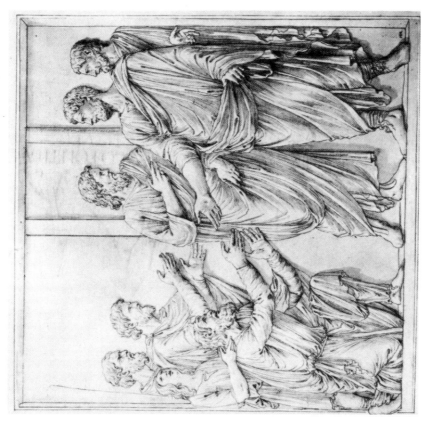

a. The submission of Barbarians to Hadrian: copy of a Roman relief in the Palazzo
Torlonia, Rome (Dal Pozzo Collection, Windsor Castle)
Reproduced by gracious permission of Her Majesty The Queen

PLATE 24

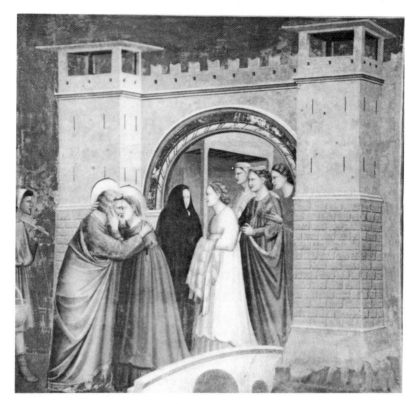

a. GIOTTO: The Meeting of St. Joachim and St. Anne at the Golden Gate of Jerusalem
(Arena Chapel, Padua)

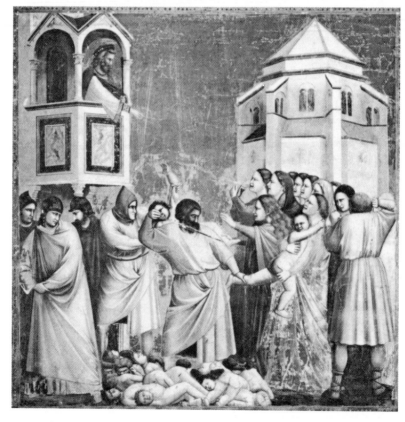

b. GIOTTO: The Massacre of the Innocents (Arena Chapel, Padua)

PLATE 25

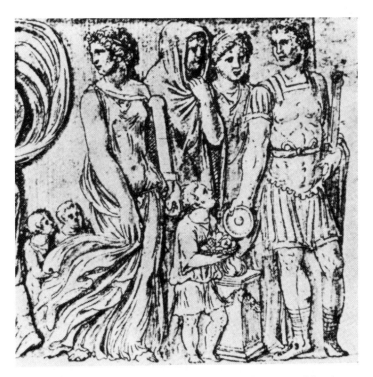

a. Drawing of a *Medea* sarcophagus (MS. Coburgensis, fol. 32)

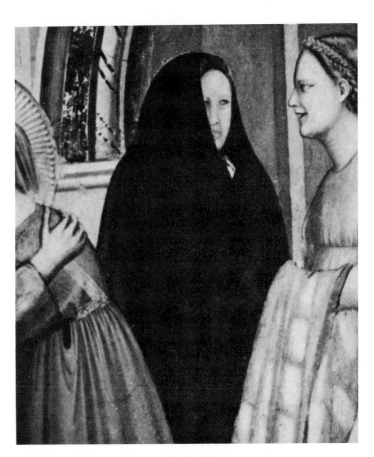

b. Detail of Pl. 24*a*

PLATE 26

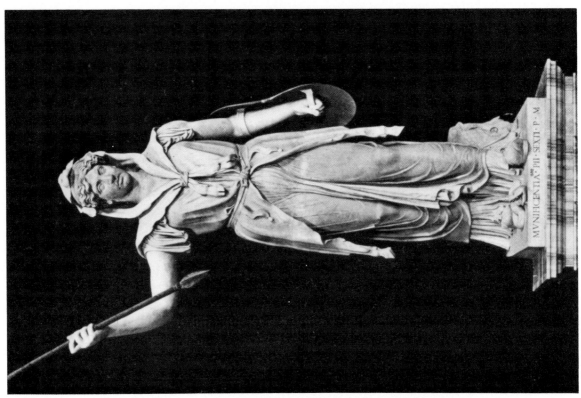

b. Juno Sospita (Vatican, Rome)

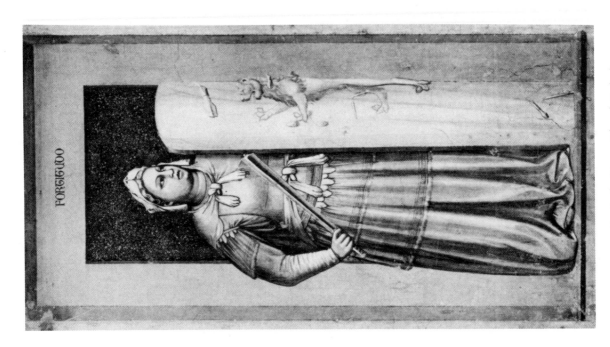

a. GIOTTO: Fortitudo (Arena Chapel, Padua)

PLATE 27

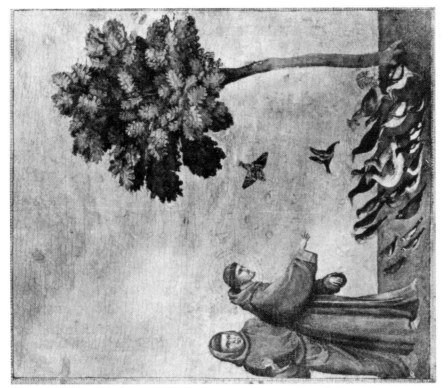

b. GIOTTO (Workshop): The Sermon to the Birds: detail of Pl. 28

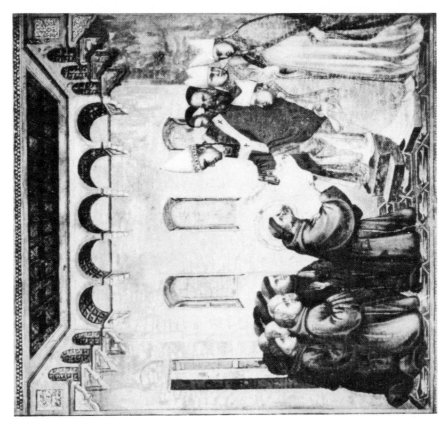

a. GIOTTO (Workshop): The Sanctioning of the Rule: detail of Pl. 28

PLATE 28

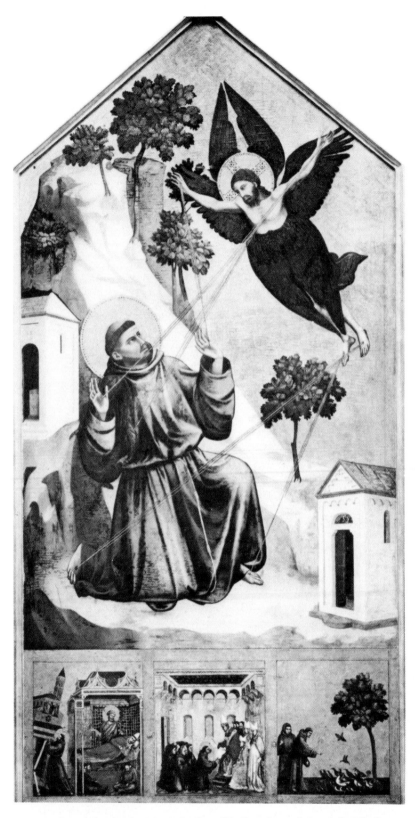

GIOTTO (Workshop): The Stigmatization of St. Francis; on the predella: The Dream of Innocent III, The Sanctioning of the Rule, The Sermon to the Birds (Louvre, Paris)

PLATE 29

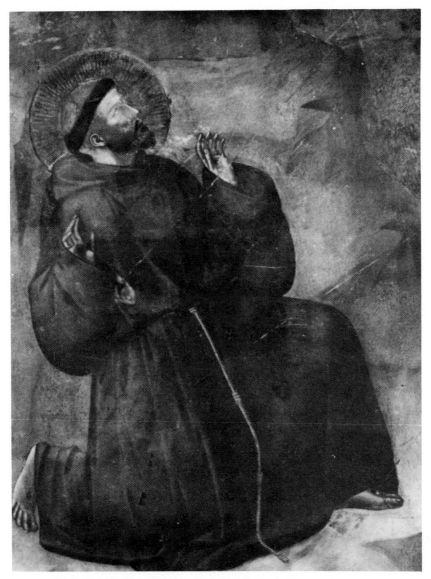

a. St. Francis receiving the Stigmata: detail of Pl. 76 (*St. Francis* Cycle, Scene XIX)

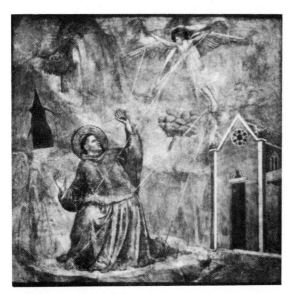

b. GIOTTO: The Stigmatization of St. Francis (entrance wall, Bardi Chapel, Santa Croce, Florence)

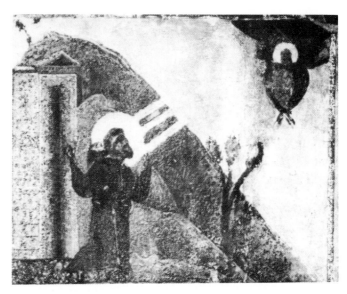

c. 'MAESTRO DEL S. FRANCESCO BARDI': The Stigmatization of St. Francis: detail of altarpiece (Bardi Chapel, Santa Croce, Florence)

PLATE 30

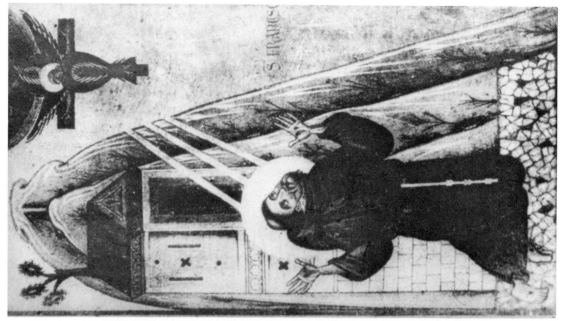

b. The Stigmatization of St. Francis (Accademia delle Belle Arti, Florence)

a. BONAVENTURA BERLINGHIERI: The Stigmatization of St. Francis: detail of altarpiece (S. Francesco, Pescia)

PLATE 31

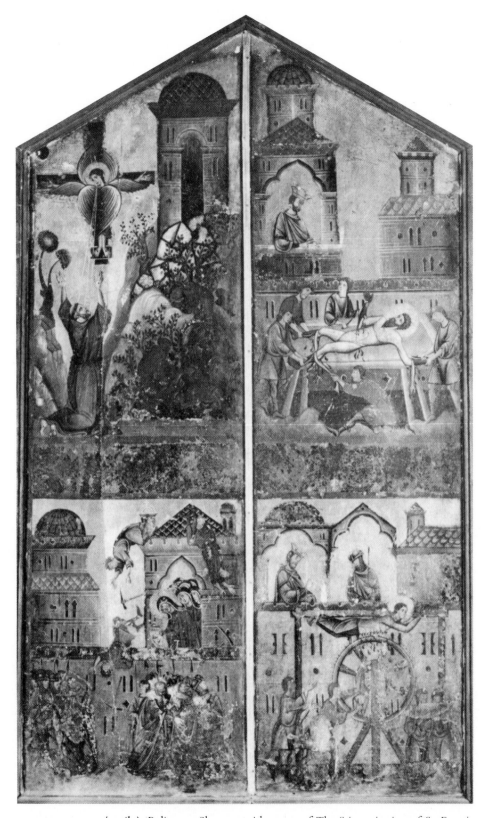

GUIDO DA SIENA (attrib.): Reliquary Shutters, with scenes of The Stigmatization of St. Francis, The Martyrdom of St. Bartholomew, St. Clare repulsing the Saracens, and The Martyrdom of St. Catherine of Alexandria (Accademia delle Belle Arti, Siena)

PLATE 32

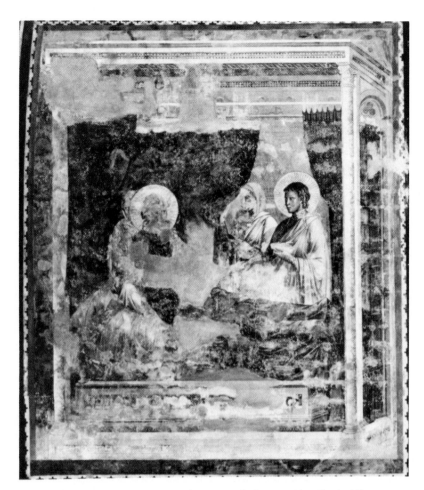

a. ISAAC MASTER: Isaac Blessing Jacob (Upper Church, Assisi)

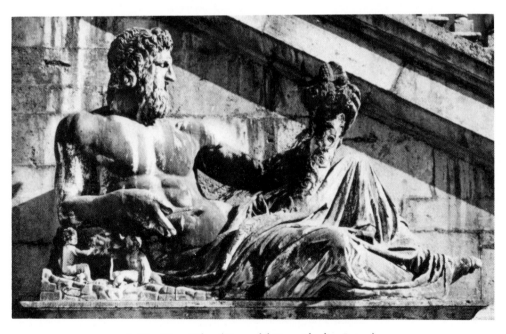

b. The River Tiber (Piazza del Campidoglio, Rome)

PLATE 33

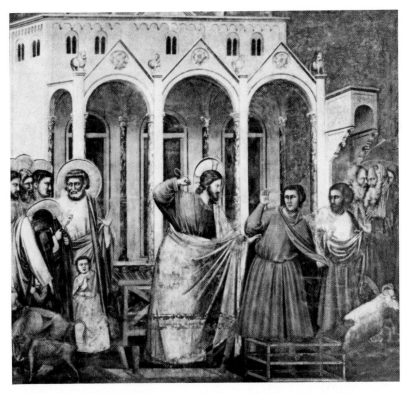

a. GIOTTO: The Expulsion of the Traders from the Temple (Arena Chapel, Padua)

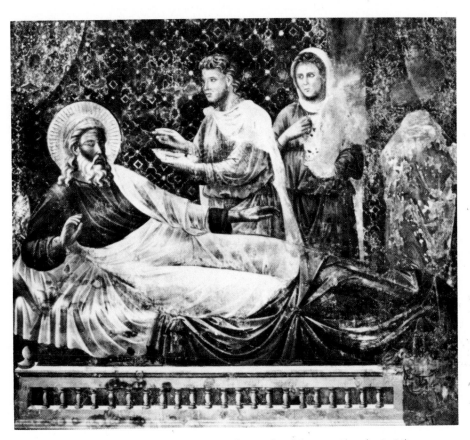

b. ISAAC MASTER: The Rejection of Esau: detail (Upper Church, Assisi)

PLATE 34

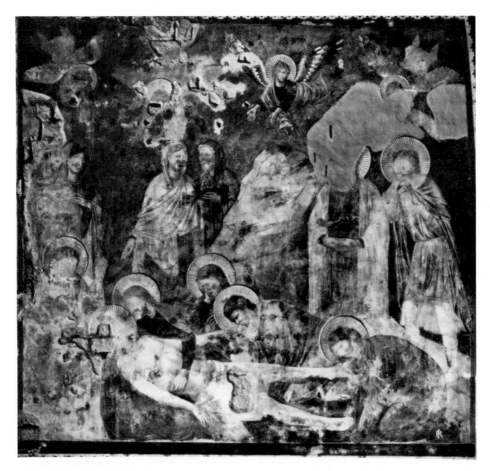

a. ISAAC MASTER: Lamentation over the Dead Christ (Upper Church, Assisi)

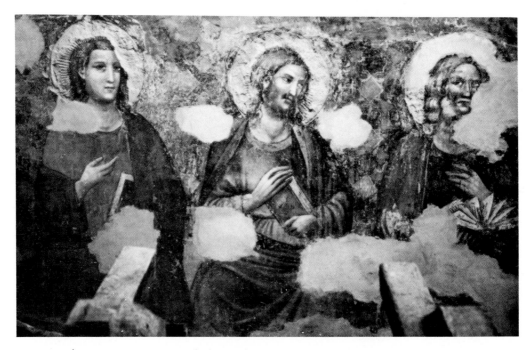

b. RIMINESE PAINTER: The Last Judgment: detail (Palazzo dell'Arengo, Rimini)

PLATE 35

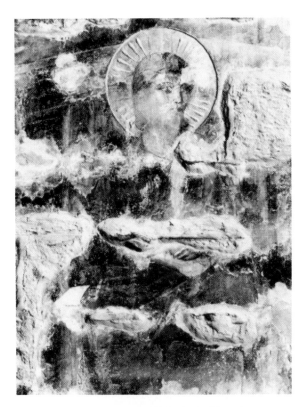

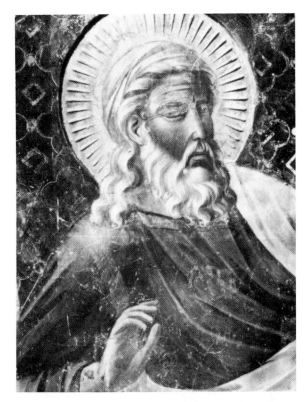

a. ISAAC MASTER: Christ in the Temple: detail (Upper Church, Assisi)

b. ISAAC MASTER: Isaac: detail of Pl. 33*b*

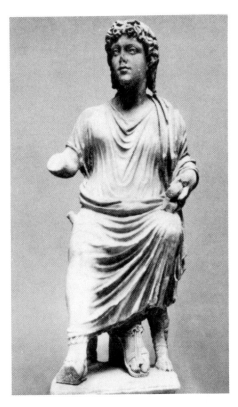

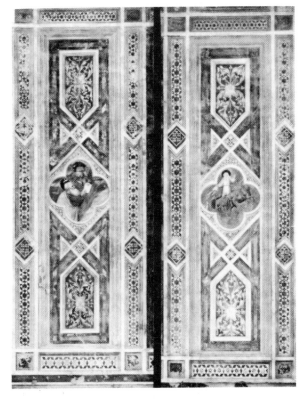

c. Christ Enthroned (Museo delle Terme, Rome)

d. GIOTTO: Decorative borders, with scenes of The Giving of the Law and The Ascension of Elijah (Arena Chapel, Padua)

PLATE 36

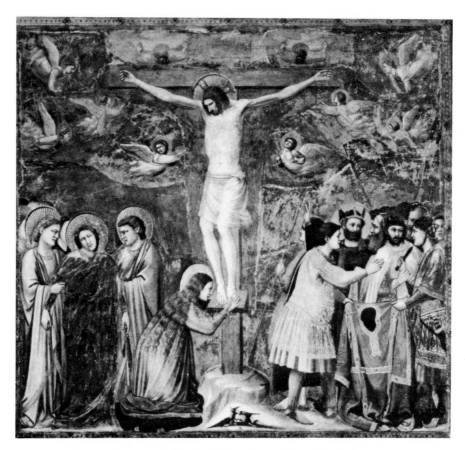

a. GIOTTO: The Crucifixion (Arena Chapel, Padua)

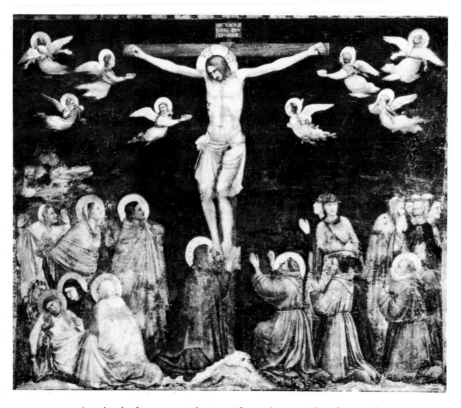

b. School of GIOTTO: The Crucifixion (Lower Church, Assisi)

PLATE 37

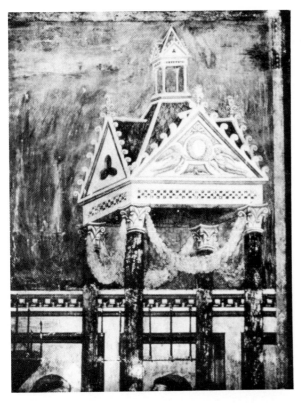

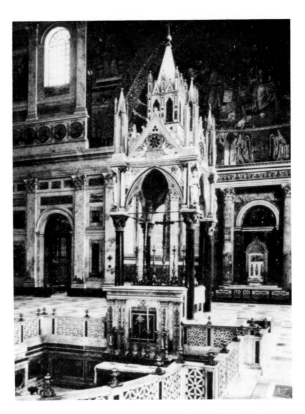

a. Detail of Pl. 63 (*St. Francis* Cycle, Scene XIII)

b. ARNOLFO DI CAMBIO: Ciborium (S. Paolo fuori le mura, Rome)

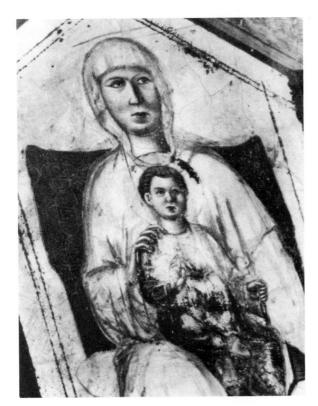

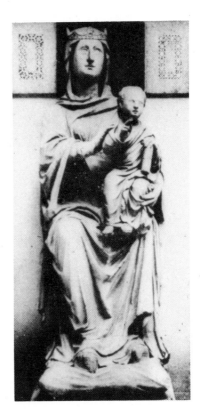

c. Detail of Pl. 82 (*St. Francis* Cycle, Scene XXII)

d. ARNOLFO DI CAMBIO: Madonna and Child (Museo dell'Opera del Duomo, Florence)

PLATE 38

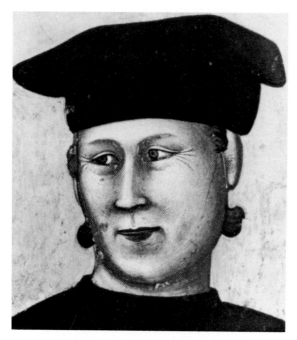

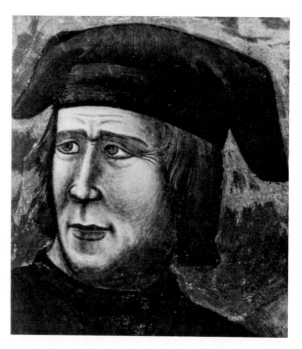

a. Detail of Frontispiece (*St. Francis* Cycle, Scene I)

b. Detail of Pl. 70 (*St. Francis* Cycle, Scene XVI)

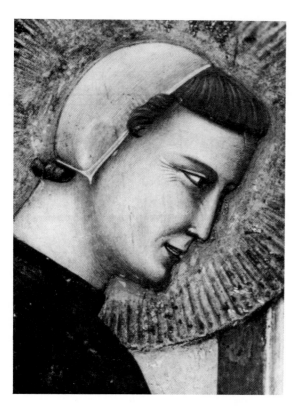

c. St. Francis: detail of Frontispiece (*St. Francis* Cycle, Scene I)

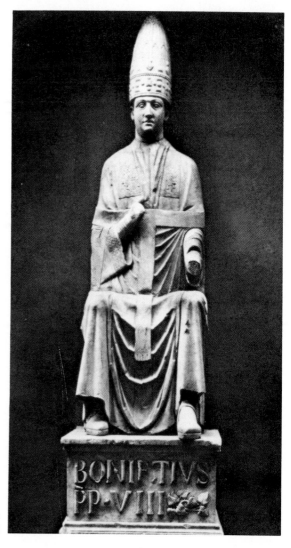

d. ARNOLFO DI CAMBIO: Pope Boniface VIII (Museo dell'Opera del Duomo, Florence)

PLATE 39

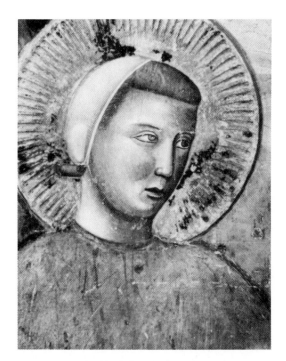

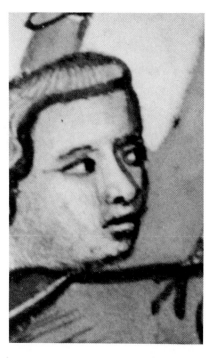

a. St. Francis: detail of Pl. 42 (*St. Francis* Cycle, Scene II)

b. PACINO DI BONAGUIDA: The Mocking of Christ: detail (Pierpont Morgan Library, New York, MS. M. 643, fol. 20)

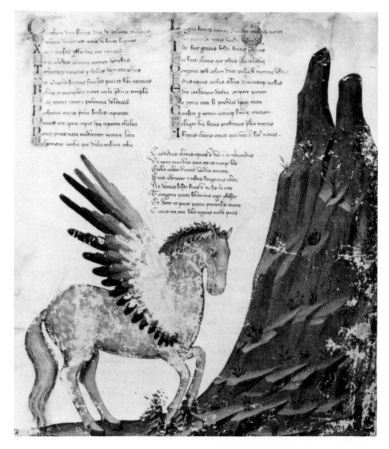

c. PACINO DI BONAGUIDA (Workshop): Pegasus (British Museum, London, Royal MS. 6 E. IX, fol. 28*v*)

PLATE 40

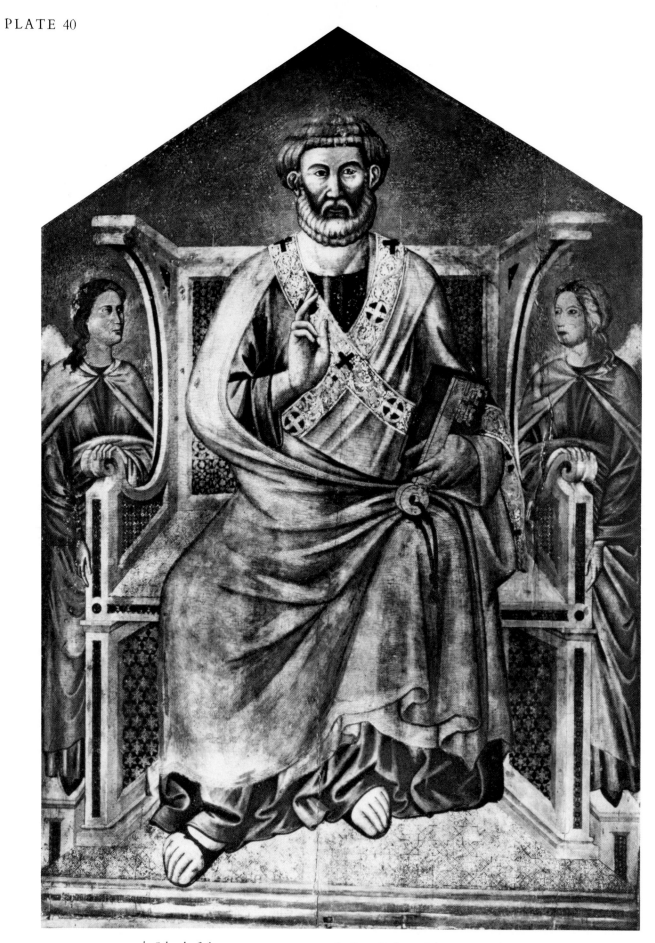

b. School of the ST. CECILIA MASTER: St. Peter Enthroned (S. Simone, Florence)

PLATE 41

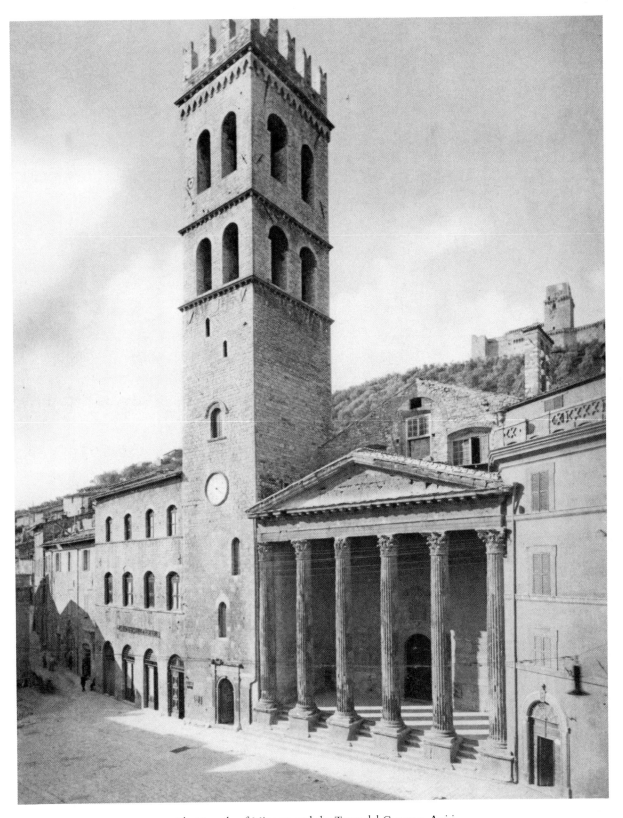

The Temple of Minerva and the Torre del Comune, Assisi

PLATE 42

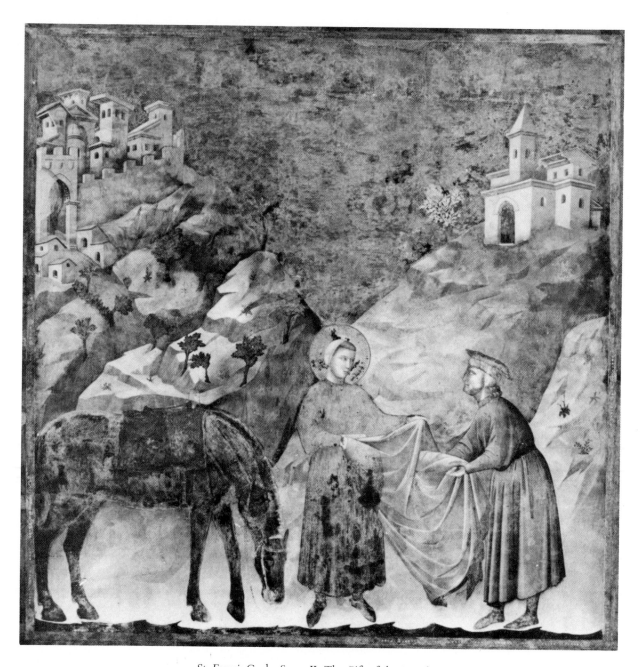

St. Francis Cycle, Scene II: The Gift of the Mantle

PLATE 43

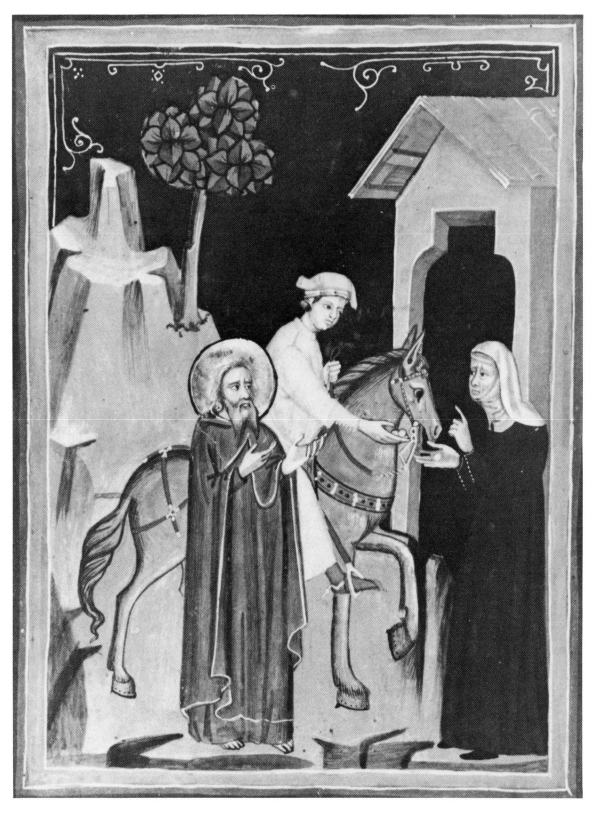

PACINO DI BONAGUIDA: The Blessed Gherardo Soliciting Alms from a Traveller (Pierpont Morgan Library, New York, MS. M 643, fol. 35)

PLATE 44

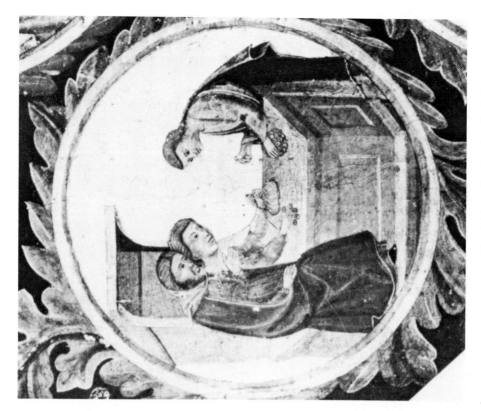

b. PACINO DI BONAGUIDA: The Hiring of Judas: detail of The Tree of Life (Accademia, Florence)

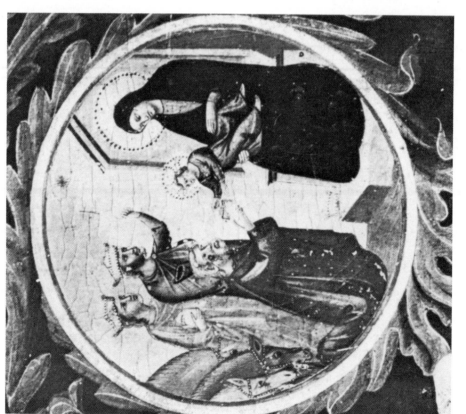

a. PACINO DI BONAGUIDA: The Adoration of the Kings: detail of The Tree of Life (Accademia, Florence)

PLATE 45

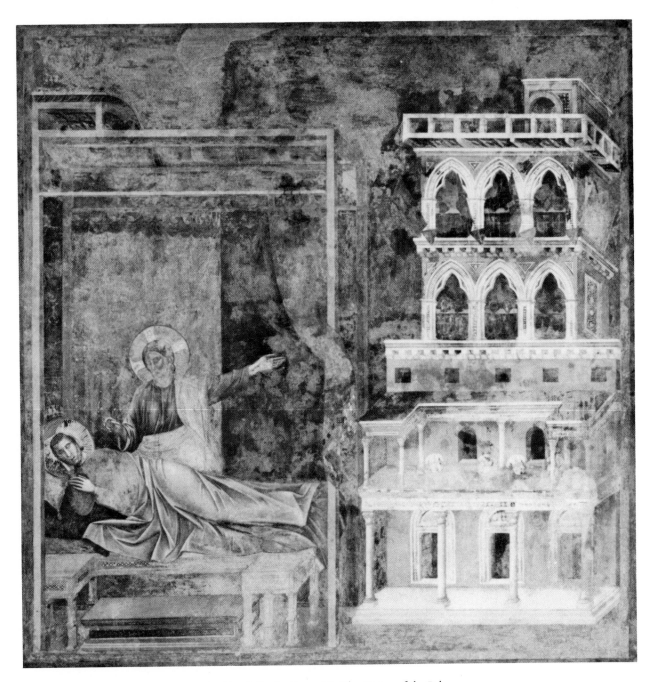

St. Francis Cycle, Scene III: The Vision of the Palace

PLATE 46

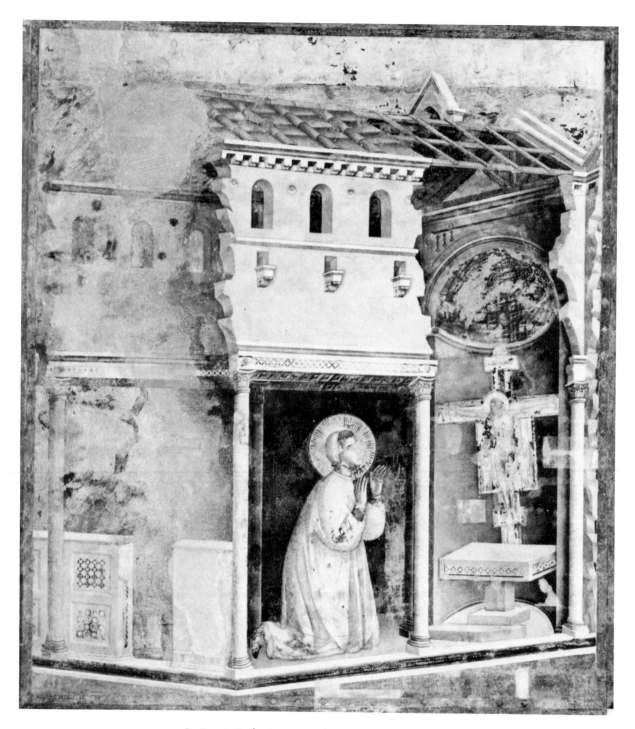

St. Francis Cycle, Scene IV: The Miracle of the Crucifix

PLATE 47

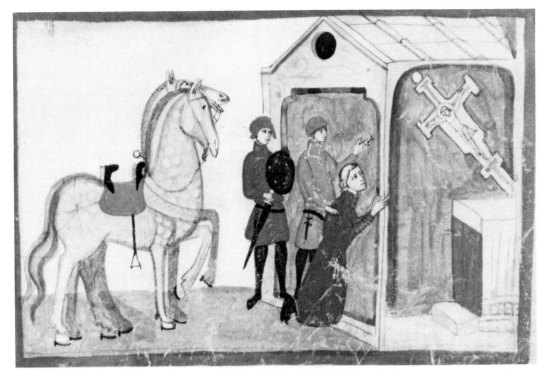

a. PACINO DI BONAGUIDA (Workshop): S. Giovanni Gualberto kneels before the Miraculous Crucifix of
S. Miniato: an illustration to Villani's *Chronicle* (Biblioteca Vaticana, Rome, Cod. Chigiano L. VIII. 296, fol. 53)

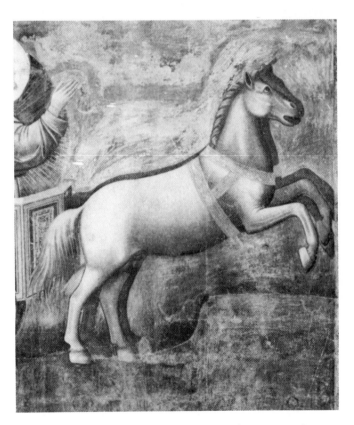

b. Detail of Plate 55 (*St. Francis* Cycle, Scene VIII)

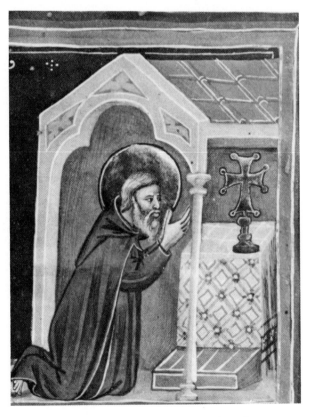

c. PACINO DI BONAGUIDA: The Blessed Gherardo at Prayer:
detail (Pierpont Morgan Library, New York, MS. M 643, fol. 36)

PLATE 48

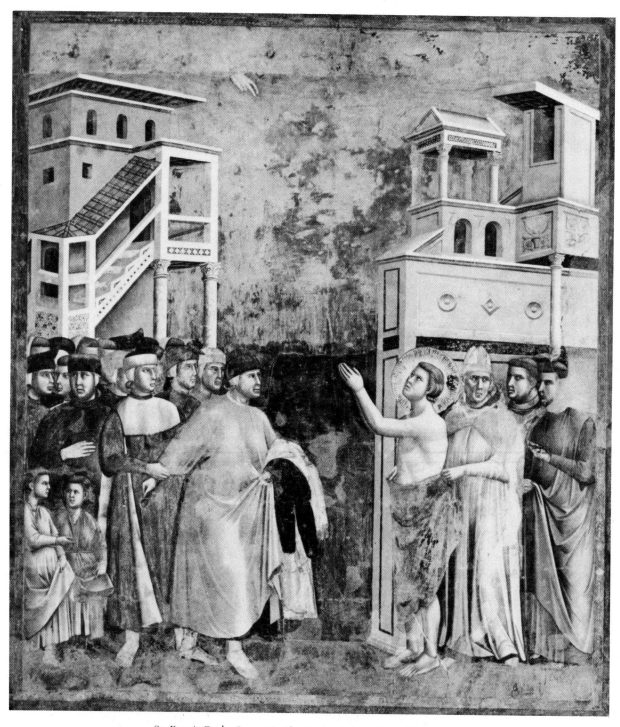

St. Francis Cycle, Scene V: The Renunciation of Worldly Goods

PLATE 49

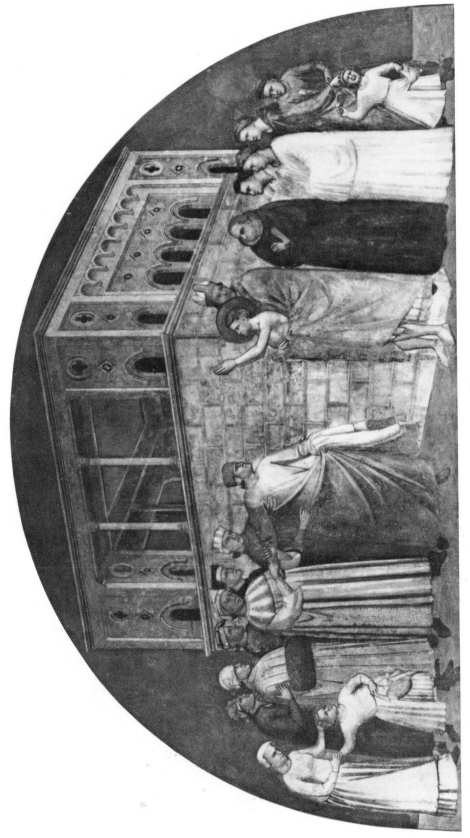

GIOTTO: The Renunciation of Worldly Goods (Bardi Chapel, Santa Croce, Florence)

PLATE 50

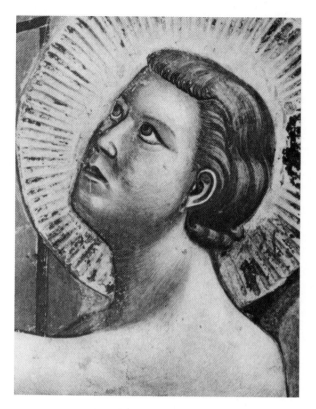

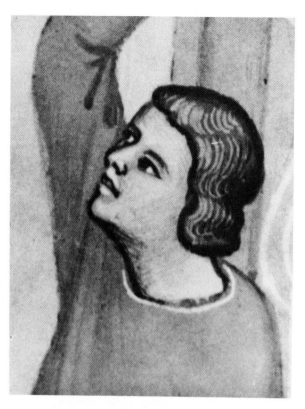

a. St. Francis: detail of Pl. 48 (*St. Francis* Cycle, Scene V)

b. PACINO DI BONAGUIDA: The Flagellation: detail (Pierpont Morgan Library, New York, MS. M 643, fol. 19)

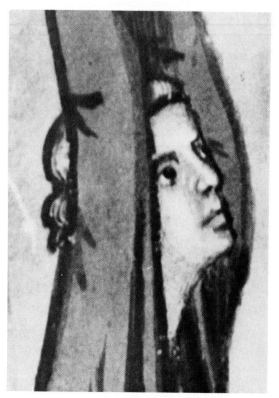

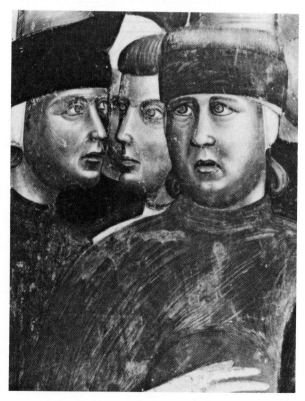

c. PACINO DI BONAGUIDA: The Flagellation: detail (Pierpont Morgan Library, New York, MS. M 643, fol. 19)

d. Detail of Pl. 48 (*St. Francis* Cycle, Scene V)

PLATE 51

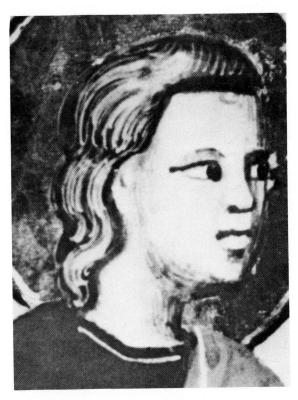

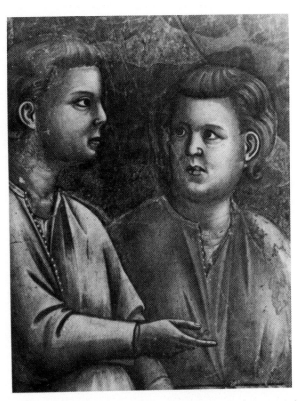

a. PACINO DI BONAGUIDA: The Supper at Emmaus: detail (Pierpont Morgan Library, New York, MS. M 643, fol. 29)

b. Two Children: detail of Pl. 48 (*St. Francis* Cycle, Scene V)

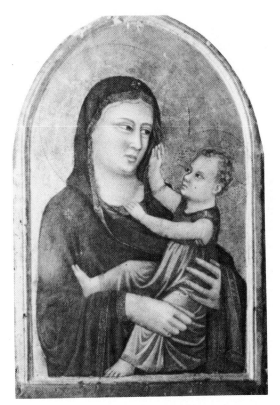

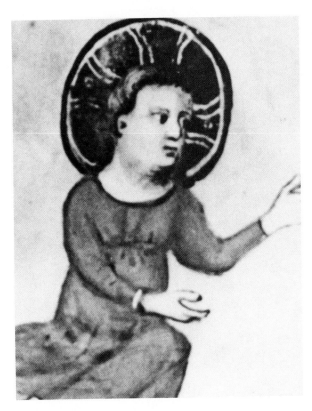

c. PACINO DI BONAGUIDA: Madonna and Child (Accademia, Florence)

d. PACINO DI BONAGUIDA: The Presentation of Christ in the Temple: detail (Pierpont Morgan Library), New York, MS. M 643, fol. 6)

PLATE 52

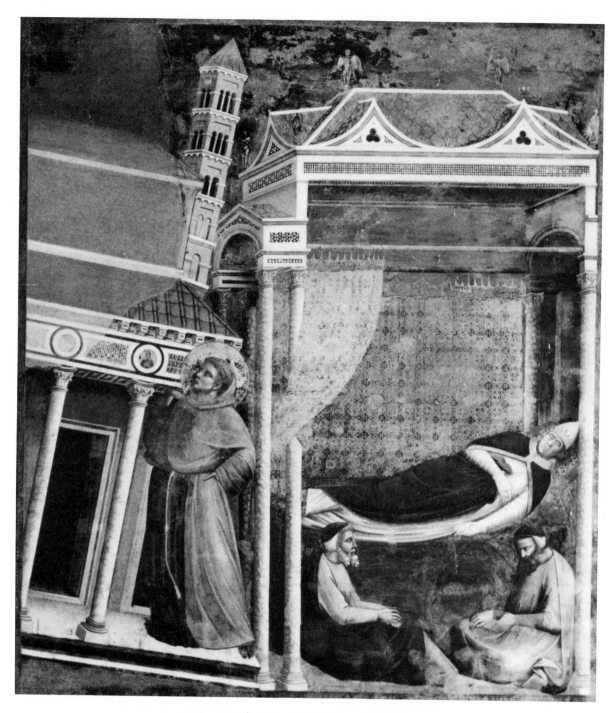

St. Francis Cycle, Scene VI: The Dream of Innocent III

PLATE 53

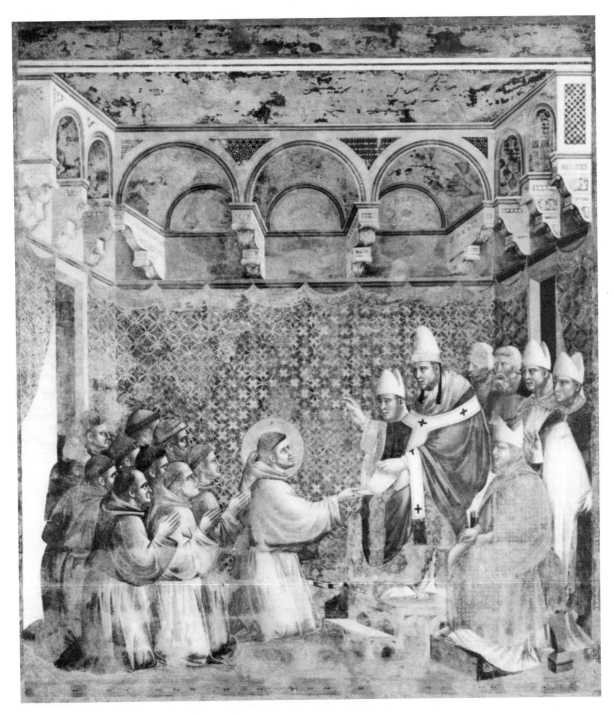

St. Francis Cycle, Scene VII: The Sanctioning of the Rule

PLATE 54

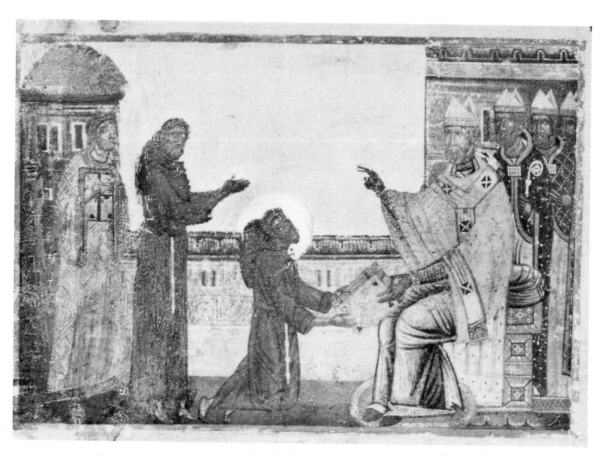

a. 'MAESTRO DEL S. FRANCESCO BARDI': The Sanctioning of the Rule: detail of altarpiece (Bardi Chapel, Santa Croce, Florence)

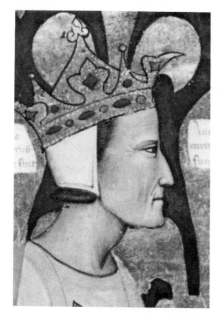

b. PACINO DI BONAGUIDA (Workshop): King Robert of Anjou: detail (British Museum, London, Royal MS. 6 E. IX, fol. 10*v*)

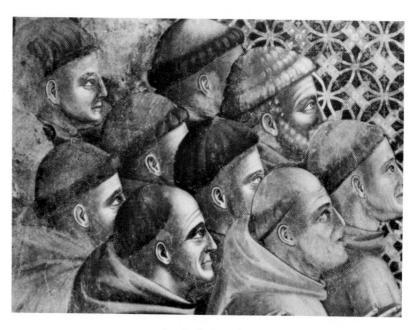

c. KNEELING FRIARS: detail of Pl. 53 (*St. Francis* Cycle, Scene VII)

PLATE·55

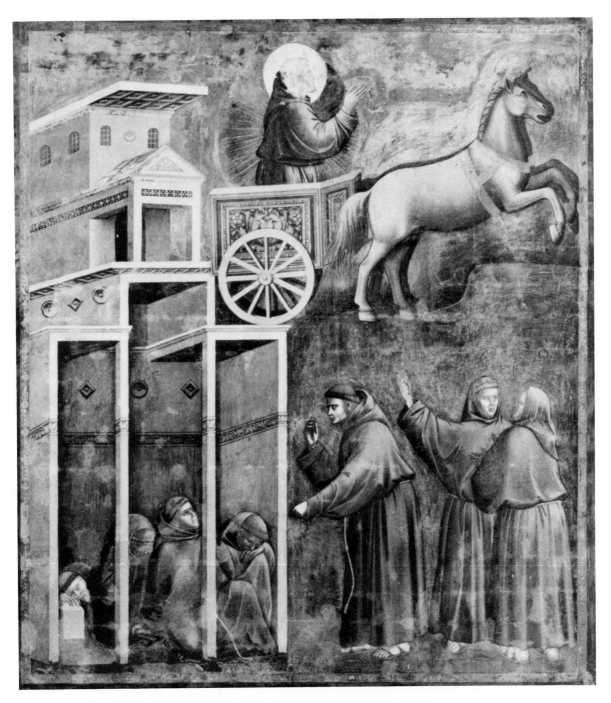

St. Francis Cycle, Scene VIII: The Vision of the Chariot

PLATE 56

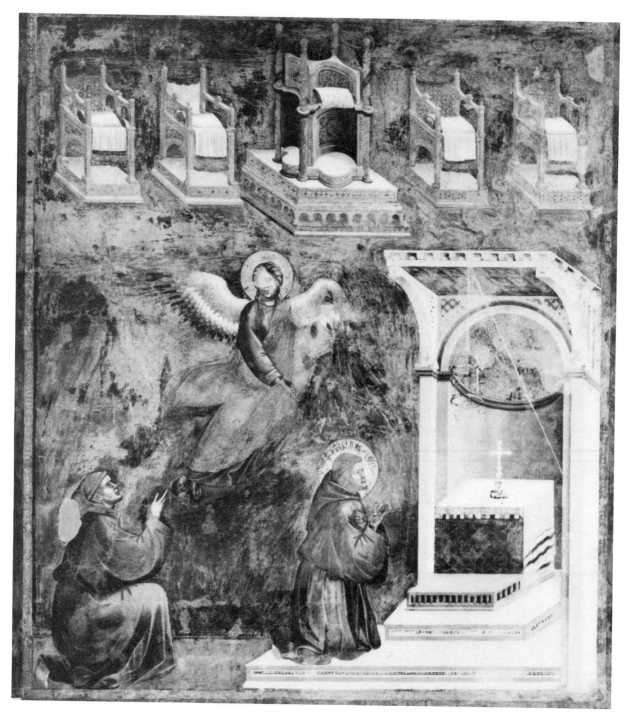

St. Francis Cycle, Scene IX: The Vision of the Thrones

PLATE 57

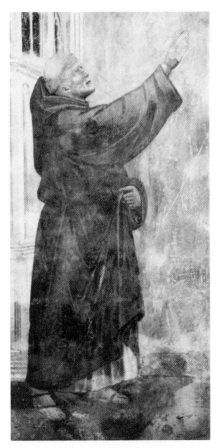

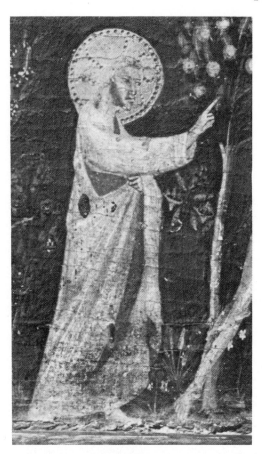

a. Brother Silvester: detail of Plate 58 (*St. Francis* Cycle, Scene X)

b. PACINO DI BONAGUIDA: The Lord: detail of The Fall and Expulsion from Paradise, from The Tree of Life (Accademia, Florence)

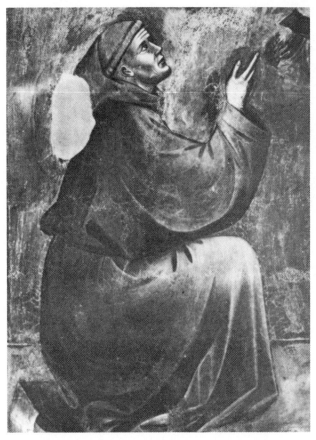

c. Detail of Plate 56 (*St. Francis* Cycle, Scene IX)

PLATE 58

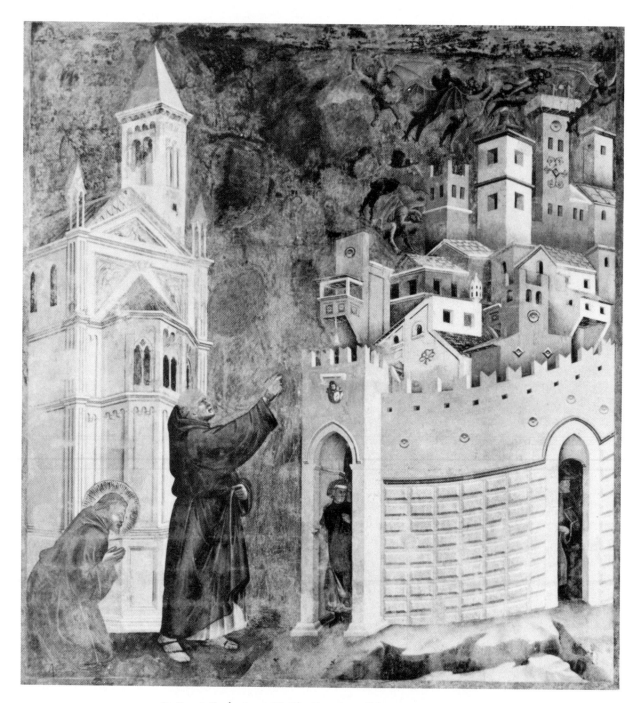

St. Francis Cycle, Scene X: The Exorcism of the Demons at Arezzo

PLATE 59

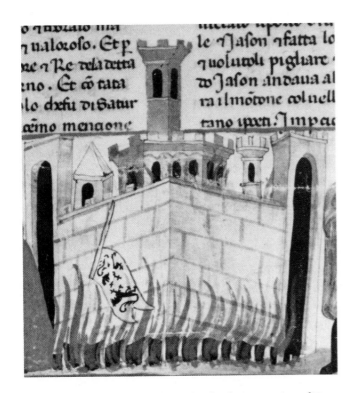

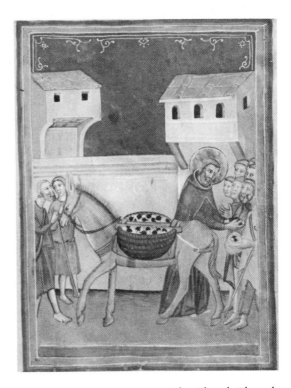

a. PACINO DI BONAGUIDA (Workshop): The Destruction of Troy: detail: an illustration to Villani's *Chronicle* (Biblioteca Vaticana, Rome, Cod. Chigiano L. VIII. 296, fol. 18*v*)

b. PACINO DI BONAGUIDA: The Blessed Gherardo Distributing Loaves of Bread to the Poor (Pierpont Morgan Library, New York, MS. M 643, fol. 34)

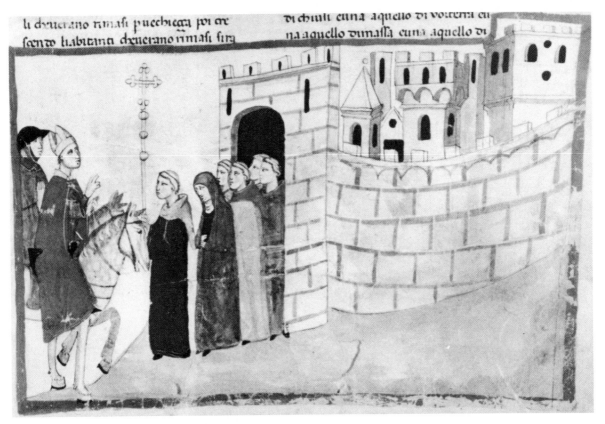

c. PACINO DI BONAGUIDA (Workshop): The Entry into Siena of its First Bishop: an illustration to Villani's *Chronicle* (Biblioteca Vaticana, Rome, Cod. Chigiano L. VIII. 296, fol. 32)

PLATE 60

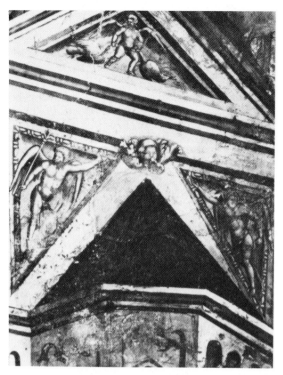

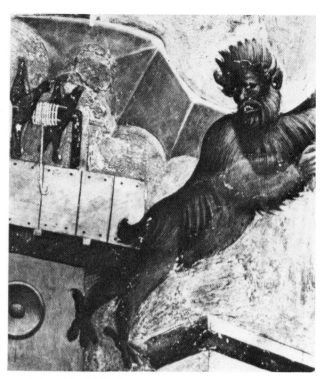

a. The reliefs on the church: detail of Pl. 56
(*St. Francis* Cycle, Scene X)

b. A Demon: detail of Pl. 58 (*St. Francis* Cycle, Scene X)

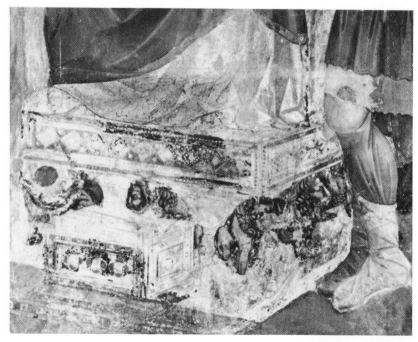

c. The base of the Sultan's throne: detail of
Pl. 61 (*St. Francis* Cycle, Scene XI)

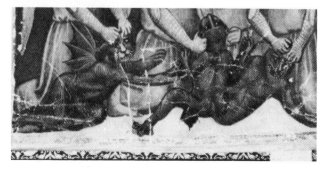

d. PACINO DI BONAGUIDA (Workshop): The Demons put
down by the Thrones, Dominions and Powers: detail (British
Museum, London, Royal MS. 6 E. IX, fol. 6*v*)

PLATE 61

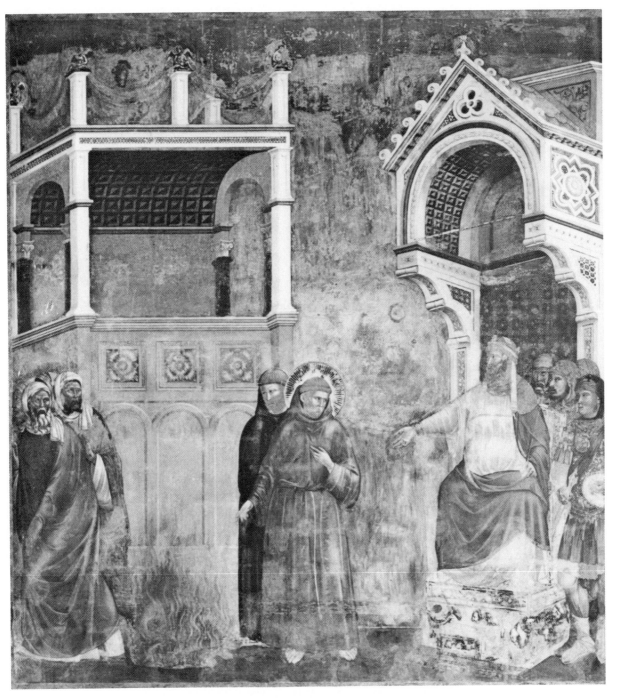

St. Francis Cycle, Scene XI: St. Francis before the Sultan

PLATE 62

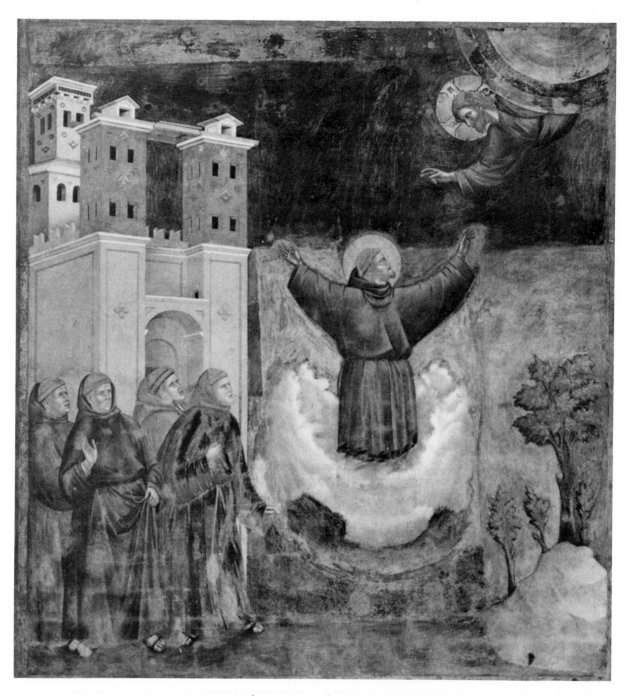

St. Francis Cycle, Scene XII: The Ecstasy of St. Francis

PLATE 63

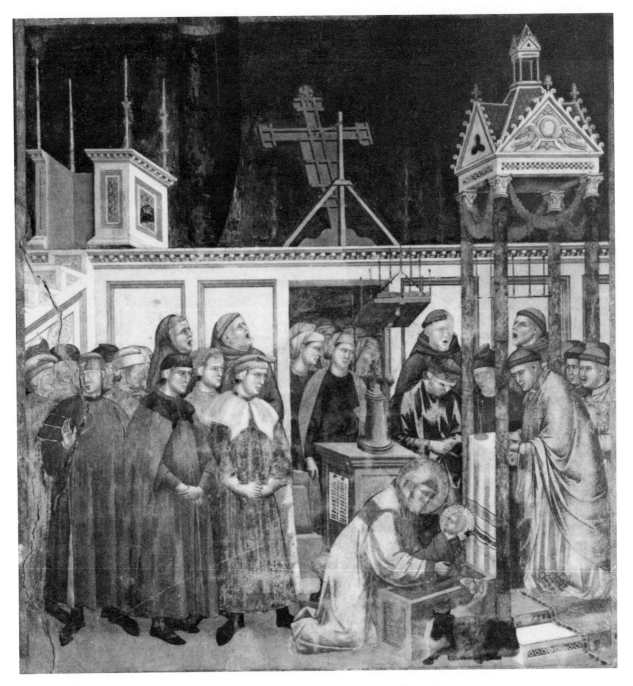

St. Francis Cycle, Scene **XIII**: The Christmas Crib at Greccio

PLATE 64

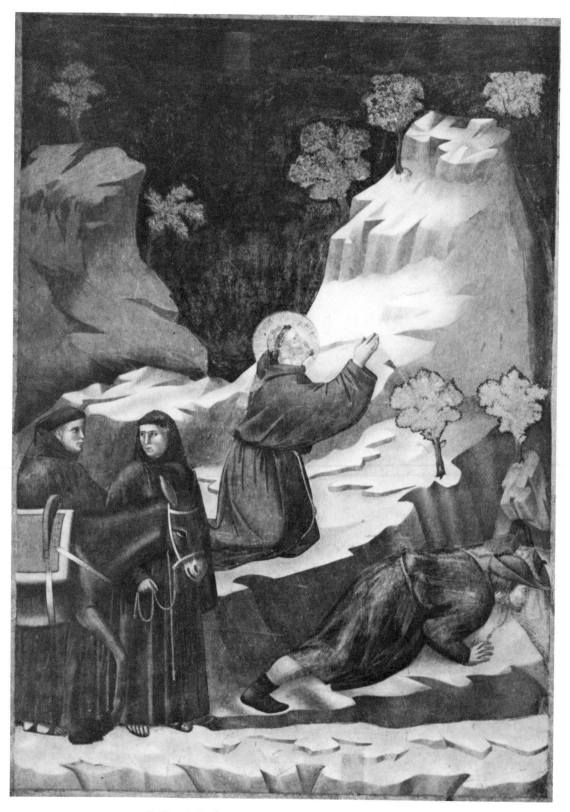

St. Francis Cycle, Scene XIV: The Miracle of the Spring

PLATE 65

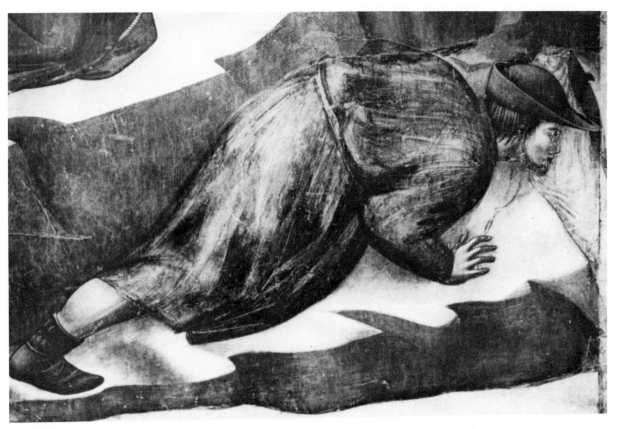

a. The thirsty muleteer: detail of Pl. 64 (*St. Francis* Cycle, Scene XIV)

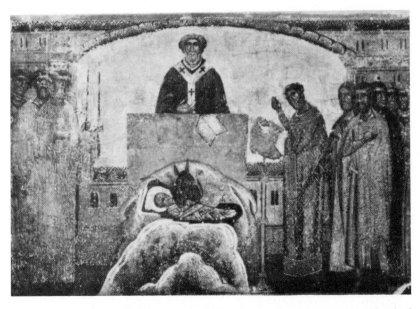

b. 'MAESTRO DEL S. FRANCESCO BARDI': The Christmas Crib at Greccio: detail of altarpiece (Bardi Chapel, Santa Croce, Florence)

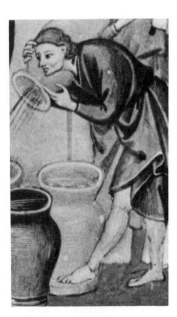

c. PACINO DI BONAGUIDA: The Miracle at Cana: detail (Pierpont Morgan Library, New York, MS. M 643, fol. 10)

PLATE 66

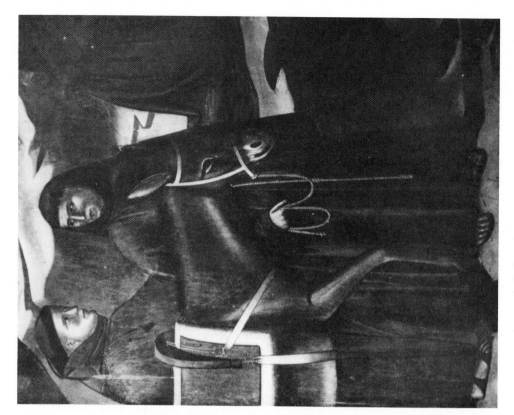

b. Detail of Pl. 64 (*St. Francis Cycle, Scene XIV*)

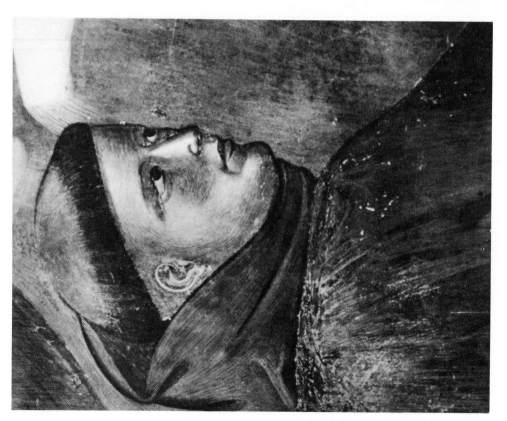

a. Detail of Pl. 64 (*St. Francis Cycle, Scene XIV*)

PLATE 67

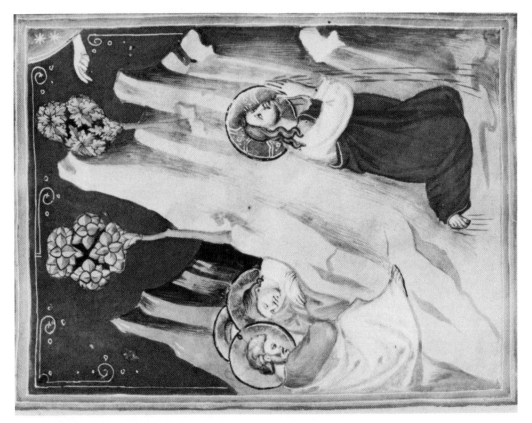

b, PACINO DI BONAGUIDA: Christ at Gethsemane (Pierpont Morgan Library, New York, MS. M 643, fol. 16)

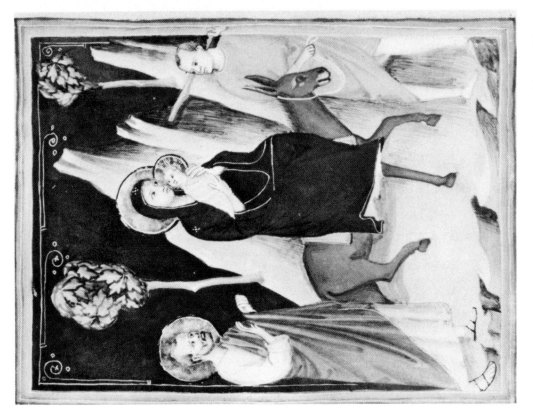

a, PACINO DI BONAGUIDA: The Flight into Egypt (Pierpont Morgan Library, New York, MS. M 643, fol. 7)

PLATE 68

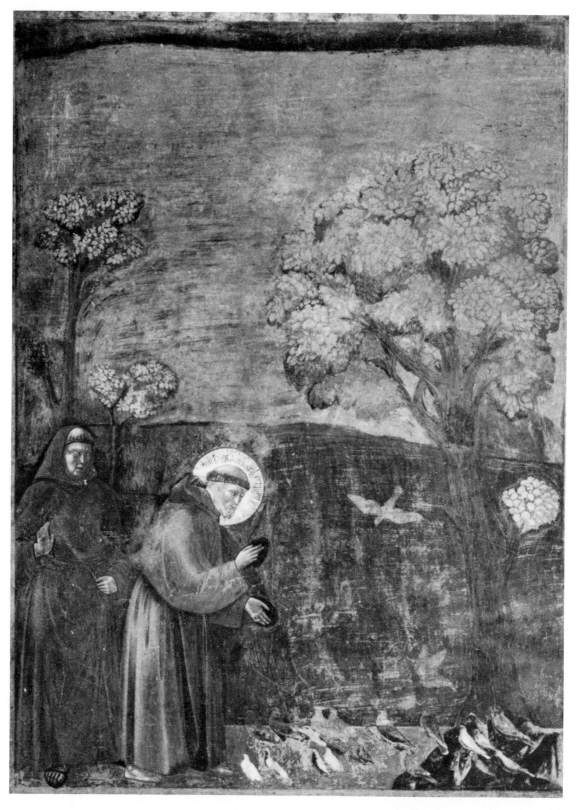

St. Francis Cycle, Scene XV: The Sermon to the Birds

PLATE 69

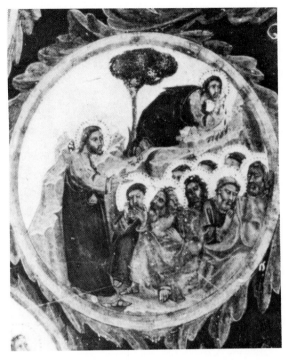

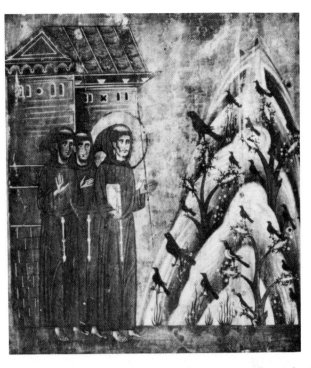

a. PACINO DI BONAGUIDA: Christ at Gethsemane, from
The Tree of Life (Accademia, Florence)

b. BONAVENTURA BERLINGHIERI: The Sermon to the Birds:
detail of altarpiece (S. Francesco, Pescia)

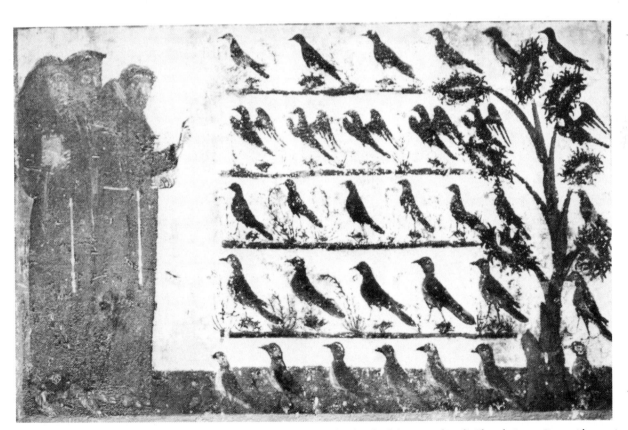

c. 'MAESTRO DEL S. FRANCESCO BARDI': The Sermon to the Birds: detail of altarpiece (Bardi Chapel, Santa Croce, Florence)

PLATE 70

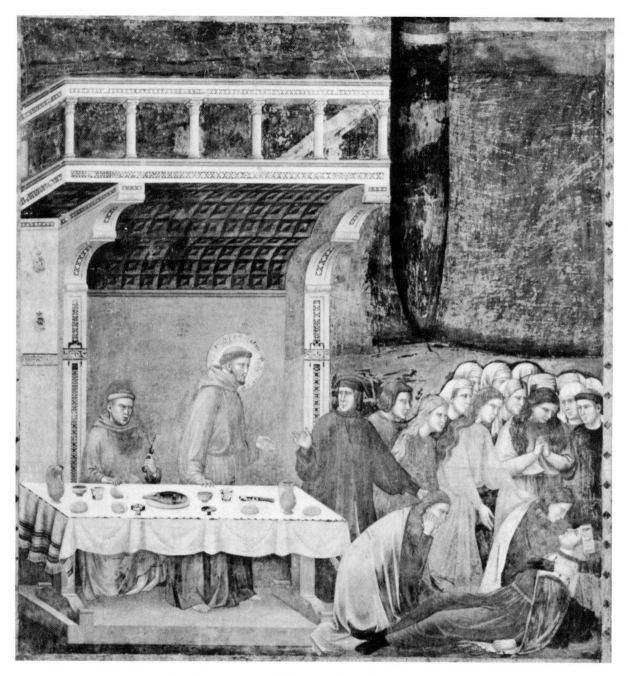

St. Francis Cycle, Scene XVI: The Death of The Knight of Celano

PLATE 71

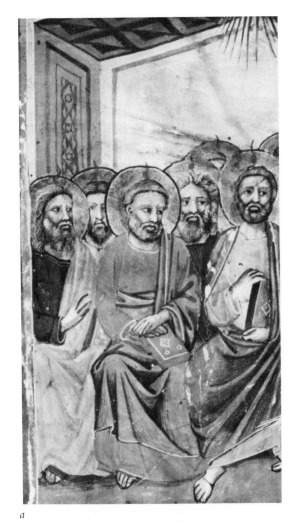

a

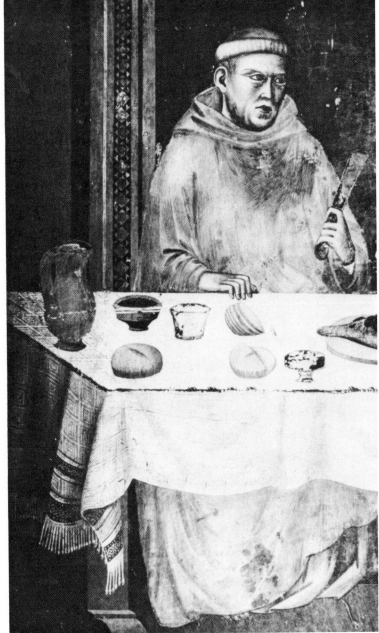

b

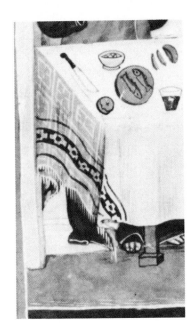

c

a. PACINO DI BONAGUIDA: Pentecost: detail (Pierpont Morgan Library, New York, MS. M 643, fol. 32)

b. Detail of Pl. 70 (*St. Francis* Cycle, Scene XVI)

c. PACINO DI BONAGUIDA: The Supper at Emmaus: detail (Pierpont Morgan Library, New York, MS. M 643, fol. 29)

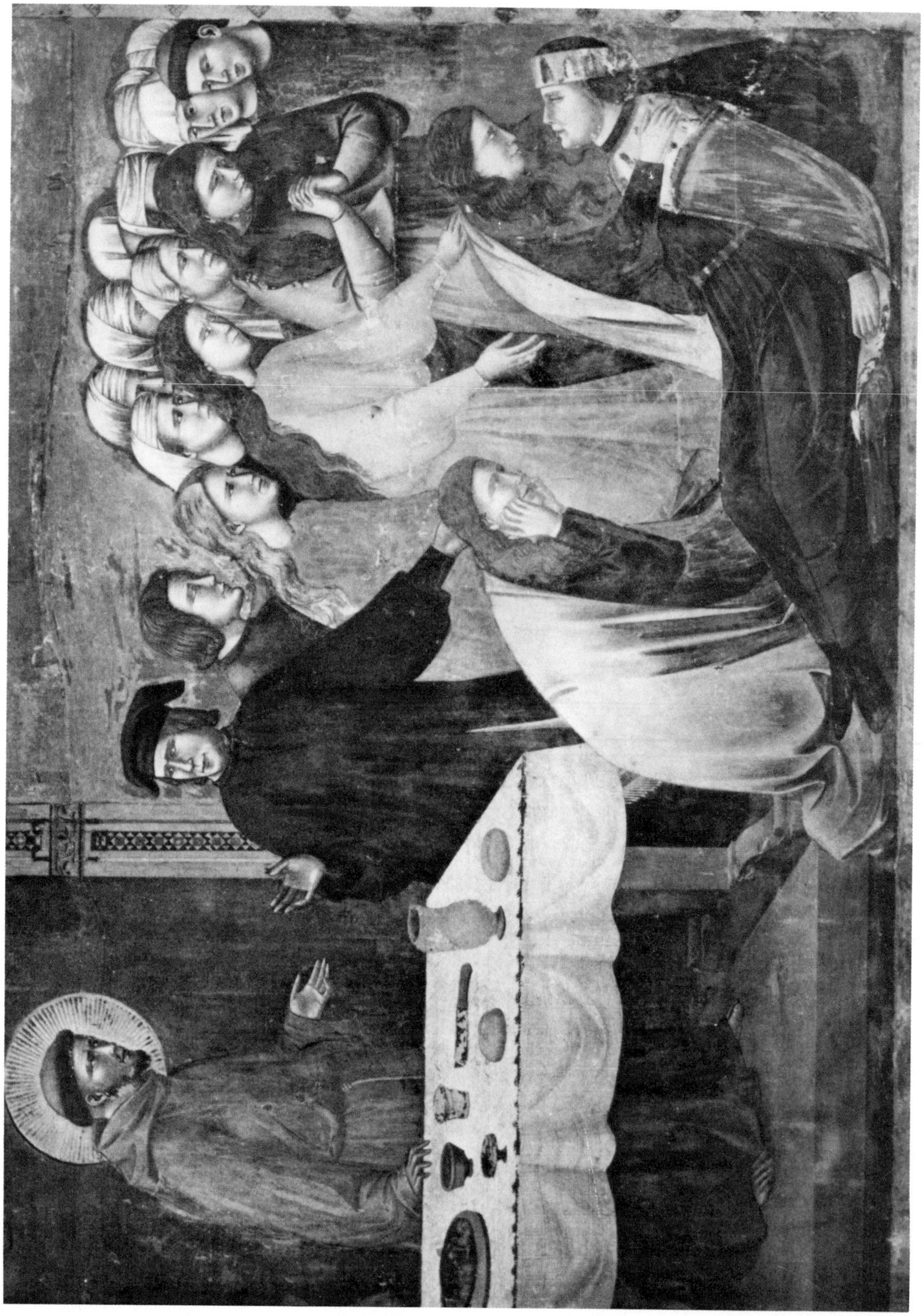

PLATE 72

Detail of Plate 70 (*St. Francis Cycle, Scene XVI*)

PLATE 73

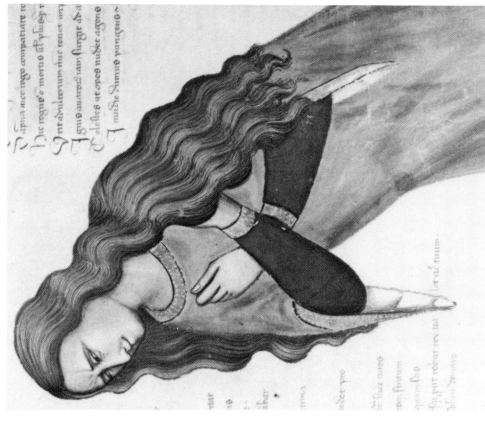

b. PACINO DI BONAGUIDA (Workshop): Italia in the Act of Prostrating Herself
(British Museum, London, Royal MS. 6 E. IX, fol. 11r)

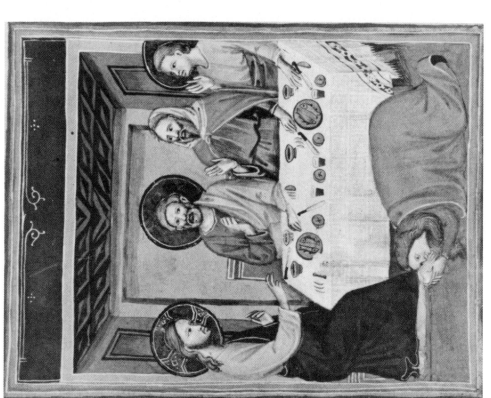

a. PACINO DI BONAGUIDA: Christ in the House of Simon the Pharisee
(Pierpont Morgan Library, New York, MS. M 643, fol. 11)

PLATE 74

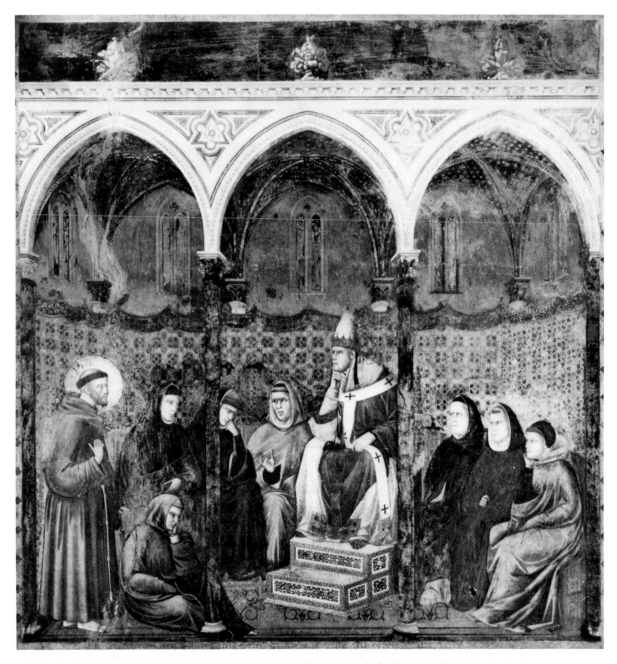

St. Francis Cycle, Scene XVII: The Sermon before Honorius III

PLATE 75

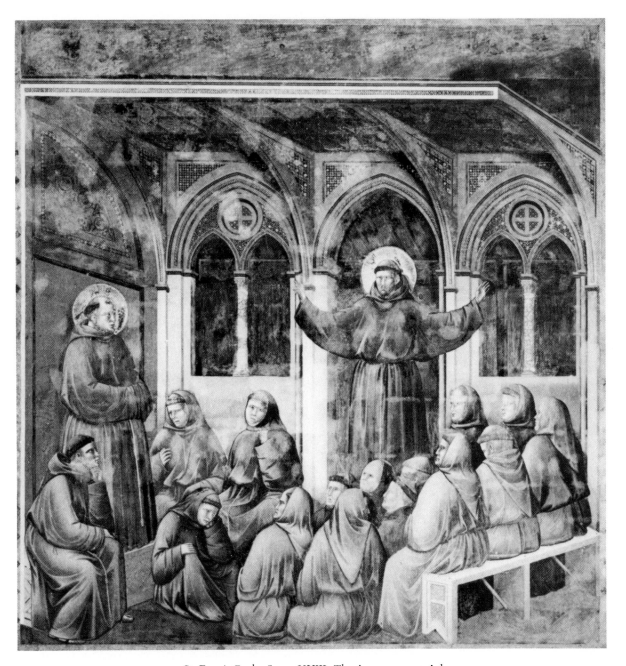

St. Francis Cycle, Scene XVIII: The Appearance at Arles

PLATE 76

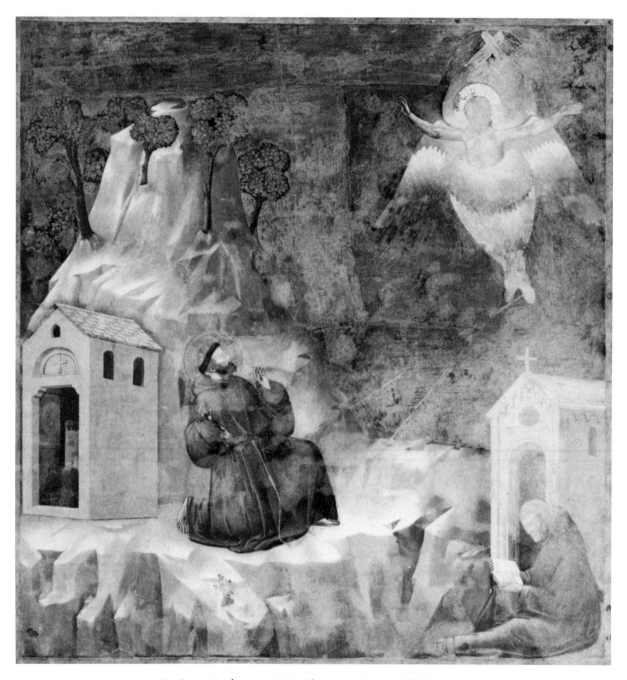

St. Francis Cycle, Scene XIX: The Stigmatization of St. Francis

PLATE 77

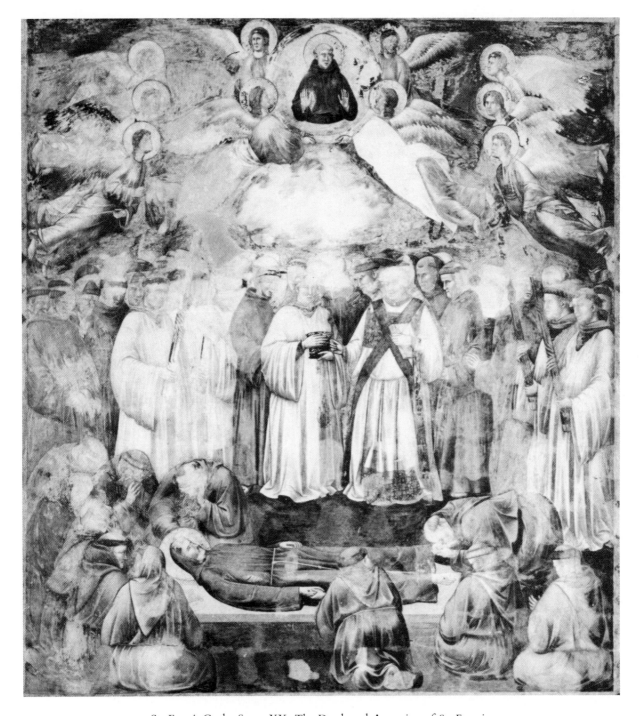

St. Francis Cycle, Scene XX: The Death and Ascension of St. Francis

PLATE 78

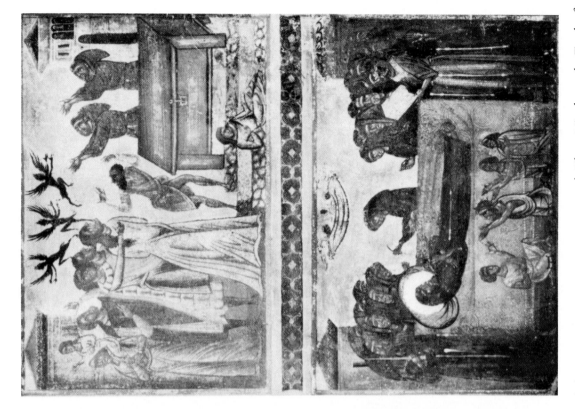

b. 'MAESTRO DEL S. FRANCESCO BARDI': Three Miracles at the Tomb of St. Francis; and The Death and Ascension of St. Francis: detail of altarpiece (Bardi Chapel, Santa Croce, Florence)

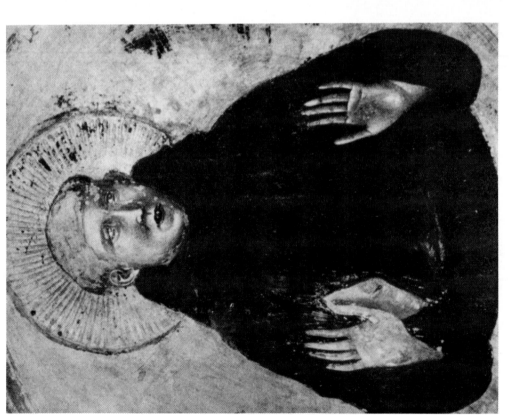

a. St. Francis: Detail of Plate 77 (St. Francis Cycle, Scene XX)

PLATE 79

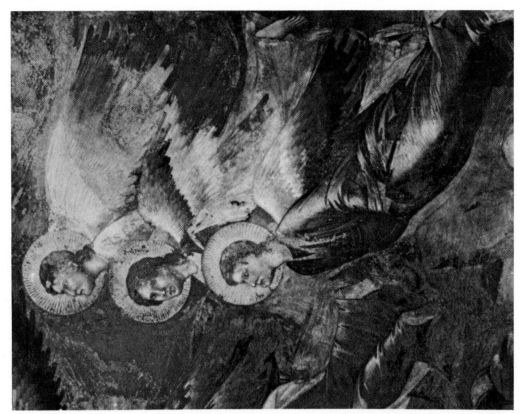

b. Angels: detail of Plate 77 (*St. Francis Cycle*, Scene XX)

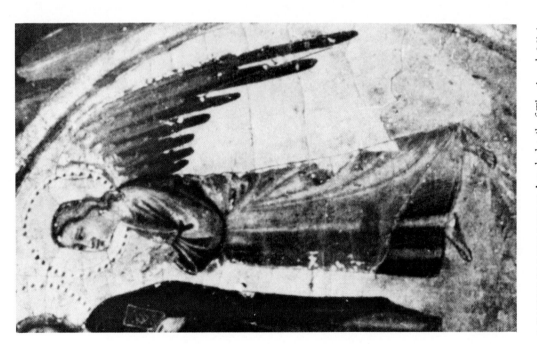

a. PACINO DI BONAGUIDA: Angel: detail of The Angels Ministering to Christ, from The Tree of Life (Accademia, Florence)

PLATE 80

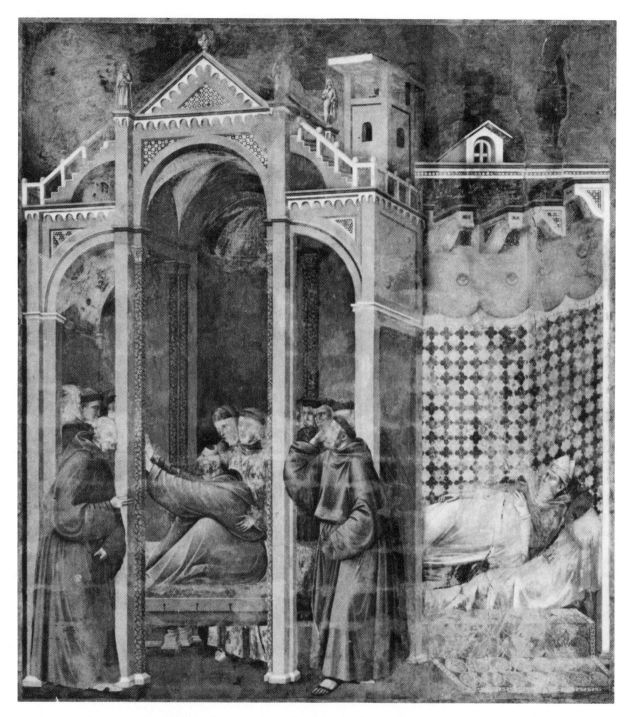

St. Francis Cycle, Scene XXI: The Vision of the Ascension of St. Francis

PLATE 81

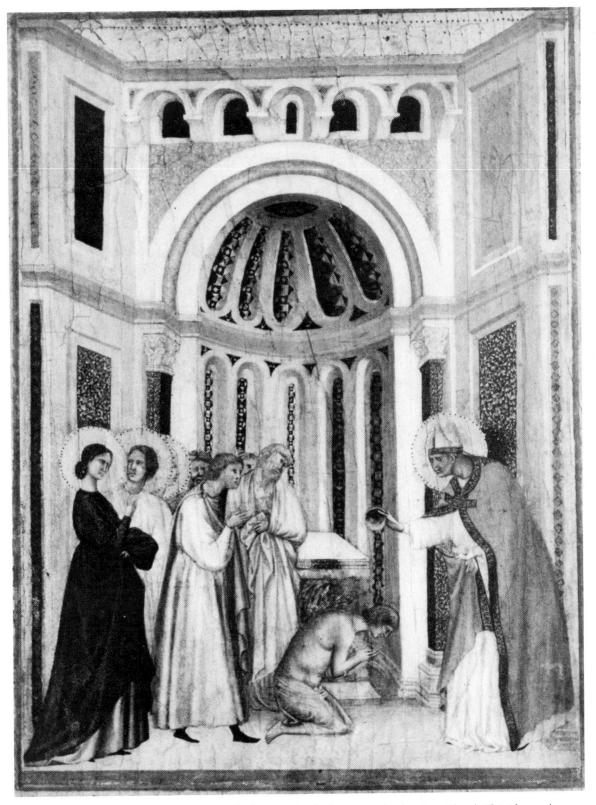

ST. CECILIA MASTER: The Baptism of Tiburtius: detail of *Santa Cecilia* altarpiece, Pl. 8 (Uffizi, Florence)

PLATE 82

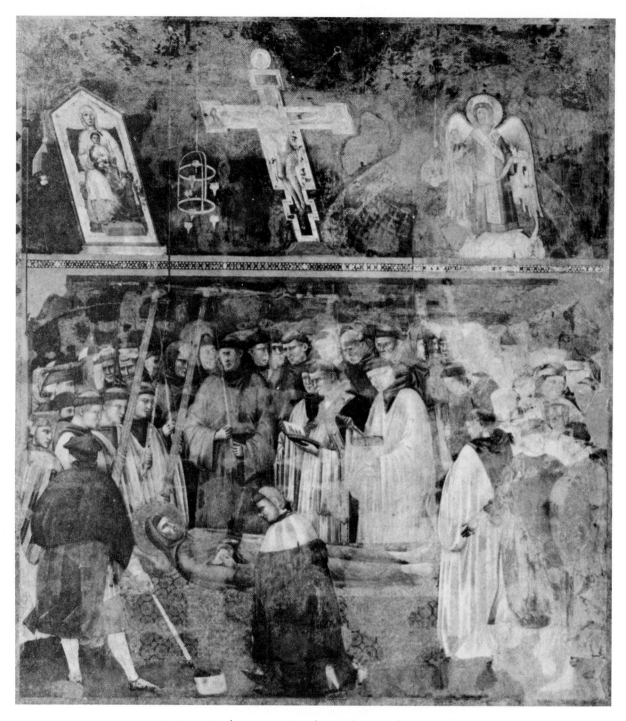

St. Francis Cycle, Scene XXII: The Verification of the Stigmata

PLATE 83

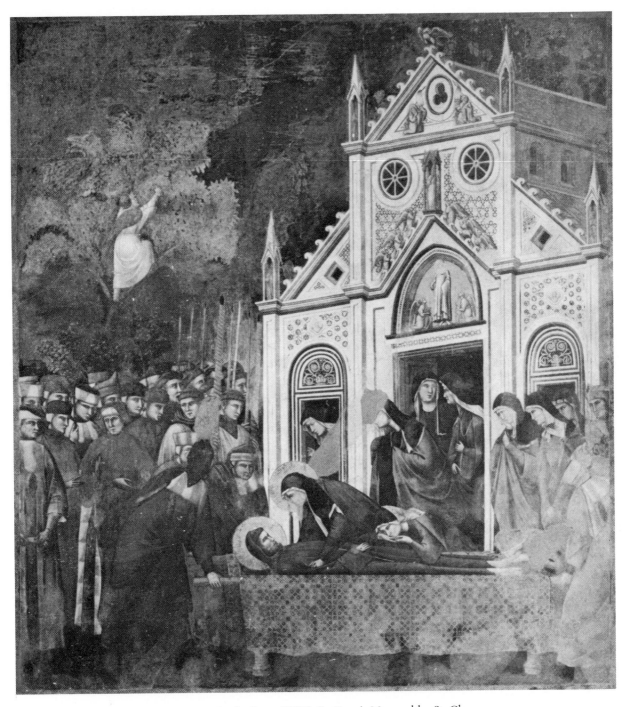

St. Francis Cycle, Scene XXIII: St. Francis Mourned by St. Clare

PLATE 84

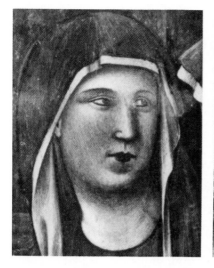

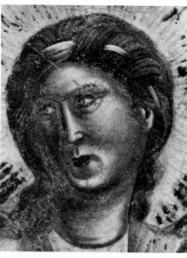

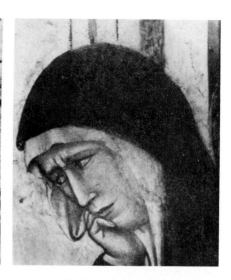

a. Detail of Pl. 83 (*St. Francis* Cycle, Scene XXIII)

b. Detail of Pl. 90 (*St. Francis* Cycle, Scene XXVI)

c. Detail of Pl. 83 (*St. Francis* Cycle, Scene XXIII)

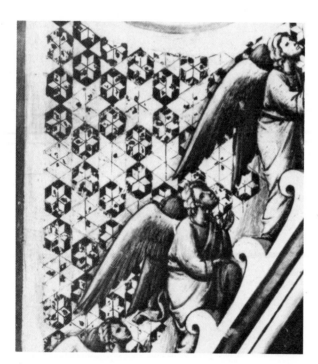

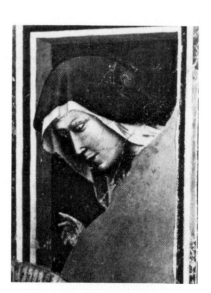

d. Decorations on the exterior of the church of San Damiano: detail of Pl. 83 (*St. Francis* Cycle, Scene XXIII)

e. Detail of Pl. 83 (*St. Francis* Cycle, Scene XXIII)

PLATE 85

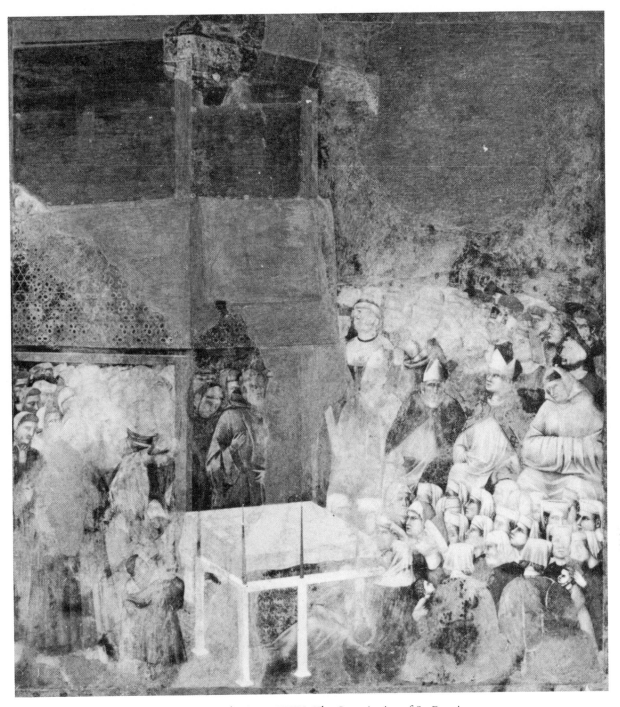

St. Francis Cycle, Scene XXIV: The Canonization of St. Francis

PLATE 86

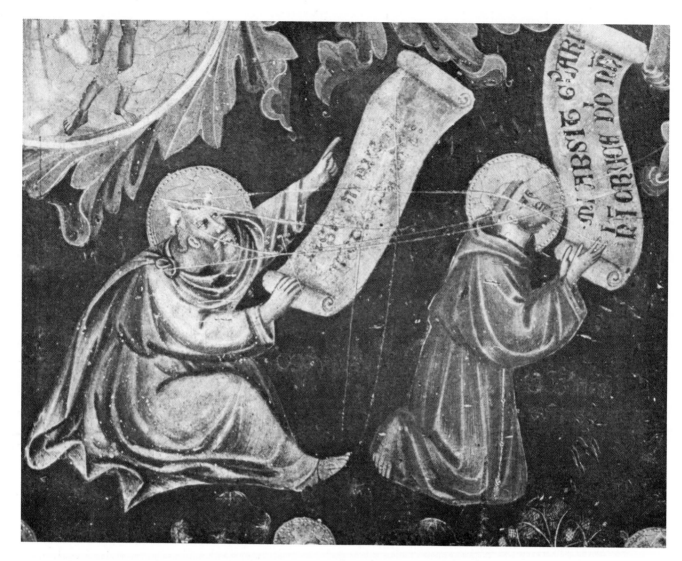

PACINO DI BONAGUIDA: Moses and St. Francis: detail of The Tree of Life

PLATE 87

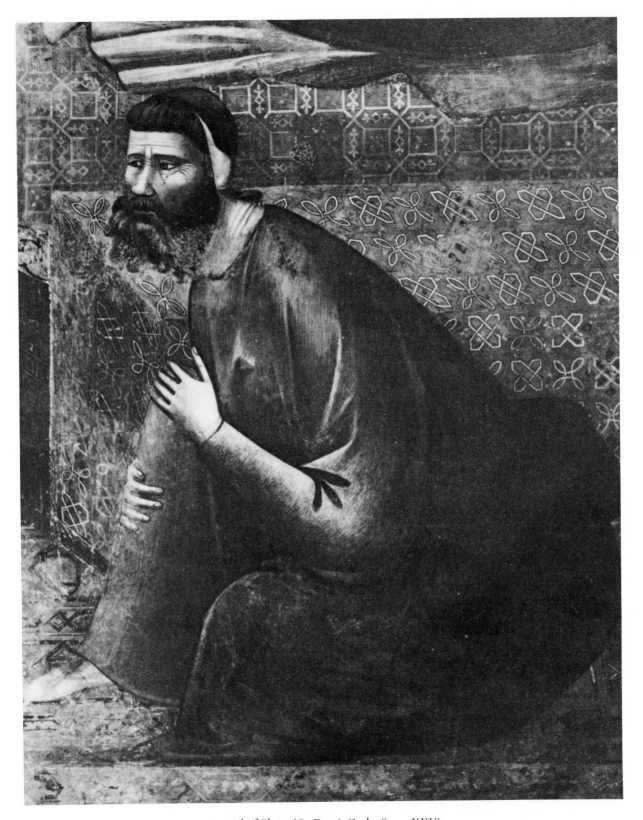

Detail of Pl. 88 (*St. Francis* Cycle, Scene XXV)

PLATE 88

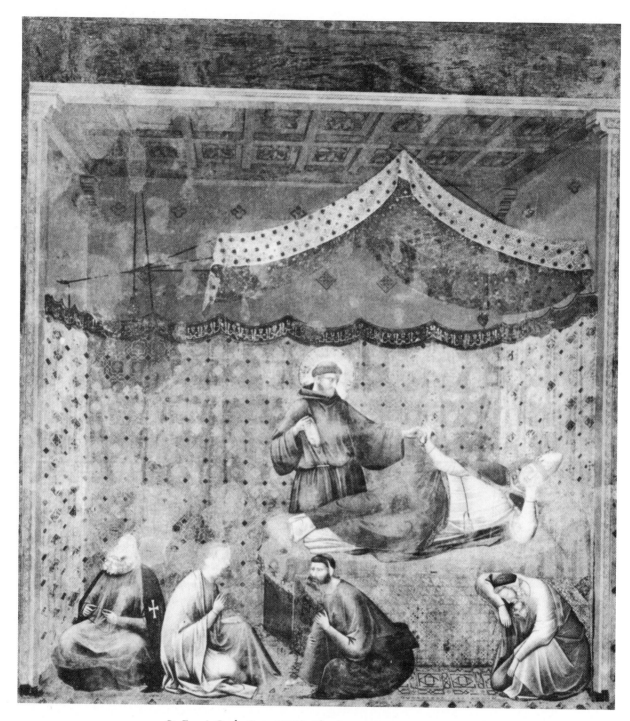

St. Francis Cycle, Scene XXV: The Appearance to Gregory IX

PLATE 89

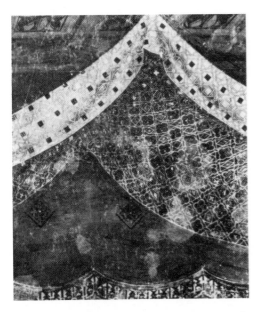

a. Detail of Pl. 88 (*St. Francis* Cycle, Scene XXV)

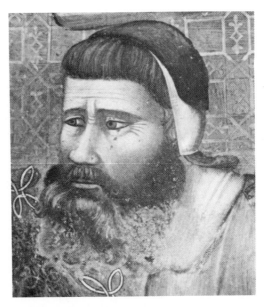

b. Detail of Pl. 88 (*St. Francis* Cycle, Scene XXV)

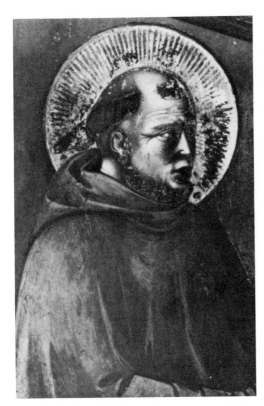

c. St. Anthony: detail of Pl. 75 (*St. Francis* Cycle, Scene XVIII)

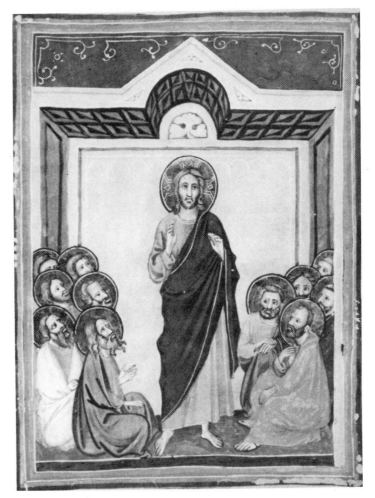

d. PACINO DI BONAGUIDA: Christ's Appearance to the Disciples (Pierpont Morgan Library, New York, MS. M 643, fol. 30)

PLATE 90

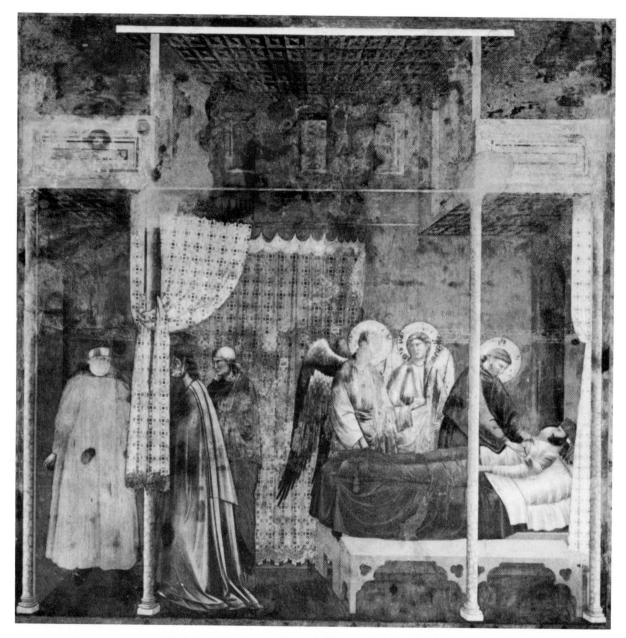

St. Francis Cycle, Scene XXVI: The Healing of the Wounded Man

PLATE 91

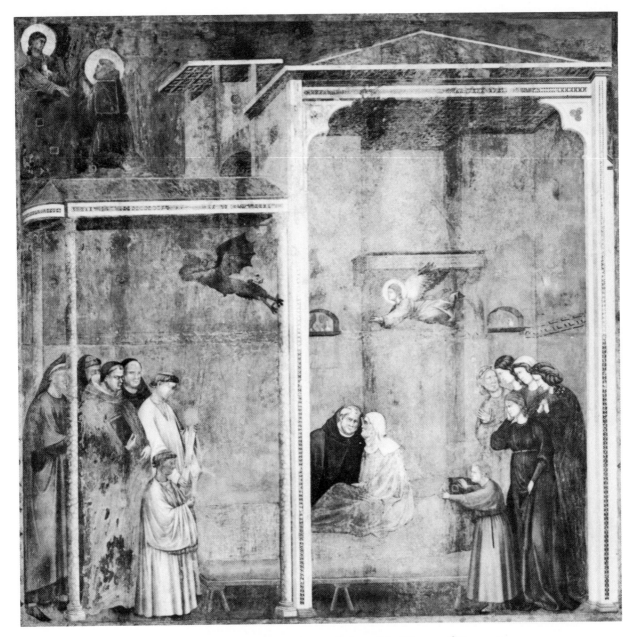

St. Francis Cycle, Scene XXVII: The Confession of the Woman of Benevento

PLATE 92

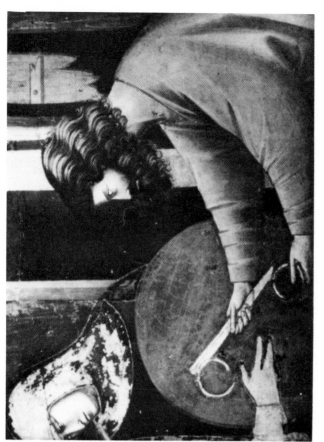

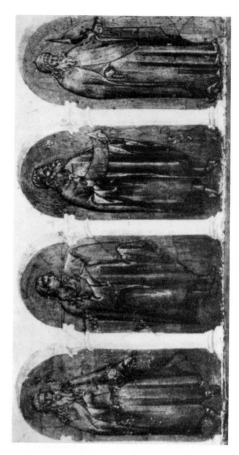

b. Detail of Pl. 93 (*St. Francis* Cycle, Scene XXVIII)

c. The Statues of Prophets: detail of Pl. 93 (*St. Francis* Cycle, Scene XXVIII)

a. St. Francis in supplication before Christ: detail of Pl. 91 (*St. Francis* Cycle, Scene XXVII)

PLATE 93

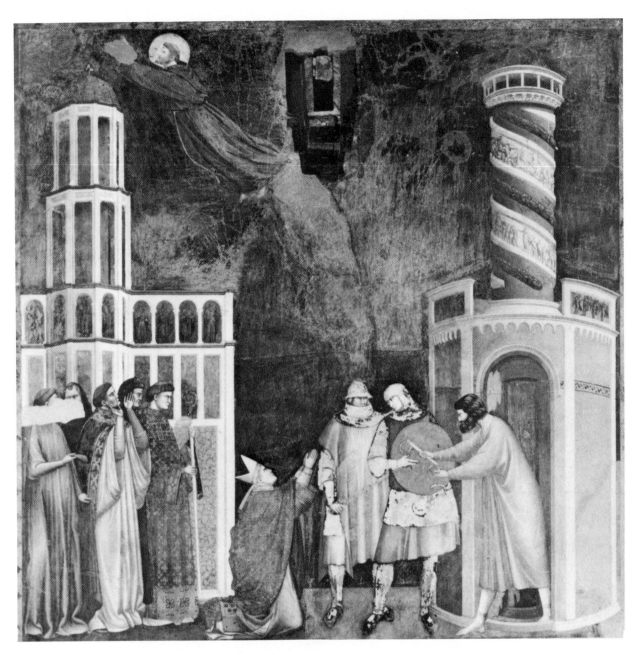

St. Francis Cycle, Scene XXVIII: The Liberation of the Prisoner

PLATE 94

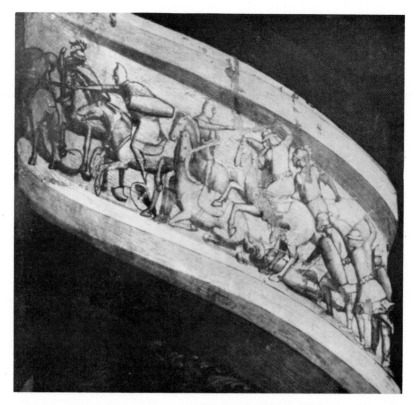

a. The upper relief on the column: detail of Pl. 93 (*St. Francis* Cycle, Scene XXVIII)

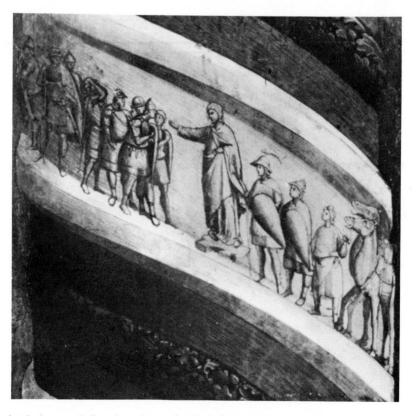

b. The lower relief on the column: detail of Pl. 93 (*St. Francis* Cycle, Scene XXVIII)

PLATE 95

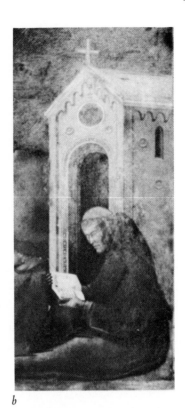

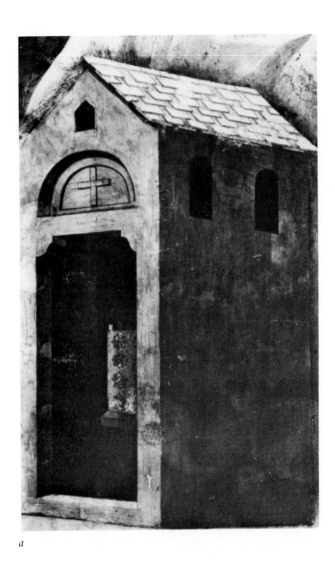

a

b

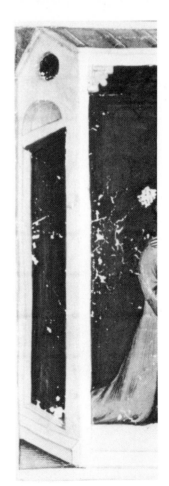

a. The chapel at La Verna: detail of Pl. 76 (*St. Francis* Cycle, Scene XIX)

b. The Saint's cell: detail of Pl. 76 (*St. Francis* Cycle, Scene XIX)

c. PACINO DI BONAGUIDA and Workshop: Scene from an Antiphonary (detail) (Collegiata di Santa Maria, Impruneta, near Florence)

c

PLATE 96

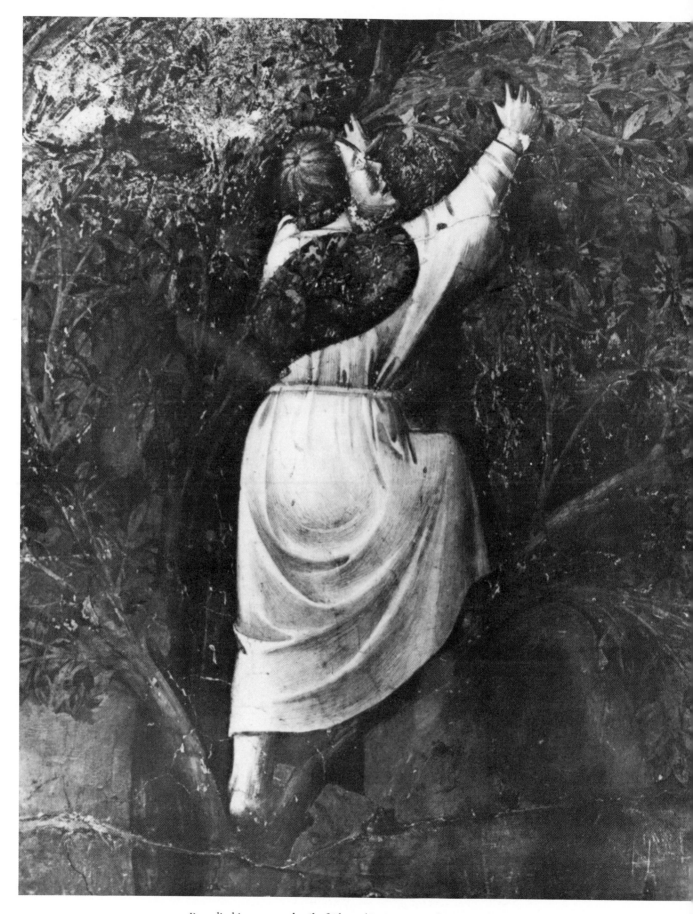

Boy climbing a tree: detail of Pl. 83 (*St. Francis* Cycle, Scene XXIII)

PLATE 97

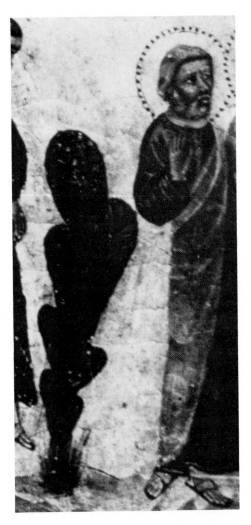

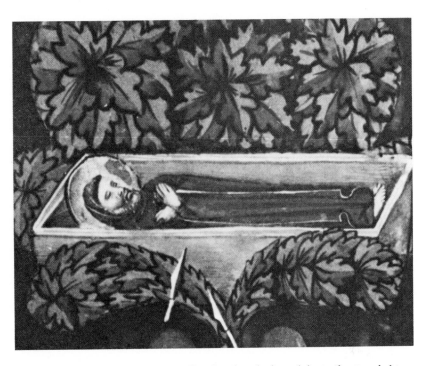

b. PACINO DI BONAGUIDA (assisted): The Blessed Gherardo's Coffin Guarded in a Tree: detail (Pierpont Morgan Library, New York, MS. M 643, fol. 36)

a. PACINO DI BONAGUIDA: The Suicide of Judas: detail; from The Tree of Life (Accademia, Florence)

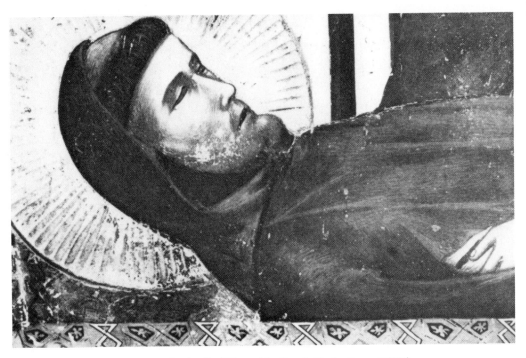

c. St. Francis: detail of Pl. 83 (*St. Francis* Cycle, Scene XXIII)

PLATE 98

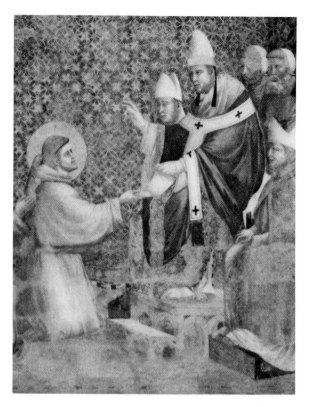

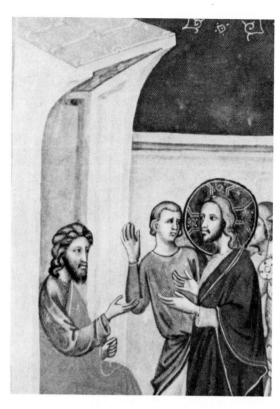

a. Detail of Pl. 53 (*St. Francis* Cycle, Scene VII)

b. PACINO DI BONAGUIDA: Christ before Pilate: detail (Pierpont Morgan Library, New York, MS. M 643, fol. 18)

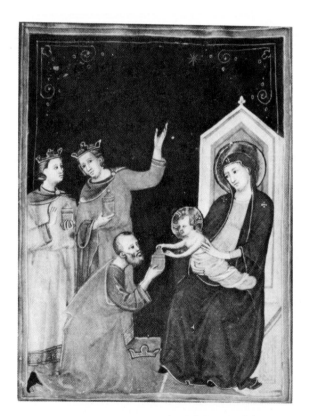

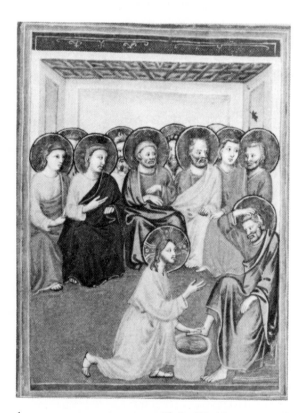

c. PACINO DI BONAGUIDA: The Adoration of the Kings (Pierpont Morgan Library, New York, MS. M 643, fol. 5)

d. PACINO DI BONAGUIDA: Christ Washing St. Peter's Feet (Pierpont Morgan Library, New York, MS. M 643, fol. 15)

PLATE 99

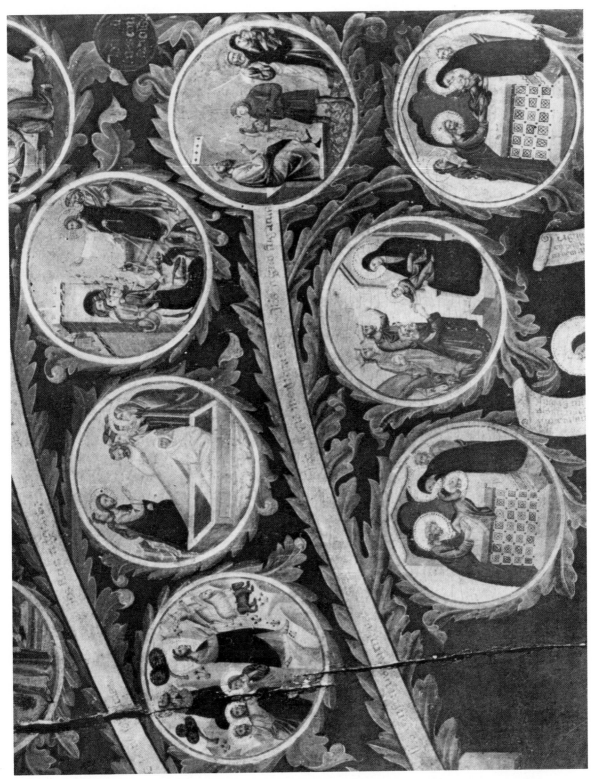

PACINO DI BONAGUIDA: The Tree of Life: detail (Accademia, Florence)

PLATE 100

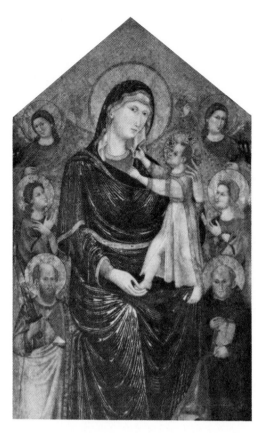

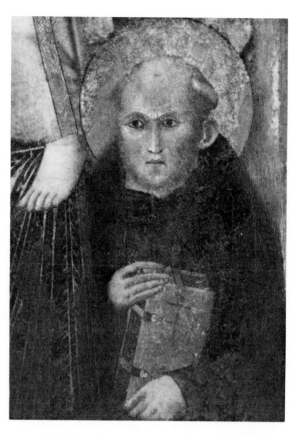

a. MARINO DA PERUGIA: Madonna and Child with Saints (Galleria Nazionale dell'Umbria, Perugia)

b. MARINO DA PERUGIA: St. Benedict (?): detail of Pl. 100*a*

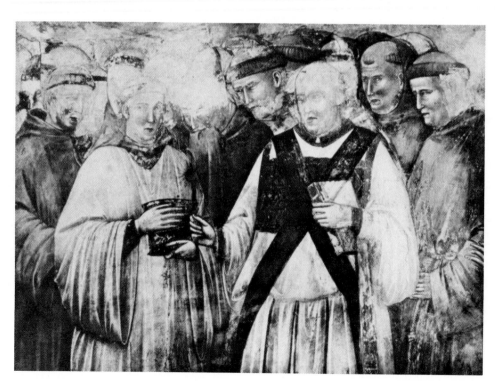

c. Detail of Pl. 77 (*St. Francis* Cycle, Scene XX)

PLATE 101

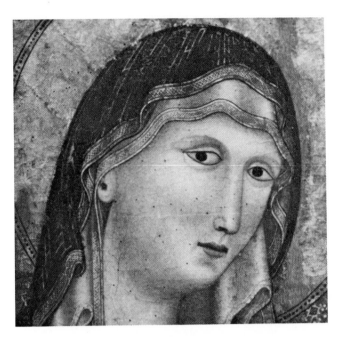

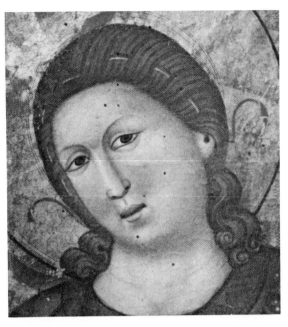

a. MARINO DA PERUGIA: The Virgin: detail of Pl. 100*a*

b. MARINO DA PERUGIA: An Angel: detail of Pl. 100*a*

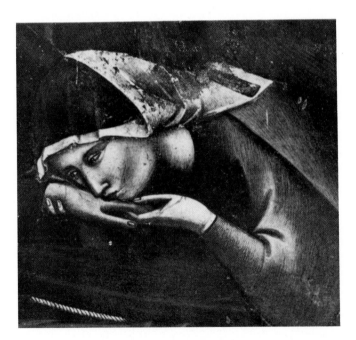

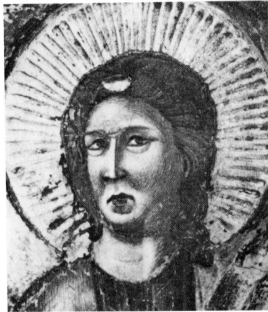

c. A companion of St. Clare: detail of Pl. 83 (*St. Francis* Cycle, Scene XXIII)

d. An Angel: detail of Pl. 77 (*St. Francis* Cycle, Scene XX)

PLATE 102

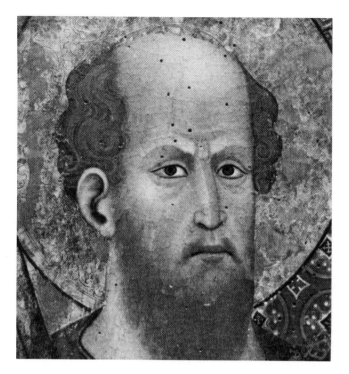

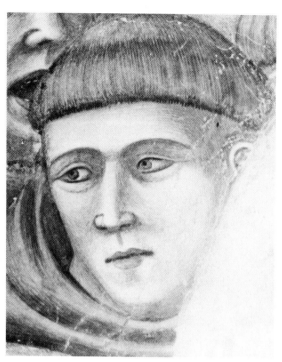

a. MARINO DA PERUGIA: St. Paul: detail of Pl. 100*a*

b. Detail of Pl. 83 (*St. Francis* Cycle, Scene XXIII)

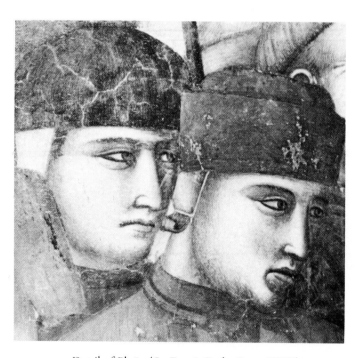

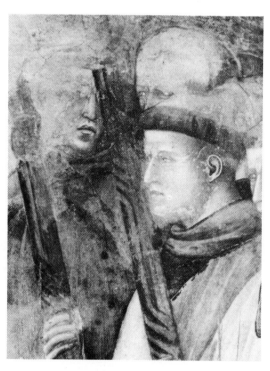

c. Detail of Pl. 83 (*St. Francis* Cycle, Scene XXIII)

d. Detail of Pl. 77 (*St. Francis* Cycle, Scene XX)

PLATE 103

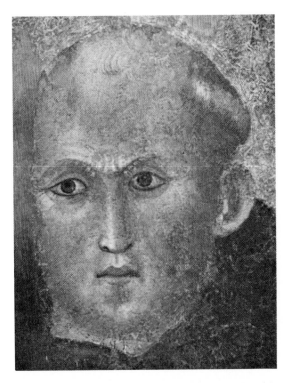

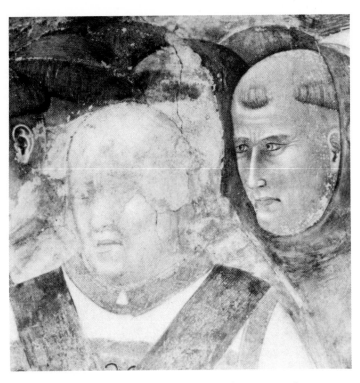

a. MARINO DA PERUGIA: Head of St. Benedict (?): detail of Pl. 100*a*

b. Detail of Pl. 77 (*St. Francis* Cycle, Scene XX)

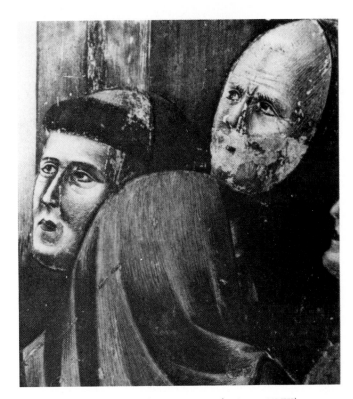

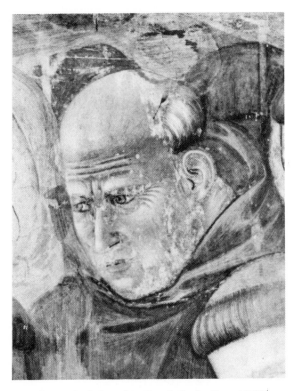

c. Detail of Pl. 75 (*St. Francis* Cycle, Scene XVIII)

d. Detail of Pl. 82 (*St. Francis* Cycle, Scene XXII)

PLATE 104

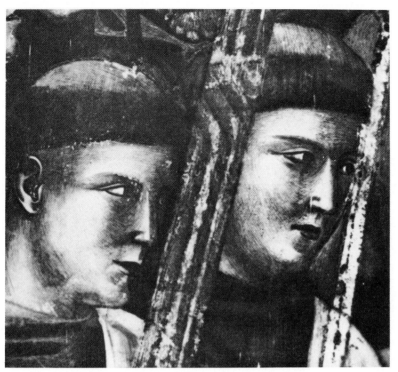

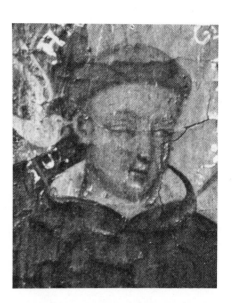

b. MASTER OF THE DOMINICAN EFFIGIES:
St. Ambrose of Siena: detail of Pl. 106

a. Detail of Pl. 82 (*St. Francis* Cycle, Scene XXII)

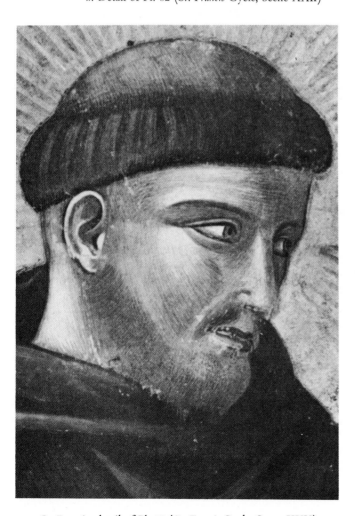

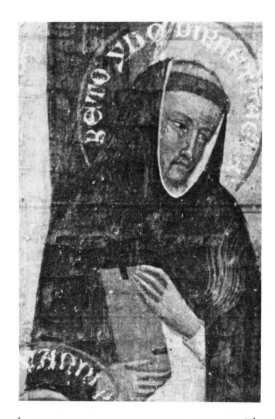

d. MASTER OF THE DOMINICAN EFFIGIES: The
Blessed Ives of Brittany: detail of Pl. 106

c. St. Francis: detail of Pl. 88 (*St. Francis* Cycle, Scene XXV)

PLATE 105

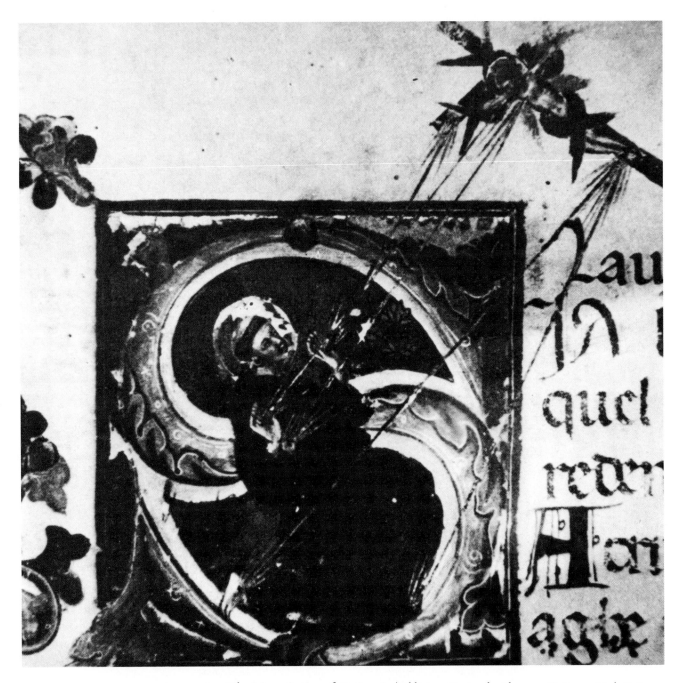

MASTER OF THE DOMINICAN EFFIGIES: The Stigmatization of St. Francis (Biblioteca Nazionale, Florence, B. R. 19, Cod. II, I. 212, fol. 52r)

PLATE 106

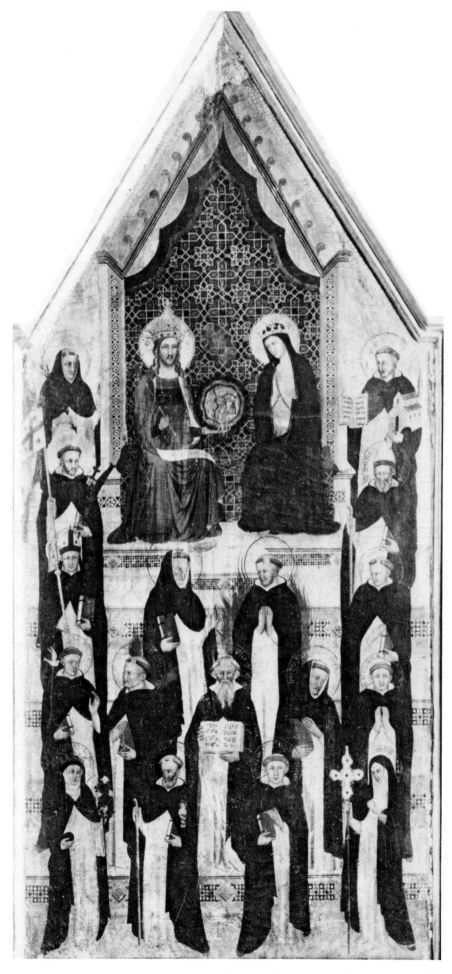

MASTER OF THE DOMINICAN EFFIGIES: Christ and the Virgin Enthroned, attended by
Seventeen Dominican Saints (Santa Maria Novella, Florence)

PLATE 107

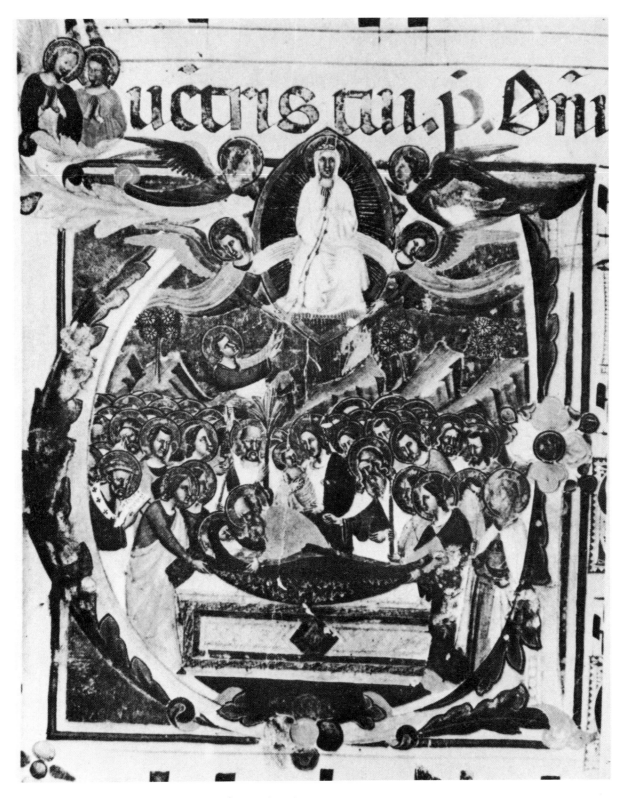

MASTER OF THE DOMINICAN EFFIGIES: The Death and Assumption of the Virgin: detail from an illuminated page in an Antiphonary (Collegiata di Santa Maria, Impruneta, Cod. A–V, fol. 158r)

PLATE 108

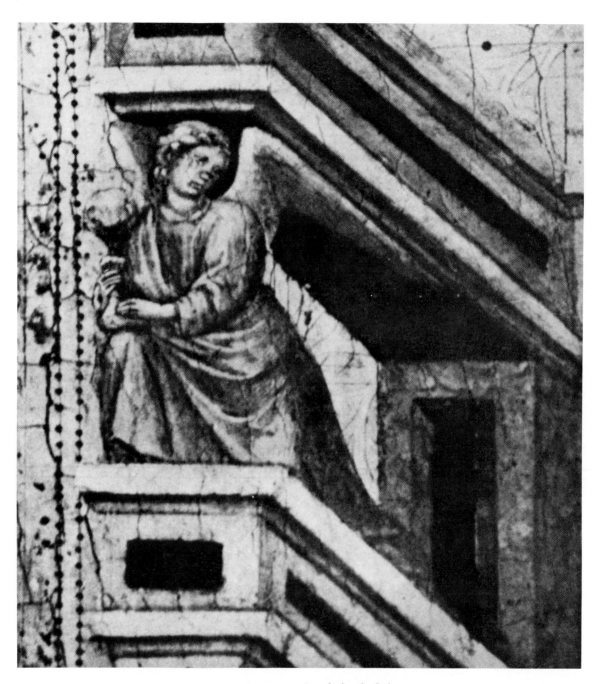

ST. CECILIA MASTER: Angel: detail of Pl. 8

PLATE 109

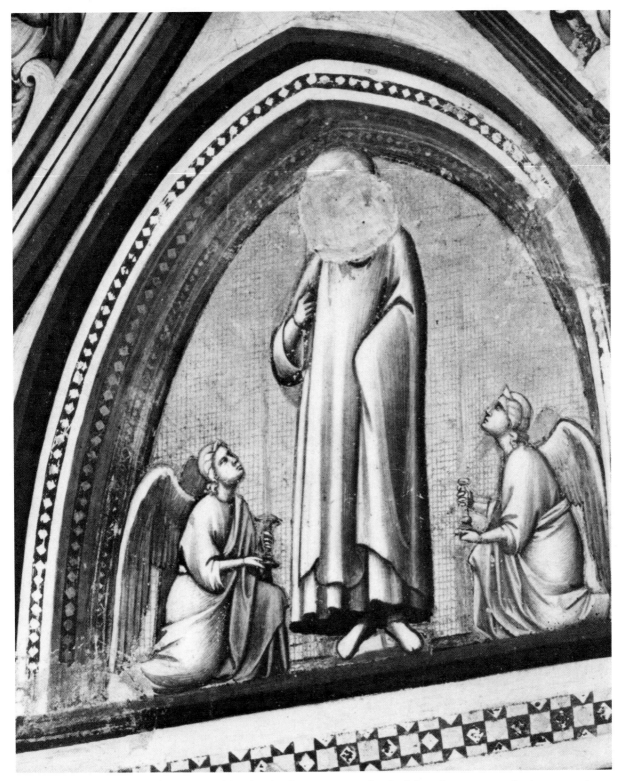

Sculptural decorations on the exterior of the church of San Damiano: detail of Pl. 83 (*St. Francis* Cycle, Scene XXIII)

PLATE 110

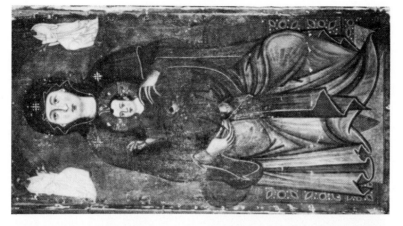

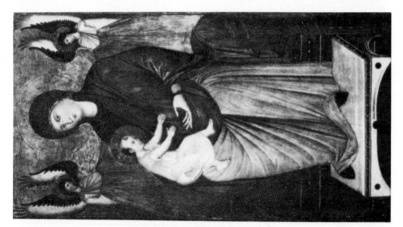

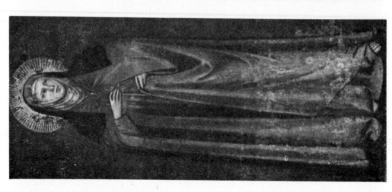

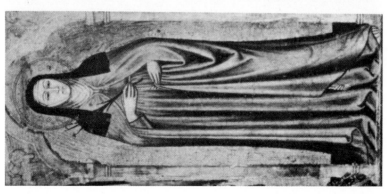

a. Follower of MEO DI GUIDO DA SIENA: St. Clare: detail of altarpiece (Galleria Nazionale dell'Umbria, Perugia)

b. ST. NICHOLAS MASTER: St. Clare: detail of fresco (Orsini Chapel, Lower Church, Assisi)

c. Florentine School, late 13th century: Madonna and Child (S. Andrea, Mosciano)

d. 'MAESTRO DELLA MADDALENA': Madonna and Child (S. Donato a Torri, Compiobbi)